# The City of God

PETER LANG
New York • Washington, D.C./Baltimore • San Francisco
Bern • Frankfurt am Main • Berlin • Vienna • Paris

# The City of God

## A Collection of Critical Essays

Edited with an Introduction by

## Dorothy F. Donnelly

PETER LANG
New York • Washington, D.C./Baltimore • San Francisco
Bern • Frankfurt am Main • Berlin • Vienna • Paris

**Library of Congress Cataloging-in-Publication Data**

The City of God: a collection of critical essays/
edited with an introduction by Dorothy F. Donnelly.
p. cm.
Includes bibliographical references.
1. Augustine, Saint, Bishop of Hippo. De civitate Dei.
2. Kingdom of God. 3. Apologetics. I. Donnelly, Dorothy F.
BR65.A65C58   239'.3—dc20   94-15185
ISBN 0-8204-1726-2


**Die Deutsche Bibliothek-CIP-Einheitsaufnahme**

The city of God: a collection of critical essays/
ed. with an introd. by Dorothy F. Donnelly. - New York; Washington, D.C./
Baltimore; San Francisco; Bern; Frankfurt am Main;
Berlin; Vienna; Paris: Lang.
ISBN 0-8204-1726-2
NE: Donnelly, Dorothy F. [Hrsg.]

Cover design by James F. Brisson.


The paper in this book meets the guidelines for permanence and durability
of the Committee on Production Guidelines for Book Longevity
of the Council of Library Resources.

© 1995 Peter Lang Publishing, Inc., New York

Printed in the United States of America.

# Acknowledgments

It is a pleasure to thank those individuals and institutions who have helped me in the preparation of this book. I am especially grateful to the three colleagues who contributed original essays to this collection—Phillip Pulsiano, chair of the English department at Villanova University and editor of the *Proceedings of the PMR Conference*; Joanna Scott, chair of the department of Political Science at Eastern Michigan University; and Frederick Van Fleteren of the Philosophy Department at LaSalle University and the Augustinian Historical Institute. I am also greatly indebted to Michael Flamini, Senior Acquisitions Editor at Peter Lang Publishing, for his early encouragement in planning this project and his suggestions about possible directions for the book.

For their help and support I want to thank Joseph Schnaubelt, OSA, and John M. Quinn, OSA, Director and Associate Director respectively of the Augustinian Historical Institute at Villanova University. I also want to express my appreciation to colleagues who have shared their ideas with me about Augustine, and innumerable other topics, in gatherings we have had over the years at professional conferences. I owe special thanks to Judith Chelius Stark, Frederick Russell, Thomas Losoncy, Robert Merrix, Patricia Silber, and James Reilly.

I would like to express my deep gratitude to Ethel Thompson for her invaluable assistance and outstanding work on this book and without whom it could not have been completed. I also owe special thanks to Roberta King and Nicole Tremblay for their important contribution in the preparation of the manuscript. I am indebted to Professor Stephen C. Wood of the University of Rhode Island who generously gave his time and expertise at critical points in the completion of this volume. Jean Sheridan of the reference department at the URI Library was extremely helpful in conducting comprehensive computer searches. Allan Fitzgerald, OSA, of the department of Religious Studies at Villanova and editor of *Augustinian Studies* provided expert assistance in locating obscure information relevant to this collection. Thanks go as well to Nona Reuter and Sandra Watanabe at Peter Lang Publishing for guiding the book through the production process with great skill.

Finally, I am pleased to acknowledge that the publication of this book was assisted by a research grant from the University of Rhode Island Foundation Faculty Award Program and a grant from the Dean's Office, College of Arts and Sciences, University of Rhode Island.

Dorothy F. Donnelly

# Contents

# Contents

# Preface

The first book devoted solely to essays on Augustine's *The City of God*, this collection brings together a wide range of approaches to the study of the work offered by some of the most important philosophers, theologians, historians, political theorists and literary critics who have written on Augustine's text.

The ideas of more than twenty-two scholars are presented in this volume. In Section I, "Political Thought," eight authors discuss the political and social views developed in *The City of God*. Section II, "Language and Literature," includes eight essays on literary and linguistic aspects of the text. Section III, "Philosophy and Theology," consists of discussions by several scholars on different topics concerning Augustine's philosophical and theological thinking as presented in *The City of God*. Within the separate groups, the essays are arranged alphabetically by author. Each section contains a new essay specially commissioned for the collection.

There are other excellent studies dealing with *The City of God* that could not be included in this volume. To assist the reader in pursuing further examination of scholarship dealing with *The City of God* the section, "Suggestions for Further Reading," provides comments on several of these studies.

Finally, the book includes a complete chronological list of writings by Augustine, as well as a selected bibliography of general studies on Augustine and his work. Because there is an immense literature about Augustine and his ideas, other bibliographic sources are included among the citations in the general bibliography.

D.F.D.

# Chronology

A.D.

| | |
|---|---|
| 354 | Augustine born at Tagaste (November). |
| 371 | Enters school at Carthage. |
| c.373 | Birth of son, Adeodatus. |
| 375 | Returns from Carthage to Tagaste to teach. |
| 376 | Returns to Carthage. |
| 383 | Goes from Carthage to Rome. |
| 384 | Takes up professorship in Milan. |
| 386 | Conversion (August). |
| 387 | Baptism (April). Death of mother, Monica (Autumn). |
| 389 | Returns to Africa. |
| 391 | Ordained priest in Hippo. |
| 395 | Becomes bishop of Hippo. |
| 396 | Writes *De doctrina christiana*. |
| 397/401 | Writes *Confessiones*. |
| 410 | Sack of Rome. |
| 411 | Conference at Carthage with Donatists. |
| 412 | Writes *De spiritu et littera*. |
| 413 | Begins *De civitate Dei*. Death of Marcellinus. |
| 426/27 | Finishes *De civitate Dei*. Writes *Retractationes*. |
| 430 | Death of Augustine (August). |

# Introduction

The essays in this collection demonstrate the diversity of scholarship that has appeared dealing with Augustine's *The City of God*. Perhaps not surprisingly, *The City of God* is also a work that attracts the attention of scholars from a great variety of disciplines. The multiplicity of ideas and issues presented by Augustine in his monumental treatise guarantees systematic inquiry into its meaning, on the one hand, and on the other assures the frequent appearance of new theories arising from different approaches to interpreting the text. The essays in this volume deal with the principal topics, as well as most of the secondary themes, in Augustine's work—politics, war, sin, two *civitates*, order, punishment, morality, authority, obedience, religion, language. Yet, while the individual essays may focus on different aspects of Augustine's thought as he develops it in *The City of God*, there are also, as the reader will observe, many points of connection among the ideas and theories that are proposed by the particular authors in their essays. Thus the arrangement of the essays into three sections based on major themes may seem to suggest theoretical and thematic separation whereas, in many ways, the essays demonstrate an eclecticism that is characteristic not only of modern criticism but also of contemporary scholarship on *The City of God*. The scope of the collection is wide with essays ranging from the idea of progress to Neoplatonism, from the origin of society to the role of political authority, and from the idea of language and narrative as syntactic strategies of meaning in *The City of God* to Augustine's symbolic use of number. Taken together, the essays link Augustine's thought to contemporary issues and define the influence of his work on western thought. And they constitute an exciting and challenging debate about the ideas of one of history's most important thinkers.

## I Political Thought

P. R. L. Brown begins his study, "Saint Augustine and Political Society," with the observation that classical political theory was based upon a rational myth of the state. In contrast, modern political thought, like medieval thought, proposes that the link between the individual and the state cannot be limited merely to a rational obligation. Political society does not exist as an "extrapolated, isolated ideal"; on the contrary, it exists concretely whether the primal cause is God or history. The essay proposes that medieval as well as modern thinkers are thus indebted to Augustine for signaling the end of the concept of political idealism embedded in Greek political philosophy and substituting for it an emphasis on the basic questions that deal with the "intractable reality" of the human situation. The main topic developed here is the notion that for Augustine rational control over one's political environment is very much limited. Augustinian political thought centers around problems of the individual's behavior in a political community. Human beings are not "natural political animals"; they are individuals faced with a whole range of aims and concerns, only some of which stem from living in political society. Augustine's political theory, according to Brown, "is based upon the assumption that political activity is merely symptomatic; it is merely one way in which men express orientations that lie far deeper in themselves. . . .The symptoms which tend to predominate in his description of human political activity can only be thought of as symptoms of a disease. . . . The most blatant symptom . . . is the inversion of the harmonious order established by God."

In his article, "The Problem of Service to Unjust Regimes in Augustine's *City of God*," Peter Burnell investigates the general notion of civil justice as this theme is developed in *The City of God*. Specifically, Burnell focuses his attention on Augustine's treatment of the "doctrine of compliance to unjust regimes." The author points out that numerous passages in *The City of God* show that Augustine had a "clear notion of the moral terms on which political life is lived" and, furthermore, that he understood that different political problems and issues could demand different kinds of moral action. Burnell challenges the many scholars who propose that the Augustinian doctrine of obedience calls for absolute cooperation in all civil affairs—"obedience to God's ministers" is required "no matter how impious or wicked they may be." From this point of view, the need for obedience and cooperation rules out the possibility of opposing civil injustice. Acknowledging that civil obedience is a central tenet in Augustine's thought, on the one hand, and on the other that all societies—as a consequence of original sin—will be unjust to a greater or lesser degree, Burnell argues that Augustine's attitude toward the issue of "civil life is not . . . static. It does not make endless cooperation with wickedness a necessary concomitant of a Christian's civil duties." According to this essay, Augustine's thinking on the subject of opposing the immoral actions and policies of unjust governments is more "open" than has been conventionally thought.

In "Augustine and The State: The Return of Order Upon Disorder," Herbert Deane offers a detailed discussion of Book XIX of *The City of God* in which Augustine challenges the definition of a people (*populus*) and of a commonwealth or state (*res publica*) given by Scipio in Cicero's *De Republica*. Deane observes that Augustine rejects Scipio's ideas on justice and the ideal state and that he substitutes in their place a new interpretation of true justice and a new explanation of the role and purpose of the state. In his analysis the author strongly, and at length, challenges the view of Professor Charles McIlwain who claims that Augustine actually agrees with the Ciceronian definition of the state or *res publica*. McIlwain says that Augustine's argument regarding the state "is a *reductio ad absurdum* indeed, but it is the absurdity of heathenism not of Cicero's definition which Augustine means to prove" (*The Growth of Political Thought in the West*, 157). Deane asserts that McIlwain disregards, on the one hand, Augustine's redefinition of true justice and, on the other, his alternative definition of a true *res publica* which Augustine proposes as a substitute for the Scipionic definition.According to the author, McIlwain fails to prove that Augustine really accepted Cicero's views on justice and the state. On the contrary, the essay concludes that for Augustine "the state itself—the political order—can never be truly just."

The political and social modernity of Augustine's *City of God* is the concern of Peter Kaufman's "Redeeming Politics: Augustine's Cities of God." Kaufman investigates the relationship between religion and politics in *The City of God* and concludes that, contrary to the views of many critics, Augustine actually offers "his own redeeming politics." As the author puts it, "the empire's distress unquestionably tempted [Augustine] to jettison some of sociolatry's prominent themes, but he revised others and reconstructed justifications for the current coalition between politicians and prelates." Thus, unlike the radical efforts of some of his contemporaries who sought to separate religion from politics, Augustine "insisted that the Bible promised Christianity dominion over all culture and that such dominion was unthinkable apart from a Christian political culture." In response to the argument that Augustine devalued political life (a view that has, he agrees, ample support in the text), Kaufman argues that *The City of God* is intended, first, to "repair Christian confidence" and, second, "to teach Christians the choices they had to make in the religious and political realms." Without question Augustine vividly describes the tension between religion and politics, "yet he nowhere seems to have encouraged readers to run from the tension, to closet themselves, and collect dust as if the end of Christian triumphalism were an excuse for inaction." In brief, for Augustine political culture was part of God's divine plan and it was thus absurd to stress the incompatibility between the religious and political realms.

The essay by Robert Markus, "Two Conceptions of Political Authority: Augustine, *De Civitate Dei*, XIX, 14-15, and Some Thirteenth-Century Interpretations," consists of two parts. The first part examines Augustine's views on the origins and nature of political authority and subjection as presented in Book XIX, chapters 14 and 15, of *De civitate Dei*. The second part discusses the interpretation of these chapters by some thirteenth-century writers, primarily Thomas Aquinas. Among other things, the analysis enables us to see how Augustine's meaning was modified by thirteenth-century thinkers whose ideas were influenced by the revival of Aristotelian thought. The essay begins with the acknowledgment that Augustine does not develop in any of his writings a detailed theory about the origin of the state. His fullest statement on the theme occurs in *De civitate Dei*, chapters 14 and 15. Markus proposes that Augustine emphasizes essentially two ideas in chapters 14 and 15: first, that "servitude is a condition or institution whose origin is not to be found in man's nature as created"; and, second, that "there is a way of exercising authority—and subjection—either in accordance with the order of nature or otherwise." Servitude itself originates in sin "but the exercise of authority need not be sinful." For Augustine, a desire for a harmonious social existence is natural to human beings. There is also, according to Augustine, a natural subordination among people, on the one hand, and on the other a subordination which has its origins in the punishment of sin. As Markus puts it, "political authority, coercive power and its apparatus are what transform society into a state. Society, as we may summarize Augustine's view, has its origins in the order of nature; the state is a dispensation rooted in sin." The purpose of the second section of the essay is to discuss how Augustine's views on the origin of the state and on political authority were treated by St. Bonaventure, St. Albert the Great and, in particular, St. Thomas Aquinas.

In "Augustine's Political Realism," Reinhold Niebuhr suggests that Augustine was the "first great 'realist' in western history." Unlike earlier thinkers who proposed the idea of an ideal *polis* as an achievable goal through the proper use of reason, Augustine, in contrast, gives a true "picture of social reality" in his account in the *De civitate Dei* of the factions and tensions that actually permeate the personal and political realms. The source of the difference between the classical and Augustinian viewpoints lies in "Augustine's biblical, rather than rationalistic, conception of human selfhood." For Augustine, the evil which threatens society is self-love, or *superbia*, precisely because it "corrupts the processes of the mind." The corrective to this condition is for humanity to devote itself to and be guided by the love of God. According to the author, the doctrine of love, not reason or the mind, is, for Augustine, the ultimate norm. Niebuhr concludes that Augustine, "whatever may be the defects of his approach to political reality, . . . nevertheless proves himself a more reliable guide than any known thinker." In the course of his discussion, the author touches upon the related topics of cynicism, relativism and idealism, the self's power of self-transcendence, the unity of mind and body, the Augustinian notion of a natural order, and the development in the *De civitate Dei* of Augustine's ideas about a potential world community.

The purpose of Oliver O'Donovan's essay, "Augustine's *City of God* XIX and Western Political Thought," is to demonstrate that *The City of God* is a study in social and political philosophy. In this context, the author concentrates on two features of Augustine's text. First, the way in which the work "anticipates modern Western political thought, in its separation between society and virtue." And second, the way the work appears "alien to modernity in its failure to allow for the progressive transformation of the social order." According to O'Donovan, Augustine, in his new definition of the true meaning of justice, introduced the first standard of modern political thought by "casting the political community off from its moorings in justice." This departure from classical theory results from the change Augustine makes to Cicero's definition of justice, namely, "the removal of the reference to right." Augustine breaks the link between society and virtue and substitutes in its place a view which gives "due recognition both to the reality of the moral order which makes social existence possible and to its fundamentally flawed character." The essay concludes that Augustine does not disparage the role of virtue in political life but, rather, that he demonstrates "an ability to discern shadows cast by virtue in surprising places." Augustine's political thought is least modern in perspective in that it lacks a theory of progress. In Augustinian thought human history is "a demonic history which expresses the divine purpose only as providence, following its own hidden course, and uses it to higher ends."

In "Augustine's Razor: Public vs. Private Interests in *The City of God*," Joanna Scott offers a detailed discussion of several topics central to an understanding of *De civitate Dei*. The author discusses Augustine's ideas on the institutions and communities of and within the *saeculum*, the relationship between individual free will and the order of creation and between free will and divine grace, the conflict between idealism and realism and, in this connection, Augustine's thoughts on public and private obligation, on the common good and, finally, on pluralism and public discourse. In terms of the institutions in the *saeculum*, the author points out, Augustine does not discuss social or political organizations in particular; however, he does make it clear that inequality in the *saeculum* "would not be necessary had Adam been willing to accept the divinely mandated inequality of his dependence upon God." And, individual wills, unaided by grace, Scott says, "are beset by the 'monstrosity' of impotence which renders good motivation inoperative." The author observes that public interest and common good are major themes for Augustine not only in *De civitate Dei* but also in many of his other writings. As she puts it, the public interest, for Augustine, "is the agenda of the moral communities which animate institutions of church and state." The common good in "theological terms is God, and in secular terms it is the collective goal or 'interest' which is the *civitas* or *res publica*." The essay concludes with the observation that Augustine "creates a new mode of Christian discourse" in an attempt to "forge a workable consensus" in the political and ecclesiastical realms.

## II   Language and Literature

Jeremy Adams, in "Augustine's Definitions of *Populus* and the Value of Society," systematically examines the meanings of *populus* in Augustine's writings generally, but with special focus on its usage in *The City of God*. The method used by Adams is to cite the frequency of the appearance of the word *populus*; identify the general patterns of its usage; discuss the attributes or properties of the word as it is used in different contexts; and analyze the distinctions between the meaning of *populus* and the other social and political terms used by Augustine. The aim of this study is to explore the "patristic sense of community." Tentative answers are sought to three principal questions: "Into which and what sorts of groups was mankind divided in the minds of patristic and early medieval thinkers? To which of those groups did they feel that they . . . belonged? If they felt a sense of community with several groups or kinds of groups, what did they feel about the proper hierarchy of loyalties in that regard?" The study argues that throughout Augustine's many writings his meaning of the term *populus* is consistent with his use of it in *The City of God*. When we take the whole range of his works together, "they permit us to see that that noun represents in Augustine's writings a fairly coherent notion, which the socio-political terminology of this century would describe as a legitimate polity, unified by an essentially conscious agreement."

In "St. Augustine's Two Cities as Medieval Dramatic Exempla," Robert Brawer is concerned with demonstrating that three of the Townley Corpus Christi plays develop a systematic presentation of a theological view of history similar to that in Augustine's *The City of God*. As in *The City of God*, the representation of historical events in the Corpus Christi plays is secondary to the elucidation of moral and spiritual choices. According to Brawer, the idea of the two cities provides a polarized theological construct for dramatizing the choice human beings have in this life between divine harmony and earthly discord. Following Augustine, there is in the Corpus Christi plays an implicit recognition of degrees of goodness in the individual's progress from being a sojourner in the *civitas terrena* to being a citizen of the *civitas Dei*. Thomas of India, the Second Shepherds' Play, and the trial and crucifixion scenes of the Townley cycle are chosen to support the author's ideas. Brawer also emphasizes the didactic element in the Townley Plays and points out that such performances were intended to "perfect the faith of the audience, to move it . . . toward a personal and communal integrity characteristic of 'heuen citee.'"

In my own essay, "Reconsidering the Ideal: *The City of God* and Utopian Speculation," I look at the relationship between *The City of God* and the utopian mode of thought. The article begins with a comprehensive survey of contemporary critical opinion on utopias and utopian thought to demonstrate that the term utopia has become so all-inclusive that it is now applied to any work containing elements of what is called utopian thought; that is, "any social, intellectual, political, religious, or psychological theory that speculates about the possibilities of achieving the good life in the future." In several of the studies mentioned, *The City of God* is cited as an example of a utopian work and interpreted from this point of view. The article argues, however, that utopia and *The City of God* are based upon significantly different underlying assumptions and premises, and they inevitably offer contrasting views on the value of the temporal world and conflicting ideas about an ideal *telos*. The work attempts to show this opposition through an analysis of four aspects of Augustine's work: his use of the term "city"; his ideas on the relationship between the individual and the state; his concept of time, and his views on and description of an "ideal existence." The study concludes that not only is *The City of God* not an example of utopian writing, but it may even be regarded as both a rejection of the utopian mode of thought and a mandate against utopianizing.

The minimal appearance of Augustine in Dante's *Divine Comedy*, as Peter Hawkins puts it in "Divide and Conquer: Augustine in the *Divine Comedy*," is one of the surprises of that work. Augustine's absence in the *Comedy* is not what we would expect in view of the repeated references to Augustine in many of Dante's other works. Hawkins mentions that some critics have explained this by suggesting that Dante "failed to see the importance of Augustine" . . . or that the liberties of a "poet's imagination freed Dante from having to account for anyone's presence or absence." Hawkins argues, however, that "it is more likely that Augustine's eclipse in the *Comedy* has to do with politics—with the political polemic that drives *The City of God* in direct opposition to many of Dante's own convictions." Hawkins approaches his topic by first analyzing the strategies used by Dante to counter Augustine and then discussing how Augustine emerges as an "informing presence within the text itself." As noted in the essay, there is a "profound intertextual relation" between the *Comedy* and *The City of God*. What interests Hawkins, more specifically, is how *Purgatorio* 15 "is an unmistakable paraphrase of *City of God* 15, a text whose description of the *civitas Dei* Dante gives to none other than Vergil." Thus it is not only the textual borrowing that is important but, more significantly, the implications of "Dante's decision to give this Augustinian glimpse into the city of God—in fact the poem's first view of paradise—to Vergil." Two inseparable issues concern Hawkins—the "rendering of a new account" by Dante of Augustine's thought, on the one hand, and on the other the fact that much of what is said by Augustine in *The City of God* is attributed to Vergil by Dante.

Penelope Johnson, in *"Virtus:* Transition from Classical Latin to the *De Civitate Dei,"* reviews the meanings of *virtus* from old Latin through the writings of Cicero and Sallust to Augustine. The article examines the implications of the word *virtus* in matters political and theological. Johnson sees its original meaning of "magic or miraculous power" transformed into civic virtue with the growth of the Roman republic and empire only to regain its miraculous connotation, while still highly politicized, in *De civitate Dei.* In *The City of God virtus* is a divine gift from God. "As Augustinian *virtus* had both a divine origin and a divine goal, 'miraculous power' was again functioning in it. . . . Whatever the conscious intention, *virtus* in *De civitate Dei* echoed its earliest meaning, and gave to the Christian vocabulary of the Middle Ages, *virtus* as *ordo amoris."* The three authors discussed in the essay—Cicero, Sallust, Augustine—are seen as using *virtus* in ways that parallel their own relationships to the rise and fall of Rome and the role of the individual in the temporal state.

Phillip Pulsiano's essay, "Language Theory and Narrative Patterning in *De Civitate Dei,* Books XV–XVIII," is concerned with language and narrative as syntactic structures of meaning in *De civitate Dei.* More specifically, he offers an examination of the "rhetoric of narrative" found in *De civitate Dei,* particularly in Boox XV–XVIII. The author notes the summary of Books XV–XVIII that is given by Augustine at the beginning of Book XVIII, a summary in which Augustine mentions that his narrative parallels the movement of historical events—"the two cities proceed on their course in our narrative, just as they did in history." Pulsiano argues that "although Augustine patterns his narrative on the incremental movement of historical event, he establishes a metahistorical narrative in tracing the progress of the two cities." The means by which Augustine is able to express both narratives simultaneously as realities is found, according to the author, in the "redeemed rhetoric made possible through the Incarnation of Christ." Pointing out that Augustine repeatedly returns to a discussion of the authority of the written word, Pulsiano proposes that, for Augustine, "the imperative is to move beyond the multiplicity of words to the single Word and thus closer to truth." Augustine achieves this through what the author calls a "process of 'narrowing' until, eventually, the single Word remains as the crucial link between historical and metahistorical, between temporal and atemporal."

Language thus bridges the gap between human and divine by creating a narrative that moves away from multiplicity toward the "utterance of what is 'far different' from historical narrative."

In his study, "More's *Utopia* and *The City of God*," Martin Raitiere compares Augustine's *The City of God* and More's *Utopia* to show that More's work embodies many of the same views as Augustine's. The essay discusses Augustine's and More's ideas on various subjects including the idea of community, the function of the state, natural law, patriarchalism, the concept of justice, the notion of *dominium*, Christian versus civic obligation, and the doctrine of the just war. Raitiere points out that scholars generally do not find any substantial evidence of a direct influence of Augustine's classic on More's work. The author argues, however, that conjecture about Augustinian influence on *Utopia* is justified within the context of the "metaphysical dimension" of the two works. From this perspective, *The City of God* is seen "as a possible source not of specific social doctrines but rather of More's *facetudo* vis-a-vis the realm of politics." The study concludes that the similarities between Augustine's work and More's result, finally, from the concern in both works with the relationship between the Christian imperatives and those of the *vita socialis*. It is the discontinuity between politics and Christian obligation that Augustine in *The City of God* and More in the *Utopia* wanted to illuminate.

The intention of Louis Swift's essay, "Defining *Gloria* in Augustine's *City of God*," is to demonstrate that when Augustine deals with the theme of *gloria* in *The City of God*, he uses the term in three different senses. First, *gloria* is linked with *libido dominandi* and with moral decline in the life of the Roman state. Second, Augustine defines *gloria Christiana* in a way that "reflects both a continuity with traditional Roman concepts and a sharp departure from them." In sum, whereas the Roman citizen found fulfillment in the recognition achieved in this lifetime, *gloria* is for Christians a reality outside time. Finally, in his text Augustine offers a brief delineation of *cupiditas gloriae*, the glory that is stimulated by a passion for renown. Since in historical terms divine providence works through human actions, those individuals who resist the vice of avarice and who pursue glory for noble aims are, in fact, placing limits on their own *amor sui*. And it is this which distinguishes them from those who are subject to the *libido dominandi* and from the Christian faithful. As the author notes, "from this perspective, then, it seems appropriate to speak of three types of glory, since there are, in fact, three types of *amores* (i.e., that of the *superbi*, that of the *boni sine fide*, and that of the *sancti*). Augustine's more typical view that all persons are governed by one of two *amores* (i.e., *amor sui* or *amor Dei*) and thus preoccupied with one or the other of two types of *gloria* does not easily accommodate a *tertium quid*, but it is clear that there are individuals who fall outside the categories of *sancti* or *superbi* and who practice a kind of natural virtue for which they receive a temporal reward." In the final analysis, temporal glory plays a significant role in encouraging Christian virtue.

## III   Philosophy and Theology

Vernon Bourke's study, "*The City of God* and History," discusses *The City of God* from the perspective of the philosophy of history it presents. The author points out that Augustine is "completely theocentric in his thinking" and his interpretation of human events is consistently informed by this attitude. For Augustine, the essay argues, human history, of itself, has no ultimate meaning or significance. Temporal history is given meaning only through divine providence, and the events of this world are explainable only within the context of the concepts of redemption and salvation. The study concludes that Augustine's primary purpose in writing *The City of God* was to articulate a fully developed Christian view of history. The essay also briefly contrasts Augustine's view of history with that of Thomas Aquinas. Bourke points out that Aquinas often speaks of a *communicatio divina* and of the *regnum Dei*. But he does not, it is argued, develop a theory of history, nor does he propose that divine providence is manifested in the temporal world. Unlike Augustine, in Thomas Aquinas's view, according to the author, "history is a mere chronicle of events."

Ernest Fortin, in "Augustine's *City of God* and the Modern Historical Consciousness," asks whether the modern concept of a meaningful and teleological historical movement within a linear temporal scheme has its origin in Augustine's "novel approach to history" as presented in the later books of *De civitate Dei* or whether it departs radically from it. Fortin's essay compares the views of Augustine chiefly with those of Eusebius and Orosius on the matter of Christianity, politicism and the nature of empire, and examines the perplexities posed to the human will in the light of divine providence. Through a close look at selected passages from their writings the author observes that what was a solution in the Eusebian and Orosian theories Augustine saw as an "insidious danger" because of the association of Christianity with temporal rewards and the equanimity implied toward both pagans and Christians. The article concludes that the only similarity between modern and Augustinian concepts of history is "the linear and nonrepeatable character of the historical process" discussed by Kant and which the author presents as fundamental to the Biblical view of history. Otherwise, an antagonism exists between Christianity and temporal politics and any "notion of a Christian polity . . . is at best a comforting and at worst a fatal illusion."

Patricia MacKinnon, in "Augustine's *City of God*: The Divided Self/The Divided *Civitas*," traces the governing analogy between the individual and the body politic, borrowed from Plato's *Republic*, in *The City of God*. MacKinnon argues that the Platonic analogy between the self and the *civitas* is exploited by Augustine as the key figure in his analysis of the doomed nature of the *civitas terrena*, and that it underlies the relation he perceives between fragmentation in the soul and the political fragmentation of civil and foreign wars. According to the author, what most distinguishes *The City of God* from other Augustinian texts is the extent to which it is based not merely upon the Platonic heritage but rather on one particular Platonic text, the *Republic*. MacKinnon argues that the link between the governing idea of the *Republic* and the conceptual framework of *The City of God* is found in Augustine's definition of the "two cities." His notion of two communities—*civitas terrena* and *civitas Dei*—builds upon Plato's "fundamental axiom that the relations internal to the individual soul are the index and determining factor of the form of polity." The notion of two contrasting cities competing for the individual's earthly allegiance is also found in Plato's speculation about human destiny in this life and the destination of the soul beyond historical time. And Plato's one "right" city becomes Augustine's unique *civitas Dei*. Lastly, as MacKinnon puts it, "Plato's claim that the inner rectitude of the soul is its own reward and may be judged by the happiness or unhappiness of its possessor, acquires an eschatological emphasis in Augustine upon ultimate spiritual polarities—the felicity of eternal life as opposed to the misery of damnation."

The analysis of Augustine's interpretation of the meaning and course of history offered by Theodor Mommsen in his essay, "St. Augustine and the Christian Idea of Progress," arrives at the conclusion that Augustine rejects both the cyclical theory proposed by the Platonists and the Stoics and the early Christian proposition that real temporal progress could be observed from the Incarnation onward. In addition to the cyclical theories of the Greeks, he rejected as an equally deplorable theory of history the Christian idea of "progress." In his theological explanation of the meaning of history, Augustine thus rejects the view that the world is eternal and the notion that human history is accompanied by evolutionary progress. To Augustine, history is linear, not cyclical. And in his view the notion of Christianity as a progressive factor in history is contrary to God's divine plan. The Augustinian perspective is that Christian ideals can be realized only in the spiritual community of God not in the temporal state or empire. Augustine regards the so-called "earthly achievements" as totally insignificant. Not surprisingly, he condemns his worldly-minded Christian contemporaries as "blasphemers who chase and long after things earthly and place their hopes in things earthly. When they have lost them, whether they will or not, what shall they hold and where shall they abide? Nothing within, nothing without; an empty coffer, an emptier conscience." Mommsen concludes that in *De civitate Dei* Augustine rejects practically all the conceptions of history proposed by his contemporaries and by his predecessors. He rejects the view of the imminence of the end of the world, eschews the cyclical theory of history, dismisses eschatological speculation regarding the future millennium, and denies the doctrine of progress. The author claims that "in contradistinction to all these conceptions, Augustine's own views concerning history represent a basic reiteration and systematic elaboration of Hebrew and early Christian ideas."

In "The Politics of Paradise," Elaine Pagels explores Augustine's reinterpretation of several aspects of early Christian doctrine, a reinterpretation that challenges not only traditional thinking but also his own earlier point of view on subjects concerning Christian orthodoxy. Using the ideas of John Chrysostom as representative of the views of Augustine's predecessors, Pagels contrasts that accepted interpretation with Augustine's "radical" reinterpretation of, among other things, the notion of free will on the one hand, and the nature of sin on the other. Not unexpectedly, what was earlier regarded by Chrysostom, and others, as "God's greatest gift to humankind—free will, liberty, autonomy, self-government—Augustine characterizes in [*The City of God*] in surprisingly negative terms." Augustine also offers other biblical interpretations that depart signficantly from the ideas presented by earlier Christian thinkers. In contrast to their interpretations, Augustine argues, for example, that "obedience, not autonomy, should have been Adam's true glory"; that Adam represents not "the single individual Chrysostom envisioned" but, rather, "a corporate personality" from whom humankind inherited "a universal nature irreversibly damaged by sin"; that the will is not only not free, it is inherently flawed; and that the "whole human race, including the redeemed, remains wholly incapable of self-government." Pagels points out that while Augustine and his contemporaries did not discuss government in "strictly political terms" they were nonetheless keenly aware of the political dimensions of their particular interpretation of the "story of Adam and Eve." The author concludes her analysis with a discussion of some of the social and political reasons why, in her view, Augustine's originally marginal and "idiosyncratic" interpretations, which so fundamentally transformed Christian doctrine, came to be so widely accepted.

Robert Russell points out, in his study of "The Role of Neoplatonism in St. Augustine's *De Civitate Dei*," Augustine's generally positive attitude towards Platonism. But his eventual departure from many of the Platonists' views is the main concern of Russell's essay. The author notes that while

Augustine accepts the Platonists' "natural philosophy and dialectic which viewed God, respectively, as the cause of the universe and the source of man's intellectual illumination," his primary concern in *The City of God* is to refute those Platonic "errors" that were incompatible with revealed truth. This study demonstrates that, in discussing this incompatibility, Augustine focuses upon two fundamental Platonic ideas that are at variance with Christian religion—namely, the notion of beatitude and the doctrine of mediatorship. Plato locates the cause of beatitude in the "transcendent Good or One"; however, Plato's doctrine of eternal cycles, according to the author, "eliminates what was for Augustine the one condition without which true happiness remains incompatible, namely, that it is *unending*." On the doctrine of mediatorship, for Augustine, the only way to achieve personal salvation is through Christ. Any theory that proposed a mediator other than that of Christ was, as the author says, "reason enough to turn Augustine against that philosophy." Thus Augustine found in Platonism a philosophy which lent itself to a rational explanation of revealed truth. Writing as an apologist for Christianity in *The City of God*, however, Augustine felt compelled to show "not where Platonism succeeded, but where it had *failed*."

Finally, as his title, *"De Civitate Dei*: Miscellaneous Observations," suggests, Frederick Van Fleteren's article offers a variety of thoughts on the *De civitate Dei*. Van Fleteren notes that the basic tenets of Augustinian thought in *De civitate Dei* derive principally from Scripture and that the exegetical methods Augustine uses in examining Scripture come almost entirely from Scripture itself. He points out that Augustine speaks again and again of the *auctoritas* of Scripture. And he observes that the same tension that exists between the earthly city and the Christian *politea* also lies within each individual. In this connection, according to Van Fleteren, we should not be surprised to find that the central focus of *De civitate Dei* is on "human destiny, not its origin." The article also treats two topics central to a discussion of *De civitate Dei*. First, the scope and nature of the influence of Plato, Plotinus and Porphyry on Augustine's views concerning the means to attaining wisdom and happiness. And second, the Augustinian notion that human reason is, ultimately, inadequate to the task of arriving at a complete understanding of truth. Van Fleteren concludes his "observations" with the argument that we do not find political theory in *De civitate Dei*—"though Augustine views eternal moral principle as bearing upon the conduct of the state, his purpose is not to sketch guidelines for the establishment of a political entity."

Dorothy F. Donnelly

# I  Political Thought

# Saint Augustine and Political Society†

## P. R. L. Brown

Isidore of Seville once wrote that if anyone told you he had read all the works of Augustine, he was a liar.[1] From the time of his conversion to Catholic Christianity, in 386, until his death in 430, Augustine wrote some 117 books.[2] Of these books, not a single one is devoted to political theory. Even the title of the book, in which we study his "political ideas"—"*City of God*," *De civitate Dei*—is misleading, Augustine treated this as a technical term, taken from the Psalms,[3] to express what we might call "The Communion of Saints."

The book itself took thirteen years to write, that is, from 413 to 426. Even Augustine thought it a bit too long; and we tend to dismiss it, as Henry James dismissed the Russian novels of the last century, as a "loose, baggy monster." Above all, *De civitate Dei* is a book of controversy. It should never be treated as though it were a static, complete photograph of Augustine's thought. It reads like a film of a professional boxing championship: it is all movement, ducking and weaving. Augustine is a really stylish professional: he rarely relies on the knockout; he is out to win the fight on points. It is a fight carried on in twenty-two books against nothing less than the whole of the pagan literary culture available to him.[4] Thus he is reluctant to follow an argument through to its conclusion in one move: instead, he twists a definition here, demolishes another there, proposes one to annoy an opponent, ignores it in the next few chapters, then takes it up again, no less than seventeen books further on, that is, ten whole years later.[5] To try to extract from this infinitely flexible book a rigidly coherent system of political ideas is like trying to square the circle: it is a problem that has fascinated many great minds, and baffled all of them.

Yet this book dominated the political thought of the early middle ages; and Augustine is one of the few thinkers of the Early Church who can be called "contemporary" to ourselves. In this, he is like a planet in opposition: given the vast distance of time and culture that separates him from us, he has come as close as possible to the preoccupation of our own age. Why is this so? Perhaps it is because the whole emphasis on what is fruitful in political theory has shifted. The texts which the student usually has to study for his examinations, and especially the works of the "classical" political theorists, Hobbes, Locke, and Rousseau, already belong to the past. But the attitudes of Augustine and of many medieval theorists, though expressed in a foreign language and forming part of a framework of ideas to which we are unaccustomed, somehow remain relevant.

"Classical" political theory, from the seventeenth century onwards, was based upon a Rational Myth of the State. By myth I mean the habit of extrapolating certain features of experience, isolating them, in abstraction or by imagining an original state in which only those elements were operative, and using the pellucid myth thus created as a means of explaining what should happen today. The tendency, therefore, was to extrapolate a rational man; to imagine how reason, and a necessity assessed by reason, would lead him to found a state; and to derive from this "mythical" rational act of choice a valid, rational reason for obeying, or reforming, the state as it now is. By contrast, medieval thought, like modern thought, is neither concerned with a myth of the state, nor to base the fact of political obedience upon this myth. Both regard it as impossible to extrapolate and isolate man in such a way. Political society exists concretely: whether because of God, or history, does not matter; it is there. Above all, the link between the individual and the state cannot be limited to a rational obligation. As it exists, in fact, it is mysterious. We are linked to political society by something that somehow escapes our immediate consciousness: by a whole tangled skein of pressures and motives, some rational, many more not so. It is the nature of this tangled skein that perplexed medieval, as it now perplexes modern, thinkers. A man just finds himself in a situation in which men, for all the world like himself, are in a position to kill him, or to order him to kill others. Should this be so? Is it worth it? Is it right? In what circumstances may it be resisted? By what means may it be controlled? Thus, Augustine will not give us a fully-worked-out "myth." Instead, he will do something more important when dealing with an intractable reality: he will tell us where it is worthwhile looking; and, in so doing, he will direct some very bright beams indeed into crucial areas of the human situation.

For this reason, our paper will not claim to summarize the political ideas of St. Augustine:[6] rather, it will attempt to delineate the distinctive manner in which he thought; to introduce the general reader to Augustine's assumptions, to what problems he thought were important, to the particular viewpoint from which he chose to impose meaning on the "blooming, buzzing confusion" of human political society. Augustine's spontaneous reactions, therefore, as they appear at random in his sermons and letters, will often provide us with material that throws quite as vivid a light on his basic assumptions as do his professed formulations of political theory. Such a study must also, with regret, leave to one side the problem of the sources of Augustine's ideas, and their destiny throughout the middle ages; it can only claim to be a portrait, not a landscape.

The central problem of Augustine's thought is one which we all have to face: to what extent is it possible to treat man as having a measure of rational control over his political environment? The discovery that the extent of this control is limited has revolutionized political theory. Half the world is committed to some form of Marxist determinism: and the other half, far from rallying to Hobbes, Locke and Rousseau, studies Freud, the social psychologists, and the sociologists. On this point, Augustine is quite explicit: "For no one is known to another so intimately as he is known to himself, and yet no one is so well known even to himself that he can be sure as to his own conduct on the morrow. . . ."[7] This is the specifically Augustinian contribution to the problem of free will and determinism: for him, man is so indeterminate, so discontinuous, so blind in his intentions and haphazard in his attempts to communicate, that he must be determined by some forces outside the horizon of his immediate consciousness—for Augustine, of course, by God.

For this reason, one should begin studying Augustine's political theory in Book Ten of his *Confessions*, which he wrote around 397 or 400, that is, a good thirteen years before he wrote the *City of God*. Here we have Augustine's man, revealed by meditation on his own "memory," in fact on his whole inner world: "Great is this power of memory . . . a spreading, limitless room within me. Who can reach its uttermost depths? Yet it is a faculty of my soul, and belongs to my nature. In fact, I cannot totally grasp all that I am."[8] Above all, man is discontinuous: he is incapable, by himself, of maintaining a continuous moral intention: "As for the allurement of sweet smells, I am not much troubled. . . . At least, so I seem to myself; perhaps I am deceived. For that darkness is lamentable in which the possibilities in me are hidden from myself: so that my mind, questioning itself upon its own powers, feels that it cannot rightly trust its own report."[9] And, if man is discontinuous, his communication with others remains an unfathomable mystery. It is here that we can see most plainly how Augustine must invoke God to give meaning to this mystery. Communication is like putting a trunk-call through a vast telephone exchange: God is the operator, and it is He, and He only, who puts you through to what He thinks best: "For you, O Lord, the most just ruler of the universe can so act by Your secret influence upon both those who consult and those who are consulted—neither of them knowing what they do—that when a man consults he hears what it behoves him to hear, given the hidden merits of souls, from the abyss of Your just judgement. Let no man say to You: What is this? or Why is this? He must not say it, he must not say it. For he is a man."[10] Now if man cannot determine himself entirely in consciousness, in moral intention, in communication, how much less can he claim complete self-determination in politics: how can he presume to claim to impose an intention planned by his reason on that scrambling box of human wills, presided over by God. It is

typical of Augustine that he should cite the biblical text which is central to
the Christian idea of kingship throughout the middle ages and beyond—*cor
regis in manu Dei*, "the heart of the king is in the hand of God"—but that he
should deliberately complete the quotation: *"Just like a running stream*, so is
the heart of the King in the hand of God: He deflects it wherever He
wants."[11]

It is from this direction that we must approach Augustine's contribution
to the Christian doctrine of passive obedience. He is a man for whom the
delusion of self-determination appears as far more dangerous than any
tyranny: "Hands off yourself" he says. "Try to build up yourself, and you
build a ruin."[12] It is important to note the way in which this obedience is
seen to rest on the individual. Augustine makes frequent use of the crucial
passage of the thirteenth chapter of St. Paul's Epistle to the Romans: *Omnis
anima potestatibus sublimioribus subdita sit, non enim est potestas nisi a Deo:
quae autem sunt a Deo ordinatae sunt . . .*: "Let every soul be subject to the
governing powers, for there is no power but from God; these, coming from
God, are subject to His ordering."[13] This is a free translation, in Augustine's
sense. In it, the weight shifts to the last part—*quae autem sunt a Deo ordinatae
sunt*. This does not mean that the "powers that be" are divinely sanctioned in
a crude sense: it is more that they are obeyed for the sort of reasons that
would induce a man to obey any aspect of God's ordering of the world. A
man is humble before his rulers because he is humble before God. His
political obedience is a symptom of his willingness to accept all processes and
forces beyond his immediate control and understanding. Thus, he can even
accept the exercise of power by wicked men. In this, Augustine's view of
obedience is strictly analogous to his view of illness, another phenomenon
plainly beyond man's control and constantly frustrating his intentions. What
does he do, he once wrote to a friend, when he feels depressed, and cannot
preach well? *Flectamur facile ne frangamur*—"Let us bend easily, lest we be
broken." "No man plans what he should do better than one who is more
prepared not to put into action what is checked by the divine power, than he
is avid to insist on doing what is thought out by his human calculations. For
*many are the thoughts in the heart of man, but the counsel of the Lord endureth for
ever.*"[14]

Because this obedience is based upon a religious attitude, it cannot be
absolute. After all, the Christian Church had, in Augustine's opinion, grown
because of the *pia libertas*[15]—the pious independence of the martyrs, who had
refused to obey orders to sacrifice. The cult of the martyrs was the only form
of popular devotion in the Early Church; and, in Africa, the accounts of how
these "prize fighters of the Lord" had snubbed raging governors were read
from the altar on innumerable anniversaries. But we must remember that

these accounts are all courtroom scenes; and, as in a courtroom, the individual's heroic gesture is strictly cut off from the outside world. It is framed in a straightforward protocol of correct behaviour. There is no appeal to the outside world—to political movements, to mobs, to immediate action of any kind. The martyrs remain, in the minds of late Roman bishops, courageous, but, like themselves, punctilious. Occasions for disobedience do not worry Augustine: what concerns him is the correct way to express an overriding love of God. One incident shows this plainly. That thoroughly un-Augustinian body of men, Augustine's own congregation at Hippo, had lynched the commander of the local garrison. Augustine is profoundly shocked. He agrees entirely that the man was a very wicked man; that his flock had been victimized by him. But the true, humble Christian, St. Laurence, on whose martyrdom he had been preaching, had limited his disobedience to a courteous refusal to sacrifice. Such a Christian would have nothing to do with an act of arbitrary violence, against a man set above him by God, for good or ill.[16] Perhaps no thinker except Confucius has placed so great an emphasis on obedience as being produced and determined by the need to maintain an exacting standard of personal integrity and inner equilibrium; and on the need to avoid "rancour," whose ideogram, derived from a "closed up heart," plays such a part in the opening columns of the *Classic of Filial Piety*.[17]

An acute sense of the spiritual dangers of excessive claims to self-determination lies at the root of Augustine's doctrine of passive obedience: and it forms a somewhat oppressive feature of his political activities as a bishop. But it is only the negative facet of a positive doctrine. It is the positive doctrine of *ordo*—of the divine order of the universe—that predominates in the *City of God*. Man cannot claim complete self-determination because of his place in the divine order of things: in that order, he is tuned to one pitch and to one pitch only.[18]

We need only look around us to be surprised by the beauty of this order: "*Omnis ordo a Deo*: All order is from God. We must admit that a weeping man is better than a rejoicing earthworm. But I could still expatiate in praise of the earthworm. Consider his shining complexion, his rotund body, the perfect way in which his top fits his middle, and his middle, his tail end; how, in his humble way, all his parts strive to make up a united whole. There is no single part of him so formed as not to harmonize with the proportions of any other."[19] But man, unlike the earthworm, is an extremely complicated and notoriously erratic being. Above all, he is capable of a bewildering variety of loves. In his sermons, Augustine's men appear, not as "dust and ashes," but as sturdy sinners, whose capacity to enjoy what they do strikes him as quite natural. "The world," he says, "is a smiling place."[20] Little wonder, then, that it is enjoyed immoderately. The tenacity of their affections amazes him: think of highwaymen, tortured because they will not reveal the names of their accomplices. "They could not have done this without a great capacity for love."21 Augustine is acutely aware of the juxtaposition of these two elements. On the one hand, there is the self-evidence of a divine order of supreme beauty, to be contemplated in nature and in the absolute certainties of the laws of thought: on the other hand, the fact that, in this beautiful universe, the human soul tends to disperse itself in a baffling multiplicity of intense but partial loves. Such human loves only hint at a lost harmony: and it is the reestablishment of this harmony, by finding man's proper place and rhythm, that constitutes, for Augustine, the sum total of Christian behaviour.

Augustine's moral thought, therefore, is devoted to the reestablishment of a lost harmony. Because of this, human action is judged in terms of its relations. A good action is one that is undertaken in the light of a relation to a wider framework: the word *referre*, "to refer," or "relate," is central to Augustine's discussion of human activity; and for Augustine, of course, this human activity, of whatever kind, can only reach fulfillment when it can take its place in a harmonious whole, where everything is in relation to God.22

It is from this direction, then, that Augustine approaches problems of political behaviour in a Christian ruler. The exercise of power, the establishment of order, the administration of punishment, and the fighting of wars have their place in the order of human loves and human needs: Augustine is the last man to ignore their existence. Along with art and learning, political activity is among the "great things" that human beings just do keep on doing with characteristic intensity.23 In Book Five of the *City of God*, the problem of political activity is dealt with at length in this fashion. To Augustine, his present age of Christian emperors is different from the pagan past, because the Christian emperors are aware of this true harmony, and the pagans were not. In Augustine's treatment of them, the ancient Romans emerge as undeniably heroic figures: Augustine plainly regarded them with the same sort of intense ambivalence as we now regard our own Eminent Victorians. But they were utterly unaware of the true nature of man's harmony. Instead, they set about establishing their own. It was a harmony based upon rigid self-control: they cowed their lesser vices with a stupendous pride and by a love of praise that led to exemplary public conduct.24 They had their reward. God allowed them to conquer lesser men and to establish a remarkable city; but it was a mere *forma*—a perfect, but dead, shell.25 God, who laughs the proud to scorn (with a rather bloody-minded humour characteristic of African authors), had used all this feverish activity to spell out words in a language which the old Romans could not have understood; they were to provide stirring examples of fortitude to inspire

Christian martyrs and the dispirited members of the "redeemed family," the Church,[26] "while they themselves conduct their own cases down below—whether successfully or not, is not at all relevant."[27] Thus, the pagan empires of the past grew, prospered, and fell for reasons of which the protagonists were entirely unconscious; from the point of view of God they were the incidental by-product of an experiment which, to put it mildly, has little to do with political theory.

With a Christian ruler the picture changes dramatically, to an historian, somewhat unconvincingly. Augustine's summary of the virtues of a Christian prince, and his portraits of Constantine and Theodosius, are, in themselves, some of the most shoddy passages of the *City of God*.[28] But in the framework of Augustine's ideas they are quite explicable. The Christian ruler differs from the pagan, not in the amount of power he wields, nor in the nature of the state which he maintains; he differs only in his awareness of where this power stands in God's order, to what it is related, what ends it may serve.[29] Above all, he will admit no illusion as to the ultimate source of what Augustine would have us regard as the by no means despicable "consolations"[30] of political success. In Book Five of the *City of God*, Constantine, the first Christian prince, appears very much as he appears on his coins: decked out in the massive finery of his imperial robes, but with his eyes raised to Heaven.[31]

By now it should be plain that what we call Augustine's political thought gravitates around problems of man's behaviour in politics. The Christian subjects to whom he preached, and the Christian officials to whom he wrote advice, were not, for Augustine, "natural political animals"; they were men faced with a whole range of aims and objects of love, of which those created by living in political society were only some among many others. They reacted to these aims not because they lived in a particular type of state, but because they were particular types of men. Put briefly, Augustine's political theory is based upon the assumption that political activity is merely symptomatic: it is merely one way in which men express orientations that lie far deeper in themselves. The Christian obeys the state because he is the sort of man who would not set himself up against the hidden ways of God, either in politics or in personal distress. The Christian ruler rules as he does because he is humble before God, the source of all benefits.

These remarks on the duties of the subject and the quality of the Christian ruler were welcome at the time. They showed that Christian ethics could absorb political life at a moment when pagans had begun to fear that Christianity had proved itself incompatible with Roman statecraft. They influenced the middle ages profoundly, because they provided a totally Christian criterion of political action in an unquestioningly Christian society.

They do not, however, exhaust Augustine's thought on the state: they provide no answer to the question of why this form of political life exists at all. Indeed, in Augustine's opinion, one swallow did not make a summer. When he wrote the *City of God*, he was convinced of the collective damnation of the human race, with the exception of a small few, predestined to be "snatched" from that "damned lump." The symptoms, therefore, which tend to predominate in his description of human political activity can only be thought of as symptoms of a disease. The roots of this disease go very deep indeed: it is first diagnosed, not even in Adam, but in the Fall of the Angels. The most blatant symptom of this Fall is the inversion of the harmonious order established by God.[32]

It is characteristic of Augustine that he should regard the most basic relationship in the divine order as one of dependence,[33] and so the most basic symptom of the dislocation of this order, as one of domination—of the need to secure the dependence of others.[34] Augustine's own sense of personal dependence on God is particularly acute, it provides what is, perhaps, the sharpest note in his *Confessions*: "Let the proud of heart deride me, and all who have never been brought low and broken by Thee unto salvation. . . . For, without Thee, what am I but a guide to my own destruction? Or at my best what am I but an infant suckled on Thy milk and feeding upon Thee. . . . What indeed is any man, seeing that he is a man? . . ."[35] For such a man, the only Fall could be one that upset this relationship of omnipotence and dependence. Thus, first the Devil, then Adam, chose to live on their own resources; they preferred their own *fortitudo*, their own created strength, to dependence upon the strength of God.[36] For this reason, the deranged relationships between fallen angels and men show themselves in a constant effort to assert their incomplete power by subjecting others to their will.[37] This is the *libido dominandi*, the lust to dominate, that was once mentioned in passing by Sallust, as an un-Roman vice, typical of aggressive states, such as Assyria, Babylon, and Macedon;[38] and was fastened upon by Augustine as the universal symptom *par excellence* of all forms of deranged relationships, among demons as among men. Seen in this bleak light, the obvious fact of domination, as a feature of political society, could make the world of states appear as a vast mental hospital, ranging from the unhealthy self-control of the early Romans to the *folie de grandeur* of a Babylonian tyrant. This was a bitter pill, which many lay rulers were forced to swallow in later ages. But, as always with Augustine, the outward expression of this "lust" in the form of organized states is merely a symptom. The extent, and even the admitted injustice of the state-building that Augustine observed, and commented on in blistering terms, was of purely secondary importance. A *libido*, for Augustine, was a desire that had somehow got out of control: the real problem, therefore, was why it had got out of control, what deeper dislocation this lack of moderation reflected. So, to say, as Lord Acton would, that "all power tends to corrupt, and absolute power corrupts absolutely," would have struck Augustine as being rather like saying that a man got measles from having spots.

We emphasize this aspect of Augustine's thought because we tend to treat the state in isolation. But this is something which Augustine never did, at any time. The object of his contemplation, the aspect of human activity that he sought to make intelligible and meaningful, is not the state: it is something far, far wider. For him, it is the *saeculum*. And we should translate this vital word, not by "the world," so much as by "existence"—the sum total of human existence as we experience it in the present, as we know it has been since the fall of Adam, and as we know it will continue until the Last Judgement.[39]

For Augustine, this *saeculum* is a profoundly sinister thing. It is a penal existence, marked by the extremes of misery and suffering,[40] by suicide,[41] madness,[42] by "more diseases than any book of medicine can include,"[43] and by the inexplicable torments of small children.[44] It is also marked by a disquieting inanity. Like a top set off balance, it wobbles up and down without rhyme or reason. Huge states can just happen, "like a passing mist";[45] a gang of slaves almost overturns the Roman Republic at its height;[46] elderly bishops, vowed to poverty, are tortured by their conquerors for buried treasure they have no part in.[47] There are no verbs of historical movement in the *City of God*, no sense of progress to aims that may be achieved in history.[48] The Christians are members of a far country. Even to call them "pilgrims" somewhat weakens the impact of Augustine's terminology: they are *peregrini* in the full classical sense; they are registered aliens, existing, on sufferance, *in hoc maligno saeculo*. Above all, they are in the *saeculum*, as in a vast experimental laboratory: to bring this point home, Augustine uses the familiar image of an olive press, squeezing the olives for oil.[49] The religious life of all members of the Christian Church is quite inconceivable for Augustine without this constant *pressura*—this constant pressing—inside the *saeculum*. It is important to note this. A whole study of the relations between the Catholic Church and society might be written around changes in the meaning of this one word, *saeculum*. For Augustine, it is all-embracing and inescapable: for other writers, it can become narrow, it can stand for a "lay world" outside the Church, as a sort of primeval swamp of unregenerate politics that demands reclamation by the Catholic Church. This last view would contradict Augustine's most firmly held assumptions on the religious life: the true Christian was here to be pressed in the selfsame press as the bad; to suggest anything else would be like suggesting that, in our experimental laboratory, the guinea pigs should take over control of the tadpoles.[50]

The most obvious feature of man's life in this *saeculum* is that it is doomed
to remain incomplete.[51] No human potentiality can ever reach its fulfillment
in it; no human tension can ever be fully resolved. The fulfillment of the
human personality lies beyond it; it is infinitely postponed to the end of time,
to the Last Day and the glorious resurrection. Whoever thinks otherwise,
says Augustine: "understands neither what he seeks, nor what he is who seeks
it."[52]

For Augustine, human perfection demands so much, just because human
experience covers so very wide an area, a far wider area than in most ethical
thinkers of the ancient world. It includes the physical body: this dying,
unruly thing cannot be rejected, it must be brought into its proper place and
so renewed.[53] It includes the whole intense world of personal
relationships:[54] it can only be realized, therefore, in a life of fellowship, in a
*vita socialis sanctorum*.[55] It is inconceivable that such claims can be met in
this world; only a morally obtuse man, or a doctrinaire, could so limit the
area of human experience as to pretend that its fulfillment was possible in this
life. Thus, in opening his nineteenth book of the *City of God* by enumerating
and rejecting the 288 possible ethical theories known to Marcus Varro as "all
those theories by which men have tried hard to build up happiness for
themselves actually within the misery of this life,"[56] Augustine marks the end
of classical thought. For an ancient Greek, ethics had consisted of telling a
man, not what he ought to do, but what he could do, and, hence, what he
could achieve.[57] Augustine, in the *City of God*, told him for what he must
live in hope. It is a profound change. In substituting for the classical ideal of
an available self-perfection, the idea of a man, placed as a stranger in an
uncomprehending land, a man whose virtue lies in a tension towards
something else, in hope, in faith, in an ardent yearning for a country that is
always distant, but made ever-present by the quality of his love, that "groans"
for it, Augustine could well be called the first Romantic. Thus we should
never isolate Augustine's reflections on the state and society. They are part of
an anxious search for at least some echo, for some stunted analogy, that might
lead men, in the misery of this life, to share with him some appreciation of
the fulfilment of the human being that will be achieved beyond the *saeculum*.
Anyone who reads the whole of Book Nineteen of the *City of God*—and it can
be done with a most intelligent translation in Barrow's *Introduction to St.
Augustine, The City of God*—will realize this immediately. It will be a salutary
lesson in the true perspective of Augustine's thought.

Augustine attempts deliberately and persistently to see in human society
the expression of the most basic and fundamental human needs. For only
when he has hit upon what is truly fundamental in this life, can he feel that he

has caught a partial hint of how these needs will reach fulfilment in his "most glorious City." For this reason, he is impatient with classical Roman theories of the state: these exclude too much of the realities of human behaviour. Augustine's political theory, therefore, is marked by the search for an all-embracing lowest common denominator of human needs that seek realization in social life. It is concerned with what is fundamental.

He finds this fundamental need in the human desire for peace. "So great a good is peace," he writes, "that even in earthly and mortal conditions to hear of it is pleasant, and nothing more desirable can be desired, nothing better, in fact, can be found. I should like to speak a little longer about this, and I think I shall not burden the reader: I do it because peace is the end of the city which I am describing, and also because of its inherent attractiveness, since peace is dear to all of us."[58] This *pax*, for Augustine, means far more than tranquillity, unity, and order. These things are only preconditions for its attainment. For Augustine, the obverse of peace is tension—the unresolved tension between body and soul and man and man, of which this life is so full. Peace, therefore, is the avoidance, and in its final form, the resolution of these tensions. Such a meaning of peace is characteristic of Augustine. He was a sensitive man, with an acute sense of violence and tension. His concern with peace as something absolutely fundamental to human happiness made him welcome any feature of organized society that might at least cancel out some of those tensions of which he was so intensely conscious.[59]

For this reason, Augustine could accept the domination of man over man that had arisen from the Fall. This domination at least cancelled out certain tensions: although at a terrible cost, as anyone who has witnessed judicial torture and executions would admit if he had any sense of human dignity.[60] But at least an ordered hierarchy of established powers can canalize and hold in check the human lust for domination and vengeance. For Augustine, like Hobbes, is a man for whom a sense of violence forms the firmest boundary stone of his political thought. The North Africa of his age was a notoriously "tough" province. Augustine narrowly escaped assassination by his ecclesiastical rivals.[61] What Augustine feels particularly acutely is the manner in which violence is a two-way affair, as demoralizing for the avenger as for the victim.[62] It is this that shocks him in the lynching of the commander of the garrison at Hippo. *Ordinata est respublica* he says: "The state is an ordered affair"; if he was wicked, let him be executed by a properly vested, impersonal authority, and not by the most degrading of all forms of action for all who take part in it, *privata licentia*, taking the law into one's own hands by mob violence.[63] It is a deep-seated and lasting anxiety. We in England, who can only bring ourselves to kill a man by hanging him decently in impersonal surroundings, are the direct heirs of this, Augustine's antiseptic theory of the state.

The weakness of Augustine's position is, of course, that it implies a very static view of political society. It is quite content merely to have some of the more painful tension removed. It takes an ordered political life for granted. Such an order just happens among fallen men. Largely because he feels he can take it for granted, Augustine can dismiss it. For him, it is a "peace of Babylon" that should only be "used" by the citizens of the Heavenly City. Like the Jews, they are "captives" in this Babylon, although they are urged, as Jeremiah urged the Jews, to *Let its peace be your peace*.[64] Even in a model prison all the inmates can do is to accept, gratefully, whatever benefits may come their way.

But this is only the most negative facet of his attitude. The structure of political society, its vested order of command and obedience, is what Augustine would take for granted: what really interested him deeply was the quality of such ordered societies, above all, the quality of the reasons for their coherence. He, therefore, rejects as too narrow the classical definition of the *respublica*: such a definition would make it appear as if political society were a mere structure designed to protect certain rights and interests. For Augustine, this misses the point. Men, because they are men, just do cohere and work out some form of normative agreement—an *ordinata concordia*. What cannot be taken for granted is the quality of this ordered life; and, for Augustine, this means the quality of the motives and aims of its individual members. "Suppose therefore," he writes, "that a different definition of *populus* is proposed . . . like this: A people is a gathering of a multitude of rational beings united in fellowship by sharing a common love of the same things. In that case, to see the character of each people, you have to examine what it loves . . . it is a better or a worse people as it is united in loving higher or lower things."[65]

This definition is typical of Augustine. It is deliberately fundamental and all-embracing. Such a definition is so wide that it could include a football crowd on a Saturday afternoon; indeed, the atmosphere of the Roman circuses, with their amazing manifestations of mob psychology, is never far from Augustine's discussion of the motives of human groups.[66] It hits upon a fundamental motive: *dilectio*, which, for Augustine, stands for the orientation of the whole personality, its deepest wishes and its basic capacity to love, and so it is far from being limited to purely rational pursuit of ends. It is dynamic: it is a criterion of quality that can change from generation to generation. "History tells us," he writes, of how the quality of the Roman Republic did change, "what were the things the Roman people loved in its earliest days, and in its later days."[67] In short, Augustine's definition deliberately focuses attention upon that "middle distance" of human habits, values, and instincts, which, far more than its structure, remains the greatest mystery of political society.

Today, perhaps, we can appreciate the importance of this shift of emphasis. Previously, it could be assumed that political theory was a matter of structure, in an almost mechanical sense. In discussing this structure, we had tended to analyse it into its component parts, and, hence, to isolate the individual on the one hand, and the state, on the other, as the only two parts whose relations are relevant to thought on political society. In fact, this isolation is a deliberately self-limiting myth. So much of our modern study in sociology and social psychology has shown the degree to which political obedience is, in fact, secured, and political society coheres by the mediation of a third party, of a whole half-hidden world of irrational, semiconscious, and conscious elements that can include factors as diverse as childhood attitudes to authority, crystallized around abiding inner figures, half-sensed images of security, of greatness, of the good life, and, on the conscious plane, the acceptance of certain values.[68] These make up an orientation analogous to Augustine's *dilectio*.

The problems which this perspective poses, therefore, cannot be ones of structure, so much as of the quality of the needs that seek expression in obedience and coherence. Viewed in such a way, the state becomes a symbol: it is one of the many moulds through which men might be led to express needs and orientations that lie deep in themselves; and the expression of these needs through an organized community provides a far more tenacious bond of obligation than the purely rational agreements of a social contract. For Augustine, this need to express loves through political society can be very sinister, just as human loves can be sinister: "the earthly (or fallen) city worships its own strength in its rulers."[69] But it can also provide his successors with the foundations of a theory of the Christian state. For, as it was expressed at the time, and in the middle ages, this emphasis on quality, on the direction of a *dilectio*, as the criterion of an organized society, appealed to very different preoccupations than that of a modern sociologist. It offered a way to re-create the link between a given form of political structure and what could be broadly called a civilization—a set of traditionally accepted values. Augustine is content, in Book Nineteen, to demonstrate that the quality of a state ultimately depends upon the values of its members; but the natural inference, drawn throughout the Augustinian tradition in the middle ages, was that the state exists precisely in order to maintain specific values, to preserve the true ends and loves dictated by the Christian religion.[70] Augustine did not draw this conclusion in the *City of God*, partly, I suspect, because he could, by that time, take such an inference for granted.

The Christian emperors of his generation had made the possibility of an

official Christian state seem quite natural to Augustine. They were proud to
be "limbs of the Church" as well as Roman emperors.[71] They indulged in
spectacular acts of piety, the penance of Theodosius before St. Ambrose, told
in a surprising number of Christian sources, had already begun a popular
image of Christian kingship that would have a long future.[72] Above all, they
had suppressed pagans and heretics. Augustine was deeply involved in this
last change. He is the only bishop in the early Church whom we can actually
see evolving, within ten years, towards an unambiguous belief that Christian
emperors could protect the Church by suppressing its rivals. He is the only
writer who wrote at length in defence of religious coercion; and he did this
with such cogency and frequency that he has been called *le prince et patriarche
des persécuteurs.*[73]

        Augustine is also a crucial figure in the symbiosis between bishop and
politician that is the most obvious feature of fifth-century life.[74] The
provincial governors who came from Ravenna to Carthage, most of them
good, Catholic Christians, would have found themselves obliged both to
praise "the solicitude of the bishops" in massive edicts against heretics, and,
from 415 onwards, they were expected to read presentation copies of
instalments of the *City of God*. Augustine could write to one such man: "I
tell you this: If your administration, inspired as it is by the qualities I have
just mentioned, is limited to the one aim that men should suffer no
inconveniences in their material life, and if you do not think that it is your
business to be concerned with the end . . . to which they relate this quiet, that
is, to put it bluntly, how they should worship the true God, in Whom lies the
fulfilment of all quiet in this life, all such hard work on your part cannot
advance you to the blessed life. . . ."[75] Here we have, already in Augustine's
correspondence, the subtle and all-important difference between reading the
*City of God* for oneself, and being told it by a bishop. In later centuries, in a
society where the external role of the Church will become more explicit,
Augustine's subtle, dynamic doctrine in which values form a field of forces,
linking what men really want in their hearts with what they want from a
state, will settle down as a static hierarchy of duties. In the letter of Pope
Gregory the Great to Queen Brunhilde, the *dilectio* of Augustine has become,
quite simply, *dilectio sacerdotum,*[76] and "love," "love of the see of S. Peter."[77]

        Augustine would not have said this. We are left with a dichotomy: an
acute awareness of the actual condition of man in this *saeculum*; and a
yearning for a City far beyond it. Augustine never overcame this dichotomy.
And for this reason, his most considered reflections on political society, as
they appear in the *City of God*, are no more than the anxious questioning of a
shadow; they are a hint of a full peace and of a full realization of hidden loves,
in the Heavenly Jerusalem, whose name signifies "*Visio pacis.*" In a sermon

which he preached at Carthage in the same year as he sat down to write the *City of God*, we can see, better than anywhere else, the force and the true direction of the momentum that led Augustine to pile up this great work for future ages to puzzle on: "When, therefore, death shall be swallowed up in victory, these things will not be there; and there shall be peace—peace full and eternal. We shall be in a kind of City. Brethren, when I speak of that City, and especially when scandals grow great here, I just cannot bring myself to stop."[78]

# Notes

†Reprinted, by permission of the author and publisher, from *Trends in Medieval Political Thought*. Ed. Beryl Smalley. Oxford: Basil Blackwell, 1965. Ch. 1, 1–21. (Original title: "Saint Augustine") Rpt. in *Augustine: A Collection of Critical Essays*. Ed. Robert A. Markus. New York: Doubleday, 1972. Pp. 311–35.

[1]"Mentitur qui te totum legisse fatetur,
   Aut quis cuncta tua lector habere potest?"
Lines placed above the cupboard containing the works of Augustine in the library at Seville. Migne, *Patrologia Latina*, 83 col. 1109, cf. Possidius, *Vita Augustini*, xviii, 9.

[2]See H. I. Marrou, *St. Augustine and his influence through the ages* (Men of Wisdom), New York-London, 1957, for a succinct summary of Augustine's life, thought and influence, and a full table of the usual editions and of English translations of his works, pp. 183–86. C. Andresen, *Bibliographia Augustiniana*, Darmstadt, 1962, is a full bibliography, and E. Lamirande, "Un siècle et demi d'études sur l'ecclésiologie de S. Augustin," *Revue des Etudes augustiniennes*, viii, 1, 1962, 1–124, covers exhaustively all studies of Augustine's views on Church and State. Of innumerable editions and translations of the *De civitate Dei*, the best edition is in the *Corpus Christianorum*, Series Latina, xlvii and xlviii, 1955 (cited here by book, chapter, line and page), and the best bilingual text, that of the *Bibliothèque augustinienne*, vols. 33–36. R. H. Barrow, *Introduction to St. Augustine, The City of God*, London, 1950, contains a summary, commentary and thoughtful translations of select passages, to all of which I am particularly indebted.

[3]*Gloriosa dicta sunt de te, civitas Dei*, Ps. lxxxvi, 3. Augustine deliberately chose this title, rather than the classical word for a just community, *res publica: De civ. Dei*, ii, 21, 116 (p. 55).

[4]Augustine's qualities as a writer, and the literary taste of his age, have been brilliantly characterized by H. I. Marrou, *St. Augustin et la fin de la culture antique*, Paris, 1938, esp. pp. 39–76 (with handsome modifications, pp. 665–72). J. C. Guy, *Unité et structure logique de la "Cité de Dieu,"* Paris, 1961, is an excellent introduction to the shape of the work.

[5]*De civ. Dei*, xix, 21, 2 (p. 687), of a promise made in ii, 21 (pp. 52–55), transl. Barrow, pp. 110–18.

[6]This has been done, admirably, by J. N. Figgis, *The Political Aspects of St.*

*Augustine's "City of God,"* London, 1921, and N. H. Baynes, "The Political Ideas of St. Augustine's *"De civitate Dei,"* *Historical Association Pamphlet*, No. 104, London, 1936 = *Byzantine Studies and Other Essays*, London, 1955, pp. 288–306. See also H. A. Deane, *The Political and Social Ideas of St. Augustine*, New York-London, 1963. Recent studies have emphasized the manner in which Augustine's thought on this, and on every other subject, was constantly changing: See F. E. Cranz, "The Development of Augustine's Ideas on Society before the Donatist Controversy," *Harvard Theological Review*, xlvii, 1954, pp. 255–316, [reprinted here pp. 336–403] and B. Lohse, "Augustins Wandlung i. seiner Beurteilung d. Staates," *Studia Patristica*, vi, *Texte u. Untersuchungen*, 81, 1962, pp. 447–75.

[7]*Ep.* 130, ii, 4, transl. Dods, *The Letters of Saint Augustine*, ii, Edinburgh, 1875, p. 145.

[8]*Conf.* X, viii, 15: transl. F. J. Sheed, *The Confessions of St. Augustine*, London-New York, 1944, p. 147.

[9]*Conf.* X, xxxii, 48: transl. Sheed, p. 194.

[10]*Conf.* VII, vi, 10: transl. Sheed, p. 109.

[11]*Prov.* 21, 1, in *De gratia et libero arbitrio*, c. 42 (426/7). In this, and other passages of his late works, Augustine appears to have deliberately made a study of the political history of the Old Testament, in order to show that it was God only who controlled the outcome of the policies and conscious intentions of the protagonists: see A. M. de la Bonnardire, in *Revue des Etudes augustiniennes*, ix, 1–2, 1963, pp. 77–85.

[12]*Sermon* 169, c. 11.

[13]*Rom.* xiii, 1 ff. By a characteristic slip, Augustine, quoting from memory, once wrote "Omnis *ordo* a Deo," instead of "Omnis *potestas* . . .": *De vera religione*, xli, 77; *Retractationes*, i, 12, 8.

[14]*De cathecizandis rudibus*, xiv, 20. The citation—*Prov.* xix, 2—recurs when Augustine discusses his own dealings with the Imperial authorities on behalf of a town which had been severely punished for rioting: *Ep.* 104, iii, 11.

[15]*Contra litteras Petiliani*, II, xcii, 211.

[16]*Sermon* 302, 10–17.

[17]*Hsiao Ching*, ed. Creel, Chang and Rudolph, "Literary Chinese by the Inductive Method," Chicago, 1948, p. 68.

[18]For the complex idea of *ordo* as it affects Augustine's ethical thought, see two brilliant studies, J. Burnaby, *Amor Dei*, London, 1938, esp. pp. 113–37, and R. Holte, *Béautitude et Sagesse: St. Augustin et le problème de la fin de l'homme dans la philosophie ancienne*, Paris-Worcester (U.S.A.), 1962, esp. pp. 193–300. The essentially dynamic and interior nature of this idea is well stressed by G. Madec, in *Revue des Etudes augustiniennes*, ix, 1–2, 1963, p. 140: "Or il me semble que la spéculation augustinienne ne s'appuie sur la base statique d'un univers hierarchisé que pour s'épanouir en recherche de Dieu par l'ascension spirituelle."

[19]*De vera religione*, xli, 77.

[20]*Sermon* 158, 7.

[21]*Sermon* 169, 14.

[22]The classic summary of this idea is in *De doctrina Christiana*, I, xxii, 21; transl. D. Robertson, Saint Augustine, *On Christian Doctrine*, The Library of Liberal Arts, New

York, 1958, p. 19.

[23]*De quantitate animae*, xxxiii, 72.

[24]*De civ. Dei*, V, 13 (pp. 146-47). Characteristically, Augustine allows a classical author, Sallust, *Catilina*, vii, 6, to provide the material for this description; see F. G. Maier, *Augustin u. das antike Rom*, Stuttgart, 1955, a sound, if studiously negative treatment.

[25]*De civ. Dei*, V, 19, 50-51 (p. 155): *secundum quandam formam terrenae civitatis.* The translation of Barrow, p. 56, "if judged by the rough standards of the earthly city," misses the sharpness of the word *forma*. Cf. *Sermon*, 268, 2: a baptized Christian outside the Church is like a perfectly formed, but dead, amputated limb.

[26]*De civ. Dei*, V. 18 (pp. 151-54).

[27]*De civ. Dei*, IV. 5, 19 sq. (p. 102).

[28]Esp. the sketchy and superficial panegyric of Theodosius the Great: *De civ. Dei*, V. 26 (pp. 161-62).

[29]*De civ. Dei*, V, 24 (p. 160); transl. Barrow, pp. 58-60.

[30]*De civ. Dei*, V, 24, 6 (p. 160).

[31]*De civ. Dei*, V, 25, 1-14 (pp. 160-61). For the difficulty experienced by his first biographer, Bishop Eusebius of Caesarea, in fitting Constantine into the stereotype of a pious man, see A. D. Momigliano, "Pagan and Christian Historiography in the Fourth Century A.D.," *The Conflict between Paganism and Christianity in the Fourth Century*, ed. Momigliano, Oxford, 1963, pp. 93-94.

[32]Thus, a promise of a book dedicated to the nature of the two "cities" caused by the Fall of the Angels is contained in Augustine's commentary on Genesis: *de Genesi ad litteram*, XI, xv, 20. For this reason, I would reject, with Guy, pp. 9-10, the widespread and facile opinion that the *City of God* was provoked entirely by the Sack of Rome, in 410: a "City of God" might well have been written by Augustine without such an event.

[33]Esp. *De Genesi ad litteram*, VIII, vi, 12.

[34]Esp. *De Genesi ad litteram*, XI, xv, 20.

[35]*Confessions*, IV, i, 1: transl. Sheed, p. 45.

[36]See the massive summary in *De civ. Dei*, XII, 6, 1-14 (pp. 359-60): transl. Barrow, pp. 30-32.

[37]*De civ. Dei*, XIV, 28 (pp. 451-52): transl. Barrow, pp. 36-38.

[38]Sallust, *Catilina*, ii, 2, in *De civ. Dei*, III, 14, 50 (pp. 76-77).

[39]This aspect of Augustine's thought is made particularly clear by H. I. Marrou, *L'Ambivalence du Temps de l'Histoire chez S. Augustin*, Montreal-Paris, 1950.

[40]*De Genesi ad litteram*, XI, xxxv, 48: *omnis contritio saeculi*, above all, *De civ. Dei*, XXII, 22 (pp. 842-45).

[41]*De civ. Dei*, XIX, 4, 110-31 (pp. 666-67).

[42]*De civ. Dei*, XIX, 4, 43-61 (p. 665).

[43]*De civ. Dei*, XXII, 22, 89-94 (p. 844).

[44]See a moving passage in *Contra Julianum*, V, i, 4: "There is no other reason why the mass of Christians detest your new-fangled ideas [the Pelagian denial of collective punishment for an Original Sin] . . . but that they think of God as both the Creator of men and as absolutely just, and then witness with their own eyes the sort of agonies

suffered by their own little babies. . . ."

[45]*De civ. Dei*, IV, 5, 19 (p. 102).

[46]*De civ. Dei*, IV, 5 (p. 102).

[47]*De civ. Dei*, I, 10, 70 ff. (p. 12).

[48]Augustine's view was not shared by other Christian writers of his century: v. E. Th. Mommsen, "St. Augustine and the Christian Idea of Progress," *Journ. of the History of Ideas*, xii, 1951, 346–74 = *Medieval and Renaissance Studies*, ed. E. F. Rice, Jr., Ithaca-New York, 1959, pp. 265–88.

[49]*Sermon* 19, 6.

[50]This alternative is dismissed as irrelevant: *de Trinitate*, III, iv, 9: "But since we have not reached that state [in which 'the government and direction of human affairs are in the hands of men who are devoutly and perfectly submissive to God'] (for we must be exercised in this exile after the manner of mortal men, and be forcibly instructed by scourges in meekness and patience), let us think of that higher and heavenly country itself, from which we are separated during this exile," transl. Stephen McKenna, "Saint Augustine's *The Trinity*," Catholic University of America, Washington, D.C., 1963, p. 103.

[51]See Burnaby, pp. 53–60, for a brilliant evocation of Augustine's attitude.

[52]*De consensu Evangelistarum*, II, 20. The statement is all the more poignant as Augustine in his early days had once hoped for just such fulfilment; see Burnaby, pp. 35–36.

[53]*Sermon* 115, 15. "Take away death, the last enemy, and my own flesh shall be my dear friend throughout eternity."

[54]*De civ. Dei*, XIX, 8 (pp. 672–73): transl. Barrow, pp. 78–80.

[55]*De civ. Dei*, XIX, 5, 5–6 (p. 669): transl. Barrow, p. 70.

[56]*De civ. Dei*, XIX, 1, 4 ff. (p. 657).

[57]Max Pohlenz, *Die Stoa*, i, Göttingen, 1948, p. 111.

[58]*De civ. Dei*, XIX, 11, 26 ff. (p. 675): transl. Barrow, p. 84.

[59]"His learning is too often borrowed, and his arguments are too often his own . . .," Gibbon, *Decline and Fall*, c. xxviii, note 79. The sources of Augustine's idea of peace have been exhaustively studied by M. Fuchs, *Augustin u. der antike Friedensgedanke*, Stuttgart, 1936. But the danger of treating the history of the idea *in vacuo* is that Augustine's concern, in Book XIX, is to persuade the reader of the Resurrection as a final resolution of tensions. H. J. Diesner, "Die 'Ambivalenz' des Friedensgedankens u.d. Friedenspolitik bei Augustin," *Kirche u. Staat im spätrömischen Reich*," Berlin, 1963, 46–52, in presenting this attitude as purely static and conservative, seems to have missed the subtle alchemy by which Augustine will transform a traditional *idée reçue* by incorporating it in a novel argument.

[60]*De civ. Dei*, XIX, 6 (pp. 670–71), transl. Barrow, pp. 72–76.

[61]Possidius, *Vita Augustini*, xii, 2.

[62]*Sermon*, 302, xi. 10.

[63]*Sermon*, 302, xiv, 13–17.

[64]*Jerem.* xxix, 7 in *De civ. Dei*, XIX, 26 (pp. 695–97): transl. Barrow, pp. 126–28.

[65]*De civ. Dei*, XIX, 24, 1–3 (p. 695): transl. Barrow, p. 124, *rationalis* in this case means "possessing reason," as distinct from a herd of animals.

[66]*Confessions*, VI, viii, 13: transl. Sheed, pp. 90–91, for an acute description of this reaction of his friend, Alypius, to the gladiatoral shows—"He was no longer the man who came there, but one of the crowd to which he had come, a fit companion for those who had brought him." In *De doctrina Christiana*, I, xxix, 30: transl. Robertson, pp. 24–25, he can explain the Christian fellowship in terms of the fan-club of an actor!

[67]*De civ. Dei*, XIX, 24, 11–16 (p. 695): transl. Barrow, p. 124.

[68]Among many abstract treatments, see esp. the precise study of I. Menzies, "A Case Study of the Functioning of Social Systems as a Defence against Anxiety: A Report on a Study of the Nursing System of a General Hospital." *Human Relations*, xiii, 1960, pp. 95–121.

[69]*De civ. Dei*, XIV, 28, 7–12 (p. 451): transl. Barrow, p. 36.

[70]Esp. H. X. Arquillière, *L'Augustinisime politique*, Paris, 1955.

[71]*De civ. Dei*, V, 26, 47 (p. 162).

[72]*De civ. Dei*, V, 26, 50 ff. (p. 162).

[73]This evolution took place less abruptly and with far less hesitation than many commentators would admit. See R. Joly, "S. Augustin et l'intolérance religieuse," *Revue belge de philologie et d'histoire*, xxxiii, 1, 1955, 263–94, and P. R. L. Brown, "The Attitude of St. Augustine to Religious Coercion," *Journal of Roman Studies*, 54 (1964), pp. 107–16.

[74]P. R. L. Brown, "Religious Coercion in the Later Roman Empire: the case of North Africa," *History*, xlvii, 1963, pp. 283–305.

[75]*Ep.* 155, 10.

[76]Greg., *Reg.* VIII, 4.

[77]Greg., *Reg.* VI, 5. See Arquillière, pp. 131–41.

[78]*Ennaratio in Ps.* lxxxiv, c. 10.

# The Problem of Service to Unjust Regimes in Augustine's *City of God*†

## Peter Burnell

The ethical principles of civil life were matters of great concern to Augustine, but his opinions (actual or supposed) in this area, and two in particular, have tended to be unattractive to the contemporary mind: his undoubted support of religious persecution and his apparent willingness to regard as a duty acquiescence in the civil injustices perpetrated by established authorities.[1]

These are distinct issues, the latter being the subject of this article, but they cannot be treated quite separately. They originated near the opposite extremes of Christian civil experience—the doctrine of compliance to unjust regimes (at least from St. Peter on) in the martyred church[2]; support for religious persecution in the later, privileged church of Augustine's own time (indeed, in Augustine's own writings)—and yet it was especially in justifying religious coercion (of the Donatists) that Augustine elaborated his views on the main ethical principles of civil life.[3] Since those views must be basic to any discussion of politics in his thought, an outline of them will be necessary as a preliminary here.

Augustine's general notion of justice—which applies to any society, indeed any human enterprise—is that it consists in devotion to reunion with God and ultimately in nothing else. Injustice, therefore, consists in disordered love, and Augustine describes it as a form of lust.[4] Thus he argues the general dependence of other morality on the larger morality that is religion,[5] for in the end there is no distinction between religion and morals, religion subsuming all.[6] This is the somewhat abstract notion implied by a number of passages in the *City of God*. The idea was, however, already established in his thought in a more concrete form, as specifically civil justice; for a few years earlier, in 408, in the middle of the long struggle against the Donatists, he had applied it politically in a letter which in effect builds a full-scale defense of the suppression of that sect, on the grounds that enforcing communion in the Catholic faith is the most important part of civil justice.[7] Many former Donatists, he says, are now grateful for having been coerced into the Catholic church. To have tried to stop that persecution would have been to interrupt a rescue operation.[8] Similarly, he argues, more good would be done by taking food from a hungry man than by leaving it in his reach, if by satiety he would grow oblivious to morals. This concerns priorities in governmental morality. It assumes that, other things being equal, distributive justice would lead one, for example, to let a hungry man have his food; but distributive justice is not in its own sealed compartment; so spiritual salvation can and, where threatened, does outweigh it (moral matters here again being subsumed under spiritual). Religion, provided it be true religion, thus has complete priority for him in civil affairs.[9]

Also, though in a more limited way, civil affairs have a bearing on religion. Although Augustine makes clear in the *City of God* that salvation does not necessarily depend on our living under any particular kind of government, he also makes clear that civilizations can be immoral and that their moral condition is of spiritual importance.[10] He describes the decline in the mores of antediluvian man as a decline in civilization: the first *civitas* was itself tainted, having been founded by Cain after he had killed Abel. It then went from bad to worse morally and by a process of social involvement (*concretio*) infected the originally wholesome line that stemmed from Seth.[11] As a result, most human beings were rejected by God and destroyed in the Flood.[12] That, one is led to conclude, is what comes from allowing oneself to be involved in the injustice of one's own society: one's relationship with God is jeopardized.

So the unity of religion and morality (here morality in a civil form) cuts the other way, too: the immorality of civilization can pollute people in their religion. Some human beings survived the Flood. What had been destroyed was Cain's rotten civilization and those who had rotted in it or from its effects. Thus in the *City of God* Augustine interprets human moral life (again in a continuum with religion) in partly civil terms. For rhetorical reasons his concern in this passage is only with the negative side of the connection. When reaffirming his support for coercion of the Donatists during the same period, however, he uncovers the positive side of the connection: in the letter he wrote in 417 to the Roman commander Boniface he says that kings of the earth should serve God not only as men but as kings (*in quantum sunt reges*) and that their proper way to do that is by institutionalizing religious truth at the civil level.[13] Sometimes, then, religious duty must be done by civil means.

On Augustine's thinking after about 400 the view taken here is an unconventional one. R. A. Markus has argued that in Augustine's later writings the state is secular, having no proper part in either of the two spiritually constituted "cities."[14] But though, as Markus says, the middle-aged Augustine spoke increasingly of kings rather than kingdoms, verbally down-playing the institution of the state in such contexts, the passage just mentioned says that kings in so far as they are kings have the unique duty of enforcing Christian orthodoxy, which is to say they have that duty in virtue of their kingdoms. Hence, while not denying that there is considerable further complexity in this area, one may conclude that even as late as 417 he was thinking of the state as properly an instrument of the church.[15]

While retaining this opinion, Augustine was no political perfectionist as he grew older. As Markus points out, by the time he came to favor religious persecution (that is, by 408), he had left behind his quasi-messianic, "Eusebian" idealism about Christian emperors.[16] Its place was taken, however, not only by pessimism but also by a more serviceable kind of optimism based on experience. The successful suppression of the Circumcellion terrorists and the spectacle of genuine conversions resulting from persecution had convinced him to reverse his political position and support religious coercion.[17] He came to favor a certain bluff governmental pragmatism in dealing with heretics and saw this as precedented in the methods God himself had followed with the recalcitrant children of Israel, buffeting the chosen people with privations and testings: the Roman state was doing the same for the Donatists.[18]

Yet that pragmatism raises our main question. A civil regime might provide some sort of wholesome moral and religious structure but still leave much to be desired in that respect. Given some possibility of political influence, what, if anything, should be done about the ways in which such a state falls short in this most important function (to help its citizens towards salvation)? Would Augustine's pragmatism extend only to swallowing one's moral distaste and allow no political opposition aimed at further improvement for that vital purpose?

The question is problematic, not immediately and straightforwardly answerable, as it is widely thought to be. Two of Augustine's disquisitions in the *City of God*, on the nature and origins of civil society, are especially important here.[19] These passages not only crystallize in a developed form some of the general notions outlined above but reveal three convictions of Augustine's which, taken together, make the nature of the problem clear. The first is that injustice is unavoidably part of civil life: for Augustine the consequences of original sin are always the underlying human problem, and affect civil affairs as they do all areas of experience. Because of our inherited moral enfeeblement, all civil societies will be unjust in some degree. He did not think that the establishment of a Christian empire by Constantine and Theodosius had fundamentally changed that: the label "Catholic" is not a guarantee of perfect civil justice. All civil life is lived in the middle ground between perfection, stopping well short of perfection, and utter chaos.[20]

The second conviction is that we human beings, though morally crippled and in any case having as our deepest need a beauty and order beyond this world, still have civil duties. One must officiate in a law court, for instance, when called upon. The fact that such duties must be performed in the midst of an iniquitous system—for horrible things, he points out, happen in a law court—does not mean that we may run away from them. "Human society constrains him [the wise man] and sets him plainly to his duty. To desert human society he considers unspeakable wickedness [*nefas*]."21

The third conviction is that despite the effects of original sin, civilization is susceptible of moral improvement. Augustine points out, for instance, that it can respond sensitively to natural law, as when innate human decency impelled later communities to put a legal ban on marriage between cousins, which earlier communities had to allow.22 It can also be improved by specifically Christian influence.23 (The entire work is, of course, a defence of the wholesomeness of Christianity's influence on the Roman empire.) Thus, despite the Fall, civilizations can make some moral progress at both natural and supernatural prompting. The middle ground of imperfect order that they occupy is still fertile with moral potentiality.

In the light of his general views these three convictions of Augustine's bring to the fore the dilemma of ethical principle that concerns us here: although it is spiritually disastrous to cooperate with the working of civil injustice (witness the fate of antediluvian man), one is supposed to cooperate in civil affairs, which even at the best of times entail the working of injustice. The problem is how, or whether, to avoid complicity. Should one oppose injustice by changing the system where one can? Or should one accept the complicity after all? One must do one or the other, for of the three logical possibilities—cooperating, opposing, or abstaining—abstaining is not an option: while not necessarily refusing all excuses, Augustine has refused the permanent ubiquity of social injustice as an excuse for permanent retreat from public life. Thus we are morally doomed, as we do our civil duties, to help injustice along unless opposition can be one of those duties.

Failure to face this consequence has meant that the solutions offered by the commentators who have discussed the problem do not actually work as solutions. For example, the distinction between absolute and relative natural law, which according to E. L. Fortin is Augustine's own solution, has some relevance but does not quite touch the point at issue.24 Painful and loathsome deeds are not necessarily immoral ones. To say that in an imperfect world one should sometimes resort to actions that in an ideal world one would always avoid addresses the general fact that we have melancholy duties, not the particular danger that some of them might also involve immorality. That still, therefore, leaves us with the dilemma. E. TeSelle's conclusion, that Augustine sees the church as having a duty of reforming the state, is correct, but on the particular point it begs the question.25 What norms would govern the means of reform? If, for instance, the only admissible means were preaching and example, the dilemma facing people as they do their civil duties would still be untouched. Given Augustine's presuppositions, the only resolution, short of capitulation, that would not avoid the issue would be to give general moral permission to intend reform or possibly to attempt revolution, depending on what might be necessary or feasible: that is, permission not to give perfect acceptance to the *status quo*.

It is precisely this that Augustine is commonly described as flatly refusing to countenance. "All men must give absolute obedience to God's ministers, the kings and rulers of this earth, no matter how impious or wicked they may be." That is H. A. Deane's account of Augustine's position.26 P. R. L. Brown, in an essentially similar account, politely points out the deficiency: that such a "very static view of political society" is "the weakness of Augustine's position," which, he says, "takes an ordered political life for granted."27 Though mildly phrased, this is a serious criticism. In the context of Augustine's thought, it involves the suggestion that for him it is acceptable to get one's hands morally dirty in certain kinds of human relationship, as long as one keeps one's heart religiously pure. There would be a form of cynical dualism here. The prevailing consensus is that, nevertheless, that is what Augustine thought. Henry Chadwick succinctly summarizes this accepted view: "The follower of Christ would render Caesar the obedience of his body, and to God that of his mind and soul."28

On other grounds, however, it would be surprising if Augustine took quite this position. It violates the principle of the unity of religion and morality. In his *Expositio on Romans* (written at about the time he became a bishop) the interpretation of the Pauline "be subject to the powers that be"—we must obey civil powers because we must not discard responsibilities originating in our having bodies—is part of an anti-dualistic argument.29 Furthermore, in his ninety-third letter the case for religious coercion by the state rests partly on the notion that spiritually weak people, when assailed by an unjust regime, are vulnerable to its mischievous spiritual effect.30 The coercion was thus an urgent need. Neither passage suggests a rigidly doctrinaire limitation on what is politically allowable, given the grave importance of the cause.

The scholarly consensus must therefore be looked at more closely, to see whether it has adequate grounds and gives a complete account of Augustine's position. First, it presumably addresses only the works of Augustine's middle age and old age. As E. Portalié once pointed out, the younger, preepiscopal Augustine had, by means of a clear hypothetical example, defended the propriety of using revolution to correct civil injustice.31 Secondly, it is true that Augustine the bishop on occasion forbids opposition, let alone revolution, against civil injustice; but does he do so categorically? The debatable word in Deane's "absolute obedience to kings and rulers" is "absolute." The passage he quotes from *De Catechizandis Rudibus* (written when Augustine had been a bishop for about five years) asserts indeed that one has a duty of obedience even to a wicked tyrant but does not add or imply that the injunction is absolute.[32] This is a *secundum quid* matter, for the passage does not deal with questions such as what deeper operative principle might be revealed in a time of *stasis*, where an opportunity arose for just improvement in return for bold action. Brown's argument is that for Augustine the state exists to control certain evils of social life, thus liberating human beings for higher concerns. Once it is fulfilling that necessary but minimal role, it should be left to itself and may be taken for granted. Since it is not an instrument of justice in any greater or deeper sense, one has no right to disturb it by demanding more of it. Reason has already been given here for a different view of Augustine's thinking on this matter.[33]

However, even assuming for argument's sake that this is an accurate account of his thinking, should it be taken as held without qualification? Even if one should passively accept civil mediocrity in return for continued stability, the continued stability cannot be taken for granted: it can always break down, as Augustine was aware. He might, of course, have discounted such occasions (opportunities for radical intervention, disobedience) as unimportant. Brown argues that he did. "Occasions for disobedience," he says, "do not worry Augustine."[34] They do not always worry him. Brown cites a sermon in which Augustine condemns the lynching of a tyrannical garrison-commander in Hippo.[35] This illustrates Brown's point clearly, for it recommends martyrdom in place of such blatant law-breaking. Only duly appointed people may execute. But it is not an argument against either reform or revolution, for stopping short of addressing such possibilities is not the same as precluding them; nor does he always stop short of addressing them.

Intended audience is the important factor here. When haranguing his flock Augustine is prepared to assume the existence of settled and constant government. Hence he talks in extremes: official executions (*publica supplicia*), as opposed to open banditry (*aperta latroncinia*). In the *City of God* it is a different matter. That work was written with a far more sophisticated audience in mind, and is historically and philosophically panoramic. His discussion of civil society there is correspondingly more subtle and comprehensive. In particular, as Y.-M. Duval points out, the fall of Rome to the Goths had given Augustine's cultured pagan opponents some polemical ammunition.[36] When replying to them he must face the doctrinal implications of partial breakdown in the governmental order; now there can be no taking an ordered political life for granted. Hence, many passages in that work refer to times of political instability, radical civil change and revolution.[37] Some are of particular interest because they also touch on the principles, not merely the practices, of civil life.[38] It is in those passages, if anywhere, that Augustine may be expected to give an adequate picture of his opinions, or at least his assumptions, on the question at issue.

The first of these passages, written around 415, when he was about sixty, is part of a long survey of Roman history (Book III, chapters 15-16) demonstrating the absence of any help or supervision by the pagan gods.[39] The passage concerned is about the expulsion of the Tarquins. On one level it takes an anti-revolutionary position: Junius Brutus and his companions were imprudent to expel Tarquin and establish a republic without waiting to see how the king would respond to his citizens' grievance. But a fundamental distinction applies here between a person's own political views—a prudential matter, concerned with how ethical principles are to be applied to specific circumstances—and the ethical principles themselves (with their general grounds of application).

Our problem concerns the latter. Augustine's change of mind in favor of persecuting the Donatists illustrates the distinction. (He had long before accepted the principle, that rough measures are justified as a means to bring about the true conversions. Only on prudential grounds had he opposed the practice: he had not thought that it would actually work, and on prudential grounds he changed his mind.[40]) In this passage Augustine's own political view is that the Romans were indecent in their haste for revolution. Yet in taking that view he makes the general assumption that civil revolution is a permissible kind of action in itself. Arguing that the Romans should have waited to see involves supposing that if Tarquin had then proved callous and intransigent, revolution might then have been appropriate. This is not a logical implication but a matter of practical congruency in argumentation. If, for example, one were an outright pacifist, one would be unlikely to suggest that Chamberlain should have waited longer before declaring war, to see what Hitler's plans were after Poland.

In another passage Augustine discusses the gladiators' revolt led by Spartacus in 73 B.C.—an event demonstrating that merely having got hold of some imperial power, as Spartacus had, is not a sign of virtue.[41] In a celebrated passage in the preceding chapter Augustine has conceded that one can treat societies without reference to justice, simply as organized frameworks for people to lead their lives in, but that if one does, there will logically no longer be any essential difference between kingdoms and gangs; for with such a simple and general definition, the gap between Alexander the Great and a pirate will be a matter only of degree, as a pirate once pointed out.[42] The case of Spartacus illustrates this particularly well because by a disconcerting success he briefly filled that gap. When the empire was still new and firm, his gang of gladiators got control of a large segment of Rome's power. Thus the significant event here is not Spartacus's partial overturning of Roman rule but his partial achievement of a new one.

The wider context clarifies Augustine's purpose. A main component of his argument here (Book IV, chs. 2, 3, 5) is that God inscrutably involves His providence in the history even of unjust empires. While they last, they are the "powers that be." That even applies to Spartacus's gladiators. Were they a scurvy crew? That makes no difference, argues Augustine: look what the Romans were when they started. Did the gladiators wield great power only for a little while? Well, both Augustine and his opponents agree that an individual emperor or king is divinely helped to his exalted position; yet no individual lives very long. This argumentation makes clear that for a while Spartacus and his gladiators were, for the people they controlled, the powers that be.

Establishing that a given government is the powers that be establishes also, for anyone who takes St. Paul seriously, a presumptive duty of obedience to that government. Yet it hardly needs to be added that Augustine still thought it perfectly proper to do what one could to oppose and undermine the rule of such patent riff-raff as Spartacus's gladiators while they exercised their control. Indeed the discomfited Romans and those who supported their cause did just this with eventual success. That this is so and the principle that makes it so are clear from Augustine's assertion a few chapters later that imperial interference by Rome, invasion, destruction of other political systems, and annexation are justified as occasional moral necessities.[43] One should not desire such things for themselves, but they are justified when they prevent a greater evil, the unjust, lording it over the just. This would certainly allow for fighting and unseating Spartacus. His gladiators "indulged in whatever pleasures they wished; they did whatever lust suggested": (*usi voluptatibus quibus voluerunt, quod suggessit libido fecerunt*). Even pagan Rome, by contrast, had rightly put some limit on public depravity, as Augustine concedes later in the work.[44] We may conclude that for him Roman law, albeit built into an empire itself originally built on a lust (the *libido dominandi*), was at least committed to putting some restraint on that Protean moral disease.

Thus Roman rule was better, less incompatible with devotion to God as an end, than the regime of that licentious mob. One can speculate that Augustine might have thought the conditions decisively different if the gladiators had established stable government, but then the historical events would not have provided such an instructive middle case. The inchoate government of Spartacus is an exception (for Augustine a rare one) to the rule of obedience to the powers that be. It was too powerful to be denied the title of government, too chaotic to be taken seriously as such. Exceptions to rules show the supersession of one principle by another that more rarely applies.

The principle usually applying is obedience to the powers that be; the superseding one, the duty of trying to ensure that civil power is in the hands of the least unjust persons or groups possible; and as we have seen, Augustine proceeds to point out that this may involve overturning a regime. The passage as a whole establishes an important principle that civil justice, or rather some approximation to it, is basic to a governmental system's right to be left alone. It follows that governmental systems as such are for him not sacrosanct.

Augustine returned to the same issues in a theoretical way ten years later in two passages (Book XIX) which considerably deepen our understanding of his thinking on the matter. In the first (chapter 7) the subject of just war comes up again. In the course of ridiculing the ideal of philosophical bliss in this world, he lists the grotesque and inexorable miseries of the human condition, prominent in which is war. Foreign wars are past history, he says, but civil war within the empire is not. He now reaffirms the principle established in book IV: invasion, annexation, etc. are nothing to rejoice in, but injustice in one's adversary (*iniquitas . . . partis adversae*) justifies them. As before, there would be other pre-conditions, such as the practical usefulness of violent action (for wars are fought to attain or reestablish peace); but those are matters of prudence, of where and when. What primarily justifies such action is the enemy's injustice no matter whether the war is civil or foreign.

The importance of this principle depends on how generally one may understand it. Augustine no doubt envisages such wars mainly within the range of his experience: that is, as waged by the Roman authorities to reimpose order. But as we have seen, such circumstantial considerations are not universally determinative for him. His arguments have been quite clear: Rome had not always been big, and anyway mere size is not the crucial point. In this passage, too, he has already mentioned other kinds of wars, events of the distant past. For both those reasons we may understand his statements on just war to be general ones which are not tied to a contemporary range of manifestations. All war that is justified by Augustine's specification—war that changes a society in the direction of justice—has an obvious revolutionary dimension. Thus his point about the limits to a state's right not to be subverted is a general point.

The other passage (chapter 12) takes a theoretical position on the subject of civil unrest. In the course of a disquisition on Cacus, the monster in Virgil's *Aeneid*, Augustine compares the creature's turbulent inward condition with a civil community in *stasis*.[45] The passage illustrates the doctrine that peace is the universal motive in creatures. All that the monster, that prodigy of ferocity, ever really wanted was peace (stability and well-being). This leads to the analogy with civil life: in Cacus's internal political structure mortality has

risen up and tried to force his soul out of his body. That has caused an inward
civil emergency, and reason has had to intervene and bring about a radical
alteration in internal policy. That in turn has led to disconcerting changes in
the outward actions of this microcosmic state. The crucial point is that
mortality's original rebellion arose "out of need" (*ex indigentia*):[46] the
mortality is an unavoidable and universal fact; the need, its inevitable result in
the circumstances. The consequent revolutionary intervention of reason is on
mortality's behalf. Mortality in this analogy constitutes a number of
legitimate needs. So the whole sequence of events, culminating in Cacus's
savage acts, originates in necessities involved in staying alive (*vivendi
necessitate*). The analogy provides us with a clear and simple hypothetical
case. There is no suggestion that alternative ways were open either to Cacus's
mortality or to the frantic citizens of the analogy. Thus the comparison is
with legitimate revolution and makes no sense unless there can be a necessity
that leads a downtrodden and desperate citizenry into sedition and
legitimately causes a revolution.

In principle Augustine's view of civil life is not, therefore, static. It does
not make endless cooperation with wickedness a necessary concomitant of a
Christian's civil duties. Though a long way from the sort of "liberation
theology" that regards the Gospel as predominantly political, Augustine's
position implicitly allows for considerable development in radically
reformative or even revolutionary political directions. Such development
would of course be quite foreign to his "politics" but not to his principles.
His support for religious coercion was authoritarian. But the arguments with
which he supported that coercion are quite concordant with his openness in
principle (in both the early and late books of the *City of God*) to changing the
structure of civil society by political intervention. Indeed, thinking that civil
society should above all be an efficient instrument for changing potential
"citizens of this world" into "citizens of God" practically requires thinking
that it legitimately might be shaped to such purposes when it could be. That
this ultimately is Augustine's position shows that his thinking in this area has
more openness, more internal consistency, and also rather more constancy on
essentials than has been conventionally thought.

It is important to add that by reciprocal signification the Cacus analogy
also indicates the tendency of revolutions to have regrettable moral
consequences. Cacus's internal revolution has resulted in acts of horror.
Thus even as our original dilemma is in essence resolved a second one
immediately replaces it because of the injustice that plagues radical change in
society. This second dilemma is, however, of a different nature. There is now
no implication that we are morally bound to cooperate in wrong; merely that
we are circumstantially bound to it; for it is not that we have the duty to act

out moral failure deliberately but that, as we take what few chances for enhanced moral success civil life might occasionally offer, we are in practice almost always going to fail. Presumably that consideration would in potentially revolutionary circumstances give one serious pause; but however difficult or depressing such a dilemma might be, it is still only a prudential dilemma, not one of moral principle.

As we have seen, this distinction applies to Augustine's thought precisely because he was able to consider societies and historical periods profoundly different from his own. In an article on Augustine's political pessimism O. O'Donovan attributes that rather bleak view of politics to "Augustine's foreshortened historical perspective," which "prevented him from seeing what kinds of revolution are possible in political structures."[47] Yet the passages discussed here show both that Augustine had a clear notion of the moral terms on which political life is lived and that he knew that very different conditions could pertain (conditions foreign to his experience), where the same moral terms would demand very different kinds of action. The cause of his pessimism about politics was not foreshortened historical perspective but a steady awareness that the frustrating and demoralizing effects of original sin would persist as long as the world lasted. Not much can be done about the frustration. As for the demoralization, his picture of civil man is like that of the rower in Virgil's *Georgics*, who if he slackens for an instant will be tumbled headlong downstream.[48] One is either going to achieve little practical progress, or none. Yet it is necessary to try because resignation to the perpetuation of civil wrong is an impossible ethical luxury.

# Notes

†From *The Journal of the History of Ideas* 54 (1993): 177–88. Reprinted by permission of The Johns Hopkins UP.

[1]For criticism of the first see Peter Brown, *Augustine of Hippo. A Biography* (London, 1969), 235, 239–40, and Robert Markus, *Saeculum: History and Society in the Theology of St. Augustine* (Cambridge, 1970), 142, 150. For criticism of the second see Peter Brown, "Saint Augustine," Beryl Smalley (ed.), *Trends in Medieval Political Thought* (Oxford, 1965), 14, and Oliver O'Donovan, "Augustine's *City of God* XIX and Western Political Thought," *Dionysius*, 11 (1987), 105.

[2]1 *Pet.* 2.12–17 and 3.13–17. Cf. Augustine, *City of God* (cited as *CD*—Teubner edition [Stuttgart, 1981], 2.19).

[3]See Peter Brown, "St. Augustine's Attitude to Religious Coercion," *Journal of Roman Studies*, 54 (1964), 107–16.

[4]*CD* 5.19, 5.24, 15.4,15.7. Cf. Y. M. Duval, "L'éloge de Théodose dans la *Cité de Dieu* (V, 26.1)," *Recherches Augustiniennes*, 4 (1966), 139–43.

[5]*CD* 2.25–28. Cf. Alasdair Macintyre, *Whose Justice? Whose Rationality?* (Notre Dame, 1988), 153–55.

[6]*CD* 2.19.

[7]*Epistle* 93.2.4 (J. P. Migne, *Patrologia Latina* [cited as *PL*], 33, 323). On the dates of Augustine's writings see the chronological tables in Brown, *Augustine*.

[8]Cf. *Epistle* 173.4 (PL 33, 755).

[9]For Augustine's emphasis, in this context, on the exclusive validity of the Catholic church, see W. H. C. Frend, *The Donatist Church* (Oxford, 1971), 242.

[10]For the limited bearing of politics on religion see *CD* 5.17.

[11]*CD* 15.8, 15.22.

[12]*CD* 15.24.

[13]*Epistle* 185 (*De Correctione Donatistarum*). 5.19 (*PL* 33, 801).

[14]Markus, *Saeculum*, 144. On Augustine's emphasis on the morals of individual rulers rather than of societies see Duval 1966, 175.

[15]For an extended treatment see Peter Burnell, "The Status of Politics in St. Augustine's *City of God*," *History of Political Thought* (forthcoming).

[16]Markus, *Saeculum*, 147. Cf. Frend, *The Donatist Church*, 231. For a succinct account of Augustine's earlier, "Eusebian" views, see Alfred Schindler, "Querverbindungen zwischen Augustins theologischer und kirchenpolitischer Entwicklung, 390–400," *Thelogischer Zeitschrift*, 29 (1973), 100–101. Cf. F. Edward Cranz, "The Development of Augustine's Ideas on Society before the Donatist Controversy," *Harvard Theological Review*, 47 (1954), 305.

[17]Cf. *Retractationes* 2.5 (PL 32, 632). On the Circumcellions see Brown, *Augustine*, 335, and Neal Wood, "*Populares* and *Circumcelliones*: The Vocabulary of 'Fallen Man' in Cicero and St. Augustine," *History of Political Thought*, 7 (1986), 41–47.

[18]*Epistle* 93.2.4–5 (*PL* 33, 323).

[19]*CD* 19.6 and 15.16.

[20]*CD* 19.6.

[21]*CD* 19.6. All translations are, unless otherwise noted, those of the author.

[22]*CD* 15.16.

[23]*CD* 15.16.

[24]Ernest L. Fortin, "Idéalisme politique et foi chrétienne dans la pensée de saint Augustin," *Revue des Études Augustiniennes*, 8 (1972), 255.

[25]Eugene Teselle, *Augustine the Theologian* (London, 1970), 278.

[26]Herbert A. Deane, *The Political and Social Ideas of St. Augustine* (New York and London, 1963), 145.

[27]Brown, 1965, 14.

[28]Henry Chadwick, *Augustine* (Oxford, 1986), 103.

[29]*Expositio Quarundam Propositionum ex Epistula ad Romanos* 72 (Paula Fredriksen Landes, *Augustine on Romans* [Chico, Ca., 1982], 40–41).

[30]*Epistle* 93.6.20 (*PL* 33, 331). Cf. *Epistle* 185.1.2 (*PL* 33.793).

[31]Eugene Portalié, S. J., *A Guide to the Thought of Saint Augustine*, tr. Ralph J. Bastian, S. J. (London, 1960), 282: *De Libero Arbitrio* 1.6.14 (PL 32, 1229).

[32]Deane, *The Political and Social Ideas*, 144: *De Catechizandis Rudibus* 21.37.

[33]Again, for a more extended argument see Burnell (forthcoming).

34Brown, *Augustine*, 6.

35*Sermon* 302.11.10–19.17 (*PL* 38, 1389–92).

36See Duval, "L'éloge de Théodose," 173.

37*CD* 1.1–7, 1.10–19, 1.22–30, 1.33–35, 2.3, 2.17, 2.22, 3.15, 4.5, 4.15, 5.12, 18.20, 18.45–46, 19.7, 19.12.

38*CD* 3.15–16, 4.5, 19.7, 19.12.

39*CD* 3.1–31.

40*Epistle* 185.7.25–31 (*PL* 33, 804–7). Cf. Markus, *Saeculum*, 139.

41*CD* 4.5.

42*CD* 4.4.

43*CD* 4.15.

44*CD* 12.13.

45*CD* 19.12; Virgil, *Aeneid* 8.190–305.

46Augustine, *The City of God*, tr. Henry Bettenson (Harmondsworth, 1972), 868, misleadingly rendered "because of its insatiable desires" in the Penguin translation.

47O'Donovan, "Augustine's *City of God* XIX," 105.

48Virgil, *Georgics* 1.201–3.

# Augustine and the State:
## The Return of Order Upon Disorder†

## Herbert A. Deane

In the last chapter I analyzed Augustine's conceptions of temporal peace and earthly justice as distinguished from "true" or "real" peace and justice, found only in the City of God. We saw that although earthly peace and order are frequently disturbed by conflict, and the justice they provide is often imperfect, they are essential conditions for man's continued existence and must, therefore, be maintained by a political and legal system furnished with powers of coercion. So we come at last to the central theme—Augustine's analysis of the state, its tasks, and its powers. The state operates in this world, and most of its citizens are (and always will be) those sinful men whose characteristics we have already discussed.[1] In any earthly state a small number of the citizens may be men who have been converted by God's grace; since these men have died and been born anew, their loves, their aspirations, and their behavior are completely different from those of the great mass of the unredeemed. However, as long as this world lasts there will never be a society or a state made up solely or even predominantly of the saved. Since the two cities are inextricably bound together until the Last Judgment, every earthly state will be composed primarily of sinners, with perhaps a scattering of saints living in their midst.[2] The political and legal system must, therefore, be set up and operated on the assumption that it is dealing with fallen men. The motives upon which it relies when it makes laws and imposes penalties must be the drives that impel such men to action, and its expectations should never outrun the characteristics that they can be presumed to possess.

As we have seen, the state, for Augustine, is an external order; the peace that it maintains is external peace—the absence, or at least the diminution, of overt violence. The state is also a coercive order, maintained by the use of force and relying on the fear of pain as its major sanction for compliance to its commands. It has no weapons by which it can mold the thoughts, desires, and wills of its citizens; nor is it really concerned to exert such influence. It does not seek to make men truly good or virtuous. Rather, it is interested in their outward actions, and it attempts, with some success, to restrain its citizens from performing certain kinds of harmful and criminal acts. We have also observed that the state is a non-natural, remedial institution; like private property, slavery, and other forms of domination of man over man, it is a consequence of the Fall. It is both a punishment for sin and a remedy for man's sinful condition; without it anarchy would reign, and self-centered, avaricious, power-hungry, lustful men would destroy one another in a fierce struggle for self-aggrandizement. This external, coercive, repressive, remedial order—and its main virtue is that it *is* an order—is clearly distinguished by Augustine from the order or hierarchy found among the angels and in the whole City of God; the latter is a spontaneous order of love and not an order of coercion or domination.[3]

The reader of this brief summary of Augustine's doctrine of the state may wonder whether I am talking about Augustine, or about Hobbes or Machiavelli. Certainly, this conception of the state strikes us as essentially "modern," and we may be surprised to find it in a Christian philosopher of the fifth century. Since this formulation of the gist of Augustinian political theory is one to which some of his commentators might take exception, it will be our task to show, by explicit statements from Augustine as well as by deductions from his views of the nature of man, that it is an accurate summary and that it does not do violence to what Augustine himself says throughout the whole corpus of his writings.

Let us turn first to his discussion in *The City of God* of the definitions of a people (*populus*) and of a commonwealth or state (*res publica*) given by Scipio in Cicero's *De Republica*. He first refers to these Scipionic definitions in Book II, where he notes that according to Scipio a people is not "every assemblage or mob, but an assemblage associated by a common acknowledgment of law [i.e., an agreement about right or justice], and by a community of interests [*Populum autem non omnem coetum multitudinis, sed coetum iuris consensu et utilitatis communione sociatum esse determinat*]."[4] He promises that at a later point he will demonstrate that, according to this definition, there was never a people (*populus*) in Rome, and, consequently, that Rome was never a state or commonwealth (*res publica*), since true justice never had a place in it, and Scipio—and Cicero—has made an agreement about justice (*consensus iuris*) essential to the existence of a people and a state. This, to Augustine, is an absurd conclusion; so he adds, "But accepting the more feasible [i.e., 'more probable' (*probabiliores*)] definitions of a republic, I grant there was a republic of a certain kind, and certainly much better administered by the more ancient Romans than by their modern representatives [*Secundum probabiliores autem definitiones pro suo modo quodam res publica fuit, et melius ab antiquioribus Romanis quam a posterioribus administrata est*]."[5] To make it quite clear that no other earthly state—whether pagan or Christian, ancient or modern—possessed true justice and was therefore a commonwealth according to Scipio's definition, Augustine immediately adds: "But the fact is, true justice has no existence save in that republic whose founder and ruler is Christ [*uera autem institia non est nisi in ea re publica, cuius conditor rectorque Christus est*]."[6]

In Book XIX, Augustine fulfills his promise to return to the consideration

It is difficult to see how this interpretation fits the facts. For, in the first place, Augustine had, in Book II, promised his readers "more feasible" definitions of a "people" and a "commonwealth" to replace the Scipionic definitions. It is this promise that he now fulfills by giving a careful, precise definition from which "justice" is eliminated, so that we will have a definition of the state which can be applied to the states which exist in this world, rather than one which applies to only one commonwealth, the City of God in heaven. Second, in the quotation itself, he speaks of this new definition as "this definition of ours [*istam definitionem nostram*]." Third, the definition fits perfectly with Augustine's emphasis upon love as the determining element in human action; as we have seen,19 "my weight is my love" is the central principle of his psychological analysis. It is therefore natural and fitting that he should define and differentiate states by reference to the different objects of love which the members of each state pursue. Fourth, and perhaps most important, the definition is repeated in all its essentials in a number of other places in Augustine's writings.20

It is significant that Augustine nowhere makes the distinction between heathen and Christian states that is central to McIlwain's argument.21 At no time does he say—or suggest—that while pagan states could not possibly exhibit true justice Christian states necessarily are, or at least may be, truly just. When he speaks of the possibility that all or most of the members of a state—rulers and subjects—might actually behave like Christians, he always uses the form of a condition contrary to fact; for example,

> If the kings of the earth and all the peoples, if the princes and all the judges of the earth, if young men and maidens, old and young, every age, and both sexes; if they whom John the Baptist addresses, the tax collectors and the soldiers, *were all together to hear and observe* [*audirent atque curarent*] *these precepts* [of the Christian religion] regarding justice and honesty of character, *then would the republic* [*res publica*] *adorn the lands of this life with its own felicity*, and mount the pinnacle of life eternal to reign most blessedly. But *because* this man listens, and that man scoffs, and *most are enamored of the evil blandishments of vice rather than of the beneficial severity of virtue, the servants of Christ*—whether they be kings or princes or judges, soldiers or provincials, rich or poor, bond or free, male or female—*are enjoined to endure even the most wicked and most vicious commonwealth, if so it must be* [*tolerare Christi famuli iubentur . . . etiam pessimam, si ita necesse est, flagitiosis-simamque rem publicam*], that so they may by this endurance purchase for themselves an eminent place in that most holy and august parliament of the angels and in the celestial republic, where the will of God is law [*caelestique re publica, ubi Dei uoluntas lex est*].22

It is clear that Augustine is here speaking of his own period, when the Empire is "Christian," and not of the pagan past or of the period of the persecution of

of the Scipionic definitions of a "people" and a "commonwealth." Again he notes that, according to Scipio, "a common acknowledgment of right [*consensus iuris*]" is essential to the existence of a people and of a commonwealth; this means

> that a republic cannot be administered without justice. Where, therefore, there is no true justice there can be no right. . . . Thus where there is not true justice there can be no assemblage of men associated by a common acknowledgment of right, and therefore there can be no people, as defined by Scipio or Cicero; and if no people, then no weal of the people [*res populi*], but only of some promiscuous multitude unworthy of the name of people. Consequently . . . most certainly it follows that there is no republic where there is no justice.7

After citing the traditional definition of justice as "that virtue which gives every one his due,"8 Augustine proceeds again to show that true justice was never present in the Roman commonwealth, whether we look at its early, heroic period or its later phase of decay and degeneration. "Where, then, is the justice of man, when he deserts the true God and yields himself to impure demons? Is this to give every one his due?"9 If a man does not serve God,

> what justice can we ascribe to him, since in this case his soul cannot exercise a just control over the body, nor his reason over his vices? And if there is no justice in such an individual, certainly there can be none in a community composed of such persons. Here, therefore, there is not that common acknowledgment of right which makes an assemblage of men a people whose affairs we call a republic.10

Once more, Augustine is insisting that true justice can be found only in a community or commonwealth made up of individuals who serve and love God and, *as a result*, possess true justice. However, there is only one such community—the City of God—and it has no earthly representative; so neither the Roman State nor any other state can possibly possess true justice. If, then, in agreement with Scipio, we make justice a constitutive element in the definition of the state, we will be forced to the conclusion that no state or commonwealth has ever existed or will ever exist on this earth.

At this point it is no doubt clear that I cannot accept the interpretation of these passages from *The City of God* that is offered, for example, by Professor Charles H. McIlwain in his well-known work, *The Growth of Political Thought in the West*.11 Professor McIlwain, in his criticisms of Figgis and Carlyle, admits that Augustine states that a kingdom (*regnum*) or a city (*civitas*) may exist without justice, and that he defines both of them without including the element of right or justice in the definition.12 McIlwain then goes on to argue that Augustine meant to confine these statements to *regna* and *civitates*, and did not intend them to apply to states or commonwealths (*res publicae*). For a true *res publica* there must be the bond of justice and law which Cicero required; but if there is to be true justice, God must be worshiped and given His due. Therefore, only a Christian state can be just and, as a result, a true *res publica*. Augustine's remarks about *regna* and *civitates* are now confined to heathen states, and the way is open for McIlwain's conclusion that, for Augustine,

> justice and justice alone is the only possible bond which can unite men as a true *populus* in a real *res publica*. The great states before Christianity were *regna* but they were not true commonwealths because there was no recognition in them of what was due to the one true God, and without such recognition there could be no real justice, for justice is to render to *each* his due. . . . [A *populus*] must be united *consensu juris*, by consent to law, and that law must include the law of God as well as the law of man. Such law and such justice there cannot be in any state in which the just claims of the one true God are denied. No heathen state can ever rise quite to the height of a true commonwealth.[13]

A number of difficulties must be faced by anyone who accepts McIlwain's interpretation, in which Augustine is said to have espoused exactly that Ciceronian definition of the state or *res publica* that he seems to reject. First, McIlwain ignores Augustine's clear statement, to which I have already referred, that "true justice has no existence save in that republic whose founder and ruler is Christ,"[14] that is, in the City of God. This statement surely means that no earthly state, whether a *res publica*, a *regnum*, or a *civitas*, whether ostensibly heathen or Christian, can possess true justice, unless one proposes to identify the City of God with a so-called Christian state—an identification which Augustine would never dream of making, since he will not even allow an identification between the City of God and the Church Militant.

In addition, McIlwain ignores another important statement by Augustine, where he repeats at greater length the same idea that the only true *res publica* in the Ciceronian sense is the City of God; here alone is found in *all the citizens* and therefore in the community as a whole that true justice whereby God is served and, as a consequence, the soul rules the body and reason the vices. Certainly it would be very difficult for anyone to argue that when the Roman Empire or any other state became officially "Christian," all its citizens or even all its Christian citizens became truly just and righteous in Augustine's sense of these terms. The passage from Augustine is worth quoting in full; it comes just before he gives an alternative definition to replace the Scipionic definition that he is rejecting.

> And therefore, where there is not this righteousness [*iustitia*] whereby the one supreme God rules the obedient city according to His grace, so that it sacrifices to none but Him, and whereby, in *all the citizens* of this obedient city, the soul consequently rules the body and reason the vices in the rightful order, so that, as the individual just man, so also the community and people of the just, live by faith, which works by love, that love whereby man loves God as He ought to be loved, and his neighbour as himself,—there, I say, there is not an assemblage associated by a common acknowledgment of right, and by a community of interests. But if there is not this, there is not a people, if our [lit., "this" (*haec*)] definition [i.e., the Scipionic definition] be true, and therefore there is no republic; for where there is no people there can be no republic.[15]

Immediately Augustine proceeds to give his alternative definition of a *res publica*, which he had promised in Book II when he said that, "accepting the more feasible definitions of a republic, I grant there was a republic of a certain kind"[16] in Rome. Chapter 24 of Book XIX opens with this alternative definition, which is startling to so many readers, including McIlwain, since it completely omits the idea of justice from the definition of the state. It is a completely amoral account of what a *populus* or a *res publica* is, and it is an elastic definition that permits us to include under it a wide variety of peoples and states with different goals and interests.

> But if we discard this definition [i.e., the Scipionic] of a people, and, assuming another, say that a people is an assemblage of reasonable beings bound together by a common agreement as to the objects of their love [*populus est coetus multitudinis rationalis rerum quas diligit concordi communione sociatus*], then, in order to discover the character of any people, we have only to observe what they love. Yet whatever it loves, if only it is an assemblage of reasonable beings and not of beasts, and is bound together by an agreement as to the objects of love, it is reasonably called a people and it will be a superior people in proportion as it is bound together by higher interests, inferior in proportion as it is bound together by lower. According to *this definition of ours*, the Roman people is a people, and its weal is without doubt a commonwealth or republic.[17]

This passage presents insuperable difficulties for any commentator who, like McIlwain, is trying to prove that Augustine really accepted Cicero's definition of the state in terms of justice. McIlwain attempts to meet these difficulties by expressing serious doubt as to whether this alternative definition represents Augustine's own opinion; he argues that Augustine simply assumes it as a hypothetical definition in his attempt to argue for Christianity and against heathenism.[18]

the Church by the State. Although he assumes that it is possible that emperors or kings, princes or judges may, as individuals, be Christians, this does not lead him to speak of the state as good or just or Christian. Indeed, the conclusion of his argument is almost the reverse; true Christians must be prepared "to endure even the most wicked and most vicious commonwealth."

The Emperor Constantine had been converted to Christianity almost a century before Augustine wrote *The City of God*, and it was about forty years since Theodosius I, Gratian, and Valentinian II had issued the Edict of Thessalonica (February 27, 380), in which they established Christianity as the official religion of the Roman Empire.[23] So, had Augustine wished to make the distinction between pagan and Christian states that McIlwain tries to impose upon him he could easily have done so. His failure to say that Christian states, in contrast to pagan states, are or can be truly just, when taken together with his statements that true justice exists only in the City of God, appears to be powerful evidence on the point.[24] This evidence is strengthened when we recall that he was convinced that not even the Church, to say nothing of the state, could ever be an association composed solely of men who are redeemed and, therefore, good and just. If the number of the saved is always a small minority, it is impossible to establish and maintain an earthly society made up only of men who love and serve God and who are, as a result of that love, truly just.

One of the possible sources of Professor McIlwain's difficulties in dealing with Augustine is the failure to make the distinction, so crucial to understanding his thought, between "true justice" (*vera justitia*), found only in God's kingdom, and the much inferior but still important "image of justice" or "temporal" or "earthly" justice found in all ordered earthly states, whether they are called *res publicae*, *civitates*, or *regna*.[25] A state or earthly city, for Augustine, can be called "just" only in the sense that it is what he refers to as "well-ordered" (*bene ordinata*)[26] or "well-constituted" (*bene constituta*).[27] It has, that is, a certain harmony and concord among its citizens, and a measure of temporal peace—"what the vulgar call felicity"—is secured in it. Rulers, whether kings or princes, and laws are the major elements in securing this measure of order, peace, and earthly justice, and, therefore, a well-ordered state. "For without these things no people can be well-ordered, not even a people that pursues earthly goods. Even such a people has a measure of beauty of its own."[28] On the other hand, no state or society in this world can be called "just" in the sense of embodying true justice, that is, giving to each his due. For a city or a state would be just only if the men who make up the community—king, court, ministers, and people—were just; for "individual men . . . are, as it were, the elements and seeds of cities."[29]

Since the great majority of the members of any society are men who belong to the earthly city, who place their love in the world and in the things of the world, it necessarily follows that they will be unjust as each strives to outdo the others in the unceasing struggle for material goods, power, and glory.

> For when those things are loved which we can lose against our will, we must needs toil for them most miserably; and to obtain them, amid the straitnesses of earthly cares, whilst each desires to snatch them for himself, and to be beforehand with another, or to wrest it from him, must scheme injustice.[30]

When Augustine speaks of the ungodly or the wicked, he never confines these terms to pagans or to non-Christians, but always insists that many members of the visible Church are included in the ranks of the unredeemed; this will continue to be true as long as this world lasts.[31] Even if the unredeemed have "virtues," such as modesty, continence, or civic virtue, these are not true virtues, and their justice is not true justice,[32] although they may have a certain "uprightness," sufficient to maintain an earthly state.[33]

One of Augustine's most shockingly realistic discussions of earthly states is the famous fourth chapter of Book IV of *The City of God* in which he draws the comparison between kingdoms and robber bands. It is possible to raise questions about the meaning of certain phrases in this passage, but the sense of the chapter as a whole is clear beyond any doubt. A number of different translations and interpretations can be given for the first words of the opening sentence—*"Remota itaque iustitia quid sunt regna nisi magna latrocinia? quia et latrocinia quid sunt nisi parua regna?"* "And so, justice removed, what are kingdoms but great robber bands? And what are robber bands but small kingdoms?" Does Augustine mean, "If true justice is absent—and it need not be—kingdoms are nothing but large robber bands"? That this cannot be the meaning is clear from what we have said about the impossibility of finding real or true justice in any earthly state. Or is he saying that a kingdom which does not have even earthly or temporal justice—the shadow or image of real justice—is nothing but a great robber band? Or does he perhaps mean that since all kingdoms are unjust they are nothing but great bands of robbers?[34] Perhaps the best course is to set aside the question of the correct meaning of this initial sentence and go on to consider the rest of the paragraph. After the flat statement that robber bands are nothing but small kingdoms, Augustine continues:

> The band itself is made up of men; it is ruled by the authority of a prince; it is knit together by the pact of the confederacy; the booty is divided by the law agreed on. If, by the admittance of abandoned men, this evil increases to such a degree that it holds places, fixes abodes, takes possession of cities, and subdues

peoples, it assumes the more plainly the name of a kingdom, because the reality is now mainfestly conferred on it, *not by the removal of covetousness* [*cupiditas*], *but by the addition of impunity* [*impunitas*].[35]

At every point there is a parallel between the robber band and the kingdom: both are composed of men, both are ruled by the authority of a leader or prince; both are held together by a *pactum societatis*, a pact of association; in both the spoils are divided in accordance with the rules agreed to by the group. By these means—authority, a fundamental agreement, and operating rules—both maintain a kind of order, harmony, and even "justice." The points of identity are startling enough, but we are even more surprised when Augustine points out the differences between the robber band and the kingdom. Here, if anywhere, we would expect him to tell us that it is the presence of justice that distinguishes the state from the band of robbers. If this is our expectation, we are completely disappointed. The kingdom is larger than the robber band both in numbers and in territory occupied, and it has a fixed abode. As the robber band increases in size and settles down, it assumes the more plainly the name of a kingdom, not because its cupidity has been taken away but because it now possesses the priceless advantage of the "impunity" of a "sovereign state." Kingdoms are no less avaricious than robber bands, but whereas the band of robbers may be punished by the state, there is no super-state or international police force to punish the state for its misdeeds or its depredations.[36] The somber message of the chapter is pointed up by the anecdote that Augustine relates with approval in the final sentences.

Indeed, that was an apt and true reply which was given to Alexander the Great by a pirate who had been seized. For when that king had asked the man what he meant by keeping hostile possession of the sea, he answered with bold pride, "What thou meanest by seizing the whole earth; but because I do it with a petty ship, I am called a robber, whilst thou who dost it with a great fleet art styled Emperor."[37]

A few pages later Augustine returns to this comparison when he is discussing the wars waged by Ninus, king of the Assyrians, in order to extend his empire. "But to make war on your neighbours, and thence to proceed to others, and through mere lust of dominion to crush and subdue people who do you no harm, what else is this to be called than great robbery?"[38] The similarity between the robber and the king or prince is again pointed out when he says that even the thief and murderer who is unwilling to have any associates or accomplices wants his wife and children to obey his commands, and thus he shows that he desires to have peace in his home.

And therefore, if a city or nation offered to submit itself to him, to serve him in the same style as he had made his household serve him, he would no longer lurk in a brigand's hiding-places, but lift his head in open day as a king, *though the same covetousness and wickedness should remain in him.* And thus all men desire to have peace with their own circle whom they wish to govern as suits themselves. For even those whom they make war against they wish to make their own, and impose on them the laws of their own peace.[39]

Once more, the point is driven home that the king is distinguished from the robber not by the absence of wickedness of cupidity but rather by his exalted position, his impunity, and his acceptance by the group over which he rules.

It is important to get a clear picture of what Augustine is saying about political power and about temporal rulers. He is *not* saying that all kings are wicked, evil men; indeed, in his arguments against the Donatists he clearly rejects their contention that all kings are the enemies of the righteous, and insists that many kings have proved to be the friends of the godly.[40] In many earthly commonwealths we find citizens of the City of God among its rulers and magistrates who conduct its affairs. Since the two kingdoms, the two types of man—the lovers of earthly things and the lovers of heavenly things— are mingled together as long as this world lasts,

we see now the citizen of Jerusalem, citizen of the kingdom of heaven, have some office upon earth: to wit, one weareth purple, is a Magistrate, is Aedile, is Proconsul, is Emperor, doth direct the earthly republic: but he hath his heart above, if he is a Christian, if he is a believer, if he is godly, if he is despising those things wherein he is, and trusteth in that wherein he is not yet. . . . Despair we not then of the citizens of the kingdom of heaven, when we see them engaged in any of Babylon's matters, doing something earthly in republic earthly: nor again let us forthwith congratulate all men that we see doing matters heavenly; because even the sons of pestilence sit sometimes in the seat of Moses. . . .[41]

Men are fortunate indeed if their rulers happen to be individuals who possess true piety and, therefore, true virtue. "But there could be nothing more fortunate for human affairs than that, by the mercy of God, they who are endowed with true piety of life, if they have the skill for ruling people, should also have the power."[42] Since God, in the furtherance of His plans, grants power and dominion to both the good and the wicked, it is obvious that individual kings and rulers can be good and pious men. Augustine also says that good men who have a talent for governing have an obligation to assume the burdens of rule.[43] He frequently exhorts rulers to remember their subordination to God and their heavy responsibilities and duties toward their subjects,[44] and he gives a detailed portrait of how the pious, just ruler ought to behave. When we say that certain Christian emperors were happy, we are not referring to their long reigns, their victories at home and abroad, or their succession by their sons.

> But we say that they are happy if they rule justly; if they are not lifted up amid the praises of those who pay them sublime honours, and the obsequiousness of those who salute them with an excessive humility, but remember that they are men; if they make their power the handmaid of His majesty by using it for the greatest possible extension of His worship; if they fear, love, worship God; if more than their own they love that kingdom in which they are not afraid to have partners; if they are slow to punish, ready to pardon; if they apply that punishment as necessary to government and defence of the republic, and not in order to gratify their own enmity; if they grant pardon, not that iniquity may go unpunished, but with the hope that the transgressor may amend his ways; if they compensate with the lenity of mercy and the liberality of benevolence for whatever severity they may be compelled to decree; if their luxury is as much restrained as it might have been unrestrained; if they prefer to govern depraved desires rather than any nation whatever; and if they do all these things, not through ardent desire of empty glory, but through love of eternal felicity, not neglecting to offer to the one true God, who is their God, for their sins, the sacrifices of humility, contrition, and prayer. Such Christian emperors, we say, are happy in the present time by hope, and are destined to be so in the enjoyment of the reality itself, when that which we wait for shall have arrived.[45]

This portrait of the ideal Christian ruler, which is sometimes taken as Augustine's description of how Christian kings *do* behave rather than as his view of how they *ought* to act, and is therefore used as proof that he believed that a Christian state could be truly just, is obviously in the tradition of the large body of literature known as the "Mirror of Princes." These treatises, which first appear in the Hellenistic period and continue to be produced both in the West and in Byzantium throughout the Middle Ages, are addressed to rulers by philosophers. They all assume that kingship is the best, if not the only form of government, and they confine their efforts to giving advice and counsel to the king under the guise of painting a highly idealized portrait of the kings' benevolence, magnanimity, temperance, and justice.[46] In the Hellenistic period many of these treatises on kingship were written by Stoic teachers. Seneca's *De Clementia*, addressed to Nero and praising his many virtues, is perhaps the most famous example of the genre; there is bitter irony in the fact that Nero is here presented to the world as the model of the just and merciful ruler. Augustine was certainly familiar with this kind of political writing, and his own portrait of a good and wise Christian emperor is an obvious reworking of traditional materials. One of the elements in

Augustine's picture of the ideal Christian emperor requires special comment. We see that he urges the ruler not only to be pious and humble before God, but also to make his power the handmaid of God's majesty "by using it for the greatest possible extension of His worship."[47] The good Christian ruler is bound to use his royal power to promote true religion and the worship of the one true God. In a letter written about 414 to Macedonius, Vicar of Africa, Augustine tells him: if you employ your prudence, fortitude, temperance, and justice only with the aim that "those whose welfare you have at heart may be safe in body and secure from the dishonesty of anyone, that they may enjoy peace" and material prosperity, "in that case, yours are no true virtues, and theirs no true happiness."[48] If, he continues, your actions have only the aim "that men may suffer no undue distress according to the flesh," and if you think that

> it is not incumbent on you that they should make a return for that tranquility which you try to secure for them, that is, . . . that they should worship the true God in whom is all the fruition of the peaceful life, such effort on your part will bring you no return in true happiness.[49]

How, it may be asked, can these injunctions to a Christian ruler be reconciled with Augustine's general view that it is the task of the state and of its rulers to preserve external peace and to maintain an imperfect earthly justice among sinful men? First, it is evident that absolute consistency and complete harmony are not to be expected among the hundreds of statements about the state and its functions which are scattered throughout Augustine's writings—his doctrinal and moral treatises, his sermons, and his letters—and which he never brought together into a systematic theory of the state. We can discover a generally consistent point of view, and it is this which we are trying to elaborate here, but we should not be surprised if we find certain elements or emphases that are not easily harmonized with the main thesis. Second, the question now being discussed—the Christian ruler's use of the state's power and authority for the support and extension of true religion—is a problem with which Augustine wrestled for many years, and in the course of the struggle against the Donatist heretics in Africa he answered the question in a number of different ways. Since we shall, at a later point, examine in detail his treatment of this issue of the use of state power against schism and heresy,[50] let us postpone any further consideration of the role of the Christian ruler with respect to religious worship and doctrine or of the tensions between Augustine's views on this subject and his more general theories about the state's functions. Here we need only remember that, for Augustine, the maintenance of earthly justice and temporal, external peace and order—the peace of Babylon, that is, the maintenance of "the combination of men's wills to attain the things which are helpful to this life,"51 of "a common agreement among men regarding the acquisition of the necessaries of life"52—is always the basic and fundamental task that the state is expected to perform. When he tells a Christian ruler or magistrate that he ought to use his power not only to secure peace and prosperity for the people but also to promote and foster true religion and piety among them, he is reminding him of his duties as a Christian who is seeking to win eternal salvation—he is not discussing what a state must do if it is to be a state, nor is he advising the ruler to neglect the fundamental functions of the political and legal order.

If some kings are true Christians, many more are ordinary sinful men who are exposed to more than their share of temptations to pride and arrogance, and some are wicked and cruel rulers, whom God sends to punish men for their sins. For every good ruler such as Constantine or Theodosius, who aided the church "by most just and merciful laws . . . [and] indeed, he rejoiced more to be a member of this church than he did to be a king upon the earth,"53 one can mention a number of evil emperors, such as Diocletian, Julian, and that most impious of men, Nero. The important thing for us to remember is Augustine's insistence that it will *never* be true that the world will be ruled by the wise and the godly. Life on this earth would be far happier

> if the chief rule and government of human affairs were in the hands of the wise, and of those who were piously and perfectly subject to God; but *because this is not the case as yet* (for it behoves us first to be exercised in this our pilgrimage after mortal fashion, and to be taught with stripes by force of gentleness and patience), let us turn our thoughts to that country itself that is above and heavenly, from which we here are pilgrims.54

Moreover, we must never forget that the wicked or unjust man who exercises rule is in every way as legitimate and as much entitled to absolute obedience as the most pious or just ruler.55 The goodness or badness, piety or impiety, justice or injustice of the ruler has nothing at all to do with his title to rule and to be obeyed.

Even more important is Augustine's view that while this or that man who happens to be a ruler or an official may be pious and just, the state itself—the political order—can never be truly just. Since rulers have to deal with subjects many of whom are sinful, wicked men, the actions of the state cannot be a direct embodiment of Christian precepts of righteousness. As we have seen, the state deals with its citizens only on the level of outward, external behavior. It imposes penalties upon those who violate its laws, but it and its agents have no way of affecting the hearts and wills of men or even of knowing what men's true characters and motivations are.56 Its main weapon—fear of punishment—cannot make men good or virtuous, but only less harmful to their fellows. The state cannot know whether the punishment imposed is too heavy or too light for the man who has committed this particular crime in these circumstances, and it is never sure whether those who are punished are improved or made worse by the punishment.[57] The judge can never be sure that he is not condemning an innocent man; like all other men, he is prone to regard his suspicions as knowledge and to view as true the facts that seem credible to him.[58] Frequently his judgment is distorted even further by the pride that overcomes him because he has the power to decide the fate of other men and to judge whether they are guilty or innocent.[59] And when he employs torture in order to extract the truth from suspected criminals or from witnesses, he never knows whether the confession or the testimony that he obtains may not be false, extorted from an innocent man by torture or by the fear of it.

> What shall I say of *these judgments which men pronounce on men, and which are necessary in communities, whatever outward peace they enjoy?* Melancholy and lamentable judgments they are, since the judges are men who cannot discern the consciences of those at their bar, and are therefore frequently compelled to put innocent witnesses to the torture to ascertain the truth regarding the crimes of other men. What shall I say of torture applied to the accused himself? He is tortured to discover whether he is guilty, so that, though innocent, he suffers most undoubted punishment for crime that is still doubtful, not because it is proved that he committed it, but because it is not ascertained that he did not commit it. Thus the ignorance of the judge frequently involves an innocent person in suffering. And what is still more unendurable . . . is this, that when the judge puts the accused to the question, that he may not unwittingly put an innocent man to death, the result of this lamentable ignorance is that this very person, whom he tortured that he might not condemn him if innocent, is condemned to death both tortured and innocent. . . . And when he has been condemned and put to death, the judge is still in ignorance whether he has put to death an innocent or a guilty person, though he put the accused to the torture for the very purpose of saving himself from condemning the innocent; and consequently he has both tortured an innocent man to discover his innocence, and has put him to death without discovering it. *If such darkness shrouds social life [In his tenebris uitae socialis], will a wise judge take his seat on the bench or no? Beyond question he will. For human society, which he thinks it a wickedness to abandon, constrains him and compels him to this duty.*[60]

And he thinks it no wickedness that innocent witnesses are tortured regarding the crimes of which other men are accused; or that the accused are put to the torture, so that they are often overcome with anguish, and, though innocent, make false confessions regarding themselves, and are punished; or that, though they be not condemned to die, they often die during, or in consequence of, the torture; or that sometimes the accusers, who perhaps have been prompted by a desire to benefit society by bringing criminals to justice, are themselves condemned through the ignorance of the judge, because they are unable to prove the truth of their accusations though they are true, and because the witnesses lie, and the accused endures the torture without being moved to confession. These numerous and important evils he does not consider sins; for *the wise judge does these things, not with any intention of doing harm, but because his ignorance compels him, and because human society claims him as a judge.* But though we therefore acquit the judge of malice, we must none the less condemn human life as miserable. And if he is compelled to torture and punish the innocent because his office and his ignorance constrain him, is he a happy as well as a guiltless man? Surely it were proof of more profound considerateness and finer feeling were he to recognize the misery of these necessities, and shrink from his own implication in that misery; and had he any piety about him, he would cry to God, "From my necessities deliver Thou me."[61]

It is inescapable dilemmas like these that make it impossible for a state to be truly just, no matter what the character and personality of its rulers may be at any particular moment. The justice that emerges in the well-ordered state is a most imperfect replica or image of true justice, no matter how good the intentions of the rulers may be. Most overt crimes are punished; but some are never detected and others are never solved; sometimes the wrong man is punished, and the guilty go scot free.[62] The rulers and the citizens are only men, fallible, prejudiced, and ignorant of much that they need to know. Even when they do the best that they can, their best is far from true justice; and, often, what they do is far from their best.[63] Rulers are, as St. Paul said, God's ministers, avengers against those that do evil. But a province or a state can only be ruled by instilling fear in those who are ruled, and the fear of punishment can never produce true righteousness or justice. By their fear of the laws and of the punishments attached to them, men can be kept from performing certain injurious actions, but they cannot be made good or righteous by these means. Civil laws do not "bring men to make a good user of their wealth," but "those who make a bad use of it become thereby less injurious."[64] Augustine states the kernel of the problem in one sentence: "But, ruling a province is different from ruling a Church; the former must be governed by instilling fear, the latter is to be made lovable by the use of mildness."[65]

Of course, these dilemmas would not exist and this very imperfect, rough "justice" of the state would be converted into true justice if not only the rulers but all the subjects were truly pious and just men, who obeyed the commandments of Christ, and, as a consequence, preferred common interests to their egoistic, private interests.[66] If this were possible, we could have the "Christian state," the truly just society, based on God's law, that some commentators seem to think that Augustine regarded as feasible or necessary.[67] It is perfectly clear, however, that the conditions *sine qua non* for the existence of such a state can never be realized on this earth. Moreover, if they were to be realized, the result would not be a Christian or truly just state but rather the complete absence of the state as we know it. Since the entire apparatus of law, punishment, coercion, and repression that constitutes the heart of the state would be totally unnecessary, the state would indeed "wither away" and be replaced by the anarchist's paradise—a spontaneous, noncoercive order of love, which would embody true justice, true peace, and true harmony, with no need for armies, courts, policement, judges, jailers, and hangmen.[68]

In other words, a truly just society would be the City of God brought down from heaven to earth, and that for Augustine is an absolute impossibility. Even when he is defending Christianity against pagan charges that it is incompatible with patriotism and the well-being of the state, he is careful to retain the contrary-to-fact conditional form in speaking of the possibility of a state made up of true Christians.

> Wherefore, let those who say that the doctrine of Christ is incompatible with the State's well-being, give us an army composed of soldiers such as the doctrine of Christ requires them to be; let them give us such subjects, such husbands and wives, such parents and children, such masters and servants, such kings, such judges—in fine, even such taxpayers and tax-gatherers, as the *Christian religion has taught that men should be*, and then let them dare to say that it is adverse to the State's well-being; yea, rather, let them no longer hesitate to confess that *this doctrine, if it were obeyed, would be the salvation of the commonwealth.*[69]

\*       \*       \*

These reflections about the state's purpose—the maintenance of external peace and order—and about the means that it employs to achieve this end—punishment and the deprivation of possessions, liberty, and life—exhibit one of the most characteristic features of Augustine's thoughts about man and his life on earth—his keen awareness of the paradoxes and ironies that mark every aspect of the human condition, and especially of political life. There is a constant danger that men will destroy one another as they seek to accumulate more and more possessions and power by robbing, cheating, or injuring their fellows. They are kept from this mutual injury and annihilation only by being threatened with the loss of the goods that they love and seek to acquire. The very sin of loving earthly goods thus supplies, to some extent, its own corrective and remedy, with the result that human society, which is essential to man's survival, is not completely dissolved and at least a minimum of security and peace is maintained. Throughout the entire course of the world, order is imposed, through God's Providence, even upon the willful actions of evil men who seek to disrupt or destroy the natural order.[70] Acts of political governance and the penalties imposed by the legal system represent striking examples of this process whereby order is recreated and restored out of disorder.

\*     \*     \*

# Notes

†Reprinted by permission of the publisher from *The Political and Social Ideas of St. Augustine*. New York: Columbia UP, 1963. Ch. IV, pp. 116–43; 153.

[1]See esp. Chap. II.

[2]"But while those are better who are guided aright by love, those are certainly more numerous who are corrected by fear." (*Ep.* CLXXXV, VI, 21; CSEL LVII, 19; S IV, 641). See, too, pp. 28–31 and 34–38.

[3]See DCD, XII, 9; CCSL XLVIII, 364; H I, 493, and XXII, 30; CCSL XLVIII, 863; H II, 541–42.

[4]*Ibid.*, II, 21; CCSL XLVII, 53; H I, 75.

[5]*Ibid.*, II, 21; CCSL XLVII, 55; H I, 77.

[6]*Ibid.*

[7]*Ibid.*, XIX, 21; CCSL XLVIII, 688; H II, 331.

[8]See Chap. III, note 24.

[9]DCD, XIX, 21; CCSL XLVIII, 688; H II, 331.

[10]*Ibid.*, XIX, 21; CCSL XLVIII, 689; H II, 332.

[11]McIlwain, *The Growth of Political Thought*, pp. 154–60. I have selected McIlwain's interpretation for discussion here not only because it has had great influence (see, e.g., the statements in George H. Sabine's *A History of Political Theory* [Rev. ed., New York, Henry Holt and Co., 1950], p. 192, which are based on McIlwain's analysis), but because I regard it as more persuasive and more scholarly than other versions of the "clericalist" interpretation. If it can be shown that his treatment of Augustine is not satisfactory, other statements of the view that Augustine believed that only a Christian state can be truly just and, therefore, a true commonwealth can be ignored.

[12]McIlwain, *The Growth of Political Thought*, pp. 155–56; see below, ntoes 20 and 35.

[13]*Ibid.*, pp. 158–59. Compare Figgis's statement: "So far is S. Augustine from giving a clericalist definition of the State, that he definitely discards it, and shows us that he does so with intention, and gives his grounds. It is contrary to the facts of life" (Figgis,

*The Political Aspects*, p. 64).

14DCD, II, 21; CCSL XLVII, 55; H I, 77.

15*Ibid.*, XIX, 23; CCSL XLVIII, 695; H II, 339; italics added.

16*Ibid.*, II, 21; CCSL XLVII, 55; H I, 77; see p. 118.

17*Ibid.*, XIX, 24; CCSL XLVIII, 695; H II, 339–40; italics added.

18McIlwain, *The Growth of Political Thought*, p. 157.

19See pp. 40–41.

20A state "is nothing else than a multitude of men bound together by some associating tie [*ciuitas, quae nihil est aliud quam hominum multitudo aliquo societatis uinculo conligata*]." (DCD, XV, 8; CCSL XLVIII, 464; H II, 63.) "For what is a republic but a commonwealth? Therefore its interests are common to all; they are the interests of the State. Now what is a State but a multitude of men bound together by some bond of concord? [*quid est autem ciuitas nisi hominum multitudo in quoddam uinculum redacta concordiae?*]" (*Ep.* CXXXVIII, II, 10; CSEL XLIV, 135; S I, 484.) "For the happiness of the state has no other source than the happiness of man, since the state is merely a unified group of men [*concors hominum multitudo*]." (*Ep.* CLV, III, 9; CSEL XLIV, 439–40; FCL III, 312.) "For a people is composed of men associated under one law, a temporal law, as we have said." (*De Lib. Arbit.*, I, VII, 16, 52; CSEL LXXIV, 16; Burleigh, 121.) "A population forms a city, and dissension is full of danger for it: to dissent [*dis-sentire*]—what is that, but to think diversely? An army is made up of many soldiers. And is not any multitude so much the less easily defeated in proportion as it is the more closely united? In fact, the joining is itself called a coin, a co-union, as it were." (*De Ordine*, II, 18, 48; CSEL LXIII, 181; FC I, 325.) See, too, DCD, XVII, 14; CCSL XLVIII, 578; H II, 199, and *De Genesi ad Litteram*, IX, 9; CSEL XXVIII (I), 277.

21See the statement by Gerd Tellenbach in his *Church, State and Christian Society at the Time of the Investiture Contest* (Oxford, Basil Blackwell, 1948), p. 31: Augustine "never even drew a clear distinction between the heathen and the Christian Empire."

22DCD, II, 19; CCSL XLVII, 51; translation and italics by author.

23Cochrane, *Christianity and Classical Culture*, pp. 327–36.

24Note that after his statement that the first Romans "did preserve a certain characteristic uprightness, sufficient to found, increase, and preserve an earthly city," he does not go on to say that if true religion is added the earthly state becomes truly righteous, but rather that men can then become citizens of the only truly just community, the City of God. "God showed in the rich and far-famed Roman Empire how much can be achieved by natural [i.e., civic; *ciuiles*] virtues without true religion, so that we might understand how, with this added, men can become citizens of another state whose king is truth, whose law is love, whose measure is eternity." (*Ep.* CXXXVIII, III, 17; CSEL XLIV, 145; FCL III, 50.)

25See pp. 96–104.

26DCD, XVII, 14; CCSL XLVIII, 578; H II, 199.

27*De Vera Religione*, XXVI, 48; PL XXXIV, 143; Burleigh, 249.

28*Ibid.* This reference to kings or princes as the rulers of "a well-ordered earthly city" suggests that McIlwain's distinction between a city [*civitas*] and a kingdom [*regnum*] is not one that Augustine actually follows. See, too: "So then where a king,

where a court, where ministers, where commonalty are found, there is a city [*ciuitas*]."
(*En. in Ps.*, IX, 8; CCSL XXXVIII, 62; S VIII, 35.) McIlwain's attempt to draw an even
sharper line of cleavage between a *res publica*, on the one hand, and a *civitas* or
*regnum*, on the other, is, I think, forced and, ultimately, unconvincing.

29*En. in Ps.*, IX, 8; CCSL XXXVIII, 62; S VIII, 35. "You must see how plainly the
sacred writings show that the happiness of the state has no other source than the
happiness of man. . . . Thus, in order to . . . place happiness where it truly exists, he
[the Psalmist] says: 'Happy is the people whose God is the Lord.'" (*Ep.* CLV, II, 7–8;
CSEL XLIV, 437 and 439; FCL III, 310–11.)

30*En. in Ps.*, VII, 16; CCSL XXXVIII, 47; S VIII, 26.

31See pp. 34–38.

32". . . and if the justice of the ungodly is not true justice, then whichever they have
of the virtues allied with it are not true virtues (because failure to refer the gifts of God
to their Author makes the evil men using them unjust); thus, neither the continence of
the ungodly nor their modesty is true virtue." (*Contra Julianum*, IV, III, 17; PL XLIV,
746; FC 35, 182.) See, too, DCD, XIX, 25; CCSL XLVIII, 696; H II, 340–41, and see
pp. 50–51 and, also, p. 80.

33See *Ep.* CXXXVIII, III, 17; CSEL XLIV, 144; FCL III, 50, and see pp. 50–52.

34See the discussion by Christopher Dawson, "St. Augustine and His Age," in M. C.
D'Arcy et al., *Saint Augustine* (New York, Meridian Books, 1957), p. 63.

35DCD, IV, 4; CCSL XLVII, 101; H I,139–40; italics added.

36Professor McIlwain admits the force of this paragraph, but, as we have seen, he
argues that a *regnum* or a *civitas*, which can exist without justice, is essentially different
from a *res publica*, which must possess the bond of justice and law which Cicero
required (McIlwain, *The Growth of Political Thought*, pp. 155–56). Note the similarity
between Augustine's views and those set forth by Cardinal Newman in "Sanctity the
Token of the Christian Empire," in *Sermons on Subjects of the Day*, p. 273 (first edition),
cited by Dawson, "St. Augustine and His Age."

37DCD, IV, 4; CCSL XLVII, 101–2; H I, 140. *"Manus et ipsa hominum est, imperio
principis regitur, pacto societatis astringitur, placiti lege praeda diuiditur. Hoc malum si in
tantum perditorum hominum accessibus crescit, ut et loca teneat sedes constituat, ciuitates
occupet populos subiuget, euidentius regni nomen adsumit, quod ei iam in manifesto confert
non dempta cupiditas, sed addita inpunitas. Eleganter enim et ueraciter Alexandro illi
Magno quidam comprehensus pirata respondit. Nam cum idem rex hominem interrogaret,
quid ei uideretur, ut mare haberet infestum, ille libera contumacia: Quod tibi, inquit, ut
orbem terrarum; sed quia (id) ego exiguo nauigio facio, latro uocor; quia tu magna classe,
imperator."*

38*Ibid.*, IV, 6; CCSL XLVII, 103; H I, 142. *"Inferre autem bella finitimis et in cetera
inde procedere ac populos sibi non molestos sola regni cupiditate conterere et subdere, quid
aliud quam grande latrocinium nominandum est?"*

39*Ibid.*, XIX, 12; CCSL XLVIII, 676; H II, 316; italics added.

40"But if it were not that, as a defender of the basest cause, you are hindered by the
desire of building up falsehood . . . there can be no doubt that you could, without any
difficulty, recall some good kings as well as some bad ones, and some friendly to the

saints as well as some unfriendly. . . . Why then did you thus run head-long with your eyes shut, so that when you said, 'What have you to do with the kings of this world?' you did not add, In whom Christianity has often found envy towards herself, instead of boldly venturing to say, 'In whom Christianity has never found anything save envy towards her?'" (*Contra Litt. Petil.*, II, 92, 204; CSEL LII, 127–29; S IV, 579.)

⁴¹*En. in Ps.*, LI, 6; CCSL XXXIX, 627; S VIII, 197. "For how many faithful, how many good men, are both magistrates in their cities, and are judges, and are generals, and are counts, and are kings? . . . And as if they were doing bond-service [*angariam*] in the city which is to pass away, even there by the doctors of the Holy City they are bidden to keep faith with those set over them, 'whether with the king as supreme, or with governors as though sent by God for the punishment of evil men, but for the praise of good men': or as servants, that to their masters they should be subject, even Christians to Heathens, and the better should keep faith with the worse, for a time to serve, for everlasting to have dominion. For these things do happen until iniquity do pass away." (*Ibid.*, LXI, 8; CCSL XXXIX, 779; S VIII, 253.) See p. 31.

⁴²DCD, V, 19; CCSL XLVII, 156; H I, 216–17. "Wherefore if the true God is worshipped, and if He is served with genuine rites and true virtue, it is advantageous that good men should long reign both far and wide. Nor is this advantageous so much to themselves, as to those over whom they reign. . . . In this world, therefore, the dominion of good men is profitable, not so much for themselves as for human affairs." (*Ibid.*, IV, 3; CCSL XLVII, 101; H I, 139.)

⁴³Since the believer "by making progress in Christian faith and well-doing," becomes "so much the more faithful and useful in the administration of public business" (*Ep.* CLI, 14; CSEL XLIV, 392; S I, 509), "those who, by a talent for business, are fitted for government, must for the public benefit consent to bear the burden and suffer the hardships of public life. . . ." (*Contra Faustum*, XXII, 58; CSEL XXV, 653; S IV, 294.)

⁴⁴See *Ep.* CLV, IV, 17; CSEL XLIV, 447; FCL III, 317–18, and *En. in Ps.*, II, 9–10; CCSL XXXVIII, 6.

⁴⁵DCD, V, 24; CCSL XLVII, 160; H I, 223.

⁴⁶For examples and discussion of "Mirror of Princes" literature, especially in the period before Augustine, see Ernest Barker, *From Alexander to Constantine* (Oxford, Oxford University Press, 1956), pp. 236–38, 253–56, 303–8, 361–73, and 477–79, and *Social and Political Thought in Byzantium* (Oxford, Oxford University Press, 1957), pp. 20–21, 54–63, and 151–59.

⁴⁷DCD, V, 24; CCSL XLVII, 160; H I, 223.

⁴⁸*Ep.* CLV, III, 10; CSEL XLIV, 440; FCL III, 312.

⁴⁹*Ibid.*, CSEL XLIV, 440–41; FCL III, 312–13. See, too, *ibid.*, III, 12; CSEL XLIV, 441–42; FCL III, 313–14: "If you recognize that you have received the virtues which you have, and if you return thanks to Him from whom you have received them, directing them to His service even in your secular office; if you rouse the men subject to your authority and lead them to worship God, both by the example of your own devout life and by your zeal for their welfare, whether you rule them by love or by fear; if, in working for their greater security, you have no other aim than that they should thus attain to Him who will be their happiness—then yours will be true virtues,

then they will be increased by the help of Him whose bounty lavished them on you, and they will be so perfected as to lead you without fail to that truly happy life which is no other than eternal life."

[50]See Chap. VI, esp. pp. 214-20.

[51]DCD, XIX, 17; CCSL XLVIII, 684; H II, 326.

[52]*Ibid.*, XIX, 17; CCSL XLVIII, 685; H II, 328. See Chap. III, pp. 102-03.

[53]*Ibid.*, V, 26; CCSL XLVII, 162; H I, 226.

[54]*De Trinitate*, III, IV, 9; PL XLII, 873; S III, 58; italics added.

[55]See below, in this chapter, pp. 147-50.

[56]See below, in this chapter, pp. 139-40.

[57]"How deep and dark a question it is to adjust the amount of punishment so as to prevent the person who receives it not only from getting no good, but also from suffering loss thereby! Besides, I know not whether a greater number have been improved or made worse when alarmed under threats of such punishment at the hands of men as is an object of fear. What, then, is the path of duty, seeing that it often happens that if you inflict punishment on one he goes to destruction; whereas, if you leave him unpunished, another is destroyed?" (*Ep.* XCV, 3; CSEL XXXIV [2], 508; S I, 402.)

[58]"All or almost all of us men love to call or consider our suspicions knowledge [*cognitiones*], since we are influenced by the credible evidence of circumstances; yet some credible things are false, just as some incredible ones are true." (*Ep.* CLIII, VI, 22; CSEL XLIV, 421; FCL III, 298.)

[59]See *Sermo* CCCXLII, 5; PL XXXIX, 1504.

[60]Augustine recognizes that the true Christian should avoid all recourse to legal proceedings; when St. Paul says that it is permissible to have cases between Christians decided by brethren within the Church (though not by the regular courts), "it is clear that some concession is being made here for the infirmities of the weak." (*Enchiridion*, XXI, 78; PL XL, 270; Outler, 387.) Nevertheless, Augustine not only believes that social necessity compels the judge to continue at his post, despite the inadequacies and the fallibilities of the legal system and of his own powers of judgment, he does not object if a Christian buys the right to judicial office provided that he uses his office for the good of society and in the service of justice. "You wish to be a judge, even if you do it by money since you cannot by your merits—still I do not condemn you. For perhaps you seek to be of service in human affairs, and you buy that you may be of service; in order that you may serve justice, you do not spare your money." (*Sermo* XIII, 6-7; PL XXXVIII, 110; author's translation.) But he insists that once he occupies the office, the judge must give judgment impartially and without regard to popularity; see *En. in Ps.*, XXV (2), 13; CCSL XXXVIII, 149-50. Above all, judges and witnesses must never accept payments from the parties to a case. "But when verdicts and testimony are sold, they are unfair and untrue, because just and true ones are not to be sold, and it is much more infamous for money to be taken when it is infamously even if willingly paid." (*Ep.* CLIII, VI, 23; CSEL XLIV, 423; FCL III, 300.)

[61]DCD, XIX, 6; CCSL XLVIII, 670-71; H II, 309-10; italics added. See, too, *Ep.* CXX, IV, 19; CSEL XXXIV (2), 720-21; FCL II, 315-16. Note too Augustine's expressions of his abhorrence of the use of torture in judicial inquiries in connection

with outrages perpetrated by the Donatists. "Resolving, however, not to institute inquiry in regard to the instigators, because these, perhaps, could not be ascertained without recourse to the use of tortures, from which we shrink with abhorrence, as utterly inconsistent with our aims." (*Ep.* CIV, IV, 17; CSEL XXXIV [2], 594; S I, 433.) See too, his comment on the question of investigating the instigation of the attack on Christians and the Church by the pagans of Calama: "We think that we have a suspicion of this instigation, but no truth; so let us not discuss things which cannot be found out in any other way than by putting to torture those who could be examined." (*Ep.* XCI, 9; CSEL XXXIV [2], 433-34; FCL II, 48.) However, it is not accurate to say, as Combès does (*La doctrine politique*, pp. 192-95), that Augustine "condemned" torture. While it is clear that he did not want torture to be used in any investigation or trial in which the Church was involved, particularly in proceedings against the Donatists, he never denies that the use of torture to obtain information from accused persons and witnesses is a grim necessity of criminal justice; the judge who orders the use of torture is not committing a sin and is not to be condemned (see pp. 135-36).

At several points we shall have to indicate reservations or objections to Combès's interpretations of Augustine's political doctrines. However, quite apart from any differences in interpretation of Augustine, it should be noted that Combès's volume must be used with care by the student, since it contains many errors and inaccuracies in the references to Augustine's writings. I note only a few examples: 1) on p. 77, the phrase *"ut se interim tutos ab injuriis facerent"* does not occur in the source cited, *Ep.* LIX; PL XXXIII, 226; 2) on pp. 46 and 91, Combès says that in DCD, II, 21, Augustine "adopts Scipio's thesis" and "uses the speech of Scipio in [Cicero's] *De Republica* to illustrate his own thesis" that a state cannot exist without justice; the text makes it clear that Augustine is simply reporting the arguments set forth by Scipio and Laelius; 3) on p. 92, a definition of justice is attributed to Augustine and the reference is given to *Opus imperf. contra Julianum*, I, 35; PL XLIV [should be XLV], 1063; examination of the text shows that it is Julian and not Augustine who is speaking at this point; 4) on p. 93, the phrase quoted at note 3 does not occur in DCD, XIX, 11, and the phrase quoted at note 7 is not found in *Sermo* XCII, 3; PL XXXVIII, 573; 5) on pp. 135-36, the long quotation from *Contra Faustum*, XIX, 2; PL XLII, 347-48, is from Faustus the Manichaean and not from Augustine; 6) on p. 138, note 4, the citation should be to *De Vera Religione*, XXXI, 58; PL XXXIV, 148, not to XXVI, 48; PL XXXIV, 143; 7) on p. 149, at note 1, Combès quotes Augustine as referring to the treasury as a "dragon qui dévorait tout"; the text of *En. in Ps.*, CXLVI, 17; CCSL XL, 2135, reads: "A 'fisc' is a purse. . . . Do *not* think that a fisc is some kind of dragon, because the collector of the fisc is heard with terror; the fisc is a purse—the public purse [translation and italics by author]"; 8) on p. 152, at note 2, the reference is to *Ep.* CXCV, 8; this letter is from Jerome to Augustine (see CSEL LVII, 214-16), has no paragraph 8, and does not refer to the subject mentioned; 9) on p. 176, at note 4, the reference is to *Ep.* CLIV, 6; this letter contains no paragraph 6, and column 667 of PL XXXIII contains paragraphs 1-3 of *Ep.* CLV.

[62]See DCD, XX, 2; CCSL XLVIII, 700; H II, 347.

[63]See *De Lib. Arbit.*, I, V, 12, 34-36; CSEL LXXIV, 12; Burleigh, 118-19. The punishments imposed upon children by parents and teachers and the more severe

punishments imposed upon grownups by the legal and political system are necessary to guard us against ignorance and to bridle our evil desires—"these evils with which we came into the world"—but the punishments themselves are "full of labour and sorrow." (DCD, XXII, 22; CCSL XLVIII, 843; H II, 518-19.)

64*Ep.* CLIII, VI, 26; CSEL XLIV, 426-27; FCL III, 302. See, too, pp. 139-40.

65*Ep.*CXXXIV, 3; CSEL XLIV, 86; FCL III, 10.

66See *En. in Ps.*, CV, 34; CCSL XL, 1566; S VIII, 531.

67Combès, e.g., concludes his discussion of *l'état Chrétien* by saying: "L'État chrétien, en effet, n'est pas celui où le Christ règne extérieurement sur la nation par les représentants de son culte; c'est celui où il règne intérieurement dans la conscience du chef, des magistrats et de *tous les citoyens.*" (Combés, *La doctrine politique*, p. 112; italics added.) All that one needs to add is that therefore, according to Augustine, such a state has never existed, does not now exist, and never will exist in this world.

68"Those who are happy on account of their love of eternal things I hold act under obedience to the eternal law, while on unhappy men the temporal law is imposed. . . . [T]hose who serve the temporal law cannot be set free from subjection to the eternal law. . . . *But those who with a good will cleave to the eternal law do not need the temporal law,* as apparently you well understand." (*De Lib. Arbit.*, I, XV, 31, 107; CSEL LXXIV, 32; Burleigh, 131; italics added.)

69*Ep.* CXXXVIII, II, 15; CSEL XLIV, 141-42; S I, 486; italics added. *"Yet, were our religion listened to as it deserves, it would establish, consecrate, strengthen, and enlarge the commonwealth [consecraret, firmaret augeretque rem publicam]* in a way beyond all that Romulus, Numa, Brutus, and all the other men of renown in Roman history achieved." (*Ibid.*, II, 10; CSEL XLIV, 135; S I, 484; italics added.) In another of his letters where he is defending Christianity against pagan attacks, Augustine says that in the two great commandments of Christ—"You shall love the Lord your God with all your heart, and with all your soul, and with all your mind," and "You shall love your neighbor as yourself" (Matt. xxii, 37-39, RSV)—are contained all natural science, all ethics, all logic; "herein is the praise-worthy security of the state [*laudabilis rei publicae salus*], for the best city is erected and safeguarded on no other foundation than the bond of faith and unbreakable concord [*neque enim conditur et custoditur optima ciuitas nisi fundamento et uinculo fidei firmaeque concordiae*]. This happens when the common good is loved, when God is the highest and truest good, and when men love each other most sincerely because they love themselves for the sake of Him from whom they cannot hide the true sentiment of their hearts." (*Ep.* CXXXVII, V, 17; CSEL XLIV, 122; FCL III, 34.) Again, Augustine is insisting that the only basis for "the bond of faith and unbreakable concord" which is the foundation of "the best city" is the sincere love of its members for God, the highest good, and for one another in God. Since no earthly city or state will ever be made up entirely, or even predominantly, of men who love God and their fellow men in this way, no earthly city can be maintained by "the law of love" but must rely on coercion and the fear of punishment. Only "the best city," the City of God, has as its citizens only pious and good men who are ruled by the law of love.

70[#76 in original text] See pp. 67-70.

# Redeeming Politics: Augustine's Cities of God†

## Peter Iver Kaufman

If we want to learn how the decomposition and recomposition of Christian sociolatry were related to political crisis, the place to start is the monumental *City of God*, which is still Christianity's most influential treatment of piety and politics. Sourcebooks for political theory compress it for student use as if Augustine's tale of two cities (one "at home" on earth and the other on pilgrimage to God) were easier to abridge than Dickens's. The bishop, of course, did not write his *City* for college surveys. It was composed as a sprawling response to the great crisis of the Christian empire, the invasion of Italy and sack of Rome in 410, so Augustine and his text show us quite clearly what happened when defeat and disenchantment left the claims of Christian sociolatry dangerously exposed.

Some of my colleagues have said the *City of God* does away with sociolatry. They contend that Augustine devalued political life and political culture, and there is ample support for their contention.[1] Before the so-called barbarians humiliated Roman soldiers in the very precincts of Rome, most Christians accustomed to Eusebius's triumphalism lived comfortably in Constantine's shadow. The events of 410 shocked them. The tragedy seemed to many to herald the world's end.[2] Nearly inexpressible dismay and disappointment attended the social dislocations occasioned by invaders' raids throughout Italy and the empire's other European territories. Augustine wrote to remind fugitives who crossed to North Africa as well as those Christians who remained behind that their true empire was heaven's everlasting "city," not earth's perishable provinces.[3] Unquestionably, the bishop's reminder set limits to Eusebean triumphalism, but I will argue that it hardly marked the end of Christian sociolatry in late antiquity. We will see that Augustine tried to bend rather than break the enthusiasms generated by Constantine's conversion. The *City of God* reoriented the redeeming politics of Latin Christendom; it is sociolatry in a new key, adaptable to crisis as well as conquest.

To the extent that Eusebius had conditioned Christians to think of Constantine's conversion as the signal that God intended a consummate and lasting regeneration of political culture, there existed a crisis of confidence in the new but badly bruised Christian empire. Augustine tried to assure that disillusionment would not lead to disaffection, but his task was complicated by the pagan response to the empire's misfortunes. Pagans blamed worshipers of Rome's new Christian God for the city's sack and the empire's losses, and their recriminations blended well with the widespread nostalgia for Rome's old gods that political and military reversals had triggered. Not all pagans flocked to Christianity with Constantine and his heirs. Many remained outside the official religion and seized every opportunity to clamor against the church. Christians were accused when the rains came too often and when they failed to come at all. Learned pagan critics might not have indulged in the polemics of deluge and drought, but early fifth-century defeats could surely be used, Augustine feared, to shake the faith of the faithful. Moreover, by retailing preposterous stories about Christianity's limitless culpability for the latest developments, critics were also likely to incite mobs to violence.[4] Not long before Italy was infested with "barbarians," an unauthorized pagan festival in a village known to Augustine led to the stoning of the local church, the flight of its bishop, and the death of one believer.[5]

The threat of further violence as well as the possibility of disaffection and defections prompted Augustine to answer the pagans' accusations, even as he wrote to console his coreligionists for their losses. The principal battle was against nostalgia. The *City of God* insisted that it was both impossible and undesirable to turn back the clock. The pagans' retelling of Rome's pre-Christian history needed to be demythologized; the critics of the church had fallen prey to their own campaign of misinformation and devoted themselves to the recovery of a past that had never existed. Soon after news of Rome's troubles reached North Africa with the first wave of fugitives, Augustine started his *City* as he would have started a history lesson. In the next seven years, and in ten tendentious volumes, he labored to set the record straight. Polytheism, he argued, had never proved to be a route to peace. Neither republican nor imperial Rome had enjoyed peace while the pagans' gods ruled at the city's altars. Pagans were wrong when they said that wars were shorter and more easily won when their old gods were custodians of Rome's prosperity. All Augustine had to do was recount the long wars and the military catastrophes that predated the conversion of Constantine.[6] Still, the bishop probably despaired of convincing the ruffians (*ineruditorum turbae*) chiefly responsible for the violence against Christians; he planned the initial ten books of his *City* to persuade ringleaders who might yet listen to reason. Perhaps he hoped that learned critics would come to accept the ahistoricity of their idealization of Rome's past and then renounce their intense prejudices against Christianity. Perhaps his unremitting assault on nostalgia had other objectives as well. Whatever the case, the author's strategy reinforces the impression that the *City* was also an assault on Christian sociolatry because the *City* deflated myths about Rome's pre-Christian political culture in a way that suggested the debasement of all political culture.

The best evidence for the bishop's alleged debasement of political leadership and public service may well be his remarks on Sallust's assessment of political morality. Sallust, the first governor of Africa Nova, had declared that fear was the source of public virtue. Citizens and their governments, he said, behaved commendably only when confronted by an external enemy or when they realized that injustices, resulting grievances, and lingering antagonisms weakened their cities' defenses. This made complete sense to Augustine.[7] He admitted that from time to time Rome had been blessed with bold and resourceful leaders; no history lesson, however iconoclastic its intent, dared omit the triumphs of inspirational soldiers and Caesars. Nonetheless, he carefully distinguished between the desire for fame, which spurred pagan warriors and politicians to defend their territories and to annex those of their neighbors, and the admirable passion for immortality that animated Christian martyrs and saints. The bishop staged the comparison to make the desire for reputation appear crude and ignoble, and at one point he held that the difference between eminent politicians and petty criminals was one of scale or degree. A Caesar's vast navy made him no less a pirate than the blackguard who wrought havoc on the high seas with a single boat.[8]

Censorious statements of this kind are the ingredients for a substantial case against sociolatry, and tales of political treachery are scattered through the *City of God*'s first ten books. Furthermore, the remaining twelve books develop the distinction between the corruptible terrestrial city and the glorious city of God in terms selected specifically to discountenance Eusebius. Augustine dramatized the distinction by splitting humanity into two societies at the very beginning of the fifteenth book. The first was fathered by Cain, who, according to Genesis, established a city. Augustine admitted that to speak of either of his two societies as a city was to speak metaphorically, yet he boasted scriptural warrant for the application of political imagery to Cain's kind.[9] Abel, Cain's brother and victim, built no city. Abel was a prototypical pilgrim, whose part in history was to suffer rather than rule. Early in Genesis, then, the politician squared off against the pilgrim, who was bested in the conflict. Cain's terrestrial city grew and prospered, and the righteous were tempted to join it. Floods of superstitions washed over the next generations of pilgrims, and many were carried into the terrestrial city. The city of God on earth, however, was never wholly depopulated. Faith in God's promise of an everlasting kingdom sustained pilgrims who resisted the currents that dragged others from one compromise to the next along the route to worldly power and success.[10]

Augustine's pilgrim city intrigues scholars, although scholarly discussion usually adjourns before any consensus has been reached. Whether or not, and in what ways the pilgrim city prefigures the church are questions of long-standing importance in the history of the Christian traditions. Attempts to answer them still spark controversy. Yet, whatever Abel is said to represent, no controversy surrounds Cain; most readers consider him the progenitor of political culture.[11] Cain, after all, founded a city, and Augustine's *City of God* caged timid citizens and grand Caesars into that society of the selfish and the damned, from which few escaped in this life and none in the next. Was this terrestrial city assembled deliberately to libel political culture? Some would say so, but I think otherwise.

If we read the *City of God* closely, we find most of what was written about Cain's kind applies equally well to the vast majority of humankind, governors and governed. Augustine charged that citizens of the earthly city were preoccupied with goods that gave immediate gratification. When we claim that politicians alone are Cain's heirs, we blame the pursuit of political authority for sins that, according to Augustine, most persons of his time were busy committing most of their time.

Circumstantial evidence allows only a provisional coupling of Cain's city with the political cultures of late antiquity. Recall, for instance, that political crisis impelled Augustine to compose his text, that pagans had accused Christians of failing the empire. It was said that Christians deprived Rome's trustworthy gods of citizens' adoration. Christian church officials were suspected of beguiling Rome's trusted leaders, who foolishly permitted hostile tribes to settle within Rome's frontiers. Generals steadily gave ground to intruders. Hadrian all but withdrew from the East, much to the Persians' advantage and delight. Augustine accepted parts of this description of decline, explaining, however, that his God had arranged the setbacks for a purpose. In a sermon preached just after the capital's humiliation, he went on to argue that the calamities had been divinely ordained and orchestrated to show how unstable the world's successes and pleasures actually were. Augustine decreed, moreover, that God had planned the empire's most recent political crisis as a test. Prosperity made Christians complacent; adversity put faith under fire. The fall of Rome was a furnace in which gold and dross were separated. Patient Christians, for whom tribulation was training (*exercitatio*), proved themselves pious pilgrims by relinquishing their political ambitions and by clinging tenaciously to God's promises of eternal rewards.[12]

Augustine's lecture on God's smelting met both his apologetic objectives. First, he explained to pagans why God's assent to and complicity in Rome's misfortunes did not justify their accusations against God's vigilance. The Christian God was the watchful caretaker of Christians' souls, but the Christian God had never promised to guard cities besieged by enemies. Pagan nostalgia was based on a calculated misreading of history and on the naive belief of some poets in an empire without end (*imperium sine fine*).[13] The second objective was equally important to Augustine. He repeatedly reassured refugees that their truest sovereign placed their properties and persons in peril in order to redeem their souls. God's smelting, as Augustine depicted it, made sense of their suffering.[14]

But the *City* is not simply Christian apology. It is an extended sermon exposing preoccupations that kept Cain's heirs from becoming pilgrims. The crisis of contemporary political culture provided Augustine a splendid contrast when he juxtaposed perishable political cultures with the eternal kingdom that awaited citizens who placed their mourning in the context of their faith, as pilgrims should. Their faith, in a sense, booked them passage to a realm unrivaled by any found on earth, yet the faith of many seemed rivaled by their concerns for the kingdoms, dioceses, estates, and freedoms the barbarians had taken from them. The bishop's real target in the *City*'s later books was insatiable and uncontrollable lust for mastery and glory. Augustine unambiguously associated that lust with political culture and with the political life of late antiquity. Nevertheless, he far more frequently and unequivocally identified it as the defect that fettered most citizens to their worst instincts and enslaved them to their grief for losses that were, on the whole, quite inconsequential.[15]

The *City of God* is not a direct and deliberate attack on Christian sociolatry. Political history galvanized Augustine's lessons about sin and salvation that made the history of recent mishaps meaningful sub specie aeternitatis. It was sin and salvation that most concerned the bishop. He held that faithful citizens of the pilgrim city could still know themselves as a "holy city of God." Their response to tragedy, their perseverance and unflinching desire for eternal life, were unmistakable signs of God's grace, compassion, and purpose.[16] God kept the pilgrim city on course. As long as pilgrims were alive, subject to grief and temptation, their will to subordinate sorrow and self-love to their love for and trust in God was the surest indication of God's will to save their souls. Augustine acknowledged pilgrims would still experience sorrow and fear, but those jolting feelings should only increase their diligence against sin. Citizens of that other city, however, were so shaken by their sufferings that they lived feverishly, with confusion, and without peace.[17]

Augustine suggested, almost as an afterthought, that some of the unrighteous exercised greater self-control than others. He found that these exceptional citizens of Cain's city were indifferent to everything around them, but the bishop held no brief for this kind of equanimity. The battle between self-love and the love of God was not one that could be avoided or contemplated away in some philosophically induced narcosis, any more than history could be dissolved by dreams of eternity. God staged political crisis, according to Augustine, to fortify and refocus human will, to recall it to obedience during its pilgrimage in time.

Augustine's afterthought and much of what he wrote in the second half of the *City* suggest that he wanted to forge a weapon in the battle for the human will. Though his cities originated with biblical figures, Augustine maintained that those cities were regularly reconstituted in the postbiblical age by human choice. Some elected to live according to the standards of the flesh. Others chose to live by the standard of the spirit.[18] Even when it had been identified, the correct choice could not be made easily, Augustine explained, because Adam's sin crippled human will. That primordial crime resulted in the phenomenon of the divided self, an emotional conflict that continued to plague would-be pilgrims. Hence he urged readers to accept God's grace and God's governance and to stay within the pilgrim city: to love God and neighbor, to endure disappointment patiently and with undiminished faith in divine sovereignty and benevolence, and to yearn for the consolations of faith, which restored the will to obedience.[19]

The *City* is a collection of stories and scriptural passages accumulated principally to repair Christian confidence and to teach Christians what they should expect (and should not expect) of God's sovereignty over history. The choices those Christians had to make would reconstitute Augustine's cities of

God, so the *City* was composed to dramatize their options and, as it happened, to reify the two fields of force that shaped Christians' longings and influenced their decisions. Augustine vividly depicted the tension between those two fields, yet he nowhere seems to have encouraged readers to run from the tension, to closet themselves and collect dust as if the end of Christian triumphalism were an excuse for inaction. Peter Brown is quite right: "The *City of God*, far from being a book about flight from the world . . . is a book about being otherworldly in the world."[20]

What does this appraisal mean for the evaluation of political culture? As we noted, Augustine conscientiously exposed the frauds that braced classical political teleology and pagans' hopes for an empire without end. Such disclosures were part of his polemic against his church's critics and their ways of rewriting history. It was another thing altogether—and it certainly would have been a trickier assignment—to repeal and permanently proscribe political optimism and to alter radically Christians' understanding of God's interventions in the empire's history. Eusebius's Constantine could not be purged from the church's self-presentation, or even demoted, without considerable consequence. Had Augustine wanted to unleash a frontal assault on Christian sociolatry, he would have had to edit the current stories of Constantine's piety and prosperity. Instead, he repeated what other apologists had said about the first Christian emperor. Albeit quickly and without much fanfare, he inventoried evidence usually cited to attest God's approval of Constantine's government. He singled out the emperor's designs for a new capital city, where pagan worship was purportedly forbidden. He seemed to agree with previous eulogists that the new regime and the new city signaled that history had been given a fresh start, yet he was more restrained than Eusebius.[21] Restraint, after all, was reasonable, inasmuch as the intervening century had failed to supply Christian sociolatry with material from which a record of uninterrupted good fortune could be narratively constructed. Augustine, however, did *not* hold that the failure necessitated a root-and-branch reassessment of Constantine's mission and achievement.[22]

Augustine readily, almost eagerly, conceded that developments during the fourth century made it impossible to sustain the triumphalists' unconditional optimism for the new Christian empire. Eusebius's more ecstatic pronouncements must have sounded as hollow as the pronouncements of pagan poets who thought that the *pax Romana* would forever crown Aeneas's victories. Neither Eusebius nor Virgil, however, could be utterly dismissed. They exerted too formidable an influence on Augustine's perspective, and several passages in the *City of God* show that their enthusiasms occasionally got the better of the bishop's restraint. At the end of the eighteenth book, for example, Augustine mocked the pagan prophets who had predicted Christianity's disappearance. Oracles had decreed that the new official religion would not survive beyond the year 365. But Augustine boasted that in that very year the emperor's deputies purged Carthage of pagan worship. No doubt, the parallel with Constantine and his new capital came to mind, yet Augustine was too wrapped in the irony and in his defiance of pagan prophecy to linger for another history lesson. The worship of Christ, he noted, had increased from 365 to the time of his writing. And more could be expected. The psalmist was a much more reliable prophet than the pagans' oracles when he assured Christian exegetes that Christ would "have dominion from sea to sea . . . to the ends of the earth."[23]

For a moment, then, Augustine was just as optimistic and cheerful as the Christian triumphalists had been. But, unlike them, he had to explain hardships, betrayals, and wicked officials—all the stresses and strains of the Christian empire. He tried a novel approach. He argued that the sincerity of politicians would be suspect if every Christian emperor had been rewarded as was Constantine, or every apostasy promptly punished. Magistrates would then have been tempted to convert to Christianity or to uphold the church's liberties for the wrong reasons. The *City* is a book about expectations: both those that impart a false sense of security and those that hold inner peace and eternal reward as the genuine objectives of the Christian life. Only the latter could make the magistrate or, for that matter, any citizen a pilgrim. Augustine's point was simple: uncertainties authenticated God's control over history, for they guaranteed that conversions would not be based on prudence, greed, or ambition.[24]

That the disjunction between personal piety and political success strikes at some of sociolatry's claims cannot be denied, although that seems not to have been Augustine's purpose. The bishop was faced with a dilemma; having accused others of falsifying history, he was unlikely to get away with conspicuous omissions. Readers would remember that Emperor Julian reinstated Rome's old gods and that Emperor Theodosius's record was far from immaculate. More to the point, perhaps, Augustine composed his *City* during the empire's most profound crisis. He could not honorably ascribe permanence to the *pax Romana*, to the Christian empire, or to any particular political culture, no matter how pious the politicians. Yet, as far as Augustine could tell, Constantine placed one change beyond the possibility of reversal. The Christian empire survived the first waves of invasions in the fifth century; strictly speaking, Rome did not fall—it did not even fall into the hands of the empire's enemies in 410. The barbarians came but they soon moved on. Earlier misfortunes, particularly Julian's brief pagan revival, could still be taken as interruptions. Christianity endured and quickly recaptured Rome. For Augustine, the change that was beyond change was the conversion of political culture. Magistrates might not yet be steadfastly loyal to the church. Measures for the eradication of idolatry and heresy might not yet be enforced with appropriate vigor, but God, according to Augustine, had given clear indications that the time had arrived for the persecutors of Christianity to become persecutors *for* Christianity.[25]

To understand why Augustine valued certain remnants of Eusebean sociolatry, we must reconsider problems peculiar to the North African church. From 312, dissidents, subsequently known as Donatists, had organized churches in nearly every community. They claimed that established churches had been defiled because authorities permitted sinful members to mingle with the sinless, yet the Donatists' original grievance, which carried weight to the end of the fourth century, was that church authorities themselves could be numbered among the sinful. During the long period of persecution that preceded Constantine's conversion and conquests, some bishops frequently handed over the Christians' sacred texts to hostile imperial officials. And those same bishops retained authority after peace was restored. Some of their equally culpable fellow conspirators were named to succeed them. If innocent Christians continued to mix with these soiled bishops and with bishops and priests whom they consecrated, the contagion would spread. To guard against contamination, Donatists insisted that the unsoiled separate themselves.[26]

One suspects that disagreements about the source and perpetuation of pollution could have been composed, or at least contained, without involving government powers, but one schism led to another. The record of confusion in North Africa, even the account of quarrels among Donatists in Numidia, would run to many thousands of pages. Augustine, however, was less interested in description than reconciliation, and he pinned his hopes for peace on the authority of Christian emperors and their deputies. Augustine's confidence in the government increased during the second decade of the fifth century, just at the time he was contemplating and then composing the *City of God.*

In North Africa, only the civil government remained to pull things together. Augustine's colleagues and allies were powerless to prevent further disintegration, and the Donatists could not keep their ranks in order. Augustine predictably turned Donatist disunity to his advantage. He pointed out that the Donatists were condemning one another in his time much as their ancestors had condemned Caecilian, bishop of Carthage, at the start of the schism. The charges against Caecilian, he said, were manifestly unfair, and his accusers were wrong to discount rulings that vindicated the accused. Augustine then related the origins of Donatist dissent to the internecine disputes that divided Donatism many decades later, whereby the accusers' heirs experienced the same kind of injustice from their Christian brothers as Caecilian endured from his. Yet the danger of disunity was not confined to Donatism. One schism had turned into several, and the disharmony threatened to tear to shreds the whole fabric of North African Christianity.[27]

Donatist extremists were most responsible for the growing problem. They had taken to intimidating rival bishops and their patrons. Several of Augustine's close associates had been victimized by malcontents and vagabonds who occasionally attached themselves to the Donatist cause, if not the Donatist church.[28] Augustine chronicled the violence and presumably exaggerated it to embarrass Donatist moderates who were still willing to debate him. But the debates yielded few converts, and although the instances of intimidation and savagery helped Augustine make this case against Donatist intemperance, he increasingly feared for the safety of his church. He also suspected that leading Donatist officials either encouraged or sanctioned the extremists' tactics. Augustine's apparent inability to persuade his opponents with eloquence and argument as well as the persistence of violence induced him to endorse, reluctantly, his colleagues' petitions for imperial assistance and for coercive measures against their rivals.

Admonitions that Augustine first offered from the pulpit were easily adapted to justify government intervention in religious disputes. Government officials, at the very least, should be dutiful Christians, and dutiful Christians were obliged to bring errant clergy and laymen—lost shepherds and lost sheep—back to Catholic Christianity. If Christian politicians were silent, they would seem to approve the schism. If they approved the schism, they incurred God's wrath.[29]

In their successive councils of Carthage, Augustine's colleagues could appeal to such logic as well as to the tradition of imperial concern for the realm's religious unity. For some time, government officials had been the church's champions. Periodically they passed laws against the Donatists, who were spared only because political conditions occasionally made enforcement difficult.[30] From 401, North African bishops petitioned for new, more stringent prohibitions against their rivals' worship. They also asked that old restrictions be enforced more scrupulously. After some hesitation, Augustine consented to join the campaign and then to lead it. He had once argued that religious conviction could not be coerced, and moderate Donatists, surprised by the apparent change, scolded him for trampling upon his own convictions as well as for summoning the government to legislate against theirs. As often and as contemptuously as Augustine had called to mind the offenses of violent extremists, some Donatists could not believe that rare incidents of that kind could have swayed their opponent so suddenly. Vincent of Cartenna wrote Augustine in 408 requesting an explanation.

Augustine's reply opens with a staggering claim. He admitted that his allies' appeals to the government once seemed ill-advised to him. At the time, he did not think that divine compassion could work through coercion. But Augustine now declared that his assumptions about God's work in the world had been mistaken. Donatist apostates who rejoined his colleagues' churches expressed their gratitude effusively. Their thanks for the political pressures used to pry them from their puritanical sect persuaded Augustine that God had no compunctions about using the force of law and the threat of punishment to prevent Christians from falling further into sin.[31]

Augustine built a theology of persecution with inferences drawn from the apostates' gratitude. Cruelty, he agreed, had no place in official policy or religious conversion, but if authorities had been moved by mercy or pity, moved *ex caritate*, to rescue errant Christians from their errors, Augustine now saw God's hand in the matter. Donatists, of course, perceived things differently. They made a virtue of their outcast status. From their perspective, Christianity had no room for ruling elites; authentic Christians always suffered for their faith—blessed were the persecuted. Augustine, however, would not allow the identification of suffering with righteousness to stand unchallenged. He argued that the persecuted were not always servants of God and that persecutors were not uniformly God's enemies. With consummate skill, he deployed relevant biblical verses to make and illustrate his point. To the objection that it was wrong and wicked to coerce free will, he responded that free will was chimerical. To Donatists who either blamed Catholic bishops and government officials for coercing those appreciative apostates or ridiculed them for believing that a sincere and lasting faith could actually be coerced into existence, Augustine replied that persecution and coercion were not the direct and intrusive causes of conversion. Persecution and coercion merely prompted former Donatists to contemplate their leaders' crimes and their own misconceptions. Such contemplation then led to genuine repentance and a spontaneous profession of faith. Augustine claimed that the government acted responsibly. Measures taken to restore property confiscated by Donatists were evenhanded, and measures to outlaw the worship of schismatics were pious political efforts to restore order, unity, and charity to the churches of North Africa.[32]

Some Donatists acknowledged that their party had asked for government intervention during the early stages of the quarrel with Caecilian. They denied, however, that Constantine or his deputies had issued a final verdict.[33] Augustine effectively challenged their misreading of the documentary evidence, yet he was more interested in emphasizing Donatist resistance to the idea of a Christian empire. Notwithstanding their first appeals for government arbitration, Donatists refused to recognize Constantine's conversion as a divine ruling on the legitimacy and usefulness of imperial political culture. They refused to obey the laws passed by emperors and circulated by their deputies, refused to accept that diligent public officials were God's ensigns and champions of the church. Could such refusals, Augustine wondered, amount to anything other than sedition?[34]

Had Augustine sought a compelling illustration for his argument, he could not have found one better than the Donatists furnished during the last decade of the fourth century. At that time, some leading Donatists openly supported enemies of the Roman empire in North Africa, and the Donatist bishop of Thamugadi was eventually executed as a rebel. Augustine labored in his letters to present the Donatists as a violent and dangerous faction. At hand he had evidence that would surely impress Emperor Honorius, relatively fresh evidence of Donatist subversion and treachery. He pressed Honorius to renew the partnership between the government and the church—the Catholic church—to rid North Africa of secessionists, both political and religious.[35]

There should be no secession from the kingdom that God had given the Christians; nor could there be much doubt that the Roman empire was that kingdom. To be sure, the empire was not the heavenly city walled off, so to speak, from history. But it answered to the psalmist's prophecy that Christ would have dominion "from sea to sea . . . to the ends of the earth."

Augustine repeated the psalmist's assurances in his *City of God*, perhaps because they had assumed such a prominent role in his anti-Donatist polemic. The Donatists said that the New Testament yielded no examples of Christian rulers. Augustine countered that Scripture predicted and promised a new dispensation in which emperors would collaborate with their bishops to spread the true religion to every corner of the known world. What else could the psalmist have meant? Notwithstanding their foothold in North Africa and popularity in Numidia, the Donatists were fools to presume that their church was the sole descendant of the first church in Jerusalem, while Christians elsewhere languished in sin. Christianity started with a small assembly of committed believers, Augustine admitted, but it had spread, as promised, throughout the Mediterranean world and beyond. He scoffed at the idea that Christianity must remain small and politically disadvantaged because it started that way. God had seen to the church's growth. The universal empire had abetted Christianity's progress even before Constantine's conversion. Now that the Catholic church prospered, now that emperors and their officials, as its champions, belonged to the church, to mistrust the psalmist's forecast was inexcusable.[36]

To dispel doubts and defend the degree of universality achieved by the Catholic church against provincial and sectarian Donatists, Augustine fitfully pushed his arguments to the frontiers of Eusebean triumphalism. Hence, even as he composed the first books of his *City*, he was checking the ties between political culture and providence, pleading with authorities in North Africa to make plain and incontestable the emperor's will. For his part, he would continue to explain God's will and to demonstrate that the two wills were one.

The shock of—and aftershocks from—Rome's collapse in 410 did not tempt Augustine to dissolve the partnership between church and government, probably because imperial officials in North Africa had not been immobilized by developments on the Italian peninsula; they still used their authority to assist Augustine and his colleagues against the Donatists. Moreover, Augustine's friend Marcellinus had been sent from the imperial chancery to convene and preside over a much-heralded council in Carthage. Six hundred North African bishops descended on the city for the three sessions in June 411. The Donatists' involvement in the insurrections suppressed years before led to some deterioration in their position, but they still held a slight numerical edge at the conference. Their numbers, however, did not count for much. Marcellinus made critical procedural decisions during the third session that prepared the way for a final judgment favoring Augustine and his party. The Donatists insisted that their rivals, as accusers, either substantiate or drop their charges against Donatus and his heirs. But Marcellinus resolved that the Donatists' charges against Caecilian were at issue. They had to prove their century-old case or else stand justly accused of having originated and perpetuated the accursed schism.[37]

Augustine had won. Catholic cooperation with the authorities turned out to be highly advantageous. Emperor Honorius repealed a previous edict of toleration, perhaps to lure Donatists to the negotiations by giving them a greater stake in the results. (Honorius's preemptive action made them outlaws again; they could only improve their standing.) Marcellinus circulated the emperor's call for the council and added incentives of his own. He promised that Donatist bishops who attended would be allowed to hold their positions until the council's debates were adjourned. All this occurred after Rome is said to have fallen. And from the time Emperor Honorius acceded to Augustine's request for the council to the moment Marcellinus delivered his verdict, the outcome was certain.

The council's effect on Augustine can hardly be overstressed. He so admired Marcellinus that he dedicated the *City of God* to him, and Marcellinus's honorable and shrewd management of the affair was featured prominently in the bishop's several accounts of the deliberations. If Augustine had been disillusioned by the apparent ease with which Rome capitulated in 410, he was reassured by the empire's effectiveness in bringing the Donatists to heel in 411. Of course, Augustine still produced illustrations of the empire's vulnerability in the *City*, illustrations quite compatible with the book's aim. Disappointments and defects associated with the finest political cultures were symptomatic of the impermanence of all worldly gain and glory. The disappointments and defects were drawn from fact and overdrawn for effect, because Augustine was persuaded that ambitions for gain and glory deflected Christians from the whole-hearted worship of their God. The crisis of 410, the grand empire's political and military disgrace, was an excellent example of how the mighty might fall. Nonetheless, given the course of the Donatist controversy, we can see why the crisis did not place at risk Augustine's trust in the premises that had steadied Christian sociolatry for generations. The crisis simply compelled the bishop of Hippo to make adjustments that would keep the premises sturdy.[38]

It is reasonable to assume that Augustine influenced his amanuensis Orosius, who found it possible to sustain both the optimism and the triumphalism of earliest Christian sociolatry. Orosius probably heard Augustine reiterate the psalmist's prophecy, and he heard from others that intruders in Italy were converting to Christianity. He came to believe that Rome's religion would ultimately conquer the conquerors of Rome, that the empire would rebound from its recent setbacks, and that the Christian kingdom, "from sea to sea," would soon exercise greater authority than ever before. But Orosius's expectations outdistanced those of Augustine, who dared not hope for a deliverance of that amplitude.[39]

Despite his triumphs over the Donatists at the Council of Carthage and thereafter, Augustine was no triumphalist. We shall see that the *City of God*, making its adjustments, actually took the triumphalism out of Christian sociolatry. But this does not mean that the Christian empire was an inconsequential part of Augustine's political vision. All that we have found thus far suggests the contrary. But Giovanni Garilli many years ago proposed that Augustine was partial to polyarchy and that the *City of God* reflected his fondness for the peaceable kingdoms that circled the Mediterranean before Rome obliterated their boundaries and suppressed regional autonomy.[40] As Garilli pointed out, the *City* speaks well of the way things were before imperial expansion, but it also notes that the failure of many kingdoms to keep the peace gave Rome the chance to expand. Augustine harbored no regrets; he told the Donatists that the universal empire made possible universal religion. It enabled Christianity to fulfill the psalmist's promises, promises incompatible with polyarchy. Had Augustus and his heirs not tamed the disruptive, cannibalizing tendencies that characterized tribal political life, Christianity could not have spread as quickly and efficiently as it did. On the issues of polyarchy and political pluralism, then, Augustine agreed with Eusebius, and his remarks prefigured Dante's more detailed analysis of the problems that beset a world without world monarchy. Augustine did not begrudge Rome's expansion, yet he was not mortified by its more recent contraction. In his estimation of the political problems and religious prospects of his time, continued expansion and contraction were not mutually exclusive.[41]

The place of this paradox in Augustine's program for the rehabilitation of Christian confidence is an important one. It helped Augustine accommodate the traditional themes of Christian sociolatry to historical crisis. If we eavesdrop on him as he consoles his colleague Hesychius, a bishop in Dalmatia, we hear how cleverly he works.

Hesychius had written to tell Augustine that Europe's side of the Mediterranean was in turmoil. The empire's distress was so great that the psalmist's prophecy afforded him no encouragement. He even speculated that the promise to extend Christ's dominion "from sea to sea" referred only to the apostles' preaching during the first century, not to some future condition; for Hesychius believed that the empire's military disasters doomed Christianity's chances for global influence.

Augustine first tried to avoid the implications of Rome's disasters. He informed Hesychius that the empire's authority in North Africa was expanding even while it was contracting in Europe. In North Africa, he said, Rome's soldiers were annexing new territories and new tribes. Peoples who had never heard of Christ were adopting Christianity. But fresh conquests were not enough to calm Hesychius, who predicted the end of all civilization, so Augustine introduced observations that would have seemed paradoxical to apologists like Orosius, addicted to the intoxicating political prognoses of previous Christian sociolatry. Augustine alleged that Christianity might expand even if the empire contracted. He suggested that the beleaguered empire was not God's only instrument for the spread of Christ's kingdom. Recent crises indicated that history had turned against Rome, yet history would never turn against Christianity. Augustine told Hesychius that peoples beyond the empire's frontiers had joined the new religion in the past and, he advised, others would join as the frontiers receded. Even if the empire's new

North African acquisitions failed to compensate for European losses and were themselves lost, Christians would be foolish to lose hope.[42]

Triumphalists once considered Rome's Christian empire the culmination of history, but that would no longer do. True, Romans had been agents of divine retribution. They flattened the temple in Jerusalem and razed the Jewish kingdom soon after the Jews scorned Jesus. After the conversion of Constantine, emperors shielded the church from its enemies. Honorius and Marcellinus came to Augustine's aid and put the Donatists in their place. The memories of Rome's many services need not be effaced, yet after 410, triumphalism and self-congratulation seemed untimely and excessive. Recent misadventures and misfortune made older expressions of Christian sociolatry obsolete and historically naive.

History reminded Augustine that political culture was a human phenomenon. Because humans and human societies were invariably torn by conflicting desires, justice could only be administered imperfectly. The best motives, the most prudently codified laws, often produced unwanted consequences. Enmity, dread, and anxiety were inextinguishable, despite apologists' energetic efforts to paper over political culture's inadequacies with triumphalist pronouncements.[43] Augustine did not dodge the implications of his darker view of political life (which was an extension of his understanding of the human condition after Adam's fall and without God's grace). Having formulated the darker view, however, he also offered a personalist platform for the renewal of political culture. The Christian empire was not God's only instrument and it was not a perfect instrument, but the empire had been serviceable. And, from Augustine's perspective, there were still services to be performed—recalcitrant Donatists, for instance, to be retrieved.

Augustine's personalist platform was built on admonitions, injunctions, and exhortations, the immediate objective of which was to mend and maintain the coalition between leading prelates and politicians. The ultimate objective was to rehabilitate the redeeming politics of the Christian empire so that the government might continue to help Christianity win its battles for the human will.

The *City of God* grants that the government must order citizens' lives if the church is successfully to reorder their passions and expectations. Inconstant and uncooperative public officials stymied the church's work, so Augustine urged them to reform and to oblige their bishops.[44] He also suggested that persons of proven piety be appointed to important government posts. He trusted their piety would prevent them from taking pride in their talents and promotions and that they would constitute a spectacular demonstration of the power of Christian virtue to withstand ambition and avarice.[45] While the Donatists harped on those blessings that God promised to the persecuted, Augustine blessed the government's peacemakers (*beati pacifici*), who were committed to preserving the religious character of political culture, saving the church from squalls generated by local rivalries, and protecting the church in North Africa from Vandal invaders.[46]

Augustine's pastoral concern was beyond compromise and thus, in a sense, beyond politics. As Gerhart Ladner remarked, he wanted to include "ever larger areas of human terrestrial life in the idea and reality of reform."[47] This goal prompted Augustine to pitch Christian sociolatry in a new key. Oughts and exhortations replaced triumphalists' inflated claims, lyrical descriptions, and sunny forecasts. We might say that Augustine's sociolatry was deliberately studded with subjunctives, for the bishop used the rhetoric of personal reform to address the political and religious crises of this time. He wanted to create "a spiritual earthly city" somewhere between Cain's kind and the perfected city of God. He not only encouraged politicians to greater displays of piety; he also tried to shape a political culture for that spiritual earthly city that would produce the most auspicious environment for Christians to make the choices he would have them make.[48]

Christians' political choices were limited. Augustine prohibited civil disobedience, and he counted on government, even tyrannical government, to keep the peace until the pilgrims remaining on earth could be redeemed at the end of time. The *City of God* seems to end on this note, so Peter Brown was quite right to point out that the final books betoken Augustine's pessimism. He was also right to compare the *City* with a prize fight, "all movement, ducking, and weaving," but Brown does not extend the analogy to one plausible conclusion.[49] The mammoth text bears witness to Augustine's stamina, yet the author appears weary in the later rounds. He tries neither to redeem the standing (yet unsteady) political culture of the Christian empire with a flurry of rhetoric nor to sever the government from the unregenerate world with one final and decisive blow. What Augustine fails to do in the final books, however, hardly tells against what he had done in the earlier rounds. There, without idealizing the Christian empire, he argued that it was absurd to stress the incompatibility between Christianity and successful government. Only "success" needed redefinition. The empire was successful, in Augustine's terms, if, as part of God's providential order, it protected the church from idolators and heretics, exchanged the lust for glory for the love of God, and preserved peace so that those "larger areas of terrestrial life" might be reclaimed by God—person by person and choice by choice. The pilgrim city lived in hope, and its hope was not for terrestrial expanse or some terrestrial kingdom. Yet, for Augustine, Constantine had given the empire its redeeming politics and the psalmist had given Christians the promise of dominion "from sea to sea." Recent crises taught Christians that ultimately they had to trust God's promise of a celestial city. Biblical texts, imperial edicts, and faithful government officials like Marcellinus, however, persuaded Augustine that the present political culture was part of God's saving work in the world.

# Notes

†Reprinted from *Redeeming Politics.* New Jersey: Princeton UP, 1990. Ch. 7, 130–48. Reprinted by permission of Princeton UP.

[1] Consult Robert A. Markus, *Saeculum: History and Society in the Age of Saint Augustine,* 2nd ed. (Cambridge, 1988), particularly pp. 43–46, 69–70; Franz Weissengruber, "Zu Augustins Definition des Staates," *Römische historische Mitteilungen* 22 (1980): 31–35; and Charles Norris Cochrane, *Christianity and Classical Culture* (1940; rpt. Oxford, 1980), pp. 509–10.

[2] Otto Zwierlein, "Der Fall Roms im Spiegel der Kirchenväter," *Zeitschrift für Papyrologie und Epigraphik* 32 (1978): 45–49.

[3] *CCSL* 47: 64–65 (*DCD* 2.29).

[4] *CCSL* 47: 36 (*DCD* 2.3).

[5] *CSEL* 34: 432–33.

[6] *CCSL* 47: 158–59 (*DCD* 5.22).

[7] *CCSL* 47: 48–50 (*DCD* 2.18).

[8] *CCSL* 47: 101–2 (*DCD* 4.4). For a discussion of the *City*'s brief against pagan passions and arrogance, see Klaus Thraede, "Das antike Rom in Augustins *De civitate Dei,*" *Jahrbuch für Antike und Christentum* 20 (1977): 119–20, 139–45.

[9] *CCSL* 48: 453–54 (*DCD* 15.1).

[10] *CCSL* 48: 494 (*DCD* 15.26), 521–13 (*DCD* 16.10).

[11] For controversies over the identity of the pilgrim city, see Yves Congar, "*Civitas Dei* et *Ecclesia* chez saint Augustin," *Revue des études Augustiniennes* 3 (1957): 1–14. Also consult Jean-Claude Guy, *Unité et structure logique de la "Cité de Dieu" de saint Augustin* (Paris, 1961), particularly pp. 89–93, 112, 116–20.

[12] *CCSL* 46: 260–62.

[13] *PL* 38: 622–23.

[14] Zwierlein, "Fall Roms," pp. 56–65.

[15] *CCSL* 48: 460–61 (*DCD* 15.7).

[16] *CCSL* 48: 426 (*DCD* 14.9). Cf. Reinhart Maurer, "Thesen zur politischen Theologie: Augustinische Tradition and heutige Probleme," *Zeitschrift für Theologie und Kirche* 79 (1982): 349–51.

[17] *CCSL* 48: 429–30 (*DCD* 14.9).

[18] *CCSL* 48: 414 (*DCD* 14.1).

[19] See, e.g., *CCSL* 48: 421–23 (*DCD* 14.6–7).

[20] Peter Brown, *Augustine of Hippo* (Berkeley, 1967), pp. 319, 323.

[21] *CCSL* 47: 160–61 (*DCD* 5.25).

[22] See Johannes Straub, "Augustins Sorge um die *regeneratio imperii*: Das *Imperium Romanum* als *civitas terrena,*" *Historisches Jahrbuch* 73 (1954): 53–57.

[23] *CCSL* 48: 571–72 (*DCD* 17.8), 653–56 (*DCD* 18.54).

[24] *CCSL* 47: 160 (*DCD* 5.24).

[25] *CCSL* 47: 104 (*DCD* 4.7), 162 (*DCD* 5.26); 48: 648 (*DCD* 18.50).

[26] E.g., *CSEL* 53: 66–67.

[27] *CCSL* 38: 367. For Augustine's other references to the Maximianist schism, see A. C. de Veer, "L'exploitation du schisme maximianiste par S. Augustin dans sa lutte contre le Donatisme," *Recherches augustiniennes* 3 (1965): 219–37.

[28] For Augustine's catalogue of the crimes of the Circumcellions and for the general contention that "l'Afrique fut le théâtre d'une agitation sociale relativement organisée" between 380 and 400, see Jean-Paul Brisson, *Autonisme et christianisme dans l'Afrique*

*romaine* (Paris, 1958), particularly pp. 331–41; but also note W. H. C. Frend, *The Donatist Church*, 3rd ed. (Oxford, 1985), pp. 171–77; and Emin Tengstrom, *Donatisten und Katholiken: Soziale, wirtschaftliche und politische Aspekte einer nordafrikanischen Kirchenspaltung* (Göteborg, 1964), pp. 43–52, 71–78.

29*PL* 38: 278–80.

30See Ernst Ludwig Grasmück, *Coercitio: Staat und Kirche im Donatistenstreit* (Bonn, 1964), pp. 195–97.

31*CSEL* 34: 445–46. Augustine also claimed that Vincent had no right to fuss. The Donatists, he said, were the first to appeal to political authorities. They developed their aversion to imperial intervention only after Constantine and his heirs refused to credit Donatist arguments and started to legislate in favor of their rivals. Augustine often reiterated his claims and made it impossible for his adversaries to tiptoe around documentary evidence of early Donatist petitions in the dossier compiled by Optatus, former bishop of Milevis. See, for instance, *CSEL* 26: 25–27 for Optatus's narrative report; Hubert Cancik, "Augustin als constantinischer Theologe," in *Der Fürst dieser Welt*, ed Jacob Taubes (Munich, 1983), pp. 142–43, 148; Thraede, "Antike Rom," pp. 137–38; Maurer, "Thesen," pp. 355–57; and Grasmück, *Coercito*, pp. 202–22.

32*CSEL* 34: 493–94.

33*CSEL* 53: 89–90.

34See Brisson, *Autonisme*, pp. 268–69, 288.

35Cf. Frend, *The Donatist Church*, pp. 224–26 and Tengstrom, *Donatisten*, pp. 84–86.

36E.g., *CSEL* 34: 516–20; 52: 585–86.

37For a slice of the Donatists' strategy, see *Actes de la conférence de Carthage en 411*, ed. Serge Lancel, vol. 3 (Paris, 1975), 1138–40. Also note Alberto Pincherle, *Vita di Sant'Agostino* (Rome, 1980), pp. 313–16, 360–64, and Cancik, "Augustin," pp. 146–50.

38See Grasmück's conclusion in *Coercitio*, p. 249.

39Consult, in this connection, Theodor F. Mommsen, *Medieval and Renaissance Studies*, ed. Eugene F. Rice, Jr. (Ithaca, 1959), pp. 265–98, 325–48.

40Giovanni Garilli, *Aspetti della filosofia giuridica politica e sociale di S. Agostino* (Milan, 1957), pp. 174–76.

41*CCSL* 47: 111 (*DCD* 4.15); 48: 643–44 (*DCD* 18.46).

42*CSEL* 57: 277–78, 284–85.

43*CCSL* 47: 55 (*DCD* 2.21); 48: 578 (*DCD* 17.13), 684 (*DCD* 19.17).

44*CCSL* 47: 64 (*DCD* 2.29); 48: 680–81 (*DCD* 19.14).

45*CCSL* 47: 156 (*DCD* 5.19).

46*CSEL* 57: 497.

47See Ladner's *The Idea of Reform* (New York, 1967), pp. 184–85. Also see F. Edward Cranz, "The Development of Augustine's Ideas on Society before the Donatist Controversy," *Harvard Theological Review* 47 (1954): 308–11, and Garilli, *Aspetti*, pp. 185–86.

48See Paolo Brezzi, "Una *civitas terrena spiritualis* come ideale storico-politico di Sant'Agostino," *Augustinus Magister* 2 (1954): 921.

49Peter Brown, "Saint Augustine," in *Trends in Medieval Political Thought*, ed. Beryl Smalley (Oxford, 1965), pp. 1–21.

# Two Conceptions of Political Authority: Augustine, *De Civitate Dei*, XIX. 14–15, and Some Thirteenth-Century Interpretations†

## Robert A. Markus

Thirteenth-century scholastics were addicted to quoting statements of Saint Augustine's, as of other *sancti*, as *auctoritates* in support of their opinions. The conventions of the scholastic employment of *auctoritates* are now tolerably well known. A modern scholar will not be surprised by frequent divergences between the meaning of such statements in their original setting and the meaning given them by one or other thirteenth-century theologian. Thirteenth-century theologians would have been even less worried by such divergences. Their analysis can, nevertheless, be illuminating. In this paper I shall examine the use made by a number of thirteenth-century writers of Saint Augustine's statements about the origins and nature of political authority and subjection, mainly in the *De civitate Dei*, book xix, chapters 14 and 15. This is one of the points at which we should expect the impact of Aristotelian ideas to show itself most clearly on political thought. It is here that we may best test the validity of the rival claims that the impact of these ideas revolutionized medieval political thought or, alternatively, that they stood in direct continuity with traditional, patristic and especially Augustinian thought-forms.[1]

The purpose of this paper is not directly to adjudicate on this large problem raised by the confrontation of two opposed interpretations of the history of medieval political thought. It is a much more modest one, which nevertheless lies at the centre of the larger problem. In the first part of the paper I examine the meaning of Augustine's statements concerning the origins of political authority, obligation, and subordination in these two chapters of his *De civitate Dei*, in the light of other relevant passages. In the second part I shall turn to some thirteenth-century interpretations of the same chapters by a number of writers of both the Aristotelian and what is traditionally referred to as the "Augustinian" schools. Anything like a full study of their theories of political authority is beyond my scope. An examination of their various attempts to come to grips with the Augustinian view of the origins of this authority will, however, enable us to watch at close quarters what Augustine meant as seen through thirteenth-century preoccupations, and how far this meaning was modified by Aristotelian preoccupations.

I. *De civitate Dei*, xix. 14–15

Augustine never discusses the question of the state's origin both directly and in detail. The fullest remarks on this theme occur in these two chapters of his *De civitate Dei*, and, as we shall see, even these are not wholly centered on the problem with which we are concerned. Allusions and quotations by medieval writers, when debating our problem, are most frequently to these two chapters. They make a suitable starting-point to our inquiry.

Chapter 14 begins with a statement about the ends which the two "cities" pursue, the main theme under discussion in book xix. "In the earthly city the use of temporal things is referred to the enjoyment of earthly peace; whereas in the heavenly city it is referred to the enjoyment of eternal peace." Augustine now goes on to expound what the peace is which is desired by all men. As he describes it, it is identical with what he has called "eternal peace"; this alone ultimately satisfies all human longings. He continues with an account of how man is to conduct himself so as to attain this eternal peace. He is to obey the two chief commandments of God: to love God and to love his neighbour as himself. The latter must include having consideration for one's fellow men, encouraging them to love God,[2] and being prepared to be thus encouraged by others. In this way only can men achieve "peace" with their fellows; first with those close to them "either by the order of nature, or by the bonds of society," their families and household, then with others more remote in so far as life brings them into contact with them. The chapter ends with a picture of the "domestic peace," defined as the "ordered harmony of authority and obedience of the household."[3] This is the point in the chapter at which "authority" (*imperare, imperium*) is brought into the discussion. Hitherto Augustine had been speaking of the duties of the head towards his household in terms of "care for" and "guidance" (*consulere*). This duty is now defined in terms of authority: "to guide is to exercise authority (*imperant enim qui consulunt*) . . . and to be guided is to obey (*obediunt autem quibus consulitur*) . . . ." Authority and obedience (*imperare-obedire*) are a wider notion, to which giving and receiving guidance (*consulere-consuli*) are assimilated, a little arbitrarily, as a special case of the wider pair of concepts. Authority and obedience may present a very different face from the idyllic harmony sketched here; but in the household of the just man who lives by faith, those who rule in reality serve the subjects whom they appear to be ruling; and they rule "not through a craving for power but in virtue of their obligation of caring for and guiding [their subjects] (*neque enim dominandi cupiditate imperant, sed officio consulendi*); nor with pride in lordship, but with merciful concern."

The burden of the chapter is an exhortation to men in a place of authority and particularly a place of authority in household and family, how to conduct themselves in relation to their subjects. In the heavenly city the exercise of authority must be conceived as service. Augustine does not discuss the origin of social institutions at all in his chapter. He is concerned solely with how a man is to live within social institutions, particularly of family and household, as a citizen of the heavenly city. To this extent the chapter is concerned with two ways of exercising power within any social grouping.

The following chapter shows that the fact that in any institution power can be exercised on the model of a *paterfamilias* or otherwise has no implications for Augustine concerning the origins of institutions. The opening sentence of this chapter refers back to the previous chapter: "This is what the order of nature prescribes, this is how God created man"; and referring to Gen. i. 26, Augustine explains that God did not wish man, whom he made rational and in his own image, to rule over any but irrational creatures. Man was given dominion or authority not over other men, but over beasts. Thus the first just men of old were shepherds rather than kings. The condition of servitude is rightly imposed on sinners. The origin of the servitude in which man is subjected to another in virtue of the bondage of his condition, is sin. Only in this chapter does Augustine begin to speak about the origin of any social institution, and the institution he discusses, that of slavery, is unambiguously traced to sin as its origin. Augustine stresses that it is nevertheless a just enactment of God; for although "nobody is the slave either of man or of sin by nature, as God first created man, nevertheless penal servitude is ordained by the same law as the one which enjoins the order of nature to be kept and forbids its transgression: for if nothing had been done against that law in the first place, there would be no need for the coercion of penal servitude." The chapter concludes with an exhortation to slaves, to behave so as to achieve freedom, after a manner, in their servitude, by serving their masters with loving fidelity "until iniquity shall pass away and all domination and human power shall be emptied and God shall be all in all."

It is generally not noticed that Augustine is insisting on two things in these chapters: that, on the one hand, servitude is a condition or institution whose origin is not to be found in man's nature as created; and, on the other hand, that there is a way of exercising authority—and subjection—either in accordance with the order of nature or otherwise. Augustine explicitly includes the relation between master and slave among those in which he asserts that "this [way of conducting oneself in it] is prescribed by the order of nature."[4] Although, then, the institution itself originates in sin, the exercise of authority in it need not be and ought not to be sinful but in accordance with the order of nature. We must conclude that these chapters give no ground for the opinion that for Augustine the state and political authority are, or can be, an institution of nature. Chapter 14 asserts nothing about institutions, and speaks only about the exercise of authority, and chapter 15 indicates that he thought that the natural order could be observed within an institution belonging to the order of fallen, sinful nature.

Apart from this general principle, our two chapters assert nothing explicitly about the nature of political authority. There is a phrase in chapter 14 which suggests that Augustine would have distinguished it from the kind of authority enjoyed by a father over his family; for he distinguishes within the household over which the *paterfamilias* presides those who are close to him "by the order of nature" (i.e. his family) and those who are close "by the order of society" (i.e. his household slaves, &c.). The impression given—it is no more—is that the "order of nature" is thought of as coextensive here with the family. There is nothing specific in the text to show whether political authority is to be taken, with slavery, as originating in sin, or, with the family, as arising from the order of nature. None the less, in the absence of positive grounds for excepting political authority, the most natural way of reading what Augustine says about the subjection of man to man is to take it quite generally, including within its scope the subjection of men to their rulers. The verse quoted from Genesis (i. 26), "Let them have dominion over the fish of the sea and over the birds of the air and over every creeping thing that creeps upon the earth," and Augustine's comment that God did not wish man to rule over other men, taken in their most immediately natural sense, would exclude any kind of dominion of men over other men; and the observation in the following sentence that for this reason just men were at first shepherds rather than kings clinches the appositeness of interpreting Augustine as wishing to include political dominion with his meaning. Finally, the conclusion of the chapter also suggests that Augustine thought of all institutions of human domination and power as on a level with slavery, at least in respect of their final destiny. It is at least striking that he does not dissociate political from other forms of authority, as one might expect him to have done if he had thought of it as different in origin and kind. A long passage,[5] which recalls *De civitate Dei*, xix. 15 at a number of points, gives a similar impression. Here Augustine discusses the dominion exercised by the bad over the good. What is interesting for our purpose about this passage is not Augustine's defence of such a state of affairs, which rests on his view that it is God's dispensation *ad tempus*, and will be done away with at the end; it is the equivalence between slavery and all political authority, secular power, and dignity on which some stress is laid. Though the origins of the institutions are, again, not under discussion, the effect of the passage is to reinforce the impression that slavery and other institutions of human subjection are not fundamentally distinguished in Augustine's mind.

Augustine clarifies his position to some extent when he explains[6] that a harmonious social existence is natural to man, and a desire for such an existence is implanted in man by nature. His account of such a state implies that in it men are equal before God, until perverse imitation of God disrupts the social harmony. Rejecting equality with his fellows, man wishes to impose dominion on them. Three assertions are clearly made here: that man's nature is social, not solitary; that by their original nature men are equal and subject to God, not to one another; and that subjection to one another is the consequence of sinful pride. The last assertion, we may note, is made without particular reference to slavery; and a similar argument[7] involving political subordination suggests that this should be taken as included among the results of sin. Augustine sometimes refers to man's dominion over lower creatures as *potestas naturalis*, and traces this to man's superiority to other creatures in virtue of being made to God's image and likeness.[8] Gen.i.26, invoked here as in *De civitate Dei*, xix. 15, gives no grounds for including any form of subordination of man to man within the range of this *potestas naturalis*.

None of this, however, would suffice for a conclusive refutation of the view that for Augustine the state is natural. The case for this view rests almost entirely on the twin assertions[9] that Augustine admitted a natural subordination of men to men, notably in the family, and that the state is in this respect homogeneous with the family and therefore belongs to the order of nature. It is important, therefore, to examine more closely the manner in which Augustine distinguished natural from non-natural forms of subjection between man and man, and whether political institutions really do belong with those of the family, or, rather, with slavery.

That Augustine did not exclude all forms of subjection from the order of nature in the state of primitive innocence there can be no doubt. He asserts this quite explicitly in commenting on Gen.i.26 in a work of 419.[10] It gives us to understand, he argues, that reason is to have dominion over irrational life; this subjection is just, whereas iniquity or adversity subject men to the service of others. But, Augustine goes on to observe, the verse does not exclude "a natural order [of subjection] in mankind, too, such that in virtue of it women should be subject to men and sons to their fathers; for in these cases, too, it   right that the weaker in reason should be subject to the stronger." How little inclined Augustine was to extend this "natural order of subjection" to include political subjection we may gauge from the opening remark, which began this train of reflections. There Augustine commends the patriarchs, apropos of Gen. xlvi. 32, for being shepherds—and one recalls the comparison of shepherds and kings in *De civitate Dei*, xix. 15—for "this sort of dominion and subjection, whereby beasts are subjected to men and men in charge of beasts, is undoubtedly right." It is clear that the oft-invoked text cannot serve to justify the opinion that political authority is based on a natural order of subjection among men. An analysis of the antecedents of this text, however, reveals the structure of ideas in Augustine's mind of which this theme forms a part. The view that there is a natural subordination among men is, of course, not by any means expressed here for the first time in his work. It is clearly asserted in his great commentary on Genesis, written *c.* 401–14. Commenting in this work[11] on the verse "To the woman [God] said 'I will greatly multiply thy pain in childbearing . . . and thou shalt be under thy husband's power and he shall have dominion over thee,'"[12] Augustine observes that the text clearly speaks of what woman's condition is to be as a punishment for her sin. All the same, he insists, we are not to doubt that even before sin woman was so made that she should be under man's dominion. The punishment should therefore be understood as consisting in that kind of subjection (*servitutem*) "which belongs to a certain condition rather than to love (*quae cuiusdam conditionis est potius quam dilectionis*); so that we should understand that this kind of servitude, too, whereby men afterwards began to be servants of each other, has its origin in the punishment of sin." The servitude which Augustine identifies with loving subordination belongs to the nature in which man and woman were originally created. In their fallen state, however, this mutual service in charity is over-laid by the kind of subjection by which one person owes service and obedience to another in virtue of his condition or status. And this kind of subjection is a result of sin. Within it, service and dominion can be exercised as an office of charity; but the partnership may fall short of this and be a case of one being dominated by the other. The Apostle, Augustine says, exhorts married partners to the former (Gal. v. 13), and absolutely forbids woman to dominate over man (I Tim. ii. 12). The distinction between service as required by the natural order of subordination and service as owed in virtue of status and condition is identical with the distinction alluded to in *De civitate Dei*, xix. 15.[13]

This extensive commentary on the book of Genesis contains the first germs of many of the ideas which we meet later in the *De civitate Dei*. It is important therefore to note that it gives no countenance to the suggestion that Augustine linked the institutions of marriage and the state as belonging to the natural order as created. On the contrary: it is clear that the service and subjection which a man owes another in virtue of being subject to him as to his legitimate ruler is an instance of subjection in virtue of status only; it has nothing to do with any possible moral or intellectual superiority of the ruler over his subject. This emerges with all clarity from the theory of divine providence which Augustine elaborates in book viii of the commentary, which stands, like so many of these seminal ideas, behind the applications they find in the *De civitate Dei*.

His theory of divine providence led Augustine to dissociate the authority of man over woman, and other forms of natural subordination, from purely institutional forms of subjection to authority, such as exist in the state. With the insertion of man (and angels) into the universe, an element of freedom and rational agency is introduced: as Augustine expresses it in a fine and untranslatable image, with man "the bud (*oculus*) of reason is grafted on to the world, as on to a great tree of things."[14] With this grafting, the divine gardener's operation becomes two-fold. His providence operates in two channels, through the processes of nature and through the acts of wills. In his grand catalogue of the works of man which fall under the operation of providence, Augustine mentions "the administration of societies" specifically as under God's *providentia voluntaria*. A few paragraphs later[15] he returns to the same duality of God's providence, and enumerates examples of natural subordination which God's providence secures among natures thus: "He first subjected all things to himself, then he subjected corporeal to spiritual creatures, irrational to rational, earthly to heavenly, female to male, those of lower value to those of higher, the more restricted to the more comprehensive." Neither slavery nor political subjection is mentioned here. From the two passages taken together we may infer that the subjection of woman to man, as of those inferior in some relevant respect to those superior, derives from the order of nature; whereas the subjection of men to political authority (and slavery) does not.

It is in this great commentary on Genesis that Augustine first came to grips with the idea of nature. The distinction here developed, under the impulse of that reflection, between the twin channels of providential order lies behind the later discussions of the *De civitate Dei*. It underlies, for instance, the fine chapter[16] devoted to providence in which Augustine describes, in a passage of sweeping rhetoric, the all-embracing range of God's providence in nature, and then adds that "the kingdoms of men, their dominations and their subjections (*regna hominum eorumque dominationes et servitutes*)" are in no way to be thought remote from "the laws of his providence." These laws are obviously identical with the law Augustine refers to in *De civitate Dei*, xix. 15, the law which ordains penal servitude on the one hand, and enjoins the order of nature to be observed and forbids its transgression on the other.[17] There is a clear reference embedded here to the dual operation of divine providence elaborated in the *De Genesi ad litteram*. Augustine's view that the institutional subjection of man to man is rooted in human sin and is part of a divine dispensation for sin, has deep roots in his thought about the operation of divine providence in the world. The subjection of wives to their husbands and of children to their parents is not, in the relevant sense, institutional; it is clear and generally agreed that Augustine held these to be ordinances of nature. Nor, it is also clear, is society itself institutional in this sense. For as we have seen,[18] a social existence was in Augustine's view natural to man. God had created man with a view to social existence,[19] and the saints shall live in sociable union.[20] Men are driven "by the laws of their nature" to enter a social existence; but Augustine conceives this "natural" society as a society of equals living in concord and subject only to God.[21] That he envisaged a wide variety of grades of intelligence and ability among men we need not deny. But he was certainly not so naive as to assume that political authority and subjection were in fact often based on such a hierarchy of ability, and he certainly did not seek to justify the claims of political authority on grounds of any alleged natural superiority of ruler to subject, such as he attributes to the husband or the father over his family. He did think that the superior abilities of the wise man should find expression in concern for and guidance of the less wise. This is in accordance with the order of nature, displayed by the *paterfamilias*,[22] and it should be the pattern for the conduct of anyone in a position of authority. But the institutions of government, coercion, and punishment are brought into human society by sin. They are God's just punishment for man's transgression, and they are also his providential dispensation for coping with its consequences, disorder, strife, and lack of concord. Like society, the family, too, can be disordered by sin; here, too, disobedience may require coercion and punishment.[23] The parallel between society and the family is, indeed, important to Augustine. But it does not imply that political authority is grounded in the order of nature, as is paternal. A ruler or magistrate should behave like a *paterfamilias*; but the analogy between the two men holds only in respect of family life in the fallen state of man. For the coercive power which is part of the very substance and meaning of political authority also exists in the family; it enters the family, as it enters society, through sin and disorder. But a family is a family without it—we may conceive, even in a sinful world, of a family in which paternal authority is an exercise of care and guidance without coercion. But coercive power is part of the essence of political authority. Without it the state is not a state, though we may imagine lesser societies without it. Political authority, coercive power and its apparatus are what transform society into a state. Society, so we may summarize Augustine's view, has its origins in the order of nature; the state is a dispensation rooted in sin.

It remains to consider the analogy between the authority enjoyed by the soul over its body and that enjoyed by the ruler over his subjects. The application of this analogy would clearly point away from the view I have ascribed to Augustine. It would suggest that the relations of political authority are based on a natural order of command and obedience such as Augustine undoubtedly thought obtained between soul and body. Gustave Combès, indeed, saw the force of the analogy, and quoted[24] a passage from Augustine's *Contra Julianum* to clinch his interpretation of Augustine's theory of the state as natural. As this work is likely to be not very much earlier in composition than the later books of the *De civitate Dei*, it is worth examining its use of this analogy with some care. In the passage adduced by Combès[25] Augustine is quoting Cicero's *De republica*:

> Is it not clear that nature always gives authority (*dominatum*) to the better, for the great profit of the weaker? Why else should God rule over men, the mind over the body, reason over lust and anger and the other vicious parts of the soul? . . . But we must advert to the different forms of rule and subjection. The mind is said to rule both its body and its lusts; but it rules its body as a king rules his subjects or a parent his children, whereas it rules its lusts as a master rules his slave, with coercion and repression. Kings, emperors (*imperatores*),[26] magistrates, fathers and victorious nations have authority over their subjects in the way that the mind has authority over its body. . . .

Undoubtedly, Cicero here links political authority with paternal and likens them both to the natural authority of superior over inferior, such as the mind has in relation to its body; and Augustine quotes the passage with approval. Nevertheless, Cicero's view is not Augustine's. We may begin by noting the evident reserve with which Augustine quotes Cicero against his Pelagian opponent. Secular letters are no ground—Julian had himself appealed to Cicero—on which to refute bishops charged with expounding the holy scriptures; rather should such literature be deemed to be mad ravings if such a conflict appears.[27] All the same, since worldly literature sometimes contains "traces of the truth" (*vestigia veritatis*), Julian's arguments can be answered from the very source of his own[28]—this is how Augustine introduces his appeal to Cicero. We need not lay too much weight on the views expressed in it; Augustine makes it only too clear that the passage is introduced as a polemical device. He wishes to confute Julian on his own ground, rather than by theological argument from the scriptures. Augustine's use of this Ciceronian analogy is, however, of considerable interest and repays elucidation.

Cicero is concerned with distinguishing two kinds of authority among men, one which is in accordance with nature, and one which is despotic. The analogy with the two ways in which the mind rules its body and its passions is intended to throw light on the two ways of ruling men. Augustine reverses the application of the analogy: he is concerned with the soul and bodily passions, especially in their disorganized state in man's fallen condition. It is to illuminate this relation of mind to body that he uses the analogy with political authority. Cicero's analogy would have been just as useful to him for this purpose had it contrasted only paternal authority with despotic, omitting royal authority.[29] But since Augustine was not directly concerned with discussing the nature of political and despotic authority, as Cicero had been, he saw no harm in quoting the whole passage as it stood.

The origin of royal authority was in fact one of the issues over which Augustine sharply disagreed with Cicero.[30] For Cicero, ancient kingship was wielded, in accordance with the order of nature, by the justest and wisest of men; whereas one of the themes which appears in the *De civitate Dei* with almost monotonous frequency is the theme of the origin of kingship in conquest, domination, and lust for power. And repeatedly Augustine dwells on the significance of the fact that the Old Testament patriarchs were shepherds rather than kings.[31] There can, therefore, be no justification for inferring from Augustine's use of the passage from Cicero's *De republica* that he grouped kingship—and other non-despotic forms of political authority—with paternal and other natural forms of authority. Once in the *De civitate Dei*[32] Augustine refers to Cicero's argument, using it, on this occasion, in its original sense, that is to say, as an argument justifying political authority on the analogy of the natural rule of the mind over its body, rather than in the reverse direction. But in doing so, Augustine takes every care to evacuate the argument of all its force. In earlier parts of his *De republica*, as Augustine summarizes Cicero, he had argued the case for injustice, and suggested that a commonwealth could not exist without it, for the rule of one man over others is unjust, and yet, there can be no dominion over nations without it. Now, Augustine says, Cicero changes his standpoint, and meets this argument by asserting that this subjection is justified by the fact that "it is good for such men to be subjected, for subjection is to their benefit," in that by removing from the wicked the power to hurt, they will be better off when tamed than they had been untamed. Augustine passes over this classical piece of imperialist dogma without comment—he had plenty to say about it earlier in his work—and goes on to note Cicero's further justification of such rule by invoking the analogy of nature: "Why else should God rule over men, the mind over the body, reason over lust and the other vices?" But his answer to the rhetorical question drastically deflates its Ciceronian implications, and turns its significance in another direction. Cicero's examples show, he says, modestly, that for some people subjection is good,[33] and that subjection to God is good for all. For the mind which is justly subject to God rules justly over its body; and with the Ciceronian claim for political authority and subjection quietly by-passed, Augustine returns to the point with which the present excursus had begun: the meaning of justice and the need for it in the *res publica*, defined as Cicero had defined it. His handling of Cicero's argument shows profound reserve about Cicero's aligning of political authority and subjection on the side of natural authority and subordination.

The views on the origin of political authority which I have traced in Augustine's works appear to be his settled views from about 401 onwards. Before this time he does not appear to have devoted much thought to this question. From remarks scattered through his earlier works a somewhat different view of the nature of political authority can be pieced together.[34] The strand in Augustine's reflection on society which we have been studying is only one among several which shaped his views on the state and its functions; views which sometimes gave rise to tensions in his mind, some of which he never fully resolved. In so far as our present theme can be isolated as a coherent theme in his thought, it seems very likely that his deepened study of St. Paul in the mid 390's helped to give it shape. This is the source of his consciousness of the power of sin over human nature. The shift from an early optimism is nowhere more marked than in his reflection on society. The whole complex cluster of themes which go into the making of this reflection is too wide for study here. From a wider point of view, the revolutionary effect of thirteenth-century Aristotelianism could be summed up quite simply as lying in the assertion of the innate value of the natural order as a positive force for good, as against Augustine's refusal to assign value to the things of nature, *per se*, in a sinful world. But here I shall be concerned with a narrower question: just how, precisely, did Augustine and his thirteenth-century interpreters respectively think of political society in relation to the natural order? Stating the question in these terms one does, of course, run the risk of giving Augustine's own treatment of the theme an air of spurious terminological precision. The looseness of his conception of "nature" is too notorious to require comment; and the extent to which one should speak of his conception of "political" authority, and still more of the "state," is open to debate. But we may, at any rate, summarize the result of the inquiry of this first section by saying that the terms in which Augustine came to formulate his views on politically organized society (that is to say, on society articulated within the framework of government and its agencies, law, enforcement and the machinery of their administration: roughly what we should nowadays call the "state") were those which he thought appropriate to the treatment of the institution of slavery, rather than those which he applied to the human family.

The crucial point at stake in the theological discussions of the origins of political authority is the question as to whether it is to be treated on the model of the authority of a master over his slave, or on that of a husband and father over his wife and family. These are the paradigm cases which give us a clue to the senses in which the concept of "nature" is applied to social groupings. What is meant by asserting—or by denying—that political authority belongs to the natural order depends on the meaning attached to "natural": it will clearly be something very different according as to whether, and in what sense, the "natural order" is held to include or to exclude the institution of slavery. If there is a sense in which political society was, for Augustine, "natural"—and we shall see that some of his medieval interpreters thought that there was such a sense—it is a sense very different from that in which he thought the family to be "natural." We may, therefore, conclude, without fear of distorting his view though in a language slightly more formalized than his own, that after *c.* 400 Augustine continued to think, with Cicero,[35] that man was a social animal by nature, but that he came to reject the view that he was also naturally a political animal.[36] Of this latter view there is no trace in the two chapters of the *De civitate Dei* which we have examined; and interpreted in the context of the ideas with which they belong in Augustine's thought, and particularly in the light of his *Auseinandersetzung* with Cicero's views, they clearly assert the contrary.

## 2. *Some thirteenth-century interpretations*

Although our two chapters of the *De civitate Dei* find no place in the exposition of Gen. i. 26–27 in the *Glossa ordinaria*, or in the discussion of political authority in the *Sentences* of Peter Lombard,[37] they were nevertheless common property to medieval theologians and were often invoked in debates about the origins of authority and subjection. The purpose of this second section of my paper is to shed some light on the interpretation of Augustine's views primarily by St. Thomas Aquinas. St. Thomas's first work, his commentary on the *Sentences*, though written before Aristotle had made his full impact on Aquinas's political thought with the Latin version of the *Politics*, was already marked by strong Aristotelian influence, especially of the *Ethics*. In his *Scriptum super Sententiis* we can observe Thomas in dialogue with the tradition of the schools on the one hand, and with his contemporaries, notably St. Albert the Great and St. Bonaventure, on the other.[38] To throw Thomas's views into sharper relief, I shall begin by comparing them with Bonaventure's and Albert's, referring, incidentally, to one or two other writers. The comparison with Bonaventure serves to assess St. Thomas's views in relation to a theologian less intoxicated with the new learning and more reserved about its results than was Albert, Thomas's teacher and one of the leaders of the Christian Aristotelian revival of the century.

*      *      *

[Albert's] pupil, St. Thomas Aquinas, appears from the start to have been much more anxious to relate his Aristotelian ideas on society to the Augustinian views on subjection generally current in the schools in the 1250's. Although he had not yet a complete translation of Aristotle's *Politics* at his disposal, he could learn Aristotle's view of man as *animal politicum* from the *Ethics*,61 a work already well known to him when he composed his *Scriptum super Sententiis*. In this, his earliest work, he already shows a concern to relate the two sets of ideas within a single framework.62 That his way of dealing with the problem owes something to the current debates we may guess from his very selection of texts: they include the texts from Augustine and from Gregory which we have seen being repeatedly invoked. In his answer to the question whether there would have been authority (*praelatio seu dominium*) in the state of innocence, Thomas begins with distinguishing two "modes" of authority: one is for the sake of government (*ad regimen ordinatus*), the other for the sake of domination (*ad dominandum*). With a reference to Aristotle's *Ethics* (apparently 1161a30–b10), he remarks that the second mode is analogous to a tyrant's authority over his subjects, the first to a king's: for the former dominates over his subjects for his own benefit, the latter rules them for their good. The authority of domination could therefore exist in the state of innocence only over creatures made to subserve human purposes, not over other men; for men are not made to serve human ends. This subjection comes about only in so far as their condition is assimilated, as a consequence of sin, to that of irrational creatures. Only the authority of ruling men in their own interests could have belonged to man in his creational integrity.

The distinction between two "modes" of authority is quite at home within a fundamentally Augustinian context. In *De civitate Dei*, xix. 14 Augustine had been speaking of two ways of exercising power; what Aquinas says about two "modes" of *dominium* can be translated into Augustine's less formal speech without difficulty. He uses traditional material to state the distinction between tyrannical rule (assimilated naturally to the rule of a master over his slaves) and non-tyrannical. It is essentially the same distinction as Augustine had made between the ruler who rules *dominandi cupiditate* and the ruler who rules *officio consulendi*. On the matter of the exercise of power, and its harmony or lack of harmony with the order of nature, there is no disagreement between Aquinas and Augustine. A strain begins to show as soon as Aquinas turns to answering objections based on the Augustinian view of the institutions of human subjection. To reconcile them with his views, Thomas has to confine their significance by interpreting them as referring to the exercise of authority. Thus one objection63 is based on Augustine's *dictum* that since man was made in the image of God, he was placed only above other creatures, not above his fellow men, over whom he would have no dominion but for sin; another,[64] based on the same chapter of *De civitate Dei*, asserts that since *dominium* implies *servitus* as its correlative and since the latter, as all the fathers agree, was introduced on account of sin, there could have been no *dominium* or *praelatio* in the absence of sin. Aquinas answers both together,[65] remarking that these statements refer to the second mode of authority, that of domination. This, of course, had been far from Augustine's intention; but it was a means that lay ready to hand to effect a reconciliation. But Aquinas was not content with as perfunctory and superficial a reconciliation as satisfied Albert. In the article we are considering, he goes on to examine political authority explicitly; and his procedure shows a real attempt to clarify in his own mind how far the Augustinian assessment of political authority is acceptable.

Having distinguished the two modes of *dominium*, of which only the one "ordained for the sake of government" could have belonged to nature in its original integrity, he further considers this mode of authority in respect of three functions (*usus*) enumerated as follows: first, the direction of subjects in "what is to be done"; second, the providing for needs such as common defence of the people against enemies; third, the correction of morals, "so that the wicked may be coerced to perform the actions of virtue" by punishments. Of these functions, Aquinas says, only the first would have had a place in the absence of sin, for there would have been no need for the others. Thus, to secure agreement with Aristotle, Aquinas has driven a wedge into the substance of political authority. For Aristotle, as, indeed, for Augustine, political authority was not conceivable without coercive power. This belonged to its very essence, and this was one of the reasons why Augustine thought that all earthly kingdoms were, as institutions, rooted somehow in the dispensation of sin. Aquinas wished to concede this, and he also wanted to speak, with Aristotle, of the political order as an ordinance of nature. In his attempt to reconcile the two ways of thought, he left what Augustine would have regarded as the distinctive features of political authority in the world of fallen man; but he dissociated them as in some way adventitious to the essence of political authority, which could have existed without such features. He did not notice that in doing this he was in effect rejecting Augustine's protest against assimilating political to paternal authority. What Aquinas left on the side of nature, Augustine would not have recognized as "political." For Augustine the institutional life of the Roman Empire was still a daily reality. That he thought more readily of governmental institutions in concrete terms than Aquinas need cause no surprise. Even with the great acceleration in the growth of governmental institutions in his own century, Aquinas could readily break down their institutional character into a series of "functions" which could be isolated in this way.

If Thomas purchased agreement with Augustine by almost evacuating "political authority" of meaning, his agreement with Aristotle was purchased at the same price. This appears from his manner of dealing with the objection that according to Aristotle[66] kings and other rulers had to be instituted in order to make laws with coercive power, a power lacking to mere exhortation by wise men; and that there would have been no need for this if men had remained in their original state of justice. Aquinas answers this [67] argument with the simple assertion that in respect of "that function" (he refers to the coercive function) there would have been no authority in man's original state; whereas there would have been in respect of the other governmental functions.[68] It would have been just as unreal to Aristotle as to Augustine to drive a wedge into the substance of government in this way. He would no more have recognized political authority in the guise of a citizens' advice bureau than would Augustine.

There are many signs that Aquinas was dissatisfied with this manner of solving his problem. With his deepening appreciation of Aristotle, he came to see the full force of Aristotle's view that man is by nature *animal politicum*.[69] The view that man was by nature *animal sociale* was, by itself, entirely traditional, and could be found—on occasion in almost the very words—in Augustine.[70] With growing understanding of Aristotle, Thomas came to see that Aristotle's views on man as *animal politicum* were more far-reaching than the traditional view of him as *sociale*;[71] and he was clear that from the Aristotelian point of view there could be no distinction between *politicum* and *sociale*, as if the former were no more than a particular form or species of the latter. Social existence, in Aristotle's perspective, was identical with political existence. The *polis* was not society plus political structure, and a "society" without political structure would have been even less than chimerical in his eyes: for at least a chimera could be imaginatively constructed from elements experienced separately. If for Aristotle a society which[72] was not political was meaningless, it was not so for Augustine and the Christian fathers. For Aristotle the archetypal society was the *polis*; for them it was the family of the saints in heaven. For them there could be a real distinction between that kind of society and the politically organized society which they knew in the Empire. From their point of view "social" and "political" were by no means synonymous concepts, as they had to be for Aristotle. As St. Thomas came to regard society increasingly from an Aristotelian standpoint, it is not surprising that in his vocabulary, too, *sociale* and *politicum* should have tended to lose their distinctive features. The profound significance of St. Thomas's Aristotelian view of society is entirely beyond the scope of this paper, though its growth in his mind could still profitably be mapped with more precision than it has yet received. We must return to his understanding of Augustine's

view, and consider how he interpreted it later in his career, after the
Aristotelian vision of society had established itself more deeply in his mind.

The one occasion when Aquinas returns to consider our two chapters of
Augustine's *De civitate Dei* is in connection with his restatement of his views
on the origins of authority in his *Summa theologiae*. The framework within
which he places his article[73] on man's dominion over man in the state of
innocence is entirely traditional. It follows articles devoted to man's
authority over the lower creation, original equality of men, and so forth. His
answer to the question about dominion over men is also, at first sight,
impeccably traditional. It begins with a distinction between two kinds of
*dominium* reminiscent, but not identical with, the early distinction we have
considered. Where the early work contrasted two mutually exclusive modes
of authority, one exercised for the benefit of the master, the other for that of
the subject, we now find the distinction drawn between authority as a general
concept (*secundum quod communiter refertur ad subjectum qualitercumque*),
related to any form of subjection, and authority in a special sense, understood
as the correlative of servitude. This latter could not have existed in the state
of innocence; the former could. This way of stating the distinction between
two sorts of *dominium* may be logically equivalent to the earlier manner of
speaking; but it creates a much firmer impression that Thomas wishes to
affirm, in the first place, that *dominium* does belong to the state of nature
before the fall. Instead of asserting that in one mode it did and another it did
not exist in the state of innocence, he now says that *dominium* belongs to this
state, except for one form of it, the form found in slavery. Another difference
between this and the earlier treatment is noteworthy: whereas the two
"modes" of authority distinguished had been two ways of exercising
authority, the contrast is here drawn in institutional terms: it is between
authority as existing in slavery and authority as existing, among other
institutions, in the "office of governing free men."

The crucial difference, however, between this and the earlier treatment of
the same theme is the greater simplicity and assurance with which Thomas
now speaks. The hesitations and qualifications which he had found necessary
are now gone; most significantly, the further enumeration of the three
"functions" of authority is omitted. The purpose of that enumeration had
been to discuss the extent to which authority *ad regimen ordinatus* could be
found in the institutions of political authority. Aquinas was, at the time, still
too much of a traditionalist to be prepared to throw to the winds Augustine's
insistence that these institutions, with their necessarily coercive character,
were infected with the dispensation of sin. He had sought to reconcile
Augustine and Aristotle by dividing political authority into three functions
and allocating one of these to nature, the others to sin. Now he treats

political authority as all of a piece; and it belongs to the institutions grounded in nature. What Aquinas had come to discern in the course of the ten years or so between the two works was that coercive power belonged indivisibly to the stuff of political existence. There can be no doubt that this insight came to him with his growing understanding of Aristotle's political theory.[74] The insight excluded the possibility of compromise on the lines that he had experimented with in his youth.

In his explanation for the reason of his opinion Aquinas remarks that a subject is ruled in servile fashion in so far as he is ruled for his master's benefit; and this conflicts with the primitive order of nature. A subject is governed, however, as a free man, in so far as he is directed to his own good or the common good; and this sort of dominion must have existed before the fall, for man is by nature a social animal, and social life, according to Aristotle, would be impossible without a directive authority. The appeal to Aristotle underlines what is in any case clear: Aquinas is thinking in terms of genuine political authority with the full apparatus of governmental machinery and the power of enforcement. This is what is now traced, unambiguously, to an origin in nature. The break with the Augustinian theory of the origins of political authority appears to be complete. But Aquinas invokes *De civitate Dei*, xix. 14–15 in the course of a second argument added to prove that authority over free men would have existed in the state of innocence. It would have been inconvenient, he says, if those with a superabundance of wisdom and justice could not have devoted their superior gifts to the service of others less well endowed. "Wherefore Augustine says that 'the just rule not through a desire for power but through an obligation to give guidance; this is what the order of nature prescribes, this is how God created man.'"[75] Augustine's admonition to people occupying a position of authority has been finally turned on its head: the obligation to act as a *paterfamilias* rather than as a tyrant is turned into a justification of precisely the thing Augustine wished to deny: that political society is, like a family, a natural institution. Augustine's wholesale exclusion of all human dominion of man over man from the state of innocence is quoted as an objection;[76] Aquinas's imperious reply to all the objections, that they are valid only against the first mode of authority—authority over a servile subject—conceals a radical change of attitude to political authority. It is scarcely surprising to find St. Thomas using, among his favourite models for political authority, the analogies rejected by Augustine. Without misgiving he returns, time and again, to the image of political authority as modelled on the relation of soul and body, or of God and the world.[77]

Augustine and the tradition which he helped to inspire may not have been always wholly clear about the meaning of "nature."[78] But both Augustine, and some, at least, of his followers were clear enough about a radical difference they detected between the kind of authority and subjection to be found in the family and the kind found in slavery. In its essentials, this basic dichotomy was retained by Aquinas. The real problem lay in answering the question as to which side of the dividing line political authority was to be placed. Aquinas's first answer to this question had been, in effect, to evade its force. He had tried to split political authority by drawing the line across its very substance. Later, with increasing insight into the meaning of "political authority," acquired through Aristotle, he came to discern the unsatisfactory character of his compromise. He now opted unambiguously for what, from the Augustinian standpoint, was a revolutionary view. He was too clearsighted to be unaware of this revolution in political thinking. He had understood the Augustinian theology of society clearly enough, and loyalty to its tradition made him wish to fit his Aristotelian views into its framework. His understanding of Augustine's views Thomas shared with Bonaventure; with Albert he shared the fascination of the new Aristotelian vision of human society. Without a very much fuller study of contemporary debates, his originality in the way he accomplished the revolutionary transition from the one to the other tradition cannot be assessed. It is clear, however, that of the writers here considered, at any rate, he alone combined an appreciation of the real significance of Augustine's views with a growing, and in the end triumphant, commitment to Aristotle's ideas on man as *animal civile*. As the new ideas took a deeper hold in his mind and served to crystallize his fundamental thought about man in society, the tensions proved insurmountable. He knew he had in effect broken with the old tradition, that the whole perspective of his thought had altered. It was no longer a matter of interpreting Aristotle within a traditional framework, but of fitting Augustine—by manhandling him, if need be—into the Aristotelian scheme.

*     *     *

The particular strand of Augustine's political reflection which we have considered here is one which allies him with Christian thinkers of a period before the official recognition granted to Christianity by the Empire, and with Donatist and other schismatic writers opposed to the imperial state-Church.[89] There is, of course, much in Augustine's political thought that dissociates him sharply from this tradition of thought. It is enough to refer to his tragic, if not wholly unprepared, conversion to the policy of *coge intrare*. With his endorsement of the policy of imperial coercion of heretics at least one of the main lines of his intellectual development was given a new twist. Only when the development of the whole relevant range of his thought is taken into account[90] shall we be in a position to see how far the Donatist controversy and its exigencies obscured the central core of Augustine's political thought. In any case, the complexity of its development and the variety of its themes assured Augustine of the possibility of finding a place for the state enforcement of orthodoxy and morality within a body of thought which was not, fundamentally, hospitable to ideas of this kind. His famous letter[91] to Vincent, Rogatist bishop of Cartenna, was in some ways an expression of those very views which he attacked in the *De civitate Dei*. But traces of views like those expressed in the letter to Vincent survive even in this very differently orientated work; and they find clear expression in other writings. There are elements in Augustine's mature political thought which tend to undermine his attack on any conception of human institutions, of the Roman Empire in particular, as the vehicle of salvation for men.

If Augustine was compromised on the subject of the range of legitimate political authority, on the scope to be allowed it in enforcing morality and orthodoxy, Aquinas saw the issues at stake with greater clarity. It is neither necessary nor possible to sketch here the systematic coherence between his views on its functions as an agency of enforcing Christian morality and orthodoxy, and his views on the state as a natural institution. It will scarcely be questioned that these views form, by and large, part of a single systematic exploration of the implications of this Aristotelian theory of political authority. He perceived the radical divergence between his own views on these subjects, and the views implied by Augustine's theology of authority and subjection. Nothing illustrates this divergence better than the two different conceptions of freedom involved.

Augustinian and Aristotelian theologians were agreed that any subjection which restricts the subject's liberty cannot have belonged to nature in its original state. The Augustinian tradition, in excluding political authority from this state, implied that any interference with a subject's activities constitutes a restriction of his freedom. It may be a salutary and necessary restriction; but for all that, a man is unfree to the extent that he is coerced against his will. Political authority conceived as grounded in human nature implies a totally different conception of liberty. It becomes an agent of men's true interests, which only their shortcomings conceal from them. In securing the true goal of man, authority may override his actual wishes without thereby restricting his freedom, for it will express the "free" choice of what Sir Isaiah Berlin has called[92] "his 'true,' albeit submerged and inarticulate self." St. Thomas had, of course, no difficulty in agreeing that slavery was incompatible with freedom;[93] but the grounds on which he establishes this are not that this kind of subjection is a curtailment of the range in which men can act as they wish unhindered by other men, but that it curtails it without regard to their own good.  The subjection of free men to their ruler implies no diminution of their freedom, so long as they are ruled for their own or for the common good.  In exercising this kind of dominion over his subjects, a ruler "rules over another *ut libero,*"[94] and such a ruler "is appropriately called the servant of his subjects."[95]  Augustine had exhorted rulers to act thus; but he had no illusions about political authority, even when exercised in accordance with the order of nature, amounting to a restriction of men's freedom.  His account of the origins of political authority brings into play what Sir Isaiah Berlin has called the "negative concept of freedom": the sense according to which any coercion implies a diminution of liberty.   St. Thomas's conception relies on the "positive sense," according to which the purpose for which a man is coerced determines whether his freedom is being restricted or not.  What is at stake between the two  conceptions of political authority, in the end, is the meaning of freedom.

# Notes

†Reprinted by permission of the Oxford UP from *The Journal of Theological Studies* 16 (1965): 68–100. Rpt. in Robert A. Markus.  *"Saeculum"*: *History and Society in  the Theology of Saint  Augustine.*  Cambridge: Cambridge UP, 1970.

[1]The most distinguished of the scholars who have made this claim is Otto Schilling, particularly in his *Die Staats- und Soziallehre des heiligen Thomas von Aquin,* 2nd ed., Munich, 1930 [henceforth: *SSL Thom*].  Out of innumerable statements in the book, to some of which we shall have to return, we may quote from his own summary: "The influence of Aristotelianism is unmistakable in Saint Thomas's theory of the state, whether one examines his views on the purpose and origin of the state, on the forms of the state, or on its functions or on many other topics.  But both in general and in detail he succeeded in giving his own theory a unique stamp, mainly through giving, with the aid of tradition and especially of  Augustinian ideas, the Christian element its proper significance." *SSL Thom,* p. 238.  Schilling's interpretation of Augustine's political theory is elaborated more fully in his *Die Staats- und Soziallehre des heiligen Augustinus* (Freiburg-im-Breisgau, 1910) [henceforth: *SSL Aug*].  Of the more generally held view we may take A. J. Carlyle's as representative: "To the Stoics and the Fathers the coercive control of man by man is not an institution of nature.  By nature men, being free and equal, were under no system of coercive control.  Like slavery, the introduction of this was the result of the loss of man's original innocence, and represented the need for some power which might control and limit the unreasonable passions and appetites of human nature. . . . It was not till Aristotle's *Politics* were rediscovered in the thirteenth century that Saint Thomas Aquinas under their influence recognized that the State was not merely an institution devised to correct men's vices, but rather the necessary form of a real and full human life." R. W. and A. J. Carlyle, *A History of Medieval Political Theory in the West,* iii (1915), p. 5.

Among more recent discussions, cf. W. Ullmann, *Principles of Politics and Government in the Middle Ages* (1962), p. 231 f.; I gratefully acknowledge the help I have had from Dr. Ullmann, by no means confined to his book. I have also profited from some criticisms by Dr. M. J. Wilks.

2The range of meanings and overtones brought into play by Augustine's use of *consulere* can only rarely be rendered adequately without more than one equivalent in English. I use "have consideration," "care for," "guide," "encourage."

3*ordinata imperandi obediendique concordia cohabitantium*; cf. also *De civ. Dei*, xix. 13.

4Schilling, *SSL Aug*, p. 46, n. 1, gratuitously altering the text in his footnote, takes *hoc* to refer to *officium consulendi ac providendi*. This clearly cannot be the case; *hoc* must refer to the whole of the last sentence of ch. 14, or to the argument as a whole of which it serves as the conclusion. It is noteworthy, however, that despite this, Schilling did not interpret the passage as asserting that political authority was an institution derived from the *ordo naturae*. Although he thought that this was in fact Augustine's view, his arguments for this are based on other passages, to be considered in due course. Schilling interpreted the two chapters under discussion as making a distinction between two ways of exercising power: either despotically, or as "sympathetic guidance" (*teilnehmende Fürsorge*), ibid., p. 55. What he failed to notice is the shift in chapter 15 to a discussion of institutions, that of slavery. Gustave Combès, in his *La Doctrine politique de Saint Augustin* (Paris, 1927), pp. 76 f., also appears to be clear that these passages exclude political authority from the state of man's innocence. He bases his opinion that political authority is nevertheless a natural institution for Augustine on "the intervention of a second law of nature," which impels men to associate with each other. Their original freedom, in his view, is cancelled out by this law, and characterized men only in *une vie errante et solitaire*, in which men were alone with their consciences before God. His arguments are rarely more than assertions based on quotations torn from their context and linked by innuendo. An attempt to refute them would contribute little to an understanding of Augustine's views.

5*Enarr. in Ps.* 124. 7–8.

6*De civ. Dei*, xix. 12. 2.

7Ibid. xviii. 2. 2: *hinc factum est ut non sine Dei providentia . . . quidam essent regnis praediti, quidam regnantibus subditi. . . .*

8*In Ep. Joann. Tr.* 8. 6–8.

9Cf. Schilling, *SSL Aug*, pp. 57–60; Combès, op. cit. (above, p. 71, n. 1), pp. 79–80.

10*Quaest. in Hept.* i. 153.

11*De Gen. ad litt.* xi. 37. 50.

12*ad virum tuum conversio tua et ipse tui dominabitur*—Gen. iii. 16, in Augustine's text.

13Cf. above: *rationalem . . . noluit nisi irrationalibus dominari* and the consequent duty (ch. 14) of the just man to serve those whom he rules; and the subjection of man to man *conditionis vinculo*, rooted in sin.

14*De Gen. ad litt.* viii. 9. 17.

15Ibid. viii. 23. 44.

16*De civ. Dei*, v. ii.

[17]Cf. above: *poenalis servitus ea lege ordinatur quae naturalem ordinem conservari jubet, perturbari vetat* . . .; Augustine is not speaking of a natural law, as some commentators suggest, but of a law (that of divine providence) which enjoins the observance and forbids the disturbing of the order of nature.

[18]Cf. above.

[19]*De civ. Dei*, xii. 21 (22, Dombart and Kalb); and 27 (28, Dombart and Kalb).

[20]Ibid. xix. 3. 2; 5.

[21]*De civ. Dei*, xix. 12. 2. This section is in fact only indirectly concerned with this question. Harald Fuchs's fine analysis of the chapter in *Augustin und der antike Friedensgedanke (Neue philologische Untersuchungen*, 3, Berlin, 1926), pp. 17–36, shows that Augustine is here primarily interested in the universal drive towards *pax* operative throughout nature, human and non-human. The sociable nature of man is only an illustration of this general principle. The final sentences of section 2 of the chapter, on the *perversa imitatio Dei* which seeks to subject others naturally and originally equal with oneself under God to one's own rule, is a further illustration of the natural drive towards peace operative even in this disordered state.

[22]Ibid. xix. 14, 16. This commonplace is frequent in Augustine's correspondence, e.g. in *Epp.* 104. 2. 7; 130. 12; 133. 2; 138. 2. 14, &c.

[23]*De civ. Dei*, xix. 16; 12. 1.

[24]Op. cit., p. 80.

[25]*C. Iul.* iv. 12. 61.

[26]Whatever Augustine's historical knowledge, *imperatores* here could scarcely have made him think of anything but emperors.

[27]*C. Iul.* iv. 12. 61.

[28]Ibid. iv. 12. 60.

[29]In *De civ. Dei*, xiv. 23. 2 Augustine, in the course of a similar argument, merely refers to this passage of Cicero's *De republica* without quoting it in full. It is significant that in his summary he omits mentioning royal authority, and reduces the dichotomy between the two types of authority to the basic form in which it was acceptable to him. Cicero, he writes, "when discussing the varieties of authority (*de imperiorum differentia*), took an analogy from human nature: the limbs of the body are ruled like sons, on account of their readiness to obey, whereas the vicious parts of the soul are coerced, like slaves, by a harsher kind of rule." Nothing could give a clearer indication of the sense in which he understood the analogy, and what really mattered to him in its application.

[30]This is noted by Schilling, *SSL Aug*, pp. 53–54. Schilling refers to Cicero, *De leg.* 3. 2; *De off.* 2. 12 and, by way of pointing the contrast, to *De civ. Dei*, xvi. 4. 17; xviii. 2; v. 12, &c.

[31]*De civ. Dei*, xix. 15; *Quaest. in Hept.* i. 153.

[32]xix. 21.2.

[33]This view, too, is anticipated in *De Genesi ad litteram*, where Augustine notes the value to be set upon the *ordo reipublicae in cujusdam pacis terrenae vinculum coercens etiam peccatores* (ix. 9. 14); cf. also *De doctr. christ.* ii. 25. 39–40; 39. 58. This is, of course, a commonplace of patristic literature, and finds its classical expression in Irenaeus, *Adv. haer.* v. 24. 2. There are good grounds for thinking that Augustine was

acquainted with Irenaeus's work; cf. B. Altaner, "Augustin und Irenäus," *Theol. Quartalschr.* cxxix (1949), pp. 162–72. Schilling quotes (*SSL Aug*, pp. 46 f.) several passages from other writers containing similar views on the origins of political authority; but he does not admit that the apparent similarity entitles us to infer that Augustine derives "the whole political order from sinfulness as its source" (ibid., p. 51).

[34]Cf. the penetrating study by F. E. Cranz, "The Development of Augustine's Ideas on Society before the Donatist Controversy," *Harvard Theol. Rev.* xlvii (1954), pp. 255–316.

[35]*duce natura congregabantur homines—De off.* ii. 21. 73.

[36]Ibid., and *De fin.* v. 23. 66: human nature has *quiddam ingenitum quasi civile atque populare quod Graeci* πολιτικόν *vocant....*

[37]Lib. ii, dist. 44.

[38]Cf. M. D. Chenu, *Introduction à l'étude de Saint Thomas d'Aquin*, 2nd ed. (Paris, 1954), p. 235.

*[Text for notes 39–60 not reprinted here.]

*   *   *

[61]e. g. 1097b11, 1162a18; 1169b18.

[62]*In Sent.* ii, D. 44, q. 1, a. 3.

[63]Ibid., ob. 2.

[64]Ibid., ob. 3.

[65]Ibid., ad 2 m and *similiter* ad 3 m.

[66]*Eth.* 1179a33 f.

[67]Loc. cit., ad 4 m.

[68]Aquinas speaks of these in the plural. This must be a slip, as the article only allows one *usus* in the original state of innocence.

[69]St. Thomas's terminology and its development could be investigated with profit. I can see no grounds for the suggestion by W. Ullmann, op. cit. , p. 245, n. 2, that Aquinas's addition of *sociale* to Aristotle's *politicum* may have come from Macrobius. There is no evidence adduced for this in M. Schedler, *Die Philosophie des Macrobius und ihr Einfluss auf die Wissenschaft des christlichen Mittelalters (Beitr. z. Gesch. d. Phil. d. MA.,* 12 (1), 1916), referred to on this point by Dr. Ullmann, op. cit., p. 247, n. 2. Doubtless Macrobius was the source for much of the treatment of the political virtues, but the addition of *sociale* to *politicum* seems to me to have had no significance to Aquinas. The suggestion (made to me by Dr. M. J. Wilks) that the distinction between the two adjectives was forced on Aquinas by the discovery that Augustine could speak of a primitive order of society in which there was no coercion, whereas coercion is inseparable from Aristotle's conception of *politicum*, is attractive; but it requires testing against a survey of Aquinas's usage and its development. A cursory and far from exhaustive study of his language suggests to me that it is on the whole more likely that he began with an appreciation of Augustine's view of man as social by nature, and then came to see that Aristotle meant more than this by asserting that man was naturally *animal politicum* (or *civile*); and that as he came to see man in more thoroughly Aristotelian terms, he tended to expand the meaning of *sociale* so as to

make it effectively synonymous with *politicum* (or *civile*). He uses the terms *civile*, e.g.
*In Pol.* i, lect. I, or *politicum*, e.g. *Sum. theol.* i–ii. 61. 5; *In Eth.* i, lect. 9; ix, lect. 10; but
he speaks more often of man as *animal sociale*: e. g. *Sum. theol.* i. 96. 4; i–ii. 95. 4; ii–ii.
109. 3, ad I; *Sum. c. Gent.*, iii. 117, 128, 129, 147; *In Eth.* i, lect. 1. Sometimes he uses
*sociale et* (or *vel*) *politicum*, e. g. *Sum. theol.* i–ii. 72.4; *Sum. c. Gent.* iii. 85; *De reg. princ.*
i. 1. Schilling asserts (*SSL Thom.*, pp. 80–81) that Aquinas distinguished the two
concepts and only used them as synonymous where this did not affect his argument. I
can find no support for this view in the references he gives. I am inclined to agree with
I. T. Eschmann's judgement: "Unless special reasons suggested to Aquinas the exact
textual reproduction of the Aristotelian principle [that man is a *political* animal] he
prefers to say that man is a *social* animal." (*St. Thomas on Kingship*, translated by G. B.
Phelan, with introduction and notes by I. T. Eschmann (Toronto, 1949, p. 4, n. 2).
Generally speaking, the terms appear to be used interchangeably.
[70]Cf. above.
[71]One of the many indications of his increasing appreciation of the far-reaching
implications of Aristotle's view has been noted by Fr. Eschmann, loc. cit., p. 4, n. 3,
who draws attention to the fact that St. Thomas gradually came to the view that
Avicenna's arguments for man's being naturally a social animal ceased to satisfy
Aquinas because they were "incapable of demonstrating the conclusion that man is a
*political animal*" (italics in text).
[72]I am, of course, excluding, for this purpose, lesser groupings such as the household
or small community.
[73]i. 96. 4.
[74]The extent to which the unitary conception of political authority is derived from
Aristotle appears strikingly in *Sum. theol.* i. 92. 1 ad 2 m, where *subjectio civilis* is
coupled with *subjectio oeconomica* and contrasted with *subjectio servilis*. References to
passages in which Aquinas can be seen to assume that the power of coercing refractory
subjects belongs to the essence of political authority could be multiplied. The
following must suffice here: *Sum theol.* i–ii. 95. 1; *In Eth.* x. lect. 14; *In Pol.* i, lect. 1. It
is most explicitly argued in *In Pol.* iii, lect. 5. Most revealing, perhaps, is the surprising
presence of the idea in as unhospitable a context as that provided by the pseudo-
Dionysius's speculations on the angelic hierarchy; cf. *In div. nom.*,ch. 12. Schilling
(*SSL Thom.* p. 48) recognized that coercive power was for St. Thomas included in
political authority; he refers to *Sum. theol.* i–ii. 105. 2 and *In Pol.* iii, lect. 9 to
substantiate the view that judicial and penal systems belong to the essence of the state
as conceived by St. Thomas. It is Schilling's attempt to father on Augustine the view
that all this belongs to the order of nature (ibid., p. 101) which must be rejected.
[75]*Sum theol.* i. 96. 4, quoting *De civ. Dei*, xix. 14–15; cf. above.
[76]Loc. cit., ob. 1.
[77]e.g. *De reg. princ.* i. 1, 9; ii. 1 (= i. 12); *Sum. c. Gent.* iii. 78. The analogy between
political authority and the two ways in which the mind rules its body: *Sum theol.* i. 81.
3 ad 2 m; i–ii. 58. 2; 9. 2 ad 3 m; 17. 7, &c. *In Pol.* i, lect. 3 reveals its source.
Interestingly, Aristotle's application of the analogy differs slightly from Cicero's
version found in and rejected by Augustine.
[78]This consideration has been given more weight, I believe, than it deserves in this

context by Dr. W. Ullmann, op. cit. , pp. 238 f. Whether Augustine had an adequately clear conception of "nature" or not, he was as clear as he was emphatic that subjection was of two kinds, typified by servile subjection and by subjection to parental authority respectively. Aquinas certainly drew the line more carefully in giving the concept of "nature" greater precision (as Bonaventure had also done); but the crucial break with Augustine's theory lay in transferring political authority from one side of the line to the other (as Bonaventure had refused to do).

*[Text for notes 79-88 not reprinted here.]

*     *     *

[89]On these, cf. W. H. C. Frend, "The Roman Empire in the Eyes of Western Schismatics During the Fourth Century A.D.," *Misc. hist. eccles.* (Stockholm, 1960), pp. 9–22.

[90]Despite the full and fair treatment by H. A. Deane, *The Political and Social Ideas of St. Augustine* (New York and London, 1963), we are still far from possessing such an account. On the problem of religious coercion and Augustine's attitude to it the most penetrating study is the paper read at the Fourth International Conference on Patristic Studies, Oxford, 1963, by P. R. L. Brown, *Journal of Roman Studies*, liv (1964), pp. 107–16.

[91]*Ep.* 93.

[92]*Two Concepts of Liberty* (Oxford, 1958), p. 18.

[93]The argument of *Sum. theol.* i. 96. 4 on slavery is anticipated in *In Sent.* ii, D. 44, q. 1, a. 3, ad 1 m, in reply to the famous passage of Gregory's *Moralia* (xxi. 15. 22), which asserts man's original freedom.

[94]*Sum. theol.* i. 96. 4. The phrase by itself does not, of course, imply that a man is free even though coerced. It can be taken to mean that he is free in no more than a legal sense, i.e. that he is not a slave. But St. Thomas's argument does in fact presuppose that a man remains free in being coerced, provided that it is for his own or the common good.

[95]*In Sent.* ii, D. 44, q. 1, a. 3, ad 1 m.

# Augustine's Political Realism†

## Reinhold Niebuhr

The terms "idealism" and "realism" are not analogous in political and in metaphysical theory; and they are certainly not as precise in political, as in metaphysical theory.

In political and moral theory "realism" denotes the disposition to take all factors in a social and political situation, which offer resistance to established norms, into account, particularly the factors of self-interest and power. In the words of a notorious "realist," Machiavelli, the purpose of the realist is "to follow the truth of the matter rather than the imagination of it; for many have pictures of republics and principalities which have never been seen." This definition of realism implies that idealists are subject to illusions about social realities, which indeed they are.

"Idealism" is, in the esteem of its proponents, characterized by loyalty to moral norms and ideals, rather than to self-interest, whether individual or collective. It is, in the opinion of its critics, characterized by a disposition to ignore or be indifferent to the forces in human life which offer resistance to universally valid ideals and norms. This disposition, to which Machiavelli refers, is general whenever men are inclined to take the moral pretensions of themselves or their fellowmen at face value; for the disposition to hide self-interest behind the facade of pretended devotion to values, transcending self-interest, is well-nigh universal. It is, moreover, an interesting human characteristic, proving that the concept of "total depravity," as it is advanced by some Christian realists, is erroneous. Man is a curious creature with so strong a sense of obligation to his fellows that he cannot pursue his own interests without pretending to serve his fellowmen.

The definitions of "realists" and "idealists" emphasize disposition, rather than doctrines; and they are therefore bound to be inexact. It must remain a matter of opinion whether or not a man takes adequate account of all the various factors and forces in a social situation. Was Plato a realist, for instance, because he tried to guard against the self-interest of the "guardians" of his ideal state by divesting them of property and reducing their family responsibilities to a minimum? Does this bit of "realism" cancel out the essential unrealism, inherent in ascribing to the "lusts of the body" the force of recalcitrance against the moral norm; or in attributing pure virtue to pure mind?

## The Distinctive Nature Of Augustine's Realism

Augustine was, by general consent, the first great "realist" in Western history. He deserves this distinction because his picture of social reality in his *Civitas Dei* gives an adequate account of the social factions, tensions, and competitions which we know to be well-nigh universal on every level of community; while the classical age conceived the order and justice of its *polis* to be a comparatively simple achievement, which would be accomplished when reason had brought all subrational forces under its dominion.

This difference in the viewpoints of Augustine and the classical philosophers lies in Augustine's biblical, rather than rationalistic, conception of human selfhood, with the ancillary conception of the human self, according to which the self is composed of mind and body; the mind being the seat of virtue because it has the capacity to bring all impulses into order; and the body, from which come the "lusts and ambitions," being the cause of evil. According to Augustine, the self is an integral unity of mind and body. It is something more than the mind and is able to use mind for its purposes. The self has, in fact, a mysterious identity and integrity transcending its functions of mind, memory, and will. "These three things, memory, understanding, and love are mine and not their own," he declares, "for they do what they do not for themselves but for me; or rather I do it by them. For it is I who remember by memory and understand by understanding and love by love."[1] It must be observed that the transcendent freedom of this self, including its capacity to defy any rational or natural system into which someone may seek to coordinate it (its capacity for evil), makes it difficult for any philosophy, whether ancient or modern, to comprehend its true dimension. That is why the classical wise men obscured it by fitting its mind into a system of universal mind and the body into the system of nature; and that is also why the modern wise men, for all their rhetoric about the "dignity" of the individual, try to cut down the dimension of human selfhood so that it will seem to fit into a system of nature.

This conception of selfhood is drawn from the Bible, rather than from philosophy, because the transcendent self which is present in, though it transcends, all of the functions and effects of the self is comprehensible only in the dramatic-historical mode of apprehension which characterizes biblical faith. Augustine draws on the insights of neo-Platonism to illustrate the self's power of self-transcendence; but he rejects Plotinus' mystic doctrine, in which the particular self, both human and divine, is lost in a vast realm of undifferentiated being.

Augustine's conception of the evil which threatens the human community on every level is a corollary of his doctrine of selfhood. "Self-love" is the source of evil rather than some residual natural impulse which mind has not yet completely mastered. This excessive love of self, sometimes also defined as pride or *superbia*, is explained as the consequence of the self's abandonment of God as its true end and of making itself "a kind of end." It is this powerful self-love or, in a modern term, "egocentricity," this tendency of the self to make itself its own end or even to make itself the false center of whatever community it inhabits, which sows confusion into every human community. The power of self-love is more spiritual than the "lusts of the body," of which Plato speaks; and it corrupts the processes of the mind more than Plato or Aristotle knew. That is why Augustine could refute the classical theory with the affirmation that "it is not the bad body which causes the good soul to sin but the bad soul which causes the good body to sin." At other times Augustine defines the evil in man as the "evil will," but with the understanding that it is the self which is evil in the manifestation of its will. "For he who extols the whole nature of the soul as the chief good and condemns the nature of the flesh as if it were evil, assuredly is fleshly both in love of the soul and in the hatred of the flesh."[2] This concise statement of the Christian position surely refutes the absurd charge of moderns that the Christian faith is "dualistic" and generates contempt for the body. It also establishes the only real basis for a realistic estimate of the forces of recalcitrance which we must face on all levels of the human community, particularly for a realistic estimate of the spiritual dimension of these forces and of the comparative impotence of "pure reason" against them.

Compared with a Christian realism, which is based on Augustine's interpretation of biblical faith, a great many modern social and psychological theories, which fancy themselves anti-Platonic or even anti-Aristotelian and which make much of their pretended "realism," are in fact no more realistic than the classical philosophers. Thus modern social and psychological scientists are forever seeking to isolate some natural impulse such as "aggressiveness" and to manage it; with equal vanity they are trying to find a surrogate for Plato's and Aristotle's disinterested "reason" in a so-called "scientific method." Their inability to discover the corruption of self-interest in reason or in man's rational pursuits, and to measure the spiritual dimension of man's inhumanity and cruelty, gives an air of sentimentality to the learning of our whole liberal culture. Thus we have no guidance amid the intricacies of modern power politics, except as the older disciplines, less enamored of the "methods of natural science," and the common sense of the man in the street, supply the necessary insights.

## The "City Of This World"

Augustine's description of the social effects of human egocentricity or self-love is contained in his definition of the life of the "city of this world," the *civitas terrena*, which he sees as commingled with the *civitas Dei*. The "city of this world" is dominated by self-love to the point of contempt of God; and is distinguished from the *civitas Dei* which is actuated by the "love of God" to the point of contempt of self. This "city" is not some little city-state, as it is conceived in classical thought. It is the whole human community on its three levels of the family, the commonwealth, and the world.

A potential world community is therefore envisaged in Augustine's thought. But, unlike the Stoic and modern "idealists," he does not believe that a common humanity or a common reason gives promise of an easy actualization of community on the global level. The world community, declares Augustine, "is fuller of dangers as the greater sea is more dangerous."[3] Augustine is a consistent realist in calling attention to the fact that the potential world community may have a common human reason, but it speaks in different languages and "two men, each ignorant of each other's language" will find that "dumb animals, though of a different species, could more easily hold intercourse than they, human beings though they be."[4] This realistic reminder that common linguistic and ethnic cultural forces, which bind the community together on one level, are divisive on the ultimate level, is a lesson which our modern proponents of world government have not yet learned.

Augustine's description of the *civitas terrena* includes an emphasis on the tensions, frictions, competitions of interest, and overt conflicts to which every human community is exposed. Even in the family, one cannot rely on friendship "seeing that secret treachery has often broken it up."[5] This bit of realism will seem excessive until we remember that our own generation has as much difficulty in preserving the peace and integrity in the smallest and most primordial community, the family, as in integrating community on the highest global level.

The *civitas terrena* is described as constantly subject to an uneasy armistice between contending forces, with the danger that factional disputes may result in "bloody insurrection" at any time. Augustine's realism prompts him to challenge Cicero's conception of a commonwealth as rooted in a "compact of justice." Not so, declares Augustine. Commonwealths are bound together by a common love, or collective interest, rather than by a sense of justice; and they could not maintain themselves without the imposition of power. "Without injustice the republic would neither increase nor subsist. The imperial city to which the republic belongs could not rule over provinces without recourse to injustice. For it is unjust for some men to rule over others."[6]

This realism has the merit of describing the power realities which underlie all large scale social integrations whether in Egypt or Babylon or Rome, where a dominant city-state furnished the organizing power for the Empire. It also describes the power realities of national states, even democratic ones, in which a group, holding the dominant form of social power, achieves oligarchic rule, no matter how much modern democracy may bring such power under social control. This realism in regard to the facts which underlie the organizing or governing power refutes the charge of modern liberals that a realistic analysis of social forces makes for state absolutism; so that a mild illusion in regard to human virtue is necessary to validate democracy. Realistic pessimism did indeed prompt both Hobbes and Luther to an unqualified endorsement of state power; but that is only because they were not realistic enough. They saw the dangers of anarchy in the egotism of the citizens but failed to perceive the dangers of tyranny in the selfishness of the ruler. Therefore they obscured the consequent necessity of placing checks upon the ruler's self-will.

Augustine's realism was indeed excessive. On the basis of his principles he could not distinguish between government and slavery, both of which were supposedly the rule over man by man and were a consequence of, and remedy for, sin; nor could he distinguish between a commonwealth and a robber band, for both were bound together by collective interest: "For even thieves must hold together or they cannot effect what they intend." The realism fails to do justice to the sense of justice in the constitution of the Roman Empire; or, for that matter, to the sense of justice in a robber band. For even thieves will fall out if they cannot trust each other to divide the loot, which is their common aim, equitably. But the excessive emphasis upon the factors of power and interest, a wholesome corrective to Cicero's and modern Ciceronian moralistic illusions, is not fatal to the establishment of justice so long as the dangers of tyranny are weighed as realistically as the dangers of anarchy.

Augustine's realistic attitude toward government rests partly upon the shrewd observation that social peace and order are established by a dominant group within some level of community; and that this group is not exempt from the corruption of self-interest merely because the peace of society has been entrusted to it. (One thinks, incidentally, how accurately the Augustinian analysis fits both the creative and the ambiguous character of the American hegemony in the social cohesion of the free world.)

The realism is partly determined by his conception of a "natural order" which he inherited from the early Christian fathers, who in turn took it from that part of the Stoic theory which emphasized the primordial or primitive as the natural. This Stoic and Christian primitivism has the merit of escaping the errors of those natural law theories which claim to find a normative moral order amid the wide variety of historic forms or even among the most universal of these forms. The freedom of man makes these Stoic conceptions of the "natural" impossible. But it has the weakness which characterizes all primitivism, whether Stoic, Christian, or Romantic, for it makes primitive social forms normative. A primitive norm, whether of communal property relations or unorganized social cohesion, may serve provisionally as an occasion for the criticism of the institutions of an advancing civilization, more particularly the institutions of property and government; but it has the disadvantage of prompting indiscriminate criticism. This lack of discrimination is obvious in primitivistic Stoicism, in early Christianity, in seventeenth-century Cromwellian sectarianism, in Romanticism, and in Marxism and anarchism.

Augustine expressed his idea of a primitive social norm as follows:

> This is the prescribed order of nature. It is thus that God created Man. For "let them," He says, "have dominion over the fish of the sea and the fowl of the air and over every creeping think, which creepeth on the earth." He did not intend that His rational creature, made in His image, should have dominion over anything but irrational creation—not man over man but man over beasts. And hence the righteous men of primitive times were made shepherds of cattle rather than kings of men.[7]

This primitivism avoids the later error of the absolute sanctification of government. But its indiscriminate character is apparent by his failure to recognize the difference between legitimate and illegitimate, between ordinate and inordinate subordination of man to man. Without some form of such subordination the institutions of civilization could not exist.

### The Commingling of the Two Cities

If Augustine's realism is contained in his analysis of the *civitas terrena*, his refutation of the idea that realism must lead to cynicism or relativism is contained in his definition of the *civitas Dei*, which he declares to be "commingled" with the "city of this world" and which has the "love of God" rather than the "love of self" as its guiding principle. The tension between the two cities is occasioned by the fact that, while egotism is "natural" in the sense that it is universal, it is not natural in the sense that it does not conform to man's nature as one who transcends himself indeterminately and can only have God rather than self for his end. A realism becomes morally cynical or nihilistic when it assumes that the universal characteristic in human behavior must also be regarded as normative. The biblical account of human behavior, upon which Augustine bases his thought, can escape both illusion and cynicism because it recognizes that the corruption of human freedom may make a behavior pattern universal without making it normative. Good and evil are not determined by some fixed structure of human existence. Man, according to the biblical view, may use his freedom to make himself falsely the center of existence; but this does not change the fact that love rather than self-love is the law of his existence, in the sense that man can only be healthy, and his communities at peace, if man is drawn out of himself and saved from the self-defeating consequences of self-love.

There are several grave errors in Augustine's account of love and the relation of love to self-love; but before considering them we might well first pay tribute to his approach to political problems. The virtue of making love, rather than justice, into the norm for the community may seem, at first blush, to be dubious. The idea of justice seems much more relevant than the idea of love, particularly for the collective relationships of men. The medieval tradition, which makes the justice of a rational "natural law" normative even for Christians when they consider the necessities of a sinful world, seems much more realistic than modern forms of sentimental Protestantism which regards love as a simple alternative to self-love which could be achieved if only we could preach the idea persuasively enough to beguile men from the one to the other.

Augustine's doctrine of love as the final norm must be distinguished from modern sentimental versions of Christianity which regard love as a simple possibility, and which think it significant to assert the obvious proposition that all conflicts in the community would be avoided if only people and nations would love one another. Augustine's approach differs from modern forms of sentimental perfectionism in the fact that he takes account of the power and persistence of egotism, both individual and collective, and seeks to establish the most tolerable form of peace and justice under conditions set by human sin. He inherited the tradition of monastic perfection; and he allows it as a vent for the Christian impulse toward individual perfection, without however changing the emphasis upon the duty of the Christian to perfect the peace of the city of this world. Furthermore, he raises questions about monastic perfection which, when driven home by the Reformation, were to undermine the whole system.

> I venture to say [he writes] that it is good for those who observe continence and are proud of it, to fall that they may be humbled. For what benefit is it to anyone in whom is the virtue of continence, if pride holds sway? He is but despising that by which man is born in striving after that which led to Satan's fall . . . holy virginity is better than conjugal chastity . . . but if we add two

other things, pride and humility . . . which is better, pride or humility? . . . I
have no doubt that a humble married woman is to be preferred to a proud
virgin. . . . A mother will hold a lesser place in the Kingdom of Heaven,
because she has been married, than the daughter, seeing that she is a virgin . . . .
But if thy mother has been humble and thou proud, she will have some sort of
place, but thou none.[8]

While Augustine's doctrine of love is thus not to be confused with modern
sentimentalities which do not take the power of self-love seriously, one may
well wonder whether an approach to politics which does not avail itself of the
calculations of injustice, may be deemed realistic. We have already noted that
Augustine avails himself of the theory of the "natural law," only in the
primordial version of the theory. If the primordial conditions of a "natural
order" are not to be defined as normative, the only alternative is to assume a
"rational order" to which the whole of historical life conforms. Aquinas, in
fact, constructed his theory of the natural law upon classical, and
primarily Aristotelian, foundations. It was the weakness of both classical and
medieval theories that they assumed an order in history, conforming to the
uniformities of nature. Aristotle was aware of deviations in history, greater
than those in nature; but he believed that there was nevertheless one form
"which was marked by nature as the best." There is, in other words, no place
in this theory of natural law for the endlessly unique social configurations
which human beings, in their freedom over natural necessity, construct. The
proponents of "natural law" therefore invariably introduce some historically
contingent norm or social structure into what they regard as God's inflexible
norm. That was the weakness of both classical and medieval social theory;
and for that matter of the natural law theories of the bourgeois parties of the
eighteenth century, who had found what they regarded as a more empirically
perceived "natural law." But the modern empirical intelligence was no more
able than the deductive rational processes of classical and medieval times, to
construct a social norm not colored by the interests of the constructor, thus
introducing the taint of ideology into the supposed sanctities of the law.

We must conclude, therefore, that Augustine was wise in avoiding the
alleged solution of a natural law theory, which was the basis of so much lack
of realism in both the classical and the medieval period, and which can persist
today, long after the Aristotelian idea of fixed form for historical events has
been overcome, as the dogma of a religious system which makes its supposed
sanctities into an article of faith. Augustine's conception of the radical
freedom of man, derived from the biblical view, made it impossible to accept
the idea of fixed forms of human behavior and of social organization,
analogous to those of nature, even as he opposed the classical theory of
historical cycles. Furthermore, his conception of human selfhood, and of the

transcendence of the self over its mind, made it impossible to assume the identity of the individual reason with a universal reason, which lies at the foundation of the classical and medieval natural law theories. It is in fact something of a mystery how the Christian insights into human nature and history, expressed by Augustine, could have been subordinated to classical thought with so little sense of the conflict between them in the formulations of Thomas Aquinas; and how they should have become so authoritative in Roman Catholicism without more debate between Augustinian and Thomistic emphases.

Augustine's formula for leavening the city of this world with the love of the city of God is more adequate than classical and medieval thought, both in doing justice to the endless varieties of historical occasions and configurations and in drawing upon the resources of love rather than law in modifying human behavior.

Every "earthly peace," declares Augustine, is good as far as it goes. "But they will not have it long for they used it not well while they had it." That is, unless some larger love or loyalty qualifies the self-interest of the various groups, this collective self-interest will expose the community to either an overt conflict of competing groups or to the injustice of a dominant group which "when it is victorious . . . will become vice's slave."

Let us use some examples from current national and international problems to illustrate the Augustinian thesis.

There is, or was, a marked social tension between the middle classes of industrial owners and the industrial workers in all modern industrial nations. In some of them, for instance in Germany and in France, this tension led to overt forms of the class conflict. In others such as Britain, the smaller European nations and America, this tension was progressively resolved by various accommodations of interest. Wherein lay the difference? It did not lie in the possession of more adequate formulae of justice in some nations than in others. The difference lay in the fact that in some nations the various interest groups had, in addition to their collective interest, a "sense of justice," a disposition to "give each man his due" and a loyalty to the national community which qualified the interest struggle. Now, that spirit of justice is identical with the spirit of love, except at the highest level of the spirit of love, where it becomes purely sacrificial and engages in no calculation of what the due of each man may be. Two forms of love, the love of the other and the love of the community, were potent, in short, in modifying the acerbities and injustices of the class struggle. The two forms of love availed themselves of various calculations of justice in arriving at and defining their ad hoc agreements. But the factors in each nation and in each particular issue were too variable to allow for the application of any general rules or formulas of justice. Agreements were easier, in fact, if too much was not claimed for these formulas. Certain "principles" of justice, as distinguished from formulas or prescriptions, were indeed operative, such as liberty, equality, and loyalty to covenants; but these principles will be recognized as no more than the law of love in its various facets.

In the same manner, the international community is exposed to exactly the tensions and competitions of interest which Augustine describes. There are no formulas of justice or laws which will prevent these tensions from reaching overt conflict, if the collective interest of each nation is not modified by its loyalty to a higher value, such as the common civilization of the free nations. Where this common loyalty is lacking, as in our relation with Russia, no formula can save us from the uneasy peace in which we live. The character of this peace is just as tentative as Augustine described it. Whenever common loves or loyalties, or even common fears, lay the foundation for community, it must of course be our business to perfect it by calculations of justice which define our mutual responsibilities as exactly as possible.

It must be noted that the Augustinian formula for leavening influence of a higher upon a lower loyalty or love, is effective in preventing the lower loyalty from involving itself in self-defeat. It corrects the "realism" of those who are myopically realistic by seeing only their own interests and failing thereby to do justice to their interests where they are involved with the interests of others. There are modern realists, for instance, who, in their reaction to abstract and vague forms of international idealism, counsel the nation to consult only its own interests. In a sense, collective self-interest is so consistent that it is superfluous to advise it. But a consistent self-interest on the part of a nation will work against its interests, because it will fail to do justice to the broader and longer interests, which are involved with the interests of other nations. A narrow national loyalty on our part, for instance, will obscure our long range interests where they are involved with those of a whole alliance of free nations. Thus the loyalty of a leavening portion of a nation's citizens to a value transcending national interest will save a "realistic" nation from defining its interests in such narrow and short range terms as to defeat the real interests of the nation.

## Critique Of Augustine's Realism

We have acknowledged some weaknesses in the Augustinian approach to the political order which we must now define and examine more carefully.

(1) Non-Catholics commonly criticize Augustine's alleged identification of the *civitas Dei* with the visible Church. But we must absolve him of this charge or insist on a qualification of the criticism. He does indeed accept the

Catholic doctrine, which had grown up before his day; and he defines the visible Church as the only perfect society. There are passages in which he seems to assume that it is possible to claim for the members of the Church that they are solely actuated by the *amor Dei*. But he introduces so many reservations to this assertion that he may well be defined in this, as in other instances, as the father of both Catholicism and the Reformation. Of the Church, Augustine declared, "by faith she is a virgin. In the flesh she has few holy virgins."9 Or again: "God will judge the wicked and the good. The evil cannot now be separated from the good but must be suffered for a season. The wicked may be with us on the threshing floor . . . in the barn they cannot be."10 The reservations which he made upon the identification of the Church and the kingdom laid the foundations for the later Reformation position.

(2) But these reservations about the sinners who might be present in the visible Church cannot obscure a graver error in his thought. This error is probably related to his conception of grace which does not allow for the phenomenon, emphasized by the Reformation, that men may be redeemed in the sense that they consciously turn from self to Christ as their end, and yet they are not redeemed from the corruption of egotism which expresses itself, even in the lives of the saints. This insight is most succinctly expressed in Luther's phrase *"simul justus et peccator"* (both justified and a sinner). When Augustine distinguished between the "two loves" which characterize the "two cities," the love of God and the love of self, and when he pictured the world as a commingling of the two cities, he does not recognize that the commingling is due not to the fact that two types of people dwell together, but because the conflict between love and self-love is in every soul. It is particularly important to recognize this fact in political analyses; for nothing is more obvious than that personal dedication is no guarantee against the involvement of the dedicated individual in some form of collective egotism.

(3) We have frequently referred to Augustine's definition of the "two loves" which inform the "two cities" of which "the one is selfish and the other social," the one loving self to the point of contempt of God and the other loving God to the point of contempt of self. The question is whether Anders Nygren is right in *Agape and Eros* in defining the Augustinian conception of *amor Dei* as rooted in a classical rather than a biblical concept.

In defense of Augustine it must be said that he is not insensible to the two facets of the love commandment and therefore does not define the *amor Dei* in purely mystical terms as a flight from this world. He insists on the contrary that the *amor Dei* is "social" and he offers the concord among brethren as a proof of the love of God. But nevertheless Nygren is right in suggesting that the thought of Plotinus has colored Augustine's conceptions sufficiently so that the *agape* of the New Testament is misinterpreted by

Augustine's conception of *caritas* and *amor Dei*. The *agape* form of love in the New Testament fails to be appreciated particularly in two of its facets.

First, the equality of the "two loves," the love of God and the love of the neighbor (enforced in the Scripture by the words "the second is like unto [the first]") is violated by Augustine under the influence of Plotinus, even as a later medieval Catholic mystic, St. John of the Cross, violated it when he regarded the love of the creature as a ladder which might lead us to the love of God, but must be subordinated to the latter. Augustine wants us to love the neighbor for the sake of God, which may be a correct formulation; but he wants us to prove the genuineness of our love of God in the love of the neighbor, or by leading him to God. Thus the meeting of the neighbor's need without regard to any ultimate religious intention is emptied of meaning. The love of the neighbor is for him not part of a double love commandment, but merely the instrument of a single love commandment which bids us flee all mortality, including the neighbor, in favor of the immutable good.

The second facet of the *agape* concept of the New Testament which tends to be obscured by Augustine is the notion of sacrificial love, the absurd principle of the cross, the insistence that the self must sacrifice itself for the other. It is not fair to Augustine to say that he neglects this facet of meaning, for he seems to emphasize it so constantly. He comes closest to its meaning when he deals with the relation of humility to love. Yet it seems fair to say that he was sufficiently imbued by classical mystical thought forms so that the emphasis lies always upon the worthiness or unworthiness of the object of our love; the insistence is that the only God and not some mutable "good" or person is worthy of our love. This is a safeguard against all forms of idolatry. But it does not answer another important question: when I love a person or a community do I love myself in them or do I truly love them? Is my love a form of alteregoism? The Augustinian *amor Dei* assumes that the self in its smallness cannot contain itself within itself, and therefore it is challenged to go out from itself to the most ultimate end. But it hardly reveals the full paradox of self-realization through self-giving, which is a scandal in the field of rational ethics as the cross is a scandal in the field of rational religion. Yet it is the source of ultimate wisdom. For the kind of self-giving which has self-realization as its result must have self-realization as its conscious end; otherwise the self by calculating its enlargement will not escape from itself completely enough to be enlarged.

The weakness of Augustine in obscuring these facets of the *agape* principle may be illustrated, without unfairness I hope, by referring to his treatment of family love. He questions the love of mate or children as the final form of love, but not for New Testament reasons. He does not say: "When you love your wife and children are you maybe really loving yourself in them and using them as the instruments of your self-aggrandisements?" He declares instead, in effect: "You must not love your family too unreservedly because your wife and children are mortal. They also belong to the rivers of Babylon, and, if you give them absolute devotion, the hour of bereavement will leave you desolate." Of course, Augustine is too much the Christian to engage in a consistent mystic depreciation of the responsibilities and joys of this earthly life. After all, his whole strategy for the "commingling" of the two cities revolves around the acceptance of the ordinary responsibilities of home and state, but in performing these tasks for the ultimate, rather than the immediate end. He asks:

> What then? Shall all perish who marry and are given in marriage, who till the fields and build houses? No, but those who put their trust in these things, who prefer them to God, who for the sake of these things are quick to offend God, these will perish. But those who either do not use these things or who use them as though they used them not, trusting more in Him who gave them than in the things given, understanding in them His consolation and mercy, and who are not absorbed in these gifts lest they fall away from the giver, these are they whom the day will not overtake as a thief unprepared.[11]

## Modern Illusions And "The River Of Babylon"

We must not, in criticizing Augustine for neo-Platonic elements in his thought, obscure the Christian elements which will be equally an offense to modern men who regard the world as self-sufficing and self-explanatory, who reject as absurd the Christian faith that there is not only a mystery behind and above the world of observed phenomena and intelligible meanings, but that it is a mystery whose meaning has been disclosed as a love which elicits our answering love. This modern generation, with its confidence in a world without mystery, and without meaning beyond simple intelligibility, will not be beguiled from its unbelief by a reminder that its emancipation from God has betrayed it into precisely those idolatries—the worship of false gods, the dedication to finite values as if they were ultimate—of which Augustine spoke. But it must be recorded nevertheless as a significant fact of modern history. While it is an offence to regard communism as the inevitable end-product of secularism, as some Christians would have us believe, it is only fair to point out that the vast evils of modern communism come ironically to a generation which thought it would be easy to invest all the spiritual capital of men, who mysteriously transcend the historical process, in some value or end within that process; and communism is merely the most pathetic and cruel of the idolatrous illusions of this generation.

We must be clear about the fact that all the illusions about man's character and history, which made it so difficult for either the classical or the modern age to come to terms with the vexing problems of our togetherness, seem to stem from efforts to understand man in both his grandeur and his misery by "integrating" him into some natural or rational system of coherence. Thereby they denied the mystery of his transcendence over every process which points another mystery beyond himself, without which man is not only a mystery to himself but a misunderstood being.

We cannot deny that from a Christian standpoint the world is like a "river of Babylon" to use Augustine's symbol; and that Augustine is right in suggesting that ultimately we cannot find peace if we are merely tossed down the river of time. We must find security in that which is not carried down the river. "Observe however," declares Augustine (in a simile which will seem strange to generations which have made the "rivers of Babylon," the stream of temporal events, into forces of redemption, but which will not seem so strange as the modern experience proves history as such to be less redemptive than we had believed):

The rivers of Babylon are all things which are here loved, and pass away.

For example, one man loves to practice husbandry, to grow rich by it, to employ his mind on it, to get his pleasure from it. Let him observe the issue and see that what he has loved is not a foundation of Jerusalem, but a river of Babylon.

Another says, it is a grand thing to be a soldier; all farmers fear those who are soldiers, are subservient to them, tremble at them. If I am a farmer, I shall fear soldiers; if a soldier, farmers will fear me. Madman! thou hast cast thyself headlong into another river of Babylon, and that still more turbulent and sweeping. Thou wishest to be feared by thy inferior; fear Him Who is greater than thou. He who fears thee may on a sudden become greater than thou, but He Whom thou oughtest to fear will never become less.

To be an advocate, says another, is a grand thing; eloquence is most powerful; always to have clients hanging on the lips of their eloquent advocate, and from his words looking for loss or gain, death or life, ruin or security. Thou knowest not whither thou hast cast thyself. This too is another river of Babylon, and its roaring sound is the din of the waters dashing against the rocks. Mark that it flows, that it glides on; beware, for it carries things away with it.

To sail the seas, says another, and to trade is a grand thing—to know many lands, to make gains from every quarter, never to be answerable to any powerful man in thy country, to be always travelling, and to feed thy mind with the diversity of the nations and the business met with, and to return enriched by the increase of thy gains. This too is a river of Babylon. When will the gains stop? When wilt thou have confidence and be secure in the gains thou makest? The richer thou art, the more fearful wilt thou be. Once shipwrecked, though wilt come forth stripped of all, and rightly wilt bewail thy fate *in* the rivers of Babylon, because thou wouldest not sit down and weep *upon* the rivers of Babylon.

But there are other citizens of the holy Jerusalem, understanding their captivity, who mark how human wishes and the diverse lusts of men, hurry and drag them hither and thither, and drive them into the sea. They see this, and do not throw themselves into the rivers of Babylon, but sit down upon the rivers of Babylon and upon the rivers of Babylon weep, either for those who are being carried away by them, or for themselves whose deserts have placed them in Babylon.[12]

Whatever the defects of the Augustine approach may be, we must acknowledge his immense superiority both over those who preceded him and who came after him. A part of that superiority was due to his reliance upon biblical rather than idealistic or naturalistic conceptions of selfhood. But that could not have been the only cause, else Christian systems before and after him would not have been so inferior. Or were they inferior either because they subordinated the biblical-dramatic conception of human selfhood too much to the rationalistic scheme, as was the case with medieval Christianity culminating in the thought of Thomas Aquinas, or because they did not understand that the corruption of human freedom could not destroy the original dignity of man, as was the case with the Reformation with its doctrines of sin, bordering on total depravity and resulting in Luther's too pessimistic approach to political problems?

As for secular thought, it has difficulty in approaching Augustine's realism without falling into cynicism, or in avoiding nihilism without falling into sentimentality. Hobbes' realism was based on an insight which he shared with Augustine, namely, that in all historical encounters, the mind is the servant and not the master of the self. But he failed to recognize that the self which thus made the mind its instrument was a corrupted and not a "normal" self. Modern "realists" know the power of collective self-interest as Augustine did; but they do not understand its blindness. Modern pragmatists understand the irrelevance of fixed and detailed norms; but they do not understand that love must take the place as the final norm for these inadequate norms. Modern liberal Christians know that love is the final norm for man; but they fall into sentimentality because they fail to measure the power and persistence of self-love.

Thus Augustine, whatever may be the defects of his approach to political reality, and whatever may be the dangers of a too slavish devotion to his insights, nevertheless proves himself a more reliable guide than any known thinker. A generation which finds its communities imperiled and in decay from the smallest and most primordial community, the family, to the largest

and most recent, the potential world community, might well take counsel of
Augustine in solving its perplexities.

# Notes

†Reprinted by permission of the Yale UP from *The Essential Reinhold Niebuhr:
Selected Essays and Addresses.* Ed. Robert McAfee Brown. New Haven: Yale UP,
1986. Pp. 123–41.

[1] *De Trin.*, 15.22.
[2] *De Civ. Dei*, 15.5.
[3] Ibid., 19.7.
[4] Ibid.
[5] Ibid. 19.5.
[6] Ibid., 19.21.
[7] Ibid., 19.15.
[8] Sermon cccliv, ix, 9.
[9] Sermon ccxiii, vii, 7.
[10] *Comm. on Ps.* cxi, 9.
[11] *Comm. on Ps.* cxx, 3.
[12] *Comm. on Ps.* cxxxvi, 3, 4.

# Augustine's *City of God* XIX and Western Political Thought†

## Oliver O'Donovan

My earliest encounter with Book XIX of Augustine's *City of God* took place when I was a theological student with little experience of reading the Fathers but a great confidence in my own ability to storm the citadels of the theological classics and carry off their treasures.[1] Like a self-conscious young man, bathing by the sea shore, who flexes his arms and his legs and breathes deeply to prepare for his big dive, I braced the muscles of my intelligence and stood poised for an elegant plunge into the waves of a masterpiece. And, like a swimmer who finds that he has incautiously become entangled in a mass of seaweed, I remember feeling first bewilderment and then panic at the drifting complexities of Augustine's discussion. Now that I teach this book to students approaching Augustine for the first time, I know that my experience was not unusual. Yet for nearly two decades it has shaped my mind, and I regard it as one of the unchallengeable masterpieces of Western writing. Ideally one would not try to meet Augustine through its pages, but would dare to approach it only after one was widely conversant with his work. For then one would marvel at the old man's capacity to resynthesize all the elements of a lifetime's theological culture into a new and unprecedented venture. One can say of this late work that he had never done anything like it before; and yet almost every move in the argument is familiar to those who know his earlier work. The "new and unprecedented venture" was a general theory of society from the point of view of a Christian theology of history; and it is this which makes *City of God* XIX a text of continuing interest to students of Western political thought who know nothing else of Augustine. My purpose in this lecture is to provide an account of the book which may assist some new readers to appreciate it with less difficulty than I experienced. To do this I shall first of all try to demonstrate that it is correctly read as an essay in social or political philosophy. Then I shall try to characterize the outline of a political philosophy that we find there, concentrating on two features: first, a feature in which it seems to anticipate modern Western political thought, in its separation between society and virtue; secondly, a feature in which it appears alien to modernity, in its failure to allow for the progressive transformation of the social order.

*City of God* XIX has a central place in any recent attempt to describe Augustine's contribution to Western political thought. The author whose work in this field represents the measure by which other attempts in our generation must be judged, R. A. Markus, entitled his monograph *Saeculum*,[2] thereby giving expression to the view that Augustine was the first theorist of the secular realm—a view which depends heavily on our book for this justification. But not all who write about the *City of God* are agreed that we are justified in looking for a contribution to Western political thought within it. A caution about the political pretensions of Book XIX has been widely spread by a popular commentary on it, that of R. H. Barrow, designed to introduce readers to the *City of God* as a whole.[3] Barrow repeatedly stresses that St. Augustine did not propound a carefully thought-out contribution to political theory: "He is concerned with historical criticism and not with developing a theory of the state" (pp. 249, 253).

In order to reach an opinion on this disagreement, we need to review the contents of the book. It has twenty-eight chapters. At the beginning of Chapter 21 Augustine announces what appears to be an appendix, superfluous to the agenda of the book. That agenda, developed in Chapters 1–20, is to provide an introduction to the fifth and last main section of the *City of God*, Books XIX–XXII. The first two main sections (bks. I–V, VI–X) were devoted to a polemical rebuttal of the principal objections to Christianity raised by paganism, first in its political and then in its philosophical and religious aspects. In the third to fifth sections Augustine undertook to write of the origins, history and ends of the two cities which between them comprise the totality of mankind, the *civitas Dei* and the *civitas terrena*. Their origins are dealt with in Books XI–XIV, their histories in Books XV–XVIII and with Book XIX he comes to address their ends. Books XX–XXII will tell of judgment, hell and heaven in that order, and it is the task of the nineteenth book to provide a general discussion of the "ends" (*debiti fines*) to which the two communities of mankind are destined. But because Augustine shares in the classical conception of a thing's "end" as being its "perfection" (*non quo consumatur sed quo perficiatur*), such a discussion must deal with the question of the supreme end-of-action, the *summum bonum*, that "for the sake of which all else is sought, but itself is sought for itself alone."[4] This, then, comprises the primary agenda for the book.

A recurrent feature of the *City of God* is extended line-by-line engagement with a representative pagan text. Book XIX begins with one of these passages; to the inexperienced reader, certainly one of the most formidable. The test is a section of Varro's lost *De philosophia*, in which the pagan author identifies six cardinal questions on which moral philosophers are observed to disagree, and by computing the possible combinations of answers to these six questions postulates a theoretical total of 288 different philosophical sects; then, by discounting in turn the importance of all but one of the six questions, he reduces the number of serious alternative positions in moral philosophy to three: either virtue is pursued for the sake of the immediate ends of action (pleasure, repose, health, etc.); or the immediate ends of action are pursued for the sake of virtue; or each is pursued for its own sake, the view that Varro himself prefers. This elaborate exordium (chs. 1–3) can have a most chilling impact. There is, it is true, a glint of humour in Augustine's treatment of Varro; but the joke, which extends to 321 lines of Latin in the *Bibliothèque Augustinienne* edition, is a long drawn out one. Augustine then announces his intention of giving the Christian view ("the response of the City of God") on each of Varro's six questions. Notice how he fulfils his promise. The first two questions are treated together in a long chapter (4) of 195 lines, which declares that the Christian answer is different from any that Varro has considered. Neither the immediate ends-of-action nor virtue can be the final good, for neither can overcome the miseries of historical contingency. The final good is eschatological, for only in eternal life can happiness, the true end of all action, be secure. He then turns to Varro's third question, whether or not the final good is social; and to this he devotes the main part of the book, 729 lines of Latin (chs. 5–17). The fourth question is then dispatched in 19 lines (ch. 18); the fifth and sixth are handled together in 44 lines (ch. 19), in which Augustine has only to say that the answer to them is a matter of indifference to the Christian church. A brief résumé (ch. 20) brings Augustine to what appears to be the end of the book proper, leaving only the appendix which takes up some unfinished business from Book II.

This helps us to understand why there is a disagreement about Augustine's intentions in Book XIX. He has set himself an agenda, taken from Varro's discussion of the final good; and he has then treated Varro's agenda with a strong measure of irony. Varro regards the question "whether the wise man should share the final good with a companion" as a secondary matter, not to do with the substance of the final good itself; but Augustine makes society central to it.[5] His successive reformulations of the definition of the final good aim to build into it not only the eschatological but the social determinant: "life everlasting in peace," "peace in everlasting life" (11), where "peace" stands as the most general category of the social good. He could almost, he thinks, simply say "peace," were it not that "peace" is used also, in a relative sense, of the social conditions of this life. "When they wish to say that the wise man's life is a social one, we agree, and we say it much more clearly than they do" (*nos multo amplius adprobamus*, 5).[6] Augustine has therefore challenged the classical account of the supreme good over the way it has organized the question. To grasp this is to grasp why *City of God* XIX is indeed an essay in political thought, contending for the acknowledgment that society is a primary determinant of the human good.

To this argument we may add another, based on the curious phenomenon
of what I have called the "apparent" appendix (chs. 21–25). "This is the
place," Augustine announces at the beginning of Chapter 21, having to all
appearances wound up the business of Book XIX "to fulfil as expeditiously
and clearly as I can the promise I made in Book II, showing that if we adopt
the definition advanced by Scipio in Cicero's *De re publica* there never was a
Roman commonwealth." There follows the most explicitly political section
of the book, tacked on apparently as an afterthought to take up some business
left unfinished some ten to fifteen years earlier. What does Augustine mean
by taking up this business in this place? Let us look back to Book II, where
Augustine was in the full flood of his polemic against pagan Roman religion.
Roman religion, he argued, had no inherent tradition of moral teaching.
Those pagan authors who most praised the austere virtue of the early Roman
republic witnessed most damningly to the failure of Roman culture to
perpetuate its early morality within the changing conditions of growing
national security and power. Cicero represents the hero of its second century
B.C., Scipio Africanus, as saying that the Roman commonwealth was a
commonwealth only in name and not in reality. For a commonwealth (*res
publica*) is a community welfare (*res populi*); and a community (*populus*—you
will pardon the inexactitude of the translation in order to catch the play on
words) implies association both by an agreement about right (*ius*) and by a
shared utility (*utilitas*)—two things which have altogether disappeared from
the later, degenerate Roman populace. To achieve his ostensible polemical
purpose all that Augustine needed to do with this passage (the sentiments, of
course, are Cicero's own, not those of the historical Africanus) was to quote
it. It supports his position sufficiently. In declaring that he would go further,
and demonstrate how, on Cicero-Scipio's terms, the Roman commonwealth
never existed, he clearly indicated that the polemical argument of Book II did
not form the horizon of his interest. This is the promise he takes up at
XIX.21. The argument is straightforward. True right (*ius*) implies obedience
to the true God; for "righteousness," or "justice" (*iustitia*), is the virtue which
assigns to everyone his due, and there can be no justice when the worship
owned by the creature to its creator is offered instead to unclean demons. But
if there is no righteousness or justice (*iustitia*), then there is no "right" (*ius*).
"One should not," he says, "describe as 'rights' (*iura*) what are merely the
unequal institutions of men" (21.1). And if no right, no community (*populus*)
associated by agreement about right, and therefore no commonwealth (*res
publica*).[7]

*     *     *

*II*

Augustine replaces Cicero's definition of a community—the assembly of a multitude associated by agreement about right and by a shared utility—with a definition of his own which excludes all mention of "right"; a community is "the assembly of a rational multitude associated by a harmonious sharing in the objects of its love" (*coetus multitudinis rationalis rerum aqas diligit concordi communione sociatus*—24). It is commonplace, which for the sake of our discussion we may cheerfully accept, that the great difference between ancient and modern political theory is that the modern has severed the ancient's connection between society and virtue. If that is so, then Augustine has, to all appearances, set up the first standard of modern political thought against ancient, casting the political community off from its moorings in justice to drift on the tide of popular consensus. We may welcome this implication or we may deplore it, depending on our position in the more general confrontation between the modern and the ancient; but we cannot simply dismiss it on the grounds that Augustine did not know what he was saying. I have already indicated my reasons for seeing this new definition as the goal to which Augustine's argument has been tending. I will not, therefore, delay over Barrow's uncomprehending suggestion that he introduces it merely by way of example to show how empty and vacuous a definition would have to be if it had to encompass all the polities which have been called commonwealths in the history of the world. "But he goes on at once," Barrow says, "to show how useless this definition is," a statement for which I can find no support whatever in Augustine's text.[10] What Augustine does say is that it is "not absurd" to use the term "community" (*populus*) in this value-free way, allowing that some communities love better things, others worse things; and that he himself adopts this usage because "I would not be prepared to say that [the Roman community] was no community, or that its welfare was no commonwealth" (24).

Cicero's Scipio Africanus, we remember, proposed two grounds of association in a community, both of which Augustine rejects. Most of his attention, and that of his commentators, is given to the repudiation of "right" (*ius*) as the basis of political association; we may shed some light, however, on that more controversial move if we consider his reasons for repudiating association by "shared utility" (*communio utilitatis*). There is, he says, "no utility for the affairs of life (*utilitas viventium*) for those who live impiously—as do all those who serve demons instead of God" (21). This is a perplexing reply. When we used the word "utility," we think of *means* which are neutral in respect of ends. "Utilities" are our term for those life-sustaining goods which the community affords, on the basis of which we may pursue our own ends; it perfectly expresses the modern concept that ends are private, means are shared. When Cicero/Scipio spoke of "shared utility," he probably meant something similar. But Augustine, in keeping with his practice throughout his life, will speak of "utility" only where the supreme good is in view as an end.[11] Augustine would have liked to impose the same discipline upon the noun "use." He more than once maintained that there was no "use" of things to wrong ends, but that the proper term was "abuse"; and his preferred habit was to describe the wicked as "wishing to make use" of things that they ought to enjoy rather than as actually doing so.[12] He was, however, forced to recognise a much wider practice in common speech, making it possible to speak quite generally of the "use" of things which can only be enjoyed.[13] With "utility," however, he held the line, not merely for the sake of being precise but in order to make the substantial point that there *are* no means which are simply neutral in respect of ends.

This affects the way we understand the important question of the relation between the City of God and the earthly city in their dealings with material goods. In Chapter 17 Augustine tells us that there is a *communis usus* between the two communities of mankind; but the *finis utendi* is proper to each, and very different. He then goes on: "Similarly the earthly city, which does not live by faith, seeks an earthly peace, and so determines the concord of its citizens with respect to ordering and giving orders as to ensure a kind of composition of human wills about matters of mortal life." It is the easiest mistake in the world for the casual reader to take the words rendered "similarly" (*ita etiam*) to refer to what has gone immediately before: the City of God and the earthly city get on together by having a common use and differing ends; similarly, the earthly city in itself comprises citizens with a common use but differing ends. From this misreading we would conclude that the earthly city is a neutral institution of shared means to private ends. To demonstrate that it is a misreading, I must simply ask you to read Chapter 17 in Latin from the beginning, and see how the sentence beginning *"ita etiam . . ."* picks up the first sentence of the chapter: "The household of those who do not live by faith seeks an earthly peace. . . . Similarly the city of those who do not live by faith seeks an earthly peace." Augustine does not think that the earthly city is constituted in the same was as the relation between the earthly city and the heavenly city is constituted. He would not say that there was a common use but differing ends among members of the earthly city. There is in fact a common end, eternal punishment, and no use in the proper sense at all, because there is no utility, no real final good which gives value to the pursuit of the intermediate goods.

Here the difference between Augustine and the moderns emerges at its sharpest. It is the single weakness of Markus's fine book to have obscured this difference. "Society," writes Markus of the tendency of Augustine's thought "becomes intrinsically 'secular' in the sense that it is not as such committed to any particular ultimate loyalty. It is the sphere in which different individuals with different beliefs and loyalties pursue their common objectives insofar as they coincide. His 'secularisation' of the realm of politics implies a pluralistic, religiously neutral civil community" (p. 173). So runs the modern liberal tradition—but not Augustine. For him the earthly city, with its earthly peace, did have an ultimate commitment, in which all its members shared: "love of the self to the exclusion of love of God" (XIV.28). The members of the heavenly city, therefore, are never *bona fide* members of the earthly city, however much they "preserve the composition of wills (i.e., *within* the earthly city, not between themselves and the earthly city) as much as piety allows." Furthermore, there never emerges a *tertium quid* between the two cities, a neutral space on which they meet as equal partners. Markus writes that "membership of either is compatible both with belonging to the Roman, or some other state and with belonging to the church" (p. 60f.); but this goes beyond Augustine, for who, it would seem, true Christians were never true Romans, nor false Christians true members of the Church. We observe how Markus reaches for the word "state"; we could sum up the difference by saying that Augustine simply had no conception of the state. Only the "earthly peace," "the temporal peace of the meantime, common alike to the good and to the wicked" (26)—not an institution, but simply a condition of order—is common to both communities. Each community makes, as it were, its own peace out of it. What Augustine likes to say is that the *City of God* makes use of "the peace of Babylon"; and then, quoting Jeremiah, "In her peace is your peace."

We turn, then, to the major change Augustine made to Cicero's definition, the removal of the reference to "right." He was, of course, perfectly aware that *ius* need mean no more than "a system of law." But one *ought* not, in Augustine's view, to speak of *ius* simply in that way without raising the question of its relation to justice. Cicero himself had argued that the loss of *iustitia* caused the Roman commonwealth to cease existing. "Even they admit," he says, "that *ius* is what flows from the fount of *iustitia*!" (21). One might as sensibly object to Augustine's argument on this score as complaining that Plato failed in the *Republic* to distinguish different senses of δικαιοσύνη. Augustine had argued in Book II that Rome, lacking a religious morality, lacked a unified public moral culture, having only the heterogeneous elements of a philosophical morality, a tradition of law and a flagrantly immoral public religion (II.12). Thus reflective and conscientious Romans like Cicero ended up with a sense of bad faith in regard to the public culture (II.27). A unified account of justice, which related law to religion, was for him a philosophical *sine qua non.*

We may, however, be surprised that Augustine did not embark upon an analogical treatment of justice, which would have allowed for it to be instantiated on different levels of society. This would have been to treat it in the same way as he treated peace: there is absolute peace and there is relative peace, so why not also absolute justice and relative justice? There is, in fact, a relative justice in Augustine's thought, but it does not extend downwards to embrace the ordinary legal activities of the earthly commonwealth. We notice the disparity in the treatment of peace and justice from the opening of Chapter 27: "That peace which is our special possession . . . is enjoyed here with God by faith, and will be enjoyed for ever with him by sight. Yet any peace we have here, whether that which we share or that which is special to us, is more like the consolation of our wretchedness than a delight in happiness." There are, we notice, three kinds of peace mentioned in that sentence: the final peace of heaven, the interior peace of the City of God enjoyed by faith, and the peace which is common to the two cities. He proceeds: "Similarly, the justice which is ours, though in its true justice oriented to the supreme good, consists in this life more in the forgiveness of sins than in the perfection of virtues." There we have only two kinds of justice or righteousness, both peculiar to the City of God, and there is no mention of any third kind which might be common to the two cities. As the discussion proceeds it becomes evident why. The Latin *iustitia* (like the Greek δικαιοσύνη), is notoriously translated in theological English by no fewer than three words: righteousness, justice and justification. Augustine cannot use the word without being aware of the problematic represented by the third of these, the *iustitia Dei, non qua iustus est sed qua iustus est sed qua iusti sunt homines quos iustificat,* "not in the sense of his being righteous, but in the sense of his justifying mankind."[14] He cannot, or will not, disengage a separate social or political sense of the word from his theological discussion. "Justice" must include the forgiveness of sins. That is why Chapter 27 thereupon takes an unexpected turn, prompted by mention of the forgiveness of sins, into terrain which belongs to his long-fought controversy with the Pelagians over Christian perfection.

Yet in at least two places in earlier books of the *City of God* Augustine has spoken of justice in connection with civil government. What are we to make of this? Is it a simple discrepancy attributable to the long intervening years which separated the composition of one part of the work from another? Well, it may be. I do not hold a strong brief for Augustine's verbal consistency, nor do I think it likely that in 415, when Books IV and V were composed, he had an exact conception of what he would say a decade or more later. Nevertheless, a consistent account of his views on justice can be given which respects all that we find him saying in the *City of God*; and I do not think such an account should be overlooked. On this account Augustine is held to believe two thinks: (a) that justice is a *virtue* of civil government, even though it is not a necessary criterion for it; (b) that this virtue is realised only when civil government is conducted by Christians.

*       *       *

Before we conclude, however, that Augustine simply allowed too little to political justice and paid too high a price in political theory for a unified account of *iustitia*, we must reckon with what he had on hand to put in its place. For having severed the connection between civil society and virtue, he takes a very different direction from the early modern theorists who attempted to re-found society on passion.[18] What he did, on the contrary, was to reformulate something like the traditional concept of society and morality in new terms which would give due recognition both to the reality of the moral order which makes social existence possible and to its fundamentally flawed character. Augustine embarks on the radical, but not revolutionary policy of characterising all polities in terms of their moral *dis*order, which itself provides an explanation of their political *order*, since, in Augustine's firmly Platonic view, disorder is nothing but a failure in an underlying moral order. When we read that famous statement in Chapter 25, "The virtues which they think they have . . . are in fact vices rather than virtues," we should not, certainly, make the mistake of dismissing it as empty rhetoric; nevertheless, we should set it alongside the characteristic affirmation of Chapter 12: "Even what is perverted must of necessity be in, derived from, or associated with—that is, at peace with—some part of reality in which it has its being, or of which it consists. Otherwise it would not exist at all." A vice, in other words, is a perversion of a *virtue*; it is a *dis*order which is predatory on some *order*. In the twelfth chapter of Book V Augustine has written that the Romans "checked their other lusts with single huge lust for this one thing," i.e. glory. From this sprang their "moral qualities" and "good arts," everything valuable about a civilisation, in fact, apart from "real" virtue. This theory has evoked some notable echoes in the modern period:

> This burning desire to be talked about, this yearning for distinction which keeps us almost always in a restless state is responsible for what is best and what is worst among men, for our virtues and our vices, for our sciences and our mistakes, for our conquerors and our philosophers—that is to say, for a multitude of bad things and very few good things. [Rousseau, *Discourse on Inequality* (p. 133, Penguin tr.)]

It is a remarkable theory, combining strengths of both ancient and modern political thought. It allows us to understand how manifestly vicious communities can function, and apparently function well, as organised societies; and yet permits us an absolute point of moral criticism from which we can say, as Augustine does in Chapter 24: "The better the object of its agreement, the better the community." Not the least striking feature of it is its capacity to take terrorist-groups seriously as political communities and understand their functioning in terms relevant to politics. Peter Brown has drawn our attention to a telling remark in one of the sermons, where Augustine remarks that it is love that enables a terrorist to endure torture rather than reveal the names of his accomplices.[19] "Love," we must note, is not passion. Although the objects of a community's life are as various as sin itself, love is still directed to the good, even if not always to the supreme good. What Augustine's reader carries away with him in the end is not a denigration of the role of virtue in politics (though there is a fair amount of deflation of pretension) but an ability to discern shadows cast by virtue in surprising places.

## III

This brings us to the second feature of Augustine's political thought, in which it appears least comfortable to modern assumptions: it lacks a theory of progress. A generation ago H. Richard Niebuhr implanted in the mind of every freshman student of Christian ethics that Augustine stood for a "transformation" of human culture by Christ.[20] For this interpretation there is, on the face of it, less than no evidence in Book XIX of the *City of God*. Many modern heads have been shaken sadly over the complacency with which he views the institution of slavery in Chapters 14–16.[21]

The context of that discussion is important. Augustine's theoretical foundation, laid in Chapters 11–13, has been that, while every community seeks some peace, the City of God seeks the heavenly peace and refers its use of all provisional goods to the enjoyment of that eternal society. What form does this "use" take with respect to the temporal peace of the earthly city? To justify his starting-point, that the City of God can actually interest itself in that temporal peace, he quotes, as so often, the two fold command of love to God and neighbour. Neighbour-love must take a form, which is inescapably conditioned by the order of society in which the believer is situated. This is illustrated first by a discussion of the household and second by a discussion of the next order of society on a scale of expanding size, the city. The household occupies Augustine in Chapters 14–16, and he discusses it as a *Christian* household, that is to say, with a believer at its head, seeking to love his neighbour within the social context it affords. At the beginning of Chapter 17 a mere sentence or two about the non-Christian household leads him to the city, which he treats the other way round, speaking of how the earthly city establishes its peace, and then of how the heavenly city makes use of it. It is a reasonable inference from the different approaches Augustine makes to the two levels of society that he thinks of a Christian household as achieving a concrete form in a way that a Christian city does not.

By "household" (*domus*) he means something political, "an ordered harmony about giving and receiving commands among those who live in the same house." It is the "incipient form, or component part, of the city" (16); and consequently "it takes its laws from the laws of the city." That is to say, it is a sphere of punishment and a sphere of command: not only do masters command servants but parents command children and husbands wives. The distinctive feature which Augustine discerns in the Christian household is that commands are given "not from lust for dominion but from dutiful concern for others' interest, not in price of precedence but in compassionate care" (14). And if he had stopped there, we would have concluded simply that the Christian household differs from any other only by the motive for which the authority-structure is maintained. But he goes on: "This [compassionate care and dutiful concern] is what the order of nature (i.e., creation) requires, for that is how God made mankind" (15). Creation-order allowed no place for dominion: the patriarchs were shepherds who ruled flocks, not kings who ruled subjects. And that is why before the time of Noah there were no slaves. In this almost offhand way Augustine reminds us of the patristic tradition that government and slavery were a provision of providence for a fallen world and no part of the order of creation; with it he conveys the message that the distinctive motive of the Christian householder is in fact subtly subversive of these institutions in that it reasserts the primal equality of every human being to every other. So easily missed is Augustine's allusion to the patristic tradition here that early modern thinkers such as Althusius could cheerfully quote his words about the morale of the Christian householder in support of the Thomist doctrine that *imperium* was neutral and for the benefit of all (*Politica* ch. 1). The righteous fathers, he remarks, distinguished between their slaves and their children in respect of temporal goods; but in respect of eternal goods they loved their slaves no less than any other member of their family. "This," he repeats, "is what the order of nature requires" (16). The Christian householder thus emerges in a form reminiscent of the Christian emperor: strangely detached from the earthly privilege of his position and longing for the heavenly rest where the burden of command will be taken from his shoulders, he makes himself the servant of others—and has more need of patience under his burden than his slave does under his.[22]

This seems to me to fall considerably short of what is meant if we speak of the "transformation" of cultural institutions. The authority-structure of the householder will not change before the coming of Christ's kingdom. What the Christian householder achieves is to superimpose another meaning on the relationships that arise within it, very much as the Christian emperor superimposes the righteousness of his conduct upon the tasks of dominion. They are the sign of God's purpose to restore created innocence, but not the substance of it. And we may, not unjustly, wish to excuse Augustine for going no further than this by pleading that his political experience did not extend as far as ours. We have seen slavery abolished—albeit slowly and with difficulty over the course of half a millennium or more—and he had not. His foreshortened historical perspective prevented him from seeing what kinds of revolution are possible in social structures.

Such an excuse, which, however courteously meant, concedes the right to modernity against Augustine, does not get to the root of the opposition between his expectations of politics and ours—which are based, to one degree or another, on an optimistic view of history and a belief in social malleability which derives from the revolutionary traditions of the Enlightenment. For the truth is, not that Augustine had no sense of historical development, but that he had a strong sense of it, and found it inherently ambiguous. The history of the earthly city, for Augustine, is the history of the growth of empire. There is an important chapter in Book XVIII (ch. 2) where he claims that the earthly city has taken form in "a great number of empires," of which two have emerged as the central empires of world-history, Assyria (in which he includes the subsequent Mesopotamian empires) and Rome. "All other kingdoms and kings I should describe as something like appendages of those empires." To write the history of the earthly city is to write of a destiny of world-government given to Rome. "It was God's design to conquer the world through her, to unite the world into a single community of Roman commonwealth and Roman laws, and so impose peace throughout its length and breadth" (XVIII.22). But this, we say, is nothing other than the Vergilian ideology of Roman empire! Quite—but with one significant difference, which turns it into a kind of photographic negative of Vergil, in which white is black and black is white. Guided by the prophets of Israel and the seer of the Apocalypse, Augustine sees this design of God as one which is fulfilled by the growth of Rome's overweening love of glory. God's purpose is achieved by his allowing evil to wax great. Within the first line of the *City of God* he finds an opportunity to quote the famous tag of Aeneid VI, *parcere subiectis et debellare superbos*, and to comment: "This is God's prerogative; but man's arrogant spirit in his swelling pride has claimed it as his own and delights to hear this verse quoted in his own praise" (I. *pro.*).[23]

World-history, then, has a shape, and the evolution of a pacified and civilised world-government is the key to it. Augustine is to this extent a historicist: there are no general questions of political theory left unaccounted for when he was giving us his account of the growth of Rome.[24] But this history turns out to be a demonic history, which expresses the divine purpose only as providence, following its own hidden course, uses it to higher ends.[25] Augustine's problem, then, is not to conceive of progress within the political realm, but to distance himself from it, to retain the perspective that God brings the pretensions of the proud to nought. What appears to be civilisational progress is, in fact, on the moral and spiritual level, self-defeating.

*     *     *

# Notes

†Reprinted by permission of the publisher from *Dionysius* 11 (1987): 89–110.
[1]Parts of this paper were delivered as a lecture at the kind invitation of the Faculty of Classics in Dalhousie University, Halifax, Nova Scotia, and other parts at Duke Divinity School, Durham, North Carolina. I am grateful to the members of both these institutions for their hospitality and discussion. I must also thank Professors R. A. Markus and R. D. Williams who commented on the typescript. I have not attempted to remove the marks of a *pièce d'occasion* which fit the propaedeutic aspirations of the paper—though I hope that some who have no need of a propaedeutic may find some of the exegetical remarks helpful.

[2]R. A. Markus, *Saeculum*, Cambridge 1970.

[3]R. H. Barrow, *An Introduction to Augustine's City of God*, London 1950. A more recent book by Peter Denis Bathory, *Political Theory as Public Confession*, New Brunswick 1981, has imaginatively highlighted the aspects of Augustine's thought which are of most significance for political theory; but the author's habit of adding "says Augustine" to wide-ranging speculations of his own is one of a number of disconcerting features which makes his book a treacherous tool for scholarship.

[4]XIX.1.1: "Finem boni ergo nunc dicimus, non quo consumatur, ut non sit, sed quo perficiatur, ut plenum sit; et finem mali, non quo esse desinat, sed quo usque nocendo perducat." There is need for more commentary on the paradoxical idea of *finis mali* or *summum malum*. It will be noted that Augustine's definition here is inconsistent with his definition at XIX.4.1: "respondebit aeternam vitam esse summum bonum, aeternam vero mortem summum malum: propter illam proinde adipiscendam istamque vitandam recte nobis esse vivendum." The problem is well outlined in G. Bardy's note in the *Bibliothèque Augustinienne* edition (xxxvii p. 725f). Augustine has inherited the antithesis of *fines bonorum et malorum* from Cicero and the Stoics. But the antithetical terms cannot be taken in the same sense. "Le ciel est un bien sans aucun mélange de mal; mais il reste encore du bien dans l'enfer."

[5]XIX.1.3: "Cum ergo quaeritur de sociali vita . . . non de ipso summo bono

quaestio est, sed de adsumendo vel non adsumendo socio ad huius participationem boni." I take this occasion to apologise to any whom I may have misled by a careless use of this text in *The Problem of Self-Love in St. Augustine* (New Haven, 1980) p. 115.

[6]Thus G. Combès understands these words correctly: "Nous l'approuvons et bien plus qu'eux" (*B. A.* xxxvii p. 79). Other translators (e.g. H. Bettenson in the Penguin translation, p. 858) suppose that Augustine means that on this question there is more fulsome support from the church for the philosophers than on the previous questions. But on the previous questions there was no support from the church for the philosophers at all. It is, moreover, more idiomatic to take the infinitive *socialem vitam esse sapientis* rather than the clause *quod . . . volunt* as the object of *adprobamus*.

[7]I simplify the argument slightly, omitting the move in 21.2, which takes up Cicero's argument from the subordination of the body to the soul, and of the soul to God, and arguing that only a community made up of individuals who are thus ordered can be a just community. This is not strictly necessary to Augustine's argument, but in view of his search for a unified concept of *iustitia* (see below, p. 99f.) it is of great interest, closely echoing Plato's *Republic*.

*[Text for notes 8-9 not reprinted here.]

*     *     *

[10]R. H. Barrow, *An Introduction to Augustine's City of God*, p. 253.

[11]Cf. the early *de diversis quaestionibus lxxxiii* 30.

[12]See my article "*Usus* and *Fruitio* in Augustine, *De Doctrina Christiana* I", *J.T.S.* xxxiii (1982) p. 376.

[13]*De civ. Dei* XI.25

[14]*Ep.* 140. 72. Cf. *de spiritu et littera* 32.56.

*[Text for notes 15–17 not reprinted here.]

*     *     *

[18]For what follows see the discussion by Ernest L. Fortin, *Political Idealism and Christianity in the Thought of St. Augustine*, Villanova 1972.

[19]*Sermon* 169. 11.14, cited in Brown, *loc. cit.* p. 317.

[20]H. Richard Niebuhr, *Christ & Culture*, New York 1951, pp. 206–18.

[21]For example, the head of my friend Richard N. Longenecker, in *New Testament Social Ethics for Today*, Grand Rapids 1984, pp. 63–6.

[22]"Quo donec veniatur, magis debent patres quod dominantur, quam servi tolerare quod serviunt." Again G. Combès has understood the idiomatic deferred infinitive: "les pères doivent avoir plus de patience à supporter de commander que les esclaves de servir" (p. 125).

[23]Augustine's love of Vergil has influenced much of the *City of God*, despite the severity which his polemic required of him. Vergil's great virtue, in Augustine's eyes, was that he could not suppress a "shudder of compassion" at the brutal deeds which made the empire great (III.16).

[24]Against Barrow, *op. cit.* p. 249.

25Cf. IV.33: "ipse dat regna terrena et bonis et malis . . . pro rerum ordine ac temporum occulto nobis, notissimo sibi"; V.1: "divina providentia regna constituuntur humana."

*[Text for notes 26–29 not reprinted here.]

*     *     *

# Augustine's Razor: Public vs. Private Interests in *The City of God*†

## Joanna V. Scott

## I. Introduction

In Augustine's *The City of God*, the world the Roman governing elite were in the process of losing may not really have been theirs in the first place. A dominant *leitmotif* running through Augustine's classic rendition of the decline and fall is the increasing discontinuity between the *de jure* and the *de facto*—between formal political structures and actual social life, and especially between the founding traditions of the Roman Republic and the "loves" of the diverse peoples of the Empire. While this theme originated in his earlier sermons and letters, it is in the context of his great debate with opinion leaders of Roman culture that Augustine reiterates and amplifies it to greatest effect.

In *The City of God* Augustine constructed a political theory of diversity without destabilization, forcing Roman critics of Christianity to acknowledge the reality of complex cultural, institutional and personal identifications but promising them public peace in return. Augustine even seems to slip over the precipice from the modern to the postmodern as he complicates the problem of diversity by adding spiritual communities to the list of possible identities. In Augustine's world *civitates* or *res publicae* exist within, but may be actually distinct from, the juridical structures of both *imperium* and *ecclesia*. The *saeculum* is compounded of two main invisible bodies, the *civitas Dei* and *civitas terrena*. Other, lesser, groupings are described variously as *res publicae*, civic associates, or "people." They too have their own bases of legitimacy in languages, local customs, historical memory and shared values. In turn, juridical institutional structures established by Roman or ecclesiastical law have their own parallel modes of discourse, procedures, history and civic virtue. Individuals may simultaneously incur the obligations of belief and obedience to several such *civitate* whose "loves" tragically conflict. The role of the state in Augustine's ordained *ordinatio ad unum* is to legislate, administer, punish citizens and defend the imperial perimeters. Whether led by Christian emperors or not, it legitimately commands obedience to its laws and applies sanctions to which believing Christians must submit. The "Roman" church promulgates canonic doctrine, makes will-enhancing grace accessible through its sacraments and provides common rules of worship which take precedence over culture, language and political diversity. It enforces conformity in religious practice for all who publicly profess belief, whether or not their private "dark" and "hidden" souls are animated by *caritas*.[1] In the end, Augustine tries to validate both moral *civitate* and the institutions of the *saeculum* using what might be termed "Augustine's razor." But the razor cannot cut as deeply in reality as in "confession." Whether by inadvertence or design, Augustine has bequeathed a significant ambiguity to the tradition of political thought. At issue is how, or even why, the *civitate Dei* and *terrena* and other *res publicae*, together with individuals of Christian conscience, can transcend the institutional structures in which they are conceived, nurtured and justified.

Modern classicists such as Hannah Arendt have celebrated Augustine's pivotal role as both critic and preserver of Roman political values and have used him as a sympathetic bridge from ancient to modern understandings of civic virtue. Arendt not only wrote her dissertation on Augustine under Martin Heidegger and Karl Jaspers but returned again and again in her later works to "the only philosopher the Romans ever had."[2] Augustine earned her particular approval for the "great sanity" with which he countered "the strong anti-political tendencies of early Christianity." For Arendt as for Augustine, the state was a "given." It was, she notes, with approval, not Augustine but Tertullian who declared that "no matter is more alien to us than what matters publicly" (1988, 74). Indeed, Arendt mused, Augustine must have been "the last to know at least what it once meant to be a citizen" (1958, 14).

The *City of God*, however, provides little support for the defense of individual rights based on a state of nature prior to the imposition of government. The American Founding Fathers and their academic successors have found cold comfort in Augustinianism for the proposition that inalienable rights continue to have legal status within the constitutional structure of the state, or that their abrogation constitutes the legitimate basis for recourse to revolution. Indeed, Augustine is not interested in discussing social organization or authority structures in pre-history, except to say that inequality in general and slavery particularly would not be necessary had Adam been willing to accept the divinely mandated inequality of his dependence on God. In Biblical pre-history, authority on earth and in God's natural order were completely identical and paternally based. By consigning Eden to a time before history began, Augustine eliminates the possibility of using it as the historical basis for revolutionary claims against the state. At the same time, the mythic golden age of spiritual community can remain as paradigm for reconstituting particular communities in the *saeculum*, though they must await the end of time to achieve perfection. In this preservationist approach to political culture and its institutions, Augustine's values are therefore much more similar to those of the anti-revolutionary Edmund Burke than those of the Founding Fathers of American liberalism—Hobbes, Locke and Adam Smith.

As teachers of political thought have learned to their dismay, *The City of God* cannot be read in the same way as Plato's *Republic* or Aristotle's *Politics*. Unlike these canonic texts, Augustine's great disquisition on citizenship does not contain a morphology of state forms based on their moral excellence, class basis, historical origins or any other analytic categories. In the context of liberal modernity, *The City of God* also has little in common with The Federalist Papers—though Augustine might himself have uttered Madison's famous observation that if human beings were angels no government would be necessary. It is the hypocrisy of Roman elites, in view of their past and present history, that interest him and not the details of Roman political structures or legal processes. As a result, Augustine also provides no roadmap for political change, revolutionary or otherwise. Things happen, usually for the worse, but no political lessons are drawn or plans laid. The *civitas Dei* is not the prototype for a revolutionary "committee of correspondence," organizing itself to form a constituent assembly and write a constitution. Augustine's *civitate* infiltrate but do not topple the old order.

## II. Constituting Communities

Perhaps no part of *The City of God* is more famous for its unexpected modernity than Augustine's redefinition of what constitutes a people and its public weal. In his classic puncturing of Ciceronian hypocrisy (*The City of God*. Trans. Marcus Dods. New York: Modern Library, 1950. II, 60–63; XIX, 699–700, 706–77. Cited as *CG*.) Augustine carefully uses the term *res publica* to refer only to the creation of a public association, an "assemblage" or "combination of men's wills to attain the things which are helpful to this life" (*CG* XIX, 695). Throwing out the substance of Cicero's thesis that moral probity is the measure of public authenticity, Augustine retains only its shell. What is necessary for viable public life is a consensus on the rules of justice ("a common agreement as to the objects of their love").

Augustine argues that the specific content of those values which are shared is historically contingent, institutional-specific, and generally of secondary importance to the associational act itself. The public space is constructed and sustained, even if passively, through pursuit of moral goals. "Love" bound Rome in the time of the Kings, the Republic and the Empire. It binds the Church, ethnic groups, nations within the empire, and in general all *res publicae*—including associations of thieves and scoundrels. In other words, large or small, spiritual or social, these associations constitute "public" bodies whose institutional articulation may be designated further with such terms as *res publica, civitas, imperium, ecclesia* or barbarian hordes when appropriate. "The life of the wise man must be social" writes Augustine, "for how could the city of God . . . either take a beginning or be developed or attain its proper destiny" without community? (*CG* XIX, 680) Even if the solitary lives of saints seem preferable to the chaos and ignorance that confounds "social" life, it is "wickedness to abandon" it. "Human society . . . constrains him and compels him to his duty" (*CG* XIX, 682). Even in sedition, "when men have separated themselves from community," they still are not beyond the bounds of a *res publica* of sorts. Their "love" is expressed in their particular rules of concord and "peace."

Without his new and elastic understanding of public goods, says Augustine, the counter factual conclusion must be reached that there never was a Roman public weal because there was never a people constituted by a common agreement about true justice. Augustine manages to hoist Cicero on his own elite petard by defending both Christian transcendent ethics and the concrete, experiential reality of legitimate government and civic associations which are far from genuinely Christian (*CG* XIX, 699, 706).

> But what I say of this people and of this republic I must be understood to think and say of the Athenians or any Greek state, of the Egyptians, of the early Assyrian Babylon and of every other nation, great or small, which had a public government.                                          [*CG* XIX, 706]

To measure the "character" of a "people" Augustine counsels gathering behavioral evidence rather than making assumptions. That is, "we have only to observe what they love." Flawed though the Roman republic may have been, "I would not on this account say either that it was not a people or that its administration was not a republic."

*Ordinatio ad unum* is a notoriously prevalent theme in Augustinianism, and is usually developed analogically in great chains of equivalence from the soul's "harmony" and "concord" through the "peace" of the universe. Individual free will is always present as the counterweight to the "order" of creation necessary to establish personal responsibility for sin. Of course, the will only functions efficaciously when it is healed through *caritas*, the result of contingent divine grace. Unaided by grace, individual wills are beset by the "monstrosity" of impotence which renders good motivation inoperative. Thus, whether viewed through the natural order which mandates peace or internally as the intervention of grace to heal the divided will, Augustine's understanding of providential order is based on a normative hierarchy of dependence and rule.

It is significant, however, that Augustine's strategy is to argue for individual obligation to God by analogy to the "principles" of political society by which citizen obedience is required. This pattern of reference to Roman values is consistent throughout his writings, and is paralleled by his acceptance of customary relationships between family members, between slaves and masters, and between the Empire and its provinces.[3] *The City of God* contains the classic formulation of *ordinatio ad unum* as the basis of both peace and of justice. "The peace of all things is the tranquility of order. Order is the distribution which allots things equal and unequal to its own place" (*CG* XIX, 690). Thus "domestic peace is the well-ordered concord between those of the family who rule and those who obey" and since "the house ought to be the beginning or element of the city" (*CG* XIX, 695), it follows that "civil peace is a similar concord among the citizens" (*CG* XIX, 690). In his lectures on the *Gospel of John*, Augustine speaks of the state in unmistakable authoritarian language, based on the Roman *paterfamilias*, as if the Roman Republic had never existed. "Divine right we have in the Scriptures, human right in the laws of kings." Ciceronian niceties of compact and consensus fall away in the offhand comment that "God had distributed to mankind these very rights [of property] through the emperors and kings of this world" (in Philip Schaff, ed. *A Select Library of Nicene and Post-Nicene Fathers of the Christian Church.* New York: Christian Literature Co., 1988. Vol. VI, 25, 26, 161).

In this mode of discourse, justice is simply obedience to "higher powers" the fact of whose existence and continuance is a sufficient basis of legitimacy. The ending of *dominium* and the establishment of a regime of true divine justice on earth is not the evaluative standard against which *regna* of the *saeculum* should be judged. Universal order as a contingent outcome of God's absolute will is visible in both the reigns of Christian emperors and evil tyrants. Both rule the invisibly mingled communities of the *civitas terrena* and *civitas Dei*. Augustine repeatedly urges that public order not be threatened by acts of violence or civil disobedience on the part of citizen, whether Christian or pagan. Personal morality of officials or the appropriateness, with respect to Scriptural ethics, of the imperial edicts they enforce is irrelevant to the legitimacy of the state and its function in the order of divine dispensation. All powers are from God, and the essence of public power is still the executioner. *Regnum* and *Sacerdotium* are the structural outcroppings of the saeculum, and are not coextensive with the moral communities formed by *caritas* (Christian love) and *cupiditas* (earthly love).

Augustine's minimalist approach to morality in public institutions coupled with his maximalist expectations for the belief and behavior of Christian citizens is often termed "political realism" by American commentators from a variety of disciplines, from Reinhold Niebuhr (1953) to Herbert Deane (1963) and Judith Shklar (1990).[4] However, Augustine's alleged realism never entails diminished faith in the normative priority of the public over private interests. It is the individual soul and its inner turmoil which Augustine renders with terms such as "darkness" and "hidden." These terms are meant to suggest resistance to human understanding but also the protection of the will's power of contingent action from the baleful effects of Greek and Roman philosophic determinism. Darkness is the backdrop not only for the divided will's struggle but also for its healing through the unmerited intervention of grace. Perhaps in Augustinianism there is some justification for the otherwise objectionable aphorism "Dark Ages"—though following the Saint's logic this cosmic interregnum commenced with Adam and Eve's fall from grace and will continue until the end of time.

The secret places of the soul (one's own and other's), together with the imperviousness of God's Being to human understanding, place severe limits upon human enterprise. As well as *The City of God*, the *Confessions* (Trans. John K. Ryan. New York: Image Doubleday, 1960. Cited as *Conf.*) explores the tragic consequences of the opacity of human relationships.

With the allurements of sweet odors I am not much troubled; when they are absent I do not seek them and when they are present I do not reject them, but I am prepared to do entirely without them. So do I seem to myself, but perhaps I am deceived. Within me are those lamentable dark areas wherein my own capacities lie hidden from me. Hence when my mind questions itself about its powers it is not easy for it to decide what should be believed. . . . In this life . . . no man should be sure whether one who can pass from worse to better might not pass from better to worse. One hope, one trust, one firm promise, your mercy!                                                                      (*Conf.* 260)

The *City of God* notes the "darkness which shrouds social life" (*CG* XIX, 682) in which "we . . . mistake a friend" (*CG* XIX, 684). The law whose judgments are "necessary in communities" to maintain an "outward peace," is a "melancholy and lamentable" enterprise because judges are mere "men who cannot discern the consciences of those at their bar" (*CG* XIX, 681–682).

William Connolly (*Political Theory and Modernity*. Oxford: Basil Blackwell, 1988; *The Augustinian Imperative: A Reflection on the Politics of Morality*. Los Angeles: Sage Publications, 1993) hears Augustine's voice in a peculiarly Western concern about the scope and limits of human autonomy. Augustine saved his deity from responsibility for evil by making it a byproduct of free will. The price of freedom is its unintended consequences (1988, 18). To Connolly it is hardly surprising that Augustine's belief in God's absolute contingent power combined with the experienced sense of the "darkness" and "error" which besets humanity, was a stimulus for the fourteenth century nominalism of William of Occam and other travellers on the "*via moderna*." In *The Confessions* Augustine mentions that reason had become an end in itself in the philosophy of the Academy and a manipulative trap in the hands of the Manicheans, astrologers and others who propounded a scientific religion. Augustine speaks of direct apprehension of "Truth" which is "neither Hebrew, nor Greek nor Latin nor Barbaric in speech" and is "without mouth or tongue . . . without noise of syllables" (*Conf.* 280). Rather than pure mind as the location of truth, Augustine posits *memoria* (memory) as "the dwelling place of thought" within which the dialogue of the soul with its Creator can take place wordlessly. In *The City of God*, attacking the skepticism of Varro and the New Academy, Augustine remarks that "the city of God detests such doubt as madness." The faithful must "believe also the evidence of the senses which the mind uses by aid of the body" even though the body is certainly "corruptible." For [if one who trusts the senses is sometimes deceived] he is more wretchedly deceived who fancies he should never trust them" (*Conf.* 697). Christians must "assent" to the Scriptures which are called "canonical" because they are "the source of faith by which the just live . . . whilst we are absent from the Lord." Yet the tenets of this faith, though foundational, are minimal. For the rest, considerable pragmatic adaptation seems justified.

So long as this faith remains inviolate and firm, we may without blame entertain certain doubts regarding some things which we have neither perceived by sense nor by reason, and which have not been revealed to us by the canonical Scriptures, nor come to our knowledge through witnesses whom it is absurd to disbelieve.                                        (*Conf.* 697)

Thus, Augustine's thoughts on public and private obligation are not as easily reducible to the realist theme as many theologians and political commentators have wished. A key indicator of the fact that both idealism and realism coexist in his political thought is that in *The City of God* Augustine pursues a distinctly non-pragmatic argument for the moral autonomy of citizens and public officials. He does so not only when discussing the dynamics of free will but also in justifying public action prompted by the "law written on the hearts of men." The Christian is bound to obey both the structural *ordinatio ad unum* of public institutions in society and state and the inner *ordo* imposed by his potential citizenship in the *civitas Dei*. Direct from Pauline critiques of Judaism comes Augustine's frequent observation that all Gentiles who acknowledge the law of God have no need of the written law which Moses gave to the Jews. "When the sin [original sin] is erased out of their hearts . . . the prescriptions of the law are done 'by nature'—not that by nature grace is denied but by grace nature is repaired." Such individuals are "a law unto themselves [*lex animata*] . . . ." (*De Spiritu et Lettera*, Ch. 47–48, 498–99. In Whitney Oates ed., *Basic Writings of Saint Augustine*. Vol. I. New York: Random House, 1948). In the same way, by analogy from the family to the state, Augustine reminds his pagan audience in *The City of God* that the virtuous person must act for the common good of the *saeculum*.

> To be innocent, we must not only do harm to no man, but also restrain him from sin or punish his sin so that either the man himself who is punished may profit by his experience or others warned by his example . . . [just as] if any member of the family interrupts the domestic peace by disobedience, he is correct either by word or blow or some kind of just and legitimate punishment such as society permits.                           (*CG* XIX, 695)

When discussing the functions of political institutions *per se* Augustine recognizes the necessary limits of morality in law. Given the mass of damned souls, he counsels political order and obedience to the very limits of conscience. However, in Augustine's other epistemology of grace-empowered will he is inclined to emphasize the force of moral communities and individuals, and thus the "social gospel" aspects of political order. This central, and deliberate, ambiguity in Augustine's work defies categorization as "realism" or any other ideology based on the passive acceptance of the politics of damnation. At the core of Augustine's understanding of "modern" political society, therefore, lies the hidden *libertas* of the obedient citizen, or dutiful public official, who is simultaneously *lex animata*. This tension, in turn, fueled by Medieval ambivalence about the state—the constant pull between an idealized pre-historical society before Adam's Fall recapitulated in the invisible *civitas Dei* and the mixture of "loves" in the *corpus politicum*. It is also an important source for early modern European understanding of individuality generated from, yet transcending, community and institutional contexts.

There are brief references in Augustine's works to what a Christian emperor might achieve in raising the moral tone of the *saeculum*. Significantly, however, once the influence of his mentor Bishop Ambrose receded, Augustine spoke only of the potential Christianization of politics in the subjective mood. "There can be nothing more fortunate for human affairs than that they who are endowed with true piety . . . if they have the skill for ruling people, should also have the power" (*CG* III, 79). The happiness of pious rulers is rendered with the conditional "if." Fulfillment will result from preserving and extending the faith," applying that punishment as necessary to government and defense of the republic and not in order to gratify their own enmity," and ultimately "if they prefer to govern depraved desires rather than any nation whatever" (*CG* V, 178).

More is in play here than the Platonic paradox of philosophers becoming kings. Confessing Christians are duty-bound to become public officials, but the necessity of coercive restraint does not dissipate even if administered with "love." Also unchanged is the problem of the moral community to which the citizen or public servant truly belongs, rather than that to which one gives allegiance in the "language marts" of rhetorical politics. Pagans can be good citizens but not good persons in the Christian era. Yet Christians cannot be good persons without also being good citizens—even to the point of wielding the executioner's axe. The tension between the cupidity-driven behavior of Roman elites and the cultural ideal projected by Cicero gives Augustine's commentary its notorious ironic edge. Satirizing the Roman elite's prayers to their Gods he writes,

> This is our concern, that every man be able to increase his wealth so as to supply his daily prodigalities, and so that the powerful may subject the weak for their own purposes. Let the poor court the rich for a living. . . . Let the people applaud not those who protect their interests, but those who provide them with pleasure. Let no severe duty be commanded, no impurity forbidden. Let kings estimate their prosperity not by the righteousness, but by the servility of their subjects. . . . Let the laws take cognizance rather of the injury done to another man's property, than of that done to one's own person. If a man be a nuisance to his neighbor, or injure his property . . . let him be actionable; but in his own affairs let every one with impunity do what he will in company with his family and with those who willingly join him.
>
> (*CG* II, 59)

### III. Public Interest and Private *Libertas*

The "public interest" is a major theme in Augustine's works, not only in *The City of God* but also in his earliest dialogues and in *The Confessions*.

Though it is sometimes couched in ethically neutral language, his approach more often carries strong normative implications. The *res publica* is defined literally as the public interest. It is the agenda of the moral communities which animate institutions of church and state. The frequently used term *libertas* means freedom within the context of the good of all. Its opposite is the state of mind described above, *cupiditas*, in which the meaning of liberty is privatized to justify pursuit of property, pleasure and power. The outer expression of this *mentalité* is *libido dominandi*. Without the ability to defer private gratification in the interest of the public weal, regardless of how "love" is defined in particular communities, the existence of the *civitas* is threatened. This explains Augustine's repeated backhanded honors for noble Romans such as Regulus and Scipio who defended to the death the *libertas* of the Roman *res publicae*, while suppressing their own personal *libido dominandi*. Their reward, justly authorized by divine providence, was *gloria*.

That which is "common property" in Augustine's moral epistemology is the "unchangeable good" of God's Truth. (*On Free Will*, II, 167–68. In J. Burleigh ed., *Augustine: Earlier Writings*. Philadelphia: Westminster P, 1953. Cited as *FW*.) The healed will can achieve *libertas*. Conversely,

> the will which turns from the unchangeable and common good and turns to its own private good or anything exterior or inferior, sins. It turns to its private good when it wills to be governed by its own authority; to what is exterior, when it is eager to know what belongs to others and not to itself . . . . A man becomes proud, inquisitive, licentious and is taken captive by another kind of life . . . when he wills to be governed by [his] own authority.  (*FW* II, 53)

The common good in theological terms is God, and in secular terms is the collective goal or "interest" which is the *civitas* or *res publica*. The good Christian and the good citizen approach congruence. Note too that the term "external" is used here to denigrate cupidity driven wills, and is equated with "private" or "inferior" goods. By implication that which is "common" is "higher" and a function of collective *caritas*. Such a commonality is not coercively enforced, nor designed for the personal power and pleasure of individuals, and so is not "external" or visible in the way secular corporate bodies and their values are.

At the same time, when writing in his "realistic" mode of discourse, Augustine most often advises Christian public officials to defer to higher powers lest a successful challenge to authority result in the mass of cupidity-driven citizens using the occasion to disrupt public peace. In *On Free Will* he establishes the paradigm for all his subsequent treatments of civil law. Though "there is no true liberty except the liberty of the happy who cleave to the eternal law . . . ," yet "for the moment I mean the liberty which people think they enjoy when they have no human masters" (*FW* I, 132). In the context of mixed communities,

> The law which governs a people concerns itself with the control of conduct

> sufficiently to keep the peace among a rough population so far as this can be
> achieved by man . . . . Hence it brings pressure to bear through fear, and to
> gain its end turns and twists the souls of the unhappy people for whose
> government it is fitted.                                          (*FW* I, 119; 132)

Even though the civil law "makes many concessions and leaves many things
unpunished which divine providence punishes," still it "is not to be
disapproved simply on the ground that it does not accomplish everything"
(*FW* I, 120).

Then, too, though the eternal law is "stamped on our minds," its contents
are conveniently ambiguous. It is "just that all things should be in perfect
order" (*FW* I, 121). Therefore "a good and serious minded people who
consider the public above their private interest should appoint its own
magistrates" while "a dissolute and worthless people should be deprived of
that liberty." Note that Augustine writes in the passive mood about the
presence or absence of public liberty, as though the decision rests in other
hands than those of the citizens themselves.

> For while they fear to lose these things [material goods] they exercise in their
> use a certain restraint suitable to hold together a society . . . composed of men
> of this kind. This law does not punish the sin which consists in loving the
> above objects but the sin which consists in taking them wrongfully from other
> people.                                                          (*FW* I, 121)

In his *potentia dei absoluta* mode of discourse, particularly in *The
Confessions* (Bk. 3, Ch. 8 & 9), Augustine discusses the kind of *libertas* a people
deserve as a subset of the question of God's willed "judgment" and the various
customary judgments of human legislators. Society between people in cities
and nations, and between "God and us," is violated when customary rules are
breached. "Base deeds which are contrary to human customs must be avoided
according to the diversity of customs." The "society" of God and his
creatures is violated by "perverted lust." Society is original, the result of a
natural impulse established before the Fall of Adam and Eve. The rules of
communities, customary or divine, are equally and fully "natural" and are not
vitiated by the sin of Adam. But customary rules and all routinized structures
are not only the outer evidence of God's *potential absoluta*. The will of the
individuals, legitimized by its source in the absolute will of God, can
intervene and overturn the apparent justice of established relationships and
the political order.

> But when God commands something contrary to the customs or laws of a
> people, it must be done even if it has never been done before; if it has been
> neglected, it must be restored; and if it has never been established it must be
> established.                                                      (*Conf.* 87)

The theme of *potentia dei absoluta* in God and the individual is directly connected to the secular "principle" that "it is lawful for a king to command within the city over which he rules something that neither he nor any predecessor had even ordered" (*Conf.* 87). The principle of *ordo* is hierarchical—*ad unum*—but can appear in pubic policy either as the arbitrary expression of the king's power, the decree of magistrates who are popularly elected or even in acts of public disobedience. Representation or dictatorship are institutional terms for the relative moral value of *libertas* in the body politic. Each can be justified *ex post facto* with reference either to *auctoritas* (traditional order) or to *potestas* (will or command).

Robert Markus argues (*Saeculum: History and Society in the Theology of St. Augustine.* Cambridge: Cambridge UP, 1970) that in the last decade of the fourth century, Augustine briefly flirted with Eusebius' celebration of Christian emperors inaugurating the reign of God on earth. In this post-Theodosian age, even Ambrose of Milan succumbed to a "Rome-theology." In the *Pax Romana* ". . . all men living under one single earthly sovereign, learnt to confess the sovereignty (*imperium*) of the one God Almighty" (50–51). But such a confident ordering of the *saeculum* in brilliant reflection of divine justice is never a convincing portrait of his times for Augustine. Things don't fit that neatly together. Neither Julian's vision of God whose equity is rationally explainable and easily approached through free will, Tertullian's damning of the Empire, nor Ambrose's fusion of the *civitas dei* and *terrena* matched Augustine's "dark" image of the *saeculum*.

The sack of Rome in 410 underscored for Augustine the ephemeral nature of all institutions of the *saeculum*. Rome, in his later thought, is suspended between the *civitas terrena* and the *civitas Dei*—under siege from its subject peoples and from the moral decay of its own governing elites, Christian or otherwise. In a Sermon cited by Markus, Augustine says, "The City which begat us according to the flesh still remains; thanks be to God! If only it would also be spiritually reborn, and go over with us to eternity" (39). Markus speaks of the "theological neutrality" of Augustine's view on the Empire (see 30–44, 144–153). However, neutrality suggests disengagement. Yet the language of dispassionate analysis is never dominant in any mode of Augustine's discourse. Instead of distancing himself from the public affairs of "the city," Augustine seems intent to validate simultaneous citizenship in a variety of communities which cross-cut institutional structures. This argument allows Augustine the freedom to shift influence and garner support as needed for his struggling *ecclesia* in North Africa.

Strikingly, Augustine's ambivalence towards the perfectibility of human institutions extends to the juridical Church as well. His language in discussing the *ecclesia* reflects not only an official stand in the Donatist controversy but also his own previous understanding of the "pilgrim" nature of the Christian community on earth. Toward the end of *The City of God*, Augustine struggles to express the meaning of the apocalyptic parts of the *Gospel of John* through *Revelations* in order to dissociate the Church "militant" and the state itself from an identification with transcendent categories—either damned or Godly.

His terminology slips occasionally, and he speaks of the *civitas Dei* as if it is the Church, and of Rome as if it is the *civitas terrena*. But his need to forge a new consensus on the relationships between communities and institutions is palpable, as is his unease with the wilder images of beasts and holocausts which these Gospels contain. Of course, such images were the favorites of his communicants and the tendency to identify the powers of the earth with them was an established tradition in the Late Empire, especially in North Africa. After citing the "beast" segment of Revelations complete with references to "inscriptions on their forehead or on their hand" Augustine advises caution.

> ... And what this beast is, though it requires a more careful investigation, yet it is not inconsistent with the true faith to understand it of the ungodly city itself and the community of unbelievers set in opposition to the faithful and the city of God.                                      (CG XX, 727)

To the "beast" belongs "not only the avowed enemies of the name of Christ and His . . . City," but also the apparent members of the *ecclesia* who are really worldly and are "the tares which are to be gathered out of his Kingdom, the Church, in the end of the world" (CG XX, 727). This is not the later Gregorian model of a universal Christian community ruled in *auctoritas* by the *ecclesia* and in the *potestas* by the local national states. Nor is it a Holy Roman Empire of Caesaro-Papist dimensions. And it certainly isn't the apocalypse of Satan and God facing off in the *saeculum* with the state and Church as surrogate combatants. Note the following careful effort, in *The City of God*, to bless the *ecclesia*—with reservations.

> He [Matthew] speaks of both as being in the kingdom of heaven, both the man who does not perform the commandments which He teaches . . . and the man who does and teaches as He did . . . . Consequently, where both classes exist, it is the Church as it now is, but where only the one shall exist, it is the Church as it is destined to be when no wicked person shall be in her . . . . It is then of this kingdom militant, in which conflict with the enemy is still maintained, and war carried on with warring lusts, or government laid upon them as they yield . . .that the Apocalypse speaks.                      (CG XX, 725–26)

Augustine gave the medieval tradition the phrase *"in figura ecclesia"* to express Peter's relationship to the Church. Peter is said to "represent" the Church as the *Corpus Christi*. This extremely suggestive phrase, submerged in layer upon layer of subsequent glosses, turns up in Gratian's *Decretum* and virtually every canon and civilian commentary on the ecclesiastical hierarchy from the twelfth century onward. Distinctions between the *corpus christi mysticum* (true church) and *juridicum* (institutional church), the *universitas civium* (body politic) and the *regnum* (government), were greatly facilitated by Augustine's creative synthesis of Roman legal discourse, customary social practices and the Christian community's understanding of what it meant to a citizen of the *civitas Dei*. However, exactly who Peter represented by standing *"in figura ecclesia"*—the body of the faithful, the clergy, or Christ, or all three—and which mutual obligations this entailed was a concern for later times when institutional distinctions between *regnum* and *sacerdotium* and between both and the rights of the citizen faithful were the main agenda.[5]

## IV. Pluralism and Public Discourse

Augustine's mode of discourse is almost entirely homiletic or polemical—that is, designed to exhort, persuade or defend an emergent orthodoxy in the Christian movement as it adjusts to establishment status. It is from Augustine's dedication to unity amid pluralism that much of his ambivalence on ecclesiastical as well as regnal public policies derives. The *congregatio fidelium* throughout the Empire was divided by language, liturgical traditions and a mélange of Roman and local cultural mixes. Augustine speaks of the Roman Christian *civitate* in language analogous to his description of the Roman world, emphasizing the search for *ordinatio ad unum* amidst accelerating diversity.

> This heavenly city . . . while it sojourns on earth calls citizens out of all nations, and gathers together a society of pilgrims of all languages, not scrupling about diversities in the manners, laws and institutions whereby earthly peace is secured and maintained but recognizing that, however various they are, they all tend to one and the same end of earthly peace. . . . So far from rescinding and abolishing these diversities it even preserves and adapts them, so long as only no hindrance to the worship of the one supreme and true God is thus introduced. (*CG* XIX, 696)

Augustine also speaks rhetorically of "your" Roman patriots and "our" saints and martyrs, though at the same time his pride in the glorious segments of Roman history is unmistakable. It is one of many ironies of which he is painfully aware that in defending order, both God's and the Emperor's, he is validating dual, and possibly conflicting, allegiances. To express this profound shift in Roman culture, he creates a new mode of Christian discourse which speaks to masses and hierarchy, believers and pagans in such a way as to forge a workable consensus, at least at the local level.

At the end of his life in his battles with Julian, Augustine unashamedly plays to the stalls rallying the fears and hopes of the mass of his parishioners against yet another Roman aristocrat cut from Cicero's antiquated mold.[6] Augustine's approach is classically illustrated in his confrontation with Julian, a Roman of noble lineage, who was educated as a philosopher and entered the Church as a "hammer of the Manichees" in the late fourth century, soon becoming an influential Bishop ministering to an upper class, educated constituency of converts. Courting danger, both physical and ecclesiastical, Julian ridiculed Augustine as "the African." According to Peter Brown's biography of Augustine, which seems distinctly more sympathetic to Julian than to the Saint, Julian positioned his argument on free will and divine equity as a "defense of Italy against the *latrocinium*" (provincials, Africans)—consisting of Augustine and African bishops who sought to "impose on the Italian church a set of dogmas genuinely foreign to the spirit of Christianity of their land" (*Augustine of Hippo.* Berkeley: U of California P, 1969. p. 383). Julian thundered that "the helm of reason has been wrenched from the Church so that opinions of the mob can sail ahead with all flags flying." Augustine was "the lord of all donkeys" (383-84; and in general for the Pelagian debate, 341-418).

An already authoritative orthodoxy largely articulated by Augustine finally managed to submerge, suppress or co-opt Pelagianism in a series of councils and edicts—even though at least one Emperor was sympathetic. The attempt to marginalize the Saint and divide *Latium* from the provinces was halted temporarily, in the Church as least. Given Augustine's attempt to unify rather than divide, it is doubly ironic that his writings and preachings did in fact reflect an African mentalité—one which was increasingly important in the Western Church as the Empire split between imperial seats at Constantinople and Ravenna, and the population and political significance of Rome declined. Augustine was successful in restoring unity not only because of his own intellectual prowess in the free will debate, but also because of his polemical jabs and thrusts in a public battle which reverberated throughout the Empire. He denounces Julian as an effete dilettante, an "intellectual" who disturbs the faith of simple, loyal military men and ordinary Christians. Julian is "above the healthy feelings of the man in the street," as Brown summarizes Augustine's argument—and even his unhealthy ones.

In the end Augustine's discourse is hegemonic. The one ring to enclose them all turns out to be two—Church and state. Unity is the source and result of "catholic" consent in the Church, and is symbolized by the Body of Christ from which the authority of Peter's Church is derived. Unity in the state is the source and result of civic virtue, shared political memory, a general combination of wills to pursue mutual gain, administrative coercion— or all four. It is the political manifestation of unity in social life derived from the singleness of Adam (*CG* XIX, 410-411). "Remembrance" of common ancestry, via Biblical parables and cultural narratives, can generate and preserve *civitate* (*CG* XIX, 680-81). More than establishment rhetoric can be sensed in Augustine's personal confession of obedience in *Against the Epistle of Manicheaus Called Fundamental* (In Schaff ed., Vol. IV, 4, par. 6).

> . . . The consent of the peoples and nations keeps me in this church; so does her authority, inaugurated by miracles, nourished by hope, enlarged by love, established by age. The succession of priests keeps me beginning from the very seat of the Apostle Peter, to whom the Lord after His resurrection gave it in charge to feed His sheep down to the present episcopate. And so lastly does the name of Catholic. (*Epis.*, 131)

For Augustine, the struggle against determinism—the "fate" of the astrologers and rational *logos* of the Academy—does not require abandoning obedience to "higher" authorities in the name of individual *libertas*. Nor does a defense of free will necessarily entail moral independence, which is from Augustine's perspective an untenable solipsism. His posthumous sparring partner, Cicero, had made an error which proved fatal both personally and professionally. Unable to reconcile apparently contradictory existential possibilities, he rejected ambiguity in favor of the "will." As a result, Cicero "shuts the religious mind to this alternative." Yet Augustine accepts Cicero's abhorrence of a necessity which "subverts" the "whole economy of human life" by denying human agency. It would be "in vain [that] laws [are] enacted . . . reproaches, praises, chidings . . . had recourse to" (V, 157). Also useless would be "the combination of wills" which creates the *civitas*, whether territorial or spiritual.

It is an irony that *The City of God*, which is generally considered one of the canonic texts in the history of political thought, is not really a study in "political" theory either in the ancient or modern sense. It much more closely resembles current postmodern political analyses which focus on sub-institutional and marginal groupings working within, and potentially reconstructing, hegemonic institutions. Yet, while for Augustine the clash of conscience and obedience is primarily a pre-political, moral narrative, when he moves to discussions of decisions to obey or enforce public law his greatest praise is reserved for those who find a way to do the right thing and maintain the public interest at the same time, usually at the expense of their lives. The discontinuity between public and private virtue in the fifth century appears so vast to Augustine as to constitute a chasm across which he allows the occasional public figure to pass, but only in the past tense or the subjunctive mood.

# Notes

†New essay written especially for this collection.

1In his *Reply to Faustus the Manichean*, Augustine underscores the importance of institutions by arguing for conformance to sacramental ritual. "There can be no religious society . . . without some sacrament or visible symbol to serve as a bond of union." (IV, 243 in Philip Schaff ed., 1988. *A Select Library of Nicene and Post-Nicene Fathers of the Christian Church*. New York: Christian Literature Co., Vol. IV, p. 243). The institutional church is a "sacerdotal order" distinct from the physically coercive order of domination and subservience established by the laws of the *saeculum*. Its functional mandate is the administration of sacraments. Nonetheless, the question Augustine poses to believers becomes central to the wider debate on the scope and limits of obedience to political institutions in Western civilization. "Do you believe you may be saved without having bishops and clergy, though not without the Christian religion"? Alternatively stated, can community of interest and belief take precedence over institutional order? As the basis of unity in orthodoxy, he wrote, "the importance of these sacraments cannot be "overstated."

[2]Arendt. "What is Freedom." In *Between Past and Future.* New York: Viking, 1968. (167); *The Human Condition.* Chicago: U of Chicago P, 1958. (74). See also: Joanna Scott, "A Detour Through Pietism: Hannah Arendt on St. Augustine's Philosophy of Freedom." *Polity.* Vol. XX, No. 3 (1988): 394–425; and Joanna Scott and Judith Chelius Stark, *Rediscovering Hannah Arendt: Love and Saint Augustine* (forthcoming Harcourt Brace). The latter is the first English edition, with extended commentary, of Hannah Arendt's dissertation on Augustine which she revised extensively from 1958 to 1961. Not surprisingly, her basic thesis on Augustine's pivotal role in articulating the interface between social and public life passes over the conceptual bridge from her thesis to her classic political works completed or begun during this period. In addition to those cited above, Augustine's *City of God* appears directly or implicitly in *Rahel Varnhagen* (1958 revised), *On Revolution* (1963), and *Eichmann in Jerusalem* (1961).

[3]For example, in *The Confessions* (John K. Ryan trans. New York: Image Doubleday, 1960): . . . it is against the principles of society for him (the king) not to be obeyed, for it is a general law of human society for men to obey their rulers . . . How much more must God, ruler of all creation, be obeyed without hesitation in whatever he impose on it. Just as among the authorities in human society the greater authority is set above the lesser in the order of obedience, so God stands above all the others" (3: 8, 16, pp. 87–88).

[4]See, for example, on Augustine's "realism": Harold Berman. *Law and Revolution.* Cambridge: Harvard UP, 1983; Herbert Deane. *The Political and Social Ideas of St. Augustine.* New York: Columbia UP, 1963; Peter I. Kaufman. *Redeeming Politics.* New Jersey: Princeton UP, 1990; Reinhold Niebuhr. *Moral Man and Immoral Society.* London: Scribner, 1963; Robert McAfee Brown, ed. *The Essential Reinhold Niebuhr: Selected Essays and Addresses.* New Haven: Yale UP, 1986; Elaine Pagels. *Adam, Eve, and the Serpent.* New York: Random House, 1988; Judith N. Shklar. *The Faces of Injustice.* New Haven: Yale UP, 1990; Walker Graham. *Moral Foundations of Constitutional Thought: Current Problems, Augustinian Prospects.* New Jersey: Princeton UP, 1990; George Weigel. *Tranquilitas Ordinis: The Present Failure and Future Promise of American Catholic Thought on War and Peace.* New York: Oxford UP, 1987.

[5]The paths of Augustinianism into "the tradition" of medieval speculations on Church and state are myriad and surprising. For example, according to Brian Tierney (*Foundations of Conciliar Theory: The Contribution of the Medieval Canonists from Gratian to the Great Schism.* Cambridge: Cambridge UP, 1968), Gratian referred in the *Decretum* to an influential text of Augustine's suggesting that "when Peter received the keys, he 'signified' the Church" as a whole (34). This collective mandate fueled the later fires of the Conciliarists such as Guilelmus Durandus who attacked papal monarchists in the interests of local church autonomy from Rome and cited Augustine accordingly (190–95). Ernst Kantorowicz's classic study, *The King's Two Bodies: A Study in Medieval Political Theology* (New Jersey: Princeton UP, 1957) shows that Ottonian (tenth century) celebrations of kingship drew heavily on Augustine's *Ennarationes in Psalmos,* 90 and 91. "Augustine points out . . . that 'the tabernacle of God is the Flesh . . . In this very tabernacle the Emperor [Christ] has militated for us . . . He is far above all heavens but his feet he has on earth . . . one person, two natures." The artist who created the Frontispiece of the Aachen Gospels had been

ordered to design a triumphal image of the Emperor and drew it directly from Augustine's commentary which was widely known. It is found in Bede, in the marginal glosses of the Canterbury Psalter and in Peter the Lombard's works. According to Kantorowicz, this Psalm was "irresistibly imperial" an inspired representations of Christ "in the full uniform of a Roman emperor," as opposed to images of God the Father, author of providential *ordinatio ad unum* as the imperial model. The Christ figure, as Augustine described it, was rooted in human turmoil. "Oh Christ, who sittest in heaven on the right side of the Father, but art with thy feet and thy limbs struggling on earth." The Aachen Emperor was "Christ-like as *Imperator in tabernaculo militans*" (71–77).

⁶In his classic study of religious cultural history, Christopher Dawson (*Religion and the Rise of Western Culture.* New York: Sheed and Ward, 1950. 40–41) celebrated Augustine's role in carrying forward the "new liturgical poetry" first created by Ambrose of Milan. That Augustine was aware of the novelty of this oratorical style is evident in *The Confessions* where he recounts how ". . . after the custom of the Eastern lands, hymns and canticles (were) sung so that the people would not become weak through tedium and sorrow" in the heat of the battle over Arianism. The whole city of Milan was "disturbed" and in a "wrought-up state" (IX, vi–vii) while Ambrose mobilized his willing constituency against the "heretic" mother of a boy-emperor (IX, 215). In Augustine's own battle with schismatics, he surpasses even his mentor and "abandons the whole tradition of classical poetry in a direct appeal to the popular audience" (Dawson, 40).

# II  Language and Literature

# Augustine's Definitions of *Populus* and the Value of Civil Society†

## Jeremy D. Adams

Augustine's two definitions of *populus* in books II and XIX of *The City of God* have caused considerable stirring among historians of ideas since the First World War, thanks to an assumption that the difference between them may represent a major split either in Augustine's thought about the state or between his thought and that of his Greco-Roman predecessors.

Several scholars from several national traditions have addressed themselves to that apparent split, and the argument among them has taken on a bewildering variety of issues. I think, however, that two steady questions can be discerned beneath the Protean elusiveness of the debate:

1. Are the two definitions fundamentally opposed?
2. Does Augustine in the final analysis see any moral value in civil society?

The following summary will review several scholarly interpretations according to their stand on the first question; this question has rarely, if ever, been answered without benefit of a decision on the second question. The following lineup of authorities does not pretend to be exhaustive, but I hope that it will indicate the range of opinions and traditions party to the controversy.

Prominent among the scholars who have concluded that the two definitions are significantly opposed are John Neville Figgis, Norman H. Baynes, Sergio Cotta, A. J. Carlyle, and Charles H. McIlwain.

Figgis argued in 1921 that Augustine rejected the stock Ciceronian definition of the state (as most English-speaking authors have translated *res publica*) because he saw that it did not fit the political facts of life, and based his new definition on empirical principles, which he discerned and followed with a ruthless realism that would not be surpassed until Hobbes's time (*The Political Aspects of S. Augustine's "City of God,"* pp. 59-67). Baynes saw individualism rather than empiricism as the signal intellectual virtue in this decision of Augustine's; his departure from Cicero was a consequence of "his individualistic viewpoint" which "declines to regard the State as an entity independent of those who compose it" (*The Political Ideas of St. Augustine's "De Civitate Dei,"* Historical Association Pamphlet, no. 104, pp. 7-8, II; reprinted in his *Byzantine Studies and Other Essays*, pp. 288-306).

Less interested in those British virtues, Sergio Cotta saw Augustine's originality as a triumph of descriptive over prescriptive reasoning in political philosophy. Writing a quarter-century after Baynes, he saw Augustine's definition-play not as a mere apologetic exercise, but as an integral product of his descriptive insight about society, which naturally rejected "la linea di pensiero giusnaturalistica" of practically all classical authorities, and informed his definitions of *civitas* and *regnum* as well (*La città politica di sant' Agostino*, pp. 24–39, 52–53).

Closer to Figgis and Baynes in time as well as in intellectual categories were the Scotsman Carlyle and the American McIlwain. Both agreed that Augustine had struck off into new territory with the second definition, but they disagreed rather violently about the value of that originality. Carlyle was almost scandalized by the negative character of Augustine's abandonment of the rest of Stoic and patristic tradition in this regard. As he put it in a short essay:

> Whether St. Augustine realised the enormous significance of what he was saying may be doubted; this definition [*CD* XIX, 24] is indeed practically the definition of Cicero, but with the element of law and justice left out, and no more fundamental difference could well be imagined, for Cicero's whole conception of the State turns upon this principle, that it is a means for attaining and preserving justice. ["St. Augustine and the *City of God*," *The Social and Political Ideas of Some Great Mediaeval Thinkers*, ed. F. J. C. Hearnshaw, p. 50.]

In the monumental *History of Mediaeval Political Theory in the West*, Carlyle had concluded that the second definition was not "a casual or isolated judgment of St. Augustine, corrected perhaps at other times." Referring to other passages in which the political importance of justice is asserted in terms not very alien to those of the older tradition, Carlyle declared that such agreement with Cicero on Augustine's part must be understood in the light of Augustine's "theological conception of justice—a conception which might be regarded as true upon his premises, but which can only be understood as related to those premises (I:164–70, esp. 167–68).

Harvard's McIlwain seemed quite pleased by Augustine's boldness. He asserted that Augustine's argument in *CD* II, 21 and XIX, 21 "is a *reductio ad absurdum* indeed, but it is the absurdity of heathenism not of Cicero's definition which Augustine means to prove" (*The Growth of Political Thought in the West, from the Greeks to the End of the Middle Ages*, pp. 154–59, esp. p. 157). After close analysis of the terms *civitas* and *regnum* in the famous passage likening empires to large-scale brigandage (*CD* IV, 4) and in *CD* XV, 8, McIlwain concluded that for Augustine, "Justice and justice alone is the only possible bond which can unite men as a true *populus* in a real *res publica*." Great pagan states had indeed been true *civitates* and *regna*, "but none of them, admirable as some were in other respects, could ever be a true *populus*, its association and its government could never rise to the height of a real *res populi* or *res publica*; . . . No heathen state can ever rise quite to the height of a true commonwealth" (ibid., pp. 158–59). The alternative definition in *CD* XIX, 24 is simply a rhetorical device: notice the clause *"velut si dicatur"* which introduces it. Unfortunately, McIlwain simply dismissed Augustine's outright validation of the *populi* and *res publicae* "of the Athenians, those of any other Greeks, of the Egyptians, of that earlier Babylon of the Assyrians, and of any other *gens* whatsoever" on the grounds that the definition which that validation follows is simply a debating trick. If that is so, how does he account for the phrase *"Secundum probabiliores autem definitiones"* which announces that second definition way back in II, 21? It is almost as though he had not read the few extra lines necessary.

McIlwain's argument probably represents the respectable limit of the opinion that Augustine's two definitions were really at variance. Most of the scholars sharing that view have also concluded that Augustine thereby indicated his low opinion (to put it mildly) of earthly institutions not redeemed by grace. That set of positions has come under strong attack, although most scholars who try to reconcile the two definitions have had to base their cases on distinctions of a fairly ingenious character.

In 1934, Carl-Victor von Horn asserted:

> Wichtig ist, ehe man sich an die Betrachtung der Textstelle heranmacht, festzustellen, dass Augustin hier [*CD* XIX, 21] nicht den Staatscharakter eines Staates ohne Gerechtigkeit leugnet, sondern über ihn nur ein abfälliges Werturteil spricht. Aber dies ist in der Literatur zuweilen nicht recht gesehen worden. [*Beiträge zur Staatslehre St. Augustins nach "De civitate Dei,"* pp. 26–32, esp. p. 29.]

Taken at face value, this is rather like saying, "Augustine meant that the unjust state was not just, not that it was not a state." Such a statement may reproduce the final impression of the *Textstelle* in which both definitions appear, but it evades the actual wording of the first definition. Von Horn then went on to argue that Augustine did not so much strike justice out of his new definition of the state as add to it another basis of concord, one which involved a fundamentally similar interest.

The German-trained American Jesuit, Morehouse F. X. Millar, addressed himself to the exact language of the first definition and attacked Carlyle's position on it quite directly, with the aid of a genuine and erudite distinction. In "The Significance of St. Augustine's Criticism of Cicero's Definition of the State," *Philosophia Perennis* 1:99–109, Millar maintained that Augustine's and Cicero's definitions depended on very similar standards of political value. Cicero's Stoic-pantheist conception of justice had just as much "theological bias" as Augustine's Judeo-Christian premises; Augustine's real difference from Cicero lay in his reassertion of a very traditional Roman distinction between the absolute, rational *ius naturale* and purely conventional "temporal" laws. In stressing the relevance to earthly society of the latter type of *ius*, Augustine was indicating that social justice was a matter of multilateral relationships as well as (indeed, rather than) a question of abstract, unilateral, or bilateral intention. On a more general level, the formula proposed in *CD* XIX, 24 bears the double principle that "society is natural" but the "concrete state has its basis equally in convention." So Millar recognized some personal empiricism as well as a sophisticated fidelity to Cicero in Augustine's proposing a second definition, and he saw no drastic rejection of civil society among its consequences.

Herbert A. Deane of Columbia University launched quite recently the most comprehensive attack on the tradition running from Figgis to Cotta in the course of his devastating rebuttal of McIlwain's argument in *The Political and Social Ideas of St. Augustine*, pp. 118–29, esp. pp. 120–26. Through careful analysis of *CD* IV, 4 and of several other passages in Augustine's works which McIlwain failed to consider, he shows that McIlwain's position was more artful than sound, and that the definition in XIX, 24 is entirely consistent with: (a) Augustine's distinction between *vera iustitia* and the "image of justice found in temporal states"; and (b) his fundamental preoccupation with the unitive power of love, whether divinely inspired or only on the level of selfish interest. I find Deane's argument thoroughly convincing, and only regret that, like almost all commentators on this now-famous pair of definitions, he was not able to look more deeply into the rich implications of Augustine's wider usage of *populus*. Deane does not deny the gap between the definitions. He minimizes it by saying that it corresponds to a distinction found throughout Augustine's work between two kinds of justice which, in the last analysis (or in the mind of God) merge into one; more valuably, in my opinion, he tries to shift attention away from justice to another moral good (both individual and social) which he sees as more fundamental to Augustine's total system of thought.

Several continental scholars had argued along those lines, partly looking for a prior or higher basis on which to reconcile the definitions, partly trying to shift the emphasis from justice.

Before the First World War, Ernst Troeltsch firmly maintained that for all his realism about politics, Augustine never really discarded the notion that human society was based on some kind of natural law (*Soziallehren der Christlichen Kirchen und Gruppen*, 1912; see Olive Wyon's translation, *The Social Teaching of the Christian Churches*, I:151–52, 155–58, and n. 75). In 1926 Edgar Salin concluded, not unlike Carlyle and McIlwain, that the second

definition was "für den Augenblick geformt und Augustinus hat an seinen
Wortlaut sich niemals gebunden," but instead of either dismissing or stressing
the novelty of the definition so conceived, he argued that it represented
simply a Christian variation on the notion of *Gemeinsamkeit* common to
Greek and Roman as well (*Civitas Dei*, pp. 186–87). After the Second World
War, Domenico Pesce discussed the two definitions against the background of
classical political thought and concluded that Augustine's departure from
Cicero achieved both an interiorization of Cicero's doctrine and a recovery of
the level of values which had distinguished Plato. Pesce admits that
Augustine's transformation of Cicero's definition risks becoming "dal punto
di visto del valore, neutra," but since his specific contribution to the older
definition was a strong emphasis on the social role of will, "si passa, nei
confronti della concezione ciceroniana, dell'esterno all'interno, dal piano
giuridico a quello etico, dalle azioni alle intenzione, dalla legge alla
determinazione della volontà o cioè appunto all'amore, ond' è che al concetto
di stato (*res publica*) si sostituisce quello di società (*civitas*)." [*Città terrena e
città celeste nel pensiero antico: Platone, Cicerone, S. Agostino*, pp. 150–60, esp.
p. 153.] Despite the apparent willingness to abandon *populus* and the wording
of the definition itself, Pesce reasserts the unity of both formulas, which end
up in his view returning to the solemn authority of Plato's hierarchical
conception of justice, and hence anything but a rejection of previous classical
tradition. A few years later, Paolo Brezzi stated this general position in more
moderate, accessible terms. Summarizing the views of several other authors,
he pointed out that the difference between the two definitions "non esclude
ovviamente che la *vera iustitia* (come altrove Agostino chiama quella che si
riferisce a Dio—e l'aggettivo è in questo caso davvero qualificativo al massimo)
possa completare ed integrare, attraverso l'amore, il precedente tipo di
giustizia umana . . ." After all, since Augustine's argument springs from a
consideration of human nature, its content and import have to be
ethicorational, and in some way akin to justice of some sort (*Analisi ed
interpretazione del "De Civitate Dei" di sant' Agostino*, Quaderni della Cattedra
Agostiniana, no. 2, Tolentino, 1960, pp. 47–50). Brezzi's argument reduces to
a sort of lowest common denominator the previous attempts to substitute
some other social virtue or value for justice in this pair of equations.

Deane's choice of unitive love as the substitute seems most solidly
grounded in Augustine's own theory; one can also find areas of congruence
for justice and love more easily than for justice and *Gemeinsamkeit*, "the
natural-law tradition," or even will (related as it is to love in Augustinian
psychology). In this stress on love, Deane joins the tendency of French
scholarship, which has not been as impressed by the differences between the
two definitions as by the elements underlying both. In his *thèse* of 1927, for

example, Gustave Combès saw the two definitions primarily as an opportunity to insist on the eminently spiritual nature of the harmony which Augustine saw unifying all forms of society (*La doctrine politique de Saint Augustin*, pp. 106–07, 109–12).

A quarter-century later, Henri-Xavier Arquillière shifted the center of emphasis to *pax* in his acute analysis of the question of justice in Augustinian social thought, especially as regards these two definitions. He affirms that justice, far from being rejected as a social value, is indeed the central idea of all twenty-two books of *The City of God*. To be sure, Augustine's treatment of it is predominantly in the evangelical terms "dont saint Paul a fait la théologie," but the purpose of his concern with that quality in the two definitions of *populus* is to reassert "la valeur légitime de l'Etat . . . dans toutes les nations antiques" (*L'Augustinisme politique*, 2d ed., Paris, 1955, p. 38). How can a justice so theologically conceived be operative in societies ignorant of and even hostile to God? Because of Providence, all-important to Augustine's view of these matters, and because they managed to achieve a certain degree of internal *pax*, a quality closely related to justice. In any case, Arquillière maintains that Augustine intended no rigorous opposition between the kinds of societies best suited by those two definitions (ibid., pp. 65–71).

In 1952, Gustave Bardy wrote two brief but important notes on the two definitions for the Bibliothèque Augustinienne edition of *The City of God* (*BA* 37:753–55, 759–60). He decided that the second definition represented Augustine's normal and basic thought on the legitimate rights of civil society—the alternative attitude would be obviously absurd in the practical order to which he was seriously committed. What, then, was the point of the first definition? It was an occasion for discussing justice in the abstract; it represents a successful Christianization of the lofty Platonic (as opposed to more pragmatic Roman) conception of justice; and it supported in a memorable formula Augustine's major contention in *The City of God* that states decline when their morals decay. So both definitions are basically about the state (rather than about justice), and the fact that the first explores the higher theoretical reaches of the problem of justice does not deny that quality's normal relationship to normal political life. What Anglo-Saxon scholar has exercised more common sense in coping with this Augustinian conundrum?

In the Cardinal Mercier Lectures at Louvain that same year, Etienne Gilson discussed the pair of definitions, but bypassed the interpretative tangle which I have summarized. Arguing that Augustine rejected both the traditional pagan conception of political society *and* the rigorist consequences of such a rejection, he concentrated his attention on the biblical sources of Augustine's notion of *populus* and on the applicability of the model so derived to the Roman experience and to other varieties of secular polity (*Les métamorphoses de la Cité de Dieu*, pp. 38-46). In citing these judicious pages which indicate what I consider the most fruitful direction for further discussions of this sector of Augustine's political thought, I cannot help remembering the very different but in one sense complementary remark made by Troeltsch in 1915, before the dispute about the definitions' relationship got well under way:

> Die Augustinische Ethik hat nicht bloss wie alle Väter die durchschnittliche wissenschaftliche Bildung und die politisch-soziale Wirklichkeit aufgenommen, sondern als einer der Führer hat Augustin die christliche und die stoisch-neuplatonische Religiosität verschmolzen und die politisch-soziale Theorie des antiken Naturrechts und der Ciceronianischen Staatsphilosophie in starker christlicher Umfärbung sich angeeignet. Und alles das hat er in einem grossen ethischen System des höchsten Gutes gegliedert um den Gedanken der christlichen Seligkeit und Gottesliebe. Aber das war weder eine neue Kultur . . . [*Augustin, die christliche Antike und das Mittelalter: Im Anschluss an die Schrift "De civitate Dei*," p. 185, cf. pp. 146-49.]

Unlike Gilson's more extended discussion, this statement is as idealist, abstract, and synthetic as one might expect; yet in its own way it too concentrates on the historical antecedents and consequences of the ideas considered.

One might wish that these two treatments nearly forty years apart would put to rest the definition controversy, but a quick glance at the publication dates of the arguments reviewed above shows that almost the opposite has happened. Perhaps that is justifiable, since the central problem has not really been resolved, even by Deane's well-documented and persuasive distinctions. Since none of the previous attempts to solve that problem have been able to rely on a very wide sample of the crucial terms, I venture now to propose yet another solution, based partly on a new method.

I see no need to recast the problem, although restating it in the hope of refining it somewhat through paraphrase may be of use. I prefer to translate *res publica* as "civil society" rather than as "state," however. As the problem has concerned most of the scholars cited above, it consists of two questions:

1. Are the two definitions ultimately opposed or reconcilable? In other words, does Augustine take one position or two on this issue?

2. Is, therefore, civil society inherently legitimate in Augustine's opinion? Unredeemed by the pervading presence of the City of God, or considered in the abstract, aside from the presence or absence of any such transforming influence—as Bardy points out, Augustine occasionally indulged in such speculation—is civil society morally good (at least potentially), or irretrievably

vicious? In other words, does civil society possess any inherent moral validity, and philosophically respectable legitimacy?

How should we tackle such a question? Augustine himself shows us one way, which most of the scholars cited above have for some reason preferred to ignore: that is, through analysis of the logically decisive terms of a speculative definition. I suspect that Augustine would have been rather surprised at all the flurry caused by his dialectical (not rhetorical) device fifteen centuries later, and I think that close attention to his method of argument and to his general usage of the obviously cardinal term in that argument enables us to recapture his intent.

To answer the first question, I think that the two definitions are not only reconcilable, but end up being one, in the sense that the second absorbs the first. Its terms include the terms of the former definition by an extension of their scope. Stated second, it becomes logically prior. I have stated this contention in chapter 12 of this study (see pp. 19-20); it may be useful to paraphrase it briefly here in relation to some of the previous interpretations cited in this appendix. My argument, in its most narrow statement, is this: If a *populus* of the type outlined in the second definition agrees to love ethical standards of sufficient loftiness as revealed by the true God, it can hardly help but meet the requirements of the most rigorist interpretation of the first definition. Such is the achievement of the *populus Dei*, the *res publica Christi*. Carlyle emphasized the difference between the two definitions because he thought that Augustine thought that an earthly society could never match on its own level the definition—synthesizing achievement of the *populus Dei*; Carlyle's own focus was exclusively on earthly society (only one aspect, after all, of the "political theory" arising from Augustine's speculation) and on explicit reference to *ius* or *iustitia*. But even within those limitations of the problem, is it not at least arguable that the language of the second definition contains the terms of the first, on the condition that some *consensus iuris* and some agreement about the nature of *utilitas* are among the *res quas diligit populus*? Carlyle does not seem to have considered that the question could be posed in this manner. Neither does McIlwain, who, in his eagerness to defend the importance of justice to Augustine's conception of *res publica*, simply dismissed the second definition. Deane's drawing of a distinction between two kinds of justice, a view of Augustine's intention previously expressed by John O'Meara (*Charter of Christendom: The Significance of the "City of God,"* pp. 96-101), would lend strong support to my contention that the two definitions are really two dimensions of one "definition," although neither of the last two authors puts it that way.

I agree with Bardy (rather than with McIlwain) that the first definition is the clever device, although I think the device of a pair of definitions derives

from dialectical rather than from rhetorical method. It seems to me that
Augustine is indulging here in a dialogue between definitions, making the first
statement the contrary, piquant incitement to discuss, and the second
statement the sober reply. The first statement is set in the heart of a paradox,
which Augustine half disowns after developing its consequences, by promising
the reader a *probabilior* treatment of *populus*, the heart of the definition at the
heart of the paradox. This dialogue is not a dialectical triad, since it has no
third term. The absence of that sort of reassuring capping statement has been
perhaps the most disturbing thing about these definitions to our post-Hegelian
scholarly world. Why did Augustine leave his dialogue hanging (or is it only
we modern interpreters who are caught in that embarrassing position)?

Perhaps because the first definition was designed to fit a paradox so
obvious that it did not need to be solemnly described as such. I think that
McIlwain is correct in seeing that part of the argument as a *reductio ad
absurdum*, and that both he and Bardy are right in referring to Augustine's
rhetorical habits in that connection. Marrou has pointed out the unique
importance for Augustine of the rhetorical figure of antithesis: "C'est chez lui
un mode d'expression si caractéristique qu'on ne peut se contenter de
l'inventorier parmi les procédés d'élocution empruntés à l'arsenal de la
rhétorique classique: c'est un rythme fondamental qui domine non seulement
les mots mais la pensée elle-même; il apparaît lié à la structure même de son
esprit" (*Saint Augustin et la fin de la culture classique*, p. 659; cf. pp. 79–80).
However, in matching (and topping) the first definition with the second,
Augustine moved to the sphere of dialectical discourse, a calmer atmosphere
of argument, more conducive to loosely ranging discussion, with a set of
conventions quite different from the cut-and-dried rules appropriate to
polemic disputation originally developed in the courtroom or the forum
rather than in the garden or the banquet chamber. Instead of reducing his
opponent to absurdity with the intention of leaving him in that state of
blatant confusion, Augustine in book XIX is in a mood rather like that of his
dialogues with his son or his old friends. In that context of "argument" the
master's technique is to absorb and advance the statements of his interlocutors
rather than to rebut them. Polite recognition of the evident truth by all the
civilized participants is the tone properly concluding such a discussion.

If we insist on recasting that late-antique discussion in terms more
sympathetic to our modes of argument—and much modern scholarship insists
on such recasting—then I propose a loose syllogism oriented to the second
basic question elaborated above. It goes like this:

*Major proposition*: No civil society is valid unless it is a *populus* (i.e., has
justice);

*Minor proposition*: But most (or normal) civil societies are *populi* (because they are unified by love);

*Conclusion*: Therefore most (or normal) civil societies are valid. The two-term dialectic of definitions operates within or alongside this structure, by changing the scope and hence the name of the essential constituent of a *populus*. Of course Augustine does not state the conclusion to this pseudosyllogism, just as he does not turn his dialogue of definitions into a dialectical triad. But we should be resigned to his maddening habits by now, and might do well to consider William Empson's observation, in *The Structure of Complex Words*, that "Aristotle, for that matter, pointed out that a syllogism might be regarded as a redefinition followed by a tautology" (p. 40). We can be grateful that the presence of a *populus* necessitates the presence of a valid civil society both in this syllogism and in Augustine's own statement of the rigorist paradox in *CD* II, 21. Consequently, if we wish to find out whether Augustine thought civil societies of a valid character were a widespread phenomenon or not (i.e., if we wish to establish the minor proposition), we simply have to see what sorts of society he calls *populi*. This step depends for some of its force on the premise that his usage is generally consistent with the pair of definitions, but I hope chapter 2 has established that consistency adequately.

Selecting as a sample only the work in which these definitions appear, *The City of God*, we can easily see that Augustine is faithful to the remarks about the *populi* and the *res publicae* of the Romans, Greeks, Egyptians, Assyrians, and others with which he concluded XIX, 24. A glance at columns A–H in the tabulations of Appendix B will show that Rome and other Gentile societies qualify normally for the designation *populus*, and that in books I–X such *populi* far outnumber the *populi* of Israel or the Church. Book X is something of a pivot in that regard; although *populus* is a rare word in the four books immediately following, it picks up with book XV as predominantly Israelite or Elect, in which guise it first appears massively in book X. It continues in that guise until book XIX. In the definition-dominated chapters of that book, *populus* is usually either matter-of-factly Roman or abstractly neutral rather than Jewish, Christian, or viciously Gentile. The last three books are a toss-up in regard to that noun's application, although the contemporary Church appears as a *populus* with abnormal frequency in XXII. This very sketchy summary should suffice to indicate how many quite different societies all seemed to be *populi* to Augustine, and hence probably seemed to possess the appropriate quotient of inherent legitimacy.

If further proof-texts are required, I suggest two: the last sentence of XIX, 24 and most of X, 13.

At the very end of developing his second definition, Augustine adds a final sentence insisting on the validity of his critique of pagan society uttered ten

years before in II, 21: "In general, however, the *civitas impiorum* does not
obey God's command to sacrifice to none beside Himself, and for that reason
the mind does not rightly and faithfully command the body in its midst, nor
the reason the vices, and so it lacks true justice (*caret iustitiae veritate*)."

If this qualifying remark seems to negate all the foregoing argument about
reconciling the two definitions, we should take careful note of two choices of
wording:

1. The evil, unjust society here is called a *civitas*, not a *populus*, and is
singular and universal. It should be identified with the Other City of the
damned, that transcendent society, rather than with any specific historical
state. And if Augustine had intended to reconstruct his original paradox, why
did he choose *civitas* instead of *populus*, the unmistakably cardinal term in that
paradox? It is worth noting that he makes the same shift of terminology in
the final sentence of II, 21, just after expressing his concern about current
usage of that key term (see chapter 2, p. 21).

2. To say that even such a society lacks *iustitiae veritas* is not quite
equivalent to saying that it lacks *iustitia* or even *vera iustitia*. Both Bardy and
Deane have remarked the rather elaborate character of this formulation (brief
though it is). As in the case of *civitas impiorum*, Augustine's choice of
wording seems to be both careful and an indication that he is not just
repeating himself again in either thought or vocabulary.

Book X, chapter 13 of *The City of God* seems to me an eloquent piece of
evidence that Augustine attributed at least a limited degree of genuine moral
probity to historical societies not favored by divine revelation. Book X
terminates and culminates the (near-) half of *The City of God* which is
dedicated to refuting the values of the pagans. From chapter 8 on, Augustine
pays a great deal of attention to the *populus Israel*, which will dominate much
of the second (more-than-) half of the work. Five chapters later, Augustine
returns to that *populus*, the model of true worship before Christ, the spiritual
ancestor of true worshipers since. But even that chosen people, Augustine
remarks, needed to have its unique law promulgated in unforgettably dramatic
fashion:

> Cum igitur oporteret Dei legem in edictis angelorum terribiliter dari, non uni
> homini paucisve sapientibus, sed universae genti et populo ingenti: coram
> eodem populo magna facta sunt in monte, ubi lex per unum dabatur,
> conspiciente multitudine metuenda ac tremenda quae fiebant. Non enim
> populus Israel sic Moysi credidit, quem ad modum suo Lycurgo
> Lacedaemonii, quod a Iove seu Apolline leges, quas condidit, accepisset. Cum
> enim lex dabatur populo, qua coli unus iubebatur Deus, in conspectu ipsius
> populi, quantum sufficere divina providentia iudicabat, mirabilibus rerum
> signis ac motibus apparebat ad eandem legem dandam creatori servire
> creaturam.

Here we see not only a passage heightened by rhyme and rhythm in its prose, but also most of the elements of either definition of *populus* in three sentences containing five appearances of that word. We can tell that a *populus* is (as it should be) a multitude of human beings unified by their concentrated, acutely alert attention to the spectacular effects surrounding the promulgation of their law, which as the reader knows was a law containing "civil" and "religious" regulations as well as an ultimate moral code, and endowing those who were faithful to it with an extraordinary inheritance and destiny. All five appearances of *populus* refer directly to Israel, but in the midst of them appears another group: The Lacedaemonians who surpassed the *populus Israel* in ready responsiveness when they received from Lycurgus a law said to derive from their false gods. Presumably that law was flawed in some ways besides its prescription of idolatry, but if that was the case Augustine surely does not stress it here. If he had applied a common noun to these Lacedaemonians instead of their proper name, what would he have called them?

An answer to that rhetorical question is less important than an appreciation of this group's role in this context. If I may be permitted another quasi-syllogism, I submit that this passage and this virtual *populus* occupy a middle position dialectically as well as spatially between the two definitions of *populus*, of which the former is hostile to pagan society and the latter tolerant. In II, 21 Augustine maintains that only *populi* worshiping the true God could be true *populi*; in X, 13 he remarks that some Gentile societies have in fact been truer to their false gods than Israel was to God Himself; and so we should be prepared to find in XIX, 24 that Augustine has shifted the emphasis of his critique from objective to subjective judgment.

I hope that Augustine would not object too strenuously to this latter-day, synthetic syllogism with *three* terms. I am fairly sure that he would find nothing inappropriate in the empirical character of the historical observation which constitutes the middle term.

†Reprinted by permission of the Yale UP from *The Populus of Augustine and Jerome: A Study in the Patristic Sense of Community*. New Haven: Yale UP, 1971. Appendix A, pp. 123–35.

# St. Augustine's Two Cities as Medieval Dramatic Exempla†

## Robert A. Brawer

The widespread use of Biblical exegesis to define the over-all form and aim of medieval lyrics, narratives and drama, as well as the meaning of individual passages within a given work, makes it difficult at times to know where exegesis ends and the work of art begins.[1] This is particularly so where patristic influence on medieval literature is so manifestly pervasive. The Corpus Christi plays, written and enacted in England in the fourteenth and fifteenth centuries, typify the kinship, if not indistinguishability, between exegesis and religious drama. They are related in their aim and over-all structure to St. Augustine's *City of God*, for they offer, like Augustine's work, a theological view of history, systematically presented. In chronological order, the plays record God's interventions in human history—specifically, the working out of His plan to redeem mankind from the nearly disastrous consequences of man's defections from God's law. The outline of events from beginning to end of this dramatized history play corresponds to St. Augustine's division of Christian salvation history into seven ages.[2] As in the *City of God*, too, the representation of historical events is subsidiary to the elucidation of moral and spiritual choices. The choices are those of the ancient Biblical figures from Adam to the disciples, who are shown to be torn between the claims of earthly monarchs (Pharaoh, Caesar Augustus, Herod, etc.) and of Christ to divine sovereignty. Concomitantly, the choices are those of the medieval townsmen who impersonate those figures on the stage and of the audience itself, also medieval townspeople, in whose time the individual and communal struggle between the laws of men in the earthly city and the laws of God in the heavenly city persists. Though the cycle play takes place largely in an historic past, its moral perspective, like that of St. Augustine's *City of God*, is timeless and universal.

The Towneley Corpus Christi, or cycle, play offers more specific evidence of the application of Augustinian principles than does any of its three extant sister cycles. The actor playing Noah, prior to building the ark, exposits man's creation and fall thus:

> Of the trinite bi accord/Adam and eve that woman
> To multiplie without discord/in paradise put he thaym.
> (III, ll. 30–31)[3]

This statement defines precisely what constitutes defection from God's will on the part of Adam and all of Adam's descendants. The condition of Paradise, or in a larger sense, the city of God, is "accord," for man is made in the "liknes" of the "trinite," itself characterized by perfect accord. Those who are incorrigibly evil, therefore, are, in the terms of Noah's pronouncement, in perpetual discord.

In thus providing the theological context for enactments of discord and accord throughout the dramatized history of man's redemption, the Towneley playwright follows Augustine's insistence that a self-destructive discord is characteristic of the city of men, or that part of mankind disobedient to God's law. For Augustine, Rome is the prototype of the earthly city divided against itself, as first exemplified in the discord between Romulus and Remus, its legendary founders. But he also conceives of a recurrent discord and accord in the history of Christian salvation. Hence, Cain is the founder of the earthly city in which, according to Augustine, "the wicked perpetually war with the wicked." On the other hand, Abel is the founder of the city of God, Augustine's metaphor for an ideal Christian commonwealth unified by an accord rooted in recognition of and obedience to the divine kingship. Here the peace that exists is "the peace of reasonable creatures, consisting as it does in the perfectly ordered and harmonious enjoyment of God and of one another in God."[4]

Now Augustine's dichotomy between the two cities is an absolute one, for he flatly says, "When, therefore, man lives according to man, not according to God, he is like the Devil." Conversely, while the "wicked war with the wicked . . . good men, or at least perfectly good men, cannot war"; and, by extension, the possession of goodness is increased in proportion to the concord and charity of each of those who share it.[5] Augustine's implicit recognition here of degrees of goodness is fundamental to his moral and spiritual history of man's progress from being a pilgrim or sojourner in the city of men to being a self-perfected citizen of the city of God; for while the majority of men may be good, they are by no means "perfectly good."

Of all the works in the Middle Ages that represent the Augustinian concept of discord and accord, only the cycle drama does so in other than absolute terms. The figure of Discordia in Prudentius' *Psychomachia* and, later, in Alain de Lille's *Anticlaudianus*, where Discord leads the vices in their assault upon Man, is perforce fixed as a personified abstraction of evil.[6] Similarly, at the cathedrals of Chartres, Amiens, and Paris, which contain the most fully developed iconography of the virtues and vices, the statue of Discord is consistently juxtaposed to those of the cardinal sins and frozen, as it were, in diametrical opposition to Accord and the other virtues.[7] The same is true of Middle English Biblical narratives like the *Cursor Mundi*, where discord and accord are presented as antitheses after the manner of moral exhortation:

> wiþ alkin þing þe gode sal acorde
> wiþ alkin þing þe wikked discorde.[8]

Because it, too, is didactic in aim and sometimes directly hortatory in manner, the medieval religious drama contains characterizations that are mostly simple and straightforward, so that moral distinctions between the two cities are clear cut. But the cycle play also attends with great particularity of detail, characterization, and dialogue to those whom Augustine calls sojourners in the city of men. These sojourners are shown by their words and acts to progress from discord with other sojourners into a more perfect accord with each other than would have seemed possible. Thus chastened, these figures become exemplars for the audience of the play. An examination of how they function in plays about Christ's signal appearances on man's behalf can offer us grounds for distinguishing properly between the exposition of a theological concept and the interpretation—or better, reinterpretation—of that concept through scenic representation and dialogue.

I

The Towneley play *Thomas of India*, with its representation of faith overcoming doubt, derives ultimately from John 20:29; for the moral of the episode, as expressed by the actor playing Jesus just after Thomas puts his finger in his wound, is a Biblical paraphrase:

> Thomas, for thow felys me . . .
> Mi risyng is trowed in the . . .
> All that it trowes and not se/and does after my lare,
> Euer blissid mot they be/and heuen be thaym yare!
>
> (ll. 352–55)

Within the sequence of episodes in Towneley and other cycles in which Jesus appears successively to his disciples, these words are climactic. Blinded by the spectacle of the suffering Man of Sorrows, unaware of the harrowing of hell, and beset by their fear of Christ's earthly enemies, the disciples require sensory evidence of Christ's continued dominion before they can perform their own apostolic mission. In Towneley alone, however, the efficacy of their power to save men by bringing them to a belief in Christ is shown to depend on a perfect accord among themselves, the prototype of which is the trinity. In *Thomas of India*, the problem of recognition on the part of each of the disciples is auxiliary to the resolution of the discord among them.

The play has two main parts, each of which has as its climax an appearance by Jesus in the role of peacemaker. Peter's and Paul's traditional skepticism toward the report of Mary Magdalene, here intensified into antagonism by Paul's anti-feminist diatribe (ll. 29–52), is resolved by Jesus' "peasse emangys you euer ichon!" (l. 96), and by this admonition:

> ye haue forthynkyng and shame/for your dysseferance,
> I forgif you the blame/in me now haue affyance.
>
> (ll. 144–45)

This scene prepares us for the main section of the play, for the resolution of the "dysseferance" among these three disciples is dramatically analogous to what follows. A protracted debate between Thomas and all the other disciples is resolved by Jesus' speech, "Brethere all, be with you peasse!/leaffe stryfe that now is here!" (l. 312). Thus Christ's subsequent promise to the repentant Thomas of the "blys . . . that is in heuen cytee" (l. 348) is contingent, first of all, upon Thomas' accord with his fellow disciples.

Having identified the main action of *Thomas of India* as one of discord among the disciples and its resolution by Christ as the maker of accord, we can account for the unique characterization of Thomas in this cycle and for the unique manner in which his relationship with the other disciples and with Jesus is developed. The introduction of Thomas through the distinctively dramatic device of a stage soliloquy emphasizes his aloofness from the disciples and suggests an internal conflict that underlies his altercation with the disciples. Outwardly, the Towneley Thomas is something of a self-conscious dandy—the kind of person medieval preachers often inveighed against as a type of pride. Thomas himself admits to this, but at the same time discloses his grief at Christ's death—for Thomas a sign of apparent defeat:

> If that I prowde as a pacok go,/my hart is full of care . . .
> My life wyrkys me all this wo/of blys I am full bare,
> Yit wold I nawthere freynde ne fo/wyst how wo me ware.
>
> (ll. 168, 170–71)

Like other disciples as they appear initially, Thomas grieves; yet his worldliness shows him as cut off from the other disciples and loath to believe except in his own worldly—that is, purely sensory—terms. The soliloquy thus prepares for the extended debate between Thomas and the disciples, each of whom twice tries and fails to convince Thomas of the fulfillment of Christ's redemptive plan. It has been claimed that the circularity of argument that characterizes this debate is far too long and repetitive to sustain Thomas' brief Scriptural statement, "I trow it not or that I se."[9] But this amplification of the traditional Gospel account is the very substance and—in medieval terms—*sentence* of this play. For while Thomas gives the appearance of rationality ("Bot tell me a skyll perfyte/any of you on raw . . ." [l. 217]), his replies to the disciples, especially when they testify, for Thomas' benefit, to Christ's appearances to them, are simply personal attacks:

> Waloway! ye can no good/youre resons ar defaced,
> ye ar as women rad for blood/and lightly oft solaced. . . .
>
> (ll. 232-33)

Indeed, there is a fine irony in Thomas' accusations, for when he says, "I wote your hartes was full wo/and fownd with vanyte . . ." (l. 306), he reinforces his own description of himself in his opening soliloquy. In short, the Towneley Thomas is a worldly rather than rational skeptic; and this condition produces an impasse among the disciples that only Christ, as the maker of accord, can resolve.

In the context of the dramatic presentation, then, the climax of the play has as much to do with bringing the disciples to accord with Thomas as it does with reversing Thomas' disbelief. Thomas' final speech of contrition just after touching Christ's wound is at once an appropriate resolution to his internal conflict as defined by the opening soliloquy, and to his stubbornness and aloofness toward the other disciples. The speech illustrates well the mixture of styles and interplay of genres found so often in medieval literature, yet potentially so exasperating—because so inconsistent—for a modern audience.[10] It borrows its content and tone from the mystical treatises of the late fourteenth century, and its form from the medieval lyric tradition.

> Mercy, ihesu, rew on me/my hande is blody of thi blode!
> Mercy, ihesu, for I se/thi myght that I not vnderstode!
> Mercy, ihesu, I pray the/that for all synfull died on roode!
> Mercy, ihesu, of mercy fre/for thi goodness that is so goode!
> . . . .
> Mi gyrdill gay and purs of sylk/and cote away thou shall;
> whils I am werere of swylke/the longere mercy may I call.
> Ihesu, that soke the madyns mylk/ware noght bot clothes of pall
> Thi close so can thai fro the pyke/on roode thay left the small.
> . . . .
> Mercy, ihesu, honoure of man/mercy, ihesu, mans socoure!
> Mercy, ihesu, rew thi leman/mans saull, thou boght full soure!

Mercy, ihesu, that may and can/forgif syn and be socoure!
Mercy, ihesu, as thou vs wan/forgif and gif thi man honoure.
                                   (ll. 316–19, 332–35, 336–39)

Though it contains the typical penitential motifs of hope for salvation, self-abnegation, and mystical identification with Christ as man's "leman" or lover, the Towneley "lyric" operates as a dramatic speech because it signifies a radical change in Thomas' moral character and is prompted by a specific occasion in the play: Thomas' physical contact with Christ. The disciple's words at this point emphasize the ironic reversal of his role from antagonist to spokesman for the disciples: "Mercy, ihesu, as thou *vs* wan" (italics mine). The ecstatic, ejaculatory tone, so different from Thomas' increasingly succinct, desiccated retorts to the disciples, further documents his progress toward moral and spiritual perfection—that is, toward being at one with himself, his fellow man, and God.

The progress of the Towneley Thomas is precisely the progress from the city of man to the city of God, at least for those who, like Thomas, choose to be sojourners in, not permanent citizens of the earthly city. Augustine says that the "peace of the rational soul is the harmony of knowledge and action."[11] Thomas' new-found knowledge and the action—that is, the act of faith—it produces is a case in point. By extension, the peace of the celestial city is the perfectly ordered and harmonious enjoyment of God and of one another in God. Because the audience is led to infer this principle from what it sees and hears on the stage, *Thomas of India* has an exemplary relevance that is distinctively dramatic in form. The play serves thus to perfect the faith of the audience, to move it, through the example of Thomas and the disciples, toward a personal and communal integrity characteristic of "heuen citee."

II

The artistic freedom with which the creator of *Thomas of India* borrowed and adapted non-dramatic materials for the stage is even more evident in a play that is analogous to *Thomas* in function. Reminiscent, or more accurately anticipatory, of the Thomas play in this cycle is the celebrated nativity play, the *Second Shepherds Play*. Like Thomas, the shepherds to whom the angelic announcement of the nativity is made are men of this world who require sensory evidence that the promised Advent is now a fact:

When I *se* him and *fele*,
Then wote I full weyll
It is true as steyll
That prophetys haue spokyn.                    (ll. 687–700; italics mine)

After the shepherds "se" and adore the Christ child, they, too, are enjoined to perform an apostolic function ("Tell furth as ye go" [l. 744]). Here, too, the over-all action is one of discord afflicting "good but not perfectly good" men, culminating in the appearance of Christ as the bringer of peace. If anything, the exemplary nature of the plot is even more pointed than it is in *Thomas*, because the discordant world that the shepherds and, by implication, the audience are shown to inhabit before the coming of Christ is presented at once from a detailed fifteenth-century perspective, yet within a universal framework.

The formal introductory monologues of these shepherds, each of whom appears in turn on stage, delineate, respectively, the civic discord between the shepherds and "gentlery men," including "manteners" of the king; the domestic discord between "sely wedmen" and shrewish wives; and that between "seruandys . . . that swettys and swynkys" and their "master-men." Apart from its local significance, the proliferation of civic and domestic discord in the world of the shepherds is symptomatic of the disruption of the divinely ordained universal order. According to St. Augustine:

> Peace between man and man is well-ordered concord. Domestic peace is the well-ordered concord between those of the family who rule and those who obey. Civil peace is a similar concord among the citizens. . . . The peace of all things is the tranquility of order. Order is the distribution which allots things equal and unequal, each to its own place.[12]

The lack of social and universal order in the world of the shepherds is symbolized further by the shepherds' complaints about the foul weather. The lament of the third shepherd in particular—"Was neuer syn Noe floode sich floodys seyn"—recalls the Towneley Noah's own plaintive longing for a world in which Adams' descendants might "multiplie without discord."

The *Second Shepherds Play* does more, however, than simply establish discord as a dramatic fact in order to make meaningful Christ's coming as the Prince of Peace who will remedy all.[13] In this play, the presentation of discord and its resolution by Christ provides the framework of the action only; it does not account for the playwright's interpolation of the comic episode involving the three shepherds' faltering but eventually successful efforts to recover the lost sheep that their neighbor Mak has stolen and disguised as a newborn child in order to deceive them. The placement of this episode just prior to the angelic announcement to the shepherds of the nativity suggests its significance as a false nativity illuminating, by contrastive analogy, the meaning of the divine birth.[14] But the system of analogies thus adduced does not adequately account for the function of the sheep-stealing episode specifically in respect to the shepherds' lengthy complaints of discord at the beginning and its resolution by Christ at the end of the play.

The dramatist's introduction of Mak the sheep-stealer in the opening expository section of the play provides one important structural link in the action of the play as a whole. Mak's initial appearance as a false yeoman of the king, the shepherds' upbraiding him for his foolishness, and his complaints about his unruly wife and children all occur prior to the action proper, the point at which Mak conceives his plan to hoodwink the shepherds (l. 269) and the extended dramatic conflict of the play begins. The extension of the exposition in this way allows the playwright to define Mak's role as antagonist to the three shepherds, one who embodies the shepherds' own complaints about the parasitical gentry, shrewish wives, and arrogant masters respectively. Even Mak's affectation of a Southern dialect in attempting to beguile the other shepherds may be said to suggest the prevention of concord among sojourners in earthly societies:

> . . . man is separated from man by the differences of languages. For if two men, each ignorant of the other's language, meet, and are not compelled to pass, but on the contrary, to remain in company, dumb animals, though of different species, would more easily hold intercourse than they, human beings though they be. For their common nature is no help to friendliness when they are prevented by diversity of language from conveying their sentiments to one another. . . .[15]

In short, the exposition of the *Second Shepherds Play* establishes Mak the sheep-stealer as a universal symbol of discord against whom the shepherds' efforts to remedy their woes will be concentrated in the central action of the play. The shepherds' punishment of Mak by blanket-tossing after they find him out thus represents more than a punishment for sheep-stealing. Because Mak symbolically embodies all the levels of discord that afflict the shepherds, the blanket-tossing is at once an exorcism of the spirit of discord in an unchastened world and a discovery of a new-found peace that the angel, appropriately, comes to proclaim to them at that very point in the play:

> *Angelus.*   Ryse hyrd-men heynd, for now is he borne
> That shall take fro the feynd that Adam had lorne;
> That warloo to sheynd, this nyght is he borne.
>
> (ll. 638–40)

The allusion to the "feynd" as "warloo" or warlock is echoed subsequently by the first shepherd when he hails the Christ child: "Thou has waryd, I wene, the warlo so wylde" (l. 713). In its literal, original sense, by no means ignored by writers in the fourteenth and fifteenth centuries, the term warlock means covenant-breaker, or one who breaks faith with his neighbors.[16] Christ's victory over the devil is paralleled here on an earthly level by the shepherds' victory over Mak the covenant-breaker, thus affirming their appropriateness as the ones who first meet and adore Christ.

The dramatization of how, precisely, the three shepherds come to find Mak out is no less important to the dramatic structure of the *Second Shepherds Play* than the representation of their symbolic exorcism of the sheep-stealer. Correlative to the shepherds' conflict with Mak is the incipient discord they find themselves in as good but imperfect sojourners in the earthly city and their subsequent self-amelioration in demonstrations of concerted action as a true fellowship of men.

The shepherds' soliloquies show them from the beginning as not only inert and passive, but isolated from each other, oblivious even to one another's presence on the stage, so absorbed is each in his own problems.[17] This condition is compounded by the conflict between the youngest shepherd, Daw, and his masters, the first two shepherds, who revile him as a sluggard. While the master-servant relationship as depicted here is in some sense a typical and perennial one, the playwright gets dramatic mileage from it, so to speak, by showing it as militating first against the shepherds' knowledge of the theft and then against their efforts to locate Mak as the perpetrator of the crime. When Daw intuits the truth about the theft from his nightmare after the shepherds awake from their sleep and from the "spell" that Mak has cast upon them, the second shepherd is openly contemptuous of him (ll. 368-74). Even when the shepherds discover that their sheep has indeed been stolen, the first rebukes Daw in like manner for suggesting Mak as the culprit (ll. 460-61).

The use of Daw as, ironically, the wisest of the three—a dramatic example of the familiar medieval topos of the *puer senex*—is at the same time a means of measuring the progress of the three shepherds toward a harmony of knowledge and action.[18] Despite the older shepherds' ingrained hostility toward Daw, it is he who activates the other shepherds into collectively seeking out Mak, takes the initiative in performing the act of charity which leads to Mak's exposure, and gets the others to agree on a suitable punishment that will peremptorily rid them of the spirit of discord in their midst:

> We will nawther ban ne flyte,
> Fyght nor chyte,
> Bot have done as tyte,
> And cast hym in canvas.                                    (ll. 625–28)

The representation of the change in the relationship among the three shepherds as coincident with their exorcism of the spirit of discord demonstrates, in a way that would otherwise not be possible, the need for them to act as one in order to remedy their misfortunes. The play thus gives dramatic life to St. Augustine's insistence that "the possession of goodness is increased in proportion to the concord and charity of each of those who share it." That the shepherds do indeed *act* in an efficacious way, prior to any divine intervention on their behalf, further illustrates one of the basic presuppositions of Augustine's view of redemptive history. Acknowledging God's omnipotence and foreknowledge, Augustine nonetheless says:

> Our wills . . . exist as wills, and do themselves whatever we do by willing, and which would not be done if we were unwilling. . . . It is not the case . . . that because God foreknew what would be in the power of our wills, there is for that reason nothing in the power of our wills. For He who foreknew this did not foreknow nothing. Moreover, if He who foreknew what would be in the power of our wills did not foreknow nothing, but something, assuredly, even though He did foreknow there is something in the power of our wills.[19]

In the terms of the play, even though the advent of Christ as bringer of peace is foreknown by God, the shepherds make their own peace; they use their wills to perfect themselves as far as their lot as sojourners in the city of man allows. In *Thomas of India*, the dramatic resolution is by way of a literal *deus ex machina* that demonstrates the power of Christ as spiritual healer; in the *Secunda Pastorum*, the resolution of the play consists solely in the words and acts of the shepherds as *will*ing men prior to the appearance of Christ before them. Their discovery of Christ in the manger, while itself of supreme historical significance, signifies from a dramatic point of view the shepherds' right, as a newly harmonious fellowship, to receive Christ's grace. In this lies its preeminence for the audience as a dramatic *exemplum*.

Like Augustine, too, the Towneley playwright was not insensible to the inherently comic nature of his *exemplum*:

> But who can enumerate all the great grievances with which human society abounds in the misery of this mortal state? . . . . Hear how one of their [the Romans'] comic writers makes one of his characters express the common feelings of men in this matter: "I am married; this is one misery. Children are born to me; they are additional cares." What shall I say of the miseries of love which Terence also recounts—"slights, suspicions, quarrels, war today, peace tomorrow?" Is not human life full of such things? Do they not often occur even in honorable friendships?[20]

Whether modelled after a Terentian character or not, Mak, though an agent of discord and thus akin to the devil himself, is an absurd and ineffectual character. By highlighting Mak's absurdity from the outset, the playwright assures us that the shepherds will prevail, whatever happens. The shepherds' quick perception of Mak's disguise and Southern dialect and, later, Mak's hapless deference to his wife, Gyll, show him to be an altogether foolish and inept antagonist and reduce his subsequent plot to disguise the sheep to a farce. Indeed, it is Mak who is shown to activate the shepherds and bring them into concerted action against him. The dramatic value of this strategy is considerable, for it allows the dramatist to eliminate the grounds of our concern for the shepherds and the recovery of their sheep. Because the outcome is thus never in doubt, the audience may see and understand the ease with which sojourners in the earthly city may arrive at a state of concord and charity, given the will.

The three shepherds, of course, are sympathetic characters by contrast to Mak, yet they are treated with an ironic detachment that focuses our attention upon their imperfections as sojourners in the city of men even as they complain of their hard lot. While the first shepherd is no doubt put upon beyond his just deserts, the nine stanzas of his opening monologue betray a long-winded old man whose "complaint" is for the most part a panacea for habitual loneliness:

> It does me good, as I walk thus by myn oone,
> Of this warld for to talk in maner of mone. (ll. 46–47)

Further, his diatribe against "gentlery men" does not square well with the youngest shepherd's accusation of maltreatment at his hands: "We ar oft weytt and wery when master-men wynkys" (l. 156). Similarly, the second shepherd's criticism of his wife, though doubtless true in part, is too protesting and hyperbolic to be taken seriously:

> She is as greatt as a whall,
> She has a galon of gall. (ll. 105–06)

At the same time, the modulation of the comic tone of the *Second Shepherds Play* is also a means by which to measure the progress of the three sojourners from inactive isolation to concerted action. If the shepherds are initially the objects of humor in their complaints and in their working at cross purposes with each other, they become the agents of humor and Mak the comic butt as they subject Mak's increasingly absurd attempts to conceal the sheep's lineage to their collective sarcasm:

> 1 *Pastor.*      What dewill shall be hatt, Mak? Lo, God,
>                         Makys ayre!
> 3 *Pastor.*      I know hym by the eere marke; that is a
>                         good tokyn.                                              (ll. 604, 611)

Finally, the comedy in the stable, by contrast to the raucousness of the sheep-stealing episode, is altogether tender and sympathetic in tone. The shepherds' joy in the Advent prompts them to share alike in the Christ-child's laughter, and in doing so, to purge whatever antagonisms they might have had either toward Mak or toward one another. It is important to see them at the end as, above all, good-humored men, whose unself-conscious presentation of humble gifts conveys a sense of their new-found humanity better than any entirely sober treatment of the nativity would have done.

### III

The movement toward a perfect concord among themselves on the part of the sojourners in the earthly city has its corollary in the Towneley cycle's dramatizations of those whose perpetual discord consigns them to the earthly city. St. Augustine remarks that "the wicked perpetually war with the wicked," so that "such victories as the earthly city may achieve are self-destructive and short-lived." In their incorrigible opposition to Christ and his claim to divine sovereignty in the Towneley cycle, the earthly tyrants show themselves incapable of progressing toward the kind of concord exemplified by the shepherds and disciples. The Towneley dramatization of Pilate in the trial and crucifixion scenes of this cycle epitomizes Augustinian discord, for Pilate's self-proclaimed duplicity shows him to be a sower of discord and therefore most inimical to the kind of Christian commonwealth that is an earthly paradigm of heaven's peace:

> Supporte a man to day/to-morn agans him then,
> On both parties thus I play./And fenys me to ordan the right.
>                                                              (XX, ll. 22-23)

The recurrent arguments between Pilate and his counsellors, lieutenants, and soldiers as to how best to dispose of Christ and his earthly remains, climaxed by the ironic defection of the torturers to Christ after Pilate seizes the spoils of the crucifixion for himself, all symbolize the self-destructive discord of the earthly city.[21] The dramatization of this principle—in fact, its extension into a major line of action in its own right, coordinate with the conflict between earthly and divine sovereignty—is used to represent the nature and consequences of spiritual unregeneracy.[22] These episodes are what might be called negative *exempla*, since it is in the earthly city, according to Augustine, that we see the "symbolic presence of the heavenly city."[23]

The centrality of these negative *exempla* to the cycle play in particular and to medieval tradition in general can hardly be exaggerated. The very term *Corpus Christi* by which Towneley and the other cycles are known comes to designate after the twelfth century an all-inclusive political body united under Christ.[24] Requisite to the proper functioning of the Corpus Christi, or body of Christ's faithful, is unity.[25] In the Towneley play, the attainment of such unity is made contingent on whether Adam and Eve and, by extension, mankind will "multiplie without discord."

The rulership of the earthly king is a divine privilege to be exercised for the good of the *Corpus Christi*. The king who acts in his own self-interest forfeits any claim to majesty, since he thereby foments disunity within the kingdom of God. Of all the self-serving kings guilty of misrule in the Towneley cycle, Pilate is the most reprehensible; for in sowing discord among his subjects, he subverts rather than preserves unity among the people of God. The pervasive character of discord dramatized here is symptomatic of the chaos that can infect a state whose king perverts his kingly function. Chaucer's Parson, himself the epitome of moral rectitude, states this condition succinctly and unequivocally:

> . . . the synne of men that sowen and maken discord amonges folk . . . is a synne that Crist hateth outrely. And no wonder is; for he deyde for to make concord./And moore shame do they to Crist, than dide they that hym crucifiede; for God loveth bettre that freendshipe be amonges folk, than he dide his owene body, the which that he yaf for unitee. Therfore been they likned to the devel, that euere is about to maken discord.[26]

In terms of the plot of the Towneley passion play, Pilate is the perfect antagonist for Christ, not because he is consistently evil, as one critic maintains,[27] but because he acts in a way potentially destructive to God's efforts to "make concord" among fallen men.

For a late medieval audience, the various dramatizations of discord and concord in this cycle must also have had a topical, not to say theoretical, relevance. The misery engendered by civil wars in fourteenth-century England is reflected in political poems such as "On the Corruption of the Times," with its representation of "Dyscord" as one of the widespread sins which "medelythe ful fast amonge." Hoccleve, in his *Regement of Princes* (c. 1411), specifically characterizes contemporary kings as two-faced men whose words are "hony," whose acts are "galle," and who thereby propagate "discorde" and "strife" within their realm. The sixteenth century chronicler Edward Hall still more specifically reiterates his belief that Henry IV, roughly contemporaneous with the playwrights of the Towneley cycle, was "the beginnyng and rote of the great discord and division . . . to the greate displeasure and preiudice of all the christian publike welth."[28]

Such writings affirm that the representation of ancient historical events on the stage was of immediate practical concern for a late medieval English audience. The dramatic conception of the foregoing plays as *exempla* that operate by contrast and analogy to each other points even more fundamentally to the primarily extra-historical, extra-temporal nature of the play called *Corpus Christi*. Such a system of *exempla* in a comprehensive multi-layered work is by no means peculiar to the Towneley cycle; it has notable precedent in the parallelism of exemplary figures that E. R. Curtius finds to be one of the chief organizing principles of the *Divine Comedy*.[29] But the dramatic conception and execution of a system of *exempla* defining the nature and end of the two cities of God and man for a medieval audience are unique. If St. Augustine deplored the decadence of the Roman theater, one feels he could only have respected the spirit, if not the artistic ingenuity, with which the Towneley playwrights honored his work.

# Notes

†Originally appeared in *Mediaevalia: A Journal of Mediaeval Studies* 4 (1978): 225–44. Reprinted by permission of the publisher.

[1]Typical assumptions underlying extended analyses of medieval lyric, narrative, and drama respectively are that "theology determined the aesthetic characteristics of the Middle English religious lyric" (Sarah Appleton Weber, *Theology and Poetry in the Middle English Lyric* [Columbus, Ohio, 1969], p. vii); that the Corpus Christi cycle is "one vast sermon on repentance" (Eleanor Prosser, *Drama and Religion in the English Mystery Plays* [Stanford, 1961], p. 25); and that "the general pattern which dominates medieval aesthetic ideas of all kinds is most easily discernible" in St. Augustine's "theory of figurative expression" (D. W. Robertson, Jr., *A Preface to Chaucer* [Princeton, 1962], p. 53).

[2]For general discussions emphasizing the importance of the *City of God* to an understanding of the concept of history underlying the cycle plays, see Catherine Dunn, "The Medieval Cycle as History Play: an Approach to the Wakefield Plays," *Studies in the Renaissance,* 7 (1960), pp. 78–81; and V. A. Kolve, *The Play Called Corpus Christi* (Stanford, 1966), pp. 88–92.

[3]Texts used are *The Towneley Plays,* ed. George England and Alfred W. Pollard, EETS, ES 71 (London, 1897); and, where possible, A. C. Cawley, ed., *The Wakefield Pageants in the Towneley Cycle* (Manchester, 1958).

[4]The *City of God,* trans. Marcus Dods (New York, 1950), pp. 482–83, 690.

[5]Ibid., p. 482.

[6]See esp. Bk. 8, Chap. 5; Bk. 9, Chap. 1.

[7]See Emile Mâle, *The Gothic Image*, trans. Dora Nussey (New York, 1958), pp. 109–13, 125–26; and Adolf Katzenellenbogen, *Allegories of the Virtues and Vices in Medieval Art* (New York, 1964), pp. 59, 76, 80, 83.

[8]Ed. R. Morris, EETS, 68 (London, 1892), ll. 23639–40. See also John Gower, *Confessio Amantis*, ed. Russell A. Peck (New York, 1968), p. 30, ll. 1045–47.

[9]See, e.g., Eleanor Prosser, *Drama and Religion*, p. 155.

[10]For a discussion of the mixing of genres as a principle of composition in the Middle Ages, see Ernst Robert Curtius, *European Literature and the Latin Middle Ages*, trans. Willard R. Trask, Bollingen Series, Vol. 36 (New York, 1963), p. 424.

[11]*City of God*, p. 690.

[12]Ibid., p. 690.

[13]For an alternate and more general view of the function of discord in the cycle plays, see V. A. Kolve, *The Play*, pp. 158–59.

[14]For the fullest, as well as the most recent essay on the action of the *Second Shepherds Play* as a system of analogies, see Lawrence W. Ross, "Symbol and Structure in the *Secunda Pastorum*," *Comparative Drama*, I (1967–68), 122–43.

[15]*City of God*, p. 683.

[16]See the *OED*, "warlock," 1a.

[17]See esp. l. 109, which indicates that the second shepherd has not seen the first on stage.

[18]See Rosemary Woolf, *The English Mystery Plays* (Berkeley, 1972), pp. 192–93, for a discussion of the characterization of the three shepherds in light of the fifteenth-century English background and satirical writings.

[19]*City of God*, p. 157.

[20]Ibid., pp. 680–81.

[21]See esp. Towneley XX, 150–62, 724–39; XXI, 433–41; XXII, 31–35 ff.; XXIII, 552–57; and XXIV, 400–03.

[22]For further discussion of the function of the various conflicts within the secular hierarchy in the Towneley cycle, see my "Dramatic Craftsmanship in the Towneley *Play of the Talents*," *Educational Theater Journal*, 28 (March, 1976), 79–84.

[23]*City of God*, p. 480. Augustine states further that "mention is made of it [the earthly city] so far as seemed needful to enhance the glory of the heavenly city by contrast to its opposite" (p. 488).

[24]Ernst Kantorowicz, *The King's Two Bodies: A Study in Medieval Political Theology* (Princeton, 1957) cites as the underlying reasons for such a conception, first, the "increasing tendency for secular bodies politic to become self-sufficient" (p. 194); and, second, the fact that "doctrines of corporational and organic structure of society begin to pervade anew the political theories of the West," as a result of the renewed influence of Aristotle (p. 199).

[25]For a detailed discussion of the significance of unity in thirteenth- and fourteenth-century conceptions of monarchy, see Michael Wilks, *The Problem of Sovereignty in the Later Middle Ages* (Cambridge, 1963), pp. 15–45.

[26]*Parson's Tale*, ll. 642–43. It is significant in this respect that Dante consigns sowers of discord to the eighth circle of hell (*Inferno*, Canto XXVIII), well below those guilty of ire, gluttony, and other so-called deadly sins. Such a fate conforms to the overriding

emphasis on the organic unity of mankind, as outlined above, and the paramount need for the individual to subordinate his own interests to the common good. It is further significant that the punishment of the greatest schismatic Mahomet (by whom Pilate and other tyrants of the cycle plays swear) symbolizes the way he has divided the Church, or body of Christ: for introducing a rent or breach into what may be called the organism of mankind, Mahomet has his own organism ripped open from the chin down.

[27] Arnold Williams, *The Characterization of Pilate in the Towneley Plays* (East Lansing, 1950), p. 16. It must be added here that V. A. Kolve's judgement that the Towneley Pilate is an "artistic oversimplification" (*The Play*, p. 233) is unfair without a consideration of his function in this cycle.

[28] See, respectively, Thomas Wright, ed., *Political Poems and Songs* (1857; rpt. London, 1965), p. 240; Frederick J. Furnivall, ed., EETS, ES 72 (London, 1897), ll. 2820 f., 5083–89; and *Chronicle; Containing the History of England during the Reign of Henry the Fourth, and the Succeeding Monarchs, to the End of the Reign of Henry the Eighth* (London, 1809).

[29] *European Literature*, pp. 362–64.

# Reconsidering the Ideal: *The City of God* and Utopian Speculation†

## Dorothy F. Donnelly

Interest in utopias and the utopian mode of thought has in recent years been both extensive and varied.[1] Several studies have analyzed the similarities and differences among utopias while others have compared utopia with other kinds of writings for the purpose of arriving at a synthesis. On the one hand we have attempts to demonstrate that even though utopias have a common base they can nonetheless be divided into a number of different categories, and on the other it is suggested that utopia is an all-inclusive term and that such diverse works as religious writings, the myth of the Golden Age, and various millenarianisms are properly included under the rubric of utopia. As traditionally used the term utopia refers to works which present a descriptive picture of an ideal state or commonwealth. Today however it is applied to any work containing elements of what is called utopian thought; that is, any social, intellectual, political, religious, or psychological theory that speculates about the possibilities of one's achieving the good life in the future. The tendency to draw distinctions among utopias and to divide them into opposite types gives us such categories as the soft and the hard utopia, static and dynamic utopias, utopias of escape and utopias of reconstruction, ideal utopias and practical utopias, evolutionary, scientific, and arcadian utopias, prophetic and secular utopias. The search for synthesis has resulted in classifying as utopian such distinctly different kinds of expressions as religious writings (Old and New Testaments, Augustine's *The City of God*), political and social tracts outlining plans for restructuring social arrangements (Marx's *Communist Manifesto* and Condorcet's *Sketch for the Historical Picture of the Progress of the Human Mind*), writings that set forth a plan for the redesigning of cities (Antonio Averlino's *Treatise on Architecture* and Bruni's *Laudatio Florentinae Urbis*), and fictional works presenting a picture of an ideal commonwealth (More's *Utopia* and Bacon's *New Atlantis*).[2]

This looseness in definition and classification concerning utopia runs through the literature and is found particularly in the many works on utopia and the utopian mode of thought that have appeared over the past several years. I shall not attempt to review this extensive bibliography here, but it is worth considering briefly some of the more important inquiries into the subject so that the argument I shall present in this essay—that the proliferation of reinterpretations of utopia has led to a significant diffusion of its underlying assumptions and that the classification of Augustine's *The City of*

*God* as a utopia results in a misrepresentation of Augustinian thought—will be focused within the context of the theoretical dialogue on utopia.

Two of the earlier works on utopian literature which establish both the method of assigning them to specific categories and of making the term itself an all-inclusive one are Lewis Mumford's *The Story of Utopias* and Joyce O. Hertzler's *The History of Utopian Thought*. Mumford classifies utopias as either "utopias of escape" or "utopias of reconstruction" and places works such as Augustine's *The City of God*, Morris' *News From Nowhere*, and H. G. Wells' *A Modern Utopia* in the former category and Plato's *Republic*, More's *Utopia*, and Campanella's *City of the Sun* in the latter. Mumford's categories are based upon what he finds to be two opposing functions: "One of these functions is escape or compensation; it seeks an immediate release from the difficulties or frustrations of our lot. The other attempts to provide a condition for our release in the future . . . . The first leaves the external world the way it is; the second seeks to change it so that one may have intercourse with it on one's own terms."[3] Hertzler also believes that we need to use a broad approach in the search for utopian elements and therefore argues that any "conception of social improvement either by ideas and ideals themselves or embodied in definite agencies of social change" is a utopian work. This point of view leads Hertzler to the conclusion that the utopian tradition has its roots in the prophetic tradition, namely, in the "numerous utopian expressions" of the "Hebrew prophets."[4] This merging of "secular" and "prophetic" utopias is but one of several attempts at synthesis. Other approaches are seen in the claims that there exists a relationship between utopia and the myth of the Golden Age, the Garden of Eden, the pastoral tradition, and the Arcadia of the Renaissance. S. B. Liljegren, for example, in *Studies on the Origin and Early Tradition of English Utopian Fiction*, takes the position that English utopias have their origin in the "traditions of Eden in the Bible, of the Elysian Field of Homer, of the Insulae Fortunatae or the Island(s) of the Blessed of Greek and Latin authors, [and] of Plato's Atlantis,"[5] all of which intermingle with each other and with utopias as later envisioned by English authors of the fifteenth and sixteenth centuries. And Robert C. Elliott, who traces the roots of the utopian tradition back to the myth of the Golden Age, finds that the breakdown of the belief in the historical reality of the Golden Age led philosophers to transfer "the notion of an ideal life in the irrecoverable past into utopian tales of what the world might—even should— be like; the myth, that is, provided sustenance for a conceivable reality."[6] The idea that Liljegren proposes is that utopias have in common certain "ideal" qualities; and what Elliott argues, in effect, is that "utopia is the secularization of the myth of the Golden Age."

A more ambitious study on the conceptual level is Karl Mannheim's

*Ideology and Utopia.* In his work Mannheim develops a theory of history as progressive and in this context analyzes the historical function of utopian thought. He proposes that all political thought can be divided into two classes, the ideological and the utopian. The mode of thought of those whose ideas resist social change he calls ideological and the outlook of those whose ideas work toward social change he names utopian.[7] Mannheim's theory is based on a view of society as a struggle between the desires of one group standing in opposition to those of another group. The late Paul Tillich, in his paper "Critique and Justification of Utopia," says that there exists an organic relationship between utopia and religion: "Judaism is perhaps the most momentous utopian movement in history, for directly or indirectly it has elevated all mankind to another sphere of existence through its utopia based on the coming Kingdom of God."[8] Tillich bases his ideas on the fundamental premise that utopia is "rooted in the nature of man himself."

A much different approach is taken by Frank Manuel in "Toward a Psychological History of Utopias." Writing as a philosophical and psychological historian, Manuel argues that in defining utopia the boundaries need not be narrowly drawn and his attitude, as he describes it, is "latitudinarian and ecumenical." He therefore classes as utopian any work which evokes "a vision of the life of man in an earthly paradise that would be radically different from the existing order."[9] Under this rubric Manuel includes not only works in the classical utopian tradition (Bacon, Campanella), but also modern philosophical psychologists (Fromm, Reich, Maslow) and philosophers of history (Norman O. Brown, Herbert Marcuse). Manuel's approach is to study utopias as psychological documents that tell us about the sensibility of the societies in which they were produced. Finally, mention should be made of Ernest Tuveson's important book, *Millennium and Utopia: A Study in the Background of the Idea of Progress.* Tuveson's study deals with the reappearance in the seventeenth century of a belief in a millennial end to history and the close relation between this belief and the idea of progress. As Tuveson states: "The millennium itself came to be considered as a true utopia . . . . The method of God . . . is one of progress by fixed stages of cultural development which result from the refinement of spiritual and mental faculties: the advance from the 'primitive' to the 'philosophical' stages is the story of human redemption."[10] In this secularization of the millennial theory, according to Tuveson, we find a new definition of salvation in which "evolution" and "stages of advancement of mankind" replace the theological doctrine of "grace."

This review of the critical study on the subject suggests the range of approaches taken in defining utopia. And as the survey reveals, used so variously the term becomes almost useless in our discussions of the utopian mode of thought. We see, for example, that it is used in clearly contradictory ways; on the one hand it is applied to works which speak of a *telos* outside of time—an ideal supernatural existence; and on the other to an historical *telos*— an ideal human society. Thus in the tendency to focus on similarities—in this instance on the fact of the conceptualization of the "good life"—critics have ignored basic and, it might be argued, irreconcilable differences. For regardless of what form utopias take, or however much they differ in underlying assumptions and working principles, they have in common several basic propositions: they deal with ideas about achieving an ideal *telos* in this world; they are not founded on supernatural truths; and they are not brought about by revelation or by divine intervention.[11] Thus even though the religious millennium and the Chiliastic Kingdom of God are to be established on this earth they are also in conflict with utopian thought since they too are brought about by divine intervention. Few would agree with the extreme restrictions imposed by Bertrand de Jouvenel when he suggests that "the designation of 'Utopia' should be denied to any exposition of a 'New Model' of Society which is bereft of pictures concerning daily life."[12] On the other hand, the persistent attempt by scholars to discern similarities between such different modes of thought as utopia and millennial themes has meant that no parameters are left at all. And when such similarities are assumed between utopia and *The City of God*, the fact that they are based on radically different assumptions and premises becomes completely obscured.

My purpose here is to demonstrate this opposition by turning to Augustine's own words. Although the subject is very large, the argument can be made by focusing on four aspects of Augustine's work that are central to a discussion of its relation to the utopian tradition: Augustine's use of the term "city"; his ideas about the *res publica*, or state, and more specifically the relationship between the individual and the state; his concept of time; and, finally, his views on and description of an "ideal existence."

In the *Retractations* Augustine explains that in writing *The City of God* he had a two-fold purpose in mind. The work was intended not only to refute the "worshipers of many false gods, whom we call by the customary name pagans, attempting to attribute [Rome's] destruction to the Christian religion," but also to articulate a positive theological doctrine: "But lest anyone charge that we have only argued against the beliefs of others, and have not stated our own, it is just this that the second part of this work . . . accomplishes."[13] Thus whereas the primary purpose for the utopian theorist is to analyze political, social, and economic arrangements along secular lines and within the context of the state, Augustine says forthrightly that his intention in *The City of God* is to present a descriptive analysis of the *operati Dei* and that his method is to do this within the context of an inquiry into the "origin, and progress, and deserved destinies of the two cities (the earthly and the heavenly, to wit)."[14] In the development of his argument Augustine takes care that his particular use of the term "city" remains foremost by reiterating many times and in a number of ways the distinction he makes between the City of God and the earthly city. For example, he says in Book 14, chapter 1:

> And thus it has come to pass, that though there are very many and great nations all over the earth, . . . yet there are no more than two kinds of human society, which we may justly call two cities, according to the language of our Scriptures. The one consists of those who wish to live after the flesh, the other of those who wish to live after the spirit.[15]

In chapter 1 of Book 15 it is put this way:

> This race we have distributed into two parts, the one consisting of those who live according to man, the other of those who live according to God. And these we also mystically call the two cities, or the two communities of men, of which the one is predestined to reign eternally with God, and the other to suffer eternal punishment with the devil.[16]

Augustine stresses that *civitas* is not synonymous with *res publica* or the state. On the contrary, the distinction is consistently between two societies: the society of the *civitas terrena* and the society of the *civitas Dei*. Whatever the opposing terms may be—City of God and city of human beings; heavenly city and earthly city; love of God and love of this world; love of the spirit and love of the flesh; the soul and the body—they always refer to members of a society, or *civitas*, who are distinguished not by social or political arrangements nor by allegiance to any earthly polity but, rather, by the commitment of their love: "Two cities have been formed by two loves: the earthly by the love of self, even to the contempt of God; the heavenly by the love of God, even to the contempt of self."[17] Any critique of Augustine's *The City of God* must be based on an understanding of his figurative use of the term city. It is clear that *civitas terrena* does not refer to the state; on the contrary, its sole meaning is that it represents a mystical society made up of members who are, as I have already mentioned, distinguished by the commitment of their love, not by social or political systems. And Augustine lays out this distinction unequivocally.

Yet it is this fundamental proposition in Augustine's thought—that the members of the *civitas terrena* and the *civitas Dei* are intermingled in history— which has led scholars to argue that he has therefore incorporated in his work ideas about an ideal state that human beings should aspire to achieve while they live in time in this world. Since for the utopist the state is the means through which humanity's *telos* is made possible, it is important that we understand Augustine's views on the state and the role he believes it has in the affairs of humankind. Let us see whether *The City of God* contains a model of an "ideal" state that people should aspire to establish in order to achieve the "good life."

Augustine gives his definition of a *res publica* in chapter 21 of Book 19. He begins his discussion by arguing against the definition of a people (*populus*) and of a state (*res publica*) given by Scipio in Cicero's *De Republica*. Scipio defines a republic as "the weal of the people" and a people as "an assemblage associated by a common acknowledgment of right [i.e., an agreement about justice] and by a community of interests."[18] Augustine agrees that a common acknowledgment of right or justice is essential to a true *res publica*, but the way his position differs radically from Cicero's is revealed in a critical distinction he develops in his argument. According to Augustine, since justice is the distinguishing characteristic or the first condition of a true commonwealth it follows that "where there is not true justice there can be no assemblage of men associated by a common acknowledgment of right, and therefore there can be no people, as defined by Scipio or Cicero; and if no people, then no weal of the people."[19] Augustine states the core of his argument this way: "If the republic is the weal of the people, and there is no people if it be not associated by a common acknowledgment of right, and if there is no right where there is no justice, then most certainly it follows that there is no republic where there is no justice."[20] He then poses his critical distinction: "Where, then, is the justice of man, when he deserts the true God?"[21] Thus whereas Augustine accepts the overriding principle that in a true *res publica* each individual must be "given his due," for him there is a prior consideration: "Is this to give every one his due," he asks, when a person "keeps back himself from the God who made him?"[22] The essence of Augustine's argument is that there can be no "justice" in one who "does not serve God."[23] Therefore although a kind of justice is found in that commonwealth made up of individuals who love and serve God—that is, in that society of individuals who are members of the City of God on earth—because of the Fall no earthly state can ever possess or attain true justice: "True justice has no existence save in that republic whose founder and ruler is Christ . . . [True justice reigns] in the city of which Holy Scripture says, 'Glorious things are said of thee, O City of God.'"[24] Thus from the Augustinian point of view no state—whether pagan or Christian—has ever been or can ever be a true *res publica*.

> And therefore, where there is not this righteousness whereby the one supreme God rules the obedient city according to His grace, so that it sacrifices to none but Him, [where neither the individuals nor the community] live by faith,

which works by love, that love whereby man loves God as He ought to be loved, and his neighbour as himself—there, I say, there is not an assemblage associated by a common acknowledgment of right, and by a community of interests.[25]

In summary, since the *civitas terrena* came into existence because of the Fall, since the *civitas terrena* and the *civitas Dei* are intermingled in history, since the fulfillment of the *civitas Dei* is possible only in a life beyond historical time, and since this life is for the members of the *civitas Dei* but a "pilgrimage" of the soul in the journey toward redemption, it is axiomatic that true justice, hence a true *res publica*, cannot, according to Augustine's universal theory of history, be established in the earthly world.

Are we therefore to conclude from this that Augustine agrees with those early theologians who held that there is no fundamental relationship between the citizen and the state? Tertullian, for example, argued not only that the state had no legitimate claim on the individual but also that the interests of the individual and the interests of the state were inherently antithetical. "What concord," Tertullian asks, "is there between the Academy and the Church? . . . Our instruction comes from the Porch of Solomon who taught that the Lord should be sought in simplicity of heart. Away with all attempts to produce a mottled Christianity of Stoic, Platonic, and dialectic composition."[26] Does Augustine also believe that the state must be rejected absolutely? that the state has no specific role in human history? that the interests of the individual and the interests of the state are inherently antithetical? The fact is that although Augustine believes that establishing a true *res publica* is impossible he develops at the same time a theory about the role and function of the state that stands in direct opposition to Tertullian's attitude. The question of what Augustine's views are on the place the state has in human affairs is resolved when we realize that the answer lies in the principle that the two cities "are in this present world commingled, and as it were entangled together."[27] The state is thus itself a part of God's divine providence and, as such, has a definite purpose and specific role in human history. Indeed, Augustine wonders how anyone can believe that "the kingdoms of men, their dominations and servitudes, [were left] outside of the laws of His providence."[28] On the contrary, he says, "we do not attribute the power of giving kingdoms and empires to any save to the true God, who gives happiness in the kingdom of heaven to the pious alone, but gives kingly power on earth both to the pious and the impious."[29]

Augustine makes clear that he does not reject the state; rather he conceives of it as part of God's universe and therefore as an integral part of human history. To resolve the problem raised by the idea on the one hand that a true *res publica* cannot be achieved in this life, and on the other the proposition that there exists an intrinsic relationship between the citizen and the state, Augustine gives an alternative definition of a *res publica* in which he makes a critical substitution of terms—he rejects the Ciceronian definition of justice and argues that a people is "an assemblage of reasonable beings bound together by a common agreement as to the objects of their love."[30] And for Augustine humankind can have only one "common agreement"—to love and honour God. If, however, the meaning of existence is an ultimate *telos* outside of time and if the only common agreement the members of society have is to love and honour God what function, then, can the state have? Although he devotes considerable attention to this complex subject in his text, Augustine's argument can be summarized this way: the function of the state is to maintain peace, and the state fulfills this purpose because it has the authority and the power to maintain order.[31] Order then results in peace. Thus the virtue of the temporal state is that it provides and maintains a "remedial order" which makes possible a "temporal peace." And although a temporal peace is not comparable to the true peace found only in the City of God beyond time it is, as Augustine explains, "not to be lightly esteemed, . . . for as long as the two cities are commingled, we also enjoy the peace of Babylon."[32] Thus in Augustinian thought a state with the authority to maintain order and peace is divinely ordained so that the individual will be afforded the opportunity to pursue the goal of loving and honouring God. Otherwise, if God had not created the state anarchy would reign and people would destroy each other because of their propensity toward "love of self" rather than "love of God." The corrective to this inevitability is a state conceived of as a remedial instrument which is itself part of God's divine scheme. Sheldon S. Wolin has summarized Augustine's attitude about the state this way: "To the degree that a political society promoted peace it was good; to the degree that it embodied a well-ordered concord among its members it was even better; to the extent that it encouraged a Christian life and avoided a conflict in loyalties between religious and political obligations, it had fulfilled its role within the universal scheme."[33] Thus even a state alienated from God—as all earthly states must be—is absolutely necessary; and because the state is part of God's divine scheme its instruments are God's earthly instruments for humanity's possible redemption.

On the other hand, utopia is a mode of thought which deals solely with the temporal condition and the nature of utopia is that it promises, through the establishment of an "ideal" state, the "good life" in this world. The fundamental proposition in Augustine's thought is the doctrine of divine providence and in his explication of this thesis he develops a comprehensive philosophy of universal history the ultimate end of which is the fulfillment of God's promise to humanity, the attainment of an ideal supernatural state of existence. Thus whereas the issue from the utopist's point of view is whether the individual will serve the ends of the state toward achieving the utopian *telos*, from the Augustinian viewpoint the issue is whether humankind will serve the ends of eternity. Apart from these crucial underlying philosophical differences, what has also been overlooked by critics who suggest that *The City of God* is utopian is the fact that at no point in his voluminous work does Augustine, as the utopian writer would, talk about specific social and political arrangements. The truth is that the issues of central importance to the utopist—political, social, economic, and cultural arrangements—are deliberately eschewed by Augustine.[34] At the same time, none of the central ideas he develops in his analysis—two societies, predestination, grace, divine Providence—plays any role in utopian conceptualizations.

Not unexpectedly, such opposing sets of ideas lead also to a number of contrasting emphases. For example, in utopia the focus is consistently on society—on the proper ordering of social institutions—never on the individual. The overriding value in utopia is that the state is the means by which people achieve the good life. In *The City of God* the emphasis is on the individual, not on society; it is on the integration of the individual with God, not on an integration with social institutions. In other words, self-realization in *The City of God* is shaped by an affinity with the spiritual life; in utopia it is derived solely from an active involvement with social institutions. Thus the architectonic order of utopian social structures has no place in *The City of God* where the quest for redemption is based on the idea of a life free from complex political influences.[35] Whereas in utopia there exists an intimate connection between the political order and collective fulfillment, for Augustine the peace and order the state maintains provides external conditions that are conducive to the individual's seeking personal salvation through the grace of God. For Augustine then the "ideal" temporal state is distinguished not by its political structures and social arrangements but rather by whether it fulfills the standard that those "who govern do not force [the individual] to impiety and iniquity."[36]

I want to turn now to the remaining two points mentioned earlier which, it seems to me, further support my arguments that *The City of God* and utopia are based on totally different modes of thought—Augustine's discussion of an ideal existence and his concept of time. With respect to the former, Augustine's description of the *telos* of the members of the City of God is sometimes referred to by critics as evidence that he is presenting a utopian ideal; and regarding his concept of time, it is claimed that since the City of God is to be achieved in the future, the work therefore embodies the futuristic orientation characteristic of utopias. As we have already seen, through his conceptualization of two distinctly separate societies, Augustine develops a theory of universal history that is intended to explain the doctrine of divine providence through an analysis of the origin and the destiny of the two cities, or societies. The ultimate end of divine providence is the fulfillment of God's promise to humanity; the ultimate destiny of the members of the City of God is to enjoy eternal peace with God. In chapter 30 of the concluding book of his monumental text, Augustine describes the state of blessed peace and happiness which is the destiny of the members of the City of God.

> How great shall be that felicity, which shall be tainted with no evil, which shall lack no good, and which shall afford leisure for the praises of God, who shall be all in all! For I know not what other employment there can be where no lassitude shall slacken activity, nor any want stimulate to labour. I am admonished also by the sacred song, in which I read or hear the words, "Blessed are they that dwell in Thy house, O Lord; they will be still praising Thee." All the members and organs of the incorruptible body, which now we see to be suited to various necessary uses, shall contribute to the praises of God; for in that life necessity shall have no place, but full, certain, secure, everlasting felicity.[37]

The appointed end of the City of God is an ideal life where people will enjoy everlasting and perfect peace, no longer subject to the wretchedness of mortal life. Thus unlike the utopist's description of an ideal organization of the state, Augustine's concept of an ideal existence is a vision of a mystical or spiritual state of being—in no sense is it an idealization of temporal life.

Further, for Augustine the attainment of an "ideal life" is strictly limited to an existence outside of historical time and of human events.[38] Throughout the development of his argument Augustine consistently draws a distinction between what is possible in history and what is possible outside of the temporal world. And while utopia too is conceived of as transcending historical periods, it does not transcend historical time. The "nowhere" element in utopia refers, on the one hand, to the idea that it does not presently exist, and on the other that it is not expected to be achieved. In sum, by its very nature utopia is nowhere and the ideal it contains is of a not impossible, although certainly not probable, historical future. Conversely, both the concept of "nowhere" and the quality of "wishful thinking" inherent in utopia are wholly lacking in *The City of God*. The idea uppermost in Augustine's mind is the certainty that the supernatural Heavenly City does in fact exist and that it is, for the members of the City of God, attainable at a designated time in the future. And it is the belief that human history has a *telos* outside of time which lies at the heart of his work and which he never allows us to lose sight of.

This essay has been an attempt to demonstrate from Augustine's own propositions that *The City of God* and utopia are based on opposing modes of thought. From this perspective we see that not only is *The City of God* not an example of utopian writing, but, it might even be suggested, it is a mandate against utopianizing—that is, a rejection of the utopian mode of thought. At the very least, it should be clear that those who say that *The City of God* is utopian have, on the one hand, failed to take into account the text itself, and on the other too casually reinterpreted Augustinian thought.

# Notes

†Originally published as "*The City of God* and Utopia" in *Augustinian Studies* 8 (1977): 111-23. Reprinted by permission of the publisher.

1I want to thank Professor Victor Harris, Brandeis University, for his comments and suggestions in the development of the subject presented here.

2For example, see *The Quest for Utopia: An Anthology of Imaginary Societies* (eds. G. Negley and J. M. Patrick, New York 1952). Negley and Patrick draw a distinction between "ideal" and "practical" utopias and among other examples they classify More's *Utopia* as an "ideal" utopia and works of the Italian Renaissance city-planners as "practical" utopias. Perhaps the fact that the traditional utopia is almost always presented within the framework of a well-designed city explains why critics include the works of the Italian Renaissance town-planners as utopian examples. But for the utopist the city that is described is actually the means through which the writer presents the idea of an ideal; in utopia the focus is consistently on guiding principles, not on the physical design of a city. For an excellent discussion of the "ideal city" in the Italian Renaissance see E. Garin, *Science and Civic Life in the Italian Renaissance* (trans. P. Munz, New York 1969), 21-48.

3L. Mumford, *The Story of Utopias* (New York 1922), 15.

4J. O. Hertzler, *The History of Utopian Thought* (New York 1926) 2-3, 7.

5S. B. Lilegren, *Studies on the Origin and Early Tradition of English Utopian Fiction* (Copenhagen 1961), 16.

6R. C. Elliott, *The Shape of Utopia: Studies in a Literary Genre* (Chicago 1970), 7.

7K. Mannheim, *Ideology and Utopia: An Introduction to the Sociology of Knowledge* (trans. C. Wirth and E. Shils, New York 1940), 173-181.

8P. Tillich, "Critique and Justification of Utopia," *Utopias and Utopian Thought* (ed. F. E. Manuel, Boston 1967), 298.

9F. E. Manuel, "Toward a Psychological History of Utopias," *Daedalus* 94 (Spring 1965), 293-295.

10E. L. Tuveson, *Millennium and Utopia: A Study in the Background of the Idea of Progress* (New York 1964), ix-x.

11See, for example, Raymond Ruyer, *L'utopie et les utopies* (Paris 1950); Richard Gerber, *Utopian Fantasy* (London 1955); and Darko Suvin, "Defining the Literary Genre of Utopia," *Studies in the Literary Imagination* 6 (Fall 1973), 121-145.

12B. de Jouvenel, "Utopia for Practical Purposes," *Utopias and Utopian Thought* (ed.

F. E. Manuel, Boston 1967), 221.

13Saint Augustine, *The Retractations* (trans. M. I. Bogan, R. S. M., Washington 1968), 209–210. See also the Preface to the work itself: "The glorious city of God is my theme in this work. . . . I have undertaken its defence against those who prefer their own gods to the Founder of this city."

14Saint Augustine, *The City of God* 11.1 (trans. M. Dods, New York 1950), 346. The form in which Augustine expresses the dualism of existence, that is, the conceptualization of "two cities," antedates the composition of *The City of God*. The idea is found in Stoicism, for example, in Marcus Aurelius' *Meditations*, and in Cicero and Seneca. It is also found in the Old and New Testaments. But its most explicit development is in the *Commentary on the Apocalypse* written by Tyconius, a Donatist priest. Tyconius' use of the idea is most often spoken of as Augustine's source of the overall frame for his work. See trans. note, *The Retractations, op. cit.* 213.

15*The City of God, op. cit.* 14.1.441.

16*Ibid.* 15.1.478.

17*Ibid.* 13.28.477.

18*Ibid.* 19.21.699.

19*Ibid.*

20*Ibid.*

21*Ibid.*

22*Ibid.*

23*Ibid.* 19.21.700.

24*Ibid.* 2.21.63.

25*Ibid.* 19.23.705–706.

26Quoted in C. Dawson, "Saint Augustine and His Age," *A Monument to Saint Augustine: Essays on Some Aspects of His Thought* (New York 1930), 53.

27*The City of God, op. cit.* 11.1.346.

28*Ibid.* 5.11.158.

29*Ibid.* 5.21.174.

30*Ibid.* 19.24.706.

31See book 19 of *The City of God, op. cit.*, for a full discussion of this point. In chapter 13 of book 19, for example, Augustine says: "The peace of all things is the tranquillity of order. Order is the distribution which allots things equal and unequal, each to its own place" (690).

32*The City of God, op. cit.* 19.26.707.

33S. Wolin, *Politics and Vision: Continuity and Innovation in Western Political Thought* (Boston 1960), 125.

34My emphasis here is that for Augustine political and social arrangements are of divine rather than human origin; hence the individual is impelled to accept and obey the laws of whatever kind of civil authority exists. See also Augustine's views on "obedience."

35Augustine does not argue that the political order is unimportant but rather that it must be understood within the context of a universal whole. In Augustinian thought order is an hierarchical and distributive principle which creates an harmonious whole. Thus although the diverse parts may intersect they do not absorb each other.

36*The City of God, op. cit.* 5.17.166.

37*Ibid.* 22.30.864.

38In his study of Western political thought Wolin states: "In the Augustinian conception of time one of the most original and significant contributions of Christian thought was given its classic statement. There were enormous political implications in the new notion of time, implications which did much to delineate the contrasts between the classical and Christian attitudes towards political problems" (*op. cit.* 123). See also K. Löwith, *Meaning in History: The Theogical Implications of the Philosophy of History* (Chicago 1949). Löwith says that Augustine's "final argument against the classical concept of time is . . . a moral one: the pagan doctrine is hopeless, for hope and faith are essentially related to the future and a real future cannot exist if past and future times are equal phases within a cyclic recurrence without beginning and end" (163).

# Divide and Conquer: Augustine in the *Divine Comedy*†

## Peter S. Hawkins

One of the surprises in the *Divine Comedy* is the virtual absence of the figure of Augustine. He does appear briefly at the end of *Paradiso* to take his eternal place in the heavenly rose, directly below the saints Francis and Benedict (32.35); but while Benedict is encountered at length in the sphere of Saturn (22) and Francis is praised for almost an entire canto by no less an authority than Thomas Aquinas (11), the Bishop of Hippo is only glimpsed in passing, in the eleventh hour of the poem's penultimate canto. He neither speaks nor is spoken about. It is almost as if, despite his choice seating in paradise, he were judged to be some minor citizen of the city of God rather than the theologian who described it at such imposing length.

This minimal presentation in the *Comedy* is not what Dante's other works might have led one to expect.[1] At the outset of the *Convivio*, for instance, it is to the Augustine of the *Confessions* that Dante appeals when he seeks a warrant for speaking about the course of his life as moving "di [non] buono in buono, e di buono in migliore, e di migliore in ottimo" (1.2)—a curriculum vitae from bad to best that foreshadows the tripartite itinerary of the *Comedy*. In the Letter to Can Grande della Scala, Dante uses Augustine to authorize another kind of boldness: should readers have difficulty with Dante's claims to have been taken up into paradise (as was Paul), then let them turn to Augustine's *De quantitate anime* and no longer begrudge Dante the experience ("et non invidebunt" [351]).[2] In *Monarchia*, morever, Dante cites only Augustine by name in referring to those who, although coming after Scripture, nonetheless write with something of its divine inspiration ("Sunt etiam Scripture doctorum, Augustini et aliorum, quos a Spiritu Sancto adiutos ..." [3.3]). Indeed, as Dante's impassioned letter to the Italian cardinals also argues, the church is bereft of genuine spiritual guidance in following the Bible's teaching precisely because it has discarded Augustine, along with other neglected theologians ("iacet Augustinus abiectus" [339]).

Yet it is none other than the poet of the *Comedy* who seems to have tossed Augustine away. Why this should be true has been the subject of speculation among the relative few who have taken the matter seriously. Some have argued that Dante simply failed to see the importance of Augustine; others have conjectured that Aquinas's Aristotelian bias blinded Dante to the contributions of a Christian Platonist; and at least one has contended that the dictates of a poet's imagination freed Dante from having to account for anyone's presence or absence.[3] It is far more likely, however, that

Augustine's eclipse in the *Comedy* has to do with politics—with the political polemic that drives the *City of God* in direct opposition to many of Dante's own convictions. Augustine negated pagan Rome, discredited Vergil, and refused the idea of temporal beatitude as a legitimate human "end." It was against his authoritative naysaying that Dante had to contravene in his own bid to underwrite not only a renewed Roman empire but a vision of redeemed political life on earth.[4]

But how does one take on so estimable an opponent? Though perhaps too venerable to be confronted directly (much less damned to hell as a traitor to Caesar), Augustine might nonetheless be countered by two strategies. On the one hand, Dante could more or less covertly co-opt his opponent, as he does perhaps most flagrantly both in *Convivio* 4.4 and *Monarchia* 2.5, where—without the slightest nod to the real gist of his source—he rewrites Augustine's insidiously left-handed compliment to the Romans' "greed for praise" (*City of God* 5.12) and turns it into an outright encomium of the Romans as God's chosen people. On the other hand, he could try to silence the opposition by studiously ignoring it, that is, by virtually writing the person of Augustine out of the narrative of the *Comedy*. This seems at first glance to be exactly what Dante did. The saint who by anyone's estimation should merit at least a canto's discourse in the *Paradiso* becomes instead a beatific face in the crowd, a name barely mentioned.[5]

What critics have gradually come to recognize, however, is that the Augustine who is all but excluded from the narrative surface of the poem functions as an extensive, even an informing presence within the text itself. Late in the last century Edward Moore ended his brief discussion of the two writers by acknowledging that he found himself, despite the paucity of direct Augustinian references in Dante's work, "continually coming on fresh points of resemblance," even though the possible mediation of Aquinas or Bonaventure made it difficult to decide at times exactly who Dante's primary source was (294). In the last two decades Moore's intuition of resemblance has moved closer to actual points of identification. To John Freccero in particular goes the credit for having dug deeply into the text of the *Comedy* and come up with buried treasure—not the atmospheric Augustinianism that one might find in almost any medieval work, but examples of concrete linguistic indebtedness that betoken a profound intertextual relation. In several influential essays he has stressed Dante's deep reliance on the *Confessions*; along with Francis X. Newman and Marguerite Mills Chiarenza, he has also explored the relation between the three modes of vision delineated in Augustine's *De genesi ad litteram* and both the structure and poetics of the *Comedy*'s three *cantiche*. More recently still, Ronald Martinez, Giuseppe Mazzotta, and Jeffrey Schnapp have each drawn attention to Dante's polemical reading of the *City of God*. All three have explored his vision of history as a radical reworking of both Vergil and Augustine and commented on his creation of a new notion of the earthly city to supplant the quite different constructions of Rome in his two Latin forebears.

What has not yet been noted, however, is the strategic placement of this revision at the center of the *Comedy*. For what we find undergirding *Purgatorio* 13–17 is Augustine's meditation on Cain and Abel taken out of the anti-Roman polemic of *City of God* 15 and translated into Dante's own political vernacular. It is in *Purgatorio* 15, moreover, that Augustine is introduced to us—not in person, but through an unmistakable paraphrase of *City of God* 15.5, a text whose description of the *civitas Dei* Dante gives to none other than Vergil, the *poeta nobilissmus* whom Augustine both used and abused and whose vision of Rome he so maligned. Thus, although Dante deprives us of the extended Augustinian appearance we might well have expected in paradise, he not only allows Augustine to surface textually at the heart of the poem but does so through the mediation of Vergil. The maneuver constitutes one of Dante's most outrageous acts of ideological revision, revealing yet another dimension of his will to power over his "authorities"—the politics of his poetics.

The Augustine that Dante reinvents in *Purgatorio* 13–17 is not the monastic rule maker glimpsed below Francis and Benedict in the heavenly rose. Rather, he is the great theologian of history, theorist of the earthly city, and, more specifically still, the author of the *City of God*. Halfway through that work, in the fifteenth book of his *magnum opus et arduum*, Augustine takes up the historical development of two branches of humanity, two cities, "one made up of those who live according to men, the other of those who live according to God" (1). Here he moves from Eden into history, passing through the "common door of mortality opened up in Adam" to enter the realm of Cain and Abel (21). As Adam's offspring, the brothers inherit a common legacy of sin; they are both made from the same condemned lump ("ex eadem oritur quae originaliter est tota damnata" [1]). But that is where the resemblance ends, for Augustine spins out the ramifications of his work's magisterial either/or precisely in terms of the differences between the two. Cain, the first-born, represents the flesh; he is what Paul refers to as the "old man," absorbed in things earthly and thereby blind to things divine. By contrast, Abel is the second-born, the "new man" of spiritual regeneration; he is what Paul speaks of as the "vessel of mercy for honor" (Rom. 9.22–23). This antithesis enables Augustine to understand the mystery of God's choice of the younger over the elder in Genesis 4. God received Abel's offering with favor because it was "divided" properly, because Abel had discerned the difference between the goods of the earth and the God who gave them. Cain failed to find favor because—while giving something of his own to God—he gave himself to himself ("dans aliquid suum, sibi autem se ipsum" [7]). He used God to enjoy the world, losing himself in secondary goods even as he abandoned the source of all goodness.

These familiar Augustinian themes achieve a civic focus in book 15, where Cain is shown to be mirrored in the earthly city he founded. The *civitas terrena* refers not so much to any actual urban place as to the "worldly mind" itself. Augustine sees it as the social manifestation of the same love of self (*amor sui*) that caused the expulsion of the rebel angels from paradise and of Adam and Eve from Eden. Like mortality, the spirit of the earthly city is the sinful birthright of Cain and Abel. But whereas Cain builds his life on its premises, treating it not only as his home but as his god, Abel defines himself as an alien sojourner within enemy territory. He lives in the *civitas terrena* as a pilgrim passing through, praying for its peace, perhaps, but always knowing that his citizenship is not on earth but in heaven.

Resorting to a common typology, Augustine sees Christ the Good Shepherd foreshadowed in Abel, the first keeper of sheep: "pastor ovium hominum, quem pastor ovium pecorum praefigurabat Abel" (15.7; see also 18.51). And yet, far more important to the larger purpose of Augustine's polemic is another kind of typology altogether: a blood link between Rome and the city of Cain, both founded on fratricide. Just as Cain murdered his brother out of envy and wrath before making the *civitas terrena* his refuge, so Romulus, overcome by envy, killed Remus and gave birth to what became the seat of empire. The Roman imago reflects Cain's archetype (15.5). In each case, in the words Augustine quotes from Lucan's *De bello civili* (1.95), "[f]raterno primi maduerunt sanguine muri" (the blood cries out from the city's walls).

What distinguishes Romulus's crime (and the *civitas terrena* throughout its history) is the refusal of human partnership. To maintain his sovereignty, Romulus eliminated what would have compromised his power: the threat of diminishment by a living partner ("vivo consorte"). Augustine considers this murder Rome's foundational event, the establishment of that *libido dominandi* which in time would make the city not only master of the world but victim of its own might. By refusing partnership, Romulus was choosing what was to become Rome's dead end—its fate to divide and conquer itself.

Augustine finds no escape from this death wish in Roman history. While he concedes, of course, that the city has had its civic heroes and its share of martyrs—witness the roll call of book 5—he strenuously qualifies their achievement: all Roman virtue is at best the sublimation of Roman vice, a higher version of the self-adulation that is the city's "greed for praise and passion for glory" (5.12). Even though the *civitas terrena* can at most refine its concupiscence, however, humanity is not left without an alternative. There is leaven at work within the lump, among those who live on earth, looking toward heaven as their standard and whose living therefore reflects the polity of God's kingdom. As an antidote to the cities of Cain and Romulus, therefore, Augustine offers the ethos of Abel—the ethos of community itself. Experienced here in part but known fully only in the city that is above and free, this community is a commonwealth "where there is no love of a will that is personal or, as we may say, private, but a love that rejoices in a good that is at once shared by all and unchanging, a love that makes 'one heart' out of many, a love that is the whole-hearted and harmonious obedience of mutual affection" ("ubi sit non amor propriae ac privatae quodam modo voluntatis sed communi eodemque inmutabili bono gaudens atque ex multis unum cor faciens, id est perfecte concors oboedientia caritatis" [15.3]).

What makes this *oboedientia caritatis* possible is the right priority of love. Abel chose God, not himself, as his good, and in so doing he fixed on the only object of desire that others can share without rivalry or fear of loss. Not only can they share such a love, they can actually increase it by doing so. Less can become more, and living partnership can be, not a compromise of power, but a source:

> Nullo enim modo fit minor accedente seu permanente consorte possessio bonitatis, immo possessio bonitas, quam tanto latius quanto concordius individua sociorum possidet caritas. Non habebit denique istam possessionem qui eam noluerit habere communem; et tanto eam reperiet ampliorem quanto amplius ibi potuerit amare consortem. (15.5)

> A man's possession of goodness is in no way diminished by the arrival, or the continuance, of a sharer in it; indeed, goodness is a possession enjoyed more widely by the united affection of partners in that possession in proportion to the harmony that exists among them. In fact, anyone who refuses to enjoy this possession in partnership will not enjoy it at all; and he will find that he possesses it in ampler measure in proportion to his ability to love his partner in it.

By converting the very notion of possession from the exclusive to the corporate, Augustine turns a cause of strife into the source of concord; he shows how one heart can be made out of many. What he also does, of course, is stand the values of the earthly city upside down. Pointing past the obsession with lesser goods that characterizes the children of Cain, he upholds the "possessio bonitatis" as itself the summum bonum. It alone is the source of real power, power that is not lessened with sharing but that indeed must be shared to be possessed at all. The prizing of this love of goodness above everything else makes concord instead of antagonism, abundance instead of want—and all because the end of such desire is divine and thus infinite. To divide true love is in fact to multiply it. This discovery makes it possible to imagine a new order of *civitas* entirely, one in which partnership, the concept that brackets this text from start to finish, is not only possible but necessary. *Consortio* constitutes the kingdom. This, says Augustine, is what Abel bore witness to, what Cain could not bear, and what Romulus never knew: "the united affection of partners in possession."

The passage just quoted from the *City of God*, together with the extended analysis of the *civitas terrena* that surrounds it, underwrites the central cantos of the *Purgatorio*. It is there, on the terraces of envy and wrath in cantos 13–17, that Dante gives his own account of how former citizens of Cain's city become fellow travelers with Abel. *Amor sui* having been formally renounced on the terrace of pride (10–12), Dante turns to explore the social dimensions of regeneration, the means of transforming *civitas* itself. What one finds in these cantos are pilgrims preparing themselves for life in the city of God, for partnership in goodness, by learning to reject the values Augustine associates with the earthly city.

The terraces accomplish this change of citizenship through a program of positive and negative exempla not unlike those in the *City of God*, whose readers negotiate their way through the binary opposition Augustine sustains from start to finish, confronted by the stark contrast between the two cities and implicitly asked to choose between them. On every terrace (and through a variety of media) Dante opposes exempla of virtue to those of vice, as if to dramatize within the history of the earthly city, both biblical and pagan, the perennial choice of one *civitas* or the other. His exempla of virtue, which mark the beginning of each stage of purgation, act as "the cords of the whip drawn from love" to spur on the penitents toward the contrary of the sin being expiated (13.39). Exempla of vice, in contrast, function as sin's "curb" at the end of the process (13.40).

It comes as no surprise that on the terraces of envy and wrath Cain is the paradigmatic curb to *invidia* while a New Testament version of Abel is the final spur to mercy. Thus the envious hear a voice crying out, "Anciderammi qualunque m'apprende" 'Everyone that finds me shall slay me' (14.133). The cry is a translation of the one Cain utters in Genesis 4.14 ("omnis igitur qui invenerit me, occidet me"), after he realizes his status as a fugitive and before he builds himself a city of refuge ("et aedificavit civitatem" [4.17]). Later on, in canto 15, standing in chiastic relation to Cain on the terrace of wrath— standing, that is, as the last spur to virtue rather than as the first curb to vice— is a vision of Stephen, "primus martyr pro nomine Christi," who offers a New Testament fulfillment of his prototype Abel, "in martyrio primus."6

Portrayed at the moment of his death at the hands of an angry Jerusalem mob, Stephen sinks down to the earth but keeps his eyes turned upward to the gates of heaven ("ma de li occhi facea sempre al ciel porte" [15.111]), asking God to pardon his persecutors. In a re-enactment of Christ's forgiveness on the cross, he answers their stones ("pietre" [107]) with prayers for divine mercy ("pietà" [114]). The entire scene (106–14) is not only a reprise of the biblical account in Acts 7 but a miniature of the conflict Augustine develops at length: a picture of the earthly city hurling itself in wrath against the city of God but finding its hatred answered with love. The mob's cry to kill—"Martira, martira!" (108)—coupled with the martyr's plea for "pietà" presents both the impulse to destroy the good that forever haunts the city of Cain and the transcendence of that hatred through the act of forgiveness that Augustine identifies as the mark of the city of God in pilgrimage. Murder here becomes martyrdom, for Stephen as for Abel.

This turn from one notion of *civitas* to another, presented in the *Purgatorio* by the progress from Cain to Abel-Stephen, is dramatized further on these terraces through a series of encounters and interventions. When the pilgrim first approaches a company of the envious in *Purgatorio* 13, for instance, he asks whether any soul among them is Italian ("s'anima è qui tra voi che sia latina" [92]). Posing the question in the present tense, he provokes a response that gently takes him to task for failing to realize the change of identity entailed in purgation:

> O frate mio, ciascuna è cittadina
> d'una vera città; ma tu vuo' dire
> che vivesse in Italia peregrina. (94–96)

> O my brother, each one here is a citizen of a true city:
> but you mean one that lived in Italy while a pilgrim.

Sapia, the soul who speaks here, uses the same distinctions Augustine deploys in *City of God* 15; she also makes a crucial shift in tense to bring home her point. Is anyone on the terrace of envy an Italian? The answer is both yes and no. She *is* a citizen of heaven's true city who once *lived* in Italy; yet even then she lived "in Italia peregrina." Whether she is alive or dead, her citizenship—like Abel's and like Paul's in Philippians 3.20—"in caelis est."

But is it? Sapia goes on to describe herself as once belonging to Siena ("Io fui sanese" [106]) but now, as a pilgrim, reforming the sinful disposition that formerly led her to rejoice in the defeat of her fellow citizens. And yet at the end of the canto, her request to Dante that he restore her name among the Sienese ends in her defamation of her people as "gente vana" 'vain fools,' whose future embarrassment she seems to enjoy predicting. Citizen of the true city, she continues nonetheless to bear the imprint of the *civitas terrena*—and for the poet's purpose. Because unlike Augustine, who maintains his either/or without portraying the process of conversion between one *civitas* and another, Dante shows Cain's power lingering even over those penitents who have thrown in their lot with Abel. He depicts the blur of civic allegiances rather than their neat separation, demonstrating to the reader that Augustine's two cities are intermingled in individuals as well as in history. Here the status of the soul after death reflects the confused state of the living.

A similar confusion of attachments can be seen in the next canto, where yet another of the envious, Guido del Duca, distances himself from the Romagna region in a prolonged jeremiad against its degeneracy and at the same time demonstrates the district's hold over him by the sheer weight of his loathing. The Italy he denounces may well be on its way to becoming a wasteland; but it is also true that to some extent he has strayed in its dark wood, losing sight of the "true city" to which he belongs and toward which he moves in penance. Nonetheless, Guido knows what ails the earthly community of which he himself is too much a part. He knows that what envy first unleashed from hell is the same refusal to share that Augustine saw as the curse pursuing Cain and Romulus. "O human race," Guido asks, "why do you set your hearts where there must be exclusion of partnership?" ("o gente umana, perché poni 'l core/là 'v' è mestier di consorte divieto?" [86–87]).

After this encounter—and with the word *consorte* in the air—Dante first hears Cain's cry ("Anciderammi qualunque m'apprende") and then learns from Vergil what to make of it. The "hard bit" of Cain's example, the wages of envy, is meant to keep humanity within bounds and out of Satan's trap. Instead, however, "you" take the bait, fall into the hands of the adversary, and pass beyond the help of curb or lure. Addressing Dante as "voi"—a plural broad enough to include the whole of humanity, from Cain's day until the time of the present journey—Vergil closes the canto by describing the misplaced sense of direction that all but defines what Augustine means by the *civitas terrena*:

> Chiamavi 'l cielo e 'ntorno vi si gira,
>     mostrandovi le sue bellezze etterne,
>     e l'occhio vostro pur a terra mira;
> onde vi batte chi tutto discerne.                                        (148–51)

The heavens call to you and circle about you, displaying to you their eternal splendors, and your eyes gaze only on the earth: wherefore He smites you who sees all.

So ends canto 14, with the reader's attention drawn down to the earth. But what happens from the very beginning of *Purgatorio* 15 is an abrupt volte-face that has readers suddenly looking up to discover not only the heavens but an altogether different civic reality. The first lines call attention to the play of the sun bringing evening to the Southern Hemisphere and midnight to the Northern (15.1-6). In part this opening is the poet's device for telling the passage of time in purgatory, as the pilgrim completes the cure of envy and moves on to confront the terrace of wrath. More important, it is Dante's subtle way of suggesting the joyful realities of reciprocity and harmony—between endings and beginnings, evening and midnight, north and south, there and here. These reciprocities are to be found even in the laws of physics (as in the equality of the angles of incidence and reflection referred to in the simile of lines 16-21), but they are utterly foreign to the earthly city just recalled in *Purgatorio* 14.

With the setting of this new thematic, then, readers are prepared for the dazzling arrival of one who will in effect give harmonious reciprocity a local habitation and a name: an angel sent from the "family of heaven" (15.29) who erases from Dante's brow the *P* symbolizing the *peccatum* 'sin' of *invidia* and invites him to ascend higher, toward the same celestial light from which the angel has descended. Thus introduced to the city of God in action, but still mindful of the conversation of the previous canto, Dante asks Vergil to unravel a knot in the discourse of Guido del Duca: "What did the spirit of Romagna mean when he spoke of 'exclusion' and 'partnership'?" ("'divieto' e 'consorte' menzionando?" [44-45]). Coming to the heart of the matter in these two remembered words—words that echo Augustine's indictment of envy as the refusal of partnership—Dante has Vergil respond by diagnosing an earthly problem and then pointing to its solution in the kingdom of heaven:

> Perché s'appuntano i vostri disiri
>> dove per compagnia parte si scema,
>> invidia move il mantaco a' sospiri.
> Ma se l'amor de la spera supprema
>> torcesse in suso il disiderio vostro,
>> non vi sarebbe al petto quella tema;
> ché, per quanti si dice più li "nostro,"
> tanto possiede più di ben ciascuno,
> e più di caritate arde in quel chiostro.          (49-57)

Because your desires are centered there where the portion is lessened by partnership, envy moves the bellows to your sighs. But if the love of the highest sphere turned upwards your desire, that fear would not be at your heart. For there, the more they are who say "ours," the more of good does each possess, and the more of charity burns in that cloister.

In the earthly city desire invariably focuses on what is peripheral, where division always means less and never more. But this occurs because the desire is centered down, rather than up, because the "highest sphere" is not allowed to hold sway in human affairs. If our longings were aligned with that sphere, however, another world would exist. Division of possessions would cause their growth, and the more of us who shared, who said "ours" ("nostro"), the more each of us ("ciascuno") would hold.

With the rhyme words of lines 53, 55, and 57—"vostro," "nostro," "chiostro"—Vergil presents the unfolding of "yours" into "ours" that we will find in paradise; in three tercets he takes readers from earth to heaven. But with a "fleshly" mind still oriented to the realm where "the portion is lessened by partnership," Dante cannot understand how a "good" ("un ben" [61]) can possibly be distributed so that many possessors are richer than a few. Vergil is therefore prompted to initiate him further into the economy of heaven, whereby "that infinite and ineffable Good" who is God speeds with love toward the rational creation and reaches toward it (so to speak) as light (67). Material possessions or temporal sovereignty may dwindle with division, but light (like love) augments. Giving always means gaining, at least if the recipient can reflect what has been given and thereby increase the glow. Or, as the climactic tercet of the sequence insists, the distribution of God's gifts means more—"più," "più," "più"—for all:

> E quanta gente più là sù s'intende,
> più v'è da bene amare, e più vi s'ama,
> e come specchio l'uno a l'altro rende.          (73-75)

[T]he more souls there are that are enamored there above, the more there are for loving well, and the more love is there, and like a mirror one reflects to the other.

If the bitter rancor of *Purgatorio* 14 recalls the hell of the earthly city, what readers find here is a proleptic glimpse of a paradise bounded only by love and light. No wonder that at the end of this exposition Vergil refers Dante to Beatrice for more enlightenment on the "highest sphere"—or for direct experience rather than description (76-78). Vergil's words in fact anticipate her discourse in the *Paradiso*. And yet the voice that actually resounds in his account of heaven belongs to none other than Augustine, that is, to the previously quoted passage in the *City of God* where the commonwealth of Abel, characterized by the joy of partnership, is set against the invidious cities of the fratricides Cain and Romulus:

Nullo enim modo fit minor accedente seu permanente consorte possessio bonitatis, immo possessio bonitas, quam tanto latius quanto concordius individua sociorum possidet caritas. Non habebit denique istam possessionem qui eam noluerit habere communem; et tanto eam reperiet ampliorem quanto amplius ibi potuerit amare consortem.

A man's possession of goodness is in no way diminished by the arrival, or the continuance, of a sharer in it; indeed, goodness is a possession enjoyed more widely by the united affection of partners in that possession in proportion to the harmony that exists among them. In fact, anyone who refuses to enjoy this possession in partnership will not enjoy it at all; and he will find that he possesses it in ampler measure in proportion to his ability to love his partner in it.

Dante's indebtedness to this Augustinian text was first mentioned by the earliest fourteenth-century commentators, and their successors have continued to cite the passage as the primary doctrinal source for Vergil's lines.[7] Indeed, the connections between the two are so clear that the passage from *City of God* 15.5 seems more a subtext than a source. Not only does Dante appropriate Augustine's analysis (and not of these particular lines alone but, as we have seen, of the larger discussion of book 15), he also closely translates Augustine's Latin vocabulary into his own Italian: "consortio" becomes "consorte," "bonitas" "bene," "possessio" "possiede," and "communio" "compagnia."

Merely to note the borrowing, however, is to acknowledge a debt but miss its implications; it is in fact to miss an ingenious (perhaps even an outrageous) authorial maneuver. For whatever is one to make of Dante's decision to give this Augustinian glimpse into the city of God—in fact the poem's first view of paradise—to Vergil, a pagan poet banished forever from the *civitas Dei* precisely because he lived in the time of what he himself calls "the false and lying gods" (*Inferno* 1.72)? That this phrase, "falsi e bugiardi," obviously echoes Augustine's dismissal of the "falsi et fallaces" deities of Roman religion[8]—the deities, that is, of Vergil's religion—only reinforces the irony of the transposition in *Purgatorio* 15, where the enemy speaks the accuser's lines. For Dante has given Augustine's description of the economy of heaven to the writer against whom he more or less openly polemicized: the chief poet of the *civitas terrena* of Romulus, whose characterization of Rome as an "empire without boundary" (*Aeneid* 1.279) was for Augustine nothing less than a celebration of a blasphemy, the mendacity of a venerable liar: "mendax vates erat." All the more dangerous for being revered, Vergil was for Augustine the paradigmatic "gentile," a purveyor of pagan delusion against whom the *City of God* (even from its preface) raises its massive contra.[9]

Nor is the bizarre phenomenon of an "Augustinian" Vergil limited to the single passage in the fifteenth canto. In *Purgatorio* 17, the central canto of the *Comedy*, Vergil's discourse on the moral basis of purgatory (94–105), as well as his exposition of the ordering of love according to a threefold division (106–39), is deeply indebted to passages in *City of God* 15.22 and *Christian Doctrine* 1.27.[10] Likewise, his description in the same canto of the soul's search for a good "wherein the mind may find rest" ("nel qual si queti animo" [17.128]) seems clearly to allude to the opening of the *Confessions* and the portrayal of the restless heart searching for its resting place ("inquietum est cor nostrum, donec requiescat in te").

What this concentration of subtexts and allusions may suggest is that, instead of having Augustine himself appear in the poem's narrative, Dante chose to present the theologian's teachings at the heart of the *Comedy*—but to place them all in Vergil's mouth. On the one hand, this transposition creates something like a patristic Vergil: a doctor of the church he cannot join, he can at least discern the towers of the true city, from which he is nonetheless in eternal exile, as he himself tells Statius in *Purgatorio* 21.18. On the other hand, it also offers us the possibility of a Vergilian Augustine—that is, an Augustine who is allowed to function both as architect of the city of God and as master of rightly ordered love but who has been delivered from the errors of his anti-imperial ways. Dante adopts Augustine's indictment of the *civitas terrena* and applies it, as we have seen, all along the terraces of envy and wrath. But there is no reference to Romulus or to the bloodstained walls of his city. Instead, the lust for domination Dante denounces is shown to drive the city-states of Italy; it has nothing whatsoever to do with Rome. On the contrary, Rome offers the pilgrims of purgatory example after example of virtue as well as of vice; its pagan history has the heuristic value of Scripture. Here again Dante tacitly rejects what Augustine does in *City of God* 5, where the portraits of the Roman worthies are said to demonstrate at best but a flawed and shadowy likeness of real civic virtues.[11]

Dante's reinvention of Augustine entails, therefore, a major correction of the theologian's political vision—a Roman revision. In addition to rehabilitating Vergil, moreover, Dante works toward a similar end through another figure on the terrace of wrath, one whose dialogue with the pilgrim utterly flies in the face of Augustine's teaching. For while the Bishop of Hippo rejects the notion of a political solution to the "exclusion of partnership"—and rejects as well any idea of a beatitude constituted in and of the earthly city—Marco Lombardo (and with him, of course, the author of the *Monarchia*) embraces the temporal order, discusses its redemption, and even (pace Augustine) calls its redeemer "Rome." Bracketed by what we might well regard as the "orthodox" Augustinian discourse of cantos 15 and 17 (orthodoxy voiced by Vergil), *Purgatorio* 16 presents us with a vision of Rome's place in history that is utterly antithetical to the spirit of the *City of God*:

> Soleva Roma, che 'l buon mondo feo,
>     due soli aver, che l'una e l'altra strada
>     facean vedere, e del mondo e di Deo. (106–08)

Rome, which made the world good, was wont to have two suns, which made visible both the one road and the other, that of the world and that of God.

Though rich in Augustinian analysis, Marco's extended speech turns Augustine's ideology of the earthly city against the saint.[12] Dante redeems Romulus, so to speak, by transforming him from a descendant of Cain into a figure for Abel. He changes a symbol of civic self-destruction into one that promises earthly beatitude, a Rome from whose ramparts one might well discern the towers of the true city ("la vera cittade" [16.96]). Later in the *Purgatorio* Dante even goes so far as to have Beatrice identify the "highest sphere" of the empyrean as none other than "that Rome where Christ is a Roman" (32.102).

Although this harmonization of Augustine and Vergil is carried out at considerable expense to the integrity of both, the taking of such liberties seems never to have worried Dante. On the contrary, the drive of the poem is itself a kind of *libido dominandi*, a domination of the past (pagan or Christian) to render a new account—that is, Dante's account—of everything old. What is especially intriguing about the achievement of this *discordia concors*, however, is that it should find its focus in the fifteenth canto of the *Purgatorio*, at the same structural moment that in the other two *cantiche* the pilgrim encounters a father figure he is meant either to reject or to emulate. In *Inferno* 15, it is a classicized Ser Brunetto Latini, whose humanism represents a road not to be taken and whose reflections on politics and literature recall the greed for praise and passion for glory that Augustine denounces in the alleged heroes of Rome. At the other pole of eternity, in *Paradiso* 15–17, Dante's great-great-grandfather Cacciaguida hails his arrival in the heaven of Mars with Latin words ("O sanguis meus" [15.28]) that echo Anchises's injunction to Julius Caesar (*Aeneid* 6.835) and that here become a Christian salute as well as an imperial one. In Cacciaguida, as opposed to Brunetto, the poet finds his ideal citizen of the earthly city: a soul passionately devoted to civic life, appreciative of its joys, but under no delusions about either its permanence or its ultimacy. "Your affairs all have their death" (*Paradiso* 16.79), he tells the pilgrim, as if to correct Vergil's

Jovian prophecy of an earthly empire without end; but he does not echo Augustine's refusal of empire's providential mission.

*Purgatorio* 15 apparently breaks this pattern of father-son encounters by failing to stage any such meeting. Unless, of course, the pattern is fulfilled in some other way, one perhaps more suited to the fleeting and provisional "visions" that appear for an instructional moment all along the terraces of purgatory and then are gone. In a poem careful of its own symmetries, of the structural repetitions that signal a development, it would be surprising if the deliberately analogous father-son episodes of the *Inferno* and the *Paradiso* should lack a middle term. I suggest that what we find in *Purgatorio* 15 is a third parallel, a remarkable composite of paternal acceptance, rejection, and transposition that offers us a hybrid father suitable to the transitory "in between" space of purgatory—a father who "appears" only to disappear (like all the other "non falsi errori" [15.117]) when he has been understood. At once Roman and Catholic, he is a father who offers the pilgrim his first understanding of heaven (which Vergil alone should not be able to do), without separating that eternal hope from the vocation of earthly empire building (which Augustine himself would refuse to consider).

At the heart of the *Comedy*, then, Dante gives us the architect of the *City of God* speaking through the poet of the *Aeneid*. Disarming the Bishop of Hippo of his anti-Roman artillery simply by ignoring it, Dante lays the basis of his own work for an Augustinian vision of a redeemed secular order that does not require the fratricidal Romulus as its foil. He establishes a partnership with the goals of the earthly city that Augustine largely excluded from the *City of God*, so that pilgrimage within the *civitas terrena* becomes less a passing through alien territory than a crusade on the world's behalf. Having in different ways corrected his ancient masters on the true calling of the city and its citizens, this Italian son makes peace with his Latin fathers by transforming them into his own terms. From their constructions of the earthly city he proposes a third Rome of his own imagining; from pagan epic and sacred history he invents a "sacred poem" (*Paradiso* 25.1) to which Vergil and Augustine (as well as heaven) have each contributed a hand. Seer of the earthly city and visionary of the city of God, he reconciles the opposition between his authorities by transcending them in himself—Christian Vergil and *alter Augustinus*.[13]

# Notes

†Reprinted by permission of the Modern Language Association of America from *PMLA* 106 (1991): 471–82.

¹For enumerations of the Augustinian references and citations in Dante's work, see Pincherle; Moore 291–94; Toynbee 73; Gardner 44–76; Calcaterra 447–48; and Chioccioni 46–49.

²In discussing the theological debates over the possibility of a mortal's seeing God *per speciem*, Mazzeo emphasizes the importance of Augustine's qualifiedly positive verdict on Dante's claims (84–110). On this issue see also Foster's essay and Tonelli 207–14.

³Calcaterra gives an excellent summary of the state of the question in 1931 before advancing his own essentially aesthetic rationale that the imagination has its own reasons ("la fantasia ha i suoi diritti" [446]). For subsequent considerations see Chioccioni and also Fallani, who draws attention to the frequent references to Augustine in Pietro Alighieri's 1340 *Commentarium*, although with a caveat: "L'intero commento ha 142 citazioni dirette da S. Agostino, e non è poca cosa in confronto agli altri autori: S. Tommaso ne ha cinquanta. Arbitrarietà di Pietro Alighieri, predilezione personale a un autore, o non, piuttosto, una controllata misura, rispetto ai libri che vida più spesso in mano al padre, e da lui consultati?" 'The entire commentary has 142 direct citations from St. Augustine, and that is no small thing compared with other authors: St. Thomas has fifty. Arbitrariness on the part of Pietro Alighieri, the personal predilection of an author, or, rather, a careful estimation, with respect to the books he saw most often in his father's hand, and consulted by him?' (193). Unless otherwise indicated, all translations are my own.

⁴No one has written more powerfully about the extent of Dante's radical departure from Augustine's vision of Rome (or about the poet's indebtedness to Augustine's notion of providential history) than has Charles Till Davis (*Dante* 40–73; "*Dante's Italy*" 198–289). Davis not only clarifies Dante's revision of Augustine but considers that reworking in the light of several trecento political theorists. See also Ferrante.

⁵In addition to positioning Augustine in eternity, the *Paradiso* mentions the saint one other time, invoking his name to identify someone else in the heaven of the theologians: "quello avvocato de' tempi cristiani/del cui latino Augustin si provide" 'that defender of Christian times, of whose discourse Augustine made use' (10.120). These lines are usually taken to refer to Orosius and his *Historiarum adversum paganos libri* VII. The "Augustin" cited in *Paradiso* 12.130 is one of the earliest followers of Francis.

⁶In a number of sermons on Stephen as the first martyr for the name of Christ (Migne 38: 1425–46), Augustine emphasizes the correspondence between the protomartyr and Christ in their common return of forgiveness for wrath. The spiritual antecedent of both is said to be Abel, "quem primum iustum impius frater occidet" 'the first righteous man slain by an ungodly brother,' whose lineage continues "usque in huius saeculi finem inter persecutiones mundi et consolationes Dei" 'right up to the end of history, with the persecutions of the world on the one side and on the other the consolations of God' (*City of God* 18.51).

⁷Pietro Alighieri cites Augustine's text in his *Commentarium*, as had Jacopo della Lana more than a decade before him (c. 1324–28). The citation remains a constant in twentieth-century commentary. Nardi, for example, attributes the concept of Vergil's

speech to *City of God* 15.5 and also remarks the appearance of the term *consorte* (13). See also Gmelin 250; Sapegno 261; Marti 66; and Singleton 325–26. Some of these commentators note Gregory the Great's *Moralia* 4.31 as an intermediary source.

[8]Calcaterra, building on the work of others, observes that Augustine applies the adjectives "falsi et fallaces" to the gods of pagan Rome in *City of God* 2.29 and 4.1, as well as in *De consensu evangelistarum* 1.25: "Deus Israel . . . satis ostendit illos falsos atque fallaces . . ." (440).

[9]The accusation that Vergil was a liar comes from Augustine's sermon on the fall of Rome (Migne 38: 623), a text that Davis rightly characterizes as "revealing the abyss between Augustine and Dante in their estimates of Vergil and Rome" (*Dante* 55). See also Augustine's rewrite of *Aeneid* 1.279 ("imperium sine fine dedi" 'dominion without end have I bestowed') in *City of God* 2.29, where God's pledge of eternity to the church replaces Jupiter's corresponding promise to Rome. In the prologue to the *City of God* Augustine compares a verse of Scripture (James 4.6) with a line from the *Aeneid* (6.853) in order to contrast Christian humility with Rome's "superbae animae spiritus inflatus" 'arrogant spirit in its swelling pride.' In the opening chapters of the *City of God* (as indeed elswhere in the work) it is Vergil, as Rome's theologian-poet, whom Augustine takes to task for the delusions of an entire civilization. Or, as Charles Cochrane puts it, in Vergil "we may perceive the spiritual foundations of the City of Man, over against which Augustine was to oppose its antitype in the shape of a city not built with human hands" (71). Mazzotta's treatment of Vergil and Augustine offers perhaps the most probing exploration not only of Augustine's objections to the *poeta nobilissimus* of Rome but of Dante's transformation of those objections into his own vision of history (147–91). For an altogether different assessment, see Rand 272–77.

[10]In *City of God* 15.22 Augustine considers the mingling of the sons of God with the daughters of men (Gen. 6.2) as a seduction of the soul away from the primary good and its fall into the secondary. Using terms that seem to inform Vergil's speech in *Purgatorio* 17, he goes on to say that

> Creator autem si veraciter ametur, hoc est si ipse, non aliud pro illo quod non est ipse, ametur, male amari non potest. Nam et amor ipse ordinate amandus est quo bene amatur quod amandum est, ut sit in nobis virtus qua vivitur bene. Unde mihi videtur quod definitio brevis et vera virtutis ordo est amoris; propter quod in sancto cantico canticorum cantat sponsa Christi, civitas Dei: *Ordinate in me caritatem.*

> [i]f, however, the Creator is truly loved, that is, if he himself is loved, and not something else in his stead, then he cannot be wrongly loved. We must, in fact, observe the right order even in our love for the very love that is deserving of love, so that there may be in us the virtue which is the condition of the good life. Hence, as it seems to me, a brief and true definition of virtue is "rightly ordered love." That is why in the holy Song of Songs Christ's bride, the City of God, sings, "Set love in order in me."

Dante may also have had in mind *De doctrina Christiana* 1.27:

Ille autem iuste et sancte vivit, qui rerem integer aestimator est; ipse est autem, qui ordinatam habet dilectionem, ne aut diligat, quod non est diligendum, aut non diligat, quod diligendum est, aut amplius diligat, quod minus diligendum est, aut aeque diligat, quod vel minus vel amplius diligendum est, aut minus vel amplius, quod aeque diligendum est.

He lives in justice and sanctity who is an unprejudiced assessor of the intrinsic value of things. He is a man who has an ordinate love: he neither loves what should not be loved nor fails to love what should be loved; he neither loves more what should be loved less, loves equally what should be loved less or more, nor loves less or more what should be loved equally.

11*City of God* 5.16: "verum etiam ut cives aeternae illius civitatis, quamdiu hic peregrinantur, diligenter et sobrie illa intueantur exempla et videant quanta dilectio debeatur supernae patriae propter vitam aeternam, si tantum a suis civibus terrena dilecta est propter hominum gloriam" '[Rome] had this further purpose, that the citizens of that Eternal City, in the days of their pilgrimage, should fix their eyes steadily and soberly on those examples and observe what love they should have toward the City on high, in view of life eternal, if the earthly city had received such devotion from her citizens, in their hope of glory in the sight of men.' In 5.17 Augustine notes a similarly "shadowy resemblance" ("per umbram quandam simile") between the remission of sins in the city of God and "asylum illud Romuleum, quo multitudinem, qua illa civitas conderetur, quorumlibet delictorum congregavit inpunitas" 'that refuge of Romulus, where the offer of impunity for crimes of every kind collected a multitude which was to result in the founding of Rome.' Roman virtue provides Augustine's pilgrims with a flawed simulacrum of reality, whereas Dante makes no such qualification: Roman virtue and vice get equal billing with scriptural exempla along the terraces of purgatory (see Hawkins).

12Chioccioni draws attention to the Augustinian presence in *Purgatorio* 16 and notes the specifically Augustinian resonance of the phrase "la vera città" (124–30; see also 40–42). What he fails to register is Dante's revisionary Roman departure from the polemic of the *City of God*.

13Earlier versions of this essay were delivered first at a conference on Augustine and the Middle Ages organized by the University of the South in April 1987 and then at a session of the Modern Language Association in December 1988. I am grateful for the formal response given to my paper at Sewanee by Larry Allums of Mobile College. His thoughtful consideration of my work in its earliest stages helped me subsequently to follow its implications more deliberately. Thanks go as well to Teolinda Barolini, Rachel Jacoff, Ronald Martinez, Leslie Moore, Barbara Mowat, and Joanna Weber.

## Works Cited

Alighieri, Pietro di Dante. *Petri Alleghierii super Dantis ipsius genitoris* Comoediam *commentarium*. Ed. Vincentio Nannucci. Florence, 1846.

Augustine. *City of God.* Trans. Henry Bettenson. Harmondsworth, Eng.: Penguin, 1972.

———. *De civitate Dei. Corpus Christianorum,* Series Latina 47–48. Brepols: Turnholt, 1955.

———. *De doctrina Christiana.* Corpus Christianorum Series Latina 32. Brepols: Turnholt, 1962.

———. *On Christian Doctrine.* Trans. D. W. Robertson, Jr. Indianapolis: Bobbs, 1958.

*Biblia Sacra iuxta vulgatam Clementiniam.* Ed. Alberto Colunga and Lorenzo Turrado. 5th ed. Madrid: Autores Cristianos, 1977.

Calcaterra, Carlo. "Sant' Agostino nelle opere di Dante e del Petrarca." *Rivista di filosofia neo-scolastica.* Spec. supp. to 23 (1931): 422–99. (Rpt. in *Nella selva del Petrarca.* Bologna: Capelli, 1942.)

Chiarenza, Marguerite Mills. "The Imageless Vision and Dante's *Paradiso.*" *Dante Studies* 90 (1972): 77–92.

Chioccioni, Pietro. *L'agostinismo nella* Divina commedia. Firenze: Olschki, 1952.

Cochrane, Charles Norris. *Christianity and Classical Culture.* Rev. ed. Oxford: Oxford UP, 1972.

Dante Alighieri. *Tutte le opere.* Firenze: Sansoni, 1981.

Davis, Charles Till. *Dante and the Idea of Rome.* Oxford: Clarendon-Oxford UP, 1957.

———. *"Dante's Italy" and Other Essays.* Philadelphia: U of Pennsylvania P, 1984.

Fallani, Giovanni. "Dante e S. Agostino." *L'esperienza teologica di Dante.* Lecce: Milella, 1976. 185–203.

Ferrante, Joan M. *The Political Vision of the* Divine Comedy. Princeton: Princeton UP, 1984.

Foster, Kenelm. "Dante's Vision of God." *Italian Studies* 14 (1959): 21–39.

Freccero, John, ed. *Dante: A Collection of Critical Essays.* Englewood Cliffs: Prentice, 1965.

———. *Dante: The Poetics of Conversion.* Ed. Rachel Jacoff. Cambridge: Harvard UP, 1986.

Gardner, Edmund G. *Dante and the Mystics.* London: Dent, 1913.

Gmelin, Hermann. *Dante,* Die Göttliche Komödie. Kommentar 2. Stuttgart: Klett, 1955.

Hawkins, Peter S. "Polemical Counterpoint in *De civitate Dei.*" *Augustinian Studies* 6 (1975): 97–106.

Lucan. *The Civil War.* Trans. J. D. Duff. Cambridge: Harvard UP, 1977.

Marti, Mario. *"Purgatorio,* XV." *Realismo dantesco.* Milano: Ricciardi, 1961. 63–79.

Martinez, Ronald L. "Dante, Statius, and the Earthly City." Diss. U of California, 1977.

Mazzeo, Joseph Anthony. *Structure and Thought in the* Paradiso. New York: Greenwood, 1968.

Mazzotta, Giuseppe. *Dante, the Poet of the Desert.* Princeton: Princeton UP, 1979.

Migne, J. P., ed. *Patrologiae cursus completus, series latina.* 221 vols. Paris, 1857–1912.

Moore, Edward. *Studies in Dante.* Ser. 1. New York: Greenwood, 1968.

Nardi, Bruno. *Il Canto XV del* Purgatorio. Roma: Dante, 1953.

Newman, Francis X. "St. Augustine's Three Visions and the Strucure of the *Commedia*." *MLN* 82 (1967): 56–78.

Pincherle, Alberto. "Agostino." *Enciclopedia dantesca*. Vol. 1. Roma: Fondazione enciclopedia dantesca, 1970. 80–82.

Rand, Edward Kennard. *Founders of the Middle Ages*. Cambridge: Harvard UP, 1929.

Sapegno, Natalino, ed. *La divina commedia*. By Dante. Vol. 2. Firenze: Nuova Italia, 1983.

Schnapp, Jeffrey T. *The Transfiguration of History at the Center of Dante's* Paradise. Princeton: Princeton UP, 1986.

Singleton, Charles S., ed. and trans. *The Divine Comedy*. By Dante. Bollingen Series 80. Princeton: Princeton UP, 1970–75.

Tonelli, Luigi. *Dante e la poesia del ineffabile*. Firenze: Barbera, 1934.

Toynbee, Paget. *A Dictionary of Proper Names and Notable Matters in the Works of Dante*. Rev. Charles S. Singleton. Oxford: Clarendon-Oxford UP, 1968.

Virgil. *Ecologues, Georgics, Aeneid*. Trans. H. R. Fairclough. Cambridge: Harvard UP, 1967.

# *Virtus*: Transition From Classical Latin to the *De Civitate Dei*†

## Penelope D. Johnson

After the sack of Rome by the Goths in 410, the pagan Roman aristocrats attributed the disaster to the infiltration into Roman life of the Christian religion. St. Augustine, Bishop of Hippo, responded to the challenge of these skeptics with a massive work that took thirteen years to write: *De civitate Dei*. In designing the model of the two cities, *civitas Dei* and *civitas terrena*, Augustine did not create a new terminology. He used Roman political words and ideas which he shaped to his needs injecting a new Christian sense when necessary. One such word which assumed an important role in his work, is *virtus*. The Augustinian use of *virtus* was affected by, but is subtly different from the classical use. I want to investigate the classical sense of *virtus* through the works of Cicero and Sallust and then examine the new form it takes in Augustine's hands.

*Virtus* did not derive from *vir*, man or warrior, as is often supposed. Rather, it had as its oldest meaning, "magic or miraculous power."[1] In old Latin three usages developed: valor and manliness, the fertility of the earth, and the good quality of merchandise. All three meanings derive from the basic sense of miraculous power. A warrior gains *mana* from the defeat of his enemies while the generative power of the soil and the inherent quality of merchandise to earn money all seem magical in a primitive society. In Later Latin, *virtus* came to mean valor, merit and the generalized energy necessary to achieve glory.

The Greek word, *arete*, was often used as a synonym by Latin authors and may have contributed to the growth of *virtus* its sense of moral, frugal and chaste behavior. As Roman society became more complex, *virtus*—the goal of its leaders—changed too. The vocabulary of an aggressive tribe had now to serve a rapidly expanding sophisticated state. By the second century B.C., *virtus* had become a specialized word associated with aristocratic success: the achievement of *gloria* by the *nobiles* in public service and military commands.[2] The thrust of the word had shifted from courage and skill on the battlefield to ability in public life.

Cicero used *virtus* in this classical sense, but as a word with two characters. It was a generic name used in the plural to include the four cardinal virtues. It was also a specific quality embracing within itself all the four virtues. In *De officiis*, Cicero not only discussed the intermingling of the four virtues but also the necessity of separating them for an investigation of the moral duties which originated in different aspects of virtue.[3]

*Virtus* was not judged by Cicero to be common to all men.[4] There were brave men and wise men; but to be a virtuous man all four virtues had to be present and in harmony in the individual. Consequently there were but few men who truly possessed *virtus*.[5] However, *virtus* was not an unattainable prize. It was within the grasp of all men, not just the *nobiles*. In fact, men were drawn naturally to seek *virtus*.[6] There was a *"necessitas virtutis"* in human nature.

For Cicero, *virtus* was like speech. Unless made operational it did not truly exist. It was a pragmatic not a theoretical quality. Often in his writing when Cicero lauded a man he coupled the words *virtus et industria* to emphasize the active aspects of *virtus*.[7] "Nec vero habere virtutem satis est quasi artem aliquam, nisi utare; etsi ars quidem, cum ea non utare, scientia tamen ipsa teneri potest, virtus in usu sui tota posita est; usus autem eius est maximus civitatis gubernatio et earum ipsarum rerum. . . ."[8]

The last sentence of this passage contains the heart of Cicero's definition of *virtus*. Not only was *virtus* a practical attribute that had to be put into action, but also it had to be employed in public service. His use of *virtus* is particularly striking in his historical narrative of the early years of Rome. Only Romulus and Lucius Brutus of all the early kings of Rome are described as having *virtus*. Romulus indeed was granted divinity at the time of his death for he was famous for his *virtus* and the founder of the state, while Lucius Brutus was also "vir ingenio et virtute praestans. . . ."[9]

Those who do great deeds in the service of the state thus have a divine aspect. Cicero included in his outline of the ideal religious law the provision that *virtus* should be worshipped as a divine quality.[10] There was indeed a temple to *Virtus* in Rome and according to Cicero it served as a reminder to all those who possessed *virtus* that a part of the divine was within them.[11]

Although clearly *virtus* bore rewards by promoting its practitioner to the leadership of the state, it was not to be sought for its benefits.[12] Philosophy and law could lead to *virtus*. However those who pursued *virtus* should do so not for rewards but for the pure sake of virtue itself.

In sum therefore, Cicero used *virtus* to mean an art possessed only by a few human beings which required constant exercise. This art was most fully creative in learning of and exercising itself in government. *Virtus* was to be sought for itself alone and those who most fully attained it were best fitted to govern. The elder Africanus told Scipio in the dream that closes *De republica* "ipsa virtus trahat ad verum decus . . . ."[13]

Cicero has been said to be one of the most influential men of his time. Consequently his handling of an important term affected its subsequent Latin usage. He was however one of the *novi homines* when they were but a small minority.  A younger contemporary of Cicero, who was "more truly representative of his times than any other whose work remains to us,"[14] was Sallust.

For Sallust, *virtus,* as expressed in the prologues of the *Bellum Catilinae* and the *Bellum Jugurthinum,* was of central importance to his historical analysis.  Sallust never used *virtus* in the plural.  Instead, he used the phrase, *bonae artes,* to cover the different aspects of *virtus;* and reserved *virtus* for a particular meaning, which (as in its Ciceronian usage) implied active involvement, and was still most appropriate in the political arena.  For though Sallust used *virtus* broadly in the two prologues, the bulk of both *Bella* deals with political *virtus.*

Professor Donald Earl defines the major difference between the *virtus* of the aristocratic tradition and that of Sallust as one of direction.[15]  Earl sees Sallust as shifting *virtus* from extroverted political activity to an introverted attention springing from each person's *ingenium.*  Earl also posits that the democratizing of *virtus* begun by Cicero was carried to its logical conclusion by Sallust.  Cicero had asserted that *virtus* was attainable by all men, and was not the sole province of the *nobiles.*  Sallust categorically stated that *virtus* could be achieved by any man regardless of his class through his own worthy actions.[16]

From the mid-third century B.C., *virtus* had included qualities of mind as well as of body.  The noble was to be *"fortis vir sapiensque,"* which Sallust reasserted in the prologue to the *Bellum Catilinae.*[17]  But later when he wrote the second *Bellum,* he placed greater emphasis on the mind as the reigning force which brought men to *virtus.*[18]  This increase in stress was probably due to the writer's growing need to defend his withdrawal from public life for the purpose of writing history.

Both *Bella* have as their central theme the corruption of the Roman state resulting from moral decay.  It was the decline of *virtus* that brought this on just as it had been *virtus* operating through a few outstanding citizens that had raised Rome to her greatness.  The decline occurred when citizens began to pursue wealth instead of *virtus.*  When *avaritia* and *ambitio* became motivating forces the state suffered woefully.  This deplorable state of affairs was described in a speech Sallust composed for Cato.  He described *ambitio* running amuck, setting men at each others throats, disrupting *concordia* and usurping the rewards of *virtus*: "sed alia fuere quae illos magnos fecere, quae nobis nulla sunt; domi industria, foris iustum imperium, animus in consulendo liber neque delicto neque lubidini obnoxius.  Pro his nos habemus luxuriam atque avaritiam, publice egestatem, privatim opulentiam.  Laudamus divitias, sequimur inertiam.  Inter bonos et malos discrimen nullum, omnia virtutis praemia ambitio possidet."[19]

Before the destruction of Carthage—the rather arbitrary juncture picked by Sallust to separate virtuous from decaying Rome—only a few of the *populus Romanus* possessed *virtus*. In his own day Sallust could name only two men of outstanding virtue: Marcus Cato and Gaius Caesar.[20] Yet his view of man was not totally negative. At the end of the *Bellum Catilinae*, Catiline exhorted his troops to fight valiantly and to die honored and avenged, for they were capable of possessing *virtus* at least in the manner of their dying.[21]

To sum up, *virtus* for Sallust was the central actress in the two dramas related in the *Bella*. Yet *virtus* was a tragic heroine, for both monographs illustrate her corruption into *ambitio* and the resultant decay of the Roman state. Sallust used *virtus* with great care, shearing off a portion of its traditional meanings by only using it in the singular. He also identified *virtus* as a quality of the intellect even more than of man's physical being. It was a mental approach to human situations that was learned, not innate. Sallustian *virtus* was attainable by men of all classes (though actually achieved by very few men), and could be utilized in all spheres. Its most appropriate stage was, however, political activity.

Augustine understood this classical usage of *virtus* and adjusted its political connotation for use in his two cities. He knew the writing of Cicero and Sallust and quoted them both extensively. Yet much as he admired their eloquence and intellectual power, he had to reject their paganism. In Book 19 he examined different philosophic views of the supreme good, but then dismissed the Roman classical formulations, "for we ought to form our judgment on the actual facts of the case, instead of attaching importance to knowing what any particular individual thought about them."[22] So Augustine worked a seachange by adopting *virtus* and giving it a new Christian sense and a crucial role in the *civitas Dei*. Augustine made three major changes: in the intention, the motivation and the goal of *virtus*.

The Augustinian definition of *virtus* shifted emphasis from the act to the intention.[23] Thus Augustine could reassure women raped during the sack of Rome that if a woman's mind were pure her virtue could not be touched by any violation of her body;[24] it was the purity of will and intention that mattered. If, however, a person secretly lusted for another but never acted on those feelings, he was just as guilty of unvirtuous behavior as if he had acted out his desires.

Augustine also fashioned a new motivation for *virtus*. Instead of being a worldly quality powered by the desire for success and prestige, new Christian *virtus* had love as its driving force. In Book Fifteen of *De civitate Dei* Augustine offered a "definitio brevis et vera," that *virtus* was *ordo amoris*, or "rightly ordered love": love directed wholly and unsparingly to God.[25] The direction of all human effort was to be away from the individual's self love outward to his Creator and Savior.

The final Augustinian addition to *virtus* was a change of goal as well as motivating force. No longer was *virtus* to help men to establish a blessed life on earth. For would it not be foolish to ascribe to human *virtus* the ability to eliminate illness, death, accidents and sorrow from life? The goal for virtus would be *beatitudo*, the utter bliss of eternal life. "Ipsa est enim beatitude finalis, ipse perfectionis finis, qui consumentem, non habet finem."[26]

Thus *virtus* for Augustine was a gift of God's grace to human beings. It was powered by love that sought to glorify God and was rewarded by *beatitudo*. It was judged by the sincerity of each man's inner intention to live correctly, not by his external acts.

In this Augustinian use of *virtus,* the Ciceronian and Sallustian political denotation seems entirely lost. I believe, however, that the political sense is not lost but submerged under the Christian renovation. Augustine accepted the Roman tradition according to which *virtus* was the compelling force by which the Roman state achieved greatness. As such, he incorporated *virtus* into *De civitate Dei.* In his construction of the model of the two cities, he juxtaposed pagan *virtus* in the *civitas terrena* to Christian *virtus*, or *ordo amoris*, in the *civitas Dei.* The citizens of the two cities used political tools to order their polities. The members of the *civitas terrena* strove for glorification of themselves and their state. They were: "Haec dicuntur adversariis civitatis Dei ad Babyloniam pertinentibus, de sua virtute praesumentibus, in se, non in Domino gloriantibus."[27] They had destroyed the right ordering of life by turning *virtus* inward. The citizens of the heavenly city, in contrast, must use their political *virtus* to advance their state towards eternal felicity. This difference in ordering and directing *virtus* grew out of Augustine's conviction that obedience was the fundamental ground of all virtuous behavior.[28] Citizens of the heavenly city must seek to know God's will and conform to it. The antagonist to obedience was pride—the nurturing sin for secular, Roman *virtus.* Pride was at the root of Roman civic success and had caused man, since Adam, to use his free will sinfully.[29]

Roman *virtus* was conceded by Augustine to have some passive value as it repressed worse vice.[30] Also the glories of pagan Rome had an active role in God's master plan. Members of the *civitas Dei* could learn from examples of Roman, civic patriotism, emulating such loyalty but directing it towards the heavenly city.[31] Humility as well could be learned by Christians when considering the heights to which pagans had risen without the benefits of the teaching and example of Christ.[32] How much greater could be their self-sacrifice and total commitment with the grace of God?

The growth of the Pelagian controversy demanded clear rebuttal from Augustine. Sometime in 413 or 414 Pelagius had written a letter to the widow

Demetrias in which he urged her to believe in the individual's ability to achieve inner spiritual heights. As proof he used examples of pagans who had achieved *virtus* without God's grace.[33] This coupled with other Pelagian writing was oil to Augustine's flames. Towards the end of 417, in Book Ten Augustine responded with a "hard line" position in which he sought to expose the errors of Pelagianism and the pagan philosophical ideas which had nourished it. For Augustine had come to realize that even though the Pelagians believed in an immortal soul and the advent of *beatitudo* from God, they fell into error by denying the necessity of grace. In so doing they failed to realize true Christian *virtus* which is a gift of God's grace.

In Book Nineteen Augustine specifically rejected as *virtus* any quality not directed to God: "Nam qualis corporis atque vitiorum potest esse mens domina veri Dei nescia nec eius imperio subiugata, sed vitiosissimus daemonibus corrumpentibus prostituta? Proinde virtutes, quas habere sibi videtur, per quas imperat corpori et vitiis, ad quodlibet adipscendum vel tenendum rettulerit nisi ad Deum, etiam ipsae vitia sunt potius quam virtutes."[34]

Was Augustine urging *virtus* as a Christian goal in itself? Not at all, although *virtus* was a learned art at which men had to work. "Praemium virtutis erit ipse, qui virtutem dedit eique se ipsum, quo melius et maius nihil possit esse, promisit . . . ipse finis erit desideriorum nostrorum, qui sine fine videbitur, sine fastidio amabitur, sine fatigatione laudabitur. Hoc munus, hic affectus, hic actus profecto erit omnibus, sicut ipsa vita aeterna, communis."[35] God is truly our goal.

Augustinian *virtus* would destroy the patterns of hierarchy and dominance which mishaped earthly politics; pride would go. The new *virtus* would fashion a state motivated by a common purpose to attain godliness. With this new understanding human beings could reach the eternal kingdom: "Nam quis alius noster est finis nisi pervenire ad regnum, cuius nullus est finis?"[36]

Thus *virtus* had travelled from its earliest sense of "miraculous power" through a transmutation where first warrior ability and then political achievement were regarded by the Romans as the highest goals. When Augustine structured his two cities he employed this word in a way that somewhat recaptured its earliest meaning. In the *De civitate Dei, virtus* became a divine gift through grace to men. This gift was moved by love to return its practitioner to God as the final reward. As Augustinian *virtus* had both a divine origin and a divine goal, "miraculous power" was again functioning in it. Augustine's eclecticism had been unwittingly true to the origin of one of its Roman terms. Or perhaps Augustine, "one of the richest minds of Christian antiquity"[37] was wielding his tools with greater precision and knowledge of proper ancient usage than we expect. Whatever the conscious intention, *virtus* in *De civitate Dei* echoed its earliest meaning, and gave to the Christian vocabulary of the Middle Ages, *virtus* as *ordo amoris*.

# Notes

†Reprinted by permission of the publisher from *Augustinian Studies* 6 (1975): 117–24.

[1] A. N. Van Omme, "Virtus" *Een Semantiese Studie* (Utrecht n.d.), 109–10. Although *virtus* is related to *vir* it is not, according to Van Omme, etymologically derived from it. E. Badian, *Roman Imperialism in the Late Republic* (Ithaca 1968), 12. Badian also suggested that *virtus* may have originally carried the meaning of undifferentiated *mana*.

[2] D. Earl, *The Moral and Political Tradition of Rome* (London 1967), 22–6. Also see Badian, *op. cit.* 12–5.

[3] Cicero, *De officiis* 1.5

[4] Cicero, *De re publica* 1.34.

[5] Cicero, *De legibus* 1.10.

[6] Cic. *rep.* 1.1.

[7] Cicero, 2 *Actio in Verrem* 3.4, 5.71. Also see Cicero, *Epistolae ad familiares* 5.17; Cic. *rep.* 1.1.

[8] Cic. rep. 1.2. Laelius in *De re publica* claimed that the acquiring of political skill was "the highest duty of virtue." Cic. *rep.* 1.20.

[9] Cic. *rep.* 2.10, 2.25.

[10] Cic. *leg.* 2.8.

[11] Cic. *leg.* 2.11.

[12] Cic. *off.* 2.5. It is "the peculiar function of *virtus* to win the hearts of men and to attach them to one's own service." Attractive as these fruits of *virtus* appear, they should not be pursued for themselves. Also see Cic. *rep.* 3.28; Cic. *leg.* 1.18.

[13] Cic. *rep.* 6.23.

[14] D. Earl, *The Political Thought of Sallust* (Cambridge 1961), 121.

[15] *Ibid.* 30, 111.

[16] Sallust, *Bellum Jugurthinum* 85.38. Both Catiline and Marius were made to say that eloquent speeches would not imbue an audience with *virtus*. Rather clever planning, hard work and positive reinforcement served to train men in *virtus*. Sallust, *Bellum Catilinae* 58.1; Sal. *B.J.* 85.50, 87 1–3.

[17] Earl, *The Political Thought of Sallust*, 22. Also see Sal. *B.C.* 1.5–7.

[18] Sal. *B.C.* The mind "quo neque melius neque amplius aliud in natura mortalium est . . ." Sal. *B.J.* 2.4.

[19] Sal. *B.C.* 52.22.

[20] *Ibid.* 53.6.

[21] *Ibid.* 58.21.

[22] Augustine, *De civitate Dei*, 19.3.

[23] J. Wang Tchang-Tche, *Saint Augustin et les vertus des paiens* (Paris 1938), 8.

[24]Aug. *De civ.* 1.18.

[25]*Ibid.* 15.22.

[26]*Ibid.* 19.10.

[27]*Ibid.* 17.4.

[28]*Ibid.* 14.12.

[29]*Ibid.* 21.16.

[30]*Ibid.* 5.13.  Also see Cic. *rep.* 5.7.

[31]Aug. *De civ.* 5.16.

[32]*Ibid.* 5.18.

[33]Tchang-tche, *op. cit.* 109.

[34]Aug. *De civ.* 19.25.

[35]*Ibid.* 22.30.

[36]*Ibid.*

[37]Jeremy Adams, *The Populus of Augustine and Jerome: A Study in the Patristic Sense of Community* (New Haven 1971), 68.

# Language Theory and Narrative Patterning in *De Civitate Dei*, Books XV–XVIII†

## Phillip Pulsiano

After a detailed and somewhat labored discussion of metrics, Augustine's *De musica* unexpectedly yields in its final book a rhetoric of music that binds both language theory and narrative structure and that functions as an analogy for the limitations of human perception as it struggles to comprehend, however feebly, the nature of the divine. If the first five books can be said to offer a microcosmic view of the temporal and sequential patterning of utterances—here encapsulated in the length of the metrical foot or the sounding of syllables or notes—the final book shifts the discussion to a macrocosmic plane: the *discipulus*, now brought to understand the sequential nature of the thing sounded, "the first [sounds] by disappearing, give place to the second, the second to the third,"[1] comprehends as well the gulf that separates human and divine. "Likewise, a vital movement measures off and precedes these as they move in time-spans, a vital movement serving the Master of all things, having in its numbers no temporal spans divided out, but with a power providing times" (VI.17[58]). The point is passionately reiterated in Augustine's commentary on Psalm 76:

> While I am uttering syllables, if I shall speak two syllables, the latter does not sound until the former has gone by: in a word, in that same one syllable, if it chance to have two letters, the latter letter does not sound until the former has gone by. What then have we got of these years? These years are changeable: the eternal years must be thought on, years that stand, that are not made up of days that come and depart.[2]

It is in the silence of the soul that eternity is to be contemplated: "What are eternal years? It is a mighty thought. See whether this thought requires anything but great silence. Apart from all noise without, from all tumult of things human let him remain quiet within, that would think of those eternal years" (Ps. 76.7). The physical and temporal nature of music, like speech, functions as an analogy in Augustine's charter for the historical and temporal movement of all humankind; and like music and speech, time, too, is punctuated by those silences in which eternity is contemplated, in which, more pointedly, the ineluctable movement of the temporal is set aside and the Interior Teacher illumines the soul.[3] In those moments most especially, when human speech falls silent and the constancy of the Word is sounded within, there is established a bridge linking human and divine—a dialogue in silence where language, music, history, and time come into perspective as pale adumbrations of a greater truth and mystery.

The concern with language and narrative as syntactic structures of meaning at once temporally bound and yet atemporal as they urge their way toward signifying the divine provides a model for examining what we may call the rhetoric of narrative in Augustine's final and most comprehensive work, *De civitate Dei*, and particularly in Books XV–XVIII.[4] The formal structure of the narrative comprising these books is simple enough, and Augustine provides a summary at the beginning of Book XVIII: Book XV focuses on the period from Adam to the Flood; "[a]fter that the two cities proceeded on their course in our narrative, just as they did in history, down to the time of Abraham . . . [and] the kings of Israel" (Book XVI), "and from then to the coming of the incarnate Saviour" (Book XVII). Where Books XV–XVII are concerned with the progress of the city of God, Book XVIII turns to treat of the earthly city.   But although Augustine patterns his narrative on the incremental movement of historical event, he establishes a metahistorical narrative in tracing the progress of the two cities. George J. Lavere argues that the literary structure of the work "pivots upon the symbolic and metaphorical use of this notion of the 'two cities.' A purely literal reading would miss the whole point of the work."[5] The term "metaphor," however, may misrepresent the force of Augustine's treatment of the dual narratives unless it is understood to mean that one reality (the historical narrative, traditionally understood) reflects still another independent reality (the metahistorical narrative).  Where the historical narrative is marked by intervals of time, the metahistorical narrative may be expressed syntactically or paratactically, and may move freely between the literal and the symbolic or allegorical.  Although both narratives, of necessity, are revealed through a process of temporal unfolding in their telling, the metahistorical narrative actually exists outside of time in the eternity that is God.  The problem for Augustine resides in locating the vehicle that will allow him to express both narratives simultaneously as realities and to speak of their relationship in terms that make both comprehensible.  That vehicle, of course, is found in the redeemed rhetoric made possible through the Incarnation of Christ.  As Marcia Colish succinctly states: "God creates the world and man through his Word, and he takes on humanity in the Word made flesh so that human words may take on divinity, thereby bringing man and the work back to God."[6] The implication of the statement is that through the Incarnation language now has the potential to signify a reality beyond itself when brought into dynamic relationship with God.[7]

The problem of providing concrete illustration of such constructs pervades, even guides, the whole of *De civitate Dei*, but takes on added force in Augustine's discussion of language as a vehicle for asserting the reality of the dual narratives of the earthly city and the City of God, the latter itself a reflection of still another reality, the Heavenly City. Augustine returns repeatedly to the question of the authority of the written or spoken word in his discussion of the Hebrew, Greek, and Latin translations of Scripture (e.g., XV.10–14, XVI.11, XVIII.41–44). If these translations reflect divine communication, and if language can adumbrate higher realities, how does one account for the discrepancies that exist among these translations, especially, as Augustine states, "if the divergence is such as to preclude the possibility that [these] versions are true" (XV.14)? If the authority of these texts is undermined, so also is the authority of Augustine's text, for the (meta)history he presents depends exclusively upon scriptural history. The observation assists in explaining what may at first appear to be Augustine's pedantic treatment of such issues as whether Adam lived 700 years (as in Augustine's Latin text) or 800 years (as in the Hebrew), or whether or not Methuselah survived after the Flood another fourteen years (the subject of XV.11 and 13). Augustine adduces, first of all, that while the Hebrew text reckons its years differently than in the Latin the total is always the same in both cases. Yet, the mysterious fourteen years of Methuselah's life poses problems of a different sort, for none of the versions agree on this account; and as the Latin text is a translation of the Septuagint, which in turn is a translation of the Hebrew, such a seemingly minor discrepancy can nevertheless erode scriptural authority. In response, Augustine establishes two points, the first concerning textual transmission, the second (which he defers until Book XVIII) concerning textual interpretation. He considers in the first instance the possibility that there was a mistake made on the part of the Greek translators (XV.11); but seventy(-two) translators recording the same error suggests, rather, a defective exemplar (XV.13). Nevertheless, discrepancies exist that cannot be accounted for by recourse to the notion of a faulty exemplar. To this, Augustine responds: "where it is not a question of an error of transcription, and where the sense would be in harmony with the truth and would proclaim the truth, we should believe that under the influence of the divine Spirit the seventy chose to express the meaning differently, not in fulfillment of their task as translators but in the exercise of their liberty as prophets" (XV.14). Having answered questions of textual transmission and interpretation, Augustine can proceed later to link the work of the translators with the Spirit of God operating within:

> The tradition is that the agreement in the words of their versions was marvellous, amazing, and plainly inspired by God: so much so that although each of them sat in a separate place when they engaged on their task . . . they did not differ from one another in a single word, not even by a synonym

conveying the same meaning; they did not even vary in the order of words. There was such unity in their translations that it was as if there had been one translator; for in truth there was the one Spirit at work in them all. And this was the purpose of their receiving such a marvellous gift of God; that in this way the authority of those Scriptures should be emphasized, as being not human but divine.                                                                (XVIII.42)

In this way, Augustine is thus able to establish the authority of his texts—despite their apparent discrepancies—on both a literal-historical and interpretive plane, strengthened by a textual tradition of multiple independent witnesses. More importantly, Augustine is able to demonstrate that the seeming multiplicity of texts reflects nevertheless a single text (albeit transmitted through time). If words (and texts) are signs of the Word, in Augustine's charter, then the imperative is to move beyond the multiplicity of words to the single Word and thus closer to truth. And so Augustine in his narrative begins a process of "narrowing" until, eventually, the single Word remains as the crucial link between historical and metahistorical, between temporal and atemporal, between that which is expressed as a series of syntactical utterances in points of time and that which expresses its totality as pure esssence.[8]

Thus it is that references to Babylon and the Tower of Babel form an important part of Augustine's narrative in Book XVI where they act to frame the discussion of God's mode of speech with the angels and the primacy of Hebrew as the one language common to humankind before its splintering into diverse tongues. In Book XI.6 of *Confessiones*, Augustine comments on what Jesse M. Gellrich refers to as "self-differentiating" language (what Margaret Ferguson earlier treated under the rubric "region of unlikeness).[9] In considering the question of how God spoke the creating act ("This is my beloved Son"), Augustine begins first with the external reception of the word: "The syllables were sounded and they passed away, the second after the first, the third after the second, and the rest in order, until the last one came after all the others, and silence after the rest."[10] But such knowledge of the eternal Word, filtered, as it is, through temporality and the flesh, provides imperfect knowledge based on a "fallen" epistemology. While the outer ear receives the spoken word, the inner ear of the mind, however, senses the gulf separating human comprehension and divine utterance: "Then the mind compared these words sounding in time with your eternal Word in its silence, and said, 'It is far different; it is far different'" (XI.6). The discussion of pre- and post-Babelic language in this context becomes a demonstration of just how different the divine Word is from human language. After citing the relevant passages from *Genesis*, Augustine explains, "Since a ruler's power of domination is wielded by his tongue, it was in that organ that his pride was condemned to punishment. . . . Such was God's design; and he achieved it by ways that are to us inscrutable and incomprehensible" (XVI.4). In typical fashion, Augustine counterpoises human and divine, with language mediating between both camps. While the course of human history narrates, in the earthly city, a movement away from God into multiplicity and subsequent confusion, Augustine's carefully structured metahistorical narrative depicts a movement away from multiplicity toward the single utterance of that which is "far different" from historical narrative. It is through the tongue of the earthly adversary that punishment is meted out; it is through the "tongue" of God that Word is expressed: the one resides in time and moves further into multiplicity, the other resides in eternity and expresses its "oneness" as undefiled essence.

The point is pressed further by Augustine as he turns immediately to consider the mode of God's speech with the angels: "And God does not speak to the angels in the same way we speak to one another, or to God, or to the angels, or as angels speak to us. He speaks in his own fashion, which is beyond our describing. But his speech is explained to us in our fashion" (XVI.6). God's "own fashion" has "no sound, no transitory noise; it has a power that persists for eternity and operates in time." The forceful contrast with Babylon now opens the door to exploring that speech which is "far different" and which can be grasped but palely "with our inner ears" in the stillness of silence. Augustine thus patterns his narrative by way of contrast, with narrative blocks clearly set against one another in an effort to relate his dual narratives. With striking fluidity, Augustine establishes both narratives within the temporal framework (by the simple function of their being related through speech), but where the historical narrative increasingly ensconces itself more firmly within the temporal, syntactic process of consecutive moments, the metahistorical narrative struggles to move beyond the temporal expression toward the expressive and creative stillness of the Word. Hence Augustine's discussion of the mode of speech of the angels, although marked by the realization and frustration that it is "beyond our describing." The process of narrowing continues into XVI.11, in which Augustine recalls the image of Babylon and the existence of a single language before the Flood, contrasting that language, Hebrew, with the "multiplication and change of languages [that] came by way of punishment." Multiplicity in speech, whether of languages or of syllables, marks differentiation from God. Yet, while the pilgrims in the City of God proceed through the temporal process, the movement paradoxically mirrors a potential return to the One. Similarly, the movement of Augustine's narrative through time, syntax, and multiplicity paradoxically moves him closer to comprehending the eternal moment of the creating silence of the Word.

This movement toward the Word through a process of narrowing marks Augustine's extended discussion of the psalms in Book XVII.8–20. As a preliminary to the discussion, Augustine establishes in clear terms the framework or, more precisely, the conclusion toward which his narrative at this stage is directed, namely the significance of the Incarnation and its consequences for language and, ultimately, knowledge of the divine:

> The truth is that when God speaks through the mouth of a man he speaks in human fashion; for he uses the same way of speaking when he "seeks" us. The only-begotten Son came "to seek what was lost," although we were already so well-known to him, as well as to God the Father, that we were "chosen in him before the foundation of the world."                                                     (XVII.6)

From the stock of David the psalmist, we are told, "the mediator between God and men, the man Christ Jesus" (XVII.7) made a physical descent into the flesh. The introduction of the psalmist recalls us to the final book of Augustine's *De musica*, for in David, music, in the service of faith, "suggests the unity of a well-ordered city, welded together in harmonious variety" (XVII.14). Yet here music presses beyond temporal constraints to aspire to the abstract dimension of the poetic. The very fact that in the music and poetry of the psalms can be heard the words of Christ (for example, in Psalm 89, to which Augustine devotes chapters 9–10) through the intermediary David imparts to both a dimension that allows them to aspire to an order beyond the temporal. Hence the significance of Augustine's introduction of the Incarnation at this point in the narrative: through Christ the Word made flesh, music, poetry, and language are redeemed from the perversity and frailty of human utterance so that, as Marcia Colish writes, "man may receive the power to share in the life of God in and through the conditions of temporal existence."[11] In his role as intermediary for the Mediator, David, in essence, becomes a poet of rectitude and thus draws Augustine closer to that still-point that is the Word.

Augustine's response to the art of poetry adds yet another dimension of complexity. Earlier in *De civitate Dei*, he addresses the notion of antithesis operating within the universe. For Augustine, this idea is reflected in the larger patterns of historical movement, in which there can be seen a certain "beauty in the composition of the world's history arising from the antithesis of contraries—a kind of eloquence in events" (XI.18). This harmonious opposition within the temporal narrative Augustine sees as analogous to the "kind of antithesis that gives beauty to a poem" and that gives "an added beauty to speech" generally. But not any poetry can stand as part of the analogy. The so-called "theological poets," for instance, the subject of XVIII.14, offer a type of poetry that is but "frivolous lies" in praise of many gods, among which is numbered the one God. As such, their poetry stands at the same level as the "sweetly deceptive" fictions about which Augustine speaks in *Confessiones* (I.14). In contrast is found the art of the psalmist David, "a man who loved the harmony of music":

> But David was not the ordinary man for whom music is merely for pleasure; for it served the purpose of his faith. He used it in the service of his God, the true God, by giving a mystical prefiguration of a matter of high importance. For the concord of different sounds, controlled in due proportion, suggests the unity of a well-ordered city, welded together in harmonious variety.
>
> (XVII.14)

The music and poetry of David thus functions to mediate the Word and to reflect in their art the concord of the "well-ordered city" of God on its pilgrimage toward the divine center. It is such art, then, that provides a link between temporal and eternal, but only because the incarnate Word makes such mediation possible. Within this context can be placed Augustine's own poetic composition in Book XV.22, which appears also as the opening hexameters of *De anima*:

> These are thy gifts; they are good, for thou in thy
> goodness has made them.
> Nothing in them is from us, save for sin when,
> neglectful of order,
> We fix our love on the creature, instead of on thee
> the Creator.

Like David, Augustine becomes a poet of rectitude, casting his art in "the service of his God," himself becoming a mediator of the Word.

Where earlier, in Book XV, Augustine sought to establish the textual basis for scriptural authority as a foundation for the authority of his own narrative displayed through subsequent books, by the conclusion of Book XVII and the introduction of Book XVIII, that authority, now secured by the Word, gains assertive power when set against "false" narratives. In other words, in his treatment of pagan authorities, Augustine initially proceeded along rather cautious lines, showing due regard, even in his refutation, for Varro (e.g., VI.5ff.), pagan mythology (e.g., VI.7ff., VII.1–28), Virgil (e.g., XV.8), the Platonists (IX.16, X.1–3, 23ff.), and the like, while throughout punctuating his discussion with reference to the Mediator as the avenue to knowledge of God (e.g., IX.15, X.32, XI.2, etc.).

By Book XVIII, however, having demonstrated the textual authority of Scripture, Augustine proceeds swiftly to focus his discussion on Christ the

Word incarnate. With the Word now firmly secured at the center of authority within the narrative, Augustine can let out all stops, so to speak, in countering and dismissing other "authorities." The Word, in effect, empowers him to assert its primacy over competing false doctrines and narratives; it provides him with the authoritative voice that will permit no rebuttal.

Augustine begins Book XVIII with a discussion of the rulers of the earthly city from the time of Abraham, a history that is early marked by various cults established in the worship of deified mortals. Then begins a clear pattern that occupies chapters 1–26 whereby historical periods marked by the births and deaths of kings are punctuated by accounts of false philosophies, cults, fantastic fables, deification of particular individuals, and so on. The structure of the narrative can be set forth as follows:

1–7 kings up to Joseph's death

        8–10 establishment of cults; Varro

11 kings up to the death of Joshua

        12 cult of the false gods in Greece
        13 pagan fables
        14 the "theological" poets

15 fall of the Argive kingdom

        16 Deification of Diomede

        17–18 Varro's account of incredible
        transformations of humans

20–22 regnal succession in Israel,
kings of Latium, foundation of Rome

23 Erythracean Sibyl and prophecies
of Christ

        24 Seven Sages, Romulus deified

26 end of Jewish captivity

In this section of the narrative, Augustine works with less tolerance to render the opposition impotent: Varro, we are told, stubbornly and contradictorily "refuses to give credence to fantastic fables which dishonour the gods" and yet includes in his history the lawsuit of Neptune against Minerva (XVIII.11); the tales of false gods propagated by the cults are ridiculed as entertainments suited to poets and theaters (12), while of "fable-mongers" we are told: "words fail to express what a low opinion these fable-mongers must have formed of human nature to assume that men could endure such lies with patience" (13). The "theological" poets likewise delude others with their "frivolous lies" in numbering the true God among the gods they worship (14); accounts of Saturn are "to be regarded as poetic fictions" (15); the transformation of Diomede's companion into birds is reduced to "a baseless poetic fantasy" (17) akin to Varro's "equally incredible tales" about Circe (17). In all, asserts Augustine, such tales and practices are put forward "so that men should worship many false gods and thus insult the one true God" (18).

The prophecies of the Erythraean Sibyl (XVIII.23) mark a change in the narrative strategy, which Augustine now directs toward asserting the primacy of Christ the Word. Whereas in the narrative documenting the reigns of kings and the authority of pagan beliefs, the emphasis rests solidly upon the historical, here Augustine begins to draw together the historical and metahistorical narratives, with Christ as the bridge. From the prophecies of the Sibyl about Christ, Augustine moves to the prophecies of Hosea and Amos (XVIII.28), to those of Isaiah (29), to those of Micah, Jonah, and Joel (30), of Obadiah, Nahum, and Habbakuk (31–32), of Jeremiah and Sephaniah (33), of Daniel and Ezekiel (34), of Haggai, Zechariah, and Malachi (35), and of Esdras (36). Augustine thus collapses time into a sustained burst of prophetic utterances that draws to a climax in XVIII.46, which begins with a simple statement: "Christ was born"; prophecy is shown to be fulfilled, and equally important, its authority and its position as antedating pagan philosophy is attested by fact.

Before proceeding to the central chapter 46, however, Augustine once again takes up the issue of the authority of the scriptural textual tradition. Where in Book XV Augustine was concerned with establishing that authority against detractors who, in their defense, cited the disagreements among the versions, here Augustine proceeds from the vantage point of having proven the validity of the documents as the inspired word and thus in Book XVIII uses this now established authority as a means of confirming the falsehood of those narratives that fail to conform to narrative of scriptural history:

> Moreover, the citizens of the irreligious city, who have spread all over the world, read authors of the profoundest erudition, and see no reason for rejecting the authority of any of them. . . . In contrast, we can place our reliance on the inspired history belonging to our religion and consequently have no hesitation in treating as utterly false anything which fails to conform to it, no matter what may be the position of the other works of secular literature which, whether true or false, offer nothing of value to help us to a life of righteousness and felicity.                                    (XVIII.40)

In adopting this stance, Augustine reasserts the validity of both the historical (scriptural) narrative and the metahistorical narrative that is predicated on the Word at the same time that he divorces his own narrative from those of his predecessors who did not have access to the inspired word. God spoke through the true prophets and through the translators of the Septuagint (XVIII.43), and although his words are conveyed by mortals, they are divine words, the "utterance of God" (XVIII.41). Augustine is thus able to assert confidently that there is a language, made possible through inspiration and, later, through the Incarnation, that supersedes the language of the earthly city and that can signify a reality beyond itself (as opposed to the fictions generated by other writers). From this vantage point, Augustine comes as close as possible within his own temporally-bound narrative to expressing the dual realities simultaneously. The multiplicity of historical events, so clearly marked at the beginning of Book XVIII, now yields to the single encompassing Word, mirrored in the gift of tongues to the Apostles:

> Ten days after that [i.e., the resurrection] he sent the Holy Spirit he had promised; and the greatest and most unmistakable sign of the Spirit's coming to those who believed was that every one of them spoke in the languages of all nations; thus signifying that the unity of the Catholic Church would exist among all nations and would thus speak in all languages.          (XVIII.49)

What began in Book XVI.4 as a diversity of mutually unintelligible languages as a result of the building of the Tower of Babel is here expressed as a unity of mutually intelligible languages made possible by "the Mediator who sets men free" (XVIII.51).

Augustine concludes his narrative by projecting it through time to consider the Church militant: "In this wicked world, and in these evil times, the Church through her present humiliation is preparing for future exaltation" (XVIII.49). Yet, it is a history that will be marked by the coming of the Antichrist, who will be defeated by Christ: "This last persecution . . . which will be inflicted by Antichrist will be extinguished by Jesus himself, present in person. For the Scripture says that 'he will kill him with the breath of his mouth and annihilate him by the splendour of his coming'" (XVIII.53). In projecting future events, Augustine reestablishes the temporal movement of the narrative to come while at the same moment deferring to the unknowable of the eternal mind; on the question of when the "last persecution" will come, he can only say: "But the question is completely ill-timed. For had it been in our interest to know this, who could have been a better informant than the master God himself, when his disciples asked him?" (XVIII.53).

The narrative structure of Books XV–XVIII of *De civitate Dei* stands as complex framework for the theoretical problems Augustine examines. But the stillness of the single utterance toward which language and narrative aspires is not to be realized within the confines of *De civitate Dei*. In this enterprise, the gulf that separates the words sounding in time from the eternal word remains forcefully present, underscored, as it is, by the unfolding of the narrative of history, like Augustine's own narrative, within the temporal confines in which the earthly city exists and through which the City of God makes its pilgrimage. Confronted with this limitation of human perspective, Augustine nevertheless applies his narrative to the expression of both these realities: that of human history temporally and syntactically expressed and marked by multiplicity and that which is divine, eternal, and expressed as a single utterance of pure essence. The point of contact—the bridge spanning the gulf—resides in the Word made of flesh. The illustration of these dual realities and the attendant problems that bear on language inform and guide Augustine's narrative strategy. In broad terms, Augustine begins with a statement on the dual narratives he has set as a task for himself to depict (XV.1), then turns to establish the validity and authority of the seemingly divergent scriptural texts (XV.10ff.) and from this vantage point examines the contrary modes of speech, the first as a consequence of the Tower of Babel, the second illustrated in a discussion of God's mode of speech with the angels (XVI). Having now opened the way to a consideration of the distance between human and divine speech, Augustine begins a process of "narrowing," working through a discussion of the psalms (XVII) and arriving, at Book XVIII, at a point at which the disparities between the human history and divine metahistory and between human language and divine language are made starkly clear; where earlier in the narrative the distance between these extremes may not have seemed too great, thus allowing the reader the luxury of defending the authority of the earthly city and of challenging contrary views, by Book XVIII, any defense is vitiated, and Augustine quickly and powerfully reasserts the authority of scriptural history and the validity of the true God while at the same moment confirming how "far different" is that which pertains to the divine.

# Notes

†New essay written especially for this collection.

[1] Augustine, *De musica* VI.4. Trans. Robert Catesby Taliaferro. *Writings of Saint Augustine*. New York: Cima Publishing, 1947, 330.

[2] Augustine, *Ennarationes in psalmos*, Ps. 77.7 [76.7]. Trans. Philip Schaff. *Saint Augustin: Expositions on the Book of Psalms*. New York: Christian Literature Co., 1888, 362–63.

[3] See Marcia L. Colish, "St. Augustine's Rhetoric of Silence Revisited," *Augustinian*

*Studies* 9 (1978): 15–24; Joseph A. Mazzeo, "St. Augustine's Rhetoric of Silence," *Journal of the History of Ideas* 23 (1962): 175–96; V. Capánaga, "El silencio interior en la visión augustiniana de Ostia," *Studia Patristica* 9 (1966): 359–92.

[4]Augustine, *The City of God*. Trans. Henry Bettenson. New York: Penguin, 1972; reference is made throughout to book and chapter number.

[5]"Metaphor and Symbol in St. Augustine's *De civitate Dei*." In *Collectanea Augustiniana*. Ed. Joseph C. Schnaubelt and Frederick Van Fleteren. New York: Peter Lang, 1990. Pp. 225–243, at p. 226.

[6]*The Mirror of Language: A Study in the Medieval Theory of Knowledge*. Lincoln: U. of Nebraska, 1968, rev. ed. 1983, 26.

[7]Studies treating Augustine's theory of language, particularly in *De doctrina christiana and Confessiones*, are numerous, while those focusing on *De civitate Dei* are surprisingly few in number. Of interest are: R. A. Markus, "St. Augustine on Signs," *Phronesis* 2 (1957): 60–83; rpt. in *Augustine: A Collection of Critical Essays*. Ed. R. A. Markus. New York: Anchor Books, 1972, 61–91; B. Darrell Jackson, "The Theory of Signs in St. Augustine's *De Doctrina Christiana*," *Revue des Études augustiniennes* 15 (1969): 9–49; rpt. in *Augustine: A Collection of Critical Essays*, 92–147; Margaret W. Ferguson, "Saint Augustine's Region of Unlikeness: The Crossing of Exile and Language," *The Georgia Review* 29 (1975): 842–64; Ralph Flores, "Reading and Speech in St. Augustine's *Confessions*," *Augustinian Studies* 6 (1975): 1–13; Mark D. Jordan, "Words and Word: Incarnation and Signification in Augustine's *De Doctrina Christiana*," *Augustinian Studies* 11 (1980): 177–96; Marcia L. Colish, "The Stoic Theory of Verbal Signification and the Problem of Lies and False Statements from Antiquity to St. Anselm." *Archéologie du signe*. Ed. Lucie Brind'Amour and Eugene Vance. Toronto: Pontifical Institute of Mediaeval Studies, 1983, 17–43; Tzvetan Tordorov, "A propos de la conception augustinienne du signe," *Revue des études augustiniennes* 31 (1985): 209–14; Eugene Vance, *Mervelous Signals: Poetics and Sign Theory in the Middle Ages*. Lincoln: U. of Nebraska, 1986, esp. ch. 2, "Saint Augustine: Language as Temporality," 34–50; L. G. Kelley, "St. Augustine's Theories of the Linguistic Sign and the *grammatica speculativa* of the Thirteenth Century," *Studia Patristica* 16 (1975): 517–23; Edwin D. Craun, "'Verbum Nuncius est Rationis': Augustinian Sign Theory in Medieval Pastoral Discourse on Deviant Speech," *Augustinian Studies* 20 (1989): 143–64; see also note 1.

[8]See in this connection the important article by Margaret W. Ferguson, "Saint Augustine's Region of Unlikeness: The Crossing of Exile and Language," *op. cit.*, n. 4; of interest also is Eugene Vance, *Mervelous Signals: Poetics and Sign Theory in the Middle Ages*, *op. cit.* n. 4, and Danne W. Polk, "Temporal Impermanence and the Disparity of Time and Eternity," *Augustinian Studies* 22 (1991): 63–82.

[9]Jesse M. Gellrich, *The Idea of the Book in the Middle Ages: Language Theory, Mythology, and Fiction*. Ithaca: Cornell U., 1985, 119–20; for Ferguson, see note 4 above.

[10]John K. Ryan, trans. *The Confessions of St. Augustine*. New York: Image Books, 1960, 282.

[11]*The Mirror of Language*, 30.

# More's *Utopia* and *The City of God*†

# Martin N. Raitiere

Thomas More "read for a good space a public lecture of St. Augustine, *De civitate Dei*, in the Church of St. Lawrence in the Old Jewry" shortly after his appointment about 1501 as Utter Barrister in Lincoln's Inn.[1] Stapleton tells us that More's lectures did not treat *The City of God* "from the theological point of view, but from the standpoint of history and philosophy;"[2] but Stapleton is relatively late (1588), and it is unclear whether he was rather inferring from More's situation as a layman and a common lawyer than speaking out of any real knowledge of the content of More's lectures. The lectures are not extant, but Stapleton's report together with the humanists' anti-intellectualistic bias helps to shape conjecture on their character; Chambers thought they "may have embodied some of the criticism of social evils which More later put into *Utopia*."[3]

That these lectures are not extant does not preclude, in fact, it may encourage, that study of the influence of *The City of God* on *Utopia* which Father Surtz believes "much to be desired."[4] Father Surtz enumerates a number of possible connections between the two works, but finally characterizes the influence of *The City of God* on *Utopia* as "general and tenuous."[5] Others have linked More's lectures on Augustine to *Utopia* without speaking in any specific sense of the "influence" of Augustine's work on More's.[6] It should be kept in mind that some fifteen busy years intervene in More's career between the lectures in question and the publication of *Utopia* in 1516.

Still, there is reason to risk conjecture on the relation of Augustine's classic to More's. André Prévost suggests that "Si l'on ne retrouve pas dans l'*Utopie* nombre de détails suggérés par la *Cité de Dieu*, il est certain que rien ne pouvait mieux que le commentaire de la *Cité de Dieu* qu'il fit a St. Lawrence Jewry, ouvrir à la pensee de More les immenses perspectives de l'*Utopie*." Prévost goes on to speak of the "dimension métaphysique" of *Utopia*.[7] Clearly conjecture about Augustinian influence on *Utopia* must concern the broader and more problematic aspects, the "metaphysical dimension," of the work. For neither of the thinkers in question is concerned with expounding a coherent and transmissible politics, so that Augustine, for example, "completely ignores the problem of classifying and evaluating different forms of government."[8] It does not follow that the student of *Utopia* can afford to neglect the possible bearing of Augustine's work on More's.

I should begin with what J. H. Hexter describes as that "intensification of religious sentiment and concern that began long before 1517 and extended long beyond, that in its full span had room for Luther and Loyola, the Reformed Churches and the Jesuits, Servetus and Cranmer and Edmund Campion, Paul IV and John of Leyden."[9] It was of the essence of this "Christian Revival" to hope that the ideal of community might be something more than a purely religious ideal: that the *regnum Christi* might serve as a political ideal, as a way of life. Hexter suggests, in fact, that *Utopia* reveals the pre-occupation of the humanists with a truly Christian "practice."

But to take Christianity in this sense is to risk confusing Christian imperatives with mere moralism: there was precisely this danger implicit in the Christian Revival. If the Christian Revival represented a revolt against the rationalism of ceremony and legalism, it also contained within it the seeds of a different kind of rationalism: that which obtains when Christianity is conflated with Stoic ethics. To say that More like Erasmus "saw Christianity as a way of life"[10] is to overlook the possible confusion in that broad movement between ethics and Christianity.

This confusion arises in the implicit or explicit assertion of the Christian Revival that a Christian politics is possible. Now the great, though not entirely unambiguous, denial that there exists something called Christian politics is St. Augustine's *City of God.* I hope to make clear the relevance of Augustine's work for More's by elucidating More's concern in *Utopia* with the differences between the Christian imperatives and those of the *vita socialis.*

The confusion mentioned above is finally a confusion between two motives which, from a logical point of view, are antagonistic. One of these is the originally Stoic conception of natural law; the other is a profoundly quietistic conception of patriarchalism, exemplified in the verse from Romans XIII: "the powers that be are of God." The Christian Revival was not so Stoical—though Hexter speaks of its "widespread laic character"[11]—as to speak consistently in the idiom of natural law; but any movement which conceives of itself in opposition to an irrational-patriarchal legalism has to be moving in that direction; and even Luther, though he ended with a marked patriarchalism, spoke of *Naturrecht.* Similarly, the radical Calvinistic groups later in the century had, in their struggles with the powers that be, no choice but to speak in the Stoic and medieval idiom of natural law, although this idiom directly conflicted with the dark Calvinistic view of the abilities of fallen human reason.[12]

Thomas Aquinas and Richard Hooker subsume natural law under divine law. But there is always the danger that the ideal of community based on natural law will look more Stoic than Christian. The Christian Revival, then, posed for More the problem of the difference between the community, a social ideal resting on that expression of divine law which is natural law or reason, and the state, an irrational conglomerate of traditional and positive law whose existence, for More and Augustine alike, it was impossible to justify from the point of view of natural right. It posed, in short, the question whether man had fallen from the primitive condition.

The two opposed categories of natural law and patriarchalism organized the structure of paradox in *Utopia*. A reading of More's work which recognizes only the *naturrechtlich* aspect (that, for example, which emphasizes the streak of anti-legalism running through *Utopia*) is taking the part for the whole, no less than that which sees only the irrational and paternalistic aspect. It is this structure of paradox which constitutes the "dimension métaphysique" of *Utopia*, and toward the elaboration of which *The City of God* may well have given More some clues. Ultimately *The City of God* will be seen as a possible source not of specific social doctrines but rather of More's *facetudo* vis-à-vis the realm of politics. More's humanism furnished him with a *naturrechtlich* criterion from which to judge the obvious ethical irrationalities of contemporary Europe, but his Pauline and Augustinian attitude of patriarchalism continually qualified the validity of this criterion. He had learned from Augustine—and from experience—to view the state as a structure beyond the reach of natural law, and thus was able to consider with more detachment than seems to have been possible for Erasmus the ideal of a state founded on natural law and purged of patriarchalism.

It is time for a review of Augustinian teaching on the state.[13] My task will be to demonstrate that for Augustine a rationalistic or *naturrechtlich* criticism of the state is ultimately invalid, that the Christian's attitude with regard to the state is one not of rationalistic criticism but rather of prophecy: the *civitas Dei* comes not in time but after or beyond time. Any attempt to eliminate irrationality, i.e., original sin, of which the chief expression is the *dominium* of man over man, from politics is presumption. This is not to say that Augustine adopts that position which might be called social theodicy: the social order, given its inequalities of possession and opportunity, has been divinely ordained and established. On the contrary, it is precisely the absence—with some qualifications to be noted later—of the orthodox principle of social theodicy from both *The City of God* and *Utopia* which suggests and finally validates an imaginative affinity between the two works.

The category of *dominium* is crucial for both Augustine and More—for More in *Utopia*, in the disguised form of what Hexter calls "patriarchal familism"[14]—but More and Augustine are careful never to justify the domination of man over man by means of a metaphysics of hierarchy. To do as much, to give ontological validity to *dominium*, would be to cut away the ground on which the prophet who denounces social inequity stands. The domination of one man by another is at once necessary for some measure of social stability, and an abomination, an exact parody of that true noncoercive *ordo* which obtains in the *civitas Dei*.

The circumstances of composition of *The City of God* are well known. The sack of Rome brought up the question "how it was possible to live in the state as a Christian, and how it was possible for a state composed of Christians to endure, since the practice of the Christian virtues would infallibly bring about the ruin of the state."[15] Augustine's answer to this question in *The City of God* is ultimately that Christianity is indifferent with respect to political values (though this indifference with respect to politics is momentarily blurred in that the organization of people in heaven is called, after the earthly organization, a *civitas*): Christianity cannot have had any relation to the good or bad success of the Empire. I say "good or bad" success because Augustine found himself at odds not only with those pagans who blamed Christianity for the evil success of the Empire, but also with a number of "Christian progressivists" who thought that the Incarnation signaled a beginning of improvement in the material conditions of existence. The latter in effect identified the messianic ideal with the Pax Romana: "The mission of the Roman Empire was to become finally the Christian Empire."[16] The fall of Rome may have given the lie to these "Christian progressivists," and may seem to have justified the pagan traditionalists; but both, from the point of view of Augustine, were committing the central error of seeking a correlation of some kind between the success of Rome or the *vita socialis* on the one hand and Christianity on the other. If Augustine sought to refute the pagan conception that Christianity had vitiated the noble social ideal of the Romans, he repudiated as well the conception of some Christians that the superiority of Christian life would tell in peace and material prosperity.

It seems a necessary simplification, at this point of the argument, to speak of "the indifference of Christianity with respect to politics." Christians make good citizens. But the end of Christianity is not to make good citizens.[17] Later I shall note that Augustine's *civitas terrena* is bivalent. It signifies the *civitas diaboli*, in parodic relation to the *civitas Dei*. But it signifies as well existential earthly states the social condition of which cannot but "reflect" the *civitas Dei* in some small degree, i.e., stand in mimetic rather than parodic relation to it. The notion that the *civitas terrena* has at once a mimetic and a parodic relation to the *libera civitas* will prove useful when we come to examine *Utopia*.

The indifference of Christianity with respect to the civic virtues makes for an ambiguous attitude on Augustine's part to the Roman state. On the one hand, the reasons for the fall of Rome are to be sought in the decadent nature of the Empire itself and not in Christianity;[18] on the other hand, it is clear that Roman life, at least in the days of the Republic, is a model of healthy mores and efficient politics.[19]  And, as Gilson states:

> Far from being embarrassed by the memory of a prosperous, although pagan,
> Rome, St. Augustine sees in this prosperity the sign of a providential plan.  If
> God allowed this temporal greatness, which was obtained through civil virtues,
> it was precisely in order that no one might be deceived about the proper end of
> the Christian virtues.  Since the world can enjoy prosperity without the
> Christian virtues, then, certainly, they do not exist in the view of the world.
> 'For in the most opulent and illustrious Empire of Rome, God has shown how
> great is the influence of even civil virtues without true religion, in order that it
> might be understood that, when this is added to such virtues, men are made
> citizens of another Commonwealth, of which the king is Truth, the Law is
> Love and the duration is Eternity.'  The sufficiency of the political virtues in
> their own order testifies to the supernatural specification of the Christian
> virtues both in their essence and their end.[20]

Thus, to anticipate: "In St. Augustine's terminology we may say that in
*Utopia* More gives us such a description of a *vita socialis*, based only on the
four pagan virtues, as must forcibly remind us of our duty by means of an
ardent exercise of the three Christian virtues to prepare for the *civitas Dei*."[21]

Chambers, in employing the dichotomy of reason and grace in his
discussion of *Utopia*, nonetheless implicitly maintained a continuity between
the civic and the Christian virtues: the nominally Christian contemporary
Europe is measured by the yardstick of an efficient but pagan state (I overlook
for the moment the partial acceptance in Utopia of Christianity), the point of
the work for Chambers being that Christians should be as civic-minded as the
Utopians if not more so.[22]  But it is precisely the discontinuity between
politics and the Christian imperatives which More and Augustine wished to
demonstrate.  "Since Christians cannot, in good faith, constitute a kingdom or
*polis* of their own in this world, they cannot, in good faith, claim to have a
politics of their own."[23]  And it is precisely this claim on the part of the
Christian Revival to a Christian politics which drew More's critical attention
in *Utopia*.  The efficient *polis* he opposes to the degenerate contemporary
European scene has been constituted independently of the Christian
dispensation.

The *décalage* between the Christian and the civic virtues finds its most
explicit statement in Book 19 of *The City of God*.  I shall review the arguments
of the key chapters in this book at some length.[24]

In *The City of God* 2.21 Augustine had considered the Roman Republic in
the light of Scipio's definition in Cicero's *De Re Publica* of a republic or
commonwealth as "not any mass gathering, but a multitude bound together
by a mutual recognition of rights and a mutual cooperation for the common

good" (Populum non omnem coetum multitudinis, sed coetum juris consensu et utilitatis communione sociatum esse determinat).[25] He had to conclude that, according to Scipio's own definition, "that ancient creation [the Roman state] never was a true republic, because in it true justice was never practiced." True justice was never practiced there "because true justice is not to be found save in that commonwealth, if we may so call it, whose Founder and Ruler is Jesus Christ." But he had to admit that "according to some definitions that are nearer the truth [than Scipio's in the *De Re Publica*], it [the Roman Republic] was a commonwealth of a sort, and it was better governed by the earlier Romans than by those who came later."

Augustine had promised in this discussion to return to the problem raised by Scipio's definition of the state at a later point in his work, and he does so at 19.21. Again he says that, according to Scipio's definition, "there never was any Roman Republic, because there never was in Rome any true 'weal of the people'. . . . If a commonwealth is the weal of the people, and if there is no people save one bound together by mutual recognition of rights, and if there are no rights where there is no justice, it follows beyond question that where there is no justice there is no commonwealth." Augustine elaborates this argument in emphatically logical fashion through chapter 23: the Roman definition serves only to exclude from the class of "true republics" the Roman, indeed any historical, state. But in chapter 24 he takes a different approach to the entire problem. He finds the Scipionic definition of the state adequate to the reality of the phrase "consensus juris" be left out of it. I quote the larger part of this crucial chapter:

> It is possible to define a 'people' not as Cicero does but as 'a multitude of reasonable beings voluntarily associated in the pursuit of common interests' [populus est coetus multitudinis rationalis rerum quas diligit concordi communione sociatus]. In that case, one need only consider what these interests are in order to determine of what kind any particular people may be. Still, whatever these interests are, as long as we have a multitude of rational beings—and not of irresponsible cattle—who are voluntarily associated in the pursuit of common interests, we can reasonably call them a 'people,' and they will be better or worse people according as the interests which have brought them together are better or worse interests.
>
> This definition certainly makes the Roman people a 'people' and their weal a 'commonwealth' or 'republic.' However, we know from history what kind of interests this people had, both in primitive times and more recently, and also what kind of morals brought on the rupture and corruption of their voluntary organization (which is the health, so to speak, of any community), first, by sanguinary seditions, and, later, by social and civil war. On this subject, I had a good deal to say earlier in this work [2.18, 3.23–29]. However, I would still call the Romans a 'people' and their affairs a 'commonwealth,' so long as they

remain a multitude of reasonable beings voluntarily associated in the pursuit of common interests. . . .

A state, then, in contradistinction to the Platonic definition of the state as an embodiment of a principle of justice, can be defined, less ambitiously, as a legal organization. It is now possible to deal with an accomplishment such as the Roman one in positive terms; and there can be no question of differentiating pagan from Christian states. But of that, indeed, there never was question: "At no time does [Augustine] say—or suggest—that while pagan states could not possibly exhibit true justice Christian states necessarily are, or at least may be, truly just."[26] The "clericalist" interpretation, then, of *The City of God*—that which holds that "a people, in order to be a true people, must not only be a legal society, but also, and in the same breath, a religious society worshipping [the Christian] God in union and uniformity"—is false.[27] The distinction is not between heathen and Christian states, but between the imperatives of the efficient state on the one hand, and of Christianity on the other.

Augustine has a place, by virtue of his conception of the state as a voluntary association, in the history of the political doctrine of contract.[28] Though an early modern contractarian quotes him, Augustine's idea of contract looks backward rather than forward, to the idea of contract as it was understood in the ancient world.[29] The notion of the origin of government in consensual contract rather than in "nature," which emphasizes the artificial or "mechanical" character of government, was the property of Sophists and Epicureans and one of the principal antagonists of Platonic and Aristotelian political theory.[30] In the Sophistic and Epicurean conception, the state originates in time as a legal convention; it has none of the ontological dignity with which Plato furnishes it in the *Republic*; it embodies no principle of hierarchy which may be studied in small in the individual; the relation of ruler to ruled reflects no such "natural" inequalities as Aristotle in the *Politics* discerns between parent and child, husband and wife, master and slave. The state derives from the accommodation to each other of individual wills for the sake of law and order; what legal arrangement exists for the moment represents only a partial satisfaction of individual interests. The existing arrangement is constantly threatened as an accidental imposition of stasis on the dynamic of conflicting interests: all the more need for a Pauline legitimization of the powers that be.

I say that Augustine looks backward to contract in the Sophist and Epicurean ambience rather than forward to the seventeenth- and eighteenth-century contractarians in part for the sake of simplicity. In fact the Whig contractarians are often no less pessimistic than those of the ancient world about the discontinuity between the individual and society. But there remains a crucial difference in theory: the modern contractarians tend to view contract as a logical consequence of a doctrine of natural rights; but in the contractarians of the ancient world there is no appeal from positive to natural law: in this nominalistic view laws are purely conventional impositions upon the chaos of individualism. "The radical sophists . . . carried their views much farther than the contractarians of the seventeenth and eighteenth centuries, for they derived not only the state but also the whole of morality from convention, whereas the latter's theories, with few exceptions, were *naturrechtlich*, judging the state and its rules by a criterion beyond its scope."[31]

Augustine, in repudiating the Scipionic-Ciceronian-Platonic definition of the state as an embodiment of a principle of justice, and in substituting for it a definition of the state as a "multitude of reasonable beings voluntarily associated in the pursuit of common interests," was certainly recurring to the Sophistic-Epicurean argument.[32] I go into this in detail because it may serve as a point from which to make sense of Augustine's—or More's—ambiguous but entirely unsentimental attitude to the state. On the one hand, for the dominations of man over man that keep society in one piece there is no metaphysical justification but only sin, avarice, love of self.[33] On the other hand, any such domination made habitual ensures, if not absolute justice, at least peace and quiet, a systematic injustice. *Dominium* is an evil because an expression of *libido dominandi*, a good because a form of *ordo*.[34] The state transcends the notion of justice, but it works.

To characterize this conception of the kind of law upon which the state rests as one of "relative" natural law does not quite do justice to Augustine's ironic attitude toward the social and political order. Finally, *The City of God* confronts as few other Christian works have done the chaos of inconsistency beneath Paul's "the powers that be are of God." Augustine insists the Christian should obey even the worst state.[35] But then all *dominium* is an expression of *libido dominandi* and therefore evil.

Ultimately Augustine describes the relation of the *ordo* which obtains in earthly society to the non-compulsory *ordo* of the *civitas Dei* in one of two ways: in one way the former "reflects" the latter, much as the phenomenal world for Plato may "reflect" or participate in the ideal world, and in this sense it is fair to speak of a kind of "relative" natural law embodied in the state.[36] In the other, and more profoundly Augustinian way, the kind of *ordo* which organizes earthly society is an exact upside-down parody of the non-compulsory order of love which organizes the City of God: "Sic enim superbia perverse imitatur Deum."[37] All kings parody Christ the king, who rules over his people by love, whose body is his people. To call a river

"Anydrus" is mere learned wit; to call a king "Ademus," without a people (*Utopia* 133/9), is something more: wit loaded with the Christian wisdom that only one king contains in himself all his people.

All of this has been offered as groundwork for some suggestions about the "dimension métaphysique" of More's work. From now on I shall be able to refer more frequently to *Utopia* than has been possible in the course of my review of Augustine's teaching on the state. At this point, though, one conclusion about the nature of the state and the kind of justice of which Augustine believes it capable: the minute we think of the state in historical terms we are lost, for like as not we shall find some kind of violence at the beginning of the present peaceful regime, if not outright conquest from without or usurpation from within, then that less obviously violent adjustment of individuals to each other which precedes agreement on the exact legal nature of the state. As a seventeenth-century Augustinian, Pascal, said: he who traces the present system of justice to its historical origin, dissolves it (l'anéantit).[38] It is no accident, then, that Utopia originates in military conquest (by its eponymous King Utopus of a "rude and rustic" peninsular people). Custom, the passage of time, legitimizes the present regime: this is all the patriarchalist hopes for in saying "the powers that be are of God."

That "voluntary association of individuals" that defines the state preserves order by erecting and maintaining a juristic machinery. The very fact that positive laws are necessary, of course, implies a lapse from the Stoic-Christian primitive community: laws address the infected will, as does indeed the entire coercive order of the state. The legal order can never be truly just: it is the focus of all moral ambiguity in the structure of the state. "Since rulers have to deal with subjects many of whom are sinful, wicked men, the actions of the state cannot be a direct embodiment of Christian precepts of righteousness."[39] Augustine, like More a judge, has a striking chapter in *The City of God* on the inescapable dilemmas confronting the judge: he cannot claim that the apparatus of punishment he directs can make man virtuous. It may scare some men off from crime, but it has no way of categorically affecting—nor indeed does it attempt so to affect—men's desires, just as the judge does not pretend to categorical knowledge of men's motivations.[40]

[The judge] thinks it no wickedness that innocent witnesses are tortured regarding the crimes of which other men are accused; or that the accused are put to the torture, so that they are often overcome with anguish, and, though innocent, make false confessions regarding themselves, and are punished; or that, though they be not condemned to die, they often die during, or in consequence of, the torture; or that sometimes the accusers, who perhaps have been prompted by a desire to benefit society by bringing criminals to justice, are themselves condemned through the ignorance of the judge, because they are unable to prove the truth of their accusations though they are true, and because the witnesses lie, and the accused endures the torture without being moved to confession. These numerous and important evils he does not consider sins; for the wise judge does these things, not with any intention of doing harm, but because his ignorance compels him, and because human society claims him as a judge.[41]

"Most overt crimes are punished; but some are never detected and others are never solved; sometimes the wrong man is punished, and the guilty go scot free."[42] Nevertheless, all the apparatus of coercion and repression is necessary; even the hangman.[43] It is obvious that this Augustinian background addresses itself only to one component of *Utopia*, not to that which takes its place with the Christian Revival in a vigorous polemic against contemporary legal complexities. But let us recall that the hangman has his place in Utopia: recidivists in adultery, for example, are put to death (191/20–21).

There is an impressive theme of anti-legalism in *Utopia*: the Utopians "have very few laws because few laws are needed for persons so educated. The chief fault they find with other peoples is that almost innumerable books of laws and commentaries are not sufficient. They themselves think it most unfair that any group of men should be bound by laws which are either too numerous to be read through or too obscure to be understood by anyone" (195/8–14). Taken by itself this recalls other great accusations of legalism in the period. But in *Utopia* this theme must be considered in relation to the work as a whole. The structure of paradox of *Utopia* calls for the impression, at certain points, that Utopia is a more *naturrechtlich* community than More's Europe; it calls simultaneously for the qualification of this impression at other points with grim suggestions that "in its fundamental structure [the Utopian commonwealth] is a great social instrument for the subjugation of pride."[44]

More makes possible the impression of a *naturrechtlich* community by disguising the irrational-patriarchal element. The latter takes the form not of a system of external coercion, but rather of what Hexter somewhat deftly calls "patriarchal familism."[45] Coercion, in accord with the maxim *vanae leges sine moribus*, is internalized, made a matter of morality. Hexter's statement that the family "is one of the means by which Utopians counteract the possible disruptive effects of their egalitarianism"[46] does not recognize the thematic nature of the tension between natural right and patriarchalism that More has built into his work. More's emphasis on the importance of the family for political morale arises rather from his dialectical play in *Utopia* with the opposition between reason and authority than from English domestic sentiment (as some critics have thought).[47] That aspect of More's work that emphasizes the family foretells what Christopher Hill has called the Protestant-Puritan "spiritualization of the household."[48] In *Utopia* an element of humor and exaggeration qualifies and controls this aspect. (Compare the great—and unsmiling—emphasis on the family in Bacon's *New Atlantis*.) "[M]ale children and then grandchildren," upon coming of age, "remain in the family and are subject to the oldest parent, unless he has become a dotard with old age. In the latter case the next oldest is put in his place" (135/31-34). The family is the political unit, since thirty families choose a magistrate (123/8-9). "Wives wait on their husbands, children on their parents, and generally the younger on the elders" (137/31-33). "On the Final-Feasts, before they go to the temple, wives fall down at the feet of their husbands, children at the feet of their parents" in order to confess their faults and beg pardon for their offense (233/24-26). The most serious crime is adultery (190). Families fight together in war (209/37-211/10). And "If anyone is seized with the desire of exploring the country belonging to his own city, he is not forbidden to do so, provided he obtain his father's leave and his wife's consent" (147/13-15). The family is the root of patriarchalism, and there is no escape from it in Utopia.

Augustine often expresses through analogy his paternalistic conception of political authority. "Most [citizens] are willful, passionate children, who must remain permanently under the firm tutelage of a stern master."[49] There is the striking passage in the beginning of the *Confessions* where he speaks of the need for disciplining the infinite pride and rebelliousness of infants: "This shows that, if babies are innocent, it is not for lack of will to do harm, but for lack of strength."[50] Complete egotism is impossible, as Socrates pointed out to Thrasymachus. But for Augustine as well as for More, there is a radical discontinuity between the individual and the social: society and civilization are achieved only by means of intervention upon the infected will. We recognize throughout *Utopia* an implicit criticism of natural right.

But, as I suggested above, the two antagonistic elements of individual reason[51] and patriarchal authority, erected wit and infected will, balance throughout the work. Thus, in opposition to the emphasis on authority, More hints that the Utopians are Platonists, or primitives with a *prisca theologia*, who escape of their own from reason into grace: "They never have a discussion of happiness without uniting certain principles taken from religion as well as from philosophy, which uses rational arguments. Without these principles they think reason insufficient and weak by itself for the investigation of true happiness" (161/32-37). More shares with Augustine his admiration here for the erected wit of the *Phaedrus*; and it is with Augustinian misgiving that he finally has to admit that the Utopian *prisca theologia* has not entirely rid itself of gross pagan superstition: "Nor is there any doubt that the other beliefs [superstitions, such as that which identifies God with a planet] would all have disappeared long ago had not an untoward event, which chance brought upon one of their number when he was deliberating a change of religion, been construed by fear as not having happened by chance but as having been sent by heaven—as if the deity whose worship he was forsaking were thus avenging an intention so impious against himself" (217/29–35; tr. retouched). This passage "suggests more superstition in the Utopians than is ascribed to them anywhere else."[52] It might be paralleled by a number of passages in *The City of God* where Augustine, after expressing admiration for pagan philosophers and in particular the Platonists, admits that the Christian mystery was a stumbling block to their wit: "Some of them, as far as they were hindered by human nature, fell into error, especially when Divine Providence justly thwarted their pride in order to show them, even by opposition, that the path of virtue starts from humility and rises to higher things."[53]

But it is the infected will rather than the erected wit which especially colors *Utopia*. (I agree with the Yale editors that "it would take a very fine mesh indeed to sift out of *Utopia* any discernible residue of Renaissance Neoplatonism."[54]) I have already noticed that the hangman has a place in Utopia no less than in More's England: the fabric of law expresses society's (evil but necessary) death-impulse in domestic matters, just as war expresses it in international matters. Augustine has a fully developed doctrine of the just war. "His analysis of war closely parallels his discussion of punishment and earthly justice within the state. The just war is the punishment imposed upon a state and upon its rulers when their behavior is so aggressive or avaricious that it violates even the norms of temporal justice. Other states then have not merely the right but the duty to punish these crimes and to act in the same fashion as the judge, policeman, jailer, and executioner act within the state."[55] For Augustine the just war no more than for the Utopians is limited to the defensive war. Two kinds of offensive war are just: that against a state which refuses to make reparation for wrongs committed by its citizens; and that against a state which fails to return property that has been wrongfully appropriated. It is just to employ ruses and ambushes against the enemy in just war (compare *Utopia* 203/18–27, 203/36–205/38).[56] "Always, Augustine's central point is the same—war is evil and dreadful, and yet, like the work of the jailer and the hangman in any society, it is sometimes necessary if wrongdoing and rank injustice are not to be permitted to flourish."[57] Augustine's opinions on war represent a rejection of the tradition of antimilitarism and pacifism of the early fathers Tertullian, Origen, and Lactantius.[58]

More could presumably have found the doctrine of the just offensive war elsewhere than in Augustine. But the uncompromising Utopian war policy hints at a malicious elaboration of paradox for which Augustine might be the best gloss: "Peace the earthly city can win only by war;" peace and war are implicated in each other.[59] Utopian war policy amounts to a parody of Erasmian pacifism: this is not to say that More, or Augustine for that matter, was not a pacifist, but rather that an unqualified pacifism could not be accommodated to the Augustinian perspective of *Utopia*, of which the central point is that the ends of groups transcend ethics. Morality is possible only within a context of coercion that transcends morality. Utopian war policy should be considered in the context of the dialectic More elaborates between natural right and the conditions of experience (rather than, say, as a reflection of incipient English imperialism).

An element of parody arises, then, in More's asking us to consider whence the Utopians derive the right to judge other nations: "They [go to war] only to protect their own territory or to drive an invading enemy out of their friends' lands or, in pity for a people oppressed by tyranny, to deliver them by force of arms from the yoke and slavery of the tyrant, a course prompted by human sympathy" (201/5-9). The Yale editors comment: "It is worth observing that, if one takes this statement on tyranny along with that on the conditions for a just law on ownership (164/19-23) and with that on contemporary law as a conspiracy of the rich against the poor (240/18-26), the Utopians are provided with the *casus belli* against any land they choose. More's failure to work out the implications of these three passages provides some justification for those who see the *Utopia* as a very revolutionary document in political and diplomatic affairs—if not *in esse*, at least *in posse*."[60] It is not a question of More's "failure to work out the implications." The point is that More as an Augustinian and a skeptic thinks such self-righteousness vicious and amusing: this work written in 1515-1516, then, has in it the cognate of More's and of Erasmus' criticism of Luther. Granted that the reformers were good readers of Augustine, it was nonetheless quintessential Augustine to argue that their claim to a personal criterion of truth was, when extended into politics, madness: for it separated the grain from the chaff before the time. To the conservative More, this kind of vicious self-righteousness made for great wit; thus "the Utopians are provided with the *casus belli* against any land they choose."[61]

Peace and war implicate each other much as do *dominium* and *libido dominandi*. There is, for example, no real criterion for separating the acts which subvert *dominium* from those which confirm it, for, in the perspective of time, how are we to know whether what seems at present to be usurpation will not in fact lead at some point in the future to new, more pervasive social regimentation? This kind of thinking underlies Augustine's famous

comparison of kingdoms to robber bands (*The City of God* 4.4, 4.6, 19.12).
More's passionate characterization in the peroration of *Utopia* of all existing
commonwealths as *quaedam conspiratio divitum* (240/20) surely glances at that
comparison of Augustine's.

More's great departure in *Utopia* from Augustine and the fathers in general
is on the crucial point of community of goods. Hythloday argues that
community of goods is the only remedy for social injustice. In this discussion
he uses the analogy—well known to the modern reader from Machiavelli and
others—of the community's well-being to the health of a biological organism.
He notes that solutions to social injustice which do not go so far as
communism can only alleviate to some extent the sickness in the state, but
cannot cure it. "There is no hope, however, of a cure and a return to a
healthy condition as long as each individual is master of his own property"
(105/37-39). The suggestion, then, is that the communistic Utopians do not
have the sickness (original sin, obviously). "[Pride] can have no place at all in
the Utopian scheme of things" (139/9-10). But it does, and they do have the
sickness.

That pride has a place in Utopia is obvious from the measures necessary
for its repression: as Augustine notes, the disciplining of children proves
error.[62] Professor Hexter, then, in suggesting that *Utopia* "has as one of its
central preoccupations not the amelioration of a sick society but the
conditions indispensable to a sane one,"[63] has taken the bait so carefully
drawn before us by Hythloday and More: love of self has not in fact been
cauterized from the Utopian personality. The reader who emphasizes the
broad streak of anti-legalism running through *Utopia* similarly takes the
*naturrechtlich* red herring at the cost of missing the meaning of the work in its
totality.

But Hythloday's emphasis on the necessity of communism as the requisite
for a "sane" society does give us a clue toward making sense of the work as a
whole. The More of Book 1 answers his argument by stating that in a
communistic society individuals would have little motive for personal gain
and would therefore be idle. He asks Hythloday: Why not admit the disease
and then speak (with Machiavelli and the Whig political tradition generally) in
terms of alleviating it to some degree (Machiavelli speaks of periodically
"purging" the social body), rather than project this agonizing picture of a
society that is at once healthy-egalitarian and sick-patriarchal? Chambers,
who did his best not to recognize inconsistency in More the individual, did
not admit a structure of paradox in *Utopia* but spoke rather of Utopian pagan
reason somehow organizing itself along the somber lines of a monastic order.
It cannot be had so easily both ways: the tension between egalitarian health
and pervasive authority threatens to pull the whole thing into pieces.

At the heart of the Utopian antinomy is the question of communism. Utopian communism epitomizes the dilemma, which is general in the work, between the claims of patriarchalism and natural right: if the individual will does not have the partial satisfaction of limited private ownership in land and goods, the terms for assent to central authority become all the more problematical. Rather than according the Utopian individual this partial satisfaction, More grants him everything and nothing: an Epicurean philosophy of pleasure along with Plato and the Aldine edition of Lucian for reading matter constitute a panorama of the modes of *eros*, including the *eros philosophikos* of the Neoplatonists: all this in a police state. The dilemma is evidently a real one.

The Utopian structure of paradox resists resolution. Its two antithetical aspects comment dialectically upon each other without subsumption in a single perspective. Thus, More means the reader to consider the mystery of Utopian patriarchalism co-existing with a political machinery which seems to guarantee that the Utopians' alienation of rights is by no means absolute. Utopia is a representative democracy (1/123–125); yet all Utopian officials "patres appellantur" (194/2). It is the point of the Augustinian-Sophistic attitude that the most liberal constitutional machinery—with the correlative idiom of the "conventional" or "mechanical" nature of government—does not abolish the fact of patriarchal control. More like Montaigne is a skeptic who would avoid modifying the social inheritance not out of any special respect for it, but because engaging to change it will like as not make things worse: compare Hythloday's story of the mariners who become imprudent as a result of having acquired the compass (53/21–29).

Hythloday will not accept More's argument for accommodation to the present irrational because, as Hexter has well said, he is a prophet rather than a reformer. His rejection of meliorism is traditional: it is Pelagian presumption to wish to remove the irrational from society. The proof is in the very society which Hythloday himself opposes to the contemporary European scene: for finally Utopia is not fundamentally less ethically irrational than that England which hangs thieves. It is an entirely practicable society, and one more "rationalized" than any in More's Europe. But Leviathan, "prince of the children of pride," symbol (among other things) of that evil but necessary tyranny of man over man which it is presumption to question, is not to be exterminated. More smuggles him back into Utopia in the form of "patriarchal familism." Hobbes preferred not to play hide-and-seek with Leviathan: in his vision, citizens alienate practically all their rights to him, as represented in one will, from the beginning.

The political order remains ethically irrational, transcending the free play of moral values which defines community.[64] The Augustinian does not recognize criticism from the point of view of natural law. "Rien n'est si fautif que ces lois qui redressent les fautes; qui leur obéit parce qu'elles sont justes, obéit à la justice qu'il imagine, mais non pas à l'essence de la loi; elle est toute remassée en soi; elle est loi, et rien davantage."[65] Franz Neumann expressed an insight similar to this when he wrote: "[E]very natural law doctrine is self-contradictory. None of the theories is capable of maintaining the validity of a system of norms derived merely from individual consent. All of them are compelled to admit into their system a non-normative element, namely power, thus overthrowing their whole elaborate structure."[66] For the "non-normative element" in Utopia we have only to consider the ubiquity of the family, the root of patriarchalism.

For the Augustinian, there is a great gulf between the ideal of natural law and the specific circumstances of experience so that ultimately the category of natural law gives way before the strict juristic machinery and a Pauline endorsement of "the powers that be." In the structure of paradox of Book 2 of *Utopia*, those details of Utopian life and conduct that encourage a *naturrechtlich* perspective compete with others that assume that no appeal is possible from positive to natural law. Thus, Utopians do not make international treaties because a positive form of an international understanding would be redundant (197/18-23), but in domestic matters Utopians are warned to observe private contracts with care (165/23-25).

More got from Augustine no particular social or political doctrine, such as that of the just offensive war, but rather a feeling for the inevitable mingling of good and bad in any social or legal order. It may be objected that he did not need to read any books to find out that politics was irrational. *The City of God*, though, may have helped him to give form to his own distaste for "politic" solutions. The "dimension métaphysique" that enabled More to gain perspective on Plato's myth of the rational state is essentially Augustinian.

Readers from Budé (Letter to Lupset, *Utopia* 12/6) to Chambers and Hexter have characterized Utopia as *Hagnopolis*, holy community. I have been concerned with More's criticism from an Augustinian point of view of the Stoic-Christian or rational version of *Hagnopolis* or the Christian state. But *Hagnopolis* may take the form not only of the Stoic-Christian community but also of the theocratic state; there is, that is to say, a fideistic as well as a rationalistic formulation of the ideal of a Christian politics. It may be well, then, to consider More's work in relation to theocracy for a moment.

The problem with a fideistic formulation of a Christian politics is no different from that with the rational one. For theocracy turns out to be only a disguised version of the rational state. To move in the direction of theocracy is, in the Augustinian perspective, to make larger claims for the state than are justified by the basic assumption that the state is an accidental legal order existing only to secure earthly peace. We have seen that Augustine was at pains to define the state in this manner in Book 19 of *The City of God*.

Augustine himself confronted this problem in connection with the Donatist controversy. As a propagandist for the Catholic Church he was necessarily concerned with bringing heretics into the fold. But it was inconsistent with his own skeptical view of *politike* to justify *on religious grounds* political compulsion to join the visible church. His final position on this question was in fact to move in the direction of theocracy, that is, to justify coercion of Donatists and others to join the Church (as any religious would) on religious grounds.[67] But in view of the fundamental Augustinian assumption that the state exists only to secure "the peace of Babylon," a theocracy such as Calvin's Geneva could be only an exact parody of the *civitas Dei*: any attempt to realize the Word in time, in society, disfigures the essential teaching of *The City of God* (no matter that *The City of God*—the idea perhaps rather than the book—may have inspired many such attempts).[68] It is a surrender of Augustine's ironic vision to claim with Calvin that regenerate agents could so order the state as to realize "in this mortal and transitory life some taste of the immortal and incorruptible beatitude."[69]

More in *Utopia* is concerned to demonstrate that a monolithic government only parodies, it cannot realize, the *libera civitas*. The terribly successful social regimentation of which an efficient monolith, call it State-Church or Church-State, is capable—Budé remarks on the Utopians' "resolute and tenacious love of peace and quiet" (*Utopia* 11/11–12), Busleyden on their "absolute singleness of purpose" (*ibid*. 35/36)—is a good achieved only at the expense of other goods, those notably of Christian foolishness. At this point theocrat has rejoined rationalist: each is equally premature in his vision of community. Theocrat no more than rationalist can translate from community into state, from absolute intention into politics.

The fideistic version of a Christian politics may be arraigned on the same charge as the rational one. The only difference between these two formulations is that the rational or Stoic-Christian version is at least theoretically egalitarian, whereas the theocrat divides society into the regenerate, who rule, and the unregenerate, who do not, and this manifestation within the natural order of the discontinuity between nature and grace More no less than Augustine would consider premature. To realize a community of the godly on earth, More will answer to reformist ecclesiology, would be like realizing a Platonic idea: the church community is not *Hagnopolis* but will include both the wheat and the tares.[70] A marginal gloss to the 1523 edition of More's *Responsio ad Lutherum* says Luther has seen his visible church of the godly "fortasse in Utopia."[71]

The Yale editors caution us against reading into *Utopia* knowledge of events after 1516. But our understanding of this work may gain with knowledge of the details of More's confrontation with Luther. John M. Headley notes that More, in opposition to Luther's agitation (early in his career) against the network of human law, will insist "upon the priority and superiority of laws to magistrates and the continuing need for a body of law. As he had observed earlier in his *Utopia*, even in a certain natural community (*in communitate quadam naturali*), where property and therefore the occasion for stealing are absent, laws, though fewer in number, would still be necessary."[72] More will argue, that is to say, against Luther's separation of *aequitas* from law: in contrast not only to Luther but also Aristotle and a late phase of Roman law, More understands equity as an integral aspect of the law. "Thus it would appear that More, the common lawyer, stands apart not only from Luther's understanding of equity but also from that of the late Roman development and, for that matter, from the contemporary revival of the Arisotelian understanding of *aequitas* . . . among the humanistically influenced jurists on the continent."[73]

Luther himself can illustrate the confusions in the perennial battle between the claims of individualism and authority. He argued *Naturrecht* but not, it seems, within the traditional conceptual context of that term;[74] and as his career progressed he moved in the direction of an Augustinian dependence upon the secular authority. He was even "to remark that no one since St. Augustine had given such validity and importance to the secular authority as had he."[75] We might note at this point that *The City of God* received critical attention from other early humanists besides More.[76]

In discussing the "dimension métaphysique" of *Utopia* I have not meant to suggest that More was an unqualified "Augustinian" in no way touched by humanist enthusiasms. I have been concerned rather with the way in which the polar categories of natural right and patriarchal authority may throw light on More's work. More was obviously caught up in and helped to shape the new attitudes, call them "Christian Humanism" or "Christian Revival." But it is difficult to grasp exactly what a modern scholar means when he refers to the "wide and luminous views of More and Erasmus."[77] At least, there is little optimism in *Utopia*.

If in *Utopia* More criticizes contemporary Europe from the point of view of a *naturrechtlich* criterion outside of it, this is only by way of focusing more surely on the peculiar circumstances of his own culture, for that criterion in its turn is criticized on Augustinian grounds.

More did not speak as easily as Aquinas the idiom of natural right; and he is far from the optimism of a later humanist like Grotius, who develops as a full political ideal the doctrine of natural right.[78] Politics had less dignity for him than for Aquinas, Grotius, the radical Calvinists. *Utopia* is finally a statement on the impossibility of circumventing Leviathan. Community, for More, was an ideal to be achieved in the sharing of the Eucharist, not in political life. In shaping this conclusion in a work of art, More may well have benefited from his reading in St. Augustine.

# Notes

†Originally appeared in *Studies in the Renaissance* XX(1973): 144–68. Reprinted by permission of the publisher.

[1]William Roper, *The Lyfe of Sir Thomas Moore*, ed. E. V. Hitchcock (London: Published for the Early English Text Society by H. Milford, Oxford Univ. Press, 1935 [for 1934]), p. 6. Also Nicholas Harpsfield, *The Life and Death of Sir Thomas Moore*, ed. E. V. Hitchcock, with historical notes by R. W. Chambers (1932; rpt. London: Published for the Early English Text Society by the Oxford Univ. Press, 1963), pp. 13–14; Thomas Stapleton, *The Life of Sir Thomas More*, trans. Philip E. Hallett and ed. E. E. Reynolds (London: Burns & Oates, 1966), pp. 7–8; More, letter to John Holt, in E. F. Rogers, ed., *The Correspondence of Sir Thomas More* (Princeton: Princeton Univ. Press, 1947), pp. 3–5, trans. by M. A. Haworth, S. J., in E. F. Rogers, ed., *Sir Thomas More: Selected Letters* (New Haven and London: Yale Univ. Press, 1961), pp. 1–2. In the letter to Holt which Rogers dates c. November 1501, More says that his Greek teacher William Grocyn "recently made a very successful start" on his lectures at St. Paul's on the *Celestial Hierarchies* of "Dionysius"; Harpsfield says that More's lectures came "about the same time" as Grocyn's. It was apparently Grocyn as vicar of St. Lawrence Jewry who invited his student's lectures; see Harpsfield's *Life*, note to 13/23–25.

[2]Stapleton, *loc. cit.*

[3]R. W. Chambers, *Thomas More* (1935; rpt. Ann Arbor: Univ. of Michigan Press, 1958), p. 83.

[4]*The Complete Works of St. Thomas More*, Vol. 4: *Utopia*, ed. Edward Surtz, S. J. and J. H. Hexter (New Haven and London: Yale Univ. Press, 1965), p. clxvi. References to *Utopia* will be to this edition.

[5]*Ibid.*, pp. clxvi–clxvii.

[6]See, e.g., A. W. Reed, "Sir Thomas More," in *The Social and Political Ideas of Some Great Thinkers of the Renaissance and the Reformation*, ed. F. J. C. Hearnshaw (1925; rpt. New York: Barnes & Noble, 1949), p. 138.

[7]A. Prévost, rev. of *Utopia*, ed. Edward Surtz, S. J. (New Haven and London: Yale Univ. Press, 1964), *Moreana*, I, no. 4 (Nov. 1964), 94. Prévost is reviewing the paper issue of the Yale *Utopia*, with its own introduction; Surtz's opinion here on the influence of *The City of God* does not differ from that in the parent edition: "Contrary to likely conjecture, Augustine's *City of God*, on which More had lectured publicly, seems to have influenced *Utopia*, only in a quite general and vague way" (p. xiii). See also Prévost, *Thomas More et la crise de la pensée européenne* (Lille: Mame, 1969), pp. 55, 193–194.

[8]Herbert A. Deane, *The Political and Social Ideas of St. Augustine* (New York and London: Columbia Univ. Press, 1963), p. 241.

[9]*Utopia*, p. xciii.

[10]*Ibid.*, p. lxxiv.

[11]*Ibid.*, p. xcviii.

[12]See J. W. Allen, *A History of Political Thought in the Sixteenth Century* (1928; rpt. London: Methuen, and New York: Barnes & Noble, 1960), p. 313.

[13]I have depended especially on Herbert A. Deane, *op. cit.* Deane's essay is also an anthology of Augustinian views on the social order.

[14]*Utopia*, p. xli.

[15]Etienne Gilson, foreword to the English translation of *The City of God* in the series called the *Fathers of the Church* (New York: Fathers of the Church, Inc., 1948– ), I (1950), xl. Quotations from this translation unless otherwise noticed.

[16]Theodor Mommsen, "St. Augustine and the Christian Idea of Progress," JHI, XII, no. 3 (June 1951), 346–374, reprinted in Mommsen, *Medieval and Renaissance Studies*, ed. E. F. Rice, Jr. (Ithaca: Cornell Univ. Press, 1959), pp. 289–290.

[17]Cf. Gilson, *op. cit.*, pp. xli–xlii.

[18]See, e.g., *The City of God* 2.18.

[19]See *The City of God* 5.12–15.

[20]Gilson, *op. cit.*, p. xliii, quoting Augustine, *Letter* 138 3.17.

[21]H. W. Donner, *Introduction to Utopia* (1946; rpt. Freeport, N. Y.: Books for Libraries Press, 1969), p. 81.

[22]R. W. Chambers, *Thomas More*, pp. 125–131. For the tradition of this interpretation of *Utopia*, see Donner, *loc. cit.*

[23]Henry Paolucci, introduction to *The Political Writings of St. Augustine* (Chicago: Henry Regnery, 1962), p. xviii.

[24]In summarizing the arguments of the crucial chapters in this Book, I follow Deane, pp. 118–126, and J. Nevill Figgis, *The Political Aspects of St. Augustine's "City of God"* (1921; rpt. Gloucester, Mass.: Peter Smith, 1963), pp. 59–67.

[25]*De re publica* 1.25.

[26]Deane, pp. 123–124.

[27]This is the conclusion of Deane, pp. 120–126, and Figgis, p. 64, from whom I have the identification of the view in question as "clericalist." The quotation comes from Sir Ernest Barker's introduction to the Everyman *City of God* (London: Dent, and New York: Dutton, 1945), I, xxxi. Sir Ernest himself does not accept the clericalist interpretation.

[28]See J. W. Gough, *The Social Contract*, 2d ed. (Oxford: Clarendon Press, 1957), pp. 23–24. I have not consulted Mario d'Addio, *L'Idea del Contratto Sociale dai Sofisti alla Riforma* (Milano: Giuffrè, 1954), to which Gough refers: d'Addio regards Augustine as the chief source of the idea of contract throughout the Middle Ages.

[29]Salamonius: See Gough, p. 47.

[30]For contract in the ancient world see Gough, chap. 1.

[31]Gough, p. 12, n. 2.

[32]Cf. Dino Bigongiari, "The Political Ideas of St. Augustine," appendix to Paolucci, ed., *The Political Ideas of St. Augustine*, p. 346.

33For the doctrine of the two loves, love of self which organizes the *civitas terrena* and love of God which organizes the *civitas Dei*, see *The City of God*, Book 14.

34See Barker, *op. cit.*, p. xviii.

35*The City of God* 2.19.

36See the texts quoted in Deane, pp. 96–99, and see p. 289, n. 84.

37*The City of God* 19.12. Cf. Gilson as quoted in Deane, p. 290, n. 93.

38From *Pensées*, fr. 294.

39Deane, p. 134.

40See Deane, pp. 134–143.

41*The City of God* 19.6, Dods tr. (many eds.).

42Deane, p. 136.

43Deane, pp. 141–142, quotes *De Ordine* II.4.12.

44J. H. Hexter, *More's Utopia: The Biography of an Idea* (Princeton: Princeton Univ. Press, 1952), p. 80.

45*Utopia*, pp. xli–xlv: "The Perdurable Milieu: *Utopia* and the Family."

46*Ibid.*, p. xlii.

47Hythloday's attitude to his relatives and friends is quite unsentimental: "As for my relatives and friends . . . I am not greatly troubled about them, for I think I have fairly well performed my duty to them already. The possessions, which other men do not resign unless they are old and sick and even then resign unwillingly when incapable of retention, I divided among my relatives and friends when I was not merely hale and hearty but actually young. I think they ought to be satisfied with this generosity from me and not to require or expect additionally that I should, for their sakes, enter into servitude to kings" (*Utopia* 55/23-31).

48*Society and Puritanism in Pre-Revolutionary England* (New York: Schocken, 1964), chap. 13.

49Deane, p. 153.

50*Confessions* 1.7. One might compare the Hobbesian theme of the *infans robustus* (preface to *De Cive*).

51Individual reason not as opposed to grace but as the competence of the individual to grasp moral notions independently of social conditioning: i.e., in the Platonic scheme, morals are not "taught"—since judgment cannot be inserted into the mind—but "recollected" with the aid of dialectic from the reservoir of Ideas. The individual erected wit, in this sense, does not oppose, in fact it is fulfilled in, grace. See below.

52*Utopia*, p. 518.

53*The City of God* 2.7; cf, 10.1, 10.3. Father Surtz refers to this passage at *Utopia*, p. clxvii. For Augustine's praise of the Platonists in *The City of God*, see 8.1–13.

54*Utopia*, pp. cix–cx.

55Deane, p. 156.

56See Deane, p. 310, n. 18, who quotes a passage from *Quaestionum in Heptateuchum*.

57Deane, p. 161. Chap. 5 generally: "War and Relations Among States."

58*Ibid.*, p. 155.

59*The City of God* 15.4, 19.12.

60*Utopia*, p. 499.

61For "the basic structure of the criterion problem" with respect to the exchange between Erasmus and Luther on freedom of will, see Richard H. Popkin, *The History of Scepticism from Erasmus to Descartes*, rev. ed. (New York: The Humanities Press, 1964), chap. 1. It may be well to distinguish More's skeptical and "Lucianic" Augustinianism from that of the reformers. The latter finds a convenient emblem in Luther's peevish rejoinder to Erasmus in the *De Servo Arbitrio* (1525): "Spiritus sanctus non est Scepticus." See Popkin.

62*The City of God* 22.22. The argument here differs from, though it may recall, the humanist formulation that education "repairs the ruin of our first parents." Similarly, in Utopia, education is a question of inspiring morale rather than of realizing potentialities, erecting the wit. Or, to be fair, it is a question of both, but one recalls especially the former. The streak of *otium* in Utopian life takes its place in the *naturrechtlich* component of the work.

63*Utopia*, p. cxiv.

64Professor Joseph A. Mazzeo has discussed the theme of the ethical irrationality of the state in connection with Machiavelli: see the essays on Machiavelli in *Renaissance and Seventeenth Century Studies* (New York: Columbia Univ. Press, and London: Routledge & Kegan Paul, 1964). A classic modern statement of this theme is Weber's essay "Politics as a Vocation" (*From Max Weber: Essays in Sociology*, trans., ed., and introd. H. H. Gerth and C. Wright Mills [New York: Oxford Univ. Press, 1946], chap. 4). Weber was perfectly aware he was secularizing a Christian attitude: "the early Christians knew full well the world is governed by demons and that he who lets himself in for politics, that is, for power and force as means, contracts with diabolical powers and for his action it is *not* true that good can follow only from good and evil from evil, but that often the opposite is true. Anyone who fails to see this is, indeed, a political infant" (*ibid.*, p. 123).

65Pascal, *Pensées*, fr. 294.

66"Types of Natural Law," in *The Democratic and the Authoritarian State* (Glencoe, Ill.,: The Free Press, 1957), p. 77.

67For a review of Augustine and the Donatist controversy, see Deane, pp. 174–211. Deane remarks on this contradiction in Augustine between his general view of the state and a theocratic element: "Is there a fundamental inconsistency between the view to which Augustine was driven by the exigencies of the struggle against the Donatists—that is, that Christian rulers have the obligation as well as the right to punish those whom the Church discovers to be heretics or schismatics, and, in general, that it is the duty of Christian kings to serve God by making and enforcing laws to prevent sinful men from offering insult to God's majesty and to protect and promote true religion—and Augustine's general theory of the nature and function of the State—that it is an imperfect, though essential, organization made necessary by the Fall of man, whose primary purpose it is to guarantee, by the use of the external instruments of coercion and the fear of punishment, the maintenance of earthly peace, security, and justice?" (p. 216).

68Cf. Gilson in the foreword cited above and in *Les Métamorphoses de la Cité de Dieu* (Louvain: Publications universitaires de Louvain, 1952).

69From *Institutes* (1541), as quoted in Allen, *A History of Political Thought in the*

*Sixteenth Century*, p. 69.

70*The Complete Works of St. Thomas More*, Vol. 5: *Responsio ad Lutherum*, ed. John
M. Headley (New Haven and London: Yale Univ. Press, 1969), 167/21-28, 201/33-
205/5, etc. See, in Headley's introduction, pp. 760-765. More in this work (rightly or
wrongly) understands reformist ecclesiology to center on the notion of a pure Church,
a community of believers which would apparently reject the sinful from membership.
His objection to this notion is basically Augustine's, that the two cities are *perplexae* on
this earth. More draws a parallel between reform and Donatist definitions of the
Church: both are, in effect, Puritan and rigorist. See 118/22 and note, and 205/3-5.
More uses Augustine extensively throughout the *Confutation of Tyndale* against the
rigorism of Tyndale and Robert Barnes, e.g., "both Saint Cipriane and Saint Augustine
to, dyd take the churche for none other then the knowen Catholike church, and knew
the church right wel, not for a company of onely good men, but of good and bad both,
and so they be still what ever Tyndall saye" (*English Works* [1557], 689H). Barnes,
according to More, projects "such a church as our Logiciens do *intentionem secundam*,
that is a thyng that is no where" (*ibid.*, 7488); on the satirical view of "second
intentions," cf. *Utopia* 159/31-35. On the connection between *Utopia* and More's
ecclesiology, see P. A. Sawada, "Toward the Definition of Utopia," *Moreana*, VIII, nos.
31-32 (Nov. 1971), 143-144.

71The *Responsio*, 118/11. Either the publisher Pynson or More is responsible for
the gloss. Headley notes: "If the gloss originated with More, it represents one of his
few later references to that work which has become his chief claim to literary
greatness" (p. 887).

72Headley, introduction to the *Responsio*, p. 754, referring to 276/2-5.

73*Ibid.*, p. 756. For Aristotle's understanding of the relation between law and
equity, see *Nic. Ethics* 1137a, b.

74Luther's *Naturrecht* does not appeal to the rational faculty.

75Headley, op. cit., referring to *Werke* (Weimar, 1883- ), 30/2: 109-110. Weber
and others have thought Protestantism "legitimated the authoritarian state." *From Max
Weber: Essays in Sociology*, p. 124.

76Besides the fact of More's lectures, there is Vives' edition, with full critical
apparatus, published at Basel in 1522. Bernard André, the humanist imported by
Henry VII, wrote a commentary on *The City of God* which survives in manuscript
(noticed in William Nelson, *John Skelton: Laureate* [New York, Columbia Univ. Press,
1939], Appendix I: "Bernard Andre's Works," p. 239). For Augustine's influence on
the early humanists, see P. O. Kristeller, "Augustine and the Early Renaissance,"
*Review of Religion*, VIII, no. 4 (May 1944), 339-358, reprinted in *Studies in Renaissance
Thought and Letters* (Rome: Edizioni di storia e letteratura, 1956), pp. 355-372.Vives'
commentary, which I have consulted in John Healey's Elizabethan translation (1610,
actually), has little relevance to the subject being discussed here, except insofar as the
whole effort testifies to humanist interest in Augustine's classic: it is straight philology
or explication of theology. Vives has occasion in the notes to 2.7 to praise his friend
Thomas More. There is an amusing quibble in a dedicatory letter to Healey's
translation by Th[omas] Th[orpe], to the effect that Healey, who died before the
translation was published, now lives in the *civitas Dei*, or *Eutopia*, whereas in life he

knew only the imaginary just *civitas*, or *Utopia* (sig. A3r).

[77]G. K. Hunter, in *John Lyly: The Humanist as Courtier* (London: Routledge & Kegan Paul, and Cambridge, Mass.: Harvard Univ. Press, 1962), p. 28.

[78]Cf. Ernst Cassirer, *The Myth of the State* (New Haven and London: Yale Univ. Press, 1946), p. 166: "The political rationalism of the seventeenth century was a rejuvenation of Stoic ideas."

# Defining *Gloria* in Augustine's
## *City of God*†

## Louis J. Swift

The dichotomy which Augustine establishes in the opening lines of his *City of God* between the *gloriosissimam civitatem Dei* and the *civitatem terrenam* sets the tone for the whole apology and is a particularly apt introduction to the first five books of this *magnum opus et arduum*.[1] The celestial city, he argues, is founded not on the presumptuous efforts of man but on the gratuitous act of God who "resists the proud but gives grace to the humble" (Jas. 4:6). The *civitas terrena*, on the other hand, is the work of the *superbi* who arrogate power to themselves and who glory in that spirit of mastery which is summed up in Vergil's line "Parcere subjectis et debellare superbos" (*Aen.* 6.853). In exercising dominion over others, Augustine claims, the founders of the earthly city take what belongs to God and in the very act of asserting their power become slaves themselves to the *libido dominandi*.

The contrasts outlined here between the two *civitates* (i.e., pride/humility, self-sufficiency/dependence, domination/subservience) assume very concrete form in the first five books of Augustine's work, where the theme is the relationship between the *civitas Dei* and the *civitas Romana*,[2] and where the argument is directed toward two quite specific aims.[3] In these books Augustine seeks to demonstrate first that Rome's material growth and prosperity owed nothing to the worship of pagan deities (or conversely that physical disasters such as Alaric's sack of Rome were not caused by the rise of Christianity) and, second, that the development of Roman *imperium* was the result of divine providence. On both these points Augustine could scarcely avoid dealing with the issue of *gloria*, which was an inseparable, pervasive, and all-but-controlling force in Roman society.[4] From what he has to say on this theme in the first five books of *The City of God* we can understand more clearly what separates the celestial and the terrestrial cities and what kind of interplay there is between them in the world of time, where perforce they are linked together.

A few prefatory comments are in order about traditional Roman views of *gloria* and the role it played in social, civic, and political life. "All of us," says Cicero in a typical remark, "are driven by a zeal for praise, and the best men are attracted most of all by glory."[5] Defining the term quite simply as "the good reputation one enjoys among good men" (*bona fama bonorum* [*Sest.* 65.139]), the orator suggests that *gloria* is the most desirable of human blessings (*Phil.* 5.18.49–50; *Arch.* 11.28), that the Romans surpass all other

races in pursuing this kind of personal renown (*Manil.* 3.7), and that it is the
one consolation man has for his own mortality.[6] Cicero reflects a long-
standing tradition when he claims that there can be no true *gloria* apart from
service to others[7] (a point that is implied in the Roman aphorism that glory is
the *umbra uirtutis*)[8] and that by winning glory one provides both a model and
a stimulus to later generations. Thus, it is appropriate to speak of a *hereditas
gloriae* (Cicero, *Off.* 1.22.78; 1.33.121; *Epist.* 9.14.4) and to acknowledge, in the
words of Sallust, that "the glory of [one's] forebears is a light to posterity"
(*Iug.* 85.23).[9] "The memory of [others'] accomplishments," says the historian,
"stirs a flame in the heart of noble men, and that passion is not assuaged until
they have achieved equal fame and glory through their own virtue" (*Iug.* 4.6).
Meritorious acts, of course, entail discipline, effort, and suffering, and the
amount of glory achieved is directly proportionate to the amount of difficulty
involved.[10] In all instances great care is required to prevent one's placing
one's own personal glory above the law or above the common good, for
without such vigilance what results is *nimia cupiditas gloriae*, which is nothing
less than a kind of sickness or disorder in the soul.[11]

When Augustine deals with *gloria* in the early books of the *City of God*,
he seems to be using the term in three different senses.[12] The first of these
appears in chapters 14–15 of Book 3, where *gloria* is intimately bound up with
*libido dominandi* and with moral decline in the life of the state.[13] Following
the lead of Sallust (*Catil.* 2.1–2) Augustine argues that men of the earliest times
had lived *sine cupiditate*, but that with the advent of Cyrus and the outbreak
of wars among Greek nations *libido dominandi* became sufficient reason for
taking up arms, and the belief became widespread that "the greatest glory
resided in the greatest empire" (3.14). As a victim of this "lust for mastery"
which "afflicts many evils on the human race and wears it down,"[14] Rome
triumphed over her mother city  Alba Longa and "praised her own crime
with the name of glory." Such renown, the bishop suggests caustically, is
typical of the gladiatorial contests and serves only to hide the endless slaughter
of kinsmen and allies.[15]

The *libido dominandi* which is viewed here as the vitiating element in the
pursuit of glory waxed strong in Roman society, Augustine suggests, after the
destruction of Carthage. It sprang up in *superbissimis mentibus* as a result of
the absolute power which longevity in office conferred on particular
individuals, and that longevity was itself an outgrowth of the ambition that
arose in a society corrupted by avarice and luxury. It was to forestall such a
disastrous chain of events by means of external threats, Augustine claims, that
Scipio Nasica argued against Cato's famous dictum *Carthago delenda est*.
Nasica "thought that fear [of Carthage] would act as a curb on lust and that
lust, being curbed, would not run riot in luxury and that the restraint of

luxury would bring avarice to an end, and that with these vices out of the way virtue would flourish and increase. . ." (1.31).[16]

The inescapable connection that Augustine sees here among *auaritia, libido dominandi,* and *superbia* is clearly articulated in a well-known passage of the *De Genesi ad litteram* (11.15.19), which was composed not long before these early books of the *City of God.* Commenting on the fall of the angels, Augustine suggests that the line from Ecclesiasticus "Pride is the beginning of all sin" (10:13) and the text of 1 Timothy 6:10 "Avarice is the root of all evil" are tantamount to the same thing if one understands avarice not as the love of money but more generally as that vice by which one "desires something more than he should for the sake of his own promotion and out of love for his own concerns." It was avarice, in fact, that caused the fall of Satan, "who, to be sure, loved not money but his own personal *potestas.*"[17] The opposite of such *auaritia/superbia* is *caritas,* which "does not seek its own" (1 Cor. 13:5), i.e., "does not rejoice in its own excellence and thus is not puffed up by its own achievement." Augustine then goes on to define these *duo amores,* as he calls them, by contrasting their individual characteristics. The one (*caritas*) is social, the other (*auaritia*) private; the one looks out for the common good for the sake of the celestial society, the other subordinates that good to its own power *propter adrogantem dominationem*; the one is subject to God, the other vies with him; the one prefers truth to empty praise, the other is *auidus laudis* in every way possible; the one rules in the interests of the governed, the other for its own private gain.[18]

The two loves described here are not precisely those that separate the two cities in the later books of the *De civitate Dei* (e.g., 11.33; 12.1; 14.13 and 28), where the difference between the *iusti* and the *iniqui* is presented in more metaphysical terms (i.e., *amor Dei* vs. *amor sui*). Here the contrast is rather between the social and self-sacrificing character of *caritas* and the self-aggrandizing dimension of *auaritia,* which looks out for its own interest at the expense of others.[19] It is the *gloria* that springs from the second of these *amores* (*auaritia/superbia*) that Augustine decries in Rome's wars of conquest, and it is this type of *gloria* that leads him in the preface to counter Vergil's *debellare superbos* with the words of the Psalmist "Deus superbis resistit, humilibus autem dat gratiam."

The *gloria* that is typical of the *civitas Dei* is of another kind, as Augustine's discussion of the Christian apostles and martyrs in Book 5 makes clear. In assessing their achievements Augustine works with the Ciceronian definition of glory (i.e., "the favorable judgment of men who think well of other men" [5.12]) but redefines some of its constituent elements. He rejects Cicero's notion that only those activities which are held in high esteem by society at large can give rise to glory. The apostles won distinction for

themselves by preaching the name of Christ in places where it was disdained
or even detested: "Amid curses and reviling, amid bitter persecutions and
cruel tortures, they were not deterred from preaching man's salvation in spite
of all the raging of man's hatred" (5.14). Such actions, Augustine assures us,
merited for the apostles not only "the glory of their own conscience," as St.
Paul would have it (2 Cor. 1:12), but "great glory in the Church of Christ."
Augustine then goes on to define *gloria Christiana* in a way that reflects both a
continuity with traditional Roman concepts and a sharp departure from them.
Referring to the Apostles he says,

> They did not rest in that glory as if it were the goal of their virtuous endeavor.
> Instead they ascribed that very glory to the glory of God, by whose grace they
> were such as they were. And with that tinder they set fire to those whom they
> taught, so that they also burned with the love of him who had made them, too,
> such as they were. For their master had taught them not to be good for the
> sake of human glory. . . . But again lest they should take this in the wrong
> sense and be afraid to please men and so, concealing their goodness, should be
> of less help to others, he showed them what their aim ought to be in attracting
> attention: "Let your works so shine before men that they may see your good
> deeds and glorify your father who is in heaven" [Mt. 5:16]. (5.14)[20]

Whereas the Roman might be expected to find fulfillment in the recognition
accorded him in his own lifetime and in the expectation of living on in the
memory of posterity, the Christian ascribes the glory he receives to the source
of his power, thereby stirring others to a love of that same source. This
amounts to transforming one's own subjective glory (i.e., the renown an
individual attains through virtuous acts) into an objective glory (i.e., praise of
God for enabling one to perform such acts). The reason for this change,
Augustine argues, is that the perspective of Christian heroes is different from
that of their Roman counterparts. As dwellers in an earthly city the latter
were concerned about a kingdom on earth, and because for them there was no
eternal life but only a continuous cycle of generations of men, the only thing
they could love was a glory that would survive their death on "the lips of
those who sang their praises." The Christian's destiny is an eternal city where
no man is born or dies (5.16), which is "as far removed from [Rome] as heaven
is from earth, eternal life from temporal joys, solid glory from hollow praise,
the company of angels from that of mortals" (5.17). There God himself is
"life and salvation and sustenance and richness and glory and honor and peace
and all good things" (22.30).[21]

Thus, *gloria* is for Christians a reality outside time in which they expect to
participate in a conscious way but is also a reality in time by which men are
assisted toward that final goal. Following Matthew's words about letting

one's light shine before men (Mt. 5:16) Augustine argues that by means of their own temporal glory individuals should become an example for others who might glorify the Father, turn to him, and become what they (i.e., the Christians) are (5.14).[22] Such a view is not far removed from the ideas of Sallust and Cicero on the paradigmatic character of *gloria* which we saw above, although in their case the underlying assumptions and the final good belong to a different order of reality.

The two kinds of *gloria* we have dealt with thus far are rather easy to differentiate and to describe. Between them is a *tertium quid*, which is more difficult to categorize but equally important to Augustine's thought. After arguing at length in the first four books of the *City of God* that the growth of Roman *imperium* had nothing to do with honoring pagan deities, Augustine attempts to explain in Book 5 that this development was, in fact, part of God's providential design.[23] In historical terms that providence works through human motivation, and no less than Cicero or Sallust (*Catil.* 7.6), Augustine suggests that what lay behind Rome's rise to power and what inspired its heroes was ultimately *cupiditas gloriae*: "Hanc [i.e., gloriam] ardentissime dilexerunt, propter hanc uiuere uoluerunt, pro hac emori non dubitauerunt; ceteras cupiditates huius unius ingenti cupiditate presserunt. Ipsam denique patriam suam, quoniam seruire uidebatur inglorium dominari uero atque imperare gloriosum, prius omni studio liberam, deinde dominam esse concupiuerunt" (5.12 [*CCSL* 47:142–143]).

What follows in Augustine's text is a brief delineation of the accomplishments provoked by this passion for renown, accomplishments which Augustine acknowledges were "laudibilia scilicet atque gloriosa secundum hominum existimationem." Though the underlying motive here is still *dominatio*, Augustine's remarks on the growth of empire in this part of his work are descriptive rather than polemical and are largely free of the trenchant criticism of Rome's wars that we saw earlier.[24] He follows Sallust in recognizing that the *imperium Romanum* expanded through the arts of conquest, and then he makes an interesting comment: "Has artes illi tanto peritius exercebant quanto minus se uoluptatibus debant et eneruationi animi et corporis in concupiscendis et augendis diuitiis et per illas moribus corrumpendis, rapiendo miseris ciuibus . . ." (5.12 [*CCSL* 47:144]). Following Sallust again, Augustine introduces here an old theme in Roman historiography, i.e., the corrupting effects of avarice on a society which was originally motivated by noble aims,[25] and he harks back with some satisfaction to the heroes of an earlier day who pursued glory *per bonas artes* (i.e., the path of virtue).[26] These individuals, he argues, were motivated by *ambitio* ("a vice, which comes close to being a virtue") rather than by *auaritia*, and though few in number they managed important affairs and should be considered good men "according to their own standards."

The theme of a pristine era when Rome's leaders were free of avarice is reiterated in the next chapter, where Augustine attempts to explain why God willed that the empire should come into being: "Idque [i.e., regnum] talibus potissimum concessit hominibus ad domanda grauia mala multarum gentium qui causa honoris laudis et gloriae consuluerunt patriae in qua ipsam gloriam requirebant, salutemque eius saluti suae praeponere non dubitauerunt, pro isto uno uitio, id est amore laudis pecuniae cupiditatem et multa alia uitia conprimentes" (5.13 [*CCSL* 47:146–147]). And again in chapter 15, where the topic is God's justice in granting empire to men who practiced virtue according to their own best lights, he focuses on the absence of *auaritia*: "Sic et isti priuatas res suas pro re communi, hoc est, re publica, et pro eius aerario contempserunt, auaritiae restiterunt, consuluerunt patriae consilio libero, neque delicto secundum suas leges neque libidini obnoxii, his omnibus artibus tamquam uera uia nisi sunt ad honores imperium gloriam" (5.15 [*CCSL* 47:149]).

Throughout these comments on Roman worthies who practiced a high degree of virtue (*pro suo modo*, though it be)[27] there runs a consistent thought. Such men, Augustine argues, resisted the vice of avarice; that is, they were willing to sacrifice their own good for the good of others, their own private immediate benefit for the welfare of the community at large. In short, while pursuing personal temporal glory they were, in fact, placing limits on their own *amor sui*, and it is precisely this fact which distinguishes them both from those who are totally subject to the *libido dominandi* and from the Christian faithful. From this perspective, then, it seems appropriate to speak of three types of glory, since there are, in fact, three types of *amores* (i.e., that of the *superbi*, that of the *boni sine fide*, and that of the *sancti*). Augustine's more typical view that all men are governed by one of two *amores* (i.e., *amor sui* or *amor Dei*) and thus preoccupied with one or the other of two types of *gloria* does not easily accommodate a *tertium quid*, but it is clear that there are individuals who fall outside the categories of *sancti* or *superbi* and who practice a kind of natural virtue[28] for which they receive a temporal reward.[29]

As one might expect in an apologetic work designed both to demonstrate the uniqueness of the Christian perspective and to gain a sympathetic hearing from an audience preoccupied with what Peter Brown calls *litterata uetustas*,[30] Augustine's attitude toward these heroic figures is at once begrudging and full of admiration. Speaking of them in chapter 13 of Book 5 he says in a well-known comment: "Men who do not obtain the gift of the Holy Spirit and bridle their baser passions by pious faith and by love of intelligible beauty at any rate live better because of their desire for human praise and glory. While these men are not saints, to be sure, they are less vile [*minus turpes*]." Elsewhere, the bishop insists that such virtues, motivated as they are by human glory and oriented to a temporal reward,[31] are not to be compared with the *uera uirtus* which springs solely from Christian faith (5.19), and he does not hesitate, as we have seen (5.13), to call the love of human glory a *uitium*. Nonetheless, he can also speak of a *ueram licet humanarum laudum gloriam* (5.19),[32] and his descriptions of men like Regulus, Torquatus, Fabricius, Lucius Ualerius, and other noble *maiores* (5.18) suggest that these individuals were more than paper heroes to be dismissed or treated lightly.[33] What sets them apart from others is a resistance to the kind of *auaritial superbia* that we have seen above and a readiness to sacrifice their own interests for the benefit of others. If this is not true virtue (*uera uirtus*) in the Augustinian sense of the term, it is analogously so and, thus, worthy of commendation. What is more, Augustine frankly acknowledges that love of human glory can scarcely be eradicated from the heart of man (5.14) and, indeed, in the case of individuals wielding power, its absence can be a dangerous thing: "The man who disregards glory but is eager for rule surpasses wild beasts in vicious cruelty or in luxurious living. There have been Romans of this type, who, though they had lost interest in their reputation, were, nonetheless, not free from lust for domination" (5.19).[34] Thus, for all its limitations and for all the criticisms Augustine leveled against it, temporal glory had a laudable role to play in promoting *uirtus* and restraining *uitium*.[35]

It is partly for these reasons that Roman heroes who sought and won glory for themselves could serve as paradigms for those who seek another kind of glory. "Let us consider," Augustine says to his Christian audience, "what great things those Romans disregarded, what they endured, what passions they subdued, all to get glory in the eyes of men" (5.17), and "if in serving the glorious city of God we do not cling to the virtues that they clung to in serving the glory of the earthly city, let us be pricked to our hearts with shame" (5.18).

What separates the Christian from the pagan is not the pursuit of glory but the definition of the term and the conditions that govern its pursuit. If pagan and Christian glory are ultimately incompatible, the proportion that describes the relationship between the two in the world of time is not simply *malum* to *bonum* but human to divine, temporal to eternal, terrestrial to celestial. Thus, it is not enough to focus only on the ways in which Roman heroes in their pursuit of human glory fell short of Christian *uirtus*. Roman preoccupation with *gloria* could have salutary effects even in a Christian context, and for this reason Augustine's treatment of the theme is not just a measure of the gulf that separates the author from his pagan audience but a sign of the common ground on which they both stood.

## Notes

†Originally published in *Diakonia: Studies in Honor of Robert T. Meyer*. Ed. Thomas Halton and Joseph P. Williman. Washington, D.C.: Catholic U of America P, 1986. Pp. 133–44. Reprinted by permission of the author and publisher.

[1]The relationship between this preface and the work as a whole is discussed at length (with copious bibliography) by K. Thraede, "Das antike Rom in Augustins *De Civitate Dei*," *JbAC* 20 (1977), 103–132.

[2]For Augustine's tendency in the whole first half of the *City of God* to identify the Roman state with the *civitas terrena* see H. Hagendahl, *Augustine and the Latin Classics* (= *Studia Graeca et Latina Gothburgensia* XX.II [Göteborg, 1967]), 409–412. The complexities of Augustine's thinking on this matter are well known and are succinctly summarized in R. A. Markus' comment: "Augustine's identification of the Roman state with the earthly city is as clear in his writings as is his refusal to abide by this identification. His logic is the logic of later antique rhetoric rather than modern formal logic" (*Saeculum: History and Society in the Theology of St. Augustine* [Cambridge, 1970], 59).

[3]Augustine's purposes here are reiterated in various ways in the *City of God* itself and in other works. See, for example, *Civ.* 2.2; 3.1; 4.1–2; 5 *Praef.*; *Retract.* 2.69; *Epist.* ad *Firmum*; *Epist.* 169.1 and 184 A.5. Ultimately the specific goals of the first five books should be seen in the larger context of Augustine's overall purposes and developing ideas about the two cities. On this latter point see A. Lauras and H. Rondet, "Le thème des deux cités dans l'oeuvre de Saint Augustin" in *Études Augustiniennes* (Paris, 1953), 99–160. For a good recent survey of the historical and intellectual milieu of the *City of God* see T. D. Barnes, "Aspects of the Background of the *City of God*," *University of Ottawa Quarterly* 52 (1982), 64–80.

[4]For the importance of this dimension of Roman life see, among others, A. F. von Müller, *Gloria Bona Fama Bonorum: Studien zur sittlichen Bedeutung des Ruhmes in der frühchristlichen und mittelalterlichen Welt* (= *Historische Studien*, Heft 428 [Husum, 1977]), 28–38; A. D. Leeman, *Gloria: Cicero's Waardering van de Roem en Haar Achtergrond in de Hellenistische Wijsbegeerte en de Romeinse Samenleving* (with English summary), Rotterdam, n.d.; and especially U. Knoche, "Der römische Ruhmesgedanke," *Philologus* 89 (1934), 102–124.

[5]"Trahimur omnes studio laudis, et optimus quisque maxime gloria ducitur" (*Arch.* 11.26 [ed. Clark]); cf. Tacitus' statement to the same effect: "nam contemptu famae contemni uirtutes" (*Ann.* 4.38 [ed. C. D. Fisher]).

[6]*Phil.* 14.12.32: "Brevis a natura uita nobis data est; at memoria bene redditae uitae sempiterna. Quae si non esset longior quam haec uita, quis esset tam amens qui maximis laboribus et periculis ad summam laudem gloriamque contenderet?" (ed. Clark).

[7]*Phil.* 1.12.29: "Est autem gloria laus recte factorum magnorumque in rem

publicam fama meritorum quae cum optimi cuiusque tum etiam multitudinis testimonio comprobatur" (ed. Clark). Cf. *Marcell.* 8.26.

8See Cicero, *Tusc.* 1.45.109, and consult A. Otto, *Die Sprichwörter und sprichwörterlichen Redensarten der Römer* (Leipzig, 1890), 155.

9Cf. Q. Curtius, 4.14.25: "Ite alacres et spiritus pleni ut quam gloriam accepistis a maioribus posteris relinquatis" (ed. Bardon).

10Cf. Cicero, *de Orat.* 3.4.14; *Rhet. her.* 4.25.34; Seneca, *de Prov.* 3.9.

11Cicero, *Fin.* 1.18.59–60, *Tusc.* 4.79, *Off.* 1.20.68–69.

12For important studies dealing with various aspects of this topic see von Müller, op. cit., 58–73; V. Hand, *Augustin und das klassisch römische Selbstverständnis* (= *Hamburger Philologische Studien* 13 [Hamburg, 1970]), 16–22; W. Kamlah, *Christentum und Geschichtlichkeit*, 2d ed. (Stuttgart, 1951), esp. 281–301, and F. G. Maier, *Augustin und das antike Rom* (Tubingen, 1955), esp. 125–145.

13Augustine seems not at all consistent in his views about when and if moral decline occurred in the development of the Roman state. In 3.14 he quotes Sallust to the effect that the seeds of such decline were sown after the time of Cyrus; earlier (2.18) he had suggested that vices existed from the very beginning, and in 5.12 he will contend that, despite the truth of this latter statement, there were a few men in the early days who attained glory and honor by the path of virtue. For a thoughtful analysis of how Augustine reevaluates Sallust's ideas see G. F. Chesnut, Jr., "The Pattern of the Past: Augustine's Debate with Eusebius and Sallust," in J. Deschner et al., eds., *Our Common History as Christians: Essays in Honor of Albert C. Outler* (New York, 1975), 69–95. It seems to me, however, that Chesnut's assessment of Augustine's attitude toward Roman *uirtus* is overly pessimistic.

14And which Augustine believed was especially virulent in the Roman people. See 1.30.

153.14. Cf. Thraede, op. cit., 125. In 5.17 the bishop takes a slightly different slant on such conquests but still insists on the emptiness of human glory: "Nam quid intersit ad incolumnitatem bonosque mores, ipsas certe hominum dignitates, quod alii uicerunt, alii uicti sunt, omnino non uideo, praeter illum gloriae humanae inanissimum fastum in quo perceperunt mercedam suam, qui eius ingenti cupidine arserunt et ardentia bella gesserunt" (*CCSL* 47:150).

16With a few changes I have followed the translation of the *City of God* by G. MacCracken and W. Green in the Loeb series.

17Cf. *in Epist. Ioh.* 8.6: "Certe radix omnium malorum auaritia est: inuenimus et in superbia auaritiam esse, excessit enim modum homo. Quid esse auarum esse? Progredi ultra quam sufficit" (*PL* 35:2039). For the passage under discussion see the comments of A. Solignac, S. J., "La condition de l'homme pécheur d'après saint Augustin," *Nouvelle Revue Théologique* 78 (1956), 370–371.

1811.15: "Hi duo amores—quorum alter sanctus est, alter immundus, alter socialis, alter priuatus, alter communi utilitati consulens propter supernam societatem, alter etiam rem communem in potestatem propriam redigens propter adrogantem dominationem, alter subditus, alter aemulus deo, alter tranquillus, alter turbulentus, alter pacificus, alter seditiosus, alter ueritatem laudibus errantium praeferens, alter quoquo modo laudis auidus, alter amicalis, alter inuidus, alter hoc uolens proximo quod sibi, alter subicere proximum sibi, alter propter proximi utilitatem regens proximum, alter propter suam—praecesserunt in angelis, alter in bonis, alter in malis . . ." (*CSEL* 28:347–348). On *superbia* as the source of sin see, among others, W. J. Green, *Initium Omnis Peccati Superbia* (Berkeley, 1949); Solignac, loc. cit.; D. J. Macqueen "Augustine on *Superbia*: The Historical Background and Sources of His Doctrine," *Mélanges de Science Religieuse* 34 (1977), 193–211, and the same author's "*Contemptus Dei*: St. Augustine on the Disorder of Pride in Society and Its Remedies," *Recherches augustiniennes* 9 (1973), 227–293.

[19]See Lauras and Rondet, op. cit., 113.

[20]"Non in ea tamquam in suae uirtutis fine quieuerunt, sed eam quoque ipsam ad Dei gloriam referentes, cuius gratia tales erant, isto quoque fomite eos quibus consulebant, ad amorem illius a quo et ipsi tales fierent accendebant. Namque ne propter humanam gloriam boni essent, docuerat eos magister illorum. . . . Sed rurus ne hoc peruerse intellegentes hominibus placere metuerent minusque prodessent latendo, quod boni sunt, demonstrans quo fine innotescere deberent: 'Luceant,' inquit, opera uestra coram hominibus, ut uideant bona facta uestra et glorificent patrem uestrum, qui in caelis est" (*CCSL* 47:148).

[21]*Civ.* 22.30: "Praemium uirtutis erit ipse [Deus], qui uirtutem dedit eique se ipsum, quo melius et maius nihil possit esse, promisit. Quid est enim aliud quod per prophetam dixit: 'Ero illorum Deus, et ipsi erunt mihi plebs,' nisi: 'Ego ero unde satientur, ego ero quaecumque ab hominibus honeste desiderantur, et uita et salus et uictus et copia et gloria et honor et pax et omnia bona'? Sic enim et illud recte intellegitur quod ait apostolus: 'Ut sit Deus omnia in omnibus' [I Cor. 15:28] (*CCSL* 48:863). Cf. 14.28.

[22]On this point cf. Augustine's sermon *De Bono Uiduitatis* 22 (PL 40:448–449) and consult von Müller, 63, 70–71, and L. Buisson, *Potestas und Caritas: Die Päpstliche Gewalt in Spätmittelalter* (= *Forschungen zur Kirchlichen Rechtsgeschichte und zum Kirchenrecht*, Bd. II [Koln, 1958], 129–130). Augustine returns to this theme of the *exemplum* a little later (5.19) where he discusses what the truly virtuous man does in the face of praise. This individual, having no desire to rule, is concerned only with leading others to the celestial city, "ideoque instat ardenter ut potius ille laudatur a quo habet homo quidquid in eo iure laudatur" (*CCSL* 47:155).

[23]5.11: "Nullo modo est credendus [Deus] regna hominum eorumque dominationes et seruitutes a suae prouidentiae legibus alienas esse uoluisse" (*CCSL* 47:142).

[24]For Augustine's treatment of *gloria* in this part of the *City of God* see the helpful comments of Thraede, op. cit., 138–139 with notes.

[25]For the origins of this theme see A. W. Linott, "Imperial Expansion and Moral Decline in the Roman Republic," *Historia* 21 (1972), 626–638. See also G. Bonamente, "Il *metus Punicus* e la decadenza di Roma in Sallustio, Agostino ed Orosio," *Giornale Italiano di Filologia* 27 (1975), 137–169, where additional bibliography can be found.

[26]"Hae sunt illae bonae artes, per uirtutem scilicet, non per fallacem ambitionem ad honorem et gloriam et imperium peruenire; quae tamen bonus et ignauus aeque sibi exoptant; sed ille, id est bonus, uera uia nititur. Uia uirtus est, qua nititur tamquam ad possessionis finem, id est ad gloriam honorem imperium" (5.12 [*CCSL* 47:144]).

[27]"Sed per quosdam paucos, qui pro suo modo boni erant, magna administrabantur

atque illis toleratis ac temperatis malis paucorum bonorum prouidentia res illa crescebat. . . . Paucorum igitur uirtus ad gloriam honorem imperium eura uia, id est, ipsa uirtute, nitentium etiam a Catone laudata est. Hinc erat domi industria, quam commemorauit Cato, ut aerarium esset opulentum, tenues res priuatae. Unde corruptis moribus uitium e contrario posuit, publice egestatem, priuatim opulentiam" (5.12 [*CCSL* 47:146]).

28Whether the concept of natural virtue has any proper place in Augustine's thought is a much discussed issue. For opposing views on the matter see Maier (loc. cit.) and J. Straub, "Augustins Sorge um die *regeneratio imperii*," *Historisches Jahrbuch* 73 (1954), 36-60. Their differences on this point are part of a much larger disagreement about Augustine's attitude toward Rome as a temporal power. Maier contends that Augustine is fundamentally and pervasively negative on this score; Straub argues for a more positive outlook on the bishop's part. See also Thaede (op. cit., 141-145), who attempts to strike a middle ground on the issue. On the matter of natural virtue, it is difficult to gainsay the kind of evidence found in Augustine's letter to Marcellinus (*Epist.* 138.17) dated 412 A.D.: "Deus enim sic ostendit in opulentissimo et praeclaro imperio Romanorum quantum ualerent ciuiles etiam sine uera religione uirtutes ut intellegeretur hac addita fieri homines ciues alterius ciuitatis cuius rex ueritas, cuius lex caritas, cuius modus aeternitas" (*CSEL* 44:144-145). But see Maier, op. cit., 69-75, and F. Paschoud, *Roma Aeterna* (= *Bibliotheca Helvetica Romana* VII [Rome, 1967]), 263-275. A thoughtful and comprehensive study of the whole question of pagan virtues is that of J. Wang Tch'ang-Tche, S. J., *Saint Augustin et les vertus des paiens* (Paris, 1938).

29Augustine quotes or paraphrases Mt. 6:2 ("they have received their reward") several times in this vein when he is trying to show that temporal power was God's just recompense for those who practiced virtue *sine fide*. Cf. 5.15 and 17 and see Thraede, op. cit., 139.

30I.e., an antiquarian interest in their religious past as found in the literary monuments. See Brown's *Augustine of Hippo* (Berkeley, 1969), 299-312. E. Fortin provides an attractive and more subtle analysis of what the bishop was attempting to do in his attack on bookish religious ideas of pagan contemporaries. Fortin suggests that in place of a frontal assault on civil religion, which could prove to be excessively harmful in a time of political instability, Augustine chose to "take issue with an archaic religion for the sake of demonstrating, if only by implication, the fundamental defect of contemporary pagan religion or, for that matter, of any form of civil religion" ("Augustine and Roman Civil Religion: Some Critical Reflections," *Revue des Études Anciennes* 26 [1980], 255).

31Such glory is consistently spoken of as *humana* (5.16) or *hominum* (5.18), or as *terrena gloria* (5.15). For additional references see Hand, op, cit., 20 with notes.

32Without some distinction regarding the nature of human glory, there would be no point to Augustine's remarks (following Sallust) that some of the ancients pursued *gloria* by the *uera uia* but others through *dola atque fallacia*. See 5.12 and 19.

33In citing such *exempla* Augustine was following a long-standing Roman tradition. See V. Pöschl, "Augustinus und die römische Geschichtsauffassung," *Augustinus Magister* II (1954), 957-963, and III, 206, and for his assessment of these heroes see

Maier, op. cit., 84–93, and A. Calderini, "Riflessi di storia antica nel 'De Civitate Dei,'" *S. Agostino: Pubblicazione commemorativa del xv centenario della sua morte* (Milan, 1931), 405–421.

[34]The most prominent example, of course, was Nero, "cuius fuit tanta luxuries ut nihil ab eo putaretur uirile metuendum; tanta crudelitas ut nihil molle habere crederetur, si nesciretur" (*CCSL* 47:155). For Augustine's comments on this emperor see J. Rougè, "Nèron à la fin du IV et au début du V siècle," *Latomus* 37 (1978), 77–79.

[35]For the positive effects of *cupiditas gloriae* and for Augustine's views on the superiority of the Roman *imperium* over earlier realms see the comments of E. von Ivánka, "Römische Ideologie in der *Civitas Dei*," *Augustinus Magister* II, 411–417.

# III Philosophy and Theology

# *The City of God* and History†

# Vernon J. Bourke

"Prime Minister H. F. Verwoerd, of South Africa, was shot by David Pratt on April 9th, 1960." On the surface, this statement of recent historical fact seems easy to understand. The event occurred; the wounded man is now recovered; there is nothing more to it. It may be recorded as one of the unambiguous "facts" of twentieth-century history.

However, it is not that simple. The mere fact that a man was shot is not a memorable event in world history. Probably hundreds of men, throughout the world, are shot every month. In most cases, these acts of violence are not of historic significance. What made the shooting of the Prime Minister of South Africa important was the context. The surrounding conditions were charged with meanings which students of history in the twenty-first century may understand only with difficulty.

There is the political context: this wounded man is a key official in the government of his country. As a consequence, the shooting was an attempted assassination. There is the social and cultural context: this man is an outspoken advocate of *Apartheid*, in a country where differences of color loom large. There is the context of past but pertinent events: this man is of Dutch extraction, his assailant has an English background; we recall the Boer War. There is the context of analogous events: this incident brings to mind the assassination of an obscure archduke at Sarajevo, and the consequent holocaust of World War I. Even partially to understand such a fact of history can be a tremendously complicated matter.[1]

There are some historians who would see this fact in a still broader framework. If St. Augustine were living today, he would be vitally interested. It is quite possible that this great Christian was of Berber extraction and that he was as dark as the average Moroccan of our day. One of his first thoughts would be that this shooting shows the hand of divine Providence in human affairs. Augustine was completely theocentric in his thinking.[2] He was ever aware that nothing happens in this world that escapes God's knowledge and divine permission. His contextual framework for the interpretation of the events of history is the City of God.

To understand what the City of God meant to Augustine it is advisable to start with his general view of all reality.[3] It is a picture on three levels. At the top is God, wholly immutable, superior to all the vicissitudes of space and time. With God are the *rationes aeternae*, the eternal principles of all that is permanent in being, truth and goodness. At the bottom of the picture are all bodies, including human ones. They are mutable both in space and in time. Of themselves, bodies and bodily events are so variable and unsteady that they cannot be the objects of true knowledge. There are principles of change in living bodies (the *rationes seminales*, but these seminal reasons are not bodies. On the middle level are finite spirits (human souls and angels) which are immutable in regard to space but quite mutable in time.[4]

Now, in Augustinism man is much more clearly identified with his soul than with his body. Indeed, in an early work, Augustine speaks of man as "a soul using a body."[5] So, men are situated between the immutable and the mutable. Men have only to look up in order to contemplate the eternal truths. Likewise, they have only to glance downward to lose all notion of what is of permanent value. It is from this context that we derive the famous concepts of *conversion* and *aversion*: the soul is free to turn its gaze toward or away from its Creator. This is not merely a question of knowledge; it also makes possible two kinds of love. In a famous passage, Augustine suggests the connection between this dualism and two sorts of societies:

> These are the two loves: the first is holy, the second foul; the first is social, the second selfish; the first consults the common welfare for the sake of a celestial society, the second grasps at a selfish control of social affairs for the sake of arrogant domination; the first is submissive to God, the second tries to rival God; the first is quiet, the second restless; the first is peaceful, the second trouble-making; the first prefers truth to the praises of those who are in error, the second is greedy for praise however it may be obtained; the first is friendly, the second envious; the first desires for its neighbor what it wishes for itself, the second desires to subjugate its neighbor; the first rules its neighbor for the good of its neighbor, the second for its own advantage; and [these two loves] make a distinction among the angels, first belongs to the good angels, the second to the bad angels; and they also separate the two "cities" founded among the race of men, under the wonderful and ineffable Providence of God, administering and ordering all things that have been created; the first city is that of the just, the second is that of the wicked. And though they are now, during the course of time, intermingled, they shall be divided at the last judgment; the first, being joined by the good angels under its King, shall attain eternal life; the second in union with the bad angels under its king, shall be sent into eternal fire. Perhaps, we shall treat, God willing, of these two cities more fully in another place.[6]

This text offers a key to the understanding of the City of God. It is a society of persons under God as their Head, united in a common bond of love and cooperation, transcending differences of time, race, nationality and institutions. We need not hesitate over the source of this conception of a divine City. It is doubtless true that the point had been developed previously by the Donatist scholar, Tychonius.[7] There is a much more obvious and ultimate source than this. The City of God and the earthly City are contrasted in many verses of the Psalms.[8] Jerusalem is the heavenly City and Babylon is the earthly one.[9] In that remarkable series of sermon notes on the Psalms which we know as the *Enarrationes*, Augustine summarized his views on the two Cities:

> All who have a taste for earthly things, all who prefer earthly felicity to God, all who seek their own things and not those of Jesus Christ, belong to that one City which is metaphorically called Babylon and has the Devil for its king. But all who have a taste for the things that are above, who meditate upon heavenly things, who live in this world with care lest they offend God, who are wary of sinning, who are not ashamed to confess that they are sinners, humble, meek, holy, just, pious and good—all these belong to one City that has Christ as King . . .
>
> It delights me to speak a little more to you about this sweet City of God. For the most glorious things have been said of thee, O City of God (Ps. 86:3). And if I forget thee, O Jerusalem, let my right hand be forgotten (136:5). For, but one homeland is sweet, and truly but one homeland, the only homeland; apart from it, whatever occurs to us is but a pilgrimage . . .
>
> And these two Cities are intermixed during the present; they are to be separated in the end. They are in mutual conflict: one on the side of iniquity, the other on the side of justice; one on the side of vanity, the other on the side of verity. At times, this temporal mixture causes some who belong to the Babylonian City to take charge of matters that belong to Jerusalem; and again, some who belong to Jerusalem are made to administer things that belong to Babylon . . .
>
> You know that the citizens of the evil City administer some of the affairs of the good City. Let us see, now, whether the citizens of the good City administer some of the affairs of the bad City. Every earthly state (*res publica*) will certainly perish sometime, for its rule is to pass away when that Kingdom comes for which we pray: "Thy Kingdom come"; and of which it has been foretold, "His Kingdom will be without end." So, the earthly state has our citizens administering its affairs. Indeed, how many of the faithful, how many good men, are magistrates, judges, leaders, public officials and kings, in their cities? All these are just and good, having nothing in their hearts but the most glorious things that are said of thee, O City of God.[10]

It is these same themes that are treated in extended form in the great treatise, *On the City of God*, from Book XI to XXII.[11] The Scriptural origin of this treatment of the two Cities may even be traced back to Genesis. They are prefigured in the separation of heaven from earth, of light from darkness, of the waters from the dry land, and so on.[12] However, we must not understand such statements mechanically or in a deterministic fashion; those who belong to the heavenly City do so by their own free will, and the citizens of Babylon are such by virtue of their own voluntary commitment.

## Augustine and Philosophy of History

Now, in what sense does Augustine's concept of the City of God offer a basis for a Christian philosophy of history? Let us first of all dispose of the terminological problem presented by the word, *philosophy*. Etienne Gilson has argued forcefully that what we find in Augustine is not a philosophy but a theology of history.[13] It is quite true that we do not discover in Augustine a purely rational and naturalistic interpretation of human affairs. If this is what we mean by philosophy of history, Gilson is correct, as usual. However, Augustine did not use the term, *philosophia*, in this exclusive sense. Writing against the Pelagians, he says: "the philosophy of the non-believers (*Gentium*) is not more worthy than our Christian one, which is the one true philosophy, provided that the pursuit or love of wisdom is what is meant by this word.[14] It becomes obvious, then, that in Augustine's usage he has a philosophy of history but he would not distinguish it from a theology.

Of course, he has long been accepted, in Catholic and non-Catholic scholarship alike, as one of the founders of philosophy of history. Indeed, many modern works simply take it as accepted that he is most typical of Christian thinking in this area.[15] Perhaps it has almost been forgotten that Pope Leo XIII wrote a famous *Letter on Historical Studies*, in 1883, in which he told Cardinal Nina: "The great doctor of the Church, Augustine, was the leader of all in thinking out this philosophical art of history, and he brought it to perfection."[16] One enthusiastic writer has even suggested that a complete theory of history is found in the *City of God*.[17]

There is, then, in St. Augustine a Christian view of history and whether we call it philosophy or theology is of small consequence. Some who think on human history, today, see nothing but a string of unconnected and meaningless events.[18] Augustine, on the contrary, finds Providence manifested in all temporal events. It is not that he derives a theory of morality or value *from* history.[19] Instead, what the City of God conception means is that one must look to the eternal to find the meaning of the temporal.

Implicit in the Augustinian view of history are certain essential beliefs of Christianity: there is but one God; all men are creatures of God and have Adam as a single ancestor; all things and events come under the care of divine Providence; mankind has fallen from a more favorable original condition and is now subject to suffering and other evils; mankind has been redeemed through the Incarnation; and there is an ultimate end, a final happiness, with God in a future life in eternity, which men are free to work for and to attain.[20] Seen from the vantage point of this Christian setting, the events of temporal history become actions in the drama of redemption and salvation.

If we recall the prevailing pagan notion of human life and destiny, still widely current in Augustine's time, we can better appreciate the appeal of the City of God ideal. The dominating ancient view was that man lived like a puppet bound to the wheel of fate. Time was thought to be circular and repetitious. This is the cyclic theory of history which M. Eliade has so thoroughly studied.[21] It meant that mankind and the individual person were doomed to a perpetual recurrence of the same joys, sorrows and trials. No real progress was possible. Man was on a huge merry-go-round from which escape was utterly impossible. Toynbee has said of this cyclicism:

> We can hardly escape the conclusion that we are the perpetual victims of an everlasting cosmic practical joke, which condemns us to endure our sufferings and to overcome our difficulties and to purify ourselves of our sins—only to know in advance that the automatic and inevitable lapse of a certain meaningless measure of Time cannot fail to stultify all our human exertions.[22]

Now, Augustine's way of looking at human history broke this wheel of fate. He showed that its view of time and human destiny was wrong, that there is hope for release from the cares of this world, that human life is not a rat-race on an enclosed treadmill but a short journey to a promised land. He straightened out the movement of time, made man's temporal progress linear and real. Speaking of the problem of how temporal events occur, Augustine says:

> The philosophers of this world thought that there was no possibility or proper way of solving this problem, unless they postulated temporal cycles, whereby the same things are always renewed and repeated in the order of nature; and so they claimed that these cycles of future and past ages are to occur successively and without ending.[23]

In his criticism of this necessitarianism, Augustine is blunt. "Far be it from us," he says, "to believe such things. Christ died but once for our sins. Now that He is risen from the dead, He will die no more . . . and after the resurrection, we shall be with the Lord always."[24] Notice how this refutation relies solely on the great fact of Christ's death, not on science or on rationalized argument. This fact, thoroughly attested in sacred and secular documents, freed men's minds from the burden of determinism and fate. It gave mankind a positive goal beyond time and temporal history. Christ died but once for our sins.

More than this, Augustine's philosophy of history charted a program for world peace. This plan has nothing to do with a federation of nations, with international pacts and leagues of nations. Nor was it a charter for a Holy Roman Empire: the City of God is not a political institution.25 Augustine is not a patron of the identification of Church and State. Charlemagne's ill-fated Empire was much more the creature of the Byzantine notion of an all-embracing Christian society (as exemplified in Eusebius of Caesarea26) than of the *City of God.*

It is quite evident that what Augustine called for was a reform of the hearts of individual men, rather than of political institutions. For a better world society, we simply need better men. We see this in his famous analysis of peace:

> The peace, then, of the body lies in the ordered equilibrium of all its parts, the peace of the irrational soul, in the balanced adjustment of its appetites, the peace of the reasoning soul, in the harmonious correspondence of conduct and conviction; the peace of body and soul taken together, in the well-ordered life and health of the living whole. Peace between a mortal man and his Maker consists in ordered obedience, guided by faith, under God's eternal law; peace between man and man consists in regulated friendship. The peace of a home lies in the ordered harmony of authority and obedience among the members of a family living together. The peace of the political community is an ordered harmony of authority and obedience among citizens. The peace of the heavenly City lies in a perfectly ordered and harmonious communion of those who find their joy in God, and in one another in God. Peace, in its final sense, is the tranquillity of order in all things.27

## Thomas Aquinas and the City of God

It is interesting to see what happened to this ideal of the City of God, in the writings of St. Thomas Aquinas. The first thing that strikes the reader is that the expression, "City of God," is apparently never used by Aquinas.28 Of course, St. Thomas does discuss the *regnum Dei,* as this term is used by St. Paul.29 What he says is simply an expansion of the Pauline text:

> The Kingdom of God consists principally in interior acts but, as a consequence, all those things without which interior acts would be impossible also belong to the Kingdom of God. Thus, if the Kingdom of God is interior justice and peace and spiritual joy, then all the exterior acts that are incompatible with justice, peace and spiritual joy are also incompatible with the Kingdom of God; and so, in the Gospel they should be prohibited in the Kingdom.30

Clearly, St. Thomas is not developing any special notion of human history in such a commentary. Indeed, he has a much less sophisticated approach to history than Augustine. History is a mere chronicle of events, for Aquinas.[31]

Apart from the question of words, it may even be doubted that St. Thomas ever thought in terms of a society such as the Augustinian City of God. In some sense, Augustine's heavenly society requires to be contrasted with its opposite, the earthly City.[32] But St. Thomas appears to think of *all* men as constituting a universal community under God, by virtue of the community of human nature. In several places, he hints that, because all men have by *nature* the same ultimate end, beatitude, and because this beatitude is only attainable in that highest common good which is God, therefore all men are actually or potentially members of one vast human society, with God as Ruler. This universalism is difficult to pinpoint in the text of St. Thomas but here is one way in which he suggests it:

> Just as men who are associates in a state agree on this point, that they are subjects of one prince, by whose laws they are governed, so too do all men, to the extent that they naturally tend toward beatitude, have a certain general agreement in relation to God, as to the highest Prince of all, the Source of beatitude, the Legislator of the whole of justice . . . In the aforementioned community, in which all men agree as to the end that is beatitude, each man is considered as a part, while the common good of the whole is God Himself, in Whom the beatitude of all men lies.[33]

It is to be noted in this text, taken from a highly personal work of Aquinas, that all men are placed in this same universal society. We may well wonder whether St. Thomas could view social history as Augustine did, whether Thomism is open to that initial bifurcation of mankind which characterized the Augustinian social view. There is a short text in St. Thomas' *Exposition of the Sentences* which throws additional light on his position. There, he speaks of a divine community (*communicatio divina*) of all men in the one body of the Church. He adds that this membership is either actual or potential, and that it is a friendship in charity which extends to all, even to enemies.[34]

One can hardly avoid the conclusion that Thomas Aquinas places much less stress than Augustine on the contrast between men of good will and those who turn away from God. Sometimes we may wonder whether Aquinas was sufficiently aware of the pluralistic character of actual human societies. In his *Sermon on the Creed*, preached in Naples near the end of his life, he confidently asserted:

> It is well known, in fact, that the whole world used to worship idols and to persecute Christ's faith. To this, even the histories written by pagans give testimony. Today, however, all are converted to Christ—the wise, the nobles,

the rich, the powerful and the great—all are converted to the preaching of those who are simple and poor, of those few men who preach Christ.[35]

In view of such a statement, it seems probable that, if Aquinas said little or nothing about the City of God, he had still less to say about the earthly City. Rather, he regarded mankind on the natural level as ordered and unified in a common tendency toward happiness, and on the supernatural level as unified within the all-embracing arms of divine charity. He is not unaware that there are many men who are individually evil but he does not view them as members of an evil society. Possibly this is why St. Thomas offers us no developed philosophy of history. One may, of course, take some of the characteristic Thomistic views of human life and society and elaborate a modern scholastic theory of history. This has been done by Jacques Maritain, Martin D'Arcy, and others.[36] Such works are the personal products of present-day thinkers rather than interpretations of Thomas Aquinas.[37]

## The City of God and History Today

With certain notable exceptions of whom Christopher Dawson is an outstanding example,[38] Christian historians have failed to make full use of the Augustinian concept of the City of God. To some extent, this failure is understandable. It is very easy to pervert Augustinism. One may concentrate too much on Augustine's sweeping assertions concerning God's foreknowledge and end with something very much like Calvinistic predestination. One may exaggerate the depths to which men have fallen as a result of the sin of Adam—and thus achieve a neo-Jansenism. One might overstress his assertions that man, his actions and his world, are nothing without God—and thus repeat the errors of Ontologism.

Ironically enough, Augustine has anticipated the judgment of contemporary positivism on human history. *Of itself,* the course of human events has no ultimate meaning for Augustine. What he would add (and there is no doubt that this is authentically Christian) is that we must not try to understand human affairs and institutions, *by themselves.* There are no absolutes for those who abandon an Absolute God. Ultimate values disappear, if we deliberately turn away from the Ultimate Being. This seems to me to be the foundation stone of a Christian philosophy of history.

Human events become significant when we view them in the light of divine Providence.[39] God becomes the focal point of an ultimate explanation of the human societies through time. This explanation admits of various interpretations, even within Augustinism. To some interpreters, the high point of history is the incarnation. When God became man, humanity reached its peak. All later human events are anti-climatic.[40] A second way of interpreting the Christian view of history is the eschatological. This shifts the emphasis to the End of Time and sees humanity as in process toward a not yet attained but ultimate condition of mankind.[41] Such a view would see in temporal history a continuing and increasing fulfillment of the Redemption. It is not foreign to Augustine's thought, as any reader of the last four books of the *City of God* will realize.

To stress the role of divine Providence in history is not a narrow "Catholic" position. In his introduction to the famous *Lectures on the Philosophy of History*, the Protestant Hegel said: "Our earnest endeavor must be directed to the recognition of the ways of Providence, the means it uses, and the historical phenomena in which it manifests itself."[42] It would be difficult to state the plan of a Christian view of history more succinctly. Of course, Hegel proceeds to describe the ways of God, in accord with his own dialectic, but the point is that Hegel did not exclude some sort of providential explanation of history.

Another very informative recognition of the other-worldly context of history is to be found in the late mediaeval treatise by the Mohammedan, Ibn Khaldûn. He began his work with a terse statement of the need for history as a part of philosophy:

> The inner meaning of history, on the other hand, involves speculation and an attempt to get at the truth, subtle explanation of the causes and origins of existing things, and deep knowledge of the how and why of events. [History] therefore, is firmly rooted in philosophy. It deserves to be accounted a branch of philosophy.[43]

But Ibn Khaldûn is a theist. Within a few pages, he adds: "God is the guide to that which is correct."[44] His understanding of the work of divine Providence is not identical with a Christian one, yet there are fundamental similarities.

This brings us to a final point. A Christian view of history places political institutions in a position of secondary value; these things are not ends in themselves but means to a good human life on earth. This does not mean that the Christian historian should hold earthly peace and societal order in contempt. The relation between the City of God and the Church is not without ambiguity. Sometimes Augustine seems to suggest that they are identical; sometimes he radically distinguishes them. If we take the Church as a visible institution on earth, then the City of God is much more than that. But if we understand the Church in the broadest sense, as embracing all men of good will, from all the ages, past, present and future, we more nearly approach the limits of the heavenly City. What stands out in Augustine's

account of the progress of the City of God through history is his insistence
that the good and evil men are never separated in this world, or in time. Only
at the Last Judgment will this final separation be effected.[45] There is no
question that Augustine never expected to see complete peace in this world. I
do not think, however, that he was opposed to efforts to establish good
political order throughout the world.[46]

The citizens of God should be noteworthy for their tolerance and charity
toward all. We cannot pass a final judgment now: there are good and bad
men in every period, race, community and nation. The City of God makes
room for all, on the basis of their personal qualities of mind and heart. In this
spirit, we may close with Augustine's words:

> So long, then, as the heavenly City is wayfaring on earth, she invites citizens
> from all nations and all tongues, and unites them into a single pilgrim band.
> She takes no issue with that diversity of customs, laws, and traditions whereby
> human peace is sought and maintained. Instead of nullifying or tearing down,
> she preserves and appropriates whatever in the diversities of divers races is
> aimed at one and the same objective of human peace, provided only that they
> do not stand in the way of faith and worship of the one supreme and true
> God.[47]

# Notes

†Reprinted by permission of the publisher from *Wisdom from St. Augustine*. Texas:
U of St. Thomas P, 1984. Ch. 13, 188–205.

[1] See Etienne Gilson's discussion of the statement, "Charlemagne was crowned
emperor in 800," ("Doctrinal History and Its Interpretation," *Speculum*, XXIV [1949]
483–492) for a more thorough demonstration of this point.

[2] J. Grabowski, *The All-Present God. A Study in St. Augustine* (St. Louis: Herder,
1954).

[3] B. Cooke, "The Mutability-Immutability Principle in St. Augustine's
Metaphysics," *The Modern Schoolman*, XXIII (1946), 175–193; XXIV (1946), 37–49.

[4] *Epist.* 18, 2: "Est natura per locos et tempora mutabilis, ut corpus. Et est natura
per locos nullo modo, sed tantum per tempora etiam ipsa mutabilis, ut anima. Et est
natura quae nec per locos, nec per tempora mutari potest, hoc Deus est." Cf. *De Genesi
ad litteram*, VIII, 20, 39.

[5] *De moribus ecclesiae*, I, 27, 52: "Homo igitur, ut homini apparet, anima rationalis
est mortali atque terreno utens corpore." See Gilson, *Introduction à l'etude de s.
Augustin*, 3e éd. (Paris: Vrin, 1949), p. 58.

[6] *De Genesi ad litteram*, XI, 15, 20; as translated in Bourke, *Augustine's Quest of
Wisdom* (Milwaukee: Bruce, 1945), p. 249.

[7] Cf. H. Scholz, *Glaube und Unglaube in der Weltgeschichte* (Leipzig, 1911), p. 78.

[8] Ps. 47:1: "Great is the Lord, and exceedingly to be praised in the City of our

God . . ." Ps. 86:3: "Glorious things are said of thee: O City of God." Ps. 47:5: "For behold the kings of the earth assembled themselves . . ." Ps. 48:2–3: "Hear these things all ye nations: give ear, all ye inhabitants of the world. All you that are earthborn, and you sons of men . . ."

[9]See all of Psalm 136.

[10]*Enarr. in Ps.*, 61, 6–8.

[11]A quick summary is offered in *Augustine's Quest of Wisdom*, pp. 263–284.

[12]See *Genesis* 1:1–4, 9–17, etc.

[13]See his *Introduction to the City of God* (New York: Fathers of the Church, 1949), vol. 1; in the Image Book condensation, pp. 30–31.

[14]*Contra Fulianum Pelagianum*, IV, 14, 72: "Obsecro te, non est honestior philosophia gentium quam nostra Christiana, quae una est vera philosophia, quando quidem studium vel amor sapientiae significatur hoc nomine." Cf. *De beata vita*, 4.

[15]"St. Augustine in the *City of God* advanced the first complete philosophy of history in which the past, the present, and the future are combined in one drama, a drama of sin and redemption." J. E. Boodin, "Philosophy of History," in *Twentieth Century Philosophy* (New York: Philosophical Library, 1943), p. 97. See also, Hans Meyerhoff, *The Philosophy of History in Our Time* (New York: Doubleday Anchor Books, 1959), pp. 1–7; Roger Shinn, "Augustinian and Cyclical Views of History," *Anglican Theological Review*, 31 (1949), 133–141.

[16]"Artem ipsam historiae philosophicam magnus Ecclesiae doctor Augustinus princeps omnium excogitavit, perfecit." *Lett. al Card.* Nina, Agosto 1883; cited in C. Butti, *La mente di S. Agostino nella Citta di Dio* (Firenze: Libreria Editrice Fiorentina, 1930), pp. 84–85.

[17]"In questo concetto sintetico è tutta la teorica della filosofia della storia. La teorica originale e meravigliosa della *Citta di Dio*." Butti, *op. cit.*, p. 84

[18]Karl Popper takes this positivist position in *The Open Society and Its Enemies* (Princeton: Princeton U. Press 1950), pp. 449–458.

[19]Morris Cohen mistakenly considered that this was the aim of Augustine. See *Reason and Nature* (New York and Chicago: Free Press, 1931), p. 377.

[20]Cf. Butti, *op. cit.*, pp. 77–78.

[21]Mircea Eliade, *The Myth of the Eternal Return*, translated by W. R. Trask (New York: Pantheon Books, 1954).

[22]Arnold Toynbee, *A Study of History*, 4, 30; see the further comment on this passage, in Shinn, *art. cit.*, p. 141.

[23]"Hanc autem se philosophi mundi hujus non aliter putaverunt posse vel debere dissolvere, nisi ut circuitus temporum inducerent, quibus eadem semper fuisse renovata atque repetita in rerum natura, atque ita deinceps fore sine cessatione asseverarent volumina venientium praetereuntiumque saeculorum." *De civitate Dei*, XII, 13.

[24]"Absit, inquam, ut nos ista credamus. Semel enim Christus mortuus est pro peccatis nostris: resurgens autem a mortuis jam non moritur, et mors ei ultra non dominabitur: et nos post resurrectionem semper cum Domino erimus." *Ibid.*

[25]On this, I agree with F. E. Cranz, "*De civitate Dei*, 15, 2, and Augustine's Idea of the Christian Society," *Speculum*, 25 (1952), 215–225; see my article, "The Political Philosophy of St. Augustine," *Proc. Amer. Cath. Philos. Assoc.*, VII (1931), 45–55.

[26]Cf. Cranz, *art. cit.*, p. 220.

[27]*City of God*, 19, 11; translation of G. Walsh (Image Book edition, p. 456) with some modifications by the present writer.

[28]It is difficult to establish a negative of this kind, when one is dealing with works as vast as the *Opera Omnia* of St. Thomas. Let me simply say that *civitas Dei* is not indexed in the standard concordances (L. Schütz, the Leonine *Indices*, and Peter of Bergamo's *Tabula Aurea*) nor have I ever seen the phrase, apart from citations of Augustine's treatise, in the *Opera Omnia*.

[29]Rom. 14:17.

[30]*Summa Theologiae*, 1-2, 108, I, ad 1; cf. *Expositio Pauli Epist. ad Rom.*, 14, lectio 2.

[31]"Nam historia est . . . cum simpliciter aliquid proponitur." *S. T.*, I, 1, 10, ad 2. (This statement occurs in a discussion of the historical sense of Scripture.)

[32]I do not suggest anything of Manichean dualism in Augustine's contrast; it is simply a fact for Augustine that there are two kinds of men.

[33]*De perfectione vitae spiritualis*, c. 13 (*Opuscula Omnia*, ed. P. Mandonnet, 4, 223-224)

[34]"Quarta communicatio est divina, secundum quam omnes homines communicant in uno corpore Ecclesiae, vel actu vel potentia; et haec est amicitia caritatis quae habetur ad omnes, etiam ad inimicos." *In 3 Sententiarum*, 29, 6, resp.

[35]*Expositio devotissima super Symbolum Apostolorum, ad init.* (*Opuscula Omnia*, ed. Mandonnet, 4, 351).

[36]J. Maritain, *On the Philosophy of History*, ed. by J. W. Evans (New York: Scribners, 1957); "The Christian and History," *Jubilee*, 5 (1957), 37-40. M. D'Arcy, *The Sense of History: Secular and Sacred* (London: Faber and Faber, 1959); *The Meaning and Matter of History* (New York: Farrar, Strauss and Cudahy, 1959).

[37]From quite another point of view, that of the scientific character of the discipline of history, see B. J. Muller-Thym, "Of History as a Calculus Whose Term is Science," *The Modern Schoolman*, 19, 3 (March 1942), 41-47; 19, 4 (May 1942), 73-76.

[38]Besides his well-known historical monographs, Dawson's two essays: "The Dying World," and "The City of God," in *A Monument to Saint Augustine* (New York: Sheed and Ward, 1930), are still worth careful reading.

[39]Thus understood, history can have a special meaning for Thomas Aquinas; indeed, he has so treated the sphere of human actions and society, in the Third book of his *Summa contra Gentiles*.

[40]For this Incarnationist view, see: P. Henry, "The Christian Philosophy of History," *Theological Studies*, 13 (1952), 419-432.

[41]Nikolai Berdyaev, *Smisl Istorii* (Berlin: Obelisk, 1923); translated as *The Meaning of History*, by G. Heavey (New York: Scribners, 1956). Possibly there is some parallel in the evolutionism of Père Teilhard de Chardin; see C. Tresmontant, *P. Teilhard de Chardin, His Thought* (Baltimore: Helicon, 1959).

[42]G. W. F. Hegel, *The Philosophy of History*, translated by J. Sibree (New York: Willey Book Co., 1900), p. 14.

[43]Ibn Khaldûn, *The Muqaddimah. An Introduction to History*, translated by F. Rosenthal (Bollingen Series, 43) (New York: Pantheon Books, 1958), vol. 1, p. 6.

[44]*Ibid.*, p. 26.

45*City of God*, 18, 54.
46How else explain his admiration for the *Pax Romana?* See *City of God*, 18, 22.
47*City of God*, 19, 17; translated by G. Walsh et al., Image ed., p. 465.

# Augustine's *City of God* and the Modern Historical Consciousness†

## Ernest L. Fortin

Contemporary Augustinian scholarship is distinguished among other ways by its emphasis on Augustine's alleged contribution to the development of the modern notion of history. Except for a few sporadic references to a possible theology of history in the *City of God*, one finds little in the literature of the nineteenth and early twentieth centuries to indicate that the content of that work might be of particular relevance to the problem at hand.[1] The same is not true of the post-World War I period, which witnessed a sudden surge of interest in this hitherto neglected subject, to such an extent that there has scarcely been a major treatment of Augustine's thought written since that time which does not dwell on it at considerable length. Augustine, Langdon Gilkey has recently asserted, is "the father of the historical consciousness,"[2] the first author to exhibit an awareness of the fundamentally historical character of human existence, the only early Christian writer to have brought the whole of history within the compass of a "purposive unity."[3]

It was normal perhaps that, in the midst of what was perceived as a crisis of major proportions engulfing the whole of Western civilization—witness the extraordinary success of Spengler's *Decline of the West* or Ferrero's *Words to the Deaf*, to mention two of the most widely read books of the twenties—scholarly attention should have been drawn to the waning years of the Roman empire and the upheavals that precipitated its demise. Here was a great civilization that had not only gone under but had bequeathed to posterity a well-documented record of its own breakdown, the only corpse sufficiently well preserved to lend itself to a dissection. Among the ancient writers to whom one might turn for information about this critical period, none was better suited than Augustine, who had himself been prompted by the dramatic events of his day to meditate on the fate of empires and the destiny of the human race. From him one could hope to learn something about what conceivably lay in store for us: whether the dislocations of our own troubled times were the necessary prelude to a larger and more powerful unity or whether they portended a return to the barbarism that had once plunged Europe into darkness for centuries; whether, as Ferrero put it, our fate was "that of the generations of Caesar and Augustus or that of the generations of Diocletian and Constantine."[4]

Yet the conflicting results to which this intensive research eventually led suggest that the quarry may be more elusive than had been anticipated.

Heinrich Scholz's earlier case for the presence of an incipient philosophy of history in Augustine[5] was countered by U.A. Padovani's contention that, since Augustine's unifying principle is derived from Revelation, his views are best described as a theology rather than a philosophy of history.[6] Scholz's Hegelian account of the *City of God* was followed some years later by Kamlah's Heideggerian or individualistic interpretation of the same work,[7] itself soon to be challenged by Ratzinger's forceful insistence on the properly ecclesial and sacramental dimension of Augustine's thought.[8] The protracted debate, whatever else may be said about it, has had at least one notable effect. It secured accreditation for the notion of a theology of history in academic circles and enshrined it as a kind of theological *locus communis*, decked out with the aura of a tradition supposedly dating back to the early Christian centuries and the authority of no less a figure than Augustine himself.

To be sure, few people would go so far as to say that Augustine's speculations on this theme measure up to modern standards. By comparison to our own fully developed sense of history, they remain deficient and represent at best a feeble anticipation of what was to emerge with total clarity only at a much later date. What is still lacking in them, Gilkey tells us, is an appreciation of "the creativity of freedom in time and above all the sense that the course of history itself, the 'destiny' of its institutional structures, can constitute an intrinsic part of the unfolding meaning of history."[9] Accordingly, "the consciousness of history [had to] shift before this initial sense of history's meaning under God [could become] the modern consciousness of history." It is all the more remarkable that, in spite of these manifest shortcomings, Augustine should have been able to view time and the historical process as "linear, teleological, and meaningful,"[10] thereby endowing them with "an intelligibility . . . which they had not possessed before."[11] To him, more than to anyone else, belongs the honor of having laid the groundwork for a more perfect understanding of this all-important concept.

Gilkey's subtle analysis nevertheless leaves unanswered a number of basic questions that continue to perplex the assiduous reader of Augustine and of the literature of Christian antiquity. We need not concern ourselves with the issue of the superiority of the modern over the premodern conception of history, inasmuch as any decision in that regard presupposes that one has achieved an adequate grasp of both positions—a task which clearly lies beyond the modest scope of the present study and perhaps beyond the reach of all but the greatest talents. My own more limited question is whether the modern conception to which Gilkey points as the culmination of an intellectual development originated by Augustine did in fact emerge on the basis of

Augustine's novel approach to history or whether it should not rather be seen as a radical departure from it.

It is worth noting, first of all, that Augustine himself employs the word *history* only sparingly (certainly much less frequently than some widely circulated translations of his works might lead us to think) and that when he does, it is without reference to an overall meaning with which the course of human events might be invested. The only thematic discussion of it to occur anywhere in his works, that of the *De Doctrina Christiana*, defines history in traditional terms as the accurate and useful narration of past events: *historia facta narrat fideliter atque utiliter*.[12] As opposed to the false art of soothsaying, it does not pretend to tell us what ought to be done but only what has been done and hence cannot be undone. As such, it is not unlike the account that one might give of the world around us or what is sometimes called natural history.[13] To the extent to which grammarians resort to it to explicate literary texts, it bears some relationship to the liberal arts;[14] but since its function is merely to record the actions of human beings, it is not itself an art or a product of the human mind;[15] and since the objects to which it addresses itself pertain to the realm of bodily perception, it cannot be reckoned as a science either.[16] Moreover, the information that it supplies is not altogether reliable. Historians often contradict one another or deliberately seek to mislead their readers. It stands to reason that, when such contradictions occur, only the facts that accord with Sacred scripture are to be credited.[17] Yet its importance is far from negligible, for it not infrequently sheds light on the events of sacred history and furnishes us with a store of examples from which there is occasional profit to be derived.[18] At no point in the discussion do we encounter the faintest allusion to some humanly decipherable plan which a careful study of the past could help to unveil.

Granted that Augustine never uses the word *history* in that precise sense, one may be tempted to argue that the reality associated with it in the modern mind is not foreign to his thought. Even this, however, is open to serious question. Seen from the perspective of the Bible, human events no doubt form part of a providential order that comprises the whole of history;[19] but in the absence of any specific knowledge of the workings of divine providence, one is at a loss to say how they are related to one another or to the pre-established end to which they supposedly conduce. Anyone contemplating the sequence of these events is struck first and last not by its rationality but its patent irrationality. Civilizations flourish at one moment and then vanish just as mysteriously. While we have it on the authority of Scripture that all power wielded by human beings ultimately comes from God, the reasons for which in the course of time it passed from one people to

another have not been imparted to us. What is more, there is no correlation
between just or unjust rule on the one hand and earthly prosperity or
misfortune on the other. Constantine, the first Christian emperor, enjoyed a
long reign and the certainly no less pious Jovian a very short one.[20] God
grants dominion "to whom he pleases," to Augustus one day and to Caligula
or Nero the next, for motives which, though never unjust, remain
impenetrable; so much so that even after the fact human reason is unable to
determine why he does it or how precisely what he does contributes to the
furtherance of the goal that he pursues among human beings.[21]

Any attempt to reduce the total succession of temporal events to the unity
of an intelligible order is further thwarted by the fact that these events, to the
degree to which they have their source in, or are decisively influenced by, the
undetermined human will, are largely unamenable to scientific treatment.
That there is such a thing as free choice is attested to by the common practice
of enacting laws, engaging in exhortation, bestowing praise and blame, and
administering rewards and punishments, none of which would make sense if
human beings were not accountable for their actions.[22] It can likewise be
shown that this freedom has its source in God himself, who confers on all
creatures the power not only to act but to act in accordance with their proper
mode, whether it be natural or voluntary.[23]

What is not completely clear is how, despite their radical contingency,
human acts are used by God for purposes to which they are not intrinsically
ordered. The least that can be said in answer to this admittedly complex
question is that there is nothing contradictory in the assertion that a rational
agent may be the determinate cause of events that others perceive as
fortuitous. I may, for example, arrange a meeting between two strangers who
have no reason to suspect that what they take to be a chance encounter was in
fact premeditated by someone else. The analogy is of course imperfect, since,
having no final control over the doings of others, I can never be sure that the
plan will succeed. Either one of the two parties involved could turn down my
invitation or suffer a heart attack before the projected meeting took place.
Not so with God, the supreme ruler and architect of the universe, who
weaves into the fabric of history a pattern which from a higher vantage point
may yet prove to be coherent: *architectus aedificat per machinas transituras
domum manentem.*[24] But to say this is to admit that the rationality of the
divine plan is not in the materials used but in the mind of the user, or, less
metaphorically stated, that the teleology in question remains extrinsic to the
events themselves. No analysis of these events will ever lead to the discovery
of an end which is at once present and operative in the process from the
beginning and destined to be progressively actualized through it.

It follows that the future course of human history is totally unpredictable.

History will come to an end at the appointed time, not because of anything that human beings have done or may yet do, but because God will have chosen to bring it to a close.[25] As far as anyone can tell, its completion is in no way related to emergent political structures or the general state of human affairs at any given moment. This obviously does not rule out the possibility of substantial and even "spectacular" (*stupenda*) advances in knowledge and the arts as time goes on. But if, as Augustine argues, the gains registered on this limited front are as likely to be used for destructive as for constructive purposes,[26] one fails to see how they could provide a reliable standard by which to measure the progress accomplished by the human race in the course of its long history.

*     *     *

Not only from the time of Christ but from that of Abel the Church has gone forth on pilgrimage, amid both the persecutions of the world and the consolations of God; and so it will be "until the end of time."[45] As far as the prospects for the future are concerned, they remain as uncertain as always; for "in the very great mutability of human affairs, no people has even been granted such security as would free it from the dread of invasions hostile to this life."[46] Neither is it true that the rise and decline of the great world empires fall into anything like the symmetrical pattern into which Orosius had unscrupulously tried to nudge them. The Assyrian empire, for example, endured, not 1,400 years, but 1,240 years or, if one includes the reign of Belus, 1,305 years.[47] No juggling of the historical data will allow us to uncover an intimation of rational design in this random succession of worldly powers.

The same skepticism pervades Augustine's reinterpretation of the notion of a Christian era "—*tempora christiana*—which had recently been injected into the debate as a term of derogation by the pagan adversaries of Christianity."[48] Orosius had seized upon it not only to vindicate the Christian faith—others had done as much—but to bolster his own incremental conception of the development of Roman history: "Behold how under Christian kings and in these Christian times (*tempora christiana*) civil wars, even when they prove unavoidable, are brought to a happy issue. The victory has been won, the city stands intact, the tyrant has been laid low."[49] Augustine is a good deal more cautious. However beneficial he may have considered the spread of Christianity to be in other respects, he certainly did not think that it carried with it any guarantee of earthly prosperity. It has been proposed, most recently by R. A. Markus, that Augustine, too, had once succumbed to a "triumphant" assessment of the emergence of Christianity and viewed the present age as the long-awaited fulfillment of the Old Testament prophecies, only to retract himself in his later writings and subject his initial understanding of the *tempora christiana* to a "drastic devaluation" in the light of the reverses of the first decades of the fifth century.[50] Whether or not this is the case remains somewhat debatable.[51] There is little reason to believe that Augustine ever sought to endow the Christian empire with quasi-messianic attributes, and even less reason to believe that he had second thoughts about ascribing a temporal meaning to the prophetic utterances of the Old Testament.[52] I know of no text in which he denies that *any* of these prophecies refer to temporal events. What he does deny, in his early as well as in his later works, is that they contain only glad tidings. The truth of the matter, as he sees it, is that both happy and unhappy events have been foretold by the prophets and the Gospel. Commenting again on the convulsions of this time, he writes:

> These things should make us weep but not wonder; and we ought to cry unto God that, not for our merit but according to his mercy, he may deliver us from such great evils. For, what else was to be expected by the human race, seeing that these things were so long ago foretold both by the prophets and in the Gospel? We ought not, therefore, be so inconsistent as to believe these Scriptures when they are read by us, and to complain when they are fulfilled. It is rather those who refused to believe when they read or heard these things in Scripture who ought to become believers now that they behold the word fulfilled. Just as this great pressure of the Lord God's olive-press brings forth the dregs of unbelieving murmurs and blasphemies, so, too, it should produce a steady outpouring of pure oil in the confessions and prayers of believers. For, to those who never tire of hurling their impious complaints at the Christian faith and claim that, prior to the time when this doctrine was proclaimed throughout the world, the human race was not subjected to such great evils, an answer can readily be given from the Gospel. Indeed, as the Lord says, "That servant who does not know his master's will and does what deserves a beating shall receive a light beating, whereas the servant who does know his master's will and does what deserves a beating shall receive a severe beating" (Luke 22:47–48). Is it surprising that, in these Christian times (*christianis temporibus*), this world, like the servant who knows his master's will and yet does what deserves a beating should be punished severely? These people notice the rapidity with which the Gospel is propagated, but not the perversity with which it is despised by many.[53]

If the new times, then, are not necessarily better or more peaceful than the old, one cannot claim for Christianity the politically redemptive role that Orosius and his mentor, Eusebius, had assigned to it.

The attractiveness of Eusebius' *Reichstheologie* and its Orosian analogue is that it offered what was far and away the most elegant solution yet devised to the problem of the Christian's involvement in Roman public life. As long as this involvement entailed the risk of complicity in a manifestly iniquitous rule, the Christian conscience could feel justified in adopting an attitude of uncompromising opposition to it. One is reminded in this connection of the bitter invectives of an earlier generation of Christian extremists, represented pre-eminently by Hippolytus of Rome, who had been taught by the Book of Revelation to identify the Roman Empire with the harlot "seated upon the seven hills" and "drunk with the blood of the saints and martyrs of Jesus."[54] Under such adverse conditions, it might well be asked what indeed the Church had to do with Caesar. The accession of a Christian, or of someone partial to Christianity, to the imperial throne had brought about a complete reversal of the situation. Little wonder that this unexpected turn of events should have been hailed as the most important milestone in the history of Christianity since the birth of Christ.[55] If public affairs were henceforth to be administered in accordance with the rules of strict justice, if wars were destined to disappear altogether, if the only wars remaining to be waged were demonstrably just wars, and if the newly converted empire was but an earthly reflection of God's eternal kingdom,[56] any qualms that one might have had about lending one's support to it could be laid to rest. The conflict between the moral ideal of the Sermon on the Mount and the harsh necessities of the political life had happily come to an end.

*          *          *

There is yet another, perhaps more cogent reason for which, upon reflection, Eusebius' imperial theology in any of its forms appeared fraught with peril. If, as Eusebius and Orosius seem to have been persuaded, political institutions are bound to improve with passing of time and if, along with this improvement, the evils to which they invariably gave rise are to vanish from the scene, one wonders what is to become of human excellence and virtue once the process reaches its completion. Later generations would be spared the trouble of overcoming the obstacles that had previously stood in the path of right action. The success of their endeavors would be assured without their having to make any of the efforts required of their less fortunate predecessors. One could look forward to the day when one need not shoulder the burden of virtue in order to reap its rewards.

Augustine's question is whether virtue can still be called virtue if success is always guaranteed. There is surely nothing wrong in following a charted course of action whose outcome is never in doubt, but there is nothing particularly glorious in it either. What gives to virtue its distinctively human character is precisely the uncertainty with which in all interesting cases one is compelled to act. People are at best responsible for the goodness or badness of their deeds, not for their results. They may deserve to be successful, but whether or not they are depends in large measure on circumstances that lie beyond their control and may not even be known to them at the time of action. A just judge who has done everything in his power to ascertain the facts of the case cannot be held to account for unwittingly condemning an innocent person, however wrong his judgment may be.[64] The paradox is that were it not for the possibility of evil, virtue itself would be in serious jeopardy. Prudence loses its raison d'être once one is relieved of the need to discern right from wrong, as does moderation once all the impediments to the accomplishment of what has been judged right are removed.[65] The function of virtue is not to do away with evil but to conquer it.[66] Even as it does so, its victory is never secure; for "as long as the vices against which it struggles resist, the battle remains precarious, and even when defeated they do not permit a triumph of carefree ease."[67]

Nowhere is this inner struggle more appparent than when the deliberations bear on the use of force as a means of opposing injustice. For the sake of preserving the purity of one's soul, one would doubtless prefer to see an end to all wars, but even this will never be more than a pious wish. A weak justice is hardly an appropriate response to the injustices of the world. It only leads to greater injustice by allowing the wicked to prevail over the just.[68] Complete peace is not part of man's mortal conditon. It belongs to that "other life" which alone is free from the corruption of sin and death and in which nothing either in ourselves or in others will be at war with any of us.[69]

Against the background of these ideas one is in a better position to measure the gulf that separates the Augustinian from the modern view of history. The philosophy of history came into being with Kant at the end of the eighteenth century and the early years of the nineteenth century in the wake of Rousseau's epoch-making attack on bourgeois morality. Its basic thrust was not only to restore genuine morality but to insure that its exercise would not be obstructed by oppressive political structures. With typical modern realism it assumed that human good will alone could not be relied upon to overturn these evil structures and that the necessary reform would come about only through the operation of a hidden "teleology" at work in the historical process. Progress was assured neither by the simple diffusion of scientific knowledge, as others had once thought, nor by the deliberate pursuit of moral purposes on the part of human beings, but by the free interplay of the essentially immoral or self-regarding passions.[70] By their incessant preying on one another human beings had created a situation from which they could extricate themselves only by desisting from any further attempt at aggrandizement at the expense of their fellow human beings.[71] Wars would diminish in frequency and intensity, not because their irrationality offended mankind's moral sense, but because they were proving ever more costly and suicidal.[72] An invisible hand of nature had seen to it that the antagonisms which characterize human intercourse would constrain even evildoers to accept a civic constitution recognizing the rights of all human beings and granting to each individual as much freedom as is consistent with the freedom of others.[73] The conflict between private and public morality once resolved, no one would run the risk of being punished for complying with unconditionally binding moral law.[74]

To be sure, the whole process, although morally desirable, did not of itself lead to a higher degree of morality; for, the free society that it was calculated to produce could still theoretically be made up entirely of devils.[75] To that extent, Kant's solution called for a series of correctives that others after him would attempt to supply. But if the good citizen need not be a good man, at least there was nothing to prevent the good man from being at the same time a good citizen. One was henceforth spared the ignominy of having to suffer unjustly at the hands of an immoral society.

Augustine was at once more hopeful for the destiny of the individual and less hopeful for that of society at large. To repeat what was said earlier, the *City of God* was first conceived as an effort to refurbish the argument by which Christian apologetics had traditionally sought to reconcile Christianity with the legitimate demands of the political life. It soon became apparent, however, that the incisive issue was not whether civil society could survive Christianity but whether Christianity itself could survive its integration into civil society. The problem was the more acute as the new faith was never envisaged as a purely private concern but was rather called upon to play within society a role similar to that which had once devolved upon pagan religion. Before the work was completed, the conventional defense with which it began had developed into a highly original attack on some of Augustine's fellow Christians and a far more probing analysis of the political implications of the Christian faith than any that had hitherto been undertaken.

The solution adopted by Eusebius and his followers was based on the assumption that a converted Roman empire could live up to the ethical standards of the Gospel or that a perfectly just social order was possible. Augustine destroyed the ground of the argument by insisting that no society had ever conformed to the requirements of strict justice or was likely to do so. The very notion of a Christian polity, whether it be upheld seriously or for reasons of expediency, is at best a comforting and at worst a fatal illusion.

Christian wisdom and political power are not only distinct but always more or less at odds with each other in accordance with the vicissitudes of history and the mostly evil inclinations of the human heart. Some regimes may be superior to others but there is no reason to think that the regime under which one happens to live will necessarily be followed by a better one, or, more importantly, that any of them is at all capable of fulfilling man's longing for wholeness.[76] In short, the history of which the *City of God* speaks is anything but an inside history. Its goal remains transcendent and wholly independent of any observable improvement in the political sphere.

In view of Augustine's pessimism regarding the perfectibility of human institutions and the structural foundations of society, one is entitled to ask what, if anything, the modern philosophy of history owes to him. The one point on which both views would appear to be in agreement, even though it is never explicitly discussed by Kant, concerns the linear and nonrepeatable character of the historical process. That this central premise should have been so easily taken for granted by modern philosophers of history is perhaps an indirect tribute to the persuasive power of the *City of God*. But then the notion that history takes its course along a straight line can hardly be considered an Augustinian innovation. It underlies the whole of the biblical account of human existence, for which both Kantian and Hegelian philosophy were intended as a substitute. One is still left to wonder in what specific sense Augustine might qualify as the first philosopher of history or the father of the modern historical consciousness.

# Notes

†Originally published in *The Review of Politics* 41 (1979): 323–43. Reprinted by permission of the publisher.

[1]H.-I. Marrou, "Geschichtsphilosophie," in *Reallexicom für Antike und Christentum*, vol. 10 (forthcoming).

[2]L. Gilkey, *Reaping the Whirlwind* (New York, 1956), p. 175. Cf. *ibid.*, p. 162: "With Augustine the Western, and so the modern, sense of temporal passage comes to definitive and formative expression"; p. 163: "With him (Augustine) begins the tradition of philosophy of history."

[3]*Ibid.*, p. 164.

[4]G. Ferrero, *Words to the Deaf*, trans. B. R. Redman (New York, 1926), p. 159.

[5]H. Scholz, *Glaube und Unglaübe in der Weltgeschichte* (Leipzig, 1911).

[6]U.A. Padovani, "*La Città di Dio* di Sant'Agostino: teologia e non filosofia della storia," *Rivista di filosofia neo-scolastica, Supplemento speciale al vol.* XXIII (Milano, 1931), pp. 220–263.

[7]W. Kamlah, *Christentum und Geschichtlichkeit*, 2nd ed. (Cologne-Stuttgart, 1951).

[8]J. Ratzinger, *Volk und Haus Gottes in Augustins Lehre von der Kirche* (Munich,

1954); *idem*, "Herkunft und Sinn der Civitas-Lehre Augustins," *Augustinus Magister*, vol. 2 (Paris, 1954), 965-979.

9L. Gilkey, *Reaping the Whirlwind*, p. 175. Cf. *ibid.*, p. 174: "In the end, Augustine is not even interested in the kind or level of order and justice among social institutions."

10*Ibid.*, p. 163.

11*Ibid.*, p. 162.

12*De Doctrina Christiana* 2.28.44.

13*Ibid.*, 2.29.45.

14Cf. *De Ordine* 2.12.37; *Epist.* 101.2.

15*De Doctrina Christiana* 2.28.44.

16*Ibid.*, 2.27.41.

17*De Civ. Dei* 18.40. Cf. *Contra Faust. Manich.* 18.4; *Epist.* 101.2.

18*De Doctrina Christiana* 2.28.42; *De Vera Religione* 26.49.

19Cf. *De Civ. Dei* 5.11.

20*Ibid.*, 5.25. Jovian's reign lasted less than eight months, from June 363 to February 364.

21*Ibid.*, 5.21; cf. 5.19 and 4.33. On the limits of historical knowledge according to Augustine, see A. W. Ziegler, "Die Grenzen geschichtlicher Erkenntnis: Beiträge zur augustinischen Geschichtstheologie," *Augustinus Magister*, vol. 2 (Paris, 1954), 981-989.

22*De Civ. Dei* 5.9.2 and 5.10.2.

23*Ibid.*, 5.9.4.

24*Sermo* 362.7.

25Cf. *De Civ. Dei* 18.53.1.

26*Ibid.*, 12.24.3.

*[Text for notes 27-44 not reprinted here.]

\*      \*      \*

45*Ibid.*, 18.51.2.

46*Ibid.*, 17.13.

47*Ibid.*, 4.6 and 18.21. Cf. Marrou, "Saint Augustin, Orose et l'augustinisme historique," p. 75; E. Corsini, *Introduzione alle "Storie" di Orosio* (Turin, 1968), pp. 203-204.

48Cf. P. Courcelle, "Propos antichrétiens rapportés par saint Augustin," *Recherches augustiniennes*, 1 (Paris, 1958), 178-183.

49*Hist. adv. Paganos* 7.33.

50R. A. Markus, *Saeculum: History and Society in the Theology of St. Augustine* (Cambridge, 1970), p. 35.

51See the recent discussion of Markus's thesis by G. Madec, "*Tempora christiana*: Expression du triomphalisme chrétien ou récrimination païenne," in *Scientia Augustiniana: Studien über Augustinus, den Augustinismus und den Augustinerorden*, eds. P. Mayer and W. Eckermann (Wurzburg, 1975), pp. 112-136.

52For examples of Old Testament prophecies that may be thought to have been realized in New Testament times, see *De Civ. Dei* 18.46-50.

53*Epist.* 111.2. See also *De Catechizandis Rudibus* 27.53-54; *Sermo* 81.7-9; *Sermo*

*Denis* 24.10–13; Madec, "*Tempora christiana*," pp. 124–125.

[54]Cf. Hippolytus *In Danielem* 4.8–9. J. W. Swain, "The Theory of the Four Monarchies: Opposition History under the Roman Empire," *Classical Philology*, 35 (1940), 1–21; R. A. Markus, "The Roman Empire in Early Christian Historiography," p. 342; *idem, Saeculum*, pp. 48–49.

[55]For a detailed account of the initial enthusiasm provoked by the Christianization of the Empire and the subsequent reaction against it, see G. Williams, "Christology and Church-State Relations in the Fourth Century," *Church History*, 20, no. 3 and 20, no. 4 (1951), 3–33 and 3–26.

[56]Cf. Eusebius *Laus Constantini* 1.6; 3.5–6, *passim*, and the discussion by E. Cranz, "Kingdom and Polity in Eusebius of Caesarea," *Harvard Theological Review*, 45 (1952), 47–66.

*[Text for notes 57–63 not reprinted here.]

*     *     *

[64]Cf. *De Civ. Dei* 19.6.

[65]*Ibid.*, 19.4.4

[66]*Ibid.*, 19.4.3.

[67]*Ibid.*, 19.27.

[68]*Ibid.*, 19.7.

[69]*Ibid.*, 19.27; cf. *Enar. in Psalm.* 148.1–2.

[70]Cf. I. Kant, *The Idea for a Universal History from a Cosmopolitan Point of View*, Fourth Thesis, in Immanuel Kant, *On History*, ed. L. W. Beck (Indianapolis, 1963), p. 15: "Thus man expects opposition on all sides because, in knowing himself, he knows that he, on his own part, is inclined to oppose others. This opposition it is which awakens all his powers, brings him to conquer his inclination to laziness and, propelled by vainglory, lust for power, and avarice, to achieve a rank among his fellows whom he cannot tolerate but from whom he cannot withdraw." *Idem, Perpetual Peace*, First Supplement, *ibid.*, p. 106: "The guarantee of perpetual peace is nothing less than that great artist, nature (*natura daedala rerum*). In her mechanical course we see that her aim is to produce a harmony among men, against their will and indeed through their discord. As a necessity working according to laws we do not know, we call it destiny. But, considering its design in world history, we call it 'providence,' inasmuch as we discern in it the profound wisdom of a higher cause which predetermines the course of nature and directs it to the objective final end of the human race."

[71]*Idea for a Universal History*, p. 16: "Man wishes concord; but Nature knows better what is good for the race; she wills discord. He wishes to live comfortably and pleasantly; Nature wills that he should be plunged from sloth and passive contentment into labor and trouble, in order that he may find means of extricating himself from them. The natural urges to this, the sources of unsociableness and mutual opposition from which so many evils arise, drive men to new exertions of their forces and thus to the manifold development of their capacities."

[72]*Ibid.*, Seventh Thesis, p. 18: "The friction among men, the inevitable antagonism, which is a mark of even the largest societies and political bodies, is used by Nature as a means to establish a condition of quiet and security. Through war, through the taxing

and never-ending accumulation of armament, through the want which any state, even in peacetime, must suffer internally, Nature forces them to make at first inadequate and tentative attempts; finally, after devastations, revolutions, and even complete exhaustion, she brings them to that which reason could have told them at the beginning and with far less sad experience, to wit, to step from the lawless condition of savages into a league of nations."

73*Ibid.*, Fifth Thesis, p. 16: "The highest purpose of Nature, which is the development of all the capacities which can be achieved by mankind, is attainable only in society, and more specifically in the society with the greatest freedom. Such a society is one in which there is an all-pervasive opposition among the members, together with the most exact definition of freedom and fixing of its limits so that it may be consistent with the freedom of others."

74*Perpetual Peace*, Appendix I, p. 117: "Taken objectively, morality is in itself practical, being the totality of unconditionally mandatory laws according to which we ought to act. It would obviously be absurd, after granting authority to the concept of duty, to pretend that we cannot do our duty, for in that case this concept would itself drop out of morality (*ultra posse nemo obligatur*). Consequently, there can be no conflict of politics, as a practical doctrine of right, with ethics, as a theoretical doctrine of right."

75*Perpetual Peace*, First Supplement, pp. 111–112: "Now the republican constitution is the only one entirely fitting to the rights of man. But it is the most difficult to establish and even harder to preserve, so that many say a republic would have to be a nation of angels, because men with their selfish inclinations are not capable of a constitution of such sublime form. But precisely with these inclinations nature comes to the aid of the general will established on reason, which is revered even though impotent in practice. Thus it is only a question of a good organization of the state (which does lie in man's power), whereby the powers of each selfish inclination are so arranged in opposition that one moderates or destroys the ruinous effect of the other. The consequence for reason is the same as if none of them existed, and man is forced to be a good citizen even if not morally a good man. The problem of organizing a state, however hard it may seem, can be solved even for a race of devils, if only they are intelligent."

76Cf. *De Civ. Dei* 2.21; 19.21 and 24.

# Augustine's *City of God*:
# The Divided Self/The Divided *Civitas*†

## Patricia L. MacKinnon

The *locus classicus* of the analogy between the individual and the body politic is Plato's *Republic*. The body politic analogy is introduced in Book II (368d–369a) as a heuristic device to facilitate the discovery of the true nature of justice, the virtue upon which the integrity of the individual, and consequently, of society as a whole, depends. Socrates likens the difficulty of discerning the invisible workings of justice in the depths of the individual human soul to that of trying to read an inscription of tiny letters with poor vision at a distance. He observes that the same elements or letters (*stoicheia*)—that is, the interior disposition of the souls—are present in their externalized aspect, magnified and, therefore, legible in the political life of the city. The city *qua* inscription is composed of citizens who are its "letters." Epigrammatically put, the City is the Soul writ large.[1]

The writer most influential (after Plato) in his application of the analogical form of Platonic analysis to the interpretation and representation of history is St. Augustine in the *City of God*. In his monumental account of human history, Augustine vociferously attacks the claims and classical political theory concerning the perfective function of the state. Yet at the same time he ransacks classical thought abstracting countless ideas to form a new Christian synthesis.[2] As Augustine himself acknowledges, no other philosophy exercised so profound and lasting an influence upon him as that of Plato.

Indeed, the exceptional regard in which Augustine held Plato (and subsequent Platonic and Neoplatonic thought) issues from the belief that of all the various philosophical schools, it is that of Plato which most closely approximates to the truth. In his earliest Christian work, *Against the Academicians*, Augustine unreservedly characterizes Platonism "as the one absolutely true philosophical culture."[3] According to his testimony in the *Confessions* (VII.x), the role played by "certain Platonic books" in his conversion was pivotal. The texts to which Augustine alludes in the *Confessions*, it is generally agreed, were Neoplatonic. The writings of Plotinus and perhaps, Porphyry, initiated Augustine into a world of heightened understanding which enabled him, he says, for the first time to conceive of the spiritual nature of God. Although Platonic thought was capable of attaining such lofty insights—including the understanding of the immortality of the soul, the creation, and the providential order of the cosmos—what the

Platonists lacked, according to Augustine (*Confessions* VII.ix), was an understanding of the Incarnation of the *Logos*. In the *City of God*, written toward the end of his life, Augustine continues to affirm the remarkable affinities between Christianity and Platonism. But he also regards it as his duty to correct the Platonists' errors. At the end of Book I (chapter xxxvi) he outlines the nature of his polemical dialogue with the Platonists, specifying several of the points which the Platonists hold in common, as well as their fundamental disagreement, with the Christians:

> Quae, nisi fallor, questio multo erit operosior et subtiliore disputatione dignior, ut et contra philosophos in ea disseratur, non quoslibet, sed qui apud illos excellentissima gloria clari sunt et nobiscum multa sentiunt, et de animae inmortalitate et quod Deus verus mundum condiderit et de providentia eius, qua universum quod condidit regit. Sed quoniam et ipsi in illis, quae contra nos sentiunt, refellendi sunt, deesse huic officio non debemus, ut refutatis impiis contradictionibus pro viribus, quas Deus inpertiet, asseramus civitatem Dei veramque pietatem et Dei cultum, in quo uno veraciter sempiterna beatitudo promittitur.

> Unless I am mistaken, this argument will be more difficult and will require discussion of greater subtlety. We shall have to engage with philosophers, and philosophers of no ordinary sort, but those who enjoy the most eminent reputation amongst our adversaries and who are in agreement with us on many points—on the immortality of the soul, on God's creation of the universe, and on his providence which governs his creation. But even these must be rebutted on the points on which they disagree with us; and therefore we must not fail in our duty, so that, when we have refuted their impious attacks—in so far as God gives us strength—we may establish the City of God, and true religion, and the true worship of God. For in this alone is the genuine promise of eternal bliss.[4]

What distinguishes the *City of God* from other Augustinian texts is the extent to which it is based not merely upon the Platonic heritage but rather on one particular Platonic text, the *Republic*. As Werner Jaeger stated, Augustine "created the philosophy of history which the Middle Ages were to adopt, by taking Plato's *Republic* and Christianizing it into his *City of God*."[5]

To assert that Augustine's philosophy of history in the *City of God* is directly based upon the assimilation of Plato's *Republic* within a Christian frame of reference, one has to assume that Augustine read Plato's work. Robert E. Cushman points out that among those writings of Plato which Augustine is likely to have read, the *Republic* was available in the Latin translation of Apuleius of Madaura.[6] Augustine's familiarity with the writings of Apuleius—a fellow North African, rhetorician and Platonist, and author of the satirical romance popularly known as *The Golden Ass*—is attested to in the *City of God* where Augustine refers to him at some length.[7]

Fortunately ₁Augustine has left us a clue to the actual method of appropriation and the rationale he employed in incorporating Plato. In *On the True Religion* (IV.vii), Augustine confidently asserts that all that is needed to "convert" the Platonists is the modification of a few words and formulae. The particular Platonic formula of the body politic analogy is not difficult to discern in its new Augustinian vesture.[8] Rather it serves prominently, as it does in Plato, as a unifying principle of organization. In this chapter, I shall try to show how the application of the body politic analogy in the *City of God* serves as the keystone of Augustine's pessimistic vision of the inevitable symmetry between human nature and the destiny of humankind.

### Two Cities/Two Loves

Augustine's transformation of the governing trope of the *Republic* into the conceptual keystone of the *City of God* is discernible in his definition of the "two cities." The antithetical identities of the two communities are not only typified but constituted by the inner orientation of their respective citizens. In the final chapter of Book XIV, Augustine expounds the underlying relationship between each *civitas* and its members. The nature of every community is determined by what the citizens set their hearts upon or, more simply put, what the citizens love. This definition is clearly a development of Plato's fundamental axiom that the relations internal to the individual soul are the index and determining factor of the form of polity.

Fecerunt itaque civitates duas amores duo, terrenam scilicet amor sui usque ad contemptum Dei, caelestem vero amor Dei usque ad contemptum sui. Denique illa in se ipsa, haec in Domino gloriatur. Illa enim quaerit ab hominibus gloriam; huic autem Deus conscientiae testis maxima est gloria. Illa in gloria sua exaltat caput suum; haec dicit Deo suo: Gloria mea et exaltans caput meum. Illi in principibus eius vel in eis quas subiugat nationibus dominandi libido dominatru; in hac serviunt invicem in caritate et praepositi consulendo et subditi obtemperando. Illa in suis potentibus diligit virtutem suam; haec dicit Deo suo: Diligam te, Domine, virtus mea. Ideoque in illa sapientes eius secundum hominem viventes aut corporis aut animi sui bona aut utriusque sectati sunt, aut qui potuerunt cognoscere Deum, non ut Deum honoraverunt aut gratias egerunt, sed evanuerunt in cogitationibus suis, et obscuratum est insipiens cor eorum; dicentes se esse sapientes (id est dominante sibi superbia in sua sapientia sese extollentes) stulti facti sunt et inmutaverunt gloriam incorruptibilis Dei in similitudinem imaginis corruptibilis hominis et volucrum et quadrupedum et serpentium (ad huiusce modi enim simulacra adoranda vel duces populorum vel sectatores fuerunt), et coluerunt atque servierunt creaturae potius quam Creatori, qui est benedictus in saecula; in hac

autem nulla est hominis sapientia nisi pietas, qua recte colitur versus Deus, id
expectans praemium in societate sanctorum non solum hominum, verum etiam
angelorum, ut sit Deus omnia in omnibus.[9]

We see then that the two cities were created by two kinds of love: the earthly
city was created by self-love reaching the point of contempt of God, the
Heavenly City by the love of God carried as far as contempt of self. In fact,
the earthly city glories in itself, the Heavenly City glories in the Lord. The
former looks for glory from men, the latter finds its highest glory in God, the
witness of a good conscience. The earthly lifts up its head in its own glory, the
Heavenly City says to its God: "My glory: you lift up my head." In the
former, the lust for domination lords it over its princes as over the nations it
subjugates: in the other both those put in authority and those subject to them
serve one another in love, the rulers by their counsel, the subjects by
obedience. The one city loves its own strength shown in its powerful leaders;
the other says to its god, "I will love you, my Lord, my strength."

Consequently, in the earthly city its wise men who live by men's standards
have pursued the good of the body or of their own mind, or of both. Or those
of them who were able to know God "did not honour him as God, nor did
they give thanks to him, but they dwindled into futility in their thoughts, and
their senseless heart was darkened: in asserting their wisdom:—that is, exalting
themselves in their wisdom, under the domination of pride—"they became
foolish, and changed their glory of the imperishable God into an image
representing a perishable man, or birds or beasts or reptiles"—for in the
adoration of idols of this kind they were either leaders or followers of the
general public—"and they worshipped and served created things instead of the
Creator, who is blessed for ever." In the Heavenly City, on the other hand,
man's only wisdom is the devotion which rightly worships the true God, and
looks for its reward in the fellowship of the saints, not only holy men but also
holy angels, "so that God may be all in all."[10]

I have quoted this passage at length not only because it establishes the
analogical definition governing the correspondence between "soul" and "city,"
but also because it does so through the use of *antithesis*, the other key
rhetorical strategy prominent throughout the work. The figure of *antithesis*
as Henri Marrou aptly notes "dépasse le simple procédé rythmique et devient
une forme logique, un des cadres essentiels où s'enferme sa pensée."[11] Indeed,
the example cited above represents on a miniature scale the conceptual and
structural order of the work as a whole which may be described as an example
of *syncrisis*, or concatenated antitheses, on a grand scale. Implicitly
Augustine's reliance upon this rhetorical strategy is an imitation of the
creative signature of God discernible within the logic of human history.
Augustine's methodology is based upon his understanding of the significance

of *antithesis* which he describes in Book XI (chapter xviii) as follows:

> Neque enim Deus ullum, non dico angelorum sed vel hominum crearet, quem
> malum futurem esse praescisset, nisi pariter nosset quibus eos bonorum usibus
> commodaret atque ita ordinem saeculorum tamquam pulcherriumum carmen
> etiam ex quibusdam quasi antithetis honestaret. Antitheta enim quae
> appellantur in ornamentis elocutionis sunt decentissima, quae Latine ut
> appellentur opposita, vel, quod expressius dicitur, contraposita, non est apud
> nos huius vocabuli consuetudo, cum tamen eisdem ornamentis locutionis etiam
> sermo Latinus utatur, immo linguae omnium gentium . . . Sicut ergo ista
> contraria contrariis opposita sermonis pulcritudinem reddunt: ita quadam non
> verborum, sed rerum eloquentia contrariorum oppositione saeculi pulcritudo
> componitur. Apertissime hoc positum est in libro ecclessiastico isto modo:
> "Contra malum bonum est et contra mortem vait; sic contra pium peccator.
> Et sic intuere in omnia oper Altissimi, bina bina, unum contra unum."[12]

> For God would never have created a man, let alone an angel, in foreknowledge
> of his future evil state, if he had not known at the same time how he would put
> such creatures to good use, and thus enrich the course of the world history by
> the kind of antithesis which gives beauty to a poem. "Antithesis" provides the
> most attractive figures in literary composition: the Latin equivalent is
> "opposition," or more accurately, "contraposition". . . . The opposition of such
> contraries gives an added beauty to speech; and in the same way there is beauty
> in the composition of the world's history arising from the antithesis of
> contraries—a kind of eloquence in events, instead of in words. This point is
> made very clearly in the book Ecclesiasticus, "Good confronts evil, life
> confronts death: so the sinner confronts the devout. And in this way you
> should observe all the works of the Most High; two by two; one confronting
> the other."[13]

The concept of two opposing cities competing for the individual's earthly
allegiance, to which all humankind anagogically belong, is also present in
Plato's speculations about the nature of human destiny in this life and the
final destination of the soul in eternity. In the *Theatetus* (176e–177a), Socrates
describes two contrasting societies, one of beatitude and one of misery, and
the ultimate folly of human injustice:

> There are two patterns, my friend, in the changing nature of things, one of
> divine happiness, the other of godless misery—a truth to which their folly
> makes them utterly blind, unaware that in doing injustice they are growing less
> like one of these patterns and more like the other. The penalty they pay is the
> life they lead, answering to the pattern they resemble. But if we tell them that,
> unless they rid themselves of their superior cunning, that other region which is
> free from all evil will not receive them after death, but here on earth they will

dwell for all time in some form of life resembling their own and in the society
of things as evil as themselves, all this will sound like foolishness to such strong
and unscrupulous minds.14

The typology of the two contrary paradigms set out in the *Theatetus*
appears in an elaborated, hierarchical version in the *Republic* VIII(543c–545b).
Between the opposition of the best and the worst person who, respectively,
represent the unique ideal city and that city's most extreme aberration,
Socrates introduces a graduated scale of related types of polity and personality.
As in the *Theatetus*, the ultimate index of the condition of the soul and the
city to which the individual belongs, is "the happiness and unhappiness of the
possessor." Socrates asks to be reminded where they left off, and Glaucon
responds:

> That is easy, he said, for at that time, almost exactly as now, on the supposition
> that you had finished the description of the city, you were going on to say that
> you assumed such a city as you then described and the corresponding type of
> man to be good, and that too though as it appears, you had a still finer city and
> type of man to tell of, but at any rate you were saying that the others are
> aberrations, if this city is right. But regarding the other constitutions, my
> recollection is that you said there were four species worth speaking of and
> observing their defects and the corresponding types of men, in order that when
> we had seen them all and come to an agreement about the best and worst man,
> we might determine whether the best is the happiest and the worst most
> wretched or whether it is otherwise. . . .

> Now we have already described the man corresponding to aristocracy or the
> government of the best, whom we aver to be the truly good and just man.

> We have.

> Must we not, then, after this, survey the inferior types, the man who is
> contentious and covetous of honor, corresponding to the Laconian
> constitution, and the oligarchic man in turn, and the democratic and
> tyrannical, in order that, after observing the most unjust of all, we may oppose
> him to the most just, and complete our inquiry as to the relation of pure justice
> to injustice in respect of the happiness and unhappiness of the possessor. . . . 15

Here *in nuce* is the basis of the Augustinian dichotomy between contrary
analogical types: Plato's "best" and "worst" person corresponds to
Augustine's godly and ungodly person; Plato's one "right" city versus its
multiple degenerate forms becomes Augustine's unique *civitas Dei* as opposed
to the multiplicity of exemplars characterizing the history of the *civitas*

*terrena.* Lastly, Plato's claim that the inner rectitude of the soul is its own reward and may be judged by the happiness and unhappiness of its possessor, acquires an eschatological emphasis in Augustine upon ultimate spiritual polarities—the felicity of eternal life as opposed to the misery of damnation.

Augustine is also concerned with the existential value of happiness to the soul and society. For example, in chapter iii of Book IV, Augustine reduces the two cities to their opposing character types and describes their respective internal conditions, external relations and ends. In place of the comprehensive Platonic virtue of justice, Augustine substitutes an analogical notion of temperance as a condition of right order in the individual soul from which issues the experience of peace not only in the individual but also in the body politic at all levels. Peace both subjectively and objectively in the Augustinian transposition of Plato's argument becomes the absolute measure of existential happiness, in keeping with Augustine's eschatological aspirations.[16]

In framing his discussion of the existential value of peace in the self and in society in Book IV (chapter iii), Augustine strives to educate the reader in the analytic method and significance of his argument by making explicit the analogical procedure or *regula.* It is apparent that Augustine's linguistic comparison of the relation of the individual to the city—*ut in sermone una littera*—is a conspicuous allusion to the original Socratic explication of the body politic analogy at *Republic* II.368d–369 where Socrates argues that the individual citizens stand in the same relation to the city-state as the *stoicheia* to an inscription.

> sed duos constituamus homines (nam singulus quisque homo, ut in sermone una littera, ita quasi elementum est civitatis et regni, quantali bet terrarum occupatione latissimi), quorum duorum hominum unum pauperem vel potius mediocrem, alium praedivitem cogitemus; sed divitem timoribus anxium, maeroribus tabescentem cupiditate flagrantem, numquam securum semper inquietum, perpetuis inimicitiarum contentionibus anhelantem, augentem sane his miseriis patrimonium suum in inmensum modum atque illis augmentis curas quoque amarissimas aggerantem; mediocrem vero illum re familiari parva atque succinta sibi sufficientem, carissimum suis, cum cognatis vicinis amicis dulcissima pace guadentem, pietate religiosum, benignum mente, sanum corpore, vita parcum, moribus castum, conscientia securum. Nescio utrum quisquam ita desipiat, ut audeat dubitare quem praeferat. Ut ergo in his duobus hominibus, ita in duabus familiis, ita in duobus populis, ita in duobus regnis regula sequitur aequitatis, qua vigilanter adhibita si nostra intentio corrigatur, facillime videbimus ubi habitet vanitas et ubi felicitas.[17]

Let us set before our mind's eye two men; for the individual man is, like a single letter in a statement, an element, as it were, out of which community or realm is built up, however vast its territorial possessions. Let us imagine one of the two to be poor, or, better, in a middle station of life, while the other is excessively rich. But the rich man is tortured by fears, worn out with sadness, burnt up with ambition, never knowing serenity of repose, always panting and sweating in his struggles with opponents. It may be true that he enormously swells his patrimony, but at the cost of those discontents, while by this increase he heaps up a load of further anxiety and bitterness. The other man, the ordinary citizen, is content with his strictly limited resources. He is loved by family and friends; he enjoys the blessing of peace with his relations, neighbors, and friends; he is loyal, compassionate, and kind, healthy in body, temperate in habits, of unblemished character and enjoys the serenity of good conscience. I do not think anyone would be fool enough to hesitate about which he would prefer.

It is the same with two families, two peoples, or two realms. The same canon of judgment applies as in the case of the two men. If we apply the canon scrupulously, without allowing our judgment to be warped, we shall not have the slightest difficulty in seeing where true happiness lies, and where an empty show.[18]

## Two Men, Two Families, Two Nations, Two Kingdoms

The graduated progression in Augustine's analogical series appearing at the end of the passage just cited (IV.3) exploits the methodology inherent in the Platonic body politic analogy. The susceptibility of the binary form of the analogy to interpolation did not escape Plato himself. Toward the end of the first book of the *Republic* (351d–352a), in the context of a discussion contrasting the integrative function of justice which engenders love as opposed to the divisive effect of injustice which engenders hatred, Socrates introduces an intermediate term—the family—to more concretely link the individual and the body politic. Delineating a series of graduated analogies linking individuals, the family, and the city, Socrates argues:

... because injustices generate hatred, quarrels, and factions. Only justice can create unity and love ....

So it will be with any two individuals. Injustice will make them hate each other and so divide them. They will be enemies to one another and to all just men as well.

Agreed.

The same will hold for a single individual. Injustice will once again manifest its divisive effects and will put a man at odds with himself.

Let it be as you say.

Then it becomes apparent that wherever justice appears—in the city, in the
family, or in the individual—it first spawns factions and disunion and then
excites enmity among the divided parts. Finally, anything so at odds with itself
must become its own enemy as well as the enemy of all who are just.[19]

The extrapolation of the Platonic analogy was formulated by the later
Roman Stoics in response to the new magnitude of polity represented by the
idea of world empire. The Stoics tended to think of the levels of human
society in terms of a series of concentrically related circles: the *domus* or
household constituted the innermost circle; the *civitas* or city came next,
composed of the totality of households, and all the cities together were
conceived of as forming the *orbis terrae*. The all-embracing circumference of
society according to this conception is the *mundus* or cosmopolis which links
all the lesser human communities with the soul of the departed and with the
daemons.[20]

Augustine's totalistic panorama of human history depends upon the
Platonic-Stoic analogical view of the individual as organically linked through a
graduated series of increasingly inclusive forms of familial, civic, and political
relations to humankind as a whole. As Ronald Martinez concluded of
Augustine's analogical method, it represents "a systematic, structuring feature,
linking the single person to the great collectivities both partitively and
microcosmically."[21]

The graduated articulation of increasingly comprehensive and
concentrically related forms of collectivity in which every level is
microcosmically and synechdochically related to all others, is
diagrammatically suggested in this representative passage from *De civitate Dei*
XIX (chapter 16):

Quia igitur hominis domus initium sive particula debet esse civitatis, omne
autem initium ad aliquem sui generis finem et omnis pars ad universi, cuius
pars est, integritatem refertur, satis apparet esse consequens, ut ad pacem
civicam pax domestica referatur, id est, ut ordinata imperandi oboediendique
concordia cohabitantium referatur ad ordinatam imperandi oboediendique
concordiam civium.[22]

Now a man's house ought to be the beginning, or rather a small component
part of the city, and every beginning is directed to some end of its own kind,
and every component part contributes to the completeness of the whole of
which it forms a part. The implication is quite apparent, that domestic peace

contributes to the peace of the city—that is, the ordered harmony of those who live together in a house in the matter of giving and obeying orders, contributes to the ordered harmony concerning authority and obedience obtaining among the citizens.23

The diagrammatic function of this form of analysis in St. Augustine delineates a path of human energies, centrifugally and centripetally connecting the individual, family, city, empire, and world in a closed circuit of passion and action. Disordered love in the individual—the primary element in Augustine's account—is communicated centrifugally in an escalating spiral of violence through the concentrically related forms of human association, ultimately determining the sum total of disorder in the world. Conversely, the spectacle of the tragic whirlwind of human history invades the individual consciousness wherever it turns, compounding human suffering.24

The concentrically related, closed circuit of human interaction constitutes the basis of Augustine's analysis. A representative example (XIX.vii) is his discussion of the futility of unifying humankind under the direction of one authority as a means of eliminating conflict.25 The Roman Empire, Augustine observes, like all other exemplars of the *civitas terrena*, has neither pacified nor unified its conquered territories; but rather, it has generated an endless succession of wars. The expansionism of empire which imposes the bond of peace and unity through violence, begets the backlash of civil war. Augustine attacks those who take the position that the head of the Empire, a sage, will wage only just wars. Anyone, Augustine states who is insensible to the abject suffering of humankind may be said to have lost all humanity. The invasion of the individual consciousness by the tragic spectacle of history provokes an extreme mental agony:

Post civitatem vel urbem sequitur orbis terrae, in quo tertium gradum ponunt societatis humanae, incipientes a domo atque inde ad urbem, deinde ad orbem progrediendo venientes; qui utique, sicut aquarum congeries, quanto maior est, tanto periculis plenior. In quo primum linguarum diversitas hominem alienat ab homine . . . . At enim opera data est, ut imperiosa civitas non solum iugum, verum etiam linguam suam domitis gentibus per pacem societatis inponeret, per quam non deesset, immo et abundaret etiam interpretum copia. Verum est; sed hoc quam multis et quam grandibus bellis, quanta strage hominum, quanta effusione humani sanguinis comparatum est? Quibus transactis, non est tamen eorundem malorum finita miseria. Quamvis enim non defuerint neque desint hostes exterae nationes, contra quas semper bella gesta sunt et geruntur: tamen etiam ipsa imperii latitudo peperit peioris generis bella, socialia scilicet et civilia, quibus miserabilius quatitur humanum genus, sive cum belligeratur, ut aliquando conquiescant, sive cum timetur, ne rursus exsurgant. Quorum malorum multas et multiplices clades, duras et diras necessitates si ut dignum

est eloqui velim, quamquam nequaquam sicut res postulat possim: quis erat
prolixae disputationis modus? Sed sapiens, inquiunt, iusta bella gesturus est.
Quasi non, si se hominem meminit multo magis dolebit iustorum necessitatem
sibi extitisse bellorum .... Haec itaque mala tam magna, tam horrenda, tam
saeva quisquis cum dolore considerat, miseriam fateatur; quisquis autem vel
patitur ea sine animi dolore vel cogitat, multo utique miserius ideo se putat
beatum, quia et humanum perdidit sensum.26

After the city or town comes the world, which the philosophers reckon as the
third level of human society. They begin with the household, proceed to the
city, and then arrive at the world. Now the world, being like a confluence of
waters, is obviously more full of danger than the other communities by reason
of its greater size. To begin with, on this level the diversity of languages
separates man from man .... I shall be told that the Imperial City has been at
pain to impose on conquered peoples not only her yoke but her language also,
as a bond of peace and fellowship, so that there should be no lack of
interpreters but even a profusion of them. True; but think of the cost of this
achievement! Consider the scale of those wars, with all that slaughter of
human beings, all the human blood that was shed!

Those wars are now past history; and yet the misery of these evils is not yet
ended. For although there has been, and still is, no lack of enemies among
foreign nations, against whom wars have always been waged, and are still being
waged, yet the very extent of the Empire has given rise to wars of a worse
kind, namely, social and civil wars, by which mankind is more lamentably
disquieted either when fighting is going on in the hope of bringing hostilities
eventually to a peaceful end, or when there are fears that hostilities will break
out again. If I were to try to describe, with eloquence worthy of the subject,
the many and multifarious disasters, the dour and dire necessities, I could not
possibly be adequate to the theme, and there would be no end to this
protracted discussion. But the wise man, they say, will wage just wars. Surely,
if he remembers that he is a human being, he will rather lament the fact that he
is faced with the necessity of waging just wars. ... And so everyone who
reflects with sorrow on such grievous evils, in all their horror and cruelty,
must acknowledge the misery of them. And yet a man who experiences such
evils, or even thinks about them, without heartfelt grief, is assuredly in a far
more pitiable condition, if he thinks himself happy simply because he has lost
all human feeling.27

## War In The Self/War In The Body Politic

Although it is tempting to speculate on the way in which Augustine's
analysis of history mirrors the profound ambivalence of his own complex and
discordant personality, the formal rationale for the correspondence that serves

as the key conceptual principle in the *City of God* derives from Plato, as I have said. In an analogical perspective the Adamic inheritance of the individual and the history of the *civitas terrena* are formally homologous. Both are characaterized by division, conflict, and war.[28]

The source of conflict in history is the soul and its Adamic nature. For Augustine, the gift of original justice in human nature was a threefold hierarchical relation which represented a chain of command as well as a chain of being, and involved God, the soul, and the body.[29] Adam's disobedience represented a falling away of the soul from the principle of unity and life in God towards nothingness. As a consequence, human nature lost its formerly perfect integration of spiritual and material principles, its harmonious synthesis of body and soul. The aspects of the human soul itself became fragmented, divided against itself; the soul's lower powers rebelled against the higher, reduplicating within the soul the original act of disobedience against God. The ensuing fragmentation to which humanity was condemned represents a kind of *contrapassum*:

> Denique, ut breviter dicatur, in illius peccati poena quid inoboedientiae nisi inoboedientia retributa est? Nam quae hominis est alia miseria nisi adversus eum ipsum inoboedientia eius ipsius, ut, quoniam noluit quod potuit, quod non potest velit? . . . Quid interest unde, dum tamen per iustitiam dominantis Dei, cui subditi servire noluimus, caro nostra nobis, quae subdita fuerat, non serviendo molesta sit, quamvis nos Deo non serviendo molesti nobis potuerimus esse. . . .[30]

> In fact, to put it briefly, in the punishment of that sin the retribution for disobedience is simply disobedience itself. For man's wretchedness is nothing but his own disobedience to himself, so that because he would not do what he could, he now wills to do what he cannot. . . . The important point is that through the justice of God, who is our Lord and master and whom we refused to serve as his subjects, our flesh, which had been subject to us, now gives us trouble through its non-compliance, whereas we by our defiance of God have only succeeded in becoming a nuisance to ourselves. . . .[31]

As a result of disobedience to God, the immortal soul lost its sustaining authority at the lowest level over the body, which therefore became doomed to die. The final outcome of the incipient fragmentation and war in the self that was experienced as the consequence of disobedience is mortality. Of Adam and Eve's subjective apprehension of the Fall in Book XIII (chapter xiii), Augustine says:

> Senserunt ergo novum motum inoboedientis carnis suae, tamquam reciprocam poenam inobedientiae suae. Iam quippe anima libertate in perversum propria

delectata et Deo dedignata servire pristino corporis servitio destituebatur, et quia superiorem dominum suo arbitrio deseruerat, inferiorem famulum ad suum arbitrium non tenebat, nec omni modo habebat subditam carnem, sicut semper habere potuisset, si Deo subdita ipsa mansisset. Tunc ergo coepit caro concupiscere adversus spiritum, cum qua controversia nati sumus, trahentes originem mortis et in membris nostris vitiataque natura contentionem eius sive victoriam de prima praevaricatione gestantes.[32]

Thus they felt a novel disturbance in their disobedient flesh, as a punishment which answered to their own disobedience. The soul, in fact, rejoiced in its own freedom to act perversely and disdained to be God's servant; and so it was deprived of the obedient service which its body had at first rendered. At its own pleasure the soul deserted its superior and master; and so it no longer retained its inferior and servant obedient to its will. It did not keep its own flesh subject to it in all respects, as it could have kept it for ever if it had itself continued in subjection to God. This then was the time when the flesh began to "lust in opposition to the spirit," which is the conflict that attends us from birth, the beginning of our death, and with the vitiation of our nature our body is the scene of death's assault, or rather of his victory, as the result of that first disobedience.[33]

The perpetual nature of the Pauline antagonism between spirit and flesh into which all are born is the basis, for Augustine, of the experience of conflict that constitutes the norm of the human condition. In the living hell of this life (XXII.xxii), Augustine could not help but conclude that humankind is being punished by God through a condition of war against itself; and this war characterizes both our subjective as well as our objective experience:[34]

Nam quod ad primam originem pertinet, omnem omnem mortalium progenium fuisse damnatam, haec ipsa vita, si vita dicenda est, tot et tantis malis plena testatur.[35]

As for that first origin of mankind, this present life of ours (if a state full of so much grievous misery can be called a life) is evidence that all the mortal descendents of the first man came under condemnation.[36]

In Augustine's view, the cause of the war in the self is revealed in the Biblical account of the Fall. Augustine's formal analysis, however, of the experience of internal conflict oscillates between the Platonic "approximation" of disorder in the tripartite soul, and the "true" paradigm, the Pauline war of the flesh against the spirit; the Platonic psychic economy insofar as it is functionally reducible to two opposing principles—the opposition of the rational against the irrational—is identifiable with the Pauline opposition of flesh and spirit. A representative example of Augustine's rehearsal and correction of Platonic psychology in the light of Biblical authority appears at XIV.xix:

> Hinc est quod et illi philosophi, qui veritati propius accesserunt, iram atque libidinem vitiosas animi partes esse confessi sunt, eo quod turbide atque inordinate moverentur ad ea etiam, quae sapientia perpetrari vetat, ac per hoc opus habere moderatrice mente atque ratione. Quam partem animi tertiam velut in arce quadam ad istas regendas perhibent conlocatam, ut illa imperante, istis servientibus possit in homine iustitia ex omni animi parte servari. Hae igitur partes, quas et in homine sapiente ac temperante fatentur esse vitiosas, ut eas ab his rebus, ad quas iniuste moventur, mens conpescendo et cohibendo refrenet ac revocet atque ad ea permittat, quae sapientiae lege concessa sunt (sicut iram ad exerendam iustam coercitionem, sicut libidinem ad propagandae prolis officium)—hae, inquam, partes in paradiso ante peccatum vitiosae non erant. Non enim contra rectam voluntatem ad aliquid movebantur, unde necesse esset eas rationis tamquam frenis regentibus abstinere. Nam quod nunc ita moventur et ab eis, qui temperantur et iuste et pie vivunt, alias facilius, alius difficilius, tamen cohibendo et repugnando modificantur, non est utique sanitas ex natura, sed languor ex culpa.[37]

This explains why the Platonists, who approached the truth more nearly than other philosophers, acknowledged that anger and lust are perverted elements in man's character, or soul, on the ground that they are disturbed and undisciplined emotions, leading to acts which wisdom forbids, and therefore they need the control of intelligence and reason. This third rational division of the soul is located by them in a kind of citadel, to rule the other elements, so that with the rational element in command and the others subordinate, justice may be preserved in the relation between all the parts of man's soul. These philosophers therefore admit that the two divisions of the soul are perverted, even in a wise and disciplined man. Consequently, the mind by repression and restraint bridles them and recalls them from courses they are wrongly moved to follow, while it allows them to follow any line of action permitted by the law of wisdom. Anger, for example, is allowed for the purpose of imposing compulsion, when that is justified, and lust is permitted for the duty of procreation. But in paradise before man's sin these elements did not exist in their perverted state. For then they were not set in motion, in defiance of a right will, to pursue any course which made it necessary to hold them back with the guiding reins, so to speak, of reason.

The situation now is that these passions are set in motion in this fashion, and are brought under control by those who live disciplined, just, and devout lives, sometimes with comparative ease, sometimes with difficulty. But this control entails coercion and struggle, and the situation does not represent a state of health in accordance with nature, but an enfeebled condition arising from guilt.[38]

While "converting," as it were, Plato to his own point of view, Augustine, at the same time, dogmatically corrects what he regards as Plato's errors. Whereas Plato assumed that integration, justice, and virtue were the ends of the perfective process of *paideia*, it was Augustine's conviction that disorder in the soul was the result not of ignorance but of sin. Therefore the Christian could only hope through the constant vigilance of prayer and faith that God might grant the grace to reconcile the irreconcilable contraries of the human soul. So Augustine states at XIX.iv:

> neque ipsum recte vivere nobis ex nobis est, nisi credentes adiuvet et orantes qui et ipsam fidem dedit, qua nos ab illo adiuvandos esse credamus.[39]

> and it is not in our power to live rightly, unless we believe and pray we receive help from him who has given us the faith to believe that we must be helped by him.[40]

In the same context, Augustine explains how the paradisal harmony of the soul is irrecoverable in this life. The most the individual can hope for is the remission of sin, not the perfecting of virtue. Even the attainment of the virtuous condition Plato refers to as *sophrosyne*—or, as it was translated by Cicero, *temperantia*—represents no genuine inner peace but merely an armistice in a condition of perpetual civil war.

> Porro ipsa virtus, quae non est inter prima naturae, quoniam eis postea doctrina introducente supervenit, cum sibi bonorum culmen vindicet humanorum, quid hic agit nisi perpetua bella cum vitiis, nec exterioribus, sed interioribus, nec alienis, sed plane nostris et propriis, maxime illa, quae Graece σωφροσύνη, Latine temperantia nominatur, qua carnales frenantur libidines, ne in quaeque flagitia mentem consentientem trahant? Neque enim nullum est vitium, cum, sicut dicit apostolus, caro concupiscit adversus spiritum; cui vitio contraria virtus est, cum, sicut idem dicit, spiritus concupiscit adversus carnem. Haec enim, inquit, invicem adversantur, ut non ea quae vultis faciatis. Quid autem facere volumus, cum perfici volumus fine summi boni, nisi ut caro adversus spiritum non concupiscat, nec sit in nobis hoc vitium, contra quod spiritus concupiscat? Quod in hac vita, quamvis velimus, quoniam facere non valemus, id saltem in adiutorio Dei facimus, ne carni concupiscenti adversus spiritum spiritu succumbente cedamus et ad perpetrandum peccatum nostra consensione pertrahamur. Absit ergo ut, quamdiu in hoc bello intestino sumus, iam nos beatitudinem, ad quam vicendo volumus pervenire, adeptos

esse credamus. Et quis est usque adeo sapiens, ut contra libidines nullum habeat omnino conflictum?[41]

Then again, what of virtue itself, which is not one of the primary gifts, since it supervenes on them later, introduced by teaching? Although it claims the topmost place among human goods, what is its activity in this world but unceasing warfare with vices, and those not external vices but internal, not other people's vices but quite clearly our own? And this is the particular struggle of that virtue called in Greek *sophrosyne*, which is translated "temperance"—the virtue which bridles the lusts of the flesh to prevent their gaining the consent of the mind and dragging it into every kind of immorality. For it is never true, in this life, that vice does not exist, when as the Apostle says, "the desires of the flesh oppose the spirit;" but to this vice there is an opposing virtue, when, as the same Apostle says, "the desires of the spirit oppose the flesh. For these two are in mutual opposition, so that you do not achieve what you want to achieve." But what in fact, do we want to achieve, when we desire to be made perfect by the Highest Good? It can surely, only be a situation where the desires of the flesh do not oppose the spirit, and where there is in us no vice for the spirit to oppose with its desires. Now we cannot achieve this in our present life, for all our wishing. But we can at least, with God's help, see to it that we do not give way to the desires of our flesh which oppose the spirit by allowing our spirit to be overcome, and that we are not dragged to the perpetuation of sin with our own consent. God forbid, then, that, so long as we are engaged in this internal strife, we should believe ourselves to have already attained to the happiness, the end we desire to reach by our victory. And who has reached such a height of wisdom as to have no struggle to maintain against his lusts?[42]

Just as there is no true, no "original" justice, in fallen humanity, so there can be none in the *civitas terrena*. This is illustrated in Book XIX (xxi) by the example of the Roman Republic, to which Augustine applies the logic of the body politic analogy together with rhetoric that explicitly recalls the archetypal fate of Adam at the Fall:

Serviens autem Deo animus recte imperat corpori, inque ipso animo ratio Deo Domino subdita, recte imperat libidini vitiisque ceteris. Quapropter ubi homo Deo non servit, quid in eo putandum est esse iustitiae? quando quidem Deo non serviens nullo modo potest iuste animus corpori aut humana ratio vitiis imperare. Et si in homine tali non est ulla iustitia, procul dubio nec in hominum coetu, qui ex hominibus talibus constat.[43]

Now in serving God the soul rightly commands the body, and in the soul itself the reason which is subject to its Lord God rightly commands the lusts and other perverted elements. That being so, when a man does not serve God, what amount of justice are we to suppose to exist in his being? For if a soul does not serve God it cannot with any kind of justice command the body, nor can a man's reason control the vicious elements in the soul. And if there is no justice in such a man, there can be no sort of doubt that there is no justice in a gathering which consists of such men.[44]

The Adamic terminology recurs a few chapters further on (XIX.xxiv) in reference to all the avatars of the Earthly City. Since the soul and the state are analogues, the *civitas terrena* perpetually re-enacts the Fall of Man:[45]

> Quod autem de isto populo et de ista re publica dixi, hoc de Atheniensium vel quorumcumque Graecorum, hoc de Aegyptiorum, hoc de illa priore Babylone Assyriorum, quando in rebus publicis suis imperia vel parva vel magna teneurunt, et de alia quacumque aliarum gentium intellegar dixisse atque sensisse. Generaliter quippe civitas impiorum, cui non imperat Deus oboedienti sibi, ut sacrificium non offerat nisi tantummodo sibi, et per hoc in illa et animus corpori ratioque vitiis recte ac fideliter imperet, caret iustitiae veritate.[46]

> However, what I have said about the Roman people and the Roman commonwealth I must be understood to have said and felt about those of the Athenians and of any other Greeks, or of that former Babylon of the Assyrians, when they exercised imperial rule, whether on a small or a large scale, in their commonwealths—and indeed about any other nation whatsoever. For God is not the rule of the city of the impious, because it disobeys his commandment that sacrifice should be offered to himself alone. The purpose of this law was that in that city the soul should rule over the body and reason over the vicious elements, in righteousness and faith. And because God does not rule there the general characteristic of that city is that it is devoid of true justice.[47]

In keeping with the underlying homology between the condition of the Adamic soul and the nature of the *civitas terrena*, it is hardly surprising to discover in Augustine's account of human history that the primary characteristic of all polities is a chronic condition of war. Just as on countless occasions the psychological state of fragmented human nature is explicitly compared to civil war, so the habitual state of the Earthly City *adversus se ipsam . . . dividitur* (XV.iii). Regularly the human community is torn assunder as one part arms against another:

> ideo civitas ista adversus se ipsam plerumque dividitur litigando, bellando atque pugnando et aut mortiferas aut certe mortales victorias requirendo. Nam ex quacumque sui parte adversus alteram sui partem bellando surrexerit, quaerit esse victrix gentium, cum sit captiva vitiorum; et si quidem, cum vicerit,

superbius extollitur, etiam mortifera. . . .[48]

the earthly city is generally divided against itself by litigation, by wars, by battles, by the pursuit of victories that bring death with them or at best are doomed to death. For if any section of that city has risen up in war against another part, it seeks to be victorious over other nations, though it is itself the slave of base passions; and if, when victorious, it is exalted in its arrogance, that victory brings death in its train.[49]

In Augustine's view, based on the convergent perspectives of what is essentially an elaboration of the Platonic body politic analogy in conjunction with Platonic psychology, and the Hebraic notion of the corporate personality of Adam in conjunction with the Pauline concept of the divided will, war at all levels is really intestine.[50] At II.xxv Augustine quotes a pathetic example from Livy of a soldier in the Roman civil wars which perfectly illustrates Augustine's theory in which all levels of human experience are analogously interrelated; Livy's tragic *exemplum* vividly traces the dynamic trajectory of what Augustine perceives as the negative spiral of violence which manifests itself in the body politic through civil war, in the family through fratricide, and in the individual through suicide:

Iam multos moverat, quod miles quidam, dum occiso spolia detraheret, fratrem nudato cadavere agnovit ac detestatus bella civilia se ipsum ibi perimens fraterno corpori adiunxit.[51]

Many had been touched by the tale of a soldier who stripped the spoils from one of the slain, and recognized his own brother, when the corpse was bare; moved to abhorrence of such civil strife he killed himself on the spot, and fell on his brother's lifeless body.[52]

The representation of *war* as the dominant condition of the history of the Earthly City is firmly established early in Augustine's epic account. The treatment of the theme of war depends upon the reflexive criterion inherent in the Platonic analogy, whereby subjective and objective experience are correlated. Strategically in the opening book (I.xv), Augustine affirms by analogical rule that the source of happiness in the individual is the same as that in the body politic:

Neque enim aliunde beata civitas, aliunde homo, cum aliud civitas non sit quam concors hominum multitudo.[53]

For the source of a community's felicity is no different from that of one man, since a community is simply a united multitude of individuals.[54]

Felicity may be the natural motive and goal of the individual, but misery, Augustine insists, is clearly one's actual lot.[55] In terms which combine Platonic with Pauline distinctions, Augustine examines the "moral and spiritual evils" which afflict "the interior man" in Book II, while Book III treats the "evils" to which "the exterior man" is vulnerable, including all the calamities to which flesh is heir, such as famine, pestilence, pillage, captivity, massacre and war.[56] Throughout his diagnosis of disorder in the universal body politic, Augustine insists (as Plato does before him) on the primacy of the soul. For both Plato and Augustine the destiny of the eternal soul, the "interior man," far outweighs the transient events of this world in importance.[57] The superior importance of the soul is demonstrated by the relative order of topics in Books II to III, and emphasized at the discursive level by the distinction between the "interior" as opposed to the "exterior" person and in the affirmation that the afflictions of the former *quae praecipue cavenda sunt* (III.i).

Disorder in the soul causes the social and political perturbations which wrack the body politic. Indeed, Augustine catagorically affirms that the troubles which afflict the body politic "would not occur if they did not exist first in the citizens."[58] Thus in the present ruination of Rome described at II.ii, Augustine sees the symptoms of a degenerative malady in the souls of its citizens which has destroyed whatever integrity formerly bound the city together. The razing of the walls of Rome is a metaphor of the internal moral dilapidation of the Roman citizens:

> Romam quippe partam veterum auctamque laboribus foediorem stantem fecerant quam ruentem, quando quidem in ruina eius lapides et ligna, in istorum autem vita omnia non murorum, sed morum munimenta atque ornamenta ceciderunt, cum funestioribus eorum corda cupiditatibus quam ignibus tecta illius urbis arderent.[59]

> Rome was founded and extended by the labours of those men of old; their descendants made Rome more hideous while it stood than when it fell. For in the ruin of the city it was stone and timber which fell to the ground; but in the lives of those Romans we saw the collapse not of material but of moral defences, not of material but of spiritual grandeur. The lust that burned in their hearts was more deadly than the flame which consumed their dwellings.[60]

The interpretation of the physical and political collapse of Rome as symptomatic of the moral corruption of its citizens is a variation upon the reflexive logic pervading Augustine's analysis.[61] By means of this reflexive strategy, as Robert D. Cumming aptly puts it, "*external* scenes of tyranny, enslavement, and devastation" are presented as signifying "how much more enslaving and devastating is the *inner* tyranny."[62] The same strategy of interpretating political events informs Augustine's allusion to the victory of Sulla (Book II.xxiv) which is interpreted as the cause of Sulla's spiritual demise:

> Neque enim eius dignitati tantum profuit illa victoria, quantum nocuit cupiditati; qua factum est, ut inmoderatis inhians et secundis rebus elatus ac praecipitatus magis ipse periret in moribus, quam inimicos in corporibus perderet.[63]

> And that victory increased his glory less than it advanced his ambition to his hurt; its effect was to remove all restraint from his appetite for conquest. Success turned his head, and his plunge into moral degradation wrought in his own character a more grievous havoc than any he inflicted on the persons of his enemies.[64]

Adamic man, who in his post-lapsarian condition is the *libidinis servus* (XII.xxii), and the *civitas terrena* which is the Adamic soul writ large, live exclusively for the needs of the "exterior man," that is, the flesh and its desires. This idea is couched in the Pauline typology at XIV.ii:

> Una quippe est hominum secundum carnem, altera secundum spiritum vivere. . . .[65]

> There is, in fact, one city of men who choose to live by the standard of the flesh, another of those who choose to live by the standard of the spirit.[66]

Whereas in Platonic doctrine the body is ultimately the source of the war, in Christian doctrine it is the fallen will (characterized by what St. Paul sees as the inescapable conflict between the spirit and the flesh) which is the source of the wars—or for that matter, all conflict. The political implications of the Pauline doctrine of the divided will are spelled out in the *Epistle of James* (4:1):

> Unde bella et lites in vobis? Nonne hinc? ex concupiscentis vestris, quae militant in membris vestris?[67]

> From whence come wars and fightings among you? Come they not hence, even of your lusts that war in your members?[68]

In the *Phaedo*(66c–d), the other Platonic text in the Latin translation by Apuleius to which Augustine may have had access, Plato sees the tyranny of the body, to which the soul is subjected, as the cause of war in the body politic:

> Wars and revolutions and battles are due simply and solely to the body and its
> desires. All wars are undertaken for the acquisition of wealth, and the reason
> why we have to acquire wealth is the body, because we are slaves to its
> service.[69]

The history of Earthly City as exemplified by the history of Rome in
Book III (chapter x) of *The City of God* and explicitly identified with the
"exterior man," is dominated by war precisely because war is predominantly
the consequence of disordered human passion (*semper fere per humanorum
animorum motus accidunt*).[70] Augustine cites Vergil's *Aeneid* VIII(326–327) in
confirmation of his own theory of *libido dominandi*. Of humanity's
degeneration from the golden Saturnian age and the linkage of *belli rabies* with
*amor habendi*, Vergil states:

> Deterior donec paulatim ac decolor aetas/Et belli rabies et amor successit
> habendi.[71]

> But by degrees an age depraved and duller/took its place with war's insanity
> and love of gain.[72]

The history of the Earthly City, represented by its avatar, Rome, is
characterized in Book III by a continuous chain of wars, intensified by
Augustine's compressed, synoptic view which stretches back to the mythical
foundation of Rome by the remnant of Trojan survivors and forward to the
present Christian era in the aftermath of the sack of Rome by the Goths. The
rhetorical principle of *concatenatio* is employed as a structural principle in
Book III, reflecting its subject. This principle is expressly named in the
penultimate chapter (xxx) which treats the internal power struggles and
factions of the Republican period and how they begat one another. The
concatenated account is, of course, intended to call to mind the Adamic
patrimony, the ultimate cause behind all civil war:

> Crudelia bella civilia, omnibus bellis hostilibus, auctoribus etiam eorum
> fatentibus, amariora, quibus illa res publica nec adflicta, sed omnino perdita
> iudicata est, longe ante adventum Christi exorta sunt, et scelerataarum
> concatenatione causarum a bello Mariano atque Sullano ad bella Sertorii et
> Catilinae (quorum a Sulla fuerat ille proscriptus, ille nutritus), inde ad Lepidi et
> Catuli bellum (quorum alter gesta Sullana rescindere, alter defendere cupiebat),
> inde ad Pompei et Caesaris (quorum Pompeius sectator Sullae fuerat eiusque
> potentiam vel aequaverat vel iam etiam superaverat; Caesar autem Pompei
> potentium non ferebat, sed quia non habebat, quam tamen illo victo

interfectoque transcendit), hinc ad alium Caesarem, qui post Augustus
appellatus est, pervenerunt, quo imperante natus est Christus. Nam et ipse
Augustus cum multis gessit bella civilia, et in eis etiam multi clarissimi viri
perierunt. . . .[73]

The brutal Civil Wars, more bitter, on the admission of their own authors,
than any wars against foreign enemies—those Civil Wars which, in the general
judgement, brought on the republic not merely calamity but utter
destruction—broke out long before the coming of Christ. A causal chain of
criminal enormity carried the process on from the Marian and Sullan wars to
the wars of Sertorius and Catiline (the former was one of Sulla's proscribed,
the latter, one of his protégés), on to the war of Lepidus and Catulus (one of
whom wished to annul the acts of Sulla, the other to preserve them), on to the
wars of Pompey and Caesar (Pompey had been a partisan of Sulla, whose
power he equalled, and even surpassed; Caesar found Pompey's power
insufferable—because he did not wield it—but after the defeat and death of
Pompey he transcended it); and then we come to another Caesar, afterwards
called Augustus. And it was in the reign of Augustus that Christ was born.

Augustus himself carried on many wars, against many enemies, during which
many eminent men perished. . . .[74]

The Earthly City in the service of the disordered human appetite does not
submit itself to God, but rather wages war in order to gratify the desire
(*cupiditas*) for earthly goods. Yet, earthly goods, being limited, in turn
engender further conflict, rivalry, and war within as well as between every
community.[75] The things desired are good in the total scheme of goods. But
the excessive and exclusive desire for earthly goods is misdirected. The
function of polity is to moderate and channel this *cupiditas*. Otherwise, to
borrow Hobbes' phrase, individuals would destroy themselves in *bellum
omnium contra omnes*. While government strives internally to preserve itself
by restraining the greed of its members, it enacts on a higher level what
Augustine calls *cupiditas* or *libido dominandi* by directing the insatiable desires
of its citizens outward in foreign wars of conquest. The Earthly City (XV.iv)
makes war in order to purchase a peace in which human greed can enjoy its
spoils:

Non autem recte dicitur ea bona non esse, quae concupiscit haec civitas,
quando est et ipsa in suo humano genere melior. Concupiscit enim terrenam
quandam pro rebus infimis pacem; ad eam namque desiderat pervenire
bellando; quoniam si vicerit et qui resistat non fuerit, pax erit, quam non
habebant partes in vicem adversantes et pro his rebus, quas simul habere non
poterant, infelici egestate certantes. Hanc pacem requirunt laboriosa bella,

hanc adipiscitur quae putatur gloriosa victoria. Quando autem vincunt qui
causa iustiore pugnabant, quis dubitet gratulandam esse victoriam et provenisse
optabilem pacem? Haec bona sunt et sine dubio Dei dona sunt. Sed si
neglectis melioribus, quae ad supernam pertinent civitatem, ubi erit victoria in
aeterna et summa pace secura, bona ista sic concupiscuntur, ut vel sola esse
credantur vel his, quae meliora creduntur, amplius diligantur: necesse est
miseria consequatur et quae inerat augeatur.[76]

However, it would be incorrect to say that the goods which this city desires are
not goods, since even that city is better, in its own human way, by their
possession. For example, that city desires an earthly peace, for the sake of the
lowest goods; and it is that peace which it longs to attain by making war. For
if it wins the war and no one survives to resist, then there will be peace, which
the warring sections did not enjoy when they contended in their unhappy
poverty for the things which they could not both possess at the same time.
This peace is the aim of wars, with all their hardships; it is this peace that
glorious victory (so called) achieves.

Now when the victory goes to those who were fighting for the juster cause,
can anyone doubt that the victory is a matter for rejoicing and the resulting
peace is something to be desired? These things are goods and undoubtedly they
are gifts of God. But if the higher goods are neglected, which belong to the
City on high, where victory will be serene in the enjoyment of eternal and
perfect peace—if these goods are neglected and those other goods are so desired
as to be considered the only goods, or are loved more than goods which are
believed to be higher, the inevitable consequence is fresh misery, and an
increase of the wretchedness already there.[77]

The inherent contradiction at the heart of the conception of peace-making
war is linked with, and reflects, the equally contradictory characterization of
the Earthly City as based upon a kind of concordant egoism.[78] The two
contradictory notions are conjoined in Book XIX, chapter xvii:

Ita etiam terrena civitas, quae non vivit ex fide, terrenam pacem appetit in
eoque defigit imperandi oboediendique concordiam civium, ut sit eis de rebus
ad mortalem vitam pertinentibus humanarum quaedam compositio
voluntatem.[79]

So also the earthly city, whose life is not based on faith, aims at an earthly
peace, and it limits the harmonious agreement of citizens concerning the giving
and obeying of orders to the establishment of a kind of compromise between
human wills about the things relevant to mortal life.[80]

The Earthly City is at best merely a collection of imperfectly integrated wills (*compositio voluntatum*), which are reduced to a kind of *concordia* through the application of coercion (civil obedience and rule) in order to contain the anarchic force of the self-serving wills. Domenico Pesce captures the essence of Augustine's characterization of the nature of political association in relation to the motivation of its members when he says:

> Questa unione non muta la natura di queste volontà, ma lascia inalterata. Nasce de qui l'interna tensione dialettica della vita associativa, nasce di qui quella che abbiamo chiamato *discordia concors*, nasce di qui il fatto che diritto e legge constituiscono soltanto dei limiti esterni e non rappresentano perciò un principio essenzialmente diverso da quello della forza bruta, ma si risolvano in una semplice temporanea e instabile composizione di forze.[81]

### Discordia Concors/Concordia Concors

Whereas the clash of human wills constitutes the *discordia concors*, of the Earthly City, the Heavenly City assumes by contrast the perfect integration of its members in *perfecte concors oboedientia caritatis*. At XV.iii, the "children of grace, the citizens of the free city, the sharers in eternal peace," are those:

> ubi sit non amore propriae ac privatae quodam modo voluntatis, sed communi eodemque inmutabili bono gaudens atque ex multis unum cor faciens, id est perfecte concors oboedientia caritatis.[82]

> who form a community where there is no love of a will that is personal and, as we may say, private, but a love that rejoices in a good that is at once shared by all and unchanging—a love that makes "one heart" out of many, a love that is the whole-hearted and harmonious obedience of mutual affection.[83]

In this passage, the perfect *harmonia* of the Platonic conception of the ideal body politic, in which all members are "of one mind," is conveyed by the key Latin term, *concors*, a term which bears the etymon (*cor*) of Augustine's analogical definition of the ideal community of perfectly integrated wills devoted to the common good, seeing and serving God in all.[84] The Augustinian vision of the *civitas Dei* which is perfectly ordered and harmonious has its correlative in the Platonic comparison of the totally unified state to a human body. In Plato's representation of the perfect reduction of multiplicity to unity in the ideal polity, the diversity of the body politic is reduced, as Aristotle points out, to the status of a single individual;[85] the unanimity of Plato's ideal body politic is so complete that the community feels and thinks as one, and speaks in unison in the first person singular:[86]

Do we know any greater evil for a state than the thing that distracts [i.e. literally "tears it apart"] and makes it many instead of one, or a greater good than that which binds it together and makes it one?

We do not.

Is not, then, the community of pleasure and pain the tie that binds, when, so far as may be, all citizens rejoice and grieve alike at the same births and deaths?

By all means, he said.

But the individualization of these feelings is a dissolvent, when some grieve exceedingly and others rejoice at the same happenings to the city and its inhabitants?

Of course.

And the chief cause of this is when the citizens do not utter in unison such words as "mine" and "not mine" and similarly with regard to the word "alien?"

Precisely so.

That city, then, is best ordered in which the greatest number use the expression "mine" and "not mine" of the same things in the same way.

Much the best.

And the city whose state is most like that of an individual man. For example, if the finger of one of us is wounded, the entire community of bodily connections stretching to the soul for "integration" with the dominant part is made aware, and all of it with the dominant part is made aware, and all of it feels the pain as a whole, though it is a part that suffers, and that is how we come to say that the man has a pain in his finger. And for any other member of the man the same statement holds alike for a part that labors in pain or is eased by pleasure.

The same, he said, and, to return to your question, the best-governed state most nearly resembles such an organism.

That is the kind of state, then, I presume, that when anyone of the citizens suffers aught of good or evil, will be most likely to speak of the part that suffers as its own and will share the pleasure or the pain of the whole.

Inevitably, he said, if it is well governed.[87]

Only in the Heavenly City is *concordia* perfected, a *concordia concors*. For only there, in Augustine's view, does the Platonic organic metaphor of the totally unified community become a reality in the Pauline *corpus Christi* where if "one member suffers, all the members suffer with it; or one member be honoured, all the members rejoice with it" (I *Corinthians* 12:26).[88] For Augustine, the figure of the ideal body politic is in the process of being fulfilled in the Christian scheme of salvation through the mystery of incorporation in the mystical Body of Christ. Augustine's vision of the one, true community is related to Plato's in the manner of a reality to its adumbration; at best, the Earthly City is but a "shadow and prophetic image" (XV.xi) of the Heavenly. The perfect concord of the heavenly city is identified in the final chapter (XXII.xxx) of the *ingens opus* with the Pauline *corpus Christi* (see especially I *Corinthians* 12:20–21) in which:

> tamque nolet esse unusquisque quod non accepit, quamvis sit pacatissimo concordiae vinculo ei qui accepti obstrictus, quam nec in corpore vult oculus esse qui est digitus, cum membrum utrumque contineat totius corporis pacata compago.[89]

> No one will wish to be what it has not been granted him to be; and yet he will be bound in the closest bond of peaceful harmony with one to whom it has been granted; just as in the body the finger does not wish to be the eye, since both members are included in the harmonious organization of the whole body.[90]

In the *civitas Dei* all members are one Body, each member performing its own function according to the diversity of spiritual gifts; of one heart in their love of God and enjoyment of each in God; of one mind in their collective contemplation of God.[91] In this life, although its members are scattered through out this world, the *civitas Dei*, by means of the incorporative mystery of the Eucharist, is undergoing a process of embryonic formation within the matrix of a dying world. Quoting the other key Pauline passage (*Romans* 12:4–6) which describes the perfect unity of the faithful with God, Augustine says at X.vi:

> "Sicut enim in uno corpore multa membra habemus omnia autem membra non eosdem actus habent: ita multi unum corpus sumus in Christo; singuli autem alter alterius membra, habentes dona diversa secundum gratiam, quae data est nobis." Hoc est sacrificium Christianorum: multi unum corpus in Christo. Quod etiam sacramento altaris fidelibus noto frequentat ecclesia, ubi ei demonstratur, quod in ea re, quam offert, ipsa offeratur.[92]

> ". . . For just as have many members in one body, and all the members have

not the same functions, so we are many, but we make up one body in Christ; and individually we are members of one another, possessing gifts differing according to the grace which has been given us." This is the sacrifice of Christians, who are "many, making up one body in Christ." This is the sacrifice which the Church continually celebrates in the sacrament of the altar, a sacrament well-known to the faithful where is shown to the Church that she herself is offered in the offering which she presents to God.[93]

As for the Earthly City, Augustine accounts for the tragic repetition of human suffering throughout its history and for its final doom by applying the logic of the Platonic body politic analogy to Christian doctrine so the nature of the Adamic soul and the history of the *civitas terrena* are seen to be strictly, indeed causally, related. Through his assimilation and transformation of Plato's analogical form of argumentation in the *Republic*, Augustine in *De civitate Dei* represents a dire vision of human nature and history in which the divided will of the individual and a divided humanity are locked in a vortex of misdirected energy.

# Notes

†Reprinted by permission of the author from *The Analogy of the Body Politic in St. Augustine, Dante, Petrarch, and Ariosto*. Dissertation. U of California, Santa Cruz, 1988. Ch. 1, 1–57.

[1]Werner Jaeger in *Paideia: the Ideal of Greek Culture* (New York: Oxford UP, 1943), vol. II, trans. Gilbert Highet, exhaustively demonstrates through close textual analysis that the body politic analogy is not merely a strategy of argumentation but the governing thematic principle of organization which unifies the work as a whole. I am indebted to his exposition of the way in which Plato's mastertrope functions in the *Republic*.

[2]The bibliography on Augustine is voluminous. Among the general studies on Augustine's cultural and intellectual background, his life and thought, which I have consulted and found most helpful in framing this chapter but have not otherwise cited, are: Gustave Bardy, *Saint Augustin, l'homme et l'oeuvre* (Paris: Desclée de Brouwer, 1946); Vernon Joseph Bourke, *Augustine's Quest of Wisdom: Life and Philosophy of the Bishop of Hippo* (Milwaukee: Bruce Publishing Co., 1945); John Henderson Seafort Burleigh, *"The City of God": A Study of St. Augustine's Philosophy* (London: Nisbet, 1944); Charles Norris Cochrane, *Christianity and Classical Culture: A Study of Thought and Action from Augustus to Augustine* (Oxford: Clarendon P, 1940); Pierre Courcelle, *Les Lettres grecques en Occident de Macrobe à Cassiodore* (Paris: E. de Broccard, 1948) and *Recherches sur les "Confessions" de St. Augustin* (Paris: E. de Broccard, 1950); Étienne Gilson, *History of Christian Philosophy in the Middle Ages*, trans. by Cécile Gilson (New York: Random House, 1955) Pt. III, *Introduction à l'étude de Saint*

*Augustin*, 2nd ed. rev. and enl. (Paris: J. Vrim, 1943), *Les Métamorphoses de la Cité de Dieu* (Louvain: Publications universitaires de Louvain, 1952); Paul Henry, "Augustine and Plotinus," *Journal of Theological Studies*, XXXVIII (London, 1937) 1–23; Henri-Irénée Marrou, *Saint Augustin et la fin de la culture antique*, 2 vols. (Paris: E. de Broccard, 1949); R. O'Connell, *St. Augustine's "Confessions"* (Massachusetts: Harvard UP, 1969); E. Portalié, "Augustin" in *Dictionnaire de théologie catholique*, vol I, cols. 2268–2472 (Paris: Letouzey et Ané, 1909).

3*Against the Academicians* (III.xix.42) quoted and translated by Peter Brown, *Augustine of Hippo* (Berkeley and Los Angeles: U of California P, 1967), pg. 93.

4St. Augustin, *La Cité de Dieu*, Bibliothèque Augustinienne, 4th ed., 5 vols. (Paris: 1959–60) vol. 33, pg. 302. All further references to the Latin text are cited from this edition unless otherwise specified. The English translation is Henry Bettenson's in *Augustine, The City of God* (Harmondsworth, Middlesex, England: Penguin Ltd., 1972), pg. 46–47, and the same is cited throughout unless otherwise designated.

5Jaeger, *Paideia*, vol. 2, pg. 77. On Augustine's "philosophy" of history, see the studies by: Giuseppe Amari, *Il Concetto di Storia in Sant'Agostino* (Roma: Edizioni Paoline, 1951); Norman H. Baynes, *The Political Ideas of St. Augustine's "De Civitate Dei"* (London: G. Bell and Sons, Ltd., 1936); Dino Bigongiari "The Political Ideas of St. Augustine" in *Essays on Dante and Medieval Culture* (Firenze: L. S. Olschki, 1964); Edgar H. Brookes, *"The City of God" and the Politics of Crisis* (London and New York: Oxford UP, 1960); H. A. Deane, *The Political and Social Ideas of St. Augustine* (London and New York: Columbia UP, 1963); Roy J. Deferrari and M. Jerome Keeler, "St. Augustine's *City of God*: Its Plan and Development," *American Journal of Philosophy*, 1 (1929), pp. 109–37; John N. Figgis, *The Political Aspects of St. Augustine's "City of God"* (London, New York, [etc.]: Longmans, 1921) especially chapter ii; William A. Green, *Augustine on the Teaching of History*, University of California Publications in Classical Philology, xii, 18 (Berkeley: U of California P, 1944); J. C. Guy, *Unité et structure logique de la "Cité de Dieu" de Saint Augustin* (Paris: Études Augustiniennes, 1961); F. J. C. Hearnshaw and A. J. Carlyle, "St. Augustine and the *City of God*," in *The Social and Political Ideas of Some Great Medieval Thinkers*, ed. Hearnshaw (London: G. G. Harrap & Co., Ltd., 1928); G. L. Keyes, *Christian Faith and the Interpretation of History: A Study of St. Augustine's Philosophy of History* (Lincoln: U of Nebraska P, 1966); Karl Löwith, *Meaning in History* (Chicago: U of Chicago P, 1949), chapter iv; J. J. O'Meara, *Charter of Christendom* (New York: MacMillan, 1967); Joseph Rickaby, St. *Augustine's "City of God": A View of its Contents* (London: Burns Oates & Washbourne, Ltd., 1925); Giuseppe Ruotolo, *La filosofia della storia e la "Città di Dio,"* 2nd ed. (Roma: Dott. C. Cuffi, 1950); Ferdinand Schevill, *Six Historians* (Chicago: Chicago UP, 1956), pp. 33–60; Roger L. Schinn, *Christianity and the Problem of History* (New York: Scribner, 1953), chapter ii; James T. Shotwell, *The History of History* (New York: Columbia UP, 1939), vol 1, chapter xxviii; Mathinus Versfeld, *A Guide to "The City of God"* (New York: Sheed & Ward, 1959), chapters vii–viii.

6Robert E. Cushman, *Therapeia: Plato's Conception of Philosophy* (Chapel Hill: U of North Carolina P, 1958) pg. 73, fn. 11, notes that the Platonic texts available to Augustine in Latin translation included both the *Republic* and the *Phaedo* by Apuleius, and Calcidius' partial translation and commentary of the *Timaeus* which is alluded to in the *City of God* (VIII.15).

[7]Some of the views of Apuleius are summarized in Book VIII (chapters iv through xxii) *et passim.*

[8]The Platonic foundation of Augustine's vision of salvation history was formulated in the first decade of this century by Karl Vossler. In his *Medieval Culture: An Introduction to Dante and His Times*, trans. William Cranston Lawton (New York: Ungar, 1929; rpt. 1958) vol. 1, pg. 235, Vossler comments on the pilgrimage of the *civitas Dei* as it emerges out of the *civitas terrena.* The *civitas Dei* moves

> by the force of justice, away from its dark source, sin, and upward toward the superhuman goal of grace. The same poles, sin and grace, between which the pious Christian moves, are also the opposing forces of the pious state, the *civitas Dei.* Thus Plato's doctrine of the state as a man is utilized once more.

[9]*La Cité de Dieu*, vol. 35, pp. 464, 466.

[10]Bettenson, trans., *City of God*, pp. 593–594.

[11]H. -I. Marrou, *Saint Augustin et la fin de la culture antique* (E. De Broccard, Paris: 1938), pg. 80.

[12]*La Cité de Dieu*, vol. 35, pg. 86.

[13]Bettenson, trans., *The City of God*, pg. 449.

[14]Plato, *Theatetus*, trans. F. M. Cornford in *The Collected Dialogues of Plato Including the Letters,* eds. Edith Hamilton and Huntington Cairns, Bolligen Series LXXI (Princeton: Princeton UP, 1973), pg. 881.

[15]Plato, *The Republic*, trans. Paul Shorey in *The Collected Dialogues of Plato*, pp. 773–774.

[16]Cf. Augustine's famous analysis of *pax* in the *City of God* XIX.13.

[17]*La Cité de Dieu*, vol. 33, pg. 538.

[18]Bettenson, trans., *City of God*, pp. 138–139.

[19]Plato, *The Republic*, trans. Richard W. Sterling and William C. Scott (Norton: New York and London, 1985) pp. 49–50. Cf. Plato's final dialogue, the *Laws*, where in the context of a discussion of the Socratic topic of self-mastery as "the primal and subtlest victory," the Athenian applies the analogical argumentation typifying the *Republic*:

> If each individual man is master of himself, or alternatively mastered by himself, may we, or may we not say that a family, a village, a city, exhibit this same feature? [Plato, *The Laws*, trans. A. E. Taylor in *The Collected Dialogues of Plato*, pg. 1228.]

[20]Eduard Zeller, *The Stoics, the Epicureans, and Sceptics*, ed. Oswald J. Reichel, trans. (New York: Russell and Russell, 1972), pp. 330–331.

[21]I am deeply indebted throughout this chapter and those which follow to Ronald L. Martinez for his study of microcosmic theory in Augustine which appears in Chapter One of *Dante, Statius, and the Earthly City.* Dissertation. U of California, Santa Cruz, 1977, pg. 36.

22*La Cité de Dieu*, vol. 37, pg. 126.

23Bettenson, trans., *City of God*, pg. 876.

24Cf. Augustine's allusions to human passion as a hurricane at IX.iii.6.

25World unity under a supreme ruler is, of course, Dante's solution to the problem of political conflict which will be alluded to in the following chapter on "Dante's *Inferno* XIII."

26*La Cité de Dieu*, vol. 37, pp. 84, 86, 88.

27Bettenson, trans., *City of God*, pp. 861–862.

28Of his own *psychomachia*, Augustine asks in *Against Julian* (V.vii.26) quoted by Peter Brown, *Augustine of Hippo*, pg. 327: "What is it that has sown this war in me?" See also the *Confessions* (XIII.vii) where Augustine recalls the violence of his inner conflict on the brink of his conversion in terms of the Pauline antagonism inherent in the concept of the divided will. In the same work (Bk. X, xxviii–xxxi) incontinence is associated with fragmentation, continence with reintegration; the war against intemperance is a daily battle of the soul against the flux of the body.

29This formulation recurs repeatedly, e.g. at XIX.23, 24, 27.

30*La Cité de Dieu*, (XIV .xv), vol. 35, pp. 420, 422.

31Bettenson, trans., *City of God*, pg. 576.

32*La Cité de Dieu*, vol. 35, pg. 282.

33Bettenson, trans., *City of God*, pp. 522–523.

34The litany of the miseries of human life to which the individual is condemned fills all of XXII.xxii. The infernal characterization of this life at the conclusion of the litany reads as follows:

> Ab huius tam miserae quasi quibusdam inferis vitae non liberat nisi gratia Salvatoris . . . [*La Cité de Dieu*, vol. 37, pg. 652].

> From this life of misery, a kind of hell on earth, there is no liberation save through the grace of Christ our Savior . . . [Bettenson, trans., *City of God*, pg. 1068].

35*La Cité de Dieu*, vol. 37, pp. 642, 644.

36Bettenson, trans., *City of God*, pg. 1065.

37*La Cité de Dieu*, vol. 35, pp. 432, 434.

38Bettenson, trans., *City of God*, pp. 580–581.

39*La Cité de Dieu*, vol. 37, pg. 62.

40Bettenson, trans., *City of God*, pg. 852.

41*La Cité de Dieu*, vol. 37, pp. 66, 68.

42Bettenson, trans., *City of God*, pp. 853–854.

43*La Cité de Dieu*, vol. 37, pg. 142.

44Bettenson, trans., *City of God*, pg. 883.

45Bruno Nardi, "Il concetto dell'Impero nello svolgimento del pensiero dantesco" in *Saggi di filosofia dantesca* (Firenze: "La Nuova Italia," 1967) pg. 218, captures the continuity between the Adamic soul and the tenor of the history of the Earthly City thus:

... per sant' Agostino la *civitas terrena,* non solo è una conseguenza del peccato, ma del peccato conserva tutte le tracce profonde: esse è, quasi direi, la continuazione del primo peccato....

46*La Cité de Dieu,* vol. 37, pg. 164.

47Bettenson, trans., *City of God,* pp. 890–891.

48*La Cité de Dieu,* (XV.iii) vol. 36, pg. 44.

49Bettenson, trans., *City of God,* pg. 599.

50On the corporate personality of Adam, which shares with the Platonic body politic analogy the function of reducing multiplicity to unity, see *De civitate Dei* XII.xxii:

quod ex uno homine Deus ad commendandum hominibus, quam ei grata sit etiam in pluribus unitas, genus instituisset humanum. [*La Cité de Dieu,* vol. 35, pg. 232]

that God started the human race from one man to show to mankind how pleasing to him is unity in plurality. [Bettenson, trans., *City of God,* pg. 503]

51*La Cité de Dieu,* vol. 33, pg. 392.

52Bettenson, trans., *City of God,* pg. 81.

53*La Cité de Dieu,* vol. 33, pg. 242.

54Bettenson, trans., *City of God,* pg. 25.

55Cf. Aristotle's affirmation in the *Politics* III.vi (1278b23–24) that *eudaimonia* is the "chief end, both of individuals and of states." Augustine is at pains to refute the claim which identifies human perfection with secular polity.

56The distinction between the interior as opposed to the exterior individual is fundamental to Socrates' discussion of justice in the *Republic.* Cf. Augustine's *True Religion* (26.48) where the *contaminatio* of Plato and Paul also links the *vetus homo* and the "exterior man" with the *civitas terrena*:

Here is one termed "the old man" and "exterior" and "earthly" even though that one achieve what the mob calls "happiness" in a well-constituted earthly city, whether under kings, or princes, or laws, or under them all. Else a people cannot be well constituted, not even the one that pursues earthly goals, for that sort too possesses a certain measure of beauty that is proper to it.

R. A. Markus sees the Augustinian synthesis as problematic in *Saeculum: History and Society in the Theology of St. Augustine* (Cambridge: Cambridge UP, 1970), pp. 79–81.

57See Jaeger, pg. 356, on the common heritage of the Platonist and the Christian as a "citizen of two worlds," and Theodore E. Mommsen "St. Augustine and the Christian Idea of Progress," in *Medieval and Renaissance Studies,* ed. Eugene F. Rice Jr. (Ithaca: Cornell UP, 1959), pp. 265–298.

58This passage from the *Ennarationes in Psalmos* (IX.viii) is quoted by Robert Denoon Cumming, *Human Nature and History* (Chicago and London: U of Chicago

P, 1969), vol. I, pg. 316—a work from which I have learned much.

59*La Cité de Dieu*, vol. 33, pg. 312.

60Bettenson, trans., *City of God*, pg. 49.

61Pierre Courcelle, *Confessions*, pp. 11-15, argues that Augustine's reflexive technique derives from the moralizing of the Cynic-Stoic tradition. This tradition is a proximate source for Augustine, yet there is no reason to conclude that he was not familiar with its Platonic origins.

62Cumming, *Human Nature and History*, pg. 316.

63*La Cité de Dieu*, II.xxiv, vol. 33, pg. 390.

64Bettenson, trans., *City of God*, pg. 80.

65*La Cité de Dieu*, XIV.ii, vol. 35, pg. 350.

66Bettenson, trans., *City of God*, pg. 547.

67*Biblia Sacra iuxta Vulgatam Clementinam* (Madrid: Editorial Catolica, 1977), pg. 1168.

68*The Holy Bible* (Cambridge: Cambridge UP, n.d.), pg. 846.

69Plato, *Phaedo*, trans. Hugh Tredennick in *The Collected Dialogues of Plato*, pg. 49. Cf. Plato's characterization of the appetite in the *Republic* (442a):

> The appetitive part which is the mass of the soul in each of us and the most insatiate by nature of wealth. [Plato, *Republic*, trans. Paul Shorey in *The Collected Dialogues of Plato*, pg. 684]

70*La Cité de Dieu*, vol. 33, pg. 438. The pursuit of riches which is the most common cause of conflict between nations, is not regarded by Augustine as a legitimate motive for waging war. See G. Combès, *La doctrine politque de saint Augustin* (Paris: Plon, 1927), pg. 287 ff.

71*La Cité de Dieu*, vol. 33, pg. 436.

72*The Aeneid of Vergil*, trans. Allen Mandelbaum (Toronto: Bantam Books, 1971), pg. 201.

73*La Cité de Dieu*, vol. 33, pg. 516.

74Bettenson, trans., *City of God*, pg. 131.

75Cf. XV.v where Augustine alludes to the finite nature of material goods as opposed to the infinite divisibility of spiritual goods; the latter in contrast to the former are increased rather than diminished by being shared:

> Nullo enim modo fit minor accedente seu permanente consorte possessio bonitatis, immo possessio bonitas, quam tanto latius, quanto concordius individua sociorum possidet caritas. Non habebit denique istam possessionem, qui eam noluerit habere communem, et tanto eam reperiet ampliorem, quanto amplius ibi potuerit amare consortem. [*La Cité de Dieu*, vol. 36, pg. 48]

> A man's possession of goodness is in no way diminished by the arrival, or the continuance, of a sharer in it; indeed, goodness is a possession enjoyed more widely by the united affection of partners in that possession in proportion to the harmony that exists among them. In fact, anyone who refuses to enjoy this

possession in partnership will not enjoy it all; and he will find that he possesses
it in ampler measure in proportion to his ability to love his partner in it.
[Bettenson, trans., *City of God*, pg. 601]

76*La Cité de Dieu*, vol. 36, pp. 44, 46.
77Bettenson, trans., *City of God*, pp. 599–600.
78For the Aristotelian origin (*Politics*, Book VII) of the Augustinian concept of
peace-making war, which became the standard justification of war in the middle ages,
see Maurice Defourny, *Aristote: Étude sur la "Politique"* (Paris: Beauchesne, 1932).
79*La Cité de Dieu*, vol. 37, pg. 128.
80Bettenson, trans., *City of God*, pg. 877.
81Domenico Pesce, *Città Terrena e Città Celeste nel pensiero: Platone, Cicerone, S.
Agostino* (Firenze: Sansoni, 1957), pg. 165.
82*La Cité de Dieu*, vol. 36, pp. 42, 44.
83Bettenson, trans., *City of God*, pg. 599.
84See Cumming, *Human Nature and History*, pg. 314. Cumming's assumption that
Augustine had not read the *Republic* leads him to conclude that Augustine depended
upon Cicero's translation of the Platonic concept of harmony, and that therefore, his
"Platonic" application of the key term, *concordia* is merely fortuitous.  Cumming states
that the

> analogy to musical harmony Cicero salvaged from the passage where Plato had
> described the fashion in which the three parts of the individual's mind,
> corresponding to the three classes in the ideal state, could be self-controlled.
> But unlike Cicero, Augustine was not bilingual.  Cicero kept in mind the
> derivation of *concordia* from the Greek χορδή (the string of a lyre); but
> *concordia* also incorporates a Latin root, *cor* (the heart), and it is this root that
> Augustine utilizes, so that the harmony in question becomes an "inner"
> concord with respect to the things the citizens set their "hearts" on . . . .
> Augustine is not aware of the fact that his Latin etymologizing is rescuing a
> Greek thinker's analysis of internal relations from their externalization by a
> Latin statesman and translator.  But Augustine is in fact regaining the
> application of the musical analogy to the individual's mind—the application
> which had been fundamental in Plato . . . . The state is again "of one mind" in
> Augustine (as it had been in Plato) . . . . It is a "composition of wills" which
> compose a state by moving in "the uniform direction of their love."

85See Aristotle, *Politics* II.iii.
86Like Plato's ideal body politic, Augustine's *civitas Dei* also speaks as one. For an
example of the choric voice of *civitas Dei*, see the final chapter of Book XIV.  In
*Paradiso* XVIII Dante incorporates Plato's description of the ideal body politic in the
*Republic* (462a–e) to represent the unification of the universal body politic of
humankind under the Monarchy; Dante was familiar with Plato's comparison of the
ideal city to a human body through Aristotle's discussion of Plato in the *Politics*.  I am
preparing a separate essay on this subject.

[87]Plato, *Republic* 462a–3, trans. Shorey in *The Collected Dialogues*, pg. 701.

[88]Cf. Augustine, *Commentary on the Gospel of St. John*, LXV, 1, describes the true model of society in Pauline terms.

> et ex universo genere humano quod diffunditur toto orbe terrarum, facit et
> colligit populum novum, corpus novae nuptae Filii Dei unigeniti sponsae . . .
> Propter quod pro invicem sollicita sunt membra in ea; et si patitur unum
> membrum, compatiuntur omnia membra, et si glorificatur unum membrum,
> congaudent omnia membra. [*In Iohannis Evangelium Tractatus. Commento al
> Vangelo di San Giovanni*, ed. Agostino Vita, trans. Emilio Gandolfo (Roma:
> Città Nuova Editrice, 1968), Tractatus LXV.1, pg. 1140.]

> . . . and from among the universal race of man, which overspreads the whole
> world, is making and gathering together a new people, the body of the newly-
> married spouse of the only-begotten son of God. . . . Because of this, the
> members thereof have a mutual interest in one another; and if one member
> suffers, all the members suffer with it; and one member be honored all the
> members rejoice with it. [*A Select Library of the Nicene and Post-Nicene Fathers
> of the Christian Church* ed. Philip Schaff, vol. 7, *St. Augustin: Homilies on the
> Gospel of John* (New York: The Christian Literature Company, 1888), pg. 318.]

[89]*La Cité de Dieu*, vol. 37, pg. 710.

[90]Bettenson, trans., *City of God*, pg. 1088.

[91]Cf. Thomas Merton's introduction to *The City of God*, trans. Marcus Dods, (New York: Random House, 1950), pp. xi–xii:

> It may come as a surprise to some to learn that St. Augustine quite
> spontaneously regarded contemplation as a communal endeavor. Solitude may
> be necessary for certain degrees of contemplative prayer on earth, but in
> heaven contemplation is the beatitude not merely of separate individuals but of
> an entire city. The city is a living organism whose mind is the Truth of God
> and whose will is his Love and Liberty.

[92]*La Cité de Dieu*, vol. 34, pg. 448.

[93]Bettenson, trans., *City of God*, pg. 380.

# St. Augustine and the Christian Idea of Progress: The Background of *The City of God*†

## Theodor E. Mommsen

In the summer of the year 410 Rome fell to a Visigothic army under King Alaric.[1] Since the city suffered relatively little external damage, modern historians have sometimes been inclined to regard that conquest or sack of Rome as a rather insignificant incident. We should be wary, however, of any tendency to belittle the event, remembering that it impelled Augustine to write *The City of God*. In view of the impact this work has had upon the development of Christian thought, it can certainly be said that the fall of Rome in the year 410, which motivated its composition, marks a momentous date in the intellectual history of the western world.

Moreover, Augustine was not the only contemporary to be profoundly impressed by that event, as several other writings show. It may suffice here to quote a few sentences from St. Jerome, who was at that time living in Bethlehem. When he received the news of "the havoc wrought in the West and, above all, in the city of Rome" (*Epist.* 126, 2), he expressed his feelings in the preface to the first book of the *Commentaries on Ezekiel*, which he was then writing: "When the brightest light on the whole earth was extinguished, when the Roman empire was deprived of its head and when, to speak more correctly, the whole world perished in one city, then 'I was dumb with silence, I held my peace, even from good, and my sorrow was stirred' (*Psalm* 39, 2)." And in the preface to the third book of the same work, Jerome asked: "Who would believe that Rome, built up by the conquest of the whole world, has collapsed, that the mother of nations has also become their tomb?"[2]

To understand the profound consternation of Jerome and his contemporaries we must realize that the fate of Rome meant infinitely more to the people of late antiquity than the fate of any city, even the most renowned, would mean to the western world today. For many deeply rooted ideas and beliefs, and numerous superstitions, were connected with the very name and existence of that city. One need recall only the famous lines of Vergil's *Aeneid* (1, 278 f.), in which Jupiter says: "To the Romans I assign limits neither to the extent nor to the duration of their empire; dominion have I given them without end." This notion of "the eternal city," the capital of a universal empire, "the golden Rome," we find reflected in the works of almost all the pagan writers and poets of the first centuries of our era, whether they were of Latin, Greek or Oriental origin.[3] Thus, at the end of the fourth century, the pagan general and historian Ammianus Marcellinus declared

(*Histor.*, 14, 6, 3) that "as long as there are men, Rome will be victorious so that it will increase with lofty growth." And around the year 400 the Christian poet Claudianus wrote (*On the Consulate of Stilicho*, 3, 159 f.): "There will never be an end to the power of Rome, for luxury and pride resulting in vices and enmities have destroyed all other kingdoms."

During the same period the attitude of the Christians toward the Roman empire was divided. On the one hand, there ran within early Christianity an undercurrent of strong hatred of the Roman state and of everything that state stood for. This hostility, nourished by Jewish traditions and strengthened by the persecutions, manifested itself in the apparently widespread expectation that some day the prediction of the angel in the *Book of Revelation* (14, 8) would be fulfilled: "Babylon [i.e., Rome] is fallen, is fallen, that great city, because she made all nations drink of the wine of the wrath of her fornication." On the other hand, the official spokesmen of the early Church always remembered that Jesus himself had ordered his disciples to "render therefore unto Caesar the things which are Caesar's" (*Matthew*, 22, 21), and that St. Paul had demanded obedience to the empire when he wrote in his *Epistle to the Romans* (13,1): "Let every soul be subject unto the higher powers. For there is no power but of God: the powers that be are ordained of God." In accordance, then, with these explicit orders of Christ and St. Paul, every adherent of the faith had to pay his outward respect, at least, to the established authorities of the state.

But many Christians showed themselves willing to go even farther and actually hoped and prayed for the continuance of the Roman empire. This affirmative attitude grew out of certain historical and eschatological ideas which went back to both pagan and Jewish traditions.[4] In the Hellenistic era there had developed in the East a theory which saw history take its course in a sequence of great or, rather, universal monarchies. Four of these empires were to follow one another, and the series was to conclude with a fifth monarch in which, it was believed, would last to the end of the world. This idea of the four or five monarchies was adopted by some of the Roman and Greek historians, and it appeared likewise in Jewish literature. For the great image seen in a dream by Nebuchadnezzar (*Daniel*, 2, 31 ff.) and the four beasts seen by Daniel himself (7, 1 ff.), were explained by the pre-Christian tradition in terms of an interpretation of world history: these visions were believed to signify symbolically that history takes its course through the succession of four universal monarchies; the disintegration of the last of the four empires was assumed to usher in the end of the world.

In the latter part of the second century and in the first part of the third century Christian theologians like Irenaeus of Lyons, Tertullian and Hippolytus adopted these pagan and Jewish traditions and expressed their opinion that the Roman empire "which now rules" (Irenaeus, *Against Heresies*, 5, 26, 1), should be considered to be the fourth monarchy.[5] All these Christian authors shared the belief that the fall of the last empire would be a most ominous event. Thus, Tertullian said in his treatise *On the Resurrection of the Flesh* (ch. 24), in which he interpreted a passage in St. Paul's *Second Epistle to the Thessalonians* (2, 7), that the Antichrist will appear after the Roman state has been scattered into ten kingdoms. On the basis of this eschatological belief Tertullian declared very emphatically in his *Apology* (ch. 32, 1): "There is also another and greater necessity for our praying in behalf of the emperors and the whole status of the empire and Roman affairs. For we know that only the continued existence of the Roman Empire retards the mighty power which threatens the whole earth, and postpones the very end of this world with its menace of horrible afflictions." In the early fourth century Lactantius stated even more explicitly in his *Divine Institutions* (7, 25, 6–8): "The fall and the ruin of the world will shortly take place, although it seems that nothing of that kind is to be feared as long as the city of Rome stands intact. But when the capital of the world has fallen . . . who can doubt that the end will have arrived for the affairs of men and the whole world? It is that city which still sustains all things. And the God of heaven is to be entreated by us and implored—if indeed His laws and decrees can be delayed—lest sooner than we think that detestable tyrant should come who will undertake so great a deed and tear out that eye by the destruction of which the world itself is about to fall."

During the fourth century a number of commentators on the *Book of Daniel*, including Eusebius and John Chrysostom in the East, Jerome and Sulpicius Severus (*Sacred Histories*, 2, 3) in the West, continued to identify the fourth monarchy with the Roman empire. Cyril of Jerusalem (*Catechetical Lectures*, 15, 12) followed even more closely the line of Irenaeus, Tertullian and Lactantius, by declaring: "The Antichrist is to come when the time of the Roman empire has been fulfilled and the end of the world is drawing near."

In view of the persistence of this concern for the continuance of Rome it seems safe to assume that in the year 410 many contemporaries regarded Alaric's conquest of Rome as the realization of the long-dreaded "fall of Rome" and considered the end of the world to be imminent. A reflection of this superstitious fear we find, I think, even in the words of Jerome, that "the whole world has perished in one city."

Augustine was, of course, well aware of both the pagan belief in "eternal Rome" and the eschatological speculations of his fellow-Christians. He rejected emphatically the one idea as well as the other. As to the pagan notion, he pointed out (*Sermon* 105, 9) that "the earthly kingdoms have their changes" and that only of the Kingdom of Christ it can be said: "There shall be no end" (*Luke* 1, 33). He continued (*ibid.*, §10): "They who have promised this to earthly kingdoms have not been guided by truth but have lied by flattery." He quoted the famous line from Vergil—whom he calls rather slightingly "a certain poet of theirs"—and remarked: "This kingdom which you [Jupiter] have given 'without limits to its duration,' is it on earth or in heaven? Certainly it is on earth. And even if it were in heaven, yet 'heaven and earth shall pass away' (*Matthew*, 24, 35). Those things shall pass away, which God Himself has made. How much more rapidly shall that pass away which Romulus founded?" As to the meaning of the passage in St. Paul's *Second Epistle to the Thessalonians* (2, 7): "Only he who now holdeth, let him hold until he be taken out of the way,"[6] Augustine was much less certain than Tertullian, who had concluded from these words that the duration of this world is bound up with the duration of the Roman empire. Augustine knew (*City of God*, 20, 19 E–F)[7] that "some think that this refers to the Roman empire," and he granted that such an interpretation, in contrast to some others, "is not absurd." But at the same time he felt obliged to state: "I frankly confess that I do not know what St. Paul meant."

In reply to those Christian thinkers who attempted to figure out the exact date of the end of the world and connected the coming of that event with concrete developments and with definite historical incidents like "the fall of Rome," Augustine declared (*City of God*, 18, 53 A–B) that such a question "is entirely improper." For he pointed out that Christ himself told his disciples: "It is not for you to know the times and the seasons which the Father hath put in His own power" (*Acts*, 1, 7). "In vain, then," Augustine stated, "do we attempt to compute and determine the years which remain to this world." Whoever undertakes that kind of calculation, Augustine concluded, "uses human conjecture and brings forward nothing certain from the authority of the canonical Scriptures."

Another argument which in several of his sermons Augustine employed, though in a more incidental fashion, is the observation that, after all, Rome was still standing, in spite of the disaster of the year 410. For instance, in the *Sermon on the Ruin of the City* he said that Rome, unlike Sodom, was not completely destroyed, and in another discourse (*Sermon* 105, 9) he declared: "The city which has given us birth, according to the flesh, still abides, God be thanked." He added (§ 11): "An end there will be to all earthly kingdoms. If that end be now, God alone knows. Perhaps the end is not yet, and we, because of a certain weakness or mercifulness or anguish, wish that it may not yet be." Augustine confessed (§ 12) that he himself was "entreating the Lord for Rome," not because he believed the duration of that one city would guarantee the duration of the whole world, but simply because there were many fellow-Christians in Rome, dear to him as all other Christians were.[8]

Since Rome did, in fact, survive, the old belief in its eternity also survived for many centuries to come, and with it persisted the popular superstition, in spite of its rejection by Augustine, that the final "fall" of the city would signify the coming end of the world. Only one of the many testimonials to that belief may be quoted. In a British text of the early eighth century, which was wrongly ascribed to the Venerable Bede, we find the following lines:

> As long as the Colosseum stands, Rome also stands. When the Colosseum falls, Rome also will fall. When Rome falls, the world also will fall.[9]

The denial of the pagan belief in the eternity of Rome and the rejection of any connection between Christian eschatology and specific historical events occupy, however, only a rather minor place in the whole context of *The City of God*. Augustine felt justified in making short shrift of these ideas because he regarded them as either mere superstitions or futile conjectures.

The real purpose of his great book he stated in a number of places but nowhere more concisely than in the work entitled *Retractations* (2, 68, 1), which he wrote after the completion of *The City of God* in the year 426. He defined his primary objective as follows: "In the meantime Rome had been overthrown by the invasion of the Goths under king Alaric and by the vehemence of a great defeat. The worshipers of the many and false gods, whom we commonly call pagans, attempted to attribute that overthrow to the Christian religion, and they began to blaspheme the true God with even more than their customary acrimony and bitterness. It was for that reason that I, kindled by zeal for the house of God, undertook to write the books on *The City of God* against their blasphemies and errors."

The accusation was very old that Christianity was responsible for the miseries of the world. The pagans claimed that the Christians, through their refusal to honor the traditional deities, were provoking the wrath of the very gods whose favor had raised Rome to her universal power. The Christian apologists found it easy to refute the charge. One of the most precise expressions of their customary reply is contained in Tertullian's *Apology* (40, 3, 5). Tertullian addressed the pagans as follows: "Pray, tell me, how many calamities befell the world as a whole, as well as individual cities, before Tiberius reigned, before the coming, that is, of Christ?" He asked: "Where were your gods in those days when a deluge effaced the whole earth or, as Plato believed, merely its plains?" And he concluded: "The truth is that the human race has always deserved ill at God's hand. . . . Therefore one ought to know that the very same God is angry now, as he always was, long before Christians were so much as spoken of."

Augustine used exactly the same kind of argument throughout the first five books of *The City of God*, only in a much more elaborate and detailed fashion than Tertullian, Arnobius, Lactantius and other apologists of the third century had done before him. He went still further and commissioned his younger friend Orosius to write an entire history of the world from a point of view which is best described by Orosius himself in the dedication to Augustine of his *Seven Books of Histories against the Pagans*: "You bade me to discover from all the available data of histories and annals, whatever instances past ages have afforded of the burdens of war, the ravages of diseases, the horrors of famine, terrible earthquakes, extraordinary floods, dreadful eruptions of fire, thunderbolts and hailstorms, and also instances of the cruel miseries caused by murders and crimes against man's better self."[10] Orosius proved himself indeed "the true compiler of the evils of the world," as Petrarch (*Familiares*, 15, 9, 10) was to characterize him scornfully many centuries later. But in spite, or perhaps because, of their admitted prejudices and their preconceived ideas, Augustine's and Orosius' systematic expositions of the old apologist conceptions of world history in general and of Roman history in particular were to determine the historical outlook of most western writers to the time of the Italian Renaissance.

However, that traditional apology fills only one section in the first part of *The City of God*.[11] In the second half of the work (books XI to XXII) Augustine wanted to offer much more than a mere defense, as he stated himself in his *Retractations* (2, 68, 2): "In order that no one might raise the charge against me that I have merely refuted the opinions of other men but not stated my own, I devoted to this objective the second part of the work."

Of the vast number of ideas which Augustine set forth as his "own opinions," only one problem will be discussed here, that of "History": how does history take its course and is there any meaning to be found in the sequence of events from the beginning of this world to the present age and to the day of the Last Judgment?[12]

How deeply Augustine was concerned with the question of the philosophical or rather, from his point of view, the theological interpretation of the meaning and course of history, is shown by those chapters of *The City of God* in which he discussed the problems of the origin of the world and the uniqueness of its creation. He rejected the view that this world is eternal and without beginnings, and he stated that it was definitely created in time and will come to an end in another definite moment in time, a moment known to God alone. In connection with his discussion of "this controversy about the beginnings of things temporal" (12, 13 E) Augustine wrote (12, 14 A): "The philosophers of this world believed that they could or should not solve that controversy in any other way than by introducing cycles of time, in which they asserted that the revolving of coming and passing ages would always be renewed and repeated in the nature of things and would thus go on without cessation." In this sentence Augustine was obviously referring to the cyclical theory of history held by Platonists, Stoics and other Greek schools of philosophy.[13] But although he mentioned no name, it becomes evident from the context of the passage just quoted that he knew that this cyclical view was also maintained by Origen, who attempted to support it in a somewhat qualified fashion through quotations from the Scriptures, for instance the famous sentence in *Ecclesiastes* (1, 9): "There is no new thing under the sun." In his Latin translation of Origen's text Rufinus considerably modified these views, but this did not prevent Jerome from attacking them sharply. Augustine was even more emphatic in his refutation when he exclaimed in *The City of God* (12, 14 E): "Far be it from the right faith to believe that by these words of Solomon [*i.e., Ecclesiastes*] those cycles are meant in which [according to these philosophers] the revolving of the same periods and things is repeated." He found it logical that those thinkers "erroneously wandering around in cycles, find neither entrance nor exit," for he was convinced that "they do not know how the human race and this mortal condition of ours took its origin nor how it will be brought to an end" (12, 15 A). Those "false cycles which were discovered by false and deceitful sages," he believed, "can be avoided in the sound doctrine, through the path of the straight road (*tramite recti itineris*)."[14]

To Augustine, then, history takes its course, not in cycles, but along a line. That line has a most definite beginning, the Creation, and a most definite end, the Last Judgment. Within this definite period of time the greatest single event was, of course, the appearance of Christ. "For," Augustine said (12, 14 F), "Christ died once for our sins and 'raised from the dead dieth no more' (*Romans*, 6, 9); . . . and we ourselves, after the resurrection, 'shall ever be with the Lord' (*I Thessalonians*, 4, 17)." It seems that here Augustine was arguing again indirectly against Origen who, according to Jerome, "allowed himself to assert that Christ has often suffered and will often suffer, on the ground that what was beneficial once, will always be beneficial," and who also, "in his desire to confirm the most impious dogma of the Stoics through the authority of the Divine Scriptures, dared to write that man dies over and over again.[15]

From Augustine's conception of the course of history it follows that every particular event that takes place in time, every human life and human action, is a unique phenomenon which happens under the auspices of Divine Providence and must therefore have a definite meaning. The roots of this linear conception of history, as distinguished from the cyclical theories of the Greeks, went back to Hebrew ideas which had been further developed by the early Christian theologians.[16] But it was Augustine who elaborated those ideas most fully and consistently and thus determined the theology of history which prevailed throughout the Middle Ages and was to influence the philosophies of history of modern times.

When Augustine decided to combat the cyclical theories, he was probably motivated, as we have seen, by his knowledge that this pagan view was shared, to a certain extent at least, by a prominent, though suspect and even heretical, Christian thinker, Origen. But it appears that there existed still another philosophy of history at that time, which from Augustine's point of view was even more dangerous than the cyclical theory because it was very widespread among the Christians of his own as well as previous generations. To Augustine the truly problematic and the most objectionable theory of history must have been a conception which may be called "the Christian idea of progress."

When in 1920 J. B. Bury published his book *The Idea of Progress*, he wrote (20 f.) that "the idea of the universe which prevailed throughout the Middle Ages and the general orientation of men's thoughts were incompatible with some of the fundamental assumptions which are required by the idea of progress." But more recently, a number of scholars have pointed out that, to a certain degree, such an idea can actually be found among some of the early Christian thinkers.[17] A systematic treatment of this complex topic does not yet exist and it cannot be given in a brief essay. But in the following an attempt will be made at least to set forth some examples from early Christian writings, which may serve to illustrate the nature of that idea.

One might be inclined to find the first instance of the conception of progress in that part of Christian literature which dealt with the question of the Millennium. For some of the early theologians, including Justin, Irenaeus and Lactantius, interpreted the apocalyptic prediction of Christ's future reign of one thousand years in terms of a very material bliss. But this peculiar notion cannot be truly said to express a belief in "progress," because the Messianic kingdom of the future was not to come into existence through a gradual or evolutionary process but rather through the dramatically sudden second coming of Christ. Moreover, even before Augustine's time thinkers like Origen and Tychonius had successfully discredited that very materialistic notion of the Millennium and had interpreted the conception in a primarily spiritual sense.[18] This became Augustine's own opinion also, because in the writings of the later period of his life, which dealt with eschatological speculations, he made it very clear that the question of the Millennium has nothing to do with any kind of earthly prosperity but has reference only to the necessarily imperfect realization of the divine in this world.

But apart from these speculations concerning the Millennium we find that some of the most prominent Christian apologists voiced views which implied the belief that under the auspices of Christianity the world had made concrete progress in historical time and that further progress could be expected. Those writers asserted that the new creed was bringing blessings to the whole of mankind, not merely to its own adherents. They pointed to the historically undeniable fact that the birth of Christ had taken place at the time of the foundation of the Roman empire by Augustus and the establishment of the *Pax Romana* on earth. As the appearance of Christ coincided with a marked improvement of all things secular, so, the early apologists argued, the growth of the new faith will be accompanied by further progress.[19]

The first testimony to this conception is to be found in the *Apology* which Bishop Melito of Sardis addressed to Emperor Antoninus Pius in the middle of the second century. According to Eusebius' *Ecclesiastical History* (4, 26, 7–8), Melito wrote: "Our philosophy [i.e., Christianity] flourished first among the barbarians; then, during the great reign of your ancestor Augustus, it spread among your people and, above all, it has become to your own reign an auspicious blessing. For from that time the power of Rome has grown in greatness and splendor. To this power you have succeeded as the desired heir and you will continue it with your sons if you safeguard that philosophy which grew up with the empire and took its start under Augustus . . . . The best evidence that our doctrine has been flourishing for the good of an empire happily started is this: since the reign of Augustus no misfortune has befallen it; on the contrary, all things have been splendid and glorious, in accordance with the wishes of all."

Around the year 200, Tertullian expressed the same idea, though somewhat more cautiously. He wrote in his *Apology* (ch. 40, 13): "And for all that is said, if we compare the calamities of former times [with those of our own era], we find that they fall on us more lightly now, since the earth has received from God the believers of the Christian faith. For since that time innocence has put restraint on the wickedness of this world and men have begun to plead with God for the averting of His wrath."

These two apologists, then, did not merely content themselves with rejecting the pagan accusation that Christianity was responsible for the misfortunes of the era; on the contrary, they dared to take the offensive and claimed that their faith was making a positive contribution to the well-being of the Roman empire.

From this assertion there was but a single step to the expression of the belief that the universal acceptance of the Christian religion by the Roman world would lead to a still greater degree of security and prosperity. The pagan Celsus, in the middle of the third century, raised the question as to the consequences of such an event. Origen replied to Celsus' question with utmost confidence (*Against Celsus*, 4, 69): "If all the Romans were to pray together in full harmony, then they would be able to put to flight many more enemies than those who were discomfitted by the prayers of Moses when he cried to the Lord." Fifty years after Origen, around the year 300, Arnobius expressed the same belief in his treatise *Against the Pagans* (1, 6): "If all without exception, who consider themselves men, not in form of body, but in power of reason, were willing to lend, for a little while, an ear to [Christ's] salutary and peaceful prescriptions and were not, swollen with pride and arrogance, to trust to their own senses rather than to His admonitions, then the whole world, having turned the use of iron into more peaceful occupations, would live in the most placid tranquillity and would unite in blessed harmony, maintaining inviolate the sanctity of treaties."

This conviction that the appearance of Christ has led to a general improvement of the material conditions of the world and that its universal acceptance will lead to a still greater progress, was set forth by Melito and Tertullian, by Origen and Arnobius, during a period when their faith was suppressed by the official authorities of the Roman state. When, in the reign of Constantine, the great turning-point arrived and Christianity was not only tolerated but became the religion most favored by the emperor, it was natural that hope for progress rose still higher. Thus even Lactantius, once the champion of eschatological ideas in their most extreme and pessimistic form, dared to express rather optimistic expectations at the very end of his book *On the Death of the Persecutors* (ch. 52): "The Lord has destroyed and erased from the earth those proud names [of the anti-Christian rulers]. Let us therefore celebrate the triumph of God with joy. Let us frequently praise the victory of the Lord. Day and night let us offer our prayers to the Lord that He may establish for all time the peace which has been given to His people after [a warfare of] ten years."

Constantine showed himself most eager to adopt the idea that the worship of the true and omnipotent God was bound to benefit his empire in a material sense. In a letter written shortly after his decisive victory at the Milvian Bridge in the year 312, he declared (Eusebius, *Eccles. Hist.*, 10, 7, 1): "From many facts it appears . . . that the lawful recognition and observance [of the Christian faith] has bestowed the greatest success on the Roman name and singular prosperity on all affairs of mankind, blessings which were provided by the divine beneficence." Constantine's highly materialistic conception of his relationship with the Christian God was very much in accordance with the religious notions of the ancient Romans.[20] It was the old principle of *do ut des*: "I give that you may give." The emperor argued: I, Constantine, do something for you, God, so that you may do something for me; likewise, of course, God himself was assumed to expect gifts in return from those to whom he had extended favors. This idea of a commutative contract between God and man found reflection in the politico-ecclesiastical writings of quite a few of the Christian authors of the fourth century, beginning with Constantine's court-bishop, Eusebius of Caesarea. It was a complete ideological reversal: once the pagans had charged that the worship of the Christian God was the source of all the calamities of the empire; now, Constantine had the symbol of the cross displayed in the principal room of his new imperial palace in Constantinople; according to Eusebius' *Life of Constantine* (3, 49), "this symbol seemed to the beloved of God [Constantine] to have been made as a safeguard of the empire itself."

The principle of *do ut des* was most emphatically rejected by Augustine, for it was wholly contrary to his conception of the relationship between God and man, even the great of this world.[21] Thus he stated in *The City of God* (4,33) that in God's eyes earthly power and all similar things temporal are not important gifts and that therefore God "bestows them on both the good and the bad." In discussing the question of the *imperator felix*, Augustine admitted (*City of God*, 5, 25 A) that God "gave to the emperor Constantine, who was not a worshiper of demons but of the true God Himself, such fullness of earthly gifts as no one would even dare to wish for." But Augustine continued: "Lest, however, any emperor shall become a Christian in order to merit the blessed felicity of Constantine—when everyone ought to be a Christian for the sake of the eternal life—God took away [the Christian prince] Jovian far sooner than [his pagan brother, the emperor] Julian, and He allowed [the Christian emperor] Gratian to be slain by the sword of a tyrant."

These sentences in *The City of God* sound as if they were written expressly against Eusebius, who had declared in his *Life of Constantine* (1, 3, 3), with specific reference to the emperor: "God, that God who is the common Saviour of all, has treasured up with Himself, for those who love religion, far greater blessings than man can conceive, and He gives even here and now the first-fruits as a pledge of future rewards, thus assuring in some sort immortal hopes to mortal eyes."

Eusebius based his belief in the effectiveness of the principle of *do ut des* on a very definite interpretation and philosophy of history.[22] He emphasized (*Demonstratio Evangelica*, 3, 7, 139) even more strongly than Melito and other Christian thinkers during the previous centuries, that "it was not through human merit that at no other time but only since the time of Christ most of the nations were under the single rule of the Romans; for the period of His wonderful sojourn among men coincided with the period when the Romans reached their summit under Augustus, who was then the first monarch to rule over most of the nations."[23] This concurrence of the appearance of Christ on earth and the founding of the universal empire by Augustus "was not by mere human accident" but it was "of God's arrangement." Whereas the earlier interpreters of that concurrence had stated it simply as a historical fact,

Eusebius believed himself capable of adducing proof from the Scriptures that those events were long before predicted by God. Thus he quoted in all the works in which he discussed the "synchronizing" of the birth of Christ with the reign of Augustus, the following passages from the Old Testament: "In His days the righteous shall flourish and abundance of peace" (*Psalm* 72, 7); "He shall have dominion also from sea to sea, and from the river unto the ends of the earth" (*Psalm* 72, 8); "And they shall beat their swords into plowshares, and their spears into pruninghooks: nation shall not lift up sword against nation, neither shall they learn war any more" (*Isaiah*, 2, 4).

These quotations are highly remarkable. For according to tradition those prophecies were to be understood as predictions of the future Messianic Kingdom, as we can learn from their interpretation by men like Irenaeus (*Against Heresies* 4, 56, 3), Tertullian (*Against Marcion*, 3, 21) and Lactantius (*Divine Institutions*, 4, 16, 14). It seems that previous to Eusebius only Origen (*Against Celsus*, 2, 30) had ventured to refer the passage in *Psalm* 72, 7 to the *Pax Romana*.[24] But the full elaboration of Origen's suggestion was left to Eusebius, who gave the most bluntly secular interpretations to these scriptural texts. Witness the passage in Eusebius' *Praeparatio Evangelica* (1, 4): "In accordance with these predictions [*i.e.* of *Psalm* 72 and of *Isaiah*, 2, 4], the actual events followed. Immediately after Augustus had established his sole rule, at the time of our Saviour's appearance, the rule by the many became abolished among the Romans. And from that time to the present you cannot see, as before, cities at war with cities, nor nation fighting with nation, nor life being worn away in the confusion of everything." Eusebius saw a close parallel between the victory of Christian monotheism and the growth of the Roman monarchy. Thus he stated in his *Theophania* (3, 2):[25] "Two great powers sprang up fully as out of one stream and they gave peace to all and brought all together to a state of friendship: the Roman empire, which from that time appeared as one kingdom, and the power of the Saviour of all, whose aid was at once extended to and established with everyone. For the divine superiority of our Saviour swept away the authority of the many demons and gods, so that the one Kingdom of God was preached to all men, Greeks and barbarians, and to those who resided in the extremities of the earth. The Roman empire, too—since those had been previously uprooted who had been the cause of the rule by many—soon subjugated all others and quickly brought together the whole race of man into one state of accordance and agreement."

To Eusebius the greatest gains made by mankind since the days of Christ and Augustus were the abolition of wars, foreign and civil, and the establishment of peace and security, the time-hallowed ideals of the *Pax Romana*. But he saw also other improvements. For instance, he declared in his *Praeparatio Evangelica* (1, 4): "Of the benefits resulting from God's doctrines which have become manifest on earth, you may see a clear proof if you consider that at no other time from the beginning until now, and not through the merits of any of the illustrious men of old but only through Christ's utterances and teachings, diffused throughout the whole world, the customs of all nations have been set aright, even those customs which before were savage and barbarous." Because of the strict discipline of the new faith men have learned to lead a moral life, to refrain from hostility toward others and to master their own emotions and passions. Eusebius concluded his enumeration of all the improvements made in the political, legal and moral spheres by asking: "How, then, can anyone . . . refuse to admit that our doctrine has brought to all men good tidings of very great and true blessings, and has supplied to human life that which is of immediate advantage toward happiness?"

There was no doubt in Eusebius' mind that mankind, under divine guidance, had made progress from the pre-Christian era through the three centuries of the gradual ascent of the new Church to the reign of Constantine in which he himself lived. He declared in his *Praise of Constantine* (16, 8): "As those predictions concerning our Saviour [*i.e., Psalm* 72, 7-8, and *Isaiah*, 2, 4] were foretold and delivered in the Hebrew tongue many ages before, so in our own times they have become really fulfilled in the ancient testimonies of the prophets and clearly confirmed." Great as the advances made by mankind were, still further progress was expected by Eusebius. For he asserted (*ibid.*, 6): "Although the object of the Roman empire to unite all nations in one harmonious whole has already been secured to a large degree, it is destined to be still more perfectly attained, even to the final conquest of the ends of the habitable world, by means of the salutary doctrine and through the aid of that Divine Providence which facilitates and smooths the way [of the Empire]."

In his recent essay on *The Idea of Progress*, G. H. Hildebrand stated[26] that this idea includes three principles: "First, the belief that history follows a continuous, necessary, and orderly course; second, the belief that this course is the effect of a regularly operating causal law; and third, the belief that the course of change has brought and will continue to bring improvement in the condition of mankind." The first two of these principles were always implied in the Christian belief that every single event and consequently also the course of historical events as a whole take place under God's will and in accordance with the plan of Divine Providence. But it remained for Eusebius to add the third principle, the optimistic belief in continuous improvement, and thus to develop a full-fledged Christian idea of progress.

Eusebius' idea was taken up by some of the most prominent theologians of the fourth and early fifth centuries, both in the eastern and the western parts of the Church.[27] This is shown by the interpretations which John Chrysostom, Ambrose, Jerome, Cyril of Alexandria and Theodoret of Cyrus gave in their various commentaries on *Psalm* 72 and *Isaiah* (2, 4), and we may add, on the passage in *Psalm* 46 (v. 9), which reads: "He maketh wars to cease unto the end of the earth." Like Eusebius all the writers just mentioned explained these passages in terms of the *Pax Romana* and its earthly achievements, and it seems that of the great theologians of the fourth century only Athanasius and Basil expounded them in a strictly spiritual sense.

When Augustine wrote his *Enarrations on the Psalms,* he replaced the explanations of the above passages with interpretations wholly different and entirely his own. For instance, Origen, Eusebius, John Chrysostom and Ambrose had declared that the words of *Psalm* 46: "He maketh wars to end," had been realized in the reign of Augustus; Basil alone had explained that passage in exclusively religious terms. But whereas Basil had contented himself with simply setting forth his personal exposition, Augustine accompanied the commentary which he wrote in 412, two years after the fall of Rome, with a polemic directed against the interpretation given by so many of his famous predecessors.[28] For although he did not mention any name, there seems to be no doubt that he was taking issue with the current view when he denied categorically that the prediction of a reign of peace had been fulfilled in any material or historical sense: "There are still wars, wars among nations for supremacy, wars among sects, wars among Jews, pagans, Christians, heretics, and these wars are becoming more frequent" (*Enarration on Psalm* 45, 13 = 46, 9). In Augustine's opinion, external peace was not yet achieved and, in fact, it would not even matter if it actually had. Only that peace matters which, through divine grace, man finds in himself, by his complete submission to the will of God. "When man learns that in himself he is nothing and that he has no help from himself," Augustine said, "then arms in himself are broken in pieces, then wars in himself are ended. Such wars, then, destroyed that voice of the Most High out of His holy clouds whereby the earth was shaken and the kingdoms were bowed; these wars He has taken away unto the ends of the earth."

In his *Enarration on Psalm* 71, 10 (= 72, 7), Augustine commented on the passage: "In His days righteousness (*iustitia*) shall arise and abundance of peace until the moon be exalted."[29] These words, Augustine declared, "ought to be understood as if it were said: there shall arise in His days righteousness to conquer the contradiction and the rebellion of the flesh, and there shall be made a peace so abundant and increasing 'until the moon be exalted,' that is until the Church be lifted up, through the glory of the resurrection to reign with Him." Righteousness and peace in the words of the psalmist ought not to be confused, then, with the notions of *iustitia* and *pax* of the earthly state.

Those highest Christian ideals have not yet been nor will they ever be embodied in the secular organization of the Roman empire, but they will be realized in the spiritual community of the eternal church. The theologically untenable identification of the Messianic ideal with the historical reality of the *Imperium Romanum* could not have been rejected more radically than was done by Augustine in his commentary.

\*　　\*　　\*

This was the situation, from the ideological point of view a very critical situation, which motivated Augustine to write *The City of God*. He realized that one single event, the "fall of Rome," had an impact upon the thinking and the feeling of his contemporaries which went far beyond its material importance. The significance attributed to the event resulted from the central position which the destiny and fate of "eternal" Rome occupied in the existing conceptions of history, whether they were pagan or Christian. If Augustine, then, wanted to combat in a truly fundamental fashion the interpretations of that "fall of Rome," he could do so only by setting forth his own ideas concerning the course and the meaning of history. Therefore he was willing to devote thirteen years of his life to the most comprehensive study of the problem of history, a problem which up to the year 410 had been of merely incidental interest to him.

In attempting to solve that problem, Augustine found, as we have seen, that he had to reject practically all the current conceptions of history. He did not share the sentiments of those among the early Christian writers to whom any concern about history was superfluous in view of the presumably imminent end of this world, and he had no interest in eschatological speculations and calculations regarding the future Millennium. Neither could he, of course, accept the cyclical theory as it was held by some of the pagan schools of philosophy and, in a modified form, by Origen. And he saw most clearly how perilous it was for the Christian faith to proclaim, as Eusebius and others had done during the fourth century, a belief in "progress," if that notion was understood in any kind of materialistic sense. For under the existing circumstances it was inevitable that "most of the pagans," as Augustine said in his *Enarration on Psalm* 136, 9, asked the question: "Is it not true that since the coming of Christ the state of human affairs has been worse than it was before and that human affairs were once much more fortunate than they are now?"[35] Every emphasis on the idea of secular progress was bound to lay the Christian cause wide open to attacks by the pagans and to the disillusionment of the half-hearted Christians. Both groups could rightly find that all promises of worldly success were totally disproved by the catastrophe of the year 410—and there might be more and worse disasters to come.

In contradistinction to all these conceptions Augustine's own views concerning history represent a basic reiteration and systematic elaboration of Hebrew and early Christian ideas.[36] To him history was the *operatio Dei* in time, it was "a one-directional, teleological process, directed towards one goal—salvation," the salvation of individual men, not of any collective groups or organizations.[37] Ever since the creation of the world there have existed two cities, the city of God or the community of those who "wish to live after the spirit," and the earthly city or the community of those who "wish to live after the flesh" (*City of God*, 14, 1 C). Of the twelve books of the second part of *The City of God*, eight books deal with the origin (*exortus*) and the end (*finis*) of those two cities, that is with the Creation and the Last Judgment. Only the middle section (books XV to XVIII) deals with that period of time which is commonly considered to be the historical era, and even within that section Augustine gave his main attention to those men and events which belonged to "the heavenly city which is a pilgrim on earth" (18, 54 K). The fact that only one book of *The City of God* (b. XVIII) treats historical developments proper, shows clearly that Augustine regarded the purely secular aspects of the drama of mankind as relatively insignificant.

*       *       *

Eusebius and the other Christian progressivists of the fourth century had strongly stressed the coincidence of the birth of Christ and the reign of Augustus, for they saw the counterpart of the religious summit in the erection of the "eternal" Roman empire and in the establishment of the "universal" *Pax Romana*. Whereas that observation occupied a central position in their conceptions of history, Augustine passed over it in a single sentence, by simply stating (18, 46 A): "While Herod reigned in Judaea and, after the change of the republican government, Caesar Augustus was emperor in Rome and pacified the world, Christ, man manifest out of a human virgin, God hidden out of God the Father, was born of Judah in Bethlehem." Whereas according to Eusebius and his followers the history of man had taken a fresh start at that time and had "progressed" toward a new culminating point under Constantine, when the Roman empire reached the fulfillment of its mission by becoming Christian, Augustine stopped his historical account precisely with the appearance of Christ. To him the period following that event and extending to his own days and to the end to come, was not a modern era but it was "the *senectus* of the old man, the last age in which the new man is born who now lives according to the spirit."[46] God had revealed all the truth that is to be communicated to man in this world, and henceforth the history of both the heavenly and the earthly cities has no fundamentally new lessons to teach. Augustine did not share the optimism of Eusebius and others; on the contrary, he spoke of his own era as "this malignant world, these evil days" (18, 49 A), and he reckoned even with the possibility of future persecutions of the Church and the faith (18, 52). He reminded his readers (16, 24 H) that, according to Christ's own words, the terminal period of history will not be an era of secular peace and earthly prosperity but just the opposite: "About the end of this word the faithful shall be in great perturbation and tribulation, of which the Lord has said in the Gospel: 'For then shall be great tribulation, such as was not since the beginning of the world to this time, no, nor ever shall be' (*Matthew*, 24, 21)."

In Augustine's opinion, then, there is no true "progress" to be found in the course of human history. He was, of course, well aware of the fact that "the human genius has invented and put to practical use many and great arts . . . and that human industry has made wonderful and stupefying advances" (22, 24 K-L). But at the same time he pointed out a fact which has been overlooked all too often by believers in the blessings of material progress, the fact that the ingenuity and the inventiveness of man have also their destructive aspects: "And for the injury of men, how many kinds of poison, how many weapons and machines of destruction have been invented." This dual aspect of the development of human history results from the very nature of the forces determining its course. "In this river or torrent of the human race," Augustine said toward the end of *The City of God* (22, 24 A), "two things run the course together, the evil which is derived from the parent [Adam], and the good which is bestowed by the Creator."

# Notes

†Originally published in *Journal of the History of Ideas* 12 (1951): 346–74. Reprinted by permission of The John Hopkins UP. Rpt. in *Medieval and Renaissance Studies*. Ed. Eugene F. Rice, Jr. New York: Cornell 1959. Pp. 265–98.

1This article was already in the hands of the printer when I got a copy of the essay by J. Straub, "Christliche Geschichtsapologetik in der Krisis des römischen Reiches," *Historia* (1950), 52–81. Prof. Straub's article does not discuss the idea of progress and the other Christian and pagan conceptions of history which were current before and throughout the fourth century. His main objective is rather, for the period from 378 to the aftermath of the fall of Rome in 410, to deal "mit der Rolle, welche die christlichen Apologeten in jenem epochalen Umwandlungsprozess gespielt haben, in dem der römische Staat zugrundeging, aber die mit dem Staat aufs engste verbundene

Kirche ihre eigene Existenz zu behaupten und sich für die Teilnahme an der neu zu bildenden Völkergemeinschaft der Welt des Mittelalters freizumachen suchte" (p. 54). Of particular value is Prof. Straub's clarification of the views which Augustine and Orosius had concerning the Christian attitude toward the Roman empire. Unfortunately I was unable to consult the articles by H. v. Campenhausen, O. Herding, and W. Loewenich, all of which, according to Straub, *l.c.*, p. 52, n. 1, deal with Augustine's historical conceptions.

[2]Throughout this article I have based the text of my quotations from the Church Fathers on the translations in the three series of *The Select Library of the Ante-Nicene Fathers*, and of the *Nicene and Post-Nicene Fathers* (1885–1900); very frequently, however, I have found it necessary to make changes in the translations, for which I have to take the responsibility.

[3]See E. K. Rand, *The Building of Eternal Rome* (1943).

[4]The most recent treatments of this question have been given by J. W. Swain, "The Theory of the Four Monarchies: Opposition History under the Roman Empire," *Classical Philology* (1940), 1–21; H. L. Ginsberg, *Studies in Daniel* (1948), 5–23.

[5]See the list of authors who identified the fourth monarchy with the Roman empire, which has been compiled by H. H. Rowley, *Darius the Mede and the Four World Empires in the Book of Daniel* (1935), 73 ff.

[6]The above translation is based on the text of the *Itala* quoted by Augustine; the version in the *King James Bible* reads: "Only he who now letteth will let, until he be taken out of the way."

[7]My quotations from *De civitate Dei* are based on the Latin text edited by J. E. Welldon, 2 vols. (1924), and on the translation by M. Dods, *The City of God*, 2 vols. (1872); frequently, however, I have replaced Dods' translation with my own.

[8]Cf. also *Sermon* 81, 9; all three sermons mentioned were preached in the years 410 and 411: see A. Kunzelmann in *Miscellanea Agostiniana* (1931), II, 449 f., 500. On these sermons see also M. Pontet, *L'exègése de S. Augustin prédicateur* (1944), 454, 471–476.

[9]Psuedo-Bede, *Flores ex diversis, quaestiones et parabola*, ed. Migne, *Patrologia Latina*, 94, col. 543; cf. F. Schneider, *Rom und Romgedanke im Mittelalter* (1926), 66 f., 251.

[10]Quoted from J. W. Woodworth's translation of Orosius's *Seven Books* (1936), 1.

[11]The second section of the first part of the work, which consists of books VI to X, can be passed over in this article because Augustine did not deal in it with historical problems but set out to disprove the assertions of those philosophers who "maintain that polytheistic worship is advantageous for the life to come" (*Retractations*, 2, 68, 1).

[12]See the comprehensive analysis of the main body of ideas of Augustine's main work, which has been recently presented by W. J. Oates in his introduction to *Basic Writings of St. Augustine* (1948), I, ix–xl; and by E. Gilson in his introduction to D. B. Zema's and G. G. Walsh's translation of *The City of God* (1950), I, pp. xi–xcviii. Of the vast literature dealing with Augustine's historical ideas, I can list only some of the most recent treatments: R. J. Defferari and M. Keeler, "St. Augustine's City of God: Its Plan and Development," *American Journal of Philology* (1929), L, 109–137; U. A. Padovano, "La Città di Dio: teologia e non filosofia della storia," *Rivista di Filosofia Neo-scolastica* (1931), supplem. vol. to vol. XXIII, 220–263; H. I. Marrou, *S. Augustin et*

*la fin de la culture antique* (1938; see esp. 131–135, 417–419, 461–467); H. Fuchs, *Der geistige Widerstand gegen Rom in der antiken Welt* (1938); C. N. Cochrane, *Christianity and Classical Culture: A Study of Thought and Action from Augustus to Augustine* (1944; esp. 397–516); W. M. Green, "Augustine on the Teaching of History," University of California Publications in Classical Philology (1944), XII, 315–332; K. Löwith, *Meaning in History* (1949), 160–173.

13Cf. K. Löwith, *l.c.*, 162–165, 248 n. 15; J. Baillie, *The Belief in Progress* (1951), 42–57.

14*City of God*, 12; 14 B. C. N. Cochrane, l.c., 245, stated that "we find Origen, for instance, protesting vigorously against the Platonic theory of cycles." But Cochrane and, following him, R. Niebuhr, *Faith and History* (1949), 65, based their assertion exclusively on one passage in Origen's writings (*Against Celsus*, 4, 68) and neglected the much more detailed treatment of this problem in Origen's book *On First Principles*, 2, 3, 1–5; 3, 5, 3; 4, 13. P. Koetschau, in his edition of Rufinus' translation and of the Greek fragments of *On First Principles* (*Origenes Werke* [1913], V, 113f., 120), commented on Rufinus' modifications of the original text and printed the relevant remarks made by Jerome on Origen's belief in a series of many worlds: see the English translation of Koetschau's edition by G. W. Butterworth, *Origen, On First Principles* (1935), 83–89, 238 f.; J. Baillie, l.c., 74 ff., seems to overlook, too, the fact that Origen shared the cyclical theory, although in a modified form.

15See Butterworth, *l.c.*, 88 n. 4 (Jerome, *Apology*, 1, 20) and 83 n. 1 (Jerome, *Epist.*, 96, 9).

16On the Hebrew conceptions, see H. Butterfield, *Christianity and History* (1950), esp. 1–4, 57–62, 68–88; on the Christian views, see O. Cullmann, *Christus und die Zeit; die urchristliche Zeit- und Geschichtsauffassung* (1946); R. G. Collingwood, *The Idea of History* (1946), 46–52; J. Baillie, *l.c.*, 57–87; Th. Preiss, "The Vision of History in the New Testament," *Papers of the Ecumenical Institute* (1950), V, 48–66; J. Danielou, "The Conception of History in the Christian Tradition," *ibid.*, 67–79.

17See, e.g., E. K. Rand, *Founders of the Middle Ages* (1929), 13–22, 291; Rand, *The Building of Eternal Rome* (1943), 72, 189 ff.; C. N. Cochrane, *l.c.*, 242–247, 483 f.; K. Löwith, l.c., 60 f., 84, 112 f., 182 ff.; J. Baillie, l.c., 19–22, 94–96.

18On the ideas concerning the Millennium, see, e.g., E. Bernheim, *Mittelalterliche Zeitanschauungen in ihrem Einfluss auf Politik und Geschichtschreibung* (1918), esp. 63–109; A. Wikenhauser, "Das Problem des tausendjährigen Reiches in der Johannes-Apokalypse," *Romische Quartalschrift* (1932), XL, 13–36; Wikenhauser, "Die Herkunft der Idee des tausendjährigen Reiches in der Johannes-Apokalypse," *ibid.* (1937), XLV, 1–24; J. Baillie, *l.c.*, 60–64, 79–83.

19On the discussion of these arguments, see also E. Peterson, *Der Monotheismus als politisches Problem* (1935), 66–88; J. Geffcken, *Zwei griechische Apologeten* (1907), esp. 63, 92.

20On this point, see H. Berkhof, *Kirche und Kaiser; eine Untersuchung der Entstehung der byzantinischen und theokratischen Staatsauffassung im 4. Jahrhundert* (1947), esp. 14–18, 31–34, 55–59, 66, 70.

21Cf. Berkhof, *l.c.*, 205–209.

22Cf. H. Berkhof, *Die Theologie des Eusebius von Caesarea* (1939), 45–50, 55 f., 58 f.;

E. Peterson, *l.c.*, 66 ff.

[23]See the similar passages in Eusebius' *Theophania*, 3, 2; *Praeparatio Evangelica*, 5, 1.

[24]It may be noted that Origen interpreted the passage in *Isaiah*, 2, 4 in an entirely spiritual sense; see *Against Celsus*, 5, 33; *Against Heresies*, 6, 16.

[25]Translated from the Syriac by S. Lee, *Eusebius on the Theophania* (1853), 156 f.; cf. the very similar passage in Eusebius' *Praise of Constantine*, 16, 4–5.

[26]*The Idea of Progress: A Collection of Readings.* Selected by F. J. Teggart; revised edition with an introduction by G. H. Hildebrand, 4.

[27]Cf. E. Peterson, *l.c.*, 71–88.

[28]Cf. E. Peterson, *l.c.*, 97 f.; as to the date of *Enarration on Psalm* 45, cf. S. M. Zarb, "Chronologia enarrationum S. Augustini in Psalmos," in *Angelicum* (1947), XXIV, 275–283.

[29]The above translation of *Psalm* 72 is based on the text of the *Itala* used by Augustine. This *Enarration* was written between 415 and 416; see S. M. Zarb, *op. cit.*, Angelicum (1935), XII, 77–81.

*[Text for notes 30–34 not reprinted here.]

\*       \*       \*

[35]This *Enarration* was written between 410 and 413; see Zarb, *l.c.* (1939), XVI, 289 f.

[36]See above, note 16.

[37]See K. Löwith, *l.c.*, 170 f.; E. Frank, "The Role of History in Christian Thought," *The Duke Divinity School Bulletin* (1949), XIV, 74.

*[Text for notes 38–45 not reprinted here.]

\*       \*       \*

[46]Augustine, *De Genesi contra Manichaeos*, I, 23, 40, in Migne, *l.c.*, XXXIV, 192.

# The Politics of Paradise†

## Elaine Pagels

Is a human being capable of self-government? Christians who defied the Roman government that hounded them as criminals emphatically answered yes.* Early Christian spokesmen, like Jews before them and the American colonists long after, claimed to find in the biblical creation account divine sanction for declaring their independence from governments they considered corrupt and arbitrary. Unlike its Babylonian counterpart, the Hebrew creation account of Genesis 1 indicates that God gave the power of earthly rule to *adam*—not to the king or emperor, but simply to "mankind" (and some even thought this might include women).[1] Most Christian apologists from the first through the fourth centuries would have agreed with Gregory of Nyssa who, following the lead of rabbinic tradition, explains that after God created the world "as a royal dwelling place for the future king"[2] he made humanity "as a being fit to exercise royal rule" by making it "the living image of the universal King."[3] Consequently, Gregory concludes, "the soul immediately shows its royal and exalted character, far removed as it is from the lowliness of private station, in that it owns no master, and is self governed, ruled autocratically by its own will."[4] Besides dominion over the earth and animals, this gift of sovereignty conveys the quality of moral freedom:

> Preeminent among all is the fact that we are free from any necessity, and not in bondage to any power, but have decision in our own power as we please; for virtue is a voluntary thing, subject to no dominion. Whatever is the result of compulsion and force cannot be virtue.[5]

Many Christian converts of the first four centuries regarded the proclamation of αὐτεξουσία —the moral freedom to rule oneself—as virtually synonymous with "the gospel."

Yet with Augustine this message changed. The work from Augustine's later years, radically breaking with many of his predecessors, effectively transformed the teaching of the Christian faith. Instead of the freedom of the will and humanity's original royal dignity, Augustine emphasizes the bondage of the will by depicting humanity as sick, suffering, and helpless, irreparably damaged by the Fall.[6] For that "original sin," Augustine insists, involved nothing else than Adam's prideful attempt to establish his own autonomous self-government.[7] Astonishingly, Augustine's radical views prevailed, eclipsing for future generations of Western Christians the consensus of the first three centuries of Christian tradition.

As he matured, Augustine did, of course, repudiate the Manichean version of Christian doctrine he had embraced as an enthusiastic young seeker, which categorically denied the goodness of creation and the freedom of the will. The chastened convert, claiming to accept Catholic orthodoxy, came to affirm both. But, as he grasped for ways to understand his own tumultuous experience, Augustine concluded that the qualities of that original state of creation no longer applied—at least not directly—to human experience in the present. Humanity, once given the unflawed glory of creation and the freedom of the will, actually enjoyed these only in those brief primordial moments in Paradise. Ever since the Fall, they have been apprehended—and even then only partially—only in moments of inspired imagination. For all practical purposes they are wholly lost.

Given the intense inner conflicts he reveals in his *Confessions*, Augustine's decision to abandon his predecessors' emphasis on free will need not surprise us. Much more surprising, in fact, is the result. Why did the majority of Latin Christians, instead of repudiating Augustine's idiosyncratic views as marginal—or rejecting them as heretical—embrace them? For what reasons did his teaching on "original sin" move into the center of Western Christian tradition, displacing, or at least wholly recasting, the established views on creation and free will?

The situation of Christians in the fourth and fifth centuries had changed radically. Traditional declarations of human freedom, forged by martyrs defying the emperor as anti-Christ incarnate, no longer fit the situation of Christians who suddenly found themselves the emperor's "brothers and sisters in Christ." Augustine's theory, on the contrary, conformed to this new fact and interpreted the new arrangement of state, church, and believer in ways that, many agreed, made religious sense of these astonishing new political realities.

Both Augustine and his Christian opponents recognized the political dimensions of such controversy, yet none of them discussed government in what we would recognize as strictly political terms. Instead, since everyone agreed that the story of Adam and Eve offered a basic paradigm for ordering human society, argument over the role of government most often took the form of conflicting interpretations of that story. Let us consider, then, how Augustine and his predecessors—taking as their representative John Chrysostom—each read, in opposite ways, the politics of Paradise.

John Chrysostom, speaking as a priest to console believers in Antioch who were terrified of the emperor's retribution for public riots against his policies, assures his congregation that God, in the beginning, "honored our race with sovereignty." For, he asks, what does it mean that God made us in his image?

"The image of government (τῆς ἀρχῆς εἰκόνα) is what is meant; and as there is no one in the heaven superior to God, so there is no one on earth superior to humankind."[8]

What does this mean in specific political terms? Can any one man—that is, the emperor—embody the sovereignty God bestowed upon Adam? Could Caesar represent God's rule to all the rest? To this Gregory of Nyssa says no, for "any particular man is limited," and so "the entire plenitude of humanity was included" in God's gift of his own royal image:

> For the image is not in part of our nature, nor is the divine gift in any single person . . . but this power extends equally to the whole race; and a sign of this is that the mind is implanted alike in all; for all have the power of understanding and reflecting . . . they equally bear within themselves the divine image.[9]

Chrysostom agrees: God bestowed that power upon the whole human race as a natural quality inherent in our common nature. And he goes on to distinguish such natural sovereignty from the artificial sovereignty that, he says, characterizes imperial power:

> For of governments, some are natural (φυσικαί), and others artificial (χειροτονηταί): natural, such as the rule of the lion over the quadrupeds, or the eagle over the birds; artificial, as of an emperor over us; for he does not reign over his fellow slaves by any natural authority. Therefore it happens that emperors often lose their sovereignty.[10]

Although God originally intended only natural sovereignty, Chrysostom explains, sin disrupted this order: "From the beginning, God made only one sovereignty, placing man over the woman; but after our race ran headlong into extreme disorder, there appeared also other types of government."[11] The order of superiority and subordination, natural in the case of man and woman, signals a violation of nature when it enters into the relationship between man and man. Consequently, says Chrysostom, "should anyone ask, whence is slavery, and why has it entered into human life (and many, I know, want to ask such questions, and be informed concerning them), I will tell you: Slavery is the fruit of greed, of degradation and savagery . . . the thing is the result of sin."[12]

Besides changing the structure of human relationships, sin destroys their quality. Before sin Eve's submission to Adam, expressing the sexes' mutual interdependence, had nothing in common with slavery: "What if the wife be subject to us? It is as a wife, as equal in honor."[13] But after Eve persuaded Adam to sin, incurring his resentment by bringing suffering upon both of them, the distortion of slavery entered into that first relationship.[14] Eve's subjection, once voluntary, now took on the quality of punishment, becoming mandatory and hence oppressive. Wherever sin enters, Chrysostom explains, fear and coercion displace the dynamic energy of love. Spreading from that first government, man's rule over woman, fear and coercion have infected the whole structure of human relationships, from family to city and nation. Chrysostom sees everywhere the disastrous results: "Now we are subjected to one another by force and compulsion, and every day we are in conflict with one another."[15]

Imperial rule, above all, epitomizes the social consequences of sin. Chrysostom, like other Christian spokesmen, ridicules imperial propaganda which claims that the state rests upon concord, justice, and liberty. On the contrary, he declares, the state relies upon force and compulsion, often using these to violate justice and to suppress liberty. And yet, because the majority of humankind followed Adam's example in sinning, such government, however corrupt, has become indispensable and, for this reason, even divinely endorsed:

> [God] himself has armed magistrates with power. . . . God provides for our safety through them. . . . If you were to abolish the public court system, you would abolish all order from our life. . . . If you deprive the city of its rulers, we would have to live a life less rational than that of the animals, biting and devouring one another. . . . For what crossbeams are in houses, rulers are in cities, and just as, if you were to take away the former, the walls, being separated, would fall in upon one another, so, if you were to deprive the world of magistrates and the fear that comes from them, houses, cities, and nations would fall upon one another in unrestrained confusion, there being no one to repress, or repel, or persuade them to be peaceful through the fear of punishment.[16]

While granting that the imperial system preserves social order, he charges that it tolerates—or, worse, even enforces—injustice, immorality, and inequality. Roman laws, he says, "for the most part corrupt, useless, and ridiculous," expose to torture or execution the man who steals clothes or money while ignoring more damaging acts: "Who would be considered wiser, by most people, than the persons considered worthy to legislate for the cities and nations? But yet to these wise men sexual immorality seems to be nothing worthy of punishment; at least, none of the pagan laws . . . bring men to trial for this reason."[17] Chrysostom explains specifically what kind of case he has in mind: "If a married man has intercourse with a female slave, it seems to be nothing to pagan laws, nor to people in general."[18] Most people, he admits, would laugh at anyone who tried to bring such a case to court, and the judge would dismiss it. The same is true for a married man involved with an unmarried woman or with a prostitute. Although Roman law protects only the man's rights in such cases, Chrysostom declares that "we are punished, though not by the Roman laws, yet by God."[19]

Roman laws, furthermore, allow dealers to enslave children and to train them in sexual specialities for sale as prostitutes. And pagan tradition credits the legislators as "common benefactors of the city," for instituting public entertainment that features, in the theaters, prostitutes and prostituted children and, in the sports arena, contests between men and wild animals:

> Those places, too, being full of all senseless excitement, train the people to acquire a merciless and savage and inhuman kind of temperament, and give them practice in seeing people torn in pieces, and blood flowing, and the viciousness of wild beasts upsetting everything. Now all these our wise lawgivers introduced from the beginning—so many plagues—and our cities applaud and admire them.[20]

So much for the masses; what about the few who, chastened by the example of Adam's sin, resolve to exercise appropriate restraint over themselves? Such persons, Chrysostom declares, remain exempt from the punishment that falls upon the corrupt majority—exempt, in fact, from the constraints of human government as a whole: "For those who live in a state of piety require no correction on the part of the magistrates, for 'the law was not made for a righteous man.' But the more numerous, if they had no fear of these hanging over them, would fill the cities with innumerable evils."[21]

The tyranny of external government sharply contrasts, then, with the liberty enjoyed by those capable of autonomous self-rule—and, above all, by those who, through Christian baptism, have recovered the capacity for self-government. Chrysostom, like the apologists, identifies the former with the Roman empire and the latter with the emerging new society that constitutes the Christian church: "There, everything is done through fear and constraint; here, through free choice and liberty!"[22] The use of force, the driving energy of imperial society, is utterly alien to church government:

> Christians, more than all people, are not allowed to correct by force the faults of those who sin. Secular judges, indeed, when they have captured wrongdoers under the law, demonstrate that their authority is great by preventing them, even against their own will, from following their own desires; but in our case the wrongdoer must be corrected not by force, but by persuasion.[23]

What prevents church leaders from exercising the same authority as imperial magistrates, he explains, has nothing to do with lack of power, much less inferior status. On the contrary, although a priest's authority surpasses even the emperor's, what restrains a priest from attempting to use such authority is, Chrysostom declares, principle:

> For neither has the authority of this kind to restrain sinners been given to us by law, *nor, if they had been given, should we have any place to exercise our power,* since God rewards those who abstain from evil out of their own choice, and not out of necessity. . . . If a person wanders away from the right faith, great effort, perseverance, and patience are required; for he cannot be dragged back by force, nor restrained by fear, but must be led back by persuasion to the truth from which he originally swerved.[24]

The Christian leader, refraining not only from the use of force but even from the subtler pressures of fear and coercion, must evoke each member's voluntary participation. Failing that, he must respect, however misguided he considers it to be, each member's freedom of choice and action:

> We do not have "authority over your faith," beloved, nor do we command these things as your lords and masters. We are appointed for the teaching of the word, not for power, nor for absolute authority. We hold the place of counsellors to advise you. The counsellor speaks his own opinions, not forcing his listeners, but *leaving him full master of his own choice in what is said.* He is blameworthy only in this respect, if he fails to say the things that present themselves.[25]

Church government, contrary to its secular antithesis, remains wholly voluntary and, although hierarchically structured, remains essentially egalitarian, reflecting, in effect, the original harmony of Paradise.

But Chrysostom remains uncomfortably aware that the actual churches he knows in Antioch and Constantinople fall far short of such celestial harmony. Having inherited his vision of the church from such heroic predecessors as Justin, Athenagoras, Clement, and Origen, Chrysostom, measuring the church of his own day against theirs, alternatively grieves and lashes out in anger:

> Plagues, teeming with untold mischiefs, have come upon the churches. The primary offices have become marketable. Hence innumerable evils are arising, and there is no one to redress, no one to reprove them. Indeed, the disorder has taken on a kind of method and consistency of its own.[26]

Excessive wealth, enormous power, and luxury, Chrysostom charges, are destroying the integrity of the churches. Clerics, infected by the disease of "lust for authority," he charges, are fighting for candidates on the basis of family prominence, wealth, or partisanship. Others support the candidacy of their friends, relatives, or flatterers, "but no one will look to the man who is really qualified." They ignore, Chrysostom complains, the only valid qualification—"excellence of character."27 Pagans rightly ridicule the whole business: "'Do you see,' they say, 'how all matters among the Christians are full of vainglory? And there is ambition among them, and hypocrisy. Strip them,' they say, 'of their numbers, and they are nothing.'"28

Yet could the vision forged by those embattled sectarians who saw the church as an island of purity surrounded by an ocean of corruption still fit the circumstances of a state religion, a church suddenly come into imperial favor, wealth, and power? Chrysostom still sees his church contending against powerful rivals.29 He does not consider the possibility that his vision of the church, sanctioned by nearly four centuries of tradition, may no longer correspond to the situation of his fellow Christians at the turn of the fifth century. Now that the world had invaded the church, and the church the world, new questions arose: how, for example, are Christians to account for the new role of a Christian emperor and for the legitimacy of his rule, not only over unruly pagans, but over Christians themselves (notably including the increasing flood of nominal converts)? And how are Christians to account for the unsettling new prominence of the churches, in which holding episcopal office, far from making a man a likely target for torture and execution, instead guarantees tax exemptions, vastly increased income, social power, and possibly even influence at court? Where traditional answers fail, Augustine's opposite interpretation of the politics of Paradise—and, in particular, his insistence that the whole human race, including the redeemed, remains wholly incapable of self-government—offers radically new ways to interpret this unprecedented situation.

Where Chrysostom reads the proclamation of human freedom, Augustine reads in the same Genesis story the opposite—a story of human bondage. As for αὐτεξουσία, the power to rule oneself, Augustine cannot acknowledge it as a reality—or even a genuine good—in his own experience, let alone for all humanity. And Augustine begins his reflections on government, characteristically, with introspection.

Recalling in the *Confessions* his own experience, Augustine instinctively identifies the question of self-government with rational control over sexual impulses. Describing his struggle to be chaste, Augustine recalls how, "in the sixteenth year of the age of my flesh . . . the madness of raging lust exercised its supreme dominion over me."30 Augustine characterizes himself as powerless, a man without choices, a captive and victim. Through sexual desire, he says, "my invisible enemy tracked me down and seduced me."31 Of his sexual involvements, he admits that "I drew my shackles along with me, terrified to have them knocked off."[32]  Acknowledging that his friend was "amazed at my enslavement," Augustine reflects that "what made me a slave to it was the habit (*consuetudo*) of satisfying an insatiable lust."[33]

Had Augustine confessed as much to a spiritual advisor such as John Chrysostom, his mentor, after agreeing sympathetically with the young man's assessment of his own bondage, surely would have urged him to undo the chains that bound him to bad habits and to recover and strengthen, like unused muscles, his own neglected capacity for free choice (αὐτεξουσία). But Augustine in his *Confessions* directly challenges those who hold such assumptions. Free will, he insists, is only an illusion—an illusion that he admits he once shared: "As for continence, I imagined it to be in the liberty of our own power, which I, for my part, felt I did not have."[34]  Instead of indicting his own lack of faith in the power of free will, Augustine lashes out at those who assume that they do possess such power: "What man is there, who, being aware of his own weakness, dares so much as to attribute his chastity and innocence to his own virtue?"[35]  The aging Augustine then takes his own experience as paradigmatic for all human experience—indeed, for Adam's: "Being a captive," he says, "I feigned a show of counterfeit liberty,"[36] just as, he insists, Adam had done, bringing upon himself and his progeny an avalanche of sin and punishment.

No wonder, then, that the Manichean theory of human origins, which had "explained" the sense of helplessness he experienced, attracted Augustine first. He identified, too, with the way the Manicheans interpreted the tendency to sin not simply in terms of human weakness, but (as the rabbis had taught of the *yetser hara'*) of an internal energy actively resisting God's will. When he abandoned Manichean theology, Augustine says that he worked hard to understand Catholic teaching—"that free will is the cause of our doing evil. . . . But I was not able to understand it clearly." Once he began to recognize the power of his own will, he says that "I knew that I had a will . . . and when I did either will or nill anything, I was more sure of it, that I and no other did will or nill; and here was the cause of my sin, as I came to perceive."[37]  Yet, far from relinquishing entirely the role of victim, Augustine goes on to say, "But what I did *against* my will, that I seemed to suffer rather than do. That I considered not to be my fault, but  my punishment."[38]

Through the agonizing process of his conversion Augustine claims to have discovered that he was bound by conflict within his own will:

> I was bound, not with another man's chains, but with my own iron will.  The enemy held my will, and, indeed, made a chain of it for me, and constrained me.  Because of a perverse will, desire was made; and when I was enslaved to desire (*libido*) it became habit; and habit not restrained became necessity.  By

which links . . . a very hard bondage had me enthralled.[39]

Augustine sees his own will, then, far from being free, as itself divided and consequently impotent: "Myself I willed it, and myself nilled it; it was I myself. I neither willed entirely, nor nilled entirely. Therefore I was in conflict with myself, and . . . was distracted by my own self."[40] How can he account for such conflict? Augustine insists that, since he suffered much of this "against my own will, . . . I was not, therefore, the cause of it, but the 'sin that dwells in me'; from the punishment of that *more voluntary sin, because I was a son of Adam.*"[41]

Augustine himself in his earlier writings, as Edward Cranz points out, expresses views on human freedom and self-government that virtually echo those of his predecessors.[42] But in the fourteenth chapter of *The City of God* Augustine seems intent on proving that, even if Adam once had free will, he himself had never received it. Even in Adam's case Augustine's account betrays his own ambivalence or, indeed, outright hostility toward the possibility of human freedom. What earlier apologists celebrate as God's greatest gift to humankind—free will, liberty, autonomy, self-government— Augustine characterizes in surprisingly negative terms. Had not Adam received freedom as his birthright? Yet, as Augustine tells it, the first man "conceived a desire for freedom."[43] That desire for autonomy became, in Augustine's eyes, the root of sin, betraying nothing less than contempt for God. The desire to exercise mastery over one's will, far from expressing what Origen, Clement, and Chrysostom consider the true nature of rational beings, becomes for Augustine the great and fatal temptation: "The fruit of the tree of knowledge of good and evil is personal control over one's own will (*proprium voluntatis arbitrium*).[44] Augustine cannot resist reading that desire for self-government as total, obstinate perversity: "The soul, then, delighting in its own freedom *to do wickedness*, and scorning to serve God . . . willfully deserted its higher master."[45] Seduced by this desire for autonomy, Adam entered into a "life of cruel and wretched slavery instead of the freedom for which he had conceived a desire."[46]

Uncomfortably aware of a contradiction in his argument, Augustine explains that obedience, not autonomy, should have been Adam's true glory "since man has been naturally so created that it is advantageous for him to be submissive, but disastrous for him to follow his own will, and not the will of his creator."[47] Admitting that "it does, indeed, seem something of a paradox,"[48] Augustine resorts to paradoxical language to describe how God "sought to impress upon this creature, for whom free slavery (*libera servitus*) was expedient, that he was the Lord!"[49] Whatever the constraints upon Adam's freedom, however, Augustine insists that the first man still possessed a

greater degree of liberty than any of his progeny. For he believes that only the
story of Adam's misuse of free will can account for the contradictions he
discovered within himself, his own will caught in perpetual conflict, "much of
which I suffered against my own will, rather than did by my will."[50]

Yet Augustine knows that most of his Christian contemporaries would
find this claim incredible, if not heretical. John Chrysostom, indeed, warns
the fainthearted not to blame Adam for their own transgressions. Answering
one who asks "What am I to do? Must I die because of him?" he replies, "It is
not because of him; for you yourself have not remained without sin. Even
though it is not the same sin, you have, at any rate, committed others."[51]
That Adam's sin brought suffering and death upon humankind most
Christians, like their Jewish predecessors and contemporaries, would have
taken for granted. But most Jews and Christians would also have agreed that
Adam left each of his offspring free to make his or her own choice of good or
evil. The whole point of the story of Adam, most assumed, was to warn
everyone who heard it not to misuse that divinely given capacity for free
choice.

But Augustine, intending to prove the opposite point, laboriously attempts
to prove that Adam, far from being the single individual Chrysostom
envisioned, was in fact a corporate personality. Pointing out that Adam's
genesis from earth essentially differs from that of any of his progeny born
through childbirth, Augustine declares that

> The entire human race that was to pass through woman into offspring was
> contained in the first man when that married couple received the divine
> sentence condemning them to punishment, and *humanity produced what
> humanity became, not what it was when created, but when, having sinned*, it was
> punished.[52]

The punishment itself, Augustine continues, "effected in their original
nature a change for the worse." What the nature of that change was is
derived from an interpretation of Rom 5:12: δι' ἑνὸς ἀνθρώπου ἡ ἁμαρτία
εἰς τὸν κόσμον εἰσῆλθε, καὶ διὰ τῆς ἁμαρτίας ὁ θάνατος, καὶ οὕτως εἰς
πάντας ἀνθρώπους ὁ θάνατος διῆλθεν, ἐφ' ᾧ πάντες ἥμαρτον. Chrysostom's
interpretation acknowledged that Adam's sin brought upon his progeny their
common heritage of mortality. Augustine, reading the passage in the Latin
Bible (and so either ignoring or else unaware of the connotations of the Greek
original), insists instead that Adam's sin transmits to all his offspring not only
suffering and death but sin itself.[53] Consequently, he concludes, the whole
human race inherited from Adam a universal nature irreversibly damaged by
sin. "For we all were in that one man, since all of us were that one man who
fell into sin through the woman who was made from him."[54]

How can one imagine that millions of individuals not yet born were "in Adam" or, in any sense, "were" Adam? Anticipating objections that would reduce his argument to absurdity, Augustine declares triumphantly that, although "we did not yet have individually created and apportioned forms in which to live as individuals," what did exist already was the "nature of the semen from which we were to be propagated."[55] That semen itself, Augustine argues, already "shackled by the bond of death," transmits the damage incurred by sin.[56] Hence, Augustine concludes, every human being ever conceived through semen already is born contaminated with sin. Through this astonishing argument Augustine intends to prove that every human being is, in effect, in bondage not only from birth, but indeed, from the moment of conception. And since he takes Adam as a corporate personality, Augustine applies his account of Adam's experience, disrupted by the first sin, to every one of his offspring (except, of course, to Christ).

As he goes on to describe the onset of original sin in Adam, Augustine chooses, above all, political language.[57] The effects of original sin involve the internal dynamics of individual psychology. For in the beginning, when there was only one man in the world, Adam discovered within himself the first government—the rule of the rational soul, the "better part of a human being," over the body, the "inferior part." Augustine, following philosophic commonplaces, characterizes their respective roles in political terms: the soul by divine right is to subjugate every member of its "lower servant," the body, to the ruling power of its will. Within Adam as within Eve both soul and body originally obeyed the authority of rational will: "Although they bore an animal body, yet they felt in it no disobedience moving against themselves. . . . Each received the body as a servant . . . and the body obeyed God . . . in an appropriate servitude, without resistance."[58]

The primal couple soon experienced within themselves not only the first government on earth but also the first revolution. Since Adam's assertion of his own autonomy was, Augustine insists, tantamount to rebellion against God's rule, Adam's attempt to establish his own independence involved him in insubordination to his divine Master. And Augustine appreciates the aptness with which the punishment fits the crime: "The punishment for disobedience was nothing other than disobedience. For human misery consists in nothing other than man's disobedience to himself."[59] Augustine stresses, however, that the penalty for sin involves more than bodily impulses rebelling against the mind. Instead, the "flesh" that wars against the "law of the mind" includes, he says, the "whole of one's natural being."[60] The commonest experiences of frustration—mental agitation, bodily pain, aging, suffering, and death—continually prove to us our incapacity to implement the rule of our will. For who would undergo any of these, Augustine asks, if our nature "in every way and every part obeyed our will?"[61]

But what epitomizes our rebellion against God, above all, is the "rebellion in the flesh"—a spontaneous uprising, so to speak, in the "disobedient members":

> After Adam and Eve disobeyed . . . they felt for the first time a movement of disobedience in their flesh, as punishment in kind for their own disobedience to God. . . . The soul, which had taken a perverse delight in its own liberty and disdained to serve God, was now deprived of its original mastery over the body.[62]

Specifically, Augustine concludes, "the sexual desire (*libido*) of our disobedient members arose in those first human beings as a result of the sin of disobedience . . . and because a shameless movement (*impudens motus*) resisted the rule of their will, they covered their shameful members."[63] At first, the Adam and Eve whom God had created enjoyed mental mastery over the procreative process: the sexual members, like the other parts of the body, enacted the work of procreation by a deliberate act of will, "like a handshake." Ever since Eden, however, spontaneous sexual desire is, Augustine contends, the clearest evidence of the effect of original sin: this, above all, manifests passion's triumph. What impresses Augustine most is that such arousal functions independently of the will's rightful rule: "Because of this, members are rightly called *pudenda* (parts of shame) because they excite themselves just as they like, in opposition to the mind which is their master, as if they were their own masters."[64] Sexual excitement differs from other forms of passion, Augustine contends, since in the case of anger and the rest it is not the impulse which moves any part of the body, but the will which remains in control and consents to the movement. An angry man still makes a decision whether or not to strike; but a sexually aroused man may find that erection occurs with alarming autonomy. Augustine considers this irrefutable evidence that lust (*libido*), having wrested the sexual organs from the control of the will, now has "brought them so completely under its rule that they are incapable of acting if this one emotion (*libido*) is lacking."[65] So disjoined is will from desire that even a man who wills to be sexually aroused may find that *libido* deserts him.

> At times, the urge intrudes uninvited; at other times, it deserts the panting lover, and, although desire blazes in the mind, the body is frigid. In this strange way, desire refuses service, not only to the will to procreate, but also to the desire for wantonness; and though for the most part, it solidly opposes the mind's command, at other times it is divided against itself, and, having aroused the mind, it fails to arouse the body.[66]

The experience of such arousal apart from any action taken, Augustine insists, itself is sin: "Such disobedience of the flesh as this, which lies in the very excitement, even when it is not allowed to take effect, did not exist in the first man and woman."[67] Augustine admits, however, that

> the trouble with the hypothesis of a passionless procreation controlled by the will, as I am here suggesting it, is that it has never been verified in experience, not even in the experience of those who could have proved that it was possible. In fact, they sinned too soon, and brought upon themselves exile form Eden.[68]

But Augustine believes that each person can verify from experience the radical leap to which his own inner turmoil impelled him—the leap that identifies sexual desire itself as evidence of—and penalty for—original sin. That each of us experiences desire spontaneously apart from will means, Augustine assumes, that we experience it against our will. Hence, he continues, sexual desire naturally involves shame: "A man by his very nature is ashamed of sexual desire."[69] What proves the truth of such assertions, Augustine believes, is the universal practice of covering the genitals and of shielding the act of intercourse from public view.[70]

One might, of course, ask the obvious question: is it not possible to experience desire in accordance with the will (as, for example, when engaging in intercourse for the purpose of procreation)? Chrysostom would say yes; but Augustine's very definition of sexual desire excludes that possibility. Having entered into human experience through an act of rebellion against the will, desire can never cooperate with will to form, so to speak, a coalition government. For Augustine, "lust is an usurper, defying the power of the will, and tyrannizing the human sexual organs."[71]

By defining spontaneous sexual desire as the proof and penalty of original sin, Augustine believes that he has succeeded in implicating the whole human race except, of course, for Christ. Christ alone of all humankind, Augustine explains, was born without *libido*—being born, he believes, without the intervention of semen that transmits its effects. But the rest of humankind issues from a procreative process that, ever since Adam, has sprung wildly out of control, marring the whole of human nature.

What, then, can remedy human misery? How can anyone achieve internal balance, much less establish social and political harmony between man and woman, man and man? Augustine's whole theology of the Fall depends upon his radical claim that no human power can effect such restoration. Knowing, however, that many philosophically minded people (including philosophically educated Christians from Justin Martyr through Chrysostom) stand against him and would invoke, against his argument, the evidence of all who successfully practice self-control—pagan philosophers and Christian ascetics alike—Augustine seizes the offensive. There are, he admits, a few people who restrain their passions through self-control, leading temperate, just, and holy lives. But while others honor them for their achievement, Augustine dares accuse them, in effect, of neurosis: "This is by no means a healthy state due to nature (*sanitas ex natura*), but an illness due to guilt (*languor ex culpa*)."[72] For it is not only the "common mass of men, but even the most godly and righteous," he insists, that are ravaged by sin and dominated by passion. The Stoic attempt to achieve *apatheia*—mastery of passion—he dismisses as leading its practitioners into arrogance and isolation from the rest of humanity, "not tranquillity."[73] Thus ridiculing such efforts to reassert the power of the will, Augustine concludes that the "rebellion in our members . . . that proof and penalty of man's rebellion against God," is not only universal but also ineradicable. Part of our nature stands in permanent revolt against the "law of the mind"—even among the philosophers, even among the baptized and the saints. And since he insists that everyone, even the most advanced ascetic, confronts the same continual insurrection within, Augustine concludes that humankind has wholly lost its original capacity for self-government.

Augustine, in fact, draws so drastic a picture of the effects of Adam's sin that he embraces human government, even when tyrannical, as the indispensable defense against the forces sin has unleashed in human nature. His analysis of internal conflict, indeed, leads directly into his view of social conflict in general. The war within us drives us into war with one another—and no one, pagan or Christian, remains exempt. So, he explains, "while a good man is progressing to perfection, one part of him can be at war with another of his parts; hence, two good men can be at war with one another."[74]

In the beginning Augustine agrees with Chrysostom, politics began at home:

> The union of male and female is the seed-bed, so to speak, from which the city must grow. . . . Since, then a man's home (*hominis domus*) ought to be the beginning or elementary constituent of the city, and every beginning serves some end of its own, and every part serves the integrity of the whole of which it is a part, it follows clearly enough that domestic peace serves civic peace, that is, that the ordered agreement of command and obedience among those who live together in a household serves the ordered agreement of command and obedience among citizens.[75]

Recognizing that Adam and Eve originally were created to live together in a harmonious order of authority and obedience, superiority and subordination, like soul and body, "we must conclude," says Augustine, "that a husband is meant to rule over his wife as the spirit rules the flesh." But once each member of the primal couple had experienced that first internal revolt in which the bodily passions arose against the soul, they experienced analogous disruption in their relationship with one another. Although originally created equal with man in regard to her rational soul, woman's actual formation established her existentially as the "weaker part of the human couple."[76] Being closely connected with bodily passion, woman, although created to be man's helper, became his temptress and led him into disaster.[77] The Genesis account describes the result: God himself reinforced the husband's authority over his wife, placing divine sanction upon the social, legal, and economic machinery of male domination.

Apart from the relationship between the sexes, however, Augustine again agrees with Chrysostom that "God did not want a rational being, made in his image, to have dominion over any except irrational creatures; not man over men, but man over the beasts."[78] Unlike man's dominion over woman, man's dominion over other men violates their original equality; hence, "such a condition as slavery could only have arisen as a result of sin."[79] Augustine diverges sharply from Chrysostom, however, when he traces how sin, transmitted from the primal parents through sexual reproduction, infected their offspring so that now "everyone, arising as he does from a condemned stock, is, from the first necessarily evil and carnal through Adam."[80] So Cain, when another form of carnal desire, envy, overcame his rational judgment, murdered his brother, exemplifying the lust for power that now dominates and distorts the whole structure of human relationships. Those who share Augustine's vision of the disastrous results of sin must, he believes, accept as well the rule of one man over others—master over slave, ruler over subjects— as the inescapable necessity of our universal fallen nature:

> Such, as men are now, is the order of peace. Some are in subjection to others and, while humility helps those who serve, pride harms those in power. But as men once were, when their nature was as God created it, no man was a slave either to man or to sin. However, slavery is now penal in character, and planned by that law which commands the preservation of the natural order and forbids its disturbance.[81]

Human nature, Augustine explains, instinctively desires social harmony: "By the very laws of his nature man is, so to speak, forced into social relationships and peace (*societatem pacemque*) with other men, so far as possible."[82] Yet sin distorts this universal impulse, turning it instead into the enforced order that constitutes "earthly peace."

Certain scholars recently have emphasized how carefully Augustine qualifies his affirmation of secular government. The Dutch scholar Henrik Berkhof, writing during the Second World War, takes Augustine as representing what he calls the "theocratic" view which subordinates the interests of the state to those of the church. Wilhelm Kamlah, writing in Germany after the War, points out that Augustine's theory deprives the state of any claim to ultimate religious value, regarding it, in effect as a "necessary evil."[83] Augustine expresses no illusions, certainly, about the rulers' motives for enforcing peace: even a solitary criminal, he says "demands peace in his own home, and, if need be, gets it by sheer brutality. He knows that the price of peace is to have everyone subject to some one head—in this case, to himself."[84] Should such a man gain power over a larger society, Augustine continues, he would rule through the same brutal impulse:

> Thus it is that all men want peace in their own society, and they all want it on their own terms. When they go to war, what they want is to make, if they can, their enemies their own, and to impose on them the victor's will, and call it a peace. . . . Sinful man hates the equality of all men under God, and, as though he were God, loves to impose his own sovereignty upon his fellow men.[85]

Such pragmatic and negative assessments of the function of government are not, of course, original with Augustine. Justin Martyr, addressing the emperors Antonius Pius, Marcus Aurelius, and Lucius Verus two and a half centuries earlier, borrowing an image from philosophical tradition,[86] had declared that those who rule by brute force "have just as much power as robbers in a desert."[87] Marcus Aurelius uses the same image in his own *Meditations*[88]—as, indeed, does Augustine in a famous passage: "Without justice, what then are kingdoms but great robberies? For what are robberies themselves but little kingdoms?"[89] No more original is Augustine's "insistence that political authority is not natural to man, but a result of his sinful condition."[90] Justin's younger colleague, Irenaeus, had described how

> God imposed upon humankind the fear of men since they did not acknowledge the fear of God, so that, being subject to human authority and kept under restraints by their laws, they might attain to some degree of justice. . . . Earthly rule, therefore, has been appointed by God, and not by the devil, for the benefit of nations . . . so that, under fear of human rule, people may not devour one another like fishes![91]

Irenaeus was drawing in turn upon much older tradition—using, in fact, a rabbinic image to interpret Paul's warning to Christians about the positive uses of governmental coercion (Rom 13:1–6).

Yet Augustine's predecessors—Justin and Irenaeus—affirm the necessity of coercive government primarily for "those outside." Both, like Chrysostom, clearly discriminate between the coercive government necessary for outsiders and the internal rule of the church. Baptized Christians, Justin and Irenaeus agree, essentially have recovered from the damage inflicted by sin. Baptism transforms converts from their former state as "children of necessity and ignorance . . . to become children of choice and knowledge," washed clean of sin, illuminated, and, Justin says, "by our deeds, too, found to be good citizens and keepers of the commandments."[92]

Augustine agrees with his predecessors in delineating two distinct modes of relationship—one motivated by impulses of domination and submission, the other by mutually affirming love. But what sets Augustine's mature position apart from that of his predecessors is his refusal simply to identify the first with the state and the second with the church. As he redefines them, the "city of man" and the "city of God" cut across both categories. Even baptized Christians are not exempt, either from the war of conflicting impulses or from the need for external government. Augustine insists, on the contrary, that all government remains only a superstructure imposed upon the internal rebellion that sin has instigated within everyone, pagan and Christian alike. Consequently, he believes, the situation of the baptized Christian is far more complex than Chrysostom imagined. The Christian, like the unbeliever, has to contend against the enemy within that holds power over his will. Hence he too needs the help of external discipline. So even in his domestic life, Augustine says, although the Christian longs for heaven

> where there will be no further need for giving orders to other human beings, . . . meanwhile, in case anyone in the household breaks its peace by disobedience, he is disciplined by words or whipping or other kinds of punishment lawful and licit in human society, and for his own good, to readjust to the peace he has abandoned.[93]

If Christians cannot even be trusted to govern themselves, how are they to approach church government? Later in his life Augustine came to endorse, for the church as well as the state, the whole arsenal of secular government that Chrysostom had repudiated—commands, threats, coercion, penalties, and even physical force. While Chrysostom had defined his own role as that of advisor, not ruler, Augustine, like Ignatius of Antioch, sees the bishop as ruling "in God's place." One of Augustine's favorite images for church leaders, as for his model, Christ, is that of the physician ministering to those who, although baptized, are, like himself, still sick, each one infected more or less with the same ineradicable disease contracted through original sin.[94] Augustine tends, consequently, to discount the patients' opinion. It is the physician's responsibility not only to administer to sick and suffering humanity the life-giving medication of the sacraments, but also to carry out, when necessary, disciplinary procedures as a kind of surgery.

This vision of the church, advocated by others such as Alypius, also corresponds in a sense to Augustine's own experience. He admits how desperately lost, sick, or helpless he felt, believing his will morally paralyzed as he awaited the revelation of grace mediated through the church to penetrate him from without and effect his healing.[95] But other Christians surely would not have recognized their own experiences in his account. Pelagius, for one, sharply objected, criticizing Augustine's *Confessions* for popularizing a kind of pious self-indulgence. How, then, did Augustine's idiosyncratic views on the effects of original sin—and hence on the politics of church and state—come to be accepted from the fifth century on, first by the leadership of the Catholic church and then by the majority of its members? The question is, of course, wildly ambitious; but let us attempt to sketch out the beginning of an answer.

Let us consider first how the conflicting views of Chrysostom and Augustine might sound to their contemporaries. By the beginning of the fifth century Catholic Christians lived as subjects of an empire they could no longer consider alien, much less wholly evil. Having repudiated the patronage of the traditional gods some two generations earlier, the emperors now sometimes even used military force to help stamp out pagan worship. Furthermore, the two sons of Theodosius the Great, reigning since his death in 395 as emperors of East and West, continued their father's policy of withdrawing patronage from Arian Christians and placing themselves wholly in alliance with the Catholic bishops and clergy. An earlier generation of Christian bishops, notably including Eusebius of Caesarea, deeply impressed by the events they had witnessed and convinced that they lived at a turning point in history, had hailed Constantine and his successors as God's chosen rulers. Augustine, like most of his fellow Christians, once had shared that conviction. But after two generations the Christian empire and its rulers, if no longer alien, remained in many respects all too human. By the turn of the fifth century few who dealt with the government firsthand—certainly not Chrysostom and finally not Augustine either—would have identified it with God's reign on earth.[96]

The mature Augustine offers a theology of politics far more complex and compelling than any of its rivals. Against Chrysostom's claim that imperial rule is unnecessary for believers Augustine insists that God has placed everyone, whether pagan or priest, equally in subjection to external government. Yet his reasoning diverges sharply from Eusebius's. Augustine's dark vision of a human nature ravaged by the damage of original sin and overrun by lust for power rules out uncritical adulation and qualifies his endorsement of imperial rule.[97] That same dark vision impels him to reject Chrysostom's optimistic premise that imperial power is necessary for pagans, but, in effect, superfluous in the lives of pious citizens. Augustine, on the contrary, places secular government at the center of human society, indispensable for the best as well as the worst among its members. For a Christian, civic obligations rank second, certainly, to one's obligation to God (or, as this usually meant in practice, to the church). Yet apart from direct conflict of interest even the bishop must render appropriate obedience to secular authority.[98] Augustine acknowledges the emperor's rule, however limited (or even however brutal), to be, nevertheless, as permanent and ineradicable as the effects of original sin themselves. More effectively than either Eusebius, on the one hand, or Chrysostom on the other, Augustine's theory enables his contemporaries to come to terms both with the fact and with the intractably human nature of Christian empire.

If the fifth-century state no longer looked so evil as it once had, the church, in turn, no longer looked so holy. Chrysostom, holding to his by now essentially sectarian theory, deplored what had happened to the church since imperial favor first shone upon Christians: first, the massive influx of nominal converts; and second, the way that a shower of imperial privileges had radically changed the dynamics—and raised the stakes—of ecclesiastical politics. But what Chrysostom could only denounce, Augustine could interpret. Challenging the traditional model of the church and the assumption on which it rested—free will—Augustine's theory of original sin could make theologically intelligible not only the state's imperfections, but the church's imperfections as well.

Secondly, while changing the way Catholic Christians understood the psychological and religious meaning of freedom (*libertas*), Augustine's theory bore the potential for changing as well their understanding of—and relationship to—political liberty. Throughout the Roman republic men of wealth and power tended to agree that *libertas* meant living under the rule of a "good emperor," that is, an emperor of whom the senate, consisting of such men, approved. Yet, as de Ste. Croix observes,

> in the late Republic there was a totally *different kind of libertas*, and to those who held it the optimate version of *libertas*, that of Cicero & Co., was *servitus* (slavery, political subjection), while their *libertas* was stigmatized by Cicero as mere *licentia* ("licence", lawlessness)—a word used also by the Roman rhetorician Cornificius as the equivalent of the standard Greek word for freedom of speech, *parrhesia*.[99]

Christians, so long as they remained a persecuted, illegal, and minority sect, sided predictably with the latter position. Spokesmen as diverse as Justin, Tertullian, Irenaeus, Clement, Athenagoras, Minucius Felix, and Chrysostom agreed that conversion and baptism convey above all the gift of liberty, by which they meant liberation internally from the rule of the passions and externally from enslavement to custom, convention, and from coercion by imperial authority. Minucius Felix draws a bold portrait of the Christian who, undergoing torture for his faith, maintains his *libertas*:

> How beautiful is the spectacle to God when a Christian does battle with pain, when he is brought up against threats, and punishment, and torture; when, mocking the noise of death, he treads underfoot the horror of the executioner; when *he raises up his liberty against kings and princes*, and yields to God alone . . . when, triumphant and victorious, he tramples on the very one who has passed sentence upon him.[100]

Repudiating the charge that Christians are afraid for superstitious reasons to offer pagan sacrifice, Minucius declares that "it is not a confession of fear, but an assertion of our true liberty!"[101] Tertullian, too, challenging imperial authority in the name of "liberty which is (the individual's) right,"[102] assumes that the term means freedom from superior authority.[103]

Augustine, on the contrary, having denied that human beings possess any capacity whatever for free will, accepts a definition of liberty far more agreeable to the powerful and influential men with whom he himself wholeheartedly identifies. As Augustine tells it, it is the serpent who tempts Adam with the seductive lure of liberty. The forbidden fruit symbolizes, he explains, "personal control over one's own will."[104] Not, Augustine adds, "that it is evil in itself, but it is placed in the garden to teach him the primary virtue"—obedience. So, as we noted above, Augustine concludes that humanity never was really meant to be, in any sense, truly free. God allowed us to sin in order to prove to us from our own experience that "our true good is free slavery"[105]—slavery to God in the first place and in the second to his agent, the emperor. Idiosyncratic as it sounds, Augustine's paradox finds a parallel in political debate among his contemporaries. Claudian, pagan court poet and propagandist in the service of Stilicho and of Honorius the Christian emperor of the West, challenges those who call the emperor's rule slavery (*servitium*): "Never is liberty more appreciated than under a good king!"[106] During the following centuries a similar view was incorporated into the imperial Catholic mass which directs the priest to pray that, "the enemies of peace being overthrown, Roman liberty may serve Thee in security" (*secura tibi serviat Romana libertas*).[107]

Finally, anyone observing the contrast between the careers of the two bishops might well conclude that Augustine's version of the politics of Paradise proved effective in dealing with the politics of the fifth-century Roman empire where Chrysostom's version failed. Both Augustine, born in Thagaste, North Africa in 354, and John Chrysostom, born in Antioch either the same year or a few years earlier, grew up in a world ruled for more than a generation by Christian emperors—a succession interrupted only by Julian's abrupt, two-year reversion to imperial patronage of paganism. But their responses to the new constellation of imperial power were very different from Chrysostom's.

Chrysostom, having lost his father at a young age, was raised with his sister by his Christian mother and received baptism at the age of eighteen, signaling his intention to reject a secular career. Following his baptism, he chose to enter monastic solitude. One of his first publications, *Comparison between a King and a Monk*, written at a time when the world, the imperial court, and the church were mingling in unprecedented ways, demonstrates his passionate concern to draw sharp contrasts between secular and sacred power and to prove the latter's superiority. And that early writing, however naive, articulates a theme that preoccupied John throughout his lifetime—a theme intensified and deepened through his extraordinary experiences. Some twelve years later, as a priest in Antioch speaking during the crisis precipitated by public rioting against the emperor's authority, addressing a congregation waiting in terror of imperial reprisals, John dared proclaim—not as Augustine might have, that even the Christian is subject to the emperor—that the emperor himself needs the priest and is subject to the priest's superior authority: "He is himself a ruler, and a ruler of greater dignity than the other; for the sacred laws place under his hands even the royal head."[108] After the bishop's intervention with the emperor resolves the crisis, John declares that these events prove to unbelievers "that the Christians are the saviors of the city; that they are its guardians, its patrons, and its teachers. . . . Let all unbelievers learn that the fear of Christ is a bridle to every kind of authority."[109]

In 397 John received a summons to Constantinople, sudden as a bolt from heaven. Hurrying there in secret, he found himself unexpectedly appointed bishop of Constantinople and so precipitated into a position that stood at the pinnacle of ecclesiastical power. By canon law of 391, the bishop of Constantinople ranked second only to the bishop of Rome; but often a man in that position, as chief spiritual advisor to the emperor, to the imperial family, and to the whole court, proved capable of surpassing all others in actual influence. Eutropius, the brilliant and powerful eunuch who controlled much of court politics for the emperor Arcadius, his ineffectual young charge, had arranged for the appointment. Eutropius probably guessed that John, although renowned for his piety and eloquence, had neither the taste nor the talent to ingratiate himself into the intricate strategies of court politics. And Eutropius was right; John proved, in fact, to be so impolitic, so concerned with his responsibilities as moral advisor to the powerful, advocate for the destitute and oppressed, and austere guardian of clerical discipline, that within three years he had offended virtually everyone who had once welcomed his appointment. His acts of social conscience turned powerful people among the court and clergy against him. His attempt to build a hospital for lepers directly outside the city walls, for example, set off a "war" of protest that ended with his deposition.[110] One historian concludes that John "proudly disdained the favor of the court, on which the high position of his episcopate alone rested, by his foolish idealism."[111] Another considers whether the bishop deserves to be revered as a saint and martyr or condemned "comme un idéaliste dépourvu de finesse diplomatique, un zélote sans tact, ou un fanatique incapable de nuances et victime de son emportement."[112] John's admirers would have rejected such cynical assessments, attributing the bishop's actions instead to his deep religious convictions and to his uncompromising moral consciousness. Yet even they could see how those very qualities had earned him accusations of "hardness and rudeness," and of "arrogance" intolerable in a man in his position, and so played into the hands of his enemies.

After six years in office John learned that his enemies had prevailed even over his former supporters: deposed from episcopal office, perhaps narrowly escaping death, he began under heavy guard the arduous journey into exile. There, suffering from illness and isolation, covered by accusations, defended and consoled by a few loyal friends, he survived only three years before his death. But Chrysostom's convictions never swerved from the course his earliest writings had set: that secular and spiritual powers are essentially antithetical and, in effect, mutually exclusive. From exile he wrote to his friend and fellow cleric Pentadia words that expressed, no doubt, his perspective on his own suffering and apparent failure, as well as hers, on his behalf:

> I rejoice . . . and find the greatest consolation, in my solitude, in the fact that you have been so manly and steadfast, and that you have not allowed yourself to do wrong. . . . Be glad, therefore, and rejoice over your victory. For they have done everything they could against you. You, who knew only the church and your monastic cell, they have dragged out into the public eye, from there to the court, and from court to prison. They have brought false witnesses, have slandered, murdered, shed streams of blood . . . and left nothing undone to terrify you, and to obtain from you a lie. . . . But you have brought them all to shame.[113]

Consider, then, the contrast with Augustine. Born into a nonpatrician family, Augustine, unlike John, sought a secular career with intense ambition. Simultaneously, as he tells it, he plunged into the life of the city—theatrical performances, dinner parties, rhetorical competition, and numerous friendships among other relationships. Having allowed his mother to contract for him a socially advantageous marriage, he lived with a lower class woman who engaged his passions and who bore his son. Yet once he had achieved a considerable degree of recognition as a rhetor Augustine found himself divided. Although deeply attracted to the life of philosophical and religious contemplation, he felt unwilling to give up the prospects of marriage and career. But at the age of thirty-two, spurred by stories of the desert solitaries, he abruptly renounced both and accepted baptism as a sign of his transformation. Three years later, having "given up all hope in this world," Augustine went to Hippo to set up the communal monastic life he intended to enter. Later, protesting to his congregation that he had had no intention whatever of seeking church office, he expressed ambivalence about his meteoric ecclesiastical career: "I was grabbed, I was made a priest . . . and, from there, I became your bishop."[114]

The church that Augustine chose to join, as Peter Brown points out, "was not the old church of Cyprian"—not, that is, the select community of the holy, willing to risk persecution and death or, lacking the opportunity for martyrdom, eager to leave the world. On the contrary,

> it was the new, expanding church of Ambrose, rising above the Roman world like "a moon waxing in its brightness." It was a confident, international body, established in the respect of Christian Emperors, sought out by noblemen and intellectuals, capable of bringing to the masses of the known civilized world the esoteric truths of the philosophy of Plato, a church set no longer to defy society but to master it.[115]

As Augustine understood their task, himself having learned from Ambrose, church leaders participate in the divinely ordained work of government: "You teach kings to rule for the benefit of their people; and it is You who warn the people to be subservient to their kings."[116] At the time of Augustine's baptism, the Catholic church was in the process of consolidating its identification with imperial rule. Armed with support from the emperor Honorius, the leaders of the western church, intent on preventing the Arians from returning to favor, committed themselves to the polity of implementing imperial authority and so, in the process, of asserting and consolidating the primacy of Catholicism over all its Christian rivals.

Augustine's position as bishop of a provincial North African city can scarcely be compared with the position Chrysostom received three years later in the capital city of the eastern empire. Still, in accepting the episcopate, Augustine, too, became a public figure and ruler of a community. Discovering his authority challenged by the rival church of Donatists, Augustine increasingly came to appreciate—and, indeed, masterfully to manipulate—the advantages of his alliance with the repressive power of the state. Donatist Christians for their part bitterly denounced this "unholy alliance." Agreeing in this respect with the principle that Chrysostom often expressed, Donatist Christians insisted that the church must employ only spiritual sanctions and wholly abstain from the use of force.

Yet Augustine, abandoning the policy of toleration practiced by the previous bishop of Carthage, pursued the attack. He, like Chrysostom, could praise the church's use of persuasion, not force; yet he himself, beginning with polemics and propaganda, turned progressively to an escalating use of force. First came laws denying civil rights to non-Catholic Christians; then the imposition of penalties, fines, eviction from public office; and finally, denial of free discussion, exile of Donatist bishops, and the use of physical coercion. Despite earlier misgivings Augustine came to regard military force as "indispensable" in implementing the policy of suppressing the Donatists. Replying to those who criticized him for advocating persecution of his fellow Christians, Augustine "wrote the only full justification, in the history of the early church, of the right of the state to suppress non-Catholics."[117] He came to realize, he explained, that the use of fear and coercion, which Chrysostom considered necessary only to govern outsiders, was necessary within the church as well. Many Christians as well as pagans, he noted regretfully, respond only to fear.[118]

Later, contending against the Pelagians (who, despite many other differences, shared with the Donatists both a sectarian view of the church and an insistence of free will) Augustine, finding his party out-voted in the Christian synods, unhesitatingly allied himself with imperial officials against the clergy who defended Pelagius. In 416 Innocent, bishop of Rome, received from African synods two condemnations of Pelagian ideas together with a long personal letter from Augustine and his closest associates and an open letter from Augustine challenging Pelagius. Yet the documents went far beyond a condemnation of Pelagius and his followers. They went on to warn, in Brown's words, that

> the ultimate consequence of [Pelagian] ideas . . . cut at the roots of episcopal authority. . . . The documents claimed that by appeasing the Pelagians the Catholic church would *lose the vast authority it had begun to wield as the only force that could "liberate" men from themselves.*[119]

Pelagius's supporters would make the counterclaim (and with reason) that they only followed ancient tradition concerning the church and human nature—tradition most recently championed by John Chrysostom himself. But the declarations of the African synods, engineered primarily by Augustine and his associates, signaled a major turning point in the history of western

Christianity. They offered to the bishop of Rome and to his imperial patrons a clear demonstration of the political efficacy of Augustine's doctrine of the Fall. By insisting that humanity, ravaged by sin, now lies helplessly in need of outside intervention, Augustine's theory not only could validate the means and ends of secular power, but could justify as well the imposition of church authority—even by force, if necessary—as essential for human salvation.

Augustine, having outlived by twenty-seven years his exiled and disgraced colleague, achieved, unlike John Chrysostom, a position of extraordinary power and influence in the Roman world until his death on 28 August 430. Far beyond his lifetime, even for a millennium and a half, the influence of Augustine's teaching throughout western Christendom has surpassed that of any other Church Father's. Acknowledging that there are many reasons for this, I suggest as primary among them the following: It is Augustine's theology of the Fall that made the uneasily forged alliance between the Catholic churches and imperial power palatable—not only justifiable, but necessary—for the majority of Catholic Christians. Augustine's doctrine, of course, went far beyond mere expedience. Serious believers concerned with the deeper questions of theology, as well as those concerned only with political advantage, could find in Augustine's theological legacy ways of making sense out of a situation in which church and state had become inextricably interdependent.

The eventual triumph of Augustine's theology required, however, the capitulation of all who held to the classical proclamation concerning human freedom, once regarded by many as the heart of the Christian gospel. By the beginning of the fifth century those who still held to such archaic traditions—notably including those the Catholics called "Donatists" and "Pelagians"—themselves came to be condemned as heretics. Augustine's theory of Adam's Fall, once espoused in simpler forms only by marginal groups of Christians, now moved, together with the imperially supported Catholic church that proclaimed it, into the center of western history.

# Notes

†Originally appeared in *Harvard Theological Review* 78 (1985): 67–99. Reprinted by permission of the publisher.

*I am grateful to those colleagues who read this work in manuscript and helped me with their criticism: Thomas Boslooper, Peter Brown, Elizabeth Clark, James Cone, Marilyn Harran, Robert Hammerton-Kelley, Lewis Spitz, and Gilles Quispel.

1 *Vita Adae et Evae* 22.1–2; *Jubilees* 2.14; see Jacob Jervell, *Imago Dei: Gen. 1,26f. im Spagudentum, in der Gnosis, und in den paulinischen Briefen* (Göttingen: Vandenhoeck & Ruprecht, 1960) 40–41.

²*De hom. op.* 2.1.

³Ibid., 4.1. The opposite theme—that of the emperor as sole representative of God's sovereignty on earth, a theme often supported with reference to Rom 13:1—does emerge however, especially among theologians of the Byzantine era, as G. E. M. de Ste. Croix notes: *The Class Struggle in the Ancient Greek World from the Archaic Age to the Arab Conquests* (Ithaca, NY: Cornell University Press, 1981) 397–400.

⁴*De hom. op.* 4.1.

⁵Ibid., 16.11.

⁶Both themes, certainly, appear in the works of patristic theologians; for an overview, see Lewis Spitz, "Man on this Isthmus," in Carl S. Meyer, ed., *Luther for an Ecumenical Age: Essays in Commemoration of the 450th Anniversary of the Reformation* (St. Louis: Concordia, 1967) 23–66.

⁷For citations and discussion, see below 78–89.

⁸Chrysostom *Hom. ad pop. Ant.* 7.3.

⁹*De hom. op.* 16.17.

¹⁰*Hom. ad pop. Ant.* 7.3.

¹¹*Hom. in 1 Cor.* 34.7.

¹²*Hom. in Eph.* 22.9; cf. *Hom. in I Cor.* 40.6.

¹³*Hom. in I Cor.* 26.2; cf. *Hom. in Eph.* 20.33; see n. 13.

¹⁴*Hom. in I Cor.* 26.2 stresses Eve's original equality with Adam. Yet, interpreting I Cor. 11:9, Chrysostom goes on to enumerate four reasons for man's natural superiority to woman (cf. *Hom. in I Cor.* 26.4–5). Chrysostom expresses a similarly ambivalent attitude in other passages, often related to the passage he is interpreting. *Hom. in I Cor.* 34 and *Hom. in Eph.* 20, e.g., suggest that woman, essentially man's equal, was subordinated to him for practical purposes of government, to maintain social order. Commenting on I Tim 2:11–15, on the other hand, Chrysostom denounces the whole female sex for its intrinsic inferiority (*Hom. in I Tim.* 9, passim). In *Hom. in I Cor.* 34, however, Chrysostom declares that God designed a balance of power between man and woman to insure their continuing interdependence (*Hom. in I Cor.* 34.7). See the incisive discussion by Elizabeth A. Clark in *Jerome, Chrysostom and Friends: Essays and Translations* (Studies in Women and Religion 2; New York: Mellen, 1979) esp. "The Virginal *Politeia* and Plato's *Republic*," 1–34.

¹⁵*Hom. in II Cor.* 17.3.

¹⁶*Hom. ad pop. Ant.* 6.1–2.

¹⁷*Hom. in I Cor.* 12.9.

¹⁸Ibid., 12.10.

¹⁹*Hom. in I Thess.* 5.7.

²⁰*Hom. in I Cor.* 12.10.

²¹*Hom. ad pop. Ant.* 6.2.

²²Cf., e.g., Tertullian *Apol.* 4.39; Justin *I Apol.* 12.42.

²³*De sacerdot.* 2.3.

²⁴Emphasis added.

²⁵*Hom. in Eph.*11.15–16. Emphasis added.

²⁶Ibid., 6.7.

<sup>27</sup>*De sacerdot.* 3.15.

<sup>28</sup>*Hom. in Eph.* 11.15–16.

<sup>29</sup>I am grateful to Peter Brown for reminding me of this theme in Robert L. Wilken's recent book, *John Chrysostom and the Jews: Rhetoric and Reality in the Late Fourth Century* (Berkeley: University of California Press, 1983) 29–33.

<sup>30</sup>*Conf.* 2.2. Translations used here are those of William Watts (1631) in *St. Augustine's Confessions* (Cambridge: Harvard University Press, 1977) 69. In some places I have chosen to retranslate phrases for clarity or agreement with contemporary idiom (i.e., in *Conf.* 2.3, where Watts translated *calcabat* as "trod me down," I translate "tracked me down"; in *Conf.* 6.12, where Watts translates *consuetudo* as "custom," I prefer "habit").

<sup>31</sup>Ibid., 2.3.

<sup>32</sup>Ibid., 6.12.

<sup>33</sup>Ibid.

<sup>34</sup>Ibid., 6.11. For discussion of the relationships of Augustine's theology with Chrysostom, see Pier Franco Beatrice, *Tradux peccati: Alle fonti della dottrina agostiniana del peccato originale* (Studia Patristica Mediolanensia 8; Milan: Università Cattolica del Sacro Cuore, 1978) chap. 5: "Crisostomo, Agostino e i pelagiani."

<sup>35</sup>*Conf.* 2.7.

<sup>36</sup>Ibid., 2.6.

<sup>37</sup>Ibid., 7.3

<sup>38</sup>Ibid. Emphasis added.

<sup>39</sup>Ibid., 8.5.

<sup>40</sup>Ibid., 8.10.

<sup>41</sup>Ibid. Emphasis added.

<sup>42</sup>F. Edward Cranz, "The Development of Augustine's Ideas on Society before the Donatist Controversy," *HTR* 47 (1954) 254–316. I am grateful to Elizabeth Clark, as well as to Peter Brown, for mentioning this point.

<sup>43</sup>*De civ. Dei* 14.15. The translation cited generally follows that of Philip Levine in St. Augustine, *The City of God Against the Pagans* (LCL, 1966).

<sup>44</sup>Ibid., 13.21: *Lignum scientiae boni et mali proprium voluntatis arbitrium.* According to the analysis of M. Harl ("Adam et les deux Arbres du Paradis [Gen. II–III] chez Philon d'Alexandrie," *RechSR* 50 [1962] 321–87), Philo, too, saw human autonomy which exercises choice between good and evil as the alternative—and opposite—of true piety. If so, Philo might agree with Augustine that the result of the Fall is "personal control over one's own will." Unlike Augustine, however, Philo regards the daily life of a philosophically inclined person as a constant struggle of ethical decision and action (374), and assumes that humanity has a capacity to choose the good (377).

<sup>45</sup>*De civ. Dei* 13.13. Emphasis added.

<sup>46</sup>Ibid., 14.15.

<sup>47</sup>Ibid., 14.12.

<sup>48</sup>Ibid., 14.13.

<sup>49</sup>Ibid., 14.15.

<sup>50</sup>*Conf.* 7.3.

[51] *Hom. in I Cor.* 17.4.

[52] *De civ. Dei.* 13.3. Emphasis added.

[53] Chrysostom *Hom. in Rom.* 10.1; for discussion of Augustine's exegesis, see Julius Gross, *Entstehungsgeschichte des Erbsündendogmas von der Bibel bis Augustinus* (4 vols.; Munich: Reinhardt, 1960) 1.304–5; Beatrice, *Tradux Peccati,* 139–41.

[54] *De civ. Dei* 13.14.

[55] Ibid.

[56] Ibid.

[57] Cf. Wilhelm Kamlah, *Christentum und Geschichtlichkeit: Untersuchungen zur Entstehung des Christentums und zu Augustins "Bürgerschaft Gottes"* (2d ed.; Stuttgart: Kohlhammer, 1951) 322: "Wo Augustin über die politische Herrschaft spricht, verweist er immer sogleich auf diese ursprüngliche Herrschafts- und Schöpfungsordnung und auf die Scheinherrschaft derer, die in der Knechtschaft der *libido dominandi* leben."

[58] *De civ. Dei.* 2.36.

[59] Ibid., 14.15.

[60] Ibid., 14.3.

[61] Ibid., 14.15.

[62] Ibid., 13.13.

[63] Ibid., 13.24.

[64] *De pecc. merit. et rem.* 2.2; cf. *De civ. Dei* 14.17.

[65] Ibid., 14.19–20.

[66] Ibid., 14.16.

[67] *De pecc. merit. et rem.* 2.22.

[68] *De civ. Dei* 14.26.

[69] Ibid., 14.17.

[70] *Conf.* 8.5.

[71] *De civ. Dei* 14.20. Origen, too, associated intercourse with impurity, although, as Henri Crouzel points out, "the impurity inherent in the exercise of sexuality is no more than an intensification of an even more profound uncleanness, that of the bodily condition" ("Marriage and Virginity: Has Christianity Devalued Marriage?" in idem, *Mariage et divorce, celibat et charactère sacerdotaux dans l'église ancienne: Études diverses* [Torino: Bottega d'Erasmo, 1982] 57).

[72] *De civ. Dei* 14.19.

[73] Ibid., 14.9. For discussion, see Margaret Ruth Miles, *Augustine on the Body* (AARDS 31; Missoula: Scholars Press, 1979) esp. 1–98.

[74] *De civ. Dei* 15.5.

[75] Ibid., 15.16; 19.13.

[76] Ibid., 14.11.

[77] See the excellent discussion by Kari Elizabeth Børrensen, *Subordination and Equivalence: The Nature and Role of Women in Augustine and Thomas Aquinas* (trans. Charles H. Talbot; Washington, DC: University Press of America, 1981) 15–34.

[78] *De civ. Dei* 19.15.

[79] Ibid.

80Ibid., 15.1.

81Ibid., 19.15.

82Ibid., 19.12.

83I am grateful to Professor Gilles Quispel for referring me to these works: Henrik Berkhof, *Kirche und Kaiser: Eine Untersuchung der Entstehung der byzantinischen und der theokratisichen Stattsauffassung im vierten Jahrhundert* (trans. Gottfried W. Locher; Zurich: Evangelischer Verlag, 1947); Wilhelm Kamlah, *Christentum und Geschichtlichkeit* (Stuttgart: Kohlhammer, 1951).

84*De civ. Dei* 19.12.

85Ibid.

86For discussion of the image and its history, see R. MacMullen, "The Roman Concept Robber-Pretender," *Revue Internationale des Droits de l'antiquité*, series 3, 10 (1965) 221–25.

87Justin Martyr *Apol.* 1.12.

88Marcus Aurelius *Meditations* 10.10.

89*De civ. Dei* 4.4.

90As R. A. Markus rightly notes; see his discussion in *Saeculum: History and Society in the Theology of St. Augustine* (Cambridge: Harvard University Press, 1970) 84–86.

91*Adv. haer.* 55.24.2.

92*Apol.* 1.65.

93*De civ. Dei* 19.16.

94See P. R. L. Brown, "Saint Augustine's Attitude to Religious Coercion," *JRS* 54 (1964) 107–16. For a fascinating account of the incorporation of this image into the Roman liturgy, see G. M. Lukken, *Original Sin in the Roman Liturgy: Research into the Theology of Original Sin in the Roman Sacramentaria and The Early Baptismal Liturgy* (Leiden: Brill, 1973).

95We need only recall how in *Conf.* 8.12 Augustine describes the instrument of his salvation as, first, the child's voice that, he believes, directed him to "take and read" the Scriptures (a Christian version of the *bath kol*), and then the passage in Romans (13:13) to which the "Apostle's book" fell open when he obeyed God's command mediated through that voice.

96For a detailed discussion, see Markus, *Saeculum*. According to Markus's reconstruction, Augustine from 390, for 10 or 15 years, "appeared to have joined the chorus of his contemporaries in their triumphant jubilation over the victory of Christianity" (31). "For a decade or more, his historical thinking was dominated by this motif" (32). Yet from 410, Augustine became "much less ready to speak of a Christian empire . . . he became much more reserved" (36).

97Markus sees Augustine's theory as admirably balanced: "The Empire is not to be seen either in terms of the messianic image of the Eusebian tradition, or of the apocalyptic image, as the Antichrist of the Hippolytan tradition. The empire has become no more than an historical, empirical society with a chequered career. . . . It is theologically neutral" (ibid., 559). I believe that Markus overstates his case (or, perhaps, presents his own agenda as Augustine's) when he goes farther and claims that Augustine also sees the church as "theologically neutral."

98See, e.g., Hans Joachim Diesner's discussion of Ambrose, in "Kirche und Staat im ausgehenden vierten Jahrhundert: Ambrosius von Mailand," in his *Kirche und Staat im Spätromischen Reich: Aufsätze zur Spätantike und zur Geschichte der Alten Kirche* (Berlin: Evangelische Verlaganstalt, 1963) esp. 28–34.

[99]de Ste. Croix, *Class Struggle*, 368.

[100]Minucius Felix *Octavius* 37.1. Emphasis added.

[101]Ibid., 38.1.

[102]Tertullian *Apol.* 28.

[103]Another favorite Christian slogan, free will, bore similar connotations. Many of Augustine's contemporaries, hearing Christians advocate free will (*libero arbitrio*) might associate this with those who advocate revolution, or, at least, resistance against Roman rule. See J. N. L. Myres, "Pelagius and the End of Roman Rule in Britian," *JRS* 50 (1960) 21–36.

[104]*De civ. Dei* 13.21.

[105]Ibid., 14.15.

[106]*Stilicho* 3.113–15. For an informative and incisive discussion of Claudian's point of view, see Alan Cameron, *Claudian: Poetry and Propaganda of the Court of Honorius* (Oxford: Clarendon, 1970).

[107]I am grateful to Peter Brown for pointing this out, and for referring me to the discussion of *libertas* in Gerd Tellenbach, *Church, State and Christian Society at the Time of the Investiture Contest* (trans. R. F. Bennett; Studies in Medieval History 3; Oxford: Blackwell, 1959) 14–18.

[108]*Hom. ad pop. Ant.* 3.6.

[109]Ibid., 6.6.

[110]For a detailed and useful analysis, see Florent van Ommeslaeghe, "Jean Chrysostome et le peuple de Constantinople," *AnBoll* 99 (1981) 329–49: "Il est certain qu'une des raisons de l'attachement du peuple de Constantinople à son chef spirituel fut sa bonté, son amour des pauvres, de nos jours on dirait: son sens social" (348). Also see J. H. W. G. Liebeschutz, "Friends and Enemies of John Chrysostom" in Ann Moffatt, ed., *Maistor: Classical, Byzantine and Renaissance Studies for Robert Browning* (Byzantina Australiensia 5; Canberra: Australian Association for Byzantine Studies, 1984) 85–111.

[111]Otto Seeck, *Geschichte des Untergang der antiken Welt* (6 vols. in 8; Berlin: Siemenroth & Troschel, 1897–1920) 5. 336–37.

[112]Florent van Ommeslaeghe, "Jean Chrysostome en conflit avec l'impératrice Eudoxie: Le dossier et les origines d'une légende," *AnBoll* 97 (1979) 131–59.

[113]Chrysostom *Ep.* 94.

[114]*Serm.* 355.2, as cited in Peter Brown, *Augustine of Hippo* (Berkeley: University of California Press, 1965) 138.

[115]Ibid., 225.

[116]*De mor. eccl. cath.* 1.30.63.

[117]Brown, *Augustine.* 235.

[118]*De bapt.* 1.15.23–24.

[119]Brown, *Augustine*, 358. Emphasis added.

# The Role of Neoplatonism in St. Augustine's
## *De Civitate Dei*†

## Robert Russell O.S.A.

It has been aptly observed that Book Eight of *The City of God* marks "a major turning-point" in Augustine's polemic against his pagan adversaries.[1] The opening sentence already reveals a sense of urgency and a keen awareness that the challenge posed by the philosophers will call for greater effort than that expended upon the "poetic" and "civil" theologies in the earlier books.[2] Discussions on "natural theology," remarks Augustine, are not carried on with anybody at all (*non cum quibuslibet hominibus*) but only with those who are known as philosophers. Furthermore, as Augustine indicates at the end of Book One, the discussion is not conducted with any and all philosophers but only "against those among them whose superior excellence has won them wide renown."[3] These, all of the Platonic school, identified as of "more recent origin" (*recentiores*) include Plotinus, Iamblichus, Porphyry, and the Latin Platonist, Apuleius. As we shall see, however, Augustine's apologetical masterpiece is mainly directed against Porphyry, characterized as Christianity's "most bitter enemy" (*Christianorum acerrimus inimicus*) and his numerous followers in North Africa.[4]

What makes Augustine's task even more difficult as well as embarrassing is his well-known profession of Platonism found in his earliest Christian work,[5] and his characterization there of Platonism as "the one really true system of philosophy."[6] Besides, there is the open avowal of his personal indebtedness to this philosophy so vividly recalled in the *Confessions*, a work which, as he testifies, was widely known and favorably received from the outset.[7] There the bishop recounts how a reading of "certain Platonic books" led him to search for truth within the soul[8] and also how this method of interiority enabled him to grasp spiritual reality for the first time. He likewise found philosophic support for the biblical teaching on the essential goodness of the Creator and of the entire creation and thus was able to conceive of evil as privative in character, namely, a "privation of good"[9] (*privatio boni*). Furthermore, in *The City of God*, Augustine continues to reaffirm the superiority of Platonism over other philosophies, and to recognize its similarity with the Christian religion. Most important of all, these philosophers arrived at a better understanding of the one God who made heaven and earth.[10] They also share other truths with us, says Augustine, such as "the immortality of the soul, the existence of the true God who not only created the universe but who also exercises his providence over the universe."[11]

Finally, it was from these same philosophers of the Platonic school that Augustine acquired a fundamental insight that was to serve as the point of departure and unifying principle for the exposition of his own philosophy in *The City of God*. Unlike their predecessors, remarks Augustine, it was Plato and his followers who, once having come to know God, come to recognize him as "the cause of the created universe, the light in which truth is seen, and the spring from which we drink in the waters of happiness."[12] Similarly, in reference to those who followed Plato more closely and who most clearly understood his teaching, Augustine observes that these found in God "both the cause of being, the principle of intellectual knowledge and the rule of right living."[13] Although the passing of years witnessed a gradual waning of his early enthusiasm for the Platonists, he could not forget how much this philosophy had facilitated his understanding of Christian truth and therefore had no reason to suppose that it might not do for others what it had already done for him.

Most of Augustine's negative criticism of the Platonists is reserved for their moral teaching which comes under the heading of God as the source of happiness (*fons bibendae felicitatis*). He finds himself in substantial agreement, however, with their natural philosophy and dialectic which viewed God, respectively, as the cause of the universe and the source of man's intellectual illumination. As understood by Augustine, these philosophers had even caught a glimpse of that most sublime of all truths revealed by God to Moses who, having asked for God's name, received this reply: *"Ego sum qui sum."*[14] Commenting on this passage, possibly the most metaphysical in all the Bible, Augustine states that he is not aware that this truth is to be found in any writings of those philosophers who had preceded Plato.[15]

Although Augustine extols the Platonists for their having surpassed all other philosophers by their discovery of God as the cause of the universe, his apologetic concern in *The City of God* also required him to explore and refute errors which were at variance with revealed truth. These were principally two: the necessity, and by consequence, the eternity of the world. Regarding the latter, it is noteworthy that, unlike representatives of the so-called Medieval Augustinianism, Augustine does not appear to have excluded the absolute possibility of an eternally existing world, provided that one acknowledges God as its cause. He recognizes, however, that such a notion is "barely intelligible" (*modo quodam vix intelligibili*).[16] In the area of dialectic Augustine credits the Platonists with having drawn a sharp distinction between realities seen by the mind and objects perceived by the senses.[17] They had also discovered that the "Light of the mind needed to acquire a knowledge of all things is the very same God by whom all things were made."[18] It may appear strange at first sight that Augustine has relatively little to say on the subject of divine illumination in *The City of God* even though this central doctrine permeates so much of his philosophy. Here it is well to recall the apologetic aim of this work, namely, a refutation of errors opposed to the Christian religion. But with regard to the doctrine of illumination, Augustine insists that "there is no conflict on this question between us and those more eminent philosophers,"[19] namely, the Platonists.

It seems undeniable that Augustine's teaching on divine illumination, as well as its formulation, is largely inspired by Plotinus. In his Treatise, *On Perception and Memory*, Plotinus speaks of the soul's *intuiting* the intelligible "by memory,"[20] thus introducing a *memoria praesentium* which Augustine adopts in a similar context towards the end of the *De Trinitate.*[21] Plotinus likewise states that the soul knows the intelligibles "by a natural affinity with them" and that these are its natural possession. Finally, these intelligible realities are said to constitute the soul's "natural vision."[22] Because of these striking similarities it has been suggested that Augustine could have acquired the substance of his teaching from this single passage of the *Enneads.*[23] Augustine's doctrine, however, cannot be totally identified with the authentic teaching of Plotinus. For Augustine, the source of the soul's illumination is the Supreme Being whereas, for Plotinus, it is not the Plotinian First Principle, the One, but the derived and subordinated Hypostasis called the Divine Intellect (*nous*).

Although Augustine's assessment of Platonic natural philosophy is generally positive in substance and tone, his criticism of its moral philosophy is predominantly negative because of its incompatibility on fundamental points with the Christian religion. In essence, his polemic centers mainly upon two basic issues, namely the notion of beatitude and the doctrine of mediatorship.

*Beatitude.* In contrast with Stoicism and Epicureanism which had located the source of happiness within man himself, namely virtue (*virtus*) and pleasure (*voluptas*), respectively, Platonists taught that the cause of beatitude lies outside and above man, namely in the transcendent Good or One.[24] More specifically, as Augustine notes, Plato had identified the highest good with a virtuous life which is only possible for one who knows and imitates God, and that this alone makes man happy.[25]

While Plato had correctly identified God as the object and cause of happiness, his acquiescence in the theory of the eternal cycles and of metempsychosis effectively eliminated what was for Augustine the one condition without which true happiness remains impossible, namely, that it be *unending.* "And it is certain," he says, "that Plato taught that souls are doomed to return to other bodies, even to those of animals."[26] Augustine goes on to show that the Platonist notion of happiness can only give rise to a hopeless and inescapable dilemma. For either the soul knows of its eventual return to the miseries of the body or it does not. In the former case, such awareness is itself incompatible with the full enjoyment of happiness; in the latter instance, one would have to accept the absurd conclusion that ignorance is the cause of the soul's felicity.[27] In another passage on the condition of the angels before the fall, Augustine insists again that "fear" and "error" necessarily exclude a state of happiness.[28]

A further criticism of the Platonic view of happiness stems from the Platonist anthropology which, by defining man exclusively in terms of his spiritual principle, reserved both immortality and happiness to the soul alone. In the case of Augustine himself, there is a certain irony in the fact that the one Christian doctrine which more than any other accounted for his definitive notion of man as an essential composite of body and soul was the same doctrine which Porphyry and his followers found most objectionable of all, namely, the resurrection. "It was," as the late Professor Marrou observed, "a stumbling block for the men of the time, offending the sentiments of the masses as well as the reflection of the learned."[29] Concerning the latter in particular, P. Courcelle has this to say: "Le point crucial du divorce entre la pensée päienne et le dogme chretién . . . est la résurrection de la chair."[30] Yet, for Augustine, it was a deepening comprehension of this doctrine that freed him from the vestiges of Platonic anthropology so strongly suggested in early works when the Platonist influence was strongest.[31]

The philosophical root of Porphyry's opposition to the resurrection is epitomized in the well-known aphorism, *omne corpus esse fugiendum*, which Augustine had quoted anonymously and with apparent approval, in an early work[32] but had later retracted the expression as understood by Porphyry.[33] In Book Ten of *The City of God* the aphorism is ascribed to a work of Porphyry, *De regressu animae*, a title known to us only through Augustine.[34] On the one hand, Augustine commends Porphyry for having departed from his master Plotinus on several important points. Unlike Plotinus, Porphyry had thought it might be possible for the soul to achieve eventually such a level of purification that it would never again be joined with bodies,[35] or failing that optimum eventuality, that it would at worst return only to *human* bodies.[36]

In refuting Porphyry, Augustine employs an *argumentum ad hominem* in favour of the *possibility* of the resurrection by reminding him and his followers that Plato himself held that the bodies of the lower gods, once created, will forever remain uncorrupted. In Book Thirteen (ch. 16), Augustine quotes the pertinent text of the *Timaeus* translated, as he says, by Cicero.[37] This is the celebrated discourse of God to the newly created gods which includes the following passage. "Since you have had a beginning, you cannot be immortal and indestructible; yet by no means shall you ever suffer dissolution nor shall any decree of death destroy you, nor prevail over my determination which is a stronger pledge of your perpetuity than those bodies into which you were joined when you were brought into being." In another passage from the last book of *The City of God*, Augustine repeats the same testimony and then concludes as follows: "Here again Plato demolishes the assertion of those who affirm that, since the resurrection of the body is impossible, it is unworthy of credence."[38] The Christian religion therefore had done nothing more than present as a *fact* something that was already a latent possibility in Platonism itself, namely that an immortal body could share forever in the eternal happiness of the soul.

*Mediatorship.* It is readily understandable that Augustine's more extended polemic with Porphyry should involve a doctrine that struck at the very heart of the Christian religion, namely, the belief that Christ, the Incarnate Word of God, is the one and only "way" whereby men can come to the Father and thus achieve personal salvation. Although he remained convinced that Platonism, more than other philosophies, had more closely approached the Christian faith,[39] yet any doctrine that proposed a mediatorship apart from that of Christ was of itself sufficient to turn Platonism from a philosophic ally of Christianity into a formidable and dangerous enemy.

Augustine's basic indictment of Porphyry is stated in the following apostrophe addressed to the Syrian philosopher. "Now you somehow see, though from afar and with clouded vision, the Fatherland wherein we should take up our abode, but you do not embrace the way that must take us there."[40] Augustine, of course, recognizes the futility of addressing a dead man (*scio me frustra loqui mortuo*) and adds that his words are really directed to the contemporary disciples of Porphyry who, he says, "admire and love you, either through a certain love of wisdom or from a curious interest in the [magical] arts."[41]

Although Porphyry had refused to accept the mediatorship of Christ, he did at least see that some kind of a *via universalis* was a necessity for the great majority of mankind. Better perhaps than his master Plotinus, he realized that the dialectical approach to God by philosophy alone was exceedingly difficult and only available to the few (. . . *quae ardua nimis et paucorum est*).[42]

Furthermore, he could not bring himself to believe that divine providence could have so abandoned the human race as to leave it without a *via universalis* by which souls could be liberated.[43] In his search for such a "way" Porphyry has even sought instruction from the Egyptian priest Anebo concerning the way to happiness proposed by the wisdom of Egypt.[44] In the *De regressu animae* where, as Augustine testifies, Porphyry had raised the question of a *via universalis*, he was forced to conclude that he was unable to find any historical evidence for the existence of any such way either in "the truest philosophy" of Plato or in any religious sect found among the various nations.[45]

Porphyry had drawn a sharp distinction between Christ and the Christians. He regarded Christ as only a man but one whose great piety had raised him to the ranks of the immortal whereas the Christians themselves were depraved men ensnared in the web of their errors.[46] Nor could the religion they founded provide a lasting *via universalis* since, in Porphyry's view, it would prove unable to survive the persecutions.[47] This persuasion may have been strengthened by an alleged revelation obtained through magic by the apostle Peter to the effect that after 365 years the name of Christ would no longer be held in honor.[48]

In defending the true and unique mediatorship of Christ against the Porphyrians of his time, Augustine was compelled to confront them on the common ground of the Platonic tradition which they claimed to represent. Recourse to the authority of the Gospels would have been futile since, as Augustine noted in his review of an earlier work, *De consensu Evangelistarum*, many of these had accused Christ's followers of having been led into error concerning the divinity of Christ himself.[49] Besides, as we have seen, Porphyry's severe indictment of the moral integrity of the disciple was enough to strip their testimony of any credibility.

In Book Ten of *The City of God* Augustine centers his polemical attack on Porphyry's doctrine of mediatorship upon two points: (1) no philosophy can represent itself as the "truest philosophy" (*verissima philosophia*) if it merely identifies the goal of man's happiness but fails to provide him with a clear vision of the way to reach that goal; (2) Porphyry's introduction of theurgy as a means of moral purification is a departure from authentic Platonism and is, on Porphyry's own admission, a practice incapable of achieving *complete* purification of the soul.

(1) Porphyry's insistence on the necessity of a *via universalis* and his avowal that even the "truest philosophy," namely, Platonism offered no such way placed him in a dilemma that Augustine could not fail to exploit. Porphyry makes it clear enough, says Augustine, that his personal philosophy (*eam in qua philosophatus est*) is not the "truest" and also that it contains no teaching on a *via universalis*.[50] How then, continues Augustine, can it be the "truest philosophy when it contains no such way?"[51] Porphyry's predicament was further aggravated by his conviction that divine providence could not have failed to provide a *via universalis* whereby souls are to be liberated.[52] He likewise regretted that he still found himself without the help of some supreme authority that should be followed in a matter of such great

importance.[53]

As Augustine saw it, the Christian doctrine of mediatorship, if given a fair hearing, actually met all the demands laid down by Porphyry. Its teaching on the *via universalis* not only derived from authority, which Porphyry recognized as a necessity but also from divine authority itself (*divinitus impertita est*), namely that *praestantissima auctoritas* which Porphyry had demanded for a "matter of such importance." And, unlike the particularism that characterized the teaching of the Indian and Chaldean sages, whom Porphyry had consulted, Christianity had proposed a *via universalis* that transcended geographical boundaries and extended to all nations.[54]

(2) Augustine refutes the Porphyrian teaching on mediation by pointing out that it is not only un-Platonic but also that theurgic purification through recourse to demons is untrustworthy and, in any event, admittedly inefficacious to purify the intellectual soul (*nous*) for union with God. "You did not learn this doctrine from Plato" says Augustine in a direct reference to Porphyry, "but from your Chaldean masters."[55] He also chides Porphyry who, despite his profession of Platonism, is responsible for the fact that from the vast number of men disinclined towards philosophy, more are being driven to Chaldean teachers than to the schools of Plato.[56]

Augustine attacks the doctrine of theurgic purification on two fronts. First, since Porphyry, unlike Apuleius, had attributed passions even to the higher demons, making them subject to good and evil influences, and capable of deception, their intervention can be harmful as well as beneficial.[57] Secondly, theurgic purification is not an adequate alternative to the philosophical approach since, unlike the latter, its action is limited to the "imaginative" or "spiritual" level of the soul and ceases with the death of the body. As Porphyry himself admits, the intellectual soul can only be purified of its ignorance and vices by the Paternal Intellect (*patrikon noun*).[58] Furthermore, even Porphyry was aware that the theurgic rites called *teletai* were illegal and posed dangers inherent in the practice itself.[59] By contrast, the Christian doctrine of mediatorship met all the requirements laid down by Porphyry for a *via universalis* and at the same time avoided the serious deficiencies and dangers inherent in the Porphyrian doctrine. As TeSelle has noted, "Augustine has the polemical advantage, for the Christian doctrine of the Incarnation presents a different kind of mediation, one which joins God not only to the human intellect but to the life of the body and of the imagination as well."[60]

Any critical assessment of Augustine's relationship to Neoplatonism would seem to require a distinction between the respective roles of Augustine as Christian philosopher and apologist. In constructing his classical synthesis of Christian Wisdom, which finds one of its more mature expressions in *The*

*City of God*, Augustine the philosopher found in Platonism an instrument pre-eminently suited for the task of reaching a rational understanding of revealed truth. Significantly, it was from this philosophy, as we have seen, that Augustine appropriated the threefold conception of God as the source of being, truth and happiness, a fundamental metaphysical insight that became the point of departure and unifying principle in his exposition of a Christian philosophy in *The City of God*. And, as noted earlier, it was his initial encounter with Platonism that revealed to him the method of interiority and the existence of a higher world of changeless reality which, in turn, engendered a kind of certitude that left no room for doubt. With this discovery of philosophic certitude Augustine regained his confidence in the power of reason to attain a certitude without which his efforts to elaborate a Christian philosophy would have been futile.

As an apologist of the Christian religion, however, Augustine had to vindicate the unique mediatorship of Christ and his Church against a competitive soteriology that was sure to exercise a special fascination upon men of his own time. Nor would its appeal have been limited to pagans alone, or even to prospective converts from the pagan population. As is evident from sermons to the congregation at Hippo, many Christians were still instinctively attracted to pagan practices and might easily be drawn to a religious philosophy that assigned a role to polytheism in the process of moral purification. But the danger of apostasy was not Augustine's only concern. Efforts to win over intellectual pagans to Christianity could be seriously hampered by the active presence of a philosophy which proposed a way of personal salvation that might be seen as a more acceptable alternative for many who, like Porphyry himself, were repelled by certain tenets of the Christian faith. And we know from Augustine himself that Porphyry's intellectual polemic against Christianity was well known to the pagan élite of North Africa.[61] As a recent writer has noted, "The two concerns of the apologist are both present in Augustine: defense—against attack and the prevention of apostasy, and offense—the winning of converts."[62]

As an apologist, therefore, it was incumbent upon Augustine to show, not where Platonism had *succeeded*, but where it had *failed*.

## Notes

†Originally published in *Neoplatonism and Early Christian Thought*. Ed. H. J. Blumenthal and R. A. Markus. London: Variorum Publications LTD, 1981. Pp. 160–70. Reprinted by permission of the publisher.

[1]J. H. S. Burleigh, *The City of God. A Study of St. Augustine's Philosophy* (London,

1949), 81.

[2]*Nunc intentiore nobis opus est animo multo quan erat superiorum solutione quaestionum et explicatione librorum.*

[3] . . . *contra philosophos . . . non quoslibet, sed qui apud illos excellentissima gloria clari sunt . . .* (I.36).

[4]Cf. P. Courcelle, *Les lettres Grecques en Occident* (Paris, 1948): "L'apologétique de la cité de Dieu s'adresse aux disciples de Porphyre, si nombreux dans les milieux cultivés d'Afrique" (397).

[5]Cf. *C. Academicos* III.20.43.

[6]III.19.42.

[7]Cf. *Retractationes* II.6; *De dono perseverantiae* 20.53.

[8]*Et inde admonitus redire ad memetipsum intravi in intima mea . . .* VII.10.16).

[9]VII.12.18.

[10] . . . *quoniam de Deo uno, qui fecit coelum et terram, quanto melius senserunt, tanto ceteris . . .* (VIII.12).

[11] . . . *nobiscum multa sentiunt, et de immortalitate animae et quod Deus verus mundum condiderit et de providentia eius, qua universum quod condidit regit (Ibid. I.36).*

[12] . . . *isti Deo cognito reppererunt ubi esset et causa constitutae universitatis et lux percipiendae veritatis et fons bibendae felicitatis (Ibid.* VIII.10).

[13] . . . *ut in illo inveniatur et causa subsistendi et ratio intelligendi et ordo vivendi (VIII.4).*

[14]*Exodus* 3.14 (LXX).

[15]Cf. *De civitate Dei* VIII.11.

[16]*Ibid.* XI.4.

[17]*Ibid.* VIII.7.

[18]*Lumen autem mentium esse dixerunt ad discenda omnia eundem ipsum Deum, a quo facta sunt omnia. (Ibid).*

[19]*Sed non est nobis ullus cum his excellentioribus philosophis in hac quaestione conflictus (Ibid.* X.2).

[20]*Enneads* IV.6.3.

[21]XIV.11.14.

[22]*Enneads* IV.6.3.

[23]C. Boyer, *L'idée de vérité dans la philosophie de s. Augustin* (Paris, 1940[2]): "Saint Augustin a pu prendre chez Plotin l'essentiel de sa propre théorie" (213.n.1).

[24]*Sic non est ab homine, sed super hominem, quod hominem facit beate vivere. (De civitate Dei* XIX.25).

[25]*Nunc satis sit commemorare Platonem determinasse finem boni esse secundum virtutem vivere et ei soli evenire posse, qui notitiam Dei habeat et imitationem nec essse aliam ob causam beatum. (Ibid.* VIII.8).

[26]*Ibid.* X.30. Cf. *Phaedrus* 249; *Phaedo* 81E.

[27]Cf. *De civitate Dei* X.30.

[28]*Quia scientes timor, nescientes error beatos esse utique non sinebat* (XI.11).

[29]H. I. Marrou, *The Resurrection and Saint Augustine's Theology of Human Values* (Villanova, Pa. 1966), 6–7.

[30]P. Courcelle. "Propos anti-chrétiens rapportés par s. Augustin," *Recherches Augustiniennes* (1958), 163.

[31]Definitions of the soul which reveal this mentality are found, for example, in *De quantitate animae* 13.22; *De moribus ecclesiae catholicae et de moribus Manichaeorum* I.27.52; I.4.6.

[32]*Soliloquia* I.14.24.

[33]*Retractationes* I.4.3.

[34]Recently, arguments have been adduced to show that the *De regressu animae* is merely a different title for Porphyry's *Philosophy from Oracles*. J. O'Meara, *Porphyry's Philosophy from Oracles in Augustine* (Paris, 1959).

[35] . . . *tam crebro praecipere Porphyrium omne corpus esse fugiendum, ut anima possit beata permanere cum Deo* (X.29).

[36]*Ibid.* X.30.

[37]*Timaeus* 11.40.

[38]*Ubi etiam illud evertit quod dicunt, quoniam est impossibile, ideo resurrectionem carnis non esse credendum* (XXII.26).

[39]*Nulli nobis quam isti propius accesserunt* (VIII.5).

[40]*Itaque videtis utcumque, etsi de longinquo, etsi acie caligante, patriam in qua manendum est, sed viam qua eundum est non tenetis* (X.29).

[41]*Ibid.*

[42]X.27.

[43]*Providentiam quippe divinam sine ista universali via liberandae animae genus humanum relinquere potuisse non credit* (10.32).

[44]*Ibid.* X.11. Cf. A. Sodano, *Lettera ad Anebo* (Naples, 1958).

[45]*Ibid.* X.32.

[46]*Ibid.* XIX.23.

[47]*Ibid.* X.32.

[48]*Ibid.* XVIII.53. Augustine's single reference in this passage is our only source for the existence of this specific prophecy.

[49]*Retract.* II.16. The *De consensu Evangelistarum*, written about 400, is the first of Augustine's works to mention Porphyry by name.

[50]*De civ. Dei* X.32.

[51]*Et quomodo iam potest esse verissima, qua non continetur haec via? (Ibid.).*

[52]*Ibid.*

[53]*Sentiebat enim adhuc sibi deesse aliquam praestantissimam auctoritatem, quam de re tanta sequi oporteret (Ibid.).*

[54]*Quaenam ista est universalis via, nisi quae non esse cuique genti propria, sed universis gentibus quae communis esset divinitus impertita est? (Ibid.).*

[55]*Tu autem hoc didicisti non a Platone sed a Chaldeis magistris . . .* (X.27).

[56]*Ibid.*

[57]*Ibid.*

[58]*Ibid.* X.28.

[59]*Ibid.* X.9.

[60]E. TeSelle, "Porphyry and Augustine." *Augustinian Studies* 5 (1974), 133.

61Cf. *Ep.* 102.

62E. Booth, "St. Augustine's 'notitia sui'." *Augustiniana* 27.3–4 (1977), 367.

# *De Civitate Dei*: Miscellaneous Observations†

## Frederick Van Fleteren

*De civitate Dei* has long been recognized as a seminal work in secular as well as Christian history. This *magnum opus et arduum*[1] has provided a substantial part of the foundation for Western civilization. No wonder then that, when various philosophies of the past four centuries, including contemporary secular humanism, argue with their adversaries, directly or indirectly the argument is with Augustine.

Augustine stood at the end of a dying culture. Though other of his contemporaries realized the decadence of the ancient Roman culture, Augustine was among few to realize the imminence of this demise and reasons for it, inner spiritual and moral decay, and to commit the reasons for this demise to writing. *De civitate Dei* I–VII is in some ways devoted to this topic. Yet in many respects, Augustine remained Roman to the core. Virgil and Varro, Cicero and Seneca, were to varying degrees at various times in his life heroes, formed a great part of Augustine's *Lebenswelt*, and helped shape Augustine's *Weltanschauung* throughout his life. Nevertheless, the genius of Augustine spans beyond his world to other ages and indeed into the "life to come." He realized far better than most Romans that the mutable and passing nature of Rome was but a sign of the transitory character of this life. More to the point, Augustine saw Christianity as the fulfillment of the aspirations of the best in ancient Rome. The fulfillment of these aspirations, however, took Augustine and the Western world far beyond the pale of this vale of tears.

For more than eleven centuries after Augustine's death, his works provided an intellectual substructure upon which society rested.

> In earlier books we have already spoken of the human race that God willed to create men from one man, not only to be allied by the similarity of nature, but also to be bound together by a certain bond of relationship into a harmonious unity by the bond of peace. Nor would each and every member of this race have died unless the first two men, one of whom was created from no one and the other from him, had merited death by disobedience. So great a sin was committed by them that then and there human nature was changed for the worse and was transmitted to their offspring with the chain of sin and the necessity of death. The kingdom of death had such dominion over men that a due punishment would fling all headlong also into a second death of which there is no end unless then the undue grace of God would free some. And through this deed it came about that, although so many great peoples living throughout the world with diverse ceremonies and customs are distinguished

by a complex variety of languages, arms, and clothes, no more than two kinds
of human society exist which we were rightly able to call two cities according
to our Scriptures. Indeed, one is a society of men according to the flesh,
the other according to the spirit, each wanting to live in a peace of its own
kind; and when they attain what they await, each will live in a peace of its own
kind.[2]

The world had come from God the Creator and was in the process of
returning to him. The free will of human beings under the direction of a
provident God was the moving force behind human history. Sadly, from its
inception, humankind had lost its way and was in need of a guide, indeed in
need of redemption. Christ, the divine mediator, provided this salvation.
Two loves, the love of the eternal and the love of the temporal, define two
societies. Intermingled here on earth, these two societies will attain their
ultimate destiny when Christ will come the second time. Such was
Augustine's view of the world.

For the better part of the past four centuries, however, a number of
thinkers have attempted by various intellectual means to construct a universe,
and many time an utopia, upon human reason, devoid of, or at least apart
from, God and Christ. Whether Hume or Hegel, Husserl or Heidegger, Marx
or Freud, these authors directly, many times perhaps unwittingly, challenge
Augustinian principles. Hence, a reconsideration of the central tenets of
Augustine's thought as presented in *De civitate Dei* is in order.

The canons of Augustine's thought stem principally, though of course not
exclusively, from Scripture; and the standards by which he exegizes Scripture
come, by and large, from Scripture itself: the manner in which Christ himself
and the apostles, chiefly Paul, employ the revealed word from the Old
Testament to their world inspire Augustine's exegetical principles.[3]
Augustine's christological exegesis of the psalms of *Enarrationes in Psalmos*,
for example, derives from the manner in which Christ himself, the evangelists,
and Paul find christological and messianic significance in Davidic poetry.[4]
Moreover, twice Augustine cites four possible meanings for any text in sacred
or secular literature: literal, aetiological, analogical, and allegorical.[5] The
designations may derive from Greek grammarians, but the explanations and
examples given by Augustine come directly from Scripture. Augustine uses
all these exegetical methods in *De civitate Dei*, but, in Augustine's eyes,
allegorical exegesis is most helpful in attaining the spiritual meaning in the
revealed word.[6] It is a commonplace among contemporary biblical exegetes
that allegory stems from the Greek, and not the Hebrew, world. Several
exceptions may be taken to this generalization. For example, allegories do in
fact exist in the Bible.[7] The word "allegory," in verb form, appears in
Galatians 4:24 ("These things are said through allegory"), a text influential on

Augustinian exegesis. Many times Augustine's allegorical meaning is equivalent to typological meaning, as found in the Epistle to the Hebrews[8] and practiced by some contemporary exegetes. In Augustine, Noah and the ark are types of the Church. Typological (allegorical) exegesis occurs often in *De civitate Dei* XI–XVIII. Augustine himself had used this kind of exegesis (and wanted others to use it) in refuting Manichean rejection of the Old Testament. The New Testament is the fulfillment of the Old. Both in *De civitate Dei* and elsewhere, Augustine speaks of the *auctoritas* of Scripture.[9] The Latin *auctor* comes from the same root and so, in saying that Scripture was written on divine authority, Augustine means that God is its author. God, as author, gives meanings to events and words in Scripture which are only later fully discovered. Such an understanding of Scripture is close to the *sensus plenior*, a term coined by a biblical scholar in 1927[10] to indicate fulfillment of an earlier event or text by a later one, for example the Old Testament several times being explained by the New. Augustine envisions scientific and religious/theological exegesis as complementary, not opposed.

The nature of human understanding also determines the manner in which God may speak to humankind. Because of sin, our intellects do not directly intuit divine truth. In our present condition, we can understand only through signs and allegories. Paul's statement in 1 Corinthians 13:12, that "We see now through a mirror and in riddle, but then face to face," is taken by Augustine to be a statement about the nature of human knowledge, not merely about our knowledge of God. Thus God can reveal himself and his truth to us only through sign and symbol; and we can understand what he tells us only through allegorical exegesis which in turn leads us to the spiritual meaning of Scripture.[11] Not infrequently, the use of concepts borrowed from ancient philosophy, in particular Neoplatonism, helps Augustine to discover Scripture's meaning.

The Latin *"civitas"* Augustine takes, he says, from Ps. 86:3: "Glorious things are said of you, O City of God." The term may be biblical in origin, but the Greek city-state (*polis*) and the Roman notion of society stand behind Augustine's understanding of *civitas*.[12] The ancient world, and Augustine's version of it in particular, was much more amenable to the individual as part of a larger social unit than is, for example, contemporary society with its utilitarian notion of the greatest good for the greatest number of people. Significantly, Augustine uses the Latin word meaning city as a political and social entity, not *urbs* which denotes a geographical place. The Christian *politea* is comprised of all beings who love God to the contempt of self, whether angelic or human. On this earth, the city of God is the people of God, on pilgrimage through history. Unlike its Greek predecessor, however, the Christian *polis* is not an utopia ruled by philosopher-kings here on earth, but rather the product of grace, to be realized partially in this life, but fully only in the next. It is the true Israel, "those who see God," and the authentic Jerusalem, "the vision of peace." Like "eternal life" in John's Gospel, the city of God is at once a present and future reality. While the city of God and the earthly city are social realities, paradoxically they also lie within each individual. Like many another feature in Augustine's thought, the Christian *polis* is the fulfillment of the ancient Greek and Roman *polis*, not realizable by human effort alone. The justice for which the greatest of Greeks and Romans could but strive is realized alone in that city which has Christ as its head.[13] Augustine does not visualize a theocracy such as Calvin's Geneva. Rather, the two cities form an Augustinian mystical vision of the universe.

As Augustine does not fail to remind us several times in his writings, the two cities are founded upon two loves. Indeed, the centerpiece of *De civitate Dei* is human love.

> Thus two loves make two cities: namely love of self up to a contempt for God makes an earthly city, love of God up to a contempt for self makes a heavenly city. In a word, the former glories in itself, the latter in the Lord. The former seeks glory from men; but for the latter, God, the witness of its conscience, is its greatest glory. The former lifts up its own head in its own glory; the other says to its God: "You are my glory, lifting up my head" (Ps. 3:4). In the former, the lust for power reigns in its leaders and in the nations which it subjugates; in the latter, they serve one another in love, the leaders by giving good counsel, the subjects by obeying. The former loves its own strength in its own powers; the latter says to its God: "May I love you, O Lord, my strength" (Ps. 17:2). And thus in the former its wise men, living according to man, desire goods either of its body or soul or both; or they who could know God "did not honor him as God, nor gave thanks; but they vanished into their own thoughts, and their foolish heart was obscured; saying that they were wise," that is, extolling themselves in their own wisdom under the dominion of pride, "they have become foolish; and they changed the glory of an incorruptible God into the similitude of an image of corruptible man, and of birds, and of four-legged animals, and of serpents"; for they were either leaders or followers of peoples for adoration of images of this kind: "and they adored and served a creature rather than the creator, who is blessed forever" (Rm. 1:21–25). But in the latter there is no human wisdom except piety, by which the true God is rightly adored, awaiting that reward in the society of the saints, not only men but also angels, "so that God will be all in all."                    (1 Co. 15:28)[14]

Augustine's description of the loves owes much to his skill as a rhetor; the word "*contemptum*," which sounds harsh to contemporary ears, should not be taken quite so literally. The will, of course, plays a capital role in Augustine's thought. Reflection upon Ambrose's sermons,[15] upon the problem of evil, and later upon his own conversion[16] led Augustine to see the very existence of the will and its crucial importance in human life. At the core of who a person is lies what the person loves. The kind of person we are, says Augustine, is determined not so much by what we know as by what we love. What we seek defines who we are. Two of Augustine's well-known aphorisms speak of love. (*Amor meus, pondus meus*; "My love is my weight."[17] *Dilige et quod uis fac*; "Love and do what you will."[18]) The two major poles of Augustinian thought, the human will and divine grace, are both biblical in inspiration. How much Augustine's notion of love owes to the Platonic idea of *eros* must remain a matter of conjecture. But certain it is that Scripture is the source for Augustine's emphasis on grace and love. Stress on the importance of the will and grace is a fundamental inversion of ancient Greek thought where intellect, and intellect alone, predominates, and reason unaided can save humankind. Unlike the intellectualism of the ancient Greek world (Plato's division of his ideal republic into three classes according to each one's intellectual capacity[19] would be an example), Augustine divides people according to their loves. Such a division finds scriptural basis in Paul's distinction between the spiritual and carnal, the old and new, and the interior and exterior person.[20] Can John the apostle, as is many times the case, be so very far away?[21] Augustine finds symbols of the two cities in the older and younger son in the parable of the Prodigal found in Luke's Gospel.[22] That Augustine saw himself, and indeed all humanity, as prodigals in the *Confessiones* indicates to us once again a parallel between that work and *De civitate Dei*. We find analogous groupings of humankind in Tertullian[23] and Origen,[24] and in the *Epistle to Diognetus*.[25] In Augustine's writings, we find it implicitly in *De libero arbitrio* and explicitly in *De vera religione*;[26] the idea remains an almost constant theme throughout his works. In *De civitate Dei* the definition of virtue as the order of love appears;[27] the Song of Songs lies directly in the background.[28] Ultimately, acts and practices which are not ordered to love of God or to true love of others are not virtues at all, but only splendid vices.[29]

The grouping of humankind into those who love the heavenly and those who love the earthly in such a way as to take them away from the heavenly is essentially eschatological. On a phenomenological level here on earth, the two cities intermingle; only at the end of time will the membership in them be apparent to all. Scholars have speculated concerning the existence of a third city and to ask whether the Church and the *civitas Dei* on this earth are synonymous.[30] As much as some in today's secular society might want to uncover such an entity in *De civitate Dei*,[31] the existence of a *tertium quid*, a third city, a secular city, finds no textual support in the work itself. As Marrou so ably pointed out some forty years ago,[32] what we have is the empirical datum of the intertwining of the two cities prior to the eschatological separation. On another level, in a sense *De civitate Dei* may be considered the first work on ecclesiology in Church history. The people of God, as it journeys through history to its ultimate goal, is the basis for the final twelve books of the work. Augustine does not answer—nor should he be expected to do so—many questions which are asked only in later centuries. In *De civitate Dei*, the city of God on earth is many times identified with the Church, but this identification is not absolute[33]—Augustine's church is still the church of sinners, the *ecclesia permixta*.[34] The *ecclesia* here on earth is a symbol, sign, or sacrament of the kingdom. Those who love God live in his city; the city of God lies within the Church and the Church in turn is the sign here on earth of the fullness of the city to come. Throughout the *Enarrationes in Psalmos* and elsewhere, Augustine amplifies this ecclesiology by referring often to *Christus totus*, what we refer to as the mystical body.[35] And surely the indwelling of the Spirit within the individual Christian occurs often in Augustine's writings.

Much has been written on Augustinian political theory in *De civitate Dei*. Though Augustine views eternal moral principle as bearing upon the conduct of the state, his purpose is not to sketch guidelines for the establishment of a political entity. However, there are political implications in the work which have been explored since medieval times. On the one hand, Augustine quite clearly belongs to the classical Western tradition in believing that human beings are social by nature. *Civitas* is a fundamentally social notion. Likewise, justice, the underlying moral principle upon which society should be constructed, emphasizes the societal. Finally, the social nature of the origin, development, and final goal of the city of God could hardly be more apparent. On the other hand, unlike his Greek predecessors, Augustine finds the origin of the state in human sinfulness. From an early work where he off-handedly remarks that one rational being was not set except by cupidity[36] through to *De civitate Dei*, Augustine roots the necessity for government in sinfulness. Augustine is no Hobbesian: humans are social by nature. But he is no Platonist either (on this matter): prelapsarian beings did not need government. While woman is subject to man before the fall, both are made in the image of God.[37] The balanced Augustinian judgment is well captured in *De civitate Dei*: "nothing is so anti-social by perversion, or so social by nature, as the human race."[38]

Recent attempts to focus attention on the origins of humankind throughout Augustine's works notwithstanding, human destiny, not its origin, is Augustine's principal concern. From *De beata uita*, through *De libero arbitrio*,[39] to *De civitate Dei*, in Augustinian thought human beings are on a journey to a goal of happiness. *De civitate Dei* focuses our attention on this central theme. True enough, Augustine considers the origin of humanity in the preface of his first finished work, *De beata uita*.[40] Throughout his life Augustine was quite concerned with God as creator and the interpretation of the first few chapters of Genesis. The Pelagian controversy had forced Augustine to formulate more precisely his views on the fall in the garden of Eden. Augustine spends *De civitate Dei* XI–XIV speaking of the origin of the two cities. By his almost exclusive focus on preexistence and fall of the human soul in Augustine, Robert O'Connell has fundamentally skewed Augustine's thought.[41] True enough, Augustine adopts some philosophical language from his predecessors or contemporaries, especially in his earliest writings, which betray a tendency in the source authors to think of the human soul as pre-existent. Augustine admits as much in *Retractationes*.[42] But whether he presents humanity as in an ascent or on an odyssey, the ultimate goal of union with God remains paramount. In *De civitate Dei* but one end exists for the individual, the vision of peace, union with God, accomplishable solely through the grace of God. This spirit of Augustine, so ably examined in our own century by the late Henri Cardinal de Lubac,[43] can serve as a correction to the theology of nature and supernature of the last three centuries, whatever the merits of the latter understanding may be. Despite contemporary accusations of extreme eschatologism and other-worldliness made against Augustine, his theology establishes the Church as existing very much in this world.[44]

Concupiscence takes on significance in *De civitate Dei* and Augustine's later works; it is at the essence of the earthly city. The tendency toward evil which the human heart has prior to committing any personal sin is the result of Adam's sin. Biblical evidence for such a view abounds.[45] Ultimately, Augustine's conception of concupiscence owes much to St. Paul.[46] Moreover, Augustine is acutely aware that many other patristic writers, Origen, Gregory Nazianzen, and Ambrose to name but three, intimate such alienation in their own writings. As Augustine under the pressure of the Pelagian controversy develops a fuller explanation of original sin and the fall, the place of concupiscence in his theology expands. But conception of a human tendency toward evil as a punishment for sin is found as early as *De vera religione*.[47] In the Platonic tradition, the intellect has been darkened by a fall into the material. Such a fall affects the individual morally also, although the distinction between intellectual and moral is somewhat blurred in the Platonic, and indeed the entire Greek, tradition. Augustine was familiar with such thought and at times even used such terminology. Distinct differences, however, exist between the two theories, not the least of which is that the Platonic and Neoplatonic person comes to this world, according to some passages, precisely because of sin; Augustine's theology, especially in its more developed forms, derives principally from his biblical exegesis. Part of the atmosphere in which this theology develops is Neoplatonic; it would be unreasonable to maintain that such an atmosphere exercises no influence on Augustine's theology.

The works of Plato (which, save for Cicero's transation of *Timaeus*, Augustine almost certainly never read directly), of Plotinus, and of Porphyry (the precise scope and nature of the later two have been the subject of many a treatise over the past century), Augustine esteems as the best of ancient philosophy. Augustine's reading of the Platonists had helped convert him to, and ultimately found, monasticism. He learned much more from them in metaphysics, psychology, and ethics than can profitably be outlined in a short essay; but their proclamation of a *summum bonum*, of happiness as consisting in the possession of that Good, and the search for a means to attain it, inadequate though their conceptions of the way of salvation may have been, earned his greatest respect.[48] The search of the anti-Christian Porphyry (the greatest Platonist of them all) for a universal way of salvation Augustine found fulfilled in Christ. His admiration for them extends even to calling the *Platonici* of all philosophers the closest to the Christians,[49] even though they only vaguely recognized the nature of the triune God. In *Confessiones*, Augustine begins his odyssey toward Christianity by reading Cicero's *Hortensius* and is indispensably facilitated in it by his encounter with the *libri Platonicorum*. Though Cicero did not believe that human beings could attain ultimate wisdom, it was because of reading Cicero's protreptic to philosophy that the young Augustine began to pursue wisdom itself. In reading the Neoplatonists books some thirteen years later, Augustine attempted ascents of the mind to union with Light and Truth. Some years thereafter, he ascertained that the attainment of Wisdom, union with Truth, could come about only through the grace of Christ. Augustine's position on the extent to which attainment of wisdom and ascent of the mind to God was due to the grace of God evolved during the ten year period after his conversion. Though Augustine recognized the influence and even in some sense the necessity of grace in achieving salvation quite early in his works (as he repeatedly tells us in *Retractationes* I), it was *Ad Simplicianum*, in commenting on Romans 7-8, that he first wrote of the pervasive influence of grace on human redemption. Only in *Ad Simplicianum* does he finally come to a full realization that the ultimate goal in human life is attainable solely and whollly through a freely given divine gift.[50] As Augustine himself puts it in *Retractationes*, "In answering this question, I labored very much in behalf of the free choice of the human will, but the grace of God won out."[51] In *Confessiones*, begun approximately a year later and finished no later than 401, under the guise of an autobiography Augustine quite clearly writes that this goal presented him by the ancient eudaemonistic philosophical tradition could be attained only by the grace of God through the incarnation.[52] (Though Pelagius is not mentioned by name in *De civitate Dei*, no doubt Augustine's augmentation against him stands behind some of what is written in this work. Pelagius and his followers had, in Augustine's eyes, sought to contradict the African bishop's work of a lifetime.) "You resist the proud, but give grace to the humble." This phrase, taken from 1 Peter 5:5 and James 4:6 (cf. Job 22:29; Proverbs 3:4), found at the beginning of and throughout *Confessiones*,[53] and also occurring in *De civitate Dei*,[54] represents a major theme in both works. In *De civitate Dei*, he applied his theological datum to humankind as a whole: the grace of God fulfills the ancient Hellenic aspirations for salvation which reach their apex, in Augustine's view, in the writings of Porphyry. Christ was the universal way of salvation for which the *Platonici* had been looking. Augustine's own experience, reflected upon through long years and interpreted in light of Scripture and the ancient philosophical tradition, formed the basis of his interpretation of human history. As Augustine saw the fruition of his reading of Plotinus and Porphyry in the grace of God and the Scriptures, so he saw Christ's Incarnation as the means to the fulfillment of the ancient ambitions of humankind.

*De civitate Dei* stands as a monument to Augustine's belief that human reason unaided cannot achieve the desired end of complete understanding of truth. *Crede ut intelligas*[55] remains the Augustinian dictum to his final day. Faith forms the basis for all constructive human thought. The ultimate reason why the secularism and scientism of the nineteenth and twentieth centuries, from Karl Marx to Sigmund Freud, from Rudolph Bultmann to Raymond Brown find Augustine their chief antagonist is his anti-rationalist temper. Augustine looked around and saw the greatest monument to humankind, the Roman Empire, as destined to go the way of all other human constructions. Does the Western world desire to look at its decadent cities, its decaying families, and its skeptical epistemological and social philosophies, and see in these phenomena the seeds of its own destruction? Will Christianity return to its pre-Augustinian existence in the catacombs? Undoubtedly we are witnessing the struggle of the city of God and the earthly city, which Augustine foresaw so many centuries ago, worked out in our own day.

Oddly enough, one of Augustine's adversaries in *De civitate Dei* is a man of much the same temper, from whom he had learned many things, albeit most of them indirectly, Origen.[56] Augustine, as do contemporary scholars, distinguishes Origen from Origenism, the latter being an unnuanced compendium of Origen's teachings brought together by his disciples. Origenism gradually came to influence the West in the fourth century. The essential reason for Augustine's confrontation with Origen and Origenism was the latter's at times too facile concordism between Greek philosophy and Scripture. Contemporary researchers still have much to learn about the manner in which Christian communities of patristic times communicated. What methodologies and doctrines of Origen had permeated the intellectual atmosphere, let us say, of Ambrose's Milan during the ninth decade of the fourth century? How thoroughly? How is it that Ambrosian biblical exegesis comes to owe so much to Origen? Augustinian allegorical exegesis and search for spiritual meaning in Scripture is not so distant from Origen's practice, as he learned of it through Amborse. It was in confrontation with Origen that Augustine finally sorted out, at least partially, his views on the origin of the human soul.

Augustine sees God as providential overseer of events in the lives of individuals and humankind as whole. From the time of *De libero arbitrio*, Augustine recognized the existence of an eternal law.[57] An order has been established in the universe by divine providence. When Augustine recounts events, God's intervention in and through human affairs is in evidence, in his reading of *Hortensius* to the final conversion in the garden in Milan, as well as in various other conversion stories in *Confessiones*.[58] In *De civitate Dei*, Augustine writes of the same kind of divine intervention within human history. Most, though not all, of these providential interventions are found in Scripture, for example when God intervened through Abraham, Moses, David, the prophets, and finally Christ. Augustine's interpretation of divine providence in human events is influenced by sacred Scripture, the *Enneads* of Plotinus, and quite possibly *Philosophy from Oracles* of Porphyry.

Contemporary interest in peace and justice has led to several discussions of the historical development of just war theory and Augustine's part in it. Theories about war of course do not begin or end with Augustine. Soldiers constitute one of the classes in Plato's ideal republic,[59] and apparently even an offensive war for additional property was justifiable. Cicero also countenanced war as sometimes just.[60] Augustine, himself, was not a warmonger. Indeed, *De civitate Dei* I–V can not be read without realizing that Augustine saw many of ancient Rome's wars and incidents within them as morally reprehensible. But neither is Augustine a complete pacifist. Augustine, as indeed the Bible, accepts soldiers as a legitimate part of society, rendering a legitimate service in it.[61] The origin of war lies in human sinfulness. The just war theory as it comes to us principally through Robert Bellarmine is not found in Augustine in any precise sense, but the Bishop of Hippo justifies certain wars, at least potentially.[62] The goal of war—indeed the goal of all humankind—is peace, the *tranquillitas ordinis* of which the Stoics spoke.[63] War is tolerated as a means to peace.[64] The evolution of a sophisticated just war theory would demand the development of a refined theory of justification of physical and moral evil which begin to take place only in the High Middle Ages. Augustine is not the author of just war theory in any absolute sense; he is however part of a Western tradition which justifies certain wars, while not extending such justification necessarily to all deeds within those wars.

What has been said here indicates the breadth of Augustine's thought and the seminal nature of *De civitate Dei* in the history of Christianity and the world. To a secular world, largely devoid of spiritual dimensions, *De civitate Dei* points to loves found deep in the human heart. To a theological world, concentrating on the social gospel and not seeing the importance of a larger vision, *De civitate Dei* points to the cosmic nature of Christianity. To a scholarly biblical world, given to determining only the literal meaning of the text and skeptical as to its historical accuracy, *De civitate Dei* points to a fuller meaning of scriptural passages. To a political world, seeking almost exclusively the protection of individual rights and erection of an utopia on earth, *De civitate Dei* reminds us of the common good and the inability of humankind, unaided by grace, to save itself. To a society, largely devoid of moral principle and skeptical of eternal truth, *De civitate Dei* indicates the existence of a world of truth and principle. Finally, to a warring world, Augustine presents us with the Heavenly Jerusalem, the vision of peace, where Israel, "those who see God," will be brought by the grace of God. In the final analysis, *De civitate Dei*, despite its extraordinary length and its frequent reference to events completely forgotten today, presents a vision of humankind as valid now as it was more than fifteen hundred years ago.

## Notes

†New essay written especially for this collection.
[1]*De civitate Dei* I, 1.
[2]*De civitate Dei* XIV, 1: *PL* XLI, 403: *Diximus jam in superioribus libris ad humanum genus, non solum naturae similitudine sociandum, verum etiam quadam cognationis necessitudine in unitatem concordem pacis vinculo colligandum, ex homine uno Deum voluisse homines instituere: neque hoc genus fuisse in singulis quibusque moriturum, nisi duo primi, quorum creatus est unus ex nullo, altera ex illo, id inobedientia meruissent: a quibus admissum est tam grande peccatum, ut in deterius eo natura mutaretur humana, etiam in posteros obligatione peccati et mortis necessitate transmissa. Mortis autem regnum in homines usque adeo dominatum est, ut omnes in secundam quoque mortem, cujus nullus est finis, poena debita praecipites ageret, nisi inde quosdam indebita Dei gratia liberaret. At per hoc factum est, ut cum tot tantaeque gentes per terraraum orbem diversis moribusque viventes, multiplci linguarum, armorum, vestium varietatae*

*distinctae; non tamen amplius quam duo quaedam genera humanae societatis existerent, quas civitates duas secundum Scripturas nostras merito appellare possimus. Una quippe est hominum secundum carnem, altera secundum spiritum vivere in sui cujusque generis pace volentium; et cum id quod expetunt assequuntur, in sui cujusque generis pace viventium.*

3The benchmark work on Augustine's exegesis is yet to be written. In preparation is *Collectanea Augustiniana V, Augustine: Biblical Exegete* (New York: Peter Lang Inc.) in which international scholars examine the background, principles, technique, and influence of the Augustinian hermeneutic.

4Virtually every Psalm is given a christological significance by Augustine, whether referring to the person of Christ or to his body the Church. See, for example, *Enarratio in Psalmum VIII* 13: *Et haec regula* [that allegorical meanings of words in Scripture must be taken from the context] *in omni allegoria retinenda est, ut pro sententia praesentis locis consideretur quod per similitudinem dicitur; haec est enim dominica et apostolica disciplina. Enarratio in Psalmum I* I, 1; *Enarratio in Psalmum III* I, 1; *Enarratio in Psalmum IX*, 1. Places where Christ or the authors of the scriptures use Old Testament texts to refer to Christ are too numerous to mention: cf. for example Mtt.1:23; 2:6; 2:15; 2:18; 3:3; Jn. 12:15; 19:24; 19:36–37; Rm. 1:17; 3:11 ff.

5*De utilitate credendi* III, 5; *De Genesi ad litteram, imperfectus liber* II, 5.

6*De civitate Dei* XV, 2: *Haec forma intelliendi de apostolica auctoritate descendens locum nobis aperit, quemadmodum Scripturas duorum testamentorum, Veteris et Novi accipere debeamus. Pars enim quaedam terrenae civitatis imago coelestis civitatis effecta est, non se significando, sed alteram; et ideo serviens. Non propter se ipsam, sed propter aliam significandam est instituta; et praecedente alia significatione et ipsa praefigurans praefigurata est.*

7Mtt 13:4–23; 24–30; 36–43; Mk 4:1–20; Lk 8:4–15; Gal 4:24; 1 Co 10:11.

8Hb 9:9 10:1.

9The juxtaposition of *auctoritas* and its cognate *auctor* occur more than two hundred times in Augustine's writings. See, for example, *Retractationes* I, 11; *Confessiones* VI, 5; *Epistula* XXIII 7; *Epistula* XXVIII 3; *Epistula* XXIX 6; *Epistula* LIV 2; *Epistula* LV 19; *Epistula* CXLIII 7; *Epistula* CXLVII 5; *De civitate Dei* XI, 1; 3; 9; 23; 33; 34; XII, 9; XIV, 7; XV, 1; 2; 11; 23; XVIII, 42; 53.

10The *sensus plenior* was first propounded by Andrés Fernández Truyols in 1927.

11A full discussion of Augustine's exegesis and use of 1 Co 13:12 may be found in my "*Per speculum et in aenigmate.*" *Augustinian Studies* (1992): 53–98.

12Cf. *Republic*, passim; *De re publica* as cited in *De civitate Dei* II, 19.

13*De civitate Dei* II, 21; XIX, 21–24.

14*De civitate Dei* XIV, 28: *Fecerunt itaque civitates duas amores duo; terrenam scilicet amor sui usque ad contemptum Dei, coelestem vero amor Dei usque ad contemptum sui. Denique illa in se ipsa, haec in Domino gloriatur. Illa enim quaerit ab hominibus gfloriam: huic autem deus conscientiae testis, maxima est gloria. Illa in gloria sua exaltat caput suum: haec dicit Deo suo: "Gloria mea, et exaltans caput meum* (Ps. 3:4). *Illi in principibus ejus, vel in eis quas subjugat nationibus dominandi libido dominatur; in hac serviunt invicem a charitatis, et praepositi consulendo, et subditi obtemperando. Illa in suis potentibus diligit virtutem suam: haec dicit Deo suo, "Diligam te, Domine, virtus* *mea"* (Ps. 17:2). *Ideoque in illa sapientes ejus secundum hominem viventes, aut corporis aut animi sui bona, aut ultriusque sectati sunt; aut qui potuerunt cognoscere Deum, "non ut Deum honoraverunt, vel gratias egerunt; et evanuerunt in cogitationibus suis, et obscuratum est insipiens cor eorum: dicentes se esse sapientes," id est dominante sibi superbia in sua sapientia sese extollentes, "stulti facti sunt; et immutaverunt gloriam incorruptibilis Dei in similitudinem imaginis corruptibilis hominis, et volucrum, et quadrupedem, et serpentium": ad hujuscemodi enim simulacra adoranda vel duces populorum, vel sectatores fuerunt: "et coluerunt atque servierunt creaturae potius quam Creatori, qui est benedictus in saecula"* (Rm. 1:21–25). *In hac autem nulla est hominis sapientia, nisi, pietas, qua recte colitur verus Deus, id expectans praemium in societate sanctorum, non solum hominum, verum etiam Angelorum, "ut sit Deus omnia in omnibus"* (1 Co 15:28).

[15]*Confessiones* VII, iii, 5.

[16]*Confessiones* VIII, viii, 20–xi, 27.

[17]*Confessiones* XIII, ix, 10; cf. *Confessiones* IV, 14; *Epistula LV* 10–11; *Epistula CLVII* 2; *De Genesi ad litteram* IV, 4; *De civitate Dei* XI, 16; 28; *De trinitate* VI, 10.

[18]*In Iohannis epistolam ad Parthos tractatus* 7.

[19]*Republic* III.

[20]The Pauline distinction between carnal and spiritual men is found, among other places, in Rm 8:4–5 and Gal 5:17; his distinction between the old and new man is found in Eph. 4:22–24 and Col 3:9–10; Paul refers to the interior man in Rm. 7:22 and Eph. 3:16.

[21]See, for example, 1 Jn 2:15ff.; 4:7–8.

[22]*Quaestiones Evangeliorum* II, 33.

[23]*Apologeticum* XXXVII.

[24]*Contra Celsum* VII, 75.

[25]*Epistula ad Diognetum* V.

[26]*De vera religione* XXVI, 48; XXXVIII, 51.

[27]*De civitate Dei* XV, 22. See also *Sermo* XXXVII.

[28]Sg 2:4.

[29]*De civitate Dei* XIV, 9; XIX, 25.

[30]A good short expose and bibliography on these questions can be found in F. J. Thonnard, *La Cité de Dieu. Bibliothèque Augustinienne* 37, 748, n. 18 and 774, n. 28.

[31]See, for example, the writings of Charles Journet, cited in the bibliography of the previous note.

[32]H.-I. Marrou, "La thélogie de l'histoire." *Augustinius Magister*, III, 193–204.

[33]For the identification of the city of God and the Church on earth, see *Enarratio in Psalmum CLIV* 4; *De civitate Dei* XVI, ii, 3; XX, ix, 3; however, for the distinction, see *De civitate Dei* I, ii, 2; *Sermo CCXIV* 11.

[34]*Epistula CVIII* 3; *De doctrina christiana* III, 32; *Adnotationes in Iob* 38; *Sermo CCXXIII*; *Sermo CCLI*; *De diuersis quaestionibus octoginta tribus* LXXXI; *De fide et operibus* III, 4; V, 7; XXVII, 49, among many others. The term arises in Augustine at the time of the Donatist controversy. Augustine applies the various texts of the gospels speaking of the mixing of good and evil to the church; the Donatists to the Church and the world. A certain similarity exists between Donatism and Pelagianism in the sense that both view the church on earth as pure and unspotted, not the Church

of sinners. Augustine's triumph over both is a victory of the ordinary churchgoer over ecclesiastical elitism.

35In *Iohannis evangelium tractatus* XXVIII, 1; In *Epistulam Iohannis ad Parthos tractatus* 1; *Enarratio in Psalmum III* 9; *Enarratio in Psalmum XVII* 2; 51; *Enarratio in Psalmum XXVI* 2; *Enarratio in Psalmum XXX* 2; *Sermo I* 3; 4; *Sermo II* 1; *Sermo III* 5; *Enarratio in Psalmum XXXVII* 6; *Enarratio in Psalmum LIV* 3; *Enarratio in Psalmum LVI* 1; 6; *Enarratio in Psalmum LVIII, Sermo I* 2; 5; *Enarratio in Psalmum LXXIV* 4; 5; *Enarratio in Psalmum C* 3, and so forth.

36*De immortalitate animae* XIII, 21. From the very beginning of his experience with Neoplatonism, Augustine accepts the hierarchy of being. As such, one rational being, *qua* rational being, is not superior to any other. Obviously, some intellects perceive the truth more accurately than others; in this sense, one intellect is superior to another. But this superiority is a difference in degree, whereas the superiority of human beings to the beast is a difference of kind.

37*De Genesi contra Manichaeos* I (194); *De Genesis ad litteram* III, 19; 22; VI, 4; *Contra Faustum* XXIV, 2.

38*De civitate Dei* XII, 27: *Nihil enim est quam hoc genus tam discordiosum vitio, tam sociale natura.*

39*De libero arbitrio* III, 21.

40*De beata vita* I, 1–4.

41The literature on the controversy between Robert O'Connell, SJ on the one hand, and most of the Augustinian scholars in the world on the other, especially G. Madec, G. O'Daly, and myself, on the pre-existence and fall of the soul in the works of Augustine, is voluminous.

42*Retractationes* I, 1–11.

43H. de Lubac, *The Mystery of the Supernatural.* Trans. Rosemary Sheed. New York: Herder and Herder, 1967; and *Augustinianism and Modern Theology.* Trans. Lancelot Sheppard. London: Geoffrey Chapman, 1969.

44For recent accusations of extreme eschatologism, see, for example, M. Scanlon, "Augustine, A Retrieval." *Augustinian Studies* 20 (1989): 61–92.

45Romans 5:12–21 aside, see, for example, Ps. 50:7.

46See Rm 6:12; 7:7–8; Ga 5:17, 24; Co 3:5.

47*De vera religione* XII, 23; XXIII, 44; XL, 76.

48See, for example, *De civitate Dei* X, 23–32, where Augustine praises Porphyry in this regard. The best analysis of this section in Augustine remains J. J. O'Meara, *Porphyry's Philosophy from Oracles in the Works of Augustine.* Paris: Etudes Augustiniennes, 1959.

49*De vera religione* IV, 7.

50*Ad Simplicianum* I, passim.

51*Retractationes* II, i, 1: *PL* XXXII, 629: *In cujus m quaestionis solutione laboratum est quidem pro libero arbrio voluntatis humanae, sed vicit Dei gratia.*

52Among other places, see especially *Confessiones* VII, xx, 26; VIII, xi, 27.

53*Confessiones* I, i, 1; IV, 3; 15; VII, 5; 9; X, 36.

54*De civitate Dei* I, *Praefatio*; XI.33; XVII, 4; XIX, 27.

<sup>55</sup>This phrase or its equivalent is a virtual refrain in Augustine's writings. It is one of the motifs of his writings from the very beginning. See *Contra Academicos* III, xx, 43; *De libero arbitrio* I, 4; *Epistula CXX* 1; In *Iohannis evangelium tractatus* XIX, 15; XXIX, 6; *Enarratio in Psalmum CXXX* 13; *Sermo XLIII*; *Sermo LXXXIX*; *Sermo CXVIII*. Of course, it is the underlying theme of *De trinitate*.

<sup>56</sup>*De civiate Dei* XI, 23; XXI, 17. See also, *Retractationes* I, 7; II, 44; *Epistula XL* 6; *Epistula LXXXII* 3; *Epistula CLXIX* 4; *Epistula CCIIA* 4; *Quaestionum in heptateuchum* I, *quaestio* IV; *De haeresibus* 42; 43; 83; *Conta Priscillianistas et Origenistas* passim; *De gestis Pelagii* III, 10; *Contra Iulianum, opus imperfectum* V; VI. Augustine was aware of many opinions of earlier and contemporary Church writers even in his earliest writings, though he may not have been acquainted with them *qua* any particular Church writer.

<sup>57</sup>*De libero arbitrio* I, 5; 5; 14; 15; 16; *Quaestionum in heptateuchum* II, *quaestio* 55 III, *quaestio* 16; *Sermo LXXXI*; *Contra Faustum* XXII, 27; 30; 43; 44; 61; 73; 78.

<sup>58</sup>See F. Van Fleteren, "St. Augustine's Theory of Conversion." *Augustine: The Second Founder of the Faith, Collectanea Augustiniana* I. New York: Peter Lang Inc., 1990. Pp. 65–80.

<sup>59</sup>*Republic* III 373e ff.

<sup>60</sup>The justness of some wars is implicit in *De re publica*, for example.

<sup>61</sup>*De catechizandis rudibus* XXIII; *De oere monachorum* VII, 8; *De civitate Dei* II, 19.

<sup>62</sup>*De ordine* I, iv, 11–xii, 19.

<sup>63</sup>*De civitate Dei* XIX, 13.

<sup>64</sup>*Epistula CXXXVIII*; *Epistula CCXX*; *De civitate Dei* XIX, 12.

# Writings by Augustine

The standard work on the chronology of Augustine's writings is that of S. Zarb, *Chronologia operum sancti Augustini* (Rome: Pontificium Institutum "Angelicum," 1934). See also, E. Lamirande, "Un siecle et demi d'etudes sur l'ecclesiologie de S. Augustin." *Revue des études augustiniennes* 8 (1962), pp. 1–124; A. M. LaBonnardiere, *Recherches de chronologie augustinienne* (Paris: Etudes augustiniennes, 1965).

Latin texts may be found in the following series. *Sancti Aurelii Augustini, opera omnia. Patrologia Latina* (PL). General editor J. P. Migne. Vols. 32–47. Paris, 1841–1845. Also, *Corpus Scriptorum Ecclesiasticorum Latinorum* (CSEL), Vienna, 1899 —; *Corpus Christianorum, Series Latina* (CCSL), The Hague, Nijhoff, 1953 —; and *Bibliotheque Augustinienne* (BA), Paris, 1947 —.

A.D.

386      *Contra academicos* (*Against the Academics*)

386      *De beata vita* (*The Happy Life*)

386      *De ordine* (*On Order*)

386/87    *Soliloquia* (*Soliloquies*)

386/430   *Epistulae* (*Letters*)

387      *De dialectica* (*Logic*), *De grammatica* (*Grammar*)

387      *De immortalitate animae* (*The Immortality of the Soul*)

387/88    *De quantitate animae* (*The Magnitude of the Soul*)

387/89    *De moribus ecclesiae catholicae et de moribus Manichaeorum* (*The Customs of the Catholic Church and the Customs of the Manichees*)

387/90    *De musica* (*On Music*)

388/89    *De genesi contra Manichaeos* (*Commentary on Genesis Against the Manichees*)

388/95    *De diversis quaestionibus LXXXIII* (*Eighty-three Various Questions*)

388/95    *De libero arbitrio voluntatis* (*The Free Choice of the Will*)

389      *De magistro* (*The Teacher*)

391      *De vera religione* (*On True Religion*)

391/430   *Sermones* (*Sermons*)

392      *Acta contra Fortunatum Manichaeum* (*Proceedings Against Fortunatus the Manichee*)

392      *De utilitate credendi* (*The Usefulness of Belief*)

392/93    *De duabus animabus contra Manichaeos* (*On "Two Souls" Against the Manichees*)

392/426   *Enarrationes in Psalmos* (*Sermons on the Psalms*)

# Suggestions for Further Reading

As one might expect, there has been an enormous output about Augustine and his writings. The following annotated list of recommended additional readings focuses on works dealing with *The City of God*. Full information for these titles is given in the Selected Bibliography. The bibliography should also be consulted for other important studies.

In *The Sources of the First Ten Books of Augustine's* De Civitate Dei, S. Angus offers a comprehensive examination of the first ten books of Augustine's text. The work has three parts. The first part, "Literary Sources in Books I–X," provides a detailed discussion of all the sources, with the exception of the Bible, used by Augustine in Books I–X of *De civitate Dei*. The second part, "Annotations to Books I–X," contains information about Augustine's sources that did not fit into the discussion in part one. Parts one and two supplement each other. The third part of the study, "Augustine's Knowledge of Greek," discusses the extent of Augustine's use of Greek thought in his writings. In an extended six-part introduction to *The City of God*, published by Dent & Sons in 1934, Ernest Barker offers a discerning and complete discussion of the life of Augustine and the historical circumstances that gave rise to his writing of the book. He also treats the connection between Augustine's ideas about a transcendent metaphysical "city" and similar ideas expressed by earlier philosophers. Barker points out that Augustine took over from earlier thinkers the notion of four grades of human society—the *domus* or household, *civitas* or state, *orbis terrae* or whole earth, and the *mundus* or universe. Barker traces the history of this idea of four distinct grades of human collectivity and shows the similarities and differences between the views of previous writers on the subject and Augustine's use of the concept. J. H. S. Burleigh's The City of God: *A Study of St. Augustine's Philosophy*, is a useful general introduction to *The City of God*. Burleigh's approach is to delineate the arguments made by Augustine in *The City of God* by means of a running commentary on each of the work's twenty-two books. Augustine's statements are first summarized and then compared with the views and attitudes of his predecessors and his contemporaries. Burleigh concludes that while it must be admitted Augustine is essentially anti-historical in his explanation of human events, he nonetheless develops a comprehensive notion of a Christian universal history, a history that is ordained by divine providence and which follows a divine plan. Joseph Rickaby, in *St. Augustine's* City of God: *A View of the Contents*, also offers a general overview of the contents of each of the twenty-two books of *De civitate Dei*. Here too the approach in each of the commentaries is to compare Augustine's ideas with the views of his contemporaries and his predecessors on the one hand, and in relation to their historical context on the other. Two interesting appendices are included in this work. Appendix I, "Natural Wonders, As They Appeared in St. Augustine's Time," and Appendix II, "A List of Miracles, Coming Under St. Augustine's Own Notice." Christopher Dawson's "St. Augustine and His Age," originally published in 1930, remains an essential text for students of *De civitate Dei*. Divided into two parts, the first part, "The Dying World," focuses on the historical events which inspired Augustine to write *The City of God*; the second part, "The City of God," aims to show that Augustine's work "is the one great work of Christian antiquity which professedly deals with the relation of the state and of human society in general to Christian principles." Dawson concludes that the originality of *De civitate Dei* consists in the fact that "it unites in a coherent system two distinct intellectual traditions which had hitherto proved irreconcilable." The Greeks had a theory of society and a political philosophy but not a philosophy of history. The Christians, on the other hand, had no theory of society or political philosophy but they did have a theory of history. Augustine, it is suggested, reconciled these traditions in his theory of universal history based upon the concept of two universal societies which "intermingle" in human history. The important discussion by Etienne Gilson, in his Foreword to *The City of God*, published by Doubleday in 1958, cannot be overlooked. Gilson focuses his attention on what he regards as Augustine's main theme, namely, the description "of a universal religious society," a society that stands in direct contrast to temporal materialism. He concludes that Augustine cannot be called a philosopher of history; rather, since his explanation of universal history "derives its light from Revelation, he was . . . actually a theologian of history." Yet, because he develops a concept of "universal history" it can be argued that the "first theologian of history . . . [is actually] the father of all philosophies of history, even if he had no such intention."

Despite its apology that "it raises no claim to originality," the extended study by Norman Baynes, *The Political Ideas of St. Augustine's* De Civitate Dei, first published in 1936, offers a solid foundation to the problem of politics in *De civitate Dei*. The author reviews the possible sources from which Augustine seems to have borrowed the concept of two *civitates* before turning to a study of his particular use of the term *civitas*. Baynes also deals with the often neglected issue of the early misinterpretations of Augustinian political philosophy and their impact upon medieval ecclesiastical empire. The study begins with the caution, and reasserts it toward the end, against attempts at trying to seek "Augustine's views as a whole on any particular [political] subject" primarily because Augustine is in his political theory "no systematic philosopher." Consult "The Political Ideas of St. Augustine," by Dino Bigongiari, for a discussion of the idea that all of Augustine's social and political views are connected to his theory of predestination. Augustine's political pessimism, as articulated in his doctrine of predestination, is traced back to pagan antiquity. It is their self-seeking nature, the self-seeking that Augustine calls *cupiditas*, which moves people to form political communities. From this perspective, it's claimed, the state is needed because coercion is needed. The insightful and frequently cited essay by A. J. Carlyle and F. J. C. Hearnshaw, "St Augustine and *The City of God*," focuses on a discussion of the place of St. Augustine in the history of political theory. In *De civitate Dei* Augustine very carefully argues that although "the institutions of government have been made necessary by sin, the state is also a divinely appointed remedy for sin." The state, in other words, is derived directly from God and is thus a divinely ordained instrument "by which the graver vices of men may be restrained." The state is not itself "sinful, but rather the remedy for sin." See John Figgis, *The Political Aspects of St. Augustine's* De Civitate Dei, for a treatment of Augustine's ideas about the civil and religious authorities as coordinate powers in the state and how these ideas became increasingly influential and reached fruition in the Middle Ages. According to Figgis, although the impact of *De civitate Dei* declined when the medieval unity broke up, Augustine's social ideas have remained significant. The influence of *De civitate Dei* he believes is seen today not so much in particular political systems but rather in the example it provides of the individual and collective search for higher ideals. In contrast to this approach, *Studies in the Political and Socio-Religious Terminology of the* De Civitate Dei, by R. T. Marshall, examines the major collective terms used by Augustine in *De civitate Dei*— specifically, *civitas, populus, gens, regnum, societas,* and *res publica*. Marshall's method is to cite the frequency of use of the terms under consideration and to compare and contrast their usage to determine Augustine's meaning. The essay also examines the distinctions among these terms and other kinds of "collective" terms used by Augustine. The underlying premise of the study is that the *De civitate Dei* is "essentially a social document; that is, it considers man not as an individual, but as a member or element of an organized collectivity." The work by Jeremy Adams that is included in the present collection, "Augustine's Definitions of *Populus* and the Value of Society," should be consulted in connection with Marshall's conclusions. The relation of the "political dimension of theology" to the *"status quo"* of secular and ecclesiastical establishments is the primary concern of Rosemary Radford Reuther's essay, "Augustine and Christian Political Theology." The author begins by reviewing the history of this tension within the Judaic tradition and the ferment it proved to be for the emergence of Christianity. Noting that Augustine was steeped in both politico-religious extremes the author sees him as confirming the imperial *status quo* of Roman Catholicism as well as its ostensible antithesis, the empire. Thus Augustine is credited with first recognizing in theological history an autonomously valid secular political order. Yet, as Reuther observes, so far as *The City of God* presents temporal existence as inconsequential, Augustine "fails to answer the question of the ultimate meaning of the human, historical project itself."

Other approaches to examining *The City of God* can be found in the following studies. Theodor Mommsen's purpose, in his highly praised "Orosius and Augustine," is to investigate through a close textual analysis the claim that Orosius' *Seven Books of History Against the Pagans* supplied the essential material for Augustine's *City of God*. The author intends to show that the medieval opinion, "still maintained by most modern scholars," that the *Seven Books* offers an interpretation of history from the Augustinian point of view is based upon several erroneous assumptions. In fact, the differences between the two works are far greater than is generally recognized. Augustine's purpose was to "discuss fully 'the origin, the course, and the end of the two cities,' especially of the heavenly city," whereas Orosius' aim was to "tell the tale of human misery in history." The article concludes that in spite of their similarities, *Seven Books of History Against the Pagans* and *The City of God* offer radically different interpretations of the purpose and destiny of human history.    F. Edward Cranz in *"De Civitate Dei*, XV, 2, and Augustine's Idea of the Christian Society," suggests that part of the difficulty for modern readers in interpreting the character of Christian society in *De civitate Dei* stems from a semantic gap between the fifth and twentieth centuries. Arguing in direct response to the (Neo-) Platonic interpretation given in 1925 by Hans Leisengang (i.e., a tripartite hierarchy: *civitas caelestis spiritalis, civitas terrena spiritalis, civitas terrena carnalis*) Cranz proposes that, for Augustine, by analysis of his particular use of the word *ecclesia*, Christian society in the temporal world is a mixture of all three groups. Cranz further notes that the concept of a state was the product of late medieval thought and is a form of thought "which neither Augustine nor Eusebius knows." In "The Origin and Dynamic of Society and the State According to St. Augustine," D. J. MacQueen deals with Augustine's doctrine of the state, its origins and its structure. MacQueen traces Augustine's views on the origins of the *civitas terrena* and the *civitas Dei* within the context of the relationship between Augustine's *civitas terrena* and earlier definitions of and criteria for membership in a *res publica*. Such terms as society, state, commonwealth, community, fellowship, and citizenship are analyzed with respect to their similarities and differences. The author argues that Augustine, by adding the word *Dei* (of God) to *civitas*, in effect "applies a criterion or selective principle that isolates for consideration one distinctive *civitas* from the many which have existed in the past and will appear in the future." In MacQueen's view, the term which most nearly conveys what Augustine means by *societas* is fellowship. James O'Donnell's article, "The Inspiration for Augustine's *De Civitate Dei*," begins with the observation that the idea of two cities was initially an anti-heretical polemic; he thus asks, "why did [Augustine] develop an anti-heretical idea at length in a treatise ostensibly directed against paganism?" O'Donnell views the expansion of the two cities idea into *De civitate Dei* as a "stroke of genius" and sees it as directly related to the historical circumstances under which the work was written. In Augustine's day the metaphor of *peregrini* (strangers) exiled from their true *patria* (home) was a powerful concept and it carried universal significance. The fall of Rome resulted in the exodus of Romans of all religious persuasions—Christian and pagan—from Italy into North Africa. The situation of the refugees was thus "analogous, in legal terms, to the kind of behavior which [Augustine] wanted to preach as most suitable for Christians living in the earthly city." See "Platonic Justice in Aristotle and Augustine," by Mary T. Clark, for an examination of the metamorphosis of the Platonic idea of justice into the form which Augustine received it and the subsequent impact it had on *De civitate Dei*. This study concludes that Augustine "seems to follow the thinking of the young Aristotle, and the very early works of Aristotle were modelled both nominally and really on the Platonic dialogues."

Finally, on the continuing debate as to whether Augustine actually had a plan for the writing of *The City of God* see R. J. Defarrari and M. J. Keller, "St. Augustine's *City of God*: Its Plan and Development," for a persuasive argument that his original plan for the work "was actually carried out in the finished masterpiece." This study also offers an insightful discussion of the work's "defects"—e.g., digressions, repetitions, etc.—that might be thought to "mar the plan." It is pointed out that "of the 1220 Teubner pages of *The City of God*, about 246 (one fifth of the whole) contain material which has no immediate or essential connection with the subject." The work's more overt "defects" are digressions, lengthy expositions, superfluous arguments, useless details, repetitions, and overuse of symbolism. Michael Gorman's, "A Survey of the Oldest Manuscripts of St. Augustine's *De Civitate Dei*," should be consulted on two important matters: first, the listing of known manuscripts and fragments of *De civitate Dei* produced until the twelfth century and, second, the inquiry it presents into the origin of the *capitula* for *De civitate Dei*. The impetus for this compilation is the "very random sample of the oldest manuscripts" used to prepare the Dombart-Kalb edition, the source for current standard editions of *De civitate Dei*. The author's hope is that examination of the manuscripts he surveys will yield further knowledge about the transmission of *De civitate Dei*. Mary McKinley, in *"The City of God* and the City of Man: Limits of Language in Montaigne's 'Apologie,'" notes that several scholars, starting with Villey, have pointed out that *The City of God* is "a vital presence in [Montaigne's] Essais." This study, however, examines the considerable influence *The City of God* exerted on Montaigne's "Apologie." The author compares the similar views the two men held about discourse and the role of digressions in discourse. The main focus here is on Montaigne's divergence from Augustine in matters of "poetics and the way a writer views the medium of one's creation: language." In "Some Etymologies in Augustine's *De Civitate Dei* X," J. Den Boeft shows how Augustine's rhetorical tools served him in his philosophical disputation with paganism. Given Augustine's belief that (Neo-) Platonism most approximated the Christian faith, the author elucidates the manner in which Augustine's excellence in the classical *ars rhetorica* showed that "the goal to which Porphyry was vainly seeking, viz. liberation of the soul, is in reality the heavenly kingdom, and thus it is again shown how near paganism, in this case Porphyry, was to the truths of Christianity." To support his argument the author considers in detail Augustine's unique use of five terms in *De civitate Dei* X: *religio, curia, res divina,* and *heros* from the pagan tradition, and *via regalis* ultimately derived from *Numbers* 20.17. The purpose of Joseph McCallin's essay, "The Christological Unity of St. Augustine's *De Civitate Dei*," is to show how Augustine's use of numbers in *De civitate Dei* gives unity to the work. For example, McCallin points out that in Augustine's numerology, the number five refers to perfection in the Earthly City; the number ten refers to the perfection of justice and beatitude and, taken by itself, "signifies the leit-motif, the Heavenly City." The numbers three and four reveal the "Trinitarian and evangelical nature of the second part of *De civitate Dei*. And the numbers five, six, ten, and twelve signify the cruciform Body of Christ in the thought and structure of *De civitate Dei* itself." Based upon an examination of Augustine's extensive and subtle use of number in *De civitate Dei*, the author concludes that throughout the work, "the form of City of God itself is the form of the Crucified Christ."

# Selected Bibliography

Titles preceded by an asterisk are included in the present study. The literature on Augustine and his writing is voluminous. For further bibliography the following works should be consulted. *Augustinus-Lexikon*. Stuttgart: Schwabe, 1985 —. *Fichier Augustinien*. Boston: G. K. Hall, 1972—. *Revue des études augustiniennes*. Paris, 1956—.

*A Concordance of the Works of St. Augustine: A Tool for Research*, a computer-based work prepared by Professor Cornelius Mayer, O.S.A. of the University of Würzburg, is now available through the Augustinian Historical Institute and Falvey Library at Villanova University. An important resource, this collection of the critical editions of the works of Augustine is arranged so that the materials can be searched for various kinds of informaton. For example, the five million words of the works of Augustine can be electronically searched to determine the frequency, location and context of specific words or phrases in his writings, or, to locate a text that was cited without identification in another work.

Abercrombie, Nigel. *Saint Augustine and French Classical Thought*. Oxford: Clarendon, 1938. Ch. 2, "Montaigne and *The City of God*."

*Adams, Jeremy D. "Augustine's Definitions of *Populus* and the Value of Society." From *The Populus of Augustine and Jerome: A Study in the Patristic Sense of Community*. New Haven: Yale UP, 1971. Appendix A, 123–35.

Alfraic, Prosper. *L'évolution intellectuelle de Saint Augustin*. Paris: Nourry, 1918.

Angus, S. *The Sources of the First Ten Books of Augustine's* De Civitate Dei. New Jersey: Princeton UP, 1906.

Armstrong, A. Hilary. *St. Augustine and Christian Platonism*. Pennsylvania: Villanova UP, 1967. Rpt. in *Augustine: A Collection of Critical Essays*. Ed. Markus. Pp. 3–37.

_____ and Robert A. Markus. *Christian Faith and Greek Philosophy*. London: Darton, Longman, & Todd, 1960.

Arquillière, Henri X. *L'Augustinisme politique. Essai sur la formation des théories politiques du Moyen Age*. Paris: Vrin, 1934. 2nd ed. 1972.

Augustine. *The City of God*. Trans. Henry Bettenson. Harmondsworth, Eng.: Penguin, 1972.

_____. *The City of God*. Introd. by Etienne Gilson. Trans. by Gerald G. Walsh, S. J., et al. New York: Doubleday (Image Books), 1958.

_____. *The City of God*. Introd. by Ernest Barker. Trans. by John Healey.

London.: J. M. Dent & Sons Ltd., 1934.

_____. *De Civitate Dei. Corpus Christianorum*, Series Latina 47–48. Brepols: Turnholt, 1955.

Balmus, C. I. *Étude sur le style de Saint Augustin dans les Confessions et la Cité de Dieu.* Paris: Desclée, 1930.

Bardy, Gustave. *Saint Augustin, L'homme et l'oeuvre.* Paris: Desclée, 1946.

_____. "La formation du concept de 'Cité de Dieu' dans l'oeuvre de Saint Augustin." *L'année theologique Augustinienne* 12 (1952): 5–19.

Barnes, T. D. "Aspects of the Background of *The City of God.*" *Revue de L'universite D'Ottawa* 52 (1982): 64–80.

Barr, Robert R. "The Two Cities in Saint Augustine." *Laval theologique et philosophique* 18 (1962): 211–29.

Barrow, Reginald H. *Introduction to St. Augustine,* "The City of God." London: Faber and Faber, 1950.

Battenhouse, Roy W. ed. *A Companion to the Study of Saint Augustine.* New York: Oxford UP, 1955.

Baynes, Norman H. *The Political Ideas of St. Augustine's* De Civitate Dei. Historical Association Pamphlet No. 104. London: Bell, 1936. Rpt. in *Byzantine Studies and Other Essays.* London: Athlone P, 1955. Pp. 288–306.

Béné, Charles. *Érasme et Saint Augustin ou l'influence de Saint Augustin sur l'humanisme d'Érasme.* Geneve: Droz, 1969.

Berrouard, M.-F. "S. Augustin et le Ministère de la Prédication." *Recherches augustiniennes* 2 (1961): 447–501.

Bigongiari, Dino. "The Political Ideas of St. Augustine." In *The Political Writings of St. Augustine.* Ed. Henry Paolucci. Chicago: Regnery, 1962.

Blumenthal, H. J. and R. A. Markus, eds. *Neoplatonism and Early Christian Thought: Essays in Honor of A. H. Armstrong.* London: Variorum, 1981.

Bochet, Isabelle. *Saint Augustin et le désir de Dieu.* Paris: Études augustiniennes, 1982.

Boeft, J. Den. "Some Etymologies in Augustine's *De Civitate Dei* X." *Vigiliae Christianae* 33 (1979): 242–59.

Boler, John. "Augustine and Political Theory." *Mediaevalia: A Journal of Mediaeval Studies* 4 (1978): 83–97.

Bonner, Gerald I. St. *Augustine of Hippo: Life and Controversies.* London: Westminster P, 1963.

_____. *Augustine and Pelagianism in the Light of Modern Research.* Pennsylvania: Villanova UP, 1972.

_____. "Quid imperatori cum ecclesia? St. Augustine on History and Society." *Augustinian Studies* 2 (1971): 231–51.

Booth, E. "A Marginal Comment of St. Augustine on the Principle of the

Division of Labor (*De Civ. Dei* VII, 4)." *Augustiniana* 17 (1977): 249–56.

Børresen, Kari Elisabeth. *Subordination and Equivalence: The Nature and Rôle of Woman in Augustine and Thomas Aquinas.* Washington, D.C.: UP of America, 1981.

Bourke, Vernon J. *Augustine's Quest of Wisdom.* Milwaukee: Bruce, 1945.

_____. *Augustine's View of Reality.* Pennsylvania: Villanova U P, 1964.

_____. *Joy in Augustine's Ethics.* Pennsylvania: Villanova UP, 1979.

*_____. "*The City of God* and History." From *Wisdom from St. Augustine.* Texas: U of St. Thomas P, 1984. Ch. 13, 188–205.

Boyer, Charles. *Christianisme et néo-platonisme dans la formation de S. Augustin.* Paris: Beauchesne, 1920. Rpt. Rome: Libri Catholici, 1953.

_____. *L'idée de vérité dans la philosophie de S. Augustin.* Paris: Beauchesne, 1921.

Boyle, Majorie O'Rourke. "Augustine in the Garden of Zeus: Lust, Love, and Language." *Harvard Theological Review* 83 (1990): 117–39.

*Brawer, Robert A. "St. Augustine's Two Cities as Medieval Dramatic Exempla." *Mediaevalia: A Journal of Mediaeval Studies* 4 (1978): 225–44.

Brown, Peter. *Religion and Society in the Age of Saint Augustine.* New York: Harper, 1972.

_____. *Augustine of Hippo: A Biography.* California: U of California P, 1967.

Brown, Peter R. L. "St. Augustine's Attitude to Religious Coercion." *Journal of Roman Studies* 55 (1964): 107–16.

*Brown, P. R. L. "Saint Augustine and Political Society." (Original title: "Saint Augustine") In *Trends in Medieval Political Thought.* Ed. Beryl Smalley. Oxford: Blackwell, 1965. Pp. 1–21.

Brown, Robert F. "The First Evil Will Must Be Incomprehensible: A Critique of Augustine." *Journal of the American Academy of Religion* 46 (1978): 315–29.

Burleigh, John H. S. The City of God: *A Study of St. Augustine's Philosophy.* London: Nisbet & Co., 1949.

*Burnell, Peter. "The Problem of Service to Unjust Regimes in Augustine's *City of God. Journal of the History of Ideas* 54 (1993): 177–88.

_____. "The Status of Politics in St. Augustine's *City of God." Journal of the History of Political Thought* 13 (1992): 13–29.

Burt, Donald X. "St Augustine's Evaluation of Civil Society." *Augustinianum* 3 (1963): 87–94.

Bushman, Sister Rita Marie. "St. Augustine's Metaphysics and Stoic Doctrine." *New Scholasticism* 26 (1952): 283–304.

Caldwell, Ellen C. "The *loquaces muti* and the *Verbum infans*: Paradox and Language in the *Confessiones* of St. Augustine." In *Collectanea Augustiniana.* Ed. Schnaubelt and Van Fleteren. Pp. 101–11.

Carlson, Charles P., Jr. "The Natural Order and Historical Explanation in St. Augustine's *City of God.*" *Augustiniana* 21 (1971): 417–47.

Carlyle, A. J. and F. J. C. Hearnshaw. "St. Augustine and *The City of God.*" In *The Social and Political Ideas of Some Great Medieval Thinkers.* Ed. Hearnshaw. London: Harrup, 1923.

Carlyle, R. W. and A. J. Carlyle. *A History of Mediaeval Political Theory in the West.* Vol. 1. *The Second Century to the Ninth.* Edinburgh: Blackwood, 1903–1936. 6 vols.

Caton, Hiram. "St. Augustine's Critique of Politics." *New Scholasticism* 47 (1973): 433–57.

Chadwick, Henry. *Augustine.* New York: Oxford UP, 1986.

Chestnut, Glenn F. "The Pattern of the Past: Augustine's Debate With Eusebius and Sallust." In *Our Common History as Christians: Essays in Honor of Albert C. Outler.* Ed. John Deschner, et al. New York: Oxford UP, 1975. Pp. 69–95.

Clark, Elizabeth A. *Ascetic Piety and Women's Faith: Essays on Late Ancient Christianity.* New York: Mellen P, 1986.

Clark, Mary T. *Augustine, Philosopher of Freedom. A Study in Comparative Philosophy.* Paris: Desclée, 1958.

_____. *Augustinian Personalism.* Pennsylvania: Villanova UP, 1970.

_____. "Augustinian Spirituality." *Augustinian Studies* 15 (1984): 83–92.

_____. "Augustine on Justice." *Revue des études augustiniennes* 9 (1963): 87–94.

_____. "Platonic Justice in Aristotle and Augustine." *The Downside Review* 82 (1964): 25–35.

Cochrane, Charles Norris. *Christianity and Classical Culture: A Study of Thought and Action from Augustus to Augustine.* New York: Oxford UP, 1942. 2d ed. 1957.

Colbert, Mary C. *The Syntax of the* De Civitate Dei *of St. Augustine.* Washington, D.C.: Catholic U of America P, 1923.

Colish, Marcia L. "St. Augustine's Rhetoric of Silence Revisited." *Augustinian Studies* 9 (1978): 15–24.

Combès, Gustave. *La doctrine politique de Saint Augustin.* Paris: Plon, 1927.

Congar, Yves. *L'Ecclésiologie du haut Moyen Age.* Paris: Cerf, 1968.

_____. "'Civitas Dei' et 'Ecclesia' chez S. Augustin." *Revue des études augustiniennes* 3 (1957): 1–14.

Connolly, William. *Political Theory and Modernity.* Oxford: Blackwell, 1988.

Copleston, Frederick. *History of Philosophy.* Vol. 2. Maryland: Newman P, 1950. Rpt. New York: Doubleday, 1962.

Courcelle, Pierre P. *Recherches sur les 'Confessions' de S. Augustin.* Paris: De Boccard, 1950. 2nd ed. 1968.

Cranz, F. Edward. "*De Civitate Dei*, XV, 2, and Augustine's Idea of the Christian Society." In *Augustine: A Collection of Critical Essays*. Ed. Markus. Pp. 404–21. Originally in *Speculum* 25 (1950): 215–25.

_____. "The Development of Augustine's Ideas on Society Before the Donatist Controversy." *Harvard Theological Review* 47 (1954): 255–316. Rpt. in *Augustine: A Collection of Critical Essays*. Ed. Markus. Pp. 336–403.

D'Arcy, M. C. "The Philosophy of St. Augustine." In *A Monument to Saint Augustine*. M. C. D'Arcy et al. London: Sheed and Ward, 1930. Pp. 153–95. Rpt. 1945.

_____, et al. *A Monument to Saint Augustine: Essays on Some Aspects of His Thought Written in Commemoration of His 15th Centenary*. London: Sheed and Ward, 1930. Rpt. 1945.

Dawson, Christopher. *Religion and the Rise of Western Culture*. New York: Sheed and Ward, 1950.

_____. "St. Augustine and His Age." In *A Monument to St. Augustine: Essays on Some Aspects of His Thought Written in Commemoration of His 15th Centenary*. Ed. D'Arcy. Pp. 11–77.

*Deane, Herbert. "Augustine and the State: The Return of Order Upon Disorder." From *The Political and Social Ideas of St. Augustine*. New York: Columbia UP, 1963. Ch. 4, 116–43.

Deferrari, R. J. and M. J. Keeler. "St. Augustine's *City of God*: Its Plan and Development." *American Journal of Philology* 50 (1929): 109–37.

Donnelly, Dorothy F. and Mark A. Sherman. *Augustine's De Civitate Dei: An Annotated Bibliography of Modern Criticism, 1960–1990*. New York: Peter Lang, 1991.

*_____. "Reconsidering the Ideal: *The City of God* and Utopian Speculation." (Original title: "*The City of God* and Utopia") *Augustinian Studies* 8 (1977): 111–23.

_____. "Aquinas and Some Subsequent Thinkers on the Renewal of Utopian Speculation. *The Thomist* 46 (1982): 539–72.

Dougherty, James. "The Sacred City and *The City of God*." *Augustinian Studies* 10 (1979): 81–90.

Dougherty, Richard J. "Christian and Citizen: The Tension in St. Augustine's *De Civitate Dei*." In *Collectanea Augustiniana*. Ed. Schnaubelt and VanFleteren. Pp. 205–24.

Downey, Glanville. "The Ethical City, the Secular City, and the City of God." *Anglican Theological Review* 56 (1974): 34–41.

Duval, Yves-Marie. "L'éloge de Théodose dans la Cité de Dieu (V. 26.1)." *Recherches augustiniennes* 4 (1966): 135–79.

Dvornik, Francis. *Early Christian and Byzantine Political Philosophy*.

Dumbarton Oaks Studies Nine, The Dumbarton Oaks Center for Byzantine Studies, Washington, D.C., 1966, Vol. II.

Dyson, R. W. "St. Augustine's Remarks on Time." *The Downside Review* 100 (1982): 221–30.

Elshtain, Jean Bethke. *Public Man, Private Woman: Women in Social and Political Thought.* New Jersey: Princeton UP, 1981.

Ferguson, Margaret W. "Saint Augustine's Region of Unlikeness: the Crossing of Exile and Language." *The Georgia Review* 29 (1976): 842–64.

Ferrari, Leo C. "Truth and Augustine's Conversion Scene." In *Collectanea Augustiniana.* Ed. Schnaubelt and Van Fleteren. Pp. 9–19.

_____. "Some Surprising Omissions from Augustine's *City of God.*" *Augustiniana* 21 (1970): 336–46.

Figgis, John Neville. *The Political Aspects of St. Augustine's* City of God. London: Longmans, Green, 1921. Rpt., Massachusetts: Peter Smith, 1963.

Fortin, Ernest L. *Christianisme et Culture philosophique au cinquième siècle.* Paris: *Études augustiniennes,* 1959.

_____. *Political Idealism and Christianity in the Thought of St. Augustine.* Pennsylvania: Villanova UP, 1972.

*_____. "Augustine's *City of God* and the Modern Historical Consciousness." *Review of Politics* 41 (1979): 323–43.

_____. "The Patristic Sense of Community." *Augustinian Studies* 4 (1973): 179–97.

Frazier, Thomas R. "The Ethics of *The City of God.*" *The Journal of Religious Thought* 26 (1969): 23–36.

Freeman, Curtis Wynn. *Reading St. Augustine's* City of God *as a Narrative Theology.* Dissertation. Baylor U, 1991.

Frend, W. H. C. *The Donatist Church.* Oxford: Clarendon P, 1952. Rpt. 1971.

_____. "Augustine and Orosius: On the End of the Ancient World." *Augustinian Studies* 20 (1989): 1–38.

Gannon, Sister M. Ann Ida. "The Active Theory of Sensation in St. Augustine." *New Scholasticism* 30 (1956): 154–80.

Gibson, Margaret. "Lanfranc's Notes on Patristic Texts." *The Journal of Theological Studies* 22 (1971): 435–50.

Gierke, Otto. *Political Theories of the Middle Ages.* Trans. with intro. by Frederic W. Maitland. Boston: Beacon P, 1958.

Gilson, Etienne. *L'introduction à l'étude de Saint Augustin.* Paris: Vrin, 1929. Rpt. 1949. Trans. L. E. M. Lynch. *The Christian Philosophy of Saint Augustine.* New York: Knopf, 1960.

_____. "Forward to the *City of God.*" *City of God.* New York: Fathers of the Church, 1950.

_____. *Les métamorphoses de la Cité de Dieu.* Paris: Vrin, 1952.

_____. "The Future of Augustinian Metaphysics." In *A Monument to Saint Augustine*. M. C. D'Arcy et al. London: Sheed and Ward, 1930. Pp. 287–315. Rpt. 1945.

Gorman, Michael M. "A Survey of the Oldest Manuscripts of St. Augustine's *De Civitate Dei*." *The Journal of Theological Studies* 33 (1982): 398–410.

Graham, Walker. *Moral Foundations of Constitutional Thought: Current Problems, Augustinian Prospects*. New Jersey: Princeton UP, 1990.

Green, William M. "Augustine on the Teaching of History." In *University of California Publications in Classical Philology* 12 (1944): 315–42. Berkeley: U of California P, 1944.

Guy, Jean-Claude. *Unité et structure logique de la 'Cité de Dieu' de Saint Augustin*. Paris: *Études augustiniennes*, 1961.

Halpern, Richard A. *Spiritual Vision and the* City of God *in* Sir Gawain and the Green Knight. Dissertation. Princeton U, 1976.

Hartigan, Richard S. "Saint Augustine on War and Killing. The Problem of the Innocent." *Journal of the History of Ideas* 27 (1966): 195–204.

*Hawkins, Peter S. "Divide and Conquer: Augustine in the *Divine Comedy*." *PMLA* 33 (1991): 471–82.

_____. "Polemical Counterpoint in *De Civitate Dei*." *Augustinian Studies* 6 (1975): 97–106.

Hearnshaw, F. J. C., ed. *Social and Political Ideas of some Great Medieval Thinkers*. London: Harrap, 1923.

Hohensee, H. *The Augustinian Concept of Authority*. New York: Paulist P, 1954.

Holloway, Julia B., Joan Bechtold, and Constance S. Wright, eds. *Equally in God's Image*. New York: Peter Lang, 1990.

Hölscher, Ludger. *The Reality of the Mind: Augustine's Philosophical Arguments for the Human Soul as a Spiritual Substance*. London: Routledge and Kegan Paul, 1986.

Horton, John T. "The *De Civitate Dei* as Religious Satire." *The Classical Journal* 60 (1964): 193–203.

Hundert, E. J. "Augustine and the Sources of the Divided Self." *Political Theory* 20 (1992): 86–104.

Johnson, Penelope D. *Equal in Monastic Profession*. Chicago: U of Chicago P, 1991.

*_____. "*Virtus*: Transition from Classical Latin to the *De Civitate Dei*." *Augustinian Studies* 6 (1975): 117–24.

Jones, B. V. E. "The Manuscript Tradition of St. Augustine's *De Civitate Dei*." *The Journal of Theological Studies* 16 (1965): 142–45.

Kantorowicz, Ernst. *The King's Two Bodies: A Study in Medieval Political Theology*. New Jersey: Princeton UP, 1957.

*Kaufman, Peter Iver. "Redeeming Politics: Augustine's Cities of God." From *Redeeming Politics*. New Jersey: Princeton UP, 1990. Ch. 7, 130–8.

———. "Augustine, Evil, and Donatism: Sin and Sanctity Before the Pelagian Controversy." *Theological Studies* 59 (1990): 698–716.

Keenan, M. Emily. *The Life and Times of St. Augustine as Revealed in His Letters.* Washington: Catholic U of America P, 1935.

Keyes, Gordon L. *Christian Faith and the Interpretation of History: A Study of St. Augustine's Philosophy of History.* Nebraska: U of Nebraska P, 1966.

Kilzer, Ernest. "The Social Thought of St. Augustine." *The American Benedictine Review* 3 (1962): 293–335.

Korfmacher, William C. "Four Notes on the *De Civitate Dei.*" *Classical Folia* 14 (1960): 82–85.

Kuntz, Marion L. and Paul G. Kuntz. *Jacob's Ladder and the Tree of Life: Concepts of Hierarchy and the Great Chain of Being.* New York: Peter Lang, 1988.

Lambot, Cyrille. "Lettre inédite de Saint Augustin relative au *De Civitate Dei.*" *Revue Benedictine* 51 (1939): 109–21.

Lamirande, Emilien. *Church, State, and Toleration. An Intriguing Change of Mind in St. Augustine.* Pennsylvania: Villanova UP, 1974.

Lamotte, J. "But et adversaires de saint Augustin dans le 'De Civitate Dei.'" *Augustiniana* 11 (1961): 434–69.

Laoye, John A. *Augustine's Apologetic Use of the Old Testament as Reflected Especially in the* De Civitate Dei. Dissertation. Southern Baptist Theology Seminary, 1972.

Lauras, A. and H. Rondet. "Le thème des deux cités dans l'oeuvre de s. Augustin." *Études augustiniennes* (1953): 99–160.

Lavere, George J. "Metaphor and Symbol in St. Augustine's *De Civitate Dei.*" In *Collectanea Augustiniana.* Ed. Schnaubelt and VanFleteren. Pp. 225–43.

———. "The Influence of Saint Augustine on Early Medieval Political Theory." *Augustinian Studies* 12 (1981): 1–9.

Lawless, George P. *Augustine of Hippo and His Monastic Rule.* New York: Oxford UP, 1987.

Limbrick, Elaine. "Montaigne et Saint Augustine." *Bibliothèque d'Humanisme et Renaissance* 34 (1972): 49–64.

Löwith, Karl. *Meaning in History.* Chicago: U of Chicago P, 1949.

*MacKinnon, Patricia L. "Augustine's *City of God*: The Divided Self/The Divided *Civitas.*" From *The Analogy of the Body Politic in St. Augustine, Dante, Petrarch, and Ariosto.* Dissertation: U of California, 1988. Ch. 1, 1–57.

MacQueen, D. J. "St. Augustine's Concept of Property Ownership." *Recherches augustiniennes* 8 (1972): 187–229.

_____. "The Origin and Dynamics of Society and the State According to St. Augustine." *Augustinian Studies* 4 (1973): 73–101.

McCallin, Joseph A. "The Christological Unity of St. Augustine's *De Civitate Dei*." *Revue des études augustiniennes* 12 (1966): 85–109.

McElwain, Hugh T. *St. Augustine's Doctrine on War in Relation to Earlier Ecclesiastical Writers (A Comparative Analysis)*. Chicago: Regnery, 1973.

McKee, Donald K. "Augustine's Political Thought." *The Drew Gateway* 40 (1970): 80–87.

McKinley, Mary B. "*The City of God* and the City of Man: Limits of Language in Montaigne's 'Apologie.'" *Romanic Review* 71 (1980): 122–40.

Maritain, Jacques. "St. Augustine and St. Thomas Aquinas." In *A Monument to Saint Augustine*. M. C. D'Arcy et al. London: Sheed and Ward, 1930. Pp. 197–223. Rpt. 1945.

Markus, Robert A. *Conversion and Disenchantment in Augustine's Spiritual Career*. Pennsylvania: Villanova UP, 1986.

_____. *"Saeculum": History and Society in the Theology of Saint Augustine*. Cambridge: Cambridge UP, 1970.

_____. ed. *Augustine: A Collection of Critical Essays*. New York: Doubleday, 1972.

_____. *"De Civitate Dei*: Pride and the Common Good." *Proceedings of the PMR Conference* 12–13 (1987–88), 1–16. Rpt. in *Collectanea Augustiniana*. Ed. Schnaubelt and Van Fleteren. Pp. 245–59.

*_____. "Two Conceptions of Political Authority: Augustine, *De Civitate Dei*, XIX, 14–15, and Some Thirteenth Century Interpretations." *The Journal of Theological Studies* 16 (1965), 68–100. Rpt. in Markus. *"Saeculum": History and Society in the Theology of Saint Augustine*.

Marrou, Henri-Irénée. *S. Augustin et la fin de la culture antique*. Paris: DeBoccard, 1938. Rpt. 1949.

_____. *St. Augustine and His Influence Through the Ages*. London: Longmans, 1957.

_____. "La Division en Chapitres des Livres de la 'Cité de Dieu.'" *Melanges J. de Ghellinck* 1 (1951): 235–49.

_____. "Un Lieu dit 'Cité de Dieu.'" *Augustinus Magister* 1 (1954): 101–10.

_____ and Anne Marie La Bonnardiere. "Le Dogme de la Résurrection et la Théologie des Valeurs Humains selon l'Enseignement de Saint Augustin." *Revue des études augustiniennes* 12 (1966): 111–36. Trans. *The Resurrection and Saint Augustine's Theology of Human Values*. Pennsylvania: Villanova UP, 1966.

Marshall, R. T. *Studies in the Political and Socio-Religious Terminology of the De Civitate Dei*. Washington, D. C.: Catholic UP, 1952.

Martin, Rex. "The Two Cities in Augustine's Political Philosophy." *Journal of the History of Ideas* 33 (1972): 195–216.

Mazzeo, Joseph A. "St. Augustine's Rhetoric of Silence." *Journal of the History of Ideas* 23 (1962): 175-96. Rpt. in *Renaissance and Seventeenth-Century Studies.* New York: Columbia UP, 1964. Pp. 1–28.

Meagher, Robert E. *An Introduction to Augustine.* New York: New York UP, 1978.

Meynell, Hugo A. ed. *Grace, Politics and Desire: Essays on Augustine.* Calgary: U of Calgary P, 1990.

Miles, Margaret R. *St. Augustine's Idea of the Meaning and Value of the Body in Relation to the Whole Personality.* California: Graduate Theological Union Dissertation, 1977.

Mommsen, Theodor E. "Orosius and Augustine." In *Medieval and Renaissance Studies.* Ed. Eugene F. Rice, Jr. New York: Cornell UP, 1959. Pp. 325–48.

*_____. "St. Augustine and the Christian Idea of Progress. The Background of *The City of God.*" *Journal of the History of Ideas* 12 (1951): 346–74. Rpt. in *Medieval and Renaissance Studies.* Ed. Eugene F. Rice, Jr. New York: Cornell UP, 1959. Pp. 265–98.

Morrison, John L. "Augustine's Two Theories of Time." *New Scholasticism* 45 (1971): 600–10.

Mourant, John A. *Introduction to the Philosophy of St. Augustine.* Pennsylvania: Pennsylvania State UP, 1964.

_____. *Augustine on Immortality.* Pennsylvania: Villanova UP, 1969.

_____. *St. Augustine on Memory.* Pennsylvania: Villanova UP, 1980.

Niebuhr, Reinhold. *Christian Realism and Political Problems.* New York: Scribner, 1953.

_____. *Moral Man and Immoral Society: A Study in Ethics and Politics.* New York: Scribner, 1960.

*_____. "Augustine's Political Realism." From *The Essential Reinhold Niebuhr: Selected Essays and Addresses.* Ed. Robert McAfee Brown. New Haven: Yale UP, 1986. Ch. 4, 123–41.

Nugent, Donald. "*The City of God* Revisited." *Cross Currents* 19 (1969): 241–55.

O'Brien, William J. "Original Sin in Augustine's 'Confessions.'" *Thought* 49 (1974): 436–46.

O'Connell, Robert J. *St. Augustine's Early Theory of Man, A.D. 386–391.* Massachusetts: Harvard UP, 1968.

_____. *Saint Augustine's Confessions: The Odyssey of the Soul.* Massachusetts: Harvard UP, 1969.

_____. *Saint Augustine's Platonism.* Pennsylvania: Villanova UP, 1984.

_____. "*Ennead* VI, 4 and 5 in the Works of St. Augustine." *Revue des études augustiniennes* 9 (1963): 1–39.

O'Daly, Gerard, J. P. *Augustine's Philosophy of Mind*. Berkeley: U of California P, 1987.

_____. "Augustine on the Measurement of Time: Some Comparisons with Aristotelian and Stoic Texts." In *Neoplatonism and Early Christian Thought*. Ed. Blumenthal and Markus. Pp. 171–79.

O'Donnell, James J. "The Inspiration for Augustine's *De Civitate Dei*." *Augustinian Studies* 10 (1979): 75–79.

_____. *Augustine*. Boston: G. K. Hall, 1985.

*O'Donovan, Oliver. "Augustine's *City of God* XIX and Western Political Thought." *Dionysius* 11 (1987): 89–110.

_____. *The Problem of Self-Love in St. Augustine*. New Haven: Yale UP, 1980.

Ojeman, Mary R. *Sancti Augustini* De Civitate Dei *Liber Primus: A Sense-Line Arrangement, English Translation, and Rhetorical Study*. Dissertation. Saint Louis U, 1960.

O'Meara, John J. *Charter of Christendom: The Significance of* The City of God. New York: Macmillan, 1961.

_____. *The Young Augustine: The Growth of St. Augustine's Mind up to His Conversion*. London: Longmans, 1954.

_____, ed. *An Augustine Reader*. New York: Image Books, 1973.

O'Toole, Christopher J. *The Philosophy of Creation in the Writings of St. Augustine*. Washington: Catholic U of America P, 1944.

Pagels, Elaine. *Adam, Eve and the Serpent*. New York: Random House, 1988.

*_____. "The Politics of Paradise." *Harvard Theological Review* 78 (1985): 67–99.

Paolini, Shirley J. *Confessions of Sin and Love in the Middle Ages: Dante's* Commedia *and St. Augustine's* Confessions. Washington, D.C.: UP of America, 1982.

Paolucci, Henry, ed. *The Political Writings of St. Augustine*. Chicago: Regnery Co., 1962.

Parkes, Henry B. *The Divine Order. Western Culture in the Middle Ages and the Renaissance*. New York: Knopf, 1969.

Pegis, Anton C. "The Mind of St. Augustine." *Medieval Studies* 6 (1944): 1–61.

Pelikan, Jaroslav J. *The Christian Tradition: A History of the Development of Doctrine*. Vol. 1. *The Emergence of the Catholic Tradition (100–600)*. Chicago: U of Chicago P, 1971.

_____. *The Mystery of Continuity: Time and History, Memory and Eternity in the Thought of St. Augustine*. Charlottesville: UP of Virginia, 1986.

Phillips, Oliver. "St. Augustine's Lucanesque Moment: The Third Book of *The City of God*." *Augustinian Studies* 22 (1991): 157–64.

Pincherle, Alberto. "The Confessions of St. Augustine: A Reappraisal." *Augustinian Studies* 7 (1976): 119-33.

Pope, Hugh. St. *Augustine of Hippo.* Maryland: Newman P, 1949. Rpt. New York: Doubleday, 1961.

Portalié, Eugène. *A Guide to the Thought of St. Augustine.* Trans. R. J. Bastian. Chicago: Regnery, 1960.

Preus, Mary C. *Eloquence and Ignorance in Augustine's* On the Nature and Origin of the Soul. Georgia: Scholars P, 1985.

Przywara, Erich. "St. Augustine and the Modern World." In *A Monument to Saint Augustine.* M. C. D'Arcy et al. London: Sheed and Ward, 1930. Pp. 249-86. Rpt. 1945.

*Pulsiano, Phillip. "Language Theory and Narrative Patterning in *De Civitate Dei,* Books XV-XVIII." First published in this collection. Pp.241-52.

Quinn, John M., O.S.A. *Praise in St. Augustine: Readings and Reflections.* Massachusetts: Christopher Publishing House, 1987.

_____. *A Companion to the Confessions of St. Augustine.* New York: Peter Lang. (Forthcoming)

_____. "Four Faces of Time in St. Augustine." *Recherches augustiniennes* 26 (1992): 181-231.

_____. "Anti-Manichean and Other Moral Precisions in Augustine's *Confessions."* *Augustinian Studies* 19 (1988).

*Raitiere, Martin N. "More's *Utopia* and *The City of God."* *Studies in the Renaissance* 20 (1973): 144-68.

Reeves, Eileen. "Augustine and Galileo on Reading the Heavens." *Journal of the History of Ideas* 52 (1991): 563-79.

Reeves, John-Baptist. "St. Augustine and Humanism." In *A Monument to Saint Augustine.* M. C. D'Arcy et al. London: Sheed and Ward, 1930. Pp. 121-51. Rpt. 1945.

Reis, Linda M. The City of God: *St. Augustine's Christian Philosophy of History.* Master of Divinity Thesis. Phillips U, 1987.

Renna, Thomas. "Augustine's *De Civitate Dei* in John Wyclif and Thomas More." In *Collectanea Augustiniana.* Ed. Schnaubelt and Van Fleteren. Pp. 261-71.

_____. "The Idea of Peace in the Augustinian Tradition." *Augustinian Studies* 10 (1979): 105-111.

Reuther, Rosemary Radford. "Augustine and Christian Political Theology." *Interpretation* 29 (1975): 252-65.

Rickaby, Joseph. *St. Augustine's* City of God: *A View of the Contents.* London: Burns Oates & Washbourne, 1925.

Rohmer, Jean. *La finalité morale de Saint Augustin à Duns Scot.* Paris: Vrin, 1939.

Rondet, Henri. *Essais sur la théologie de la grâce.* Paris: Beauchesne, 1964.

Rowe, Trevor T. St. *Augustine, Pastoral Theologian.* London: Epworth P, 1974.

Russell, Frederick H. *The Just War in the Middle Ages.* Cambridge: Cambridge UP, 1975.

_____. "Only Something Good Can Be Evil: The Genesis of Augustine's Secular Ambivalence." *Theological Studies* 51 (1990): 698–716.

*Russell, Robert, O.S.A. "The Role of Neoplatonism in St. Augustine's *De Civitate Dei.*" In *Neoplatonism and Early Christian Thought.* Ed. Blumenthal and Markus. Pp. 160–70.

Schmidt, Mary T. *St. Augustine's Influence on St. Thomas More's English Works.* Connecticut: Yale U Dissertation, 1943.

Schnaubelt, Joseph C., O.S.A. and Frederick Van Fleteren, eds. *Collectanea Augustiniana.* New York: Peter Lang, 1990.

*Scott, Joanna V. "Augustine's Razor: Public vs. Private Interests in *The City of God.*" First published in this collection. Pp. 151–67.

_____. "A Detour Through Pietism: Hannah Arendt On Saint Augustine's Philosophy of Freedom." *Polity* 20 (1988): 394–425.

_____ and Judith Chelius Stark. *Rediscovering Hanna Arendt: Love and Saint Augustine.* New York: Harcourt Brace. (Forthcoming)

Shinn, Roger. "Augustinian and Cyclical Views of History." *Anglican Theological Review* 31 (1949): 133–41.

Shklar, Judith N. *The Faces of Injustice.* New Haven: Yale UP, 1990.

Smalley, Beryl. *English Friars and Antiquity in the Early Fourteenth Century.* New York: Barnes & Noble, 1960.

_____, ed. *Trends in Medieval Political Thought.* Oxford: Blackwell, 1965.

Smith, Sharon Off Dunlap. *Illustrations of Raoul de Praelles' Translation of St. Augustine's* City of God *Between 1375 and 1420.* Dissertation. New York U, 1974.

Stark, Judith Chelius. "The Dynamics of the Will in Augustine's Conversion." In *Collectanea Augustiniana.* Ed. Schnaubelt and Van Fleteren. Pp. 45–64.

Stevenson, William R. *Christian Love and Just War: Moral Paradox and Political Life in St. Augustine and His Modern Interpreters.* Georgia: Mercer UP, 1987.

Sticca, Sandro. "The Augustinian Tradition in the Middle Ages." *Mediaevalia: A Journal of Mediaeval Studies* 4 (1978): 1–12.

Straw, Carole E. "Augustine as Pastoral Theologian: The Exegesis of the Parables of the Field and Threshing Floor." *Augustinian Studies* 14 (1983): 129–51.

Suchocki, Marjorie. "The Symbolic Structure of Augustine's *Confessions.*"

*Journal of the American Academy of Religion* 3 (1980): 365–78.

Suter, Ronald. "Augustine on Time With Some Criticisms from Wittgenstein." *Revue internationale de philosophie* 16 (1962): 378–94.

*Swift, Louis J. "Defining *Gloria* in Augustine's *City of God*." In *Diakonia: Studies in Honor of Robert T. Meyer*. Ed. Thomas Halton and Joseph P. Williman. Washington: Catholic U of America P, 1986.

_____. "Augustine on War and Killing: Another View." *Harvard Theological Review* 66 (1973): 369–83.

Takahashi, W. "The Contemporary Significance of Augustine's *De Civitate Dei*." *Studies in Medieval Thought* 14 (1972): 1–15.

TeSelle, Eugene. *Augustine the Theologian*. New York: Herder, 1970.

_____. *Augustine's Strategy as an Apologist*. Pennsylvania: Villanova UP, 1974.

_____. "Toward an Augustinian Politics." *Journal of Religious Ethics* 16 (1988): 87–108.

_____. "The Civic Vision in Augustine's *City of God*." *Thought* 62 (1987): 268–80.

Testard, Maurice. *Saint Augustin et Cicéron*. Vol. I. *Cicéron dans la formation et dans l'oeuvre de Saint Augustin*. Paris: Études augustiniennes, 1958. 2 vols.

Thonnard, F.-J. "La Prédestination Augustinienne. Sa Place en Philosophie Augustinienne." *Revue des études augustiniennes* 10 (1964): 97–123.

van der Meer, Frederick. *Augustine the Bishop: Religion and Society at the Dawn of the Middle Ages*. Trans. B. Battershaw and G. R. Lamb. New York: Harper and Row, 1965.

Van Fleteren, Frederick, Joseph C. Schnaubelt, O.S.A., and Joseph Reino. *Augustine: Mystic and Mystagogue*. New York: Peter Lang, 1994.

_____. "St. Augustine's Theory of Conversion." In *Collectanea Augustiniana*. Ed. Schnaubelt and Van Fleteren. Pp. 65–80.

*_____. "*De Civitate Dei*: Miscellaneous Observations." First published in this collection. Pp. 415–29.

Versfeld, Marthinus. *A Guide to* The City of God. New York: Sheed and Ward, 1958.

Von Jess, Wilma G. "Augustine: A Consistent and Unitary Theory of Time." *New Scholasticism* 46 (1972): 337–51.

Watkin, E. I. "The Mysticism of Saint Augustine." In *A Monument to Saint Augustine*. M. C. D'Arcy et al. London: Sheed and Ward, 1930. Pp. 103–19. Rpt. 1945.

Watson, Thomas R. *Perversions, Originals, and Redemptions: Typological Patterns Underlining Theme in* Paradise Lost *Based Upon Augustine's* De Civitate Dei. Dissertation. U of Louisville, 1981.

Weaver, F. Ellen and Jean Laporte. "Augustine and Women: Relationships and Teachings." *Augustinian Studies* (1981).

Wegemer, Gerard. *"The City of God* in Thomas More's *Utopia." Renascence* 44 (1992): 115–35.

Weithman, Paul J. "Augustine and Aquinas on Original Sin and the Function of Political Authority." *Journal of the History of Philosophy* 30 (1992): 353–76.

West, Rebecca. *St. Augustine.* New York: Appleton, 1933.

Wetzel, James Richard. *The Augustinian Imperative: A Reflection on the Politics of Morality.* California: Sage P, 1993.

Wilks, Michael J. "Augustine and the General Will." *Studia Patristica* 9 (1966): 487–522.

_____. "Roman Empire and the Christian State in the *De Civitate Dei." Augustinus* 12 (1967): 489–510.

Willard, Charity Cannon. "Raoul de Presles's Translation of Saint Augustine's *De Civitate Dei.*" In *Medieval Translators and Their Craft.* Ed. Jeanette Beer. Kalamazoo: Western Michigan UP, 1989.

Wilson, Everett L. *"The City of God* and the Emergence of Christendom." *Covenant Quarterly* 42 (1984): 15–26.

Wilson-Kastner, Patricia. "Andreas Osiander's Theology of Grace in the Perspective of the Influence of Augustine of Hippo." *Sixteenth Century Journal* 10 (1979): 72–91.

_____. "Grace as Participation in the Divine Life in the Theology of Augustine of Hippo; Augustine's Relationships to the Greek Theological World in Respect to the Question of Grace." *Augustinian Studies* 7 (1976): 135–52.

Wolin, Sheldon S. *Politics and Vision: Continuity and Innovation in Western Political Thought.* Boston: Little Brown, 1960.